90
D1756665

Field Methods for Geologists and Hydrogeologists

Springer

Berlin
Heidelberg
New York
Hong Kong
London
Milan
Paris
Tokyo

Fakhry A. Assaad
Philip E. LaMoreaux
Travis H. Hughes (Ed.)

Field Methods for Geologists and Hydrogeologists

With 235 Figures and 74 Tables

Springer

Authors

Assaad, Fakhry A.

P. E. LaMoreaux & Associates Inc., P.O. Box 2310, Tuscaloosa, Alabama 35403, USA
E-mail: assaad_violet@earthlink.net

LaMoreaux, Philip E. Sr.

P. E. LaMoreaux & Associates Inc., P.O. Box 2310, Tuscaloosa, Alabama 35403, USA
Tel.: (205) 752-5543, E-mail: pel@dbtech.net

Hughes, Travis H. (Ed.)

H.C.I., 143 Union Boulevard, Suite 523, Lakewood, Colorado 80228, USA

ISBN 3-540-40882-7 Springer-Verlag Berlin Heidelberg New York

Library of Congress Cataloging-in-Publication Data Applied For

Bibliographic information published by Die Deutsche Bibliothek
Die Deutsche Bibliothek lists this publication in the Deutsche Nationalbibliografie;
detailed bibliographic data is available in the Internet at http://dnb.ddb.de

Springer-Verlag Berlin Heidelberg New York
a part of the Springer Science+Business Media GmbH
springeronline.com

Printed in Germany

Cover Design: Kirchner, Heidelberg
Dataconversion: Büro Stasch (*www.stasch.com*) · Uwe Zimmermann, Bayreuth

Printed on acid-free paper – 32/2132 AO – 5 4 3 2 1 0

Preface

This book is designed for scientists and engineers who want practical information to plan, manage, write, and review geologic and hydrologic projects and reports. It provides step-by-step methods to prepare more timely, readable, and technically accurate reports. Detailed guidelines are provided to prepare the different subjects included in this book. Source references, project proposals, and checklists are included to assist authors. The use of the techniques described in this book will result in less time spent in report writing, editing, rewriting, and review, which will save time and money.

This book is the result of nearly 50 years of experience in program and project development in the field of hydrogeology. The two main authors P. E. LaMoreaux and Fakhry Assaad who submitted both the idea and the major subjects of the book, have been closely associated during this period with the Geological Survey of Egypt, the General Desert Development Organization in Egypt, the U.S. Geological Survey (USGS), the Geological Survey of Alabama, the University of Alabama, and in a great variety of consulting projects in different States of America and over the world. It is based on experience from the assignment and supervision of many professionals with a great variety of academic training and experience. In the days before sand-grain charts, color charts, the American Geological Institute guidebook, and even textbooks in hydrogeology, it was often necessary to improvise and develop organizational structure charts, training programs, and even standardization by using paint chips for color charts and manufacturing with sieve analysis equipment comparative material sets for sand size and angularity.

Over the years, a great number of guidance documents have evolved, many in response to a specific need during geologic mapping, well inventories, test drilling, or quantitative pumping tests. Included were detailed instructions for field work, the development of forms, and, in some instances, the invention of specialized equipment. Many acknowledgements would therefore be needed to reflect the organizational and financial support that made all of this experience possible. P. E. LaMoreaux, the senior hydrogeologist was involved from the very beginning in the development of special short course programs for hydrogeology for the USGS and, therefore, had access to lecture notes and handout materials that ultimately were compiled at the USGS National Training Center, as well as through association with the directors of the State Geological Surveys, and through special assignment in 1959–60 by the Water Resources Division of USGS to analyze project execution and report preparation. This detailed study consisted of all active projects of the USGS, and from this study came recommendations for project planning and execution.

Much of this material with the USGS was subsequently summarized in a report, *WRD Project and Report Management Guide*, by Jack H. Green, USGS, 1991 and later incorporated in *A Guide for Preparing Hydrologic and Geologic Projects and Reports* by John E. Moore, American Institute of Hydrology. This book, therefore, has taken advantage of all of these sources of material together with other important materials and subjects from several textbooks and fieldbooks.

Special acknowledgement to engineer Tom Brunner for his guidance on updating "Drilling Technology" (Chap. 6). Also, most thanks to Ann McCarley for her efforts in finalizing the text as the manuscript manager.

Cartoons in this text were drawn by graphic artists-draftsman Fred Burnell and used by Phil LaMoreaux for lectures on project planning and report preparation for many years. Many were generated by geologists describing to Burnell the problems of being a hydrogeologist.

August 2003

Contents

Contributors

Assaad, Fakhry A.

Consultant and Data Analyst
P. E. LaMoreaux & Associates Inc., P.O. Box 2310, Tuscaloosa, Alabama 35403, USA
Tel.: (205) 556-2409, E-mail: assaad_violet@earthlink.net

Finci, Aka G.

Mission Research Corporation, 5001 Indian School Rd. NE, Albuquerque, NM 87110-3946, USA
Tel.: (505) 768-7739

Green, D.S.

P. E. LaMoreaux & Associates Inc., P.O. Box 2310, Tuscaloosa, AL 35403, USA

Jordan, Hanspeter

HGC Hydro-Geo-Consult GmbH, Halsbrücker Straße 34, D-09599 Freiberg, Germany

Kraft, Mark

LMITCO/INEEL
P.O. Box 1625, M/S 3765/5172, Idaho Falls, ID 83415, USA, Tel.: (208) 526-0357 / -6116

LaMoreaux, Philip E. Sr.

Senior Hydrogeologist
P. E. LaMoreaux & Associates, Inc., P.O. Box 2310, Tuscaloosa, AL 35403, USA
Tel.: (205) 752-5543, E-mail: pel@dbtech.net

Memon, B.A.

P. E. LaMoreaux & Associates Inc., P.O. Box 2310, Tuscaloosa, AL 35403, USA

Molek, Herward

TU Darmstadt, Institut für Angewandte Geowissenschaften, Schnittspahnstraße 9, D-64287 Darmstadt, Germany

Reuter, Fritz

HGC Hydro-Geo-Consult GmbH, Halsbrücker Straße 34, D-09599 Freiberg, Germany

Stanfill Daniel F. III

Detection Sciences Inc., 496 Heald Road, Carlisle, MA 01741-1416, USA, Tel.: (978) 369-7999

Whitmill, Larry

LMITCO/INEEL, P.O. Box 1625, M/S 3765/5172, Idaho Falls, ID 83415, USA, Tel.: (208) 526-0357/-6116

Zhou, Wanfang

Hydrogeologist
P. E. LaMoreaux & Associates Inc., 160 Administration Road, Suite 4, Oak Ridge, Tennessee 37830, USA
Tel.: (865) 483-7483

Glossary

Abrasive
Any rock, mineral, or other substance that, owing to its superior hardness, toughness, consistency, or other properties, is suitable for grinding, cutting, polishing, scouring, or similar use.

Absorption
The assimilation of fluids into interstices.

Acid precipitation
Any atmospheric precipitation, which has an acid reaction through the absorption of acid producing substances such as sulfur dioxide.

Additive
Any material other than the basic components of a grout system.

Adhesion
Shearing resistance between soil and another material under zero externally applied pressure.

Adsorbed water
Water in a soil or rock mass attracted to the particle surface by physiochemical forces, having properties that may differ from those of pore water at the same temperature and pressure due to altered molecular arrangement.

Aeolian deposits
Wind-deposited material such as dune sands and deposits.

Alluvium
Refers to material deposited by running water (gravel, sand, silt, clay).

Anaerobic condition
Characterized by absence of air or free oxygen.

Andesitic basalt
A fine-grained extrusive igneous rock composed of plagioclase feldspar and ferro-magnesian silicates.

Anticline
A fold in which the rocks are bent convex upward.

Aquiclude
A body of relatively impermeable rock that is capable of absorbing water slowly, but functions as an upper or lower boundary of an aquifer and does not transmit ground water rapidly enough to supply a well or spring.

Aqulfer
A porous, permeable, water-bearing geologic body of rock. Generally restricted to materials capable of yielding an appreciable amount of water.

Aquifuge
A rock, which contains no interconnected openings or interstices, and therefore neither absorbs nor transmits water.

Aquitard
A confining bed that retards but does not prevent the flow of water to or from an adjacent aquifer; a leaky confining bed. It does not readily yield water to wells or springs, but may serve as a storage unit for ground water.

Artesian
An adjective referring to ground water confined under sufficient hydrostatic pressure to rise above the upper surface of the aquifer.

Artesian aquifer
Confined aquifer.

Artesian head
The level to which water from a well will rise when confined in a standing pipe.

Artesian well
A well in which water from a confined aquifer rises above the top of the aquifer. Some wells may flow without the aid of pumping.

Auger mining
A method of extracting ore by boring horizontally into a seam, much like a drill cores a hole in wood.

Avalanche
A large mass of either snow, rock debris, soil, or ice, which detaches and slides down mountain slope.

Barometer
An instrument, which measures atmospheric pressure. The first liquid barometer was designed by Torricelli in 1644.

Basalt
A fine-grained, dark-colored igneous rock composed of ferromagnesian minerals.

Bedding plane
A plane, which separates or delineates layers of sedimentary rock.

Biosphere
That part of the earth system that supports life.

BOD (biochemical oxygen demand)
The oxygen used in meeting the metabolic needs of aquatic aerobic microorganisms. A high BOD correlates with accelerated eutrophication.

Brackish water
Water with a salinity intermediate between that of freshwater and seawater.

Brine
Concentrated salt solution remaining after removal of distilled product; also, concentrated brackish saline or sea waters containing more than 100 000 mg l^{-1} of total dissolved solids.

Carbon dioxide (CO_2)
A gaseous product of combustion about 1.5 times as heavy as air. A rise in CO_2 in the atmosphere increases the greenhouse effect.

Carbon monoxide (CO)
This is a product of incomplete combustion. CO is colorless and has no odor and combines with hemoglobin in the blood leading to suffocation caused by oxygen deficiency.

Cement
Chemically precipitated mineral material that occurs in the spaces among the individual grains of a consolidated sedimentary rock, thereby binding the grains together as a rigid coherent mass; it may be derived from the sediment or its entrapped waters, or it may be brought in by solution from outside sources. The most common cements are silica (quartz, opal, chalcedony), carbonates (calcite, dolomite, siderite), and various iron oxides; others include barite, gypsum, anhydrite, and pyrite. Clay minerals and other fine clastic particles should not be considered as cements.

Centipoise
A unit of viscosity based on the standard of water at 20 °C, which has a viscosity of 1.005 centipoises.

Chain reaction
This is a self-sustaining nuclear reaction, which, once started, passes from one atom to another (see also fission).

Chemical treatment
Any process involving the addition of chemicals to obtain a desired result.

Circulation
Applies to the fluid rotary drilling method; drilling fluid movement from the mud pit, through the pump, hose and swivel, drill pipe, annular space in the hole and returning to the mud pit.

Clay minerals
One of a complex and loosely defined group of finely crystalline, meta colloidal, or amorphous hydrous silicates essentially of aluminum with a monoclinic crystal lattice of the two or three layer type in which silicon and aluminum ions have tetrahedral coordination in respect to oxygen. Clay minerals are formed chiefly by chemical alteration or weathering of primary silicate minerals such as feldspars, pyroxenes, and amphiboles and are found in clay deposits, soils, shales, and mixed with sand grains in many sandstones. They are characterized by small particle size and ability to adsorb substantial amounts of water and ions on the surfaces of the particles. The most common clay minerals belong to the kaolin, montmorillonite, and illite groups.

Climate
The statistical sum total of meteorological conditions (averages and extremes) for a given point or area over a long period of time.

Coefficient of transmissibilty
The rate of flow of water in gallons per day through a vertical strip of the aquifer 30.5 cm. Under a unit hydraulic gradient.

Cold front
The boundary on the earth's surface, or aloft, along which warm air is displaced by cold air.

Colloidal dispersion
This is the process of extremely small particles (colloids) being dispersed and suspended in a medium of liquids or gases.

Colloidal grout
In grouting, a grout in which the dispersed solid particles remain in suspension (colloids).

Colloidal particles
Particles that are so small that the surface activity has an appreciable influence on the properties of the aggregate.

Colluvium
An accumulation of soil and rock fragments at the foot of a cliff or slope under the direct influence of gravity.

Compressibility
The reciprocal of bulk modules of elasticity. Its symbol is "C". Syn.: modulus of compression.

Concentration
(1) The amount of a given substance dissolved in a unit volume of solution. (2) The process of increasing the dissolved solids per unit volume of solution, usually by evaporation of the liquid.

Concentration tank
A settling tank of relatively short detention period in which sludge is concentrated by sedimentation of floatation before treatment, dewatering, or disposal.

Conceptual model
A simplified representation of the hydrogeologic setting and the response of the flow system to stress.

Conductance (specific)
A measure of the ability of the water to conduct an electric current at 25 °C. It is related to the total concentration of ionizable solids in the water. It is inversely proportional to electrical resistance. (ASTM D-5092).

Cone volcano
A steep-sided and cone-shaped volcano, which is composed of both lava flows and layers of pyroclastic materials. This type is also called a stratovolcano.

Confined aquifer
An aquifer bounded above and below by impermeable beds or beds of distinctly lower permeability than that of the aquifer itself; an aquifer containing confined ground water.

Confined ground water

A body of ground water overlain by material sufficiently impervious to sever free hydraulic connection with overlying ground water except at the intake. Confined water moves in conduits under the pressure due to difference in head between intake and discharge areas of the confined water body.

Confining bed

A body of impermeable or distinctly less permeable material stratigraphically adjacent to one or more aquifers. Cf.: aquitard; aquifuge; aquiclude.

Contaminant

An undesirable substance not normally present in water or soil.

Core barrel

(*a*) A hollow tube or cylinder above the bit of a core drill, used to receive and preserve a continuous section or core of the material penetrated during drilling. The core is recovered from the core barrel. (*b*) The tubular section of a corer, in which ocean-bottom sediments are collected either directly in the tube or in a plastic liner placed inside the tube.

Core drill

(*a*) A drill (usually a rotary drill, rarely a cable-tool drill) that cuts, removes, and brings to the surface a cylindrical rock sample (core) from the drill hole. It is equipped with a core bit and a core barrel. (*b*) A lightweight, usually mobile drill that uses drill tubing instead of drill pipe and that can (but need not) core down from grass roots.

Core recovery

Ratio of the length of core recovered to length of hole drilled, usually expressed as a percentage.

Corrasion

Wearing away of the earth's surface forming sinkholes and caves and widening them due to running water.

Corrosion

The gradual deterioration or destruction of a substance or material by chemical action, frequently induced by electrochemical processes. The action proceeds inward from the surface.

Creep

A slow movement of unconsolidated surface materials (soil, rock fragments) under the influence of water, strong wind, or gravity.

Crustal plates

In the theory of plate tectonics it is stated that the earth's crust is not continuous but is composed of many large and small plate units that are in relative motion to one another.

Cuttings

Rock chips or fragments produced by drilling and brought to the surface. The term does not include the core recovered from core drilling. Also: well cuttings; sludge; drillings. Syn.: drill cuttings.

Darcy
A standard unit of permeability, equivalent to the passage of one cubic centimeter of fluid of one centipoise viscosity flowing in one second under a pressure differential of one atmosphere through a porous medium having an area of cross-section of one square centimeter and a length of one centimeter. A millidarcy is one one-thousandth of a darcy.

Darcy's law
A derived formula for the flow of fluids on the assumption that the flow is laminar and that inertia can be neglected. The numerical formulation of this law is used generally in studies of gas, oil, and water production from underground formations.

DDT (dichlorodiphenyltrichloroethane)
An insecticide, one of several chlorinated hydrocarbons.

Debris slide
A sudden downslope movement of unconsolidated earth materials or mine waste particularly once it becomes water saturated.

Deep-well injection
A technique for disposal of liquid waste materials by pressurized infusion into porous bedrock formations or cavities.

Degradation
The general lowering of the land by erosional processes.

Desalination
Any process capable of converting saline water to potable water.

Desertification
The creation of desert-like conditions, or the expansion of deserts as a result of man's actions which include overgrazing, excessive extraction of water, and deforestation.

Desertization
A relatively new term that denotes the natural growth of deserts in response to climatic change.

Deserts
Permanently arid regions of the world where annual evaporation by far exceeds annual precipitation. They cover about 16 percent of the earth.

Detrital
Relates to deposits formed of minerals and rock fragments transported to the place of deposition.

Dip slope
Topographic slope conforming with the dip of the underlying bedrock.

Discharge
The volume of water passing a given point within a given period of time.

Downdrafts
Downward and sometimes violent cold air currents frequently associated with cumulonimbus clouds and thunderstorms.

Drainage basin
This is the area, which is drained by a river and its tributaries.

Drilling fluid

A heavy suspension, usually in water but sometimes in oil, used in rotary drilling, consisting of various substances in a finely divided state (commonly bentonitic clays and chemical additives such as barite), introduced continuously down the drill pipe under hydrostatic pressure, out through openings in the drill bit, and back up in the annular space between the pipe and the borehole walls and to a surface pit where cuttings are removed. The fluid is then reintroduced into the pipe. It is used to lubricate and cool the bit, to carry the cuttings up from the bottom, and to prevent sloughing and cave-ins by plastering and consolidating the walls with a clay lining, thereby making casing unnecessary during drilling, and also offsetting pressures of fluid and gas that may exist in the subsurface. Syn.: drilling mud.

Drill-stem test (DST)

A procedure for determining productivity of an oil or gas well by measuring reservoir pressures and flow capacities while the drill pipe is in the hole and the well is full of drilling mud. A drill stem test may be done in a cased or uncased hole.

Drought

An extended period of below-normal precipitation especially in regions of sparse precipitation. Prolonged droughts can lead to crop failures, famines, and sharply declining water resources.

Dust storm

A severe weather system, usually in dry area, which is characterized by high winds and dust-laden air. Major dust storms were observed during the 1930s in the Dust Bowl region of the United States.

Earthquake

A sudden movement and tremors within the earth's crust caused by fault slippage or subsurface volcanic activity.

Ecosystem

A functional system based on the interaction between all living organisms and the physical components of a given area.

Effective porosity

The measure of the total volume of interconnected void space of a rock, soil or other substance. Effective porosity is usually expressed as a percentage of the bulk volume of material occupied by the interconnected void space.

Effective stress

The average normal force per unit area transmitted directly from particle to particle or rock mass. It is the stress that is effective in mobilizing internal friction. In a saturated soil, in equilibrium, the effective stress is the difference between the total stress and the neutral stress of the water in the voids; it attains a maximum value at complete consolidation of the soil.

Ejecta

Solid material thrown out of a volcano. It includes volcanic ash, lapilli, and bombs.

Elastic limit

Point on stress strain curve at which transition from elastic to inelastic behavior takes place.

Emulsion

A system containing dispersed colloidal droplets.

Environmentalism
This concept, also called environmental determinism, proposes that the total environment is the most influential control factor in the development of individuals or cultures.

Evapotranspiration
The sum of evapotranspiration from wetted surfaces and of transpiration by vegetation.

Eye (of a hurricane)
The mostly cloudless, calm center area of a hurricane. This center is surrounded by near-vertical cloud walls.

Facies
A term used to refer to a distinguished part or parts of a single geologic entity, differing from other parts in some general aspect; e.g. any two or more significantly different parts of a recognized body of rock or stratigraphic composition. The term implies physical closeness and genetic relation or connection between the parts.

Facies change
A lateral or vertical variation in the lithologic or paleontologic characteristics of contemporaneous sedimentary deposits. It is caused by, or reflects, a change in the depositional environment. Cf.: facies evolution.

Facies map
A broad term for a stratigraphic map showing the gross areal variation or distribution (in total or relative content) of observable attributes or aspects of different rock types occurring within a designated stratigraphic unit, without regard to the position or thickness of individual beds in the vertical succession; specifically a lithofacies map. Conventional facies maps are prepared by drawing lines of equal magnitude through a field of numbers representing the observed values of the measured rock attributes. Cf.: vertical-variability map.

Fault
A surface or zone of rock fracture along with there has been displacement, from a few centimeters to a few kilometers.

Fault breccia
The assemblage of broken rock fragments frequently found along faults. The fragments may vary in size from centimeters to meters.

Filtrate
The liquid, which has passed through a filter.

Filtration
The process of passing a liquid through a filtering medium (which may consist of granular material, such as sand, magnetite, or diatomaceous earth, finely woven cloth, unglazed porcelain or specially prepared paper) for the removal of suspended or colloidal matter.

Fission
The splitting of an atom into nuclei of lighter atoms through bombardment with neutrons. Enormous amounts of energy are released in this process, which is used in the development of nuclear power and weapons.

Fissure eruption
A type of volcanic eruption which takes place along a ground fracture instead of through a crater.

Flank eruption

A type of volcanic eruption that takes place on the side of a volcano instead of from the crater. This typically occurs when the crater is blocked by previous lava eruptions.

Flash flood

A local and very sudden flood that typically occurs in usually dry river beds and narrow canyons as a result of heavy precipitation generated by mountain thunderstorms.

Flood crest

The peak of a flood event, also called a flood wave, which moves downstream and shows as a curve crest on a hydrograph.

Floodplain

A stretch of relatively level land bordering a stream. This plain is composed of river sediments and is subject to flooding.

Flood stage

The stage at which overflow of the natural banks of a stream begins to cause damage in the reach in which the elevation is measured.

Flow rate

The volume per time given to the flow of water or other liquid substance which emerges from an orifice, pump, turbine or passes along a conduit or channel, usually expressed as cubic feet per second (cfs), gallons per minute (gpm) or million gallons per day (mgd).

Focus

The point of earthquake origin in the earth's crust from where earthquake waves travel in all directions.

Foliation

A textural term referring to the planar arrangement of mineral grains in metamorphic rock.

Formation

A body of rock characterized by a degree of lithologic homogeneity; it is prevailingly, but not necessarily, tabular and is mappable on the earth's surface or traceable in the subsurface.

Formation water

Water present in a water-bearing formation under natural conditions as opposed to introduced fluids, such as drilling mud.

Fossil fuel

Fuels such as natural gas, petroleum, and coal that developed from ancient deposits of organic deposition and subsequent decomposition.

Geophysical logs

The records of a variety of logging tools which measure the geophysical properties of geologic formations penetrated and their contained fluids. These properties include electrical conductivity and resistivity, the ability to transmit and reflect sonic energy, natural radioactivity, hydrogen ion content, temperature, gravity, etc. These geophysical properties are then interpreted in terms of lithology, porosity, fluid content and chemistry.

Geothermal gradient

The rate of increase of temperature in the earth with depth. The gradient near the surface of the earth varies from place to place depending upon the heat flow in the region and on the thermal conductivity of the rocks. The approximate geothermal gradient in the earth's crust is about 25 °C km^{-1}.

Glacial drift

A general term applied to sedimentary material transported and deposited by glacial ice.

Glacial till (till)

Material deposited by glaciation, usually composed of a wide range of particle sizes, which has not been subjected to the sorting action of water.

Graben

A down-faulted block. May be bounded by up-thrown blocks (horsts).

Gradation

The leveling of the land through erosion, transportation, and deposition.

Granite

A light-colored, or reddish, coarse-grained intrusive igneous rock that forms the typical base rock of continental shields.

Greenhouse effect

The trapping and reradiation of the earth's infrared radiation by atmospheric water vapor, carbon dioxide, and ozone. The atmosphere acts like the glass cover of a greenhouse.

Ground fire

This is a type of fire which occurs beneath the surface and burns rootwork and peaty materials.

Ground water

That part of the subsurface water that is in the saturated zone.

Ground-water discharge

The water released from the zone of saturation; also the volume of water released.

Ground-water flow

The movement of water in the zone of saturation.

Ground-water recharge

The process of water addition to the saturated zone; also the volume of water added by this process.

Group (General)

An association of any kind based upon some feature of similarity or relationship. Stratig: Lithostratigraphic unit consisting of two or more formations; more or less informally recognized succession of strata too thick or inclusive to be considered a formation; subdivisions of a series.

Grout

A cementitious component of high water content, fluid enough to be poured or injected into spaces such as fissures surrounding a well bore and thereby filling or sealing them. Specifically a pumpable slurry of portland cement, sand, and water forced under pressure into a borehole during well drilling to seal crevices and prevent the mixing of ground water from different aquifers.

Horst

An up-faulted block. May be bounded by downthrown blocks (grabens).

Hot spot (geol.)

Excessively hot magma centers in the asthenosphere that usually lead to the formation of volcanoes.

Humus

The partially or fully decomposed organic matter in soils. It is generally dark in color and partly of colloidal size.

Hurricane

A tropical low-pressure storm (also called baguio, tropical cyclone, typhoon, willy). Hurricanes may have a diameter of up to 400 miles (640 km), a calm center (the eye), and must have wind velocities higher than 75 mph (120 km h^{-1}). Some storms attained wind velocities of 200 mph (320 km h^{-1}).

Hydrate

Refers to those compounds containing chemically combined water.

Hydraulic

Pertaining to a fluid in motion, or to movement or action caused by water.

Hydraulic action

The mechanical loosening and removal of weakly resistant material solely by the pressure and *hydraulic force* of flowing water, as by a stream surging into rock cracks or impinging against the bank on the outside of a bend, or by ocean waves and currents pounding the base of a cliff.

Hydraulic conductivity

Ratio of flow velocity to driving force for viscous flow under saturated conditions of a specified liquid in a porous medium.

Hydraulic gradient

In an aquifer, the rate of change of *total head* per unit of distance of flow at a given point and in a given direction.

Hydraulic head

(*a*) The height of the free surface of a body of water above a given subsurface point. (*b*) The water level at a point upstream from a given point downstream. (*c*) The elevation of the *hydraulic grade line* at a given point above a given point of a pressure pipe.

Hydraulics

The aspect of engineering that deals with the flow of water or other liquids; the practical application of *hydromechanics*.

Hydrocarbon

Organic compounds containing only carbon and hydrogen. Commonly found in petroleum, natural gas, and coal.

Hydrodynamics

The aspect of *hydromechanics* that deals with forces that produce motion.

Hydrogeology

The science that deals with subsurface waters and with related geologic aspects of surface waters. Also used in the more restricted sense of ground-water geology only.

The term was defined by Mead (1919) as the study of the laws of the occurrence and movement of subterranean waters. More recently it has been used interchangeably with *geohydrology*.

Hydrograph

A graph which shows the rate of river discharge over a given time period.

Hydrography

(*a*) The science that deals with the physical aspects of all waters on the earth's surface, esp. the compilation of navigational charts of bodies of water. (*b*) The body of facts encompassed by hydrography.

Hydrologic cycle

The constant circulation of water from the sea, through the atmosphere, to the land, and its eventual return to the atmosphere by way of transpiration and evaporation from the sea and the land surfaces.

Hydrologic system

A complex of related parts – physical, conceptual, or both – forming an orderly working body of hydrologic units and their man-related aspects such as the use, treatment, and reuse, and disposal of water and the costs and benefits thereof, and the interaction of hydrologic factors with those of sociology, economics, and ecology.

Hydrology

(*a*) The science that deals with global water (both liquid and solid), its properties, circulation, and distribution, on and under the earth's surface and in the atmosphere, from the moment of its precipitation until it is returned to the atmosphere through evapotranspiration or is discharged into the ocean. In recent years the scope of hydrology has been expanded to include environmental and economic aspects. At one time there was a tendency in the U.S. (as well as in Germany) to restrict the term "hydrology" to the study of subsurface waters (DeWeist 1965). (*b*) The sum of the factors studied in hydrology; the hydrology of an area or district.

Hydrosphere

The waters of the earth, as distinguished from the rocks (lithosphere), living things (biosphere), and the air (atmosphere). Includes the waters of the ocean; rivers, lakes, and other bodies of surface water in liquid form on the continents; snow, ice, and glaciers; and liquid water, ice, and water vapor in both the unsaturated and saturated zones below the land surface. Included by some, but excluded by others, is water in the atmosphere, which includes water vapor, clouds, and all forms of precipitation while still in the atmosphere.

Hydrothermal

Of or pertaining to hot water, to the action of hot water, or to the products of this action, such as a mineral deposit precipitated from a hot aqueous solution, with or without demonstrable association with igneous processes; also, said of the solution itself. "Hydrothermal" is generally used for any hot water but has been restricted by some to water of magmatic origin.

Hydrothermal processes

Those processes associated with igneous activity that involve heated or superheated water, esp. alteration, space filling, and replacement.

Hygroscopic particles

Condensation nuclei in the atmosphere that attract water molecules (carbon, sulfur, salt, dust, ice particles).

Hygroscopic water content (w_H)
The water content of an air-dried soil or rock.

Impermeable
Impervious to the natural movement of fluids.

Induction
The creation of an electric charge in a body by a neighboring body without having physical contact.

Injection well
(*a*) A recharge well. (*b*) A well into which water or a gas is pumped for the purpose of increasing the yield of other wells in the area. (*c*) A well used to dispose of fluids in the subsurface environment by allowing it to enter by gravity flow, or injection under pressure.

Intensity (earthquake)
A measurement of the effects of an earthquake on the environment expressed by the Mercalli scale in stages from I to XII.

Ion
An electrically charged molecule or atom that lost or gained electrons and therefore has a smaller or greater number of electrons than the originally neutral molecule or atom.

Ionization
The process of creating ions (see ion).

Iron Age
The period that followed the Bronze Age when mankind began the use of iron for making implements and weapons around 800 B.C. The earliest use of iron may go back to 2500 B.C.

Ironstone
A term sometimes used to describe a hardened plinthite layer in tropical soils. It is primarily composed of iron oxides bonded to kaolinitic clays.

Isopach
A line drawn on a map through points of equal thickness of a designated stratigraphic unit or group of stratigraphic units.

Isopach map
A map that shows the thickness of a bed, formation or other tabular body throughout a geographic area; a map that shows the varying true thickness of a designated stratigraphic unit or group of stratigraphic units by means of isopachs plotted normal to the bedding or other bounding surface at regular intervals.

Isotopes
Atoms of a given element having the same atomic number but differ in atomic weight because of variations in the number of neutrons.

Jet stream
A high-velocity, high-altitude (25000 to 40000 feet or 7700 to 12200 m) wind that moves within a relatively narrow oscillating band within the upper westerly winds.

Joint (geol.)
A natural fissure in a rock formation along which no movement has taken place.

Karst
A type of topography characterized by closed depressions (sinkholes), caves, and subsurface streams.

Laminar flow (streamline flow)
Flow in which the head loss is proportional to the first power of the velocity.

Landslide
A general term that denotes a rapid downslope movement of soil or rock masses.

Land-subsidence
A gradual or sudden lowering of the land surface caused by natural or man-induced factors such as solution (see karst) or the extraction of water or oil.

Leachate
The solution obtained by the leaching action of water as it percolates through soil or other materials such as wastes containing soluble substances.

Lithification
The conversion of unconsolidated material into rock.

Lithology
(*a*) The description of rocks on the basis of such characteristics as color, structures, mineralogic composition, and grain size. (*b*) The physical character of a rock.

Lithosphere
The outer solid layer of the earth which rests on the non-solid asthenosphere. The lithosphere averages about 60 miles (100 km) in thickness.

Loess
Fine silt-like soil particles which have been transported and deposited by wind action. Some loess deposits may be hundreds of thick.

Loss of circulation
The loss of drilling fluid into strata to the extent that circulation does not return to the surface (ASTM D-5092).

Magma
Naturally occurring molten rock which may also contain variable amounts of volcanic gases. It issues at the earth's surface as lava.

Magma chambers
Underground reservoirs of molten rock (magma) that are usually found beneath volcanic areas.

Mantle (geol.)
The intermediate zone of the earth found beneath the crust and resting on the core. The mantle is believed to be about 1 800 miles (2 900 km) thick.

Marl
Calcareous clay, usually containing from 35 to 65% calcium carbonate ($CaCO_3$).

Marsh
A wetland characterized by grassy surface mats which are frequently interspersed with open water by a closed canopy of grasses, sledges, or other herbaceous plants.

Mathematical model
The representation of a physical system by mathematical expressions from which the behavior of the system can be deduced with known accuracy.

Matrix
In grouting, a material in which particles are embedded, that is, the cement paste in which the fine aggregate particles of a grout are embedded.

Member
A division of a formation, generally of distinct lithologic character or of only local extent. A specially developed part of a varied formation is called a member, if it has considerable geographic extent. Members are commonly, though not necessarily, named.

Metamorphism
The process which induces physical or compositional changes in rocks caused by heat, pressure, or chemically active fluids.

Millidarcy
The customary unit of fluid permeability, equivalent to 0.001 darcy. Abbrev.: md.

Mudflow
A downslope movement of water-saturated earth materials such as soil, rock fragments, or volcanic ash.

Mud logs
The record of continuous analysis of a drilling mud or fluid for oil and gas content.

Neutralization
Reaction of acid or alkali with the opposite reagent until the concentrations of hydrogen and hydroxyl ions in the solution are approximately equal.

Overburden (spoil)
Barren bedrock or surficial material which must be removed before the underlying mineral deposit can be mined.

Oxidation
The addition of oxygen to a compound. More generally, any reaction, which involves the loss of electrons from an atom.

Packer
In well drilling, a device lowered in the lining tubes which swells automatically or can be expanded by manipulation from the surface at the correct time to produce a water-tight joint against the sides of the borehole or the casing, thus entirely excluding water from different horizons.

Percentage map
A facies map that depicts the relative amount (thickness) of a single rock type in a given stratigraphic unit.

Perched aquifer
A water body that is not hydraulically connected to the main zone of saturation.

Permafrost
Permanently frozen ground.

Permeability
The property of capacity of a porous rock, sediment, or soil for transmitting a fluid without impairment of the structure of the medium; it is a measure of the relative ease of fluid flow under unequal pressure. The customary unit of measurement is the millidarcy.

Pesticide
Any chemical used for killing noxious organisms.

pH
The negative logarithm of the hydrogen-ion concentration. The concentration is the weight of hydrogen ions, in grams per liter or solution. Neutral water, for example, has a pH value of 7 and a hydrogen ion concentration of 10.

Plugging
The act or process of stopping the flow of water, oil, or gas in strata penetrated by a borehole or well so that fluid from one stratum will not escape into another or to the surface; especially the sealing up a well that is tube abandoned. It is usually accomplished by inserting a plug into the hole, by sealing off cracks and openings in the sidewalls of the hole, or by cementing a block inside the casing. Capping the hole with a metal plate should never be considered as an adequate method of plugging a well.

Porosity
The property of a rock, soil, or other material of containing interstices. It is commonly expressed as a percentage of the bulk volume of material occupied by interstices, whether isolated or connected.

Potentiometric surface
An imaginary surface representing the static head of ground water and defined by the level to which water will rise in a well. The water table is a particular potentiometric surface.

Pressure
(1) The total load or force acting on a surface. (2) In hydraulics, without qualifications, usually the pressure per unit area or intensity of pressure above local atmospheric pressure expressed, for example, in pounds per square inch, kilograms per square centimeter.

Primary porosity
The porosity that develops during the final stages of sedimentation or that was present within sedimentary particles at the time of deposition. It includes all depositional porosity of the sediments, or the rock.

Resistivity
Refers to the resistance of material to electrical current. The reciprocal of conductivity.

Rotary drilling
A common method of drilling, being a hydraulic process consisting of a rotating drill pipe at the bottom of which is attached to a hard-toothed drill bit. The rotary motion is transmitted through the pipe from a rotary table at the surface: as the pipe turns, the bit loosens or grinds a hole in the bottom material. During drilling, a stream of drilling mud is in constant circulation down the pipe and out through the bit from where it and the cuttings from the bit are forced back up the hole outside the pipe and into pits where the cuttings are removed and the mud is picked up by pumps and forced back down the pipe.

Runoff
That part of precipitation which flows over the surface of the land as sheet wash and stream flow.

Salinization
The excessive build-up of soluble salts in soils or in water. This often is a serious problem in crop irrigation system.

Saltation
A form of wind erosion where small particles are picked up by wind and fall back to the surface in a "leap and bound" fashion. The impact of the particles loosen other soil particles rendering them prone to further erosion.

Sanitary landfill
A land site where solid waste is dumped, compacted, and covered with soil in order to minimize environmental degradation.

Sea level
This is an imaginary average level of the ocean as it exists over a long period of time. It is also used to establish a common reference for standard atmospheric pressure at this level.

Secondary porosity
The porosity developed in a rock formation subsequent to its deposition or emplacement, either through natural processes of dissolution, stress distortion, or artificially through acidization or the mechanical injection of coarse sand.

Secondary wave (S)
A body earthquake which travels more slowly than a primary wave (P). The wave energy moves earth materials at a right angle to the direction of wave travel. This type of shear wave cannot pass through liquids.

Sedimentation
The process of removal of solids from water by gravity settling.

Seismic activity
Earth vibrations or disturbances produced by earthquakes.

Seismic survey
The gathering of seismic data from an area; the initial phase of seismic prospecting.

Seismograph
This is a device that measures and records the magnitude of earthquakes and other shock waves such as underground nuclear explosions.

Seismology
The science that is concerned with earthquake phenomena.

Seismometer
An instrument, often portable, designed to detect earthquakes and other types of shock waves.

Semi-arid regions
Transition zones with very unreliable precipitation that are located between true deserts and subhumid climates. The vegetation consists usually of scattered short grasses and drought-resistant shrubs.

Septic tank system
An onsite disposal system consisting of an underground tank and a soil absorption field. Untreated sewage enters the tank where solids undergo decomposition. Liquid effluent moves from the tank to the absorption field via perforated pipe.

Shear
The movement of one part of a mass relative to another leading to lateral deformation without resulting in a change in volume.

Shear strength
The internal resistance of a mass to lateral deformation (see shear). Shear strength is mostly determined by internal friction and the cohesive forces between particles.

Sinkhole
A topographic depression developed by the solution of limestone, rock salt, or gypsum bedrock.

Sludge
(1) Mud obtained from a drill hole in boring; mud from drill cuttings. The term has also been used for the cuttings produced by drilling. (2) A semi-fluid, slushy, and murky mass or sediment of solid matter resulting from treatment of water, sewage, or industrial and mining wastes, and often appearing as local bottom deposits in polluted bodies of water.

Slurry
A very wet, highly mobile, semiviscous mixture or suspension of finely divided, insoluble matter.

Soil failure
Slippage or shearing within a soil mass because of some stress force that exceeds the shear strength of the soil.

Soil liquefaction
The liquefying of clayey soils that lose their cohesion when they become saturated with water and are subjected to stress or vibrations.

Soil salinization
The process of accumulation of soluble salts (mostly chlorides and sulfates) in soils caused by the rise of mineralized ground water or the lack of adequate drainage when irrigation is practiced.

Soil structure
The arrangement of soil particles into aggregates which can be classified according to their shapes and sizes.

Soil texture
The relative proportions of various particle sizes (clay, silt, sand) in soils.

Solution
A process of chemical weathering by which rock material passes into calcium carbonate in limestone or chalk by carbonic acid derived from rain water containing carbon dioxide acquired during its passage through the atmosphere.

Sorting
A dynamic gradational process which segregates sedimentary particles by size or shape. Well-sorted material has a limited size range whereas poorly sorted material has a large size range.

Specific conductance
The electrical conductivity of a water sample at 25 °C (77 °F), expressed in micro-ohms per centimeter ($\mu\Omega\ cm^{-1}$).

Specific gravity
The ratio of the mass of a body to the mass of an equal volume of water.

Spontaneous combustion
This type of fire is started by the accumulation of the heat of oxidation until the kindling temperature of the material is reached.

Stage
Refers to the height of a water surface above an established datum plane.

Standing wave
An oscillating type of wave on the surface of an enclosed body of water. The wave acts similar to water sloshing back and forth in an open dish.

Stock
An irregularly shaped discordant pluton that is less than 100 km^2 in surface exposure.

Storage coefficient
In an aquifer, the volume of water released from storage in a vertical column of 1.0 square foot (929 cm^2) when the water table or other potentiometric surface declines 1.0 foot (30.48 cm). In an unconfined aquifer, it is approximately equal to the specific yield.

Stratification
The structure produced by a series of sedimentary layers or beds (strata).

Stratigraphy
The study of rock strata including their age relations, geographic distribution, composition, history, etc.

Stratosphere
The part of the upper atmosphere that shows little change in temperature with altitude. Its base begins at about 7 miles (11 km) and its upper limits reach to about 22 miles (35 km).

Stream terraces
These are elevated remainders of previous floodplains; they generally parallel the stream channel.

Stress
Compressional, tensional, or torsional forces that act to change the geometry of a body.

Structure-contour map
A map that portrays subsurface configuration by means of structure contour lines; contour map; tectonic map. Syn.: structural map, structure map.

Surface casing
The first string of a well casing to be installed in the well. The length will vary according to the surface conditions and the type of well.

Surficial deposit
Unconsolidated transported or residual materials such as soil, alluvial, or glacial deposits.

Surge
A momentary increase in flow in an open conduit or pressure in a closed conduit that passes longitudinally along the conduit, usually due to sudden changes in velocity.

Swab
A piston-like device equipped with an upward-opening check valve and provided with flexible rubber suction caps, lowered into a borehole or casing by means of a wire line for the purpose of cleaning out drilling mud or of lifting oil.

Talus debris
Unconsolidated rock fragments which form a slope at the base of a steep surface.

Tectonic
Said of or pertaining to the forces involved in, or the resulting structures or features of, tectonics. Syn.: geotectonic.

Till
Unstratified and unsorted sediments deposited by glacial ice.

Topsoil
The surface layer of a soil that is rich in organic materials.

Tornado
A highly destructive and violently rotating vortex storm that frequently forms from cumulonimbus clouds. It is also referred to as a twister.

Total porosity
The measure of all void space of a rock, soil or other substance. Total porosity is usually expressed as a percentage of the bulk volume of material occupied by the void space.

Toxin
A colloidal, proteinaceous, poisonous substance that is a specific product of the metabolic activities of a living organism and is usually very unstable, notably toxic when introduced into the tissues and typically capable of inducing antibody formation.

Transmissivity
In an aquifer, the rate of which water of the prevailing kinematic viscosity is transmitted through a unit width under a unit hydraulic gradient. Though spoken of as a property of the aquifer, it embodies also the saturated thickness and the properties of the contained liquid.

Transpiration
The process by which water absorbed by plants is evaporated into the atmosphere from the plant surface.

Triangulation
A survey technique used to determine the location of the third point of a triangle by measuring the angles from the known end points of a base line to the third point.

Turbulence (meteorol.)
Any irregular or disturbed wind motion in the air.

Twister
An American term used for a tornado.

Unconfined aquifer
A ground water body that is under water table conditions.

Unconsolidated material
A sediment that is loosely arranged, or whose particles are not cemented together, occurring either at the surface or at depth.

Urbanization
The transformation of rural areas into urban areas. Also referred to as urban sprawl.

Vapor pressure
That part of the total atmospheric pressure which is contributed by water vapor. It is usually expressed in inches of mercury or in millibars.

Vesicular
A textural term indicating the presence of many small cavities in a rock.

Viscosity
The property of a substance to offer internal resistance to flow; its internal friction. Specifically, the ratio of the rate of shear stress to the rate of shear strain. This ratio is known as the coefficient of viscosity.

Wastewater
Spent water. According to the source, it may be a combination of the liquid and water-carried wastes from residence, commercial buildings, industrial plants, and institutions, together with any ground water, surface water, and storm water which may be present. In recent years, the term wastewater has taken precedence over the term sewage.

Water quality
The chemical, physical, and biological characteristics of water with respect to its suitability for a particular purpose.

Water table
The surface marking the boundary between the zone of saturation and the zone of aeration. It approximates the surface topography.

Weather
The physical state of the atmosphere (wind, precipitation, temperature, pressure, cloudiness, etc.) at a given time and location.

Well log
A log obtained from a well, showing such information as resistivity, radioactivity, spontaneous potential, and acoustic velocity as a function of depth; esp. a lithologic record of the rocks penetrated.

Well monitoring
The measurement, by on-site instruments or laboratory methods, of the water quality of a water well. Monitoring may be periodic or continuous.

Well plug
A water tight and gas tight seal installed in a borehole or well to prevent movement of fluids. The plug can be a block cemented inside the casing.

Well record

A concise statement of the available data regarding a well, such as a scout ticket; a full history or day-by-day account of a well, from the day the well was surveyed to the day production ceased.

Well stimulation

Term used to describe several processes used to clean the well bore, enlarge channels, and increase pore space in the interval to be injected thus making it possible for wastewater to move more readily into the formation. The following are well stimulation techniques: (1) surging, (2) jetting, (3) blasting, (4) acidizing, and (5) hydraulic fracturing.

Windbreak

Natural or planted groups or rows of trees that slow down the wind velocity and protect against soil erosion.

Zone of aeration

The zone in which the pore spaces in permeable materials are not filled (except temporarily) with water. Also referred to as unsaturated zone or vadose zone.

Zone of saturation

The zone in which pore spaces are filled with water. Also referred to as phreatic zone.

Standard Terminology Relating to Soil, Rock, and Contained Fluids (ASTM D-653-96)

Absorption
The assimilation of fluids into interstices.

Additive
Any material other than the basic components of a grout system.

Adhesion
Shearing resistance between soil and another material under zero externally applied pressure.

Adsorbed water
Water in soil or rock mass attracted to the particle surfaces by physiochemical forces, having properties that may differ form those of pore water at the same temperature and pressure due to altered molecular arrangement; absorbed water does not include water that is chemically combined with the clay minerals.

Aeolian deposits
Wind deposited material such as dune sands and loess deposits.

Alluvium
Soil, the constituents of which have been transported in suspension by flowing water and subsequently deposited by sedimentation.

Circulation
Applies to the fluid rotary drilling method; drilling fluid movement from the mud pit, through the pump, hose and swivel, drill pipe, annular space in the hole and returning to the mud pit.

Coefficient of transmissibility
The rate of flow of water in gallons per day through a vertical strip of the aquifer 1 ft (0.3 m) wide, under a unit hydraulic gradient.

Colloidal grout
In grouting, a grout in which the dispersed solid particles remain in suspension (colloids).

Colloidal particles
Particles that are so small that he surface activity has an appreciable influence on the properties of the aggregate.

Conceptual model
A simplified representation of the hydrogeologic setting and the response of the flow system to stress.

Conductance (specific)
A measure of the ability of the water to conduct an electric current at 77 °F (25 °C). It is related to the total concentration of ionizable solids in the water. It is inversely proportional to electrical resistance.

Connate water, *n*
Water entrapped in the voids of a sedimentary or extrusive igneous rock at the time of its deposition or emplacement.

Consolidation
The gradual reduction in volume of a soil mass resulting from an increase in compressive stress.

Contaminant
An undesirable substance not normally present in water or soil.

Core recovery
Ration of the length of core recovered to the length of hole drilled, usually expressed as a percentage.

Drain
A means for intercepting, conveying, and removing water.

Elasticity
Property of material that returns to its original form or condition after the applied force is removed.

Elastic limit
Point on stress strain curve at which transition from elastic to inelastic behavior takes place.

Electric log
A record or log of a borehole obtained by lowering electrodes into the hole and measuring any of the various electrical properties of the rock formations or materials traversed.

Emulsion
A system containing dispersed colloidal droplets.

Fault breccia
The assemblage of broken rock fragments frequently found along faults. The fragments may vary in size from inches to feet. (ISRM)

Glacial till (till)
Material deposited by glaciation, usually composed of a wide range of particle sizes, which has not been subjected to the sorting action of water.

Ground-water discharge
The water released from the zone of saturation; also the volume of water released.

Ground-water flow
The movement of water in the zone of saturation.

Ground-water level
The level of the water table surrounding a borehole or well. The ground-water level can be represented as an elevation or as a depth below the ground surface.

Ground-water recharge
The process of water addition to the saturated zone; also the volume of water added by this process.

Humus
A brown or black material formed by the partial decomposition of vegetable or animal matter, the organic portion of soil.

Hydration
Formation of a compound by the combining of water with some other substance.

Hydraulic conductivity (field aquifer tests)
The volume of water at the existing kinematic viscosity that will move in a unit time under a unit hydraulic gradient through a unit area measured at right angles to the direction of flow.

Hygroscopic capacity (hygroscopic coefficient), w_e (D)
Ratio of: (1) the weight of water absorbed by a dry soil or rock in a saturated atmosphere at a given temperature, to (2) the weight of the oven-dried soil or rock.

Hygroscopic water content, w_H (D)
The water content of an air-dried soil or rock.

Joint
A break of geological origin in the continuity of a body of rock occurring either singly, or more frequently in a set system, but not attended by a visible movement parallel the surface of discontinuity. (ISRM)

Kaolin
A variety of clay containing a high percentage of kaolinite.

Laminar flow (streamline flow) (viscous flow)
Flow in which the head loss is proportional to the first power of the velocity.

Landslide
The perceptible downward sliding or movement of a mass of earth or rock, or a mixture of both. (ISRM)

Loam
A mixture of sand, silt, or clay, or a combination of any of these, with organic matter (see humus).

Loss of circulation
The loss of drilling fluid into strata to the extent that circulation does not return to the surface.

Marl
Calcareous clay, usually containing from 35 to 65% calcium carbonate ($CaCO_3$).

Marsh
A wetland characterized by grassy surface mats which are frequently interspersed with open water or by a closed canopy of grasses, sedges, or other herbacious plants.

Mathematical model
The representation of a physical system by mathematical expressions form which the Behavior of the system can be deduced with known accuracy. (ISRM)

Matrix
In grouting, a material in which particles are embedded, that is, the cement paste in which the fine aggregate particles of a grout are embedded.

Monitoring well (observation well)
A special well drilled in a selected location of observing parameters such as liquid level or pressure changes or for collecting liquid samples.

Overburden
The loose soil, sand, silt, or clay that overlies bedrock.

Peat
A naturally occurring highly organic substance derived primarily from plant materials.

Percent fines
Amount, expressed as a percentage by weight, of a material in aggregate finer than a given sieve, usually the no. 200 (74 μm) sieve.

Perched ground water
Unconfined ground water separated from an underlying body of ground water by an unsaturated zone.

Perched water table
Ground water separated from an underlying body of ground water by unsaturated soil or rock. Usually located at a higher elevation that the ground-water table. (ISRM)

Percolation
The movement of gravitational water through soil.

Percussion drilling
A drilling technique that uses solids or hollow rods for cutting and crushing the rock by repeated blows. (ISRM)

Perforation
A slot or hole made in well casing to allow for communication of fluids between the well and the annular space.

pH, *pH* (D)
An index of the acidity or alkalinity of a soil in terms of the logarithm of the reciprocal of the hydrogen ion concentration.

Piezometric surface
The surface at which water will stand in a series of piezometers.

Plasticity
The property of a soil or rock which allows it to be deformed beyond the point of recovery without cracking or appreciable volume change.

Plastic limit, w_p, *PL*, P_w (D)
(*a*) The water content corresponding to an arbitary limit between the plastic and the semisolid states of consistency of a soil. (*b*) Water content at which a soil will just begin to crumble when rolled into a thread approximately 1/8 in. (3.2 mm) in diameter.

Plugging material
A material that has a hydraulic conductivity equal to or less than that of the geologic formation(s) to be sealed. Typical materials include portland cement and bentonite.

Porosity, *n* (D)

The ratio, usually expressed as a percentage, of: (1) the volume of voids of a given soil or rock mass, to (2) the total volume of the soil or rock mass. The ratio of the aggregate volume of voids or interstices in a rock or soil to its total volume. (ISRM)

Potentiometric surface

An imaginary surface representing the static head of ground water. The water table is a particular potentiometric surface.

Residual soil

Soil derived in place by weathering of the underlying material.

Specific yield

The ratio of the volume of water that the saturated rock or soil will yield by gravity to the volume of the rock or soil. In the field, specific yield is generally determined by tests of unconfined aquifers and represents the change that occurs in the volume of water in storage per unit area of unconfined aquifer as the result of a unit change in head. Such a change in storage is produced by the draining or filling or pore space and is, therefore, mainly dependent on particle size, rate of change of the water table, and time of drainage.

Storage coefficient

The volume of water an aquifer releases from or takes into storage per unit surface area of the aquifer per unit change in head. For a confined aquifer, the storage coefficient is equal to the product of the specific storage and aquifer thickness. For an unconfined aquifer, the storage coefficient is approximately equal to the specific yield.

Unconfined aquifer, *n*

An aquifer that has a water table.

Vadose zone

The hydrogeological region extending from the soil surface to the top of the principle water table; commonly referred to as the "unsaturated zone" or "zone of aeration".

References

American Geological Institute (1959) Glossary of geology and related sciences. Washington, DC

American Geological Institute (1996) Dictionary of mining and related terms, 2nd edn. (in corporation with the Society for Mining, Metallurgy, and Exploration Inc.)

American Geological Institute (1997) Dictionary of mining, mineral, and related terms, 2nd edn. Virginia, USA

ASTM (1996) Standard terminology relating to soil, rock, and contaminated fluids. D-653-96

DeWeist RJM (1965) Geohydrology. Wiley, New York

Mead DW (1919) Hydrology, the fundamental basis of hydraulic engineering, 1st edn. McGraw-Hill, New York

UNESCO (1990) Hydrology and water resources for sustainable development in a changing environment

Chapter 1

Introduction

1.1 Historical Aspect

In the 1970s "environment" became the password, and "silent spring" and "love canal" became the battle cry. It was thought that new protective legislation and money would solve the problem. Unfortunately, there were few scientists available with the proper training to implement the remedial programs financed by Federal and State funding. There resulted an explosion of environmental studies at universities similar to a new program in Alabama at the University of Alabama, the Environmental Institute for Waste Management Studies (EIWMS), which brought together a "think tank" of senior scientists from over the USA with experience in water resources to address the major problems facing local, State and Federal governments. These institutes and programs at universities became a part of the engineering and/or geology departments under the title of environmental studies.

During the 1940s through the 1970s, for example, at the United States Geological Survey (USGS) and the Geological Survey of Alabama and later through activities of newly formed consulting firms with geologists, engineers, chemists, biologists, and botanists, multidiscipline geoscience capabilities in environmental hydrogeology were developed to meet the nation's needs to solve a complex myriad of problems in the environment, many caused by the industrial revolution brought about by crash programs to produce materials for a world war configration. These programs incorporated a substantial number of professional women, a new element in the work force, who often were able to obtain far more information more easily during the fieldwork stages, particularly well inventories of hydrogeological work than the men.

This book summarizes many of these experiences during this early evolutionary period in the development of the field of environmental hydrogeology in the office as well as during field mapping, data collection, laboratory analyses, test drilling, and surface geophysical and downhole logging. The text includes guidelines for project objectives, purposes, and scope. It includes sample agreements, contracts, data sheets, and forms; itemization of examples of data needed and their compilation; samples of surface and subsurface mapping; types of graphics to illustrate methods of investigation; examples of equipment and supplies that can be used in ground-water investigations; and project scheduling and execution. It includes analysis and cost accounting for completion requirements. There are gaps, unintended, however, hopefully there will be few of these.

During the 1960s, the Alabama headquarters for the Ground-Water Division of the USGS was in an old barracks building behind Smith Hall on the University of Alabama campus. It housed an enthusiastic group of individuals carrying out cooperative ground-water investigations in cooperation with the State Geological Survey of Alabama. Each ground-water project had a component of geologic mapping, water, minerals, and resources evaluation. Methods employed air photography, sedimentation studies, heavy mineral analyses, spring inventories, water analyses, and quantitative testing for a series of cooperative financed reports for each county of the state. Students of the University of Alabama art department developed artwork for illustrations and the covers of reports. The resulting reports published by the Geological Survey of Alabama as bulletins, professional papers, atlases, and special reports converted older more somber traditional reports made more attractive and interesting to the general citizens, business people, and politicians. There resulted a ten-fold increase in sales, and the general public and industry became interested in geology and hydrogeology. This interest was reflected in a very rapid increase in funding and expansion of geoscience work throughout the state.

Within this manual there are a series of comic graphics by Fred Bunnel that illustrate phases of a ground-water investigation. These graphics are included for two purposes: they have been used to help organize and carry out ground-water studies by illustrating the need for proper scheduling and budgeting. They also add a bit of humor. They were developed by Bunnel to illustrate some of the problems that the hydrogeologist confronted in the field.

Finally, the manual recognizes that hydrogeology is a multidisciplinary science, including segments of engineering, physics, chemistry, biology, and botany. As our civilization demands more water for agriculture, commerce, resource development, and urban and domestic supplies, there will become a greater and greater need for knowledge about concepts and methods that will provide the needed information about water resources. It is imperative that we have imaginative, industrious, articulate scientists to convey results of their studies. It is imperative that these professionals also have a practical ability for they must work with well drillers, engineers, citizens, and politicians and be able to communicate with them. They must learn to install water level recorders, rain gages, barometers, recover a tape dropped in a well, repair a malfunctioning motor in a boat, build a monitor well house, or solve a myriad of other practical problems including handling an irate landowner. These are problems that occur everyday in the life of a hydrogeologist. For all of these reasons this manual has been prepared.

It is said that necessity is the mother of invention. This is the case on many occasions when in the early execution of work in district offices of the Ground Water Branch data and specialized equipment and new methods were required. During an early well inventory for example: when preliminary quantitative tests required pumping wells for either a specific capacity or a more detailed analysis. The Alabama district office, using surplus army equipment available after World War II, constructed a trailer mounted, portable, submersible pump. It consisted of an intake hose wound around a makeshift barrel reel. At the flip of a switch it could be lowered into the well and a preliminary pumping test carried out. Installation time was thirty minutes to begin pumping.

Another good example was the training of field geologists to standardize sample collection and description as a part of a geologic field-mapping. Standardization was needed for sand grain size analysis, shape angularity and a color guide. The staff developed a card with standard paint chip samples and with mechanical sand grain analysis equipment, i.e. sieve, shaker, and a meticulous selection of grains were mounted representative grains illustrating grain size, shape, and assortment. These ideas were subsequently developed commercially and sold. When satellite imagery became available, it was immediately applied to well inventory, geologic mapping, special karst studies, seepage loss, vegetation patterns, etc. Early satellite imagery was used in ground-water studies in a report by William J. Powell, district office in Alabama.

These are but a few examples of the need for developing a practical ability by hydrogeologists and engineers in early phases of ground-water work. There are many others, for example, "geobombs" that were developed by Petar Milanovic to study flow rates of ground water in karst. Herb Skibitzke in the USGS Water Resources Division office in Arizona, commandeered a large room, surplus equipment from the air corps and constructed an early 3-D solid-state hydrogeologic computer model. With a modern computer, we now can carry more computation power on our wrists; however, Skibitzke's computer for ground water quantitative studies was a first.

Some of the more imaginative staffs in the district offices developed laboratory and field techniques; for example, the paint chips became more scientific color charts for standardization of lithologic characteristics; sand grain samples became sand grain charts; later both were commercialized and used as a standard means of sample descriptions. Field chemistry laboratory kits were gradually updated to sophisticated laboratory analysis; and eventually, data recording evaluation and recovery evolved from computer capabilities. Portable pumping equipment was invented. Geophysical downhole logging became standard practice. Sequential air photography and satellite imagery became readily available and with these changes the character of geologic mapping, well inventory, pumping tests, geochemical studies, and report preparation change remarkably.

This book was born out of experience from work beginning in 1943 with the Ground-Water Branch (GWB) of the United States Geological Survey (USGS). This was an early period represented by studies of the geology, source, occurrence, and movement of ground water in the United States by the USGS. During this period of ground-water investigations, employees of the Water Resources Division Ground-Water Branch were under the supervision of Dr. O. E. Meinzer, who is considered the "Father of Ground Water" in the United States and one of the early ground-water scientists in the world. His Water Supply Papers 489 and 494 – *Ground-water resources of the United States* were used as a textbook for the early generations of hydrogeologist. In the 1940s, 1950s and 1960s, the Water Resources Division implemented ground-water schools at different district offices twice a year to provide training for its staff of geologists, engineers, and chemists. In these early training schools Gerry Parker was known as the "Professor of Hydrological Knowledge". These were reorganized into two-week courses at elementary and graduate level and eventually were developed into a formal program given at the USGS Denver Federal Center. Initially, there were ground-water notes and special publications supplied by leaders and professors that included C. V. Theis, Stan Lohman, C. E. Jacobs, Hilton Cooper, Bob Bennett, Bob Brown, John Ferris, Ivan Johnson, and others. Subsequently, the notes from these early lectures were formalized in two special Water Resources Series 1536–1544. The more formal training program at the Denver Federal Center with class and lecture rooms and laboratories was expanded to include a select group of international students as well as representatives from other Federal and State agencies.

It would be unacceptable to omit the fact that the early hydrogeologists learned and borrowed many techniques and equipment from the oil patch. Author LaMoreaux spent weeks with representatives of major oil companies in the field and laboratory learning methods applied to surface exploration, test drilling, sample description, well construction practices, and surface geophysical methods that could be applied to ground-water studies. This experience was combined with many days working with water well drillers, learning the practical aspects of development of ground water from wells. These methods were implemented in the Alabama district office of the USGS while working closely together with geologists of the Geologic Division – Watson Monroe, L. W. Stephenson, F. Stearnes McNeal, Hoye Eargle, Lewis Conant, and State Geologists Bob Vernon, Lyman Tolman, Furcron and others. This experience illustrated dramatically the importance of understanding the geology, structure, stratigraphy, and depositional environments as related to determining the recharge, source, and occurrence of ground water.

Hundreds of talks on geoscience and in particular water resources to elementary, high school, college, civic clubs, and social and political groups, plus teaching hydrogeology at the university for nearly 20 years, has illustrated the necessity for graphic communication about geology and hydrogeology. Clear, precise, and carefully prepared graphics were needed: photographs, columnar sections, cross sections, fence diagrams, and 3-D models. Information that the student, lay public, and politician can understand were required. There also became a need for adequate graphic material for courtroom testimony and a whole new field of communication has developed.

Finally, geoscientists are not generally known for their administrative capabilities. In the early history of ground-water studies, projects were often contracted with little planning of purpose, scope, objectives, cost, or accountability. These techniques for planning had to be borrowed from administrative procedures developed in business and commerce. Early hydrogeologic projects without proper planning and scheduling resulted in hundreds of reports overdue, over-budgeted, missed deadlines, and limited use. Many of these reports sit on shelves rarely used. Some of the basic techniques related to management are included in this manual.

1.2 Concept of Environmental Movement

In the 1970s the environmental movement resulted in State and Federal regulations to establish restrictions for location of hazardous waste and municipal, solid waste landfills. Regulations require owners/operators to demonstrate that the hydrogeology has been completely characterized at proposed landfills, and that locations for monitoring wells have been properly selected. Owners/operators are also required to demonstrate that engineering measures have been incorporated in the design of the municipal solid waste landfills, so that the site is not subject to destabilizing events, as a result of location in unstable areas.

The complexity of hydrogeologic systems, mandates thorough hydrogeologic studies to determine whether a specific site is, or can be rendered, suitable for a land disposal facility. Important components of hydrogeologic studies are field mapping of structural and stratigraphic units; interpretation of sequential aerial photographs; test drilling and geophysical analysis; fracture analysis; seasonal variation in water within aquifers; determination of control for recharge, and local base level; and evaluation of the effects of man's activities, such as pumping, dewatering and construction.

Consequently, for example the siting landfills involves collection of information necessary to answer a few questions, including those that follow: (1) Will the natural hydrogeologic system provide for isolation of wastes, so that disposal will not cause potential harm or the environment? (2) Is the site potentially susceptible to destabilizing events, such as collapse or subsidence, which will produce a sudden and catastrophic release of contaminants? (3) Will contaminants, if released from the facility, or rapidly and irrevocably transmitted to important aquifers or bodies of surface water? (4) Are the monitoring wells in proper positions to intercept ground-water flow from the facility? (5) If minor releases (leakage) occurs, will contaminants be readily detected in monitoring wells? (6) If a release is detected, is knowledge of the hydrogeologic setting sufficient to allow rapid and complete remediation of a release? (7) Is the hydrogeologic system sufficiently simple to allow interception and remediation of contaminated ground water?

Answers to the above questions depend upon the thoroughness of hydrogeologic studies, by which each site must be assessed and evaluated, prior to construction of a land-disposal facility. In the experience of the authors, most significant environmental problems, resulting from releases from land disposal facilities, occur from facilities for which preliminary, hydrogeologic studies were inadequate to answer the above questions. In many such cases, studies, designed to gain understanding of the hydrogeologic system, did not begin until after a release was detected. Compliance monitoring, "plume chasing" and remediation of ground water are costly processes, all of which can be avoided by assiduous care in selection of propre sites for land disposal.

In practice, the conceptual hydrgeologic model will be modified and improved as studies progress at the selected site. The final model should provide an accurate integration of the geologic, hydrogeologic, and geotechnical characteristics on the site that has been tested by installation of borings, piezometers and monitoring wells, measurement of water levels, and determination of the direction and rate of ground-water flow. The knowledge and understanding represented by the hydrogeologic model, and the data necessary to derive the model, serve to demonstrate suitability of the site and provide the basis for the final engineering design of the landfill.

1.3 Environmental Aspects of Karst Terrains

Some special attention is required for areas underlain by karst or areas underlain by limestone, dolomite, or gypsum or salt type of rocks, These regions constitute about 25% of the land surface of the world and are a source of abundant water supplies, minerals, and oil and gas.

Because of the complexity of karst systems, the concepts related to the movement and occurrence of ground water in karst, methods of exploration and development of water, safe engineering practices in construction of all kinds, and adequate environmental safety precautions cannot be based on one uniform set of rules.

The impact of karst terrains is great on humans and of substantial interest financially. This is documented by select references from recent publications. John Newton (1984) *Development of Sinkholes Resulting From Man's Activities in the Eastern United States* (19 states) reports that since 1950 there have been more than 6 500 sinkholes or related features that have occurred. Newton further states that the total cost of damage and associated protective measures resulting from these induced sinkholes is unknown, however, at 5 dam sites alone repair costs were in excess of U.S.$140 million. In a report of the U.S. National Research Council (1991) *Mitigating Losses from Land Subsidence in the United States* was reported that 6 states have individually sustained U.S.$10 million or more from damages from the cause.

Karst areas are dynamic as well as environmentally sensitive. The geologic structure, solubility of the rocks involved, and climatic conditions determine, to a great degree, how rapid changes can take place. Therefore, karst investigations must consider the dynamic nature of karst.

The USGS and some state surveys in the USA have special reports on karst areas. For example, the Illinois State Geological Survey has published *Karst Map Projects to Aid Ground Water Regulators* in their Summer 1994 issue of *GeoNews* (GeoNews 1994).

Other State Geological Surveys around the world have released similar materials.

In other countries, for example the GSI Ground-water Newsletter of the Geological Survey of Ireland presents guidelines for ground-water development, their problems and solutions in karst areas, preparing ground-water vulnerability maps and reports (Geological Survey of Ireland 1994). In England, reports relate *Research on Radon in British Limestone Caves and Mines, 1970–1990* (Gunn et al. 1991), and *Protecting Cumbria's Limestone Pavements* (Cumbria County Council 1993). In the western Ukraine, regulations are being developed for karst terrains, environmental changes, and human impact (1993).

Since the 1970s, the environmental movement in the USA has progressed from adolescence to maturity. The Resource Conservation and Recovery Act (RCRA) and Comprehensive Emergency Compensation and Liability Act (CERCLA) were enacted.

The range of environmental issues are diverse and encompass local, regional, and global problems involving pesticides and toxic substances, hazardous and solid waste disposal, water quality and quantity, urban and rural air pollution, resource use and management, soil erosion and stability, degradation of aquatic and terrestrial ecological systems, marine pollution, loss of biological diversity, and climate change.

Federal laws in the USA that protect ground-water statutes in the USA include:

- Clean Water Act
- Safe Drinking Water Act
- Clean Air Act
- Comprehensive Environmental Response, Compensation and Liability Act
- Federal Insecticide, Fungicide, and Rodenticide Act
- Toxic Substances Control Act
- Coastal Zone Management Act
- Endangered Species Act
- Magnuson Fisheries Act
- Resources Conservation Recovery Act
- Forest Land Management Planning Act
- Renewable Natural Resources Planning Act
- Disaster Relief Act
- Marine Plastics Pollution Research and Control Act
- Marine Protection, Research and Sanctuaries Act
- Ocean Dumping Ban Act
- Shore Protection Act
- National Earthquakes Hazards Reduction Act
- Energy Act
- Global Climate Change Protection Act
- Global Change Research Act
- Oil Pollution Act
- National Environmental Policy Act
- Weather Service Modernization Act
- Federal Emergency Management Act

References

Cumbria County Council (1993) Protecting Cumbria's limestone pavements, what Limestone Pavement Orders are, why and how they are made, and their legal effects. Planning Department of Cumbria County Council, Dixon Printing Co., Ltd., Kendal, Cumbria

Geological Survey of Ireland (1994) GSI Ground Water Newsletter. Dublin 25:22

Gunn J, Feltcher S, Prime D (1991) Research on radon in British limestone caves and mines (1970–1990). (BCRA) Science 18(2):63–66 (British Cave Research Assosciation, e-mail: j.gunn@hud.ac.uk)

Newton JG (1984) Natural and induced sinkhole development – eastern United States. International Association of Hydrological Sciences Proceedings, Third International Symposium on Land Subsidence, Venice, Italy

Part I

Surface Geological and Geophysical Field Studies

Chapter 2

Geology of Indurated Rocks, Unconsolidated Sedimentary Deposits and Karst Terrains

2.1 Introduction

Geology and hydrogeology are broad-based multidisciplines developed from many different sciences. The origin of hydrogeology required concepts from mathematics, physics, chemistry, hydrology, and geology. Meinzer (1942), who subdivided the science of hydrology, noted that hydrology could not be understood unless the basic concepts of geology, weathering, and soils were incorporated. Knowledge of rock type, stratigraphy, and structure is imperative as a basis of understanding ground water, recharge, storage, and discharge characteristics. An understanding of geology is a prerequisite to the understanding of the source, occurrence, availability, and movement of ground water.

State and Federal agencies have established regulations and guidelines as an effort to protect our environment and to aid environmental planning and development. The implementation of these regulations and guidelines must be based on a thorough understanding of the geology, hydrology, hydrogeology, and geochemistry of an area.

2.2 Rock Composition and Rock Types

2.2.1 Rock Composition

Rocks and soils are composed of aggregates of one or more minerals that constitute the largest part of the earth's crust. A mineral is composed of elements or groups of elements that unite in nature to form an inorganic crystalline substance with a definite internal structure. Each mineral has unique physical properties, which constitute the fundamental criteria for mineral identification.

The most abundant minerals include varieties of the silica group including quartz, the feldspar group, and the clay minerals. Another important group is represented by the carbonate minerals (e.g. calcite and dolomite). They are considered to be the key rock-forming minerals and may be summarized as follows.

2.2.1.1 *The Feldspar Group*

The feldspars represent the most abundant group of minerals in the earth's crust. They provide a basic constituent in many igneous, sedimentary and metamorphic rocks. There are two sub-groups of feldspars: potash feldspars ($KAlSi_3O_8$), and the plagioclase feldspars, which include both sodium feldspars or albite ($NaAlSi_3O_8$), and calcium feldspars or anorthite ($CaAl_2Si_2O_8$). Plagioclase feldspars are represented by a complete solid solution between the end members: albite ($NaAlSi_3O_8$) and anorthite ($CaAl_2Si_2O_8$). The plagioclase feldspars can be divided into six members according to the percent of sodium and calcium in each member and can be differentiated by means of a petrographic microscope, X-ray diffraction techniques, or chemical analysis.

Potash feldspars are predominant in granites and the associated rocks. They comprise two principal members, orthoclase and microcline, which can be differentiated by crystal structure and color. Orthoclase is usually white or light pink. Microcline is characteristically darker pink or green and occurs in coarse-grained igneous dykes, veins and some metamorphic rocks. Plagioclase is dominant in basalts and related rocks but is also present in acidic and intermediate igneous rocks. Unlike quartz, the feldspars readily decompose to form clay minerals.

2.2.1.2 *The Silica Group*

The silica group (quartz) includes many minerals that are composed of silicon and oxygen (SiO_2). Some varieties of quartz form at high temperatures and develop crystals that differ from those that are formed at lower temperature. Crystalline quartz is characterized by a high hardness (7 on Mohs hardness scale) and by conchoidal fracture. However, some cryptocrystalline varieties have hardnesses as low as 5 (e.g. unweathered chert, chalcedony, etc.).

Quartz comprises 10–25% of granite and its associated rock types. It is chemically very stable, and resists mechanical breakdown. It is present in sandstone, siltstone and in many other clastic sedimentary rocks. It often forms well-developed hexagonal crystals. Pure quartz is colorless to white. Impurities lead to many hues. Two main groups of quartz are known as crystalline and cryptocrystalline.

1. *Crystalline quartz* can be distinguished on the basis of composition, hardness, and Crystal forms as follows: *Milky quartz* – milky white, translucent to nearly opaque; *Rose quartz* – pink to red-rose, transparent to translucent; *Smoky quartz* – light to dark gray, transparent to translucent; and pure quartz crystals are typically euhedral, generally transparent and colorless.
2. *Cryptocrystalline quartz* can sometimes be distinguished under high magnification. Their varieties are known as follows: (1) *Chalcedony* may appear to be fibrous under the microscope. However, in a hand specimen it is translucent and has a waxy luster. It has a variety of colors; its color-banding gives rise to *agate and onyx*. The banding of agate is due to successive periods of deposition and may alternate with layers of opal. *Onyx* is a banded type of chalcedony in which the bands are parallel and straight rather than conforming to the walls of the cavity as in the agate. (2) *Granular cryptocrystalline quartz* exhibits a granular appearance under the microscope although it is similar to chalcedony in hand specimen. Three types are known: flint, which resembles chalcedony but is dull and often dark colored; chert may precipitate directly from sea water in areas where volcanism releases abundant silica. Most chert originates from silica shells of organisms. It is similar to flint but lighter in color. Flint and chert are common constituents in carbonate rocks and occur as lenses, thin beds, fracture fillings, and as elongate nodules parallel to the bedding. Jasper is a variety of chert that is red or brown in color due to hematite inclusions.
3. *Amorphous silica* is an uncrystallized type of silica (e.g. opal). It contains variable amounts of water (usually 3 to 10%; $SiO_2 \cdot nH_2O$). It is present in a wide variety of environments such as hot spring deposits, fossil shells and chert. It is distinguished by its less waxy and more glassy luster than chalcedony or chert.

2.2.1.3 *The Carbonate Minerals – Calcite and Dolomite*

1. The mineral calcite: Calcite ($CaCO_3$) is mainly characterized by its perfect rhombohedral cleavage, reaction with dilute hydrochloric acid and by its solubility. Both surface and ground waters are able to dissolve large quantities of this mineral in geologic time as indicated by the great number of caves and solution valleys in some limestone terrains.

   Crystalline calcite has well developed clear crystals referred to as "spar" and may be present as linings in voids, cavities, fractures, and veins. Calcite is also present in sedimentary rocks such as limestone and its derivatives.

   Aragonite, which is a polymorph of calcite commonly developed in warm shallow seas, as linings in shells or in caverns where it changes to calcite with time (Hamblin and Howard 1965).
2. The mineral dolomite: Dolomite, $CaMg(CO_3)$, is the main constituent of dolostone, which is generally formed by replacement of calcite, $CaCO_3$, presumably soon after burial. The reduction in volume in this replacement may produce irregular voids and may obliterate fossils. Dolomite is pink, colorless, white, or dark gray of rhombohedral cleavage and reacts, only if powdered, with dilute hydrochloric acid.

   Calcite and dolomite are two common constituents of carbonate rocks and can be metamorphosed into marble by heat and pressure forming a hard compact rock.

2.2.2 Rock Types

Rocks are classified into three major groups: igneous, sedimentary, and metamorphic: (*a*) Igneous rocks, mainly form the original crust of the earth and solidify from magma or lava that is composed of silicates, oxides, water, gases, and minor sulfides. (*b*) Sedimentary rocks are composed of rock fragments and chemical precipitates, the components of which are derived by weathering and erosion of some former rock mass and deposited in sedimentary basins, such as marshes, lakes and seas, or by the accumulation of organic materials. Organic remains, such as coral reefs, shells of marine invertebrates and vegetation, act also as a source of sediment, e.g. coal and certain limestones composed of organic remains. (*c*) Metamorphic rocks are those that are transformed by heat, pressure, and hydrothermal solution to an extent that their original structures such as bedding are largely destroyed and the mineralogy is modified to form new minerals that are stable in the higher temperature and pressure environment.

Soils constitute the loose residual or transported mantle on the surface of the earth and may be chemically defined as multi-component and biogeochemical systems, see Sec. 2.3.2.

2.2.2.1 *Igneous Rocks*

Texture and mode of occurrence: Igneous rocks occur in two ways, either as intrusive bodies or as extrusive rocks.

The ultimate source of igneous magma is probably deep in the crust or in the upper part of the mantle.

Intrusive igneous rocks are concordant if the contacts of the intrusive body are more or less parallel to the layering of the intruded rocks, and discordant if the intrusive body cuts across the older rocks. The largest discordant bodies are called batholiths (e.g. mountain ranges of the Sierra Nevada in California, USA). Smaller bodies of coarse-grained igneous rocks are termed stocks or plutons. Dikes are tabular, discordant intrusive bodies and range in thickness from a few inches to several thousand feet. Sills and laccoliths are concordant intrusive bodies intruded between sedimentary beds.

The *extrusive rocks* result from lava flows and pyroclastic deposits and sometimes from other types of volcanic activity.

The principle elements in magma are oxygen, silica, aluminum, iron, calcium, sodium, potassium and magnesium. These elements combine to form feldspars, pyroxenes, amphibole, quartz, mica and other minor minerals. Magmas, rich in iron, magnesium and calcium (basic igneous rocks), produce greater amounts of pyroxene, amphibole and calcium plagioclase and are usually dark in color because of the abundant ferromagnesium minerals. Magmas, rich in silica, (acidic or siliceous igneous rocks), tend to produce more quartz, orthoclase and sodium feldspars and generally form light colored rocks. Therefore, the mineral composition of igneous rocks ca be identified by its color.

Many igneous rocks are a mixture of coarse and fine crystals, and its texture is called porphyritic. Texture in igneous rocks refers to the size, shape and arrangement of mineral grains. It is largely controlled by rate of cooling, composition and temperature of the magma. Textures are subdivided into different types as follows: (1) fragmental texture that consists of broken and angular pyroclastic rocks and range from large blocks to fine dust; (2) glassy texture (cryptocrystalline) that is similar to ordinary glass and results from rapid chilling of lava; (3) aphanic texture that cannot be distinguished without the aid of a microscope (microcrystalline); and (4) phaneritic texture (crystalline) that includes large crystals plainly visible to the naked eye.

All igneous rocks may be classified on the basis of texture, which reflects the history of cooling, and mineral composition, which reflects the nature of the magma. Igneous rocks of different composition but similar texture (and vice versa) can be grouped. Figures 2.1a and 2.1b are charts showing the classification of igneous rocks where composition is indicated vertically, and texture is indicated horizontally (Foster 1979; Tennissen 1983). The upper part of Fig. 2.1a shows the range in mineral composition of each rock type.

2.2.2.2 *Sedimentary Rocks*

Sedimentary rocks are derived from debris of other rocks and accumulate at or near the earth's surface under normal temperatures and pressure. There are four successive processes involved in their genesis: (1) physical and chemical weathering; (2) transportation of the weathered products; (3) deposition of the material in a sedimentary basin; and (4) compaction and cementation of the sediment into solid rock (Hamblin and Howard 1965).

Classification of Sedimentary Rocks

Sedimentary rocks can be classified according to their genesis, e.g. marine, lacustrine (lake deposited), glacial, eolian (wind deposited), fluvial (river deposited), etc. They can also be classified by their mode of origin as clastic (transported and deposited by mechanical agents) or as non-clastic (chemical and organic precipitate) as follows (Foster 1979; Pettijohn 1975; Gilluly 1959):

(a) Clastic Rocks

Clastic rocks or fragments of rock debris, are defined according to texture and composition. Texture includes grain size, roundness, sorting, and cementation (Hamblin and Howard 1965, Table 2.1a; Tennissen 1983, Table 2.1b). *Roundness* is a measure of angularity of the grains that range from angular to well rounded. Both grain size and roundness are a rough measure of distance over which the particles have been transported. *Sorting*, on the other hand, refers to the distribution of the various sizes of particles (see Chap. 5). *Sorting* gives an indication of the transporting medium and environment of deposition. Ice and mudflows do not sort materials. Wind and moving water are the best sorting agents giving rise to sand dunes, beaches, and bars.

Conglomerates and breccias: A conglomerate or its unconsolidated equivalent may be mainly sand sized with an abundance of coarse grains of rounded gravels, pebbles and cobbles exceeding two millimeters in diameter (see Chap. 5). An accumulation of fragments exhibiting high angularity is commonly referred to as "breccia". Conglomerates and breccias have a wide range in color, depending on the type of matrix, the composition of the fragments, and the degree of weathering. The thickness of conglomerates and breccias ranges from inches to hundreds of feet. These rocks frequently represent the basal beds of many formations and therefore may serve as criteria for recognizing unconformable relationships.

Sandstones: Sands and sandstones represent the medium-grained clastic sediments. They are composed primarily of quartz grains of various rocks and miner-

Fig. 2.1a.
Chart showing the classification of the igneous rocks. Composition is indicated vertically, and texture is indicated horizontally. The upper part of the chart shows the range in mineral composition of each rock type (after Foster 1979, adapted by permission of Charles Merril Publishing Co., Columbus, OH)

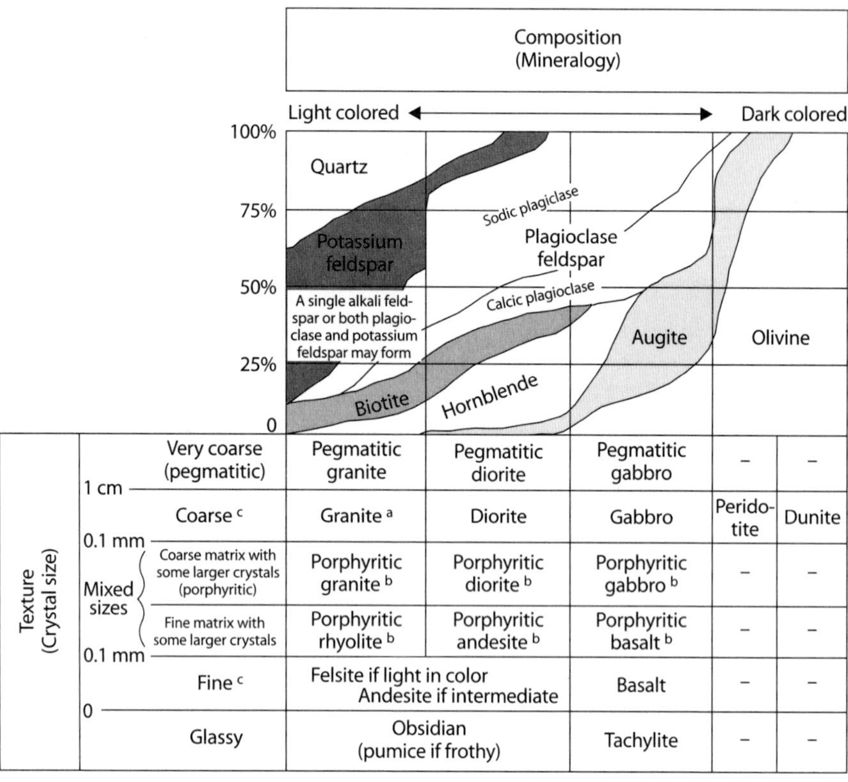
Composition
(Mineralogy)
Light colored
Dark colored
100%
75%
50%
25%
0
Quartz
Potassium feldspar
A single alkali feldspar or both plagioclase and potassium feldspar may form
Sodic plagioclase
Plagioclase feldspar
Calcic plagioclase
Biotite
Hornblende
Augite
Olivine
Texture (Crystal size)
1 cm
0.1 mm
Mixed sizes
0.1 mm
0
Very coarse (pegmatitic)
Pegmatitic granite
Pegmatitic diorite
Pegmatitic gabbro
Coarse [c]
Granite [a]
Diorite
Gabbro
Peridotite
Dunite
Coarse matrix with some larger crystals (porphyritic)
Porphyritic granite [b]
Porphyritic diorite [b]
Porphyritic gabbro [b]
Fine matrix with some larger crystals
Porphyritic rhyolite [b]
Porphyritic andesite [b]
Porphyritic basalt [b]
Fine [c]
Felsite if light in color
Andesite if intermediate
Basalt
Glassy
Obsidian
(pumice if frothy)
Tachylite

Minor accessory minerals are omitted.

[a] Granite is used in the widest sense. Several names are common in use, depending on the type of feldspar.

[b] Modifier porphyritic is generally omitted unless crystals are very prominent.

[c] Coarse and fine are used in the sense that phaneritic aphanitic are used in petrography.

als ranging from 0.063 to 2.0 mm in diameter. Sandstones are classified according to the degree of sorting and composition. They may be composed almost entirely of quartz sand and may also be associated with accessory components of heavy minerals such as pyrite, hornblende, pyroxenes, olivine, magnetite, garnet, tourmaline, zircon, mica, staurolite and glauconite.

The term *arenite* is used for relatively well-sorted sandstones; and the *wacke* is used for more poorly-sorted sandstones. *Graywacke* is known as strongly indurated dark-colored wacke. It is fine to coarse grained with marked graded bedding and is usually marine in origin. It is composed of very angular grains, mainly quartz, feldspar and rock fragments, which are set in a "clay" matrix that may be converted on low-grade metamorphism to a matrix of chlorite and sericite. An *orthoquartzite* is a sedimentary quartzite in which pore spaces of the sandstone have been filled with quartz without the impress of metamorphism. An *arkose* or arkosic sandstone, is usually coarse grained, light in color (pink or light gray), cross bedded, and contains 25% or more of feldspar derived from the disintegration of acidic igneous rock of granitoid texture. Arkoses are typically deposited in intracratonic basins, whereas graywackes accumulate dominantly within geosynclines (LeRoy 1950; Pettijohn 1975).

Siltstones: the indurated equivalent of silts, are fine-grained clastics and contain particles ranging in size from 0.063 to 0.004 mm. These rocks vary considerably in color and structure. They frequently contain organic matter and heavy minerals as accessories. They may also contain significant amounts of sand and be classified as sandy siltstones.

Shale and mudstone constitute the finest clastic materials and their particle sizes are below 0.004 mm. The primary constituents of these rocks are represented by the complex clay minerals where silica is the dominant element and is present either as free silica (quartz) or in the form of silicates such as clay minerals that include kaolinite, montmorillonite and illite. Other elements include iron, manganese, calcium, etc. Alumina is next in importance to silica.

Hybrid types of argillaceous rocks include marlstones (50–80% carbonate), clay ironstones (rich in siderite) and black shale (rich in organic matter). Important accessory minerals in the laminated shales and the massive thick layers of mudstones include mica, glauconite, pyrite, silt and sand. Cementing materials may be a siliceous, ferruginous, calcareous, or carbonaceous.

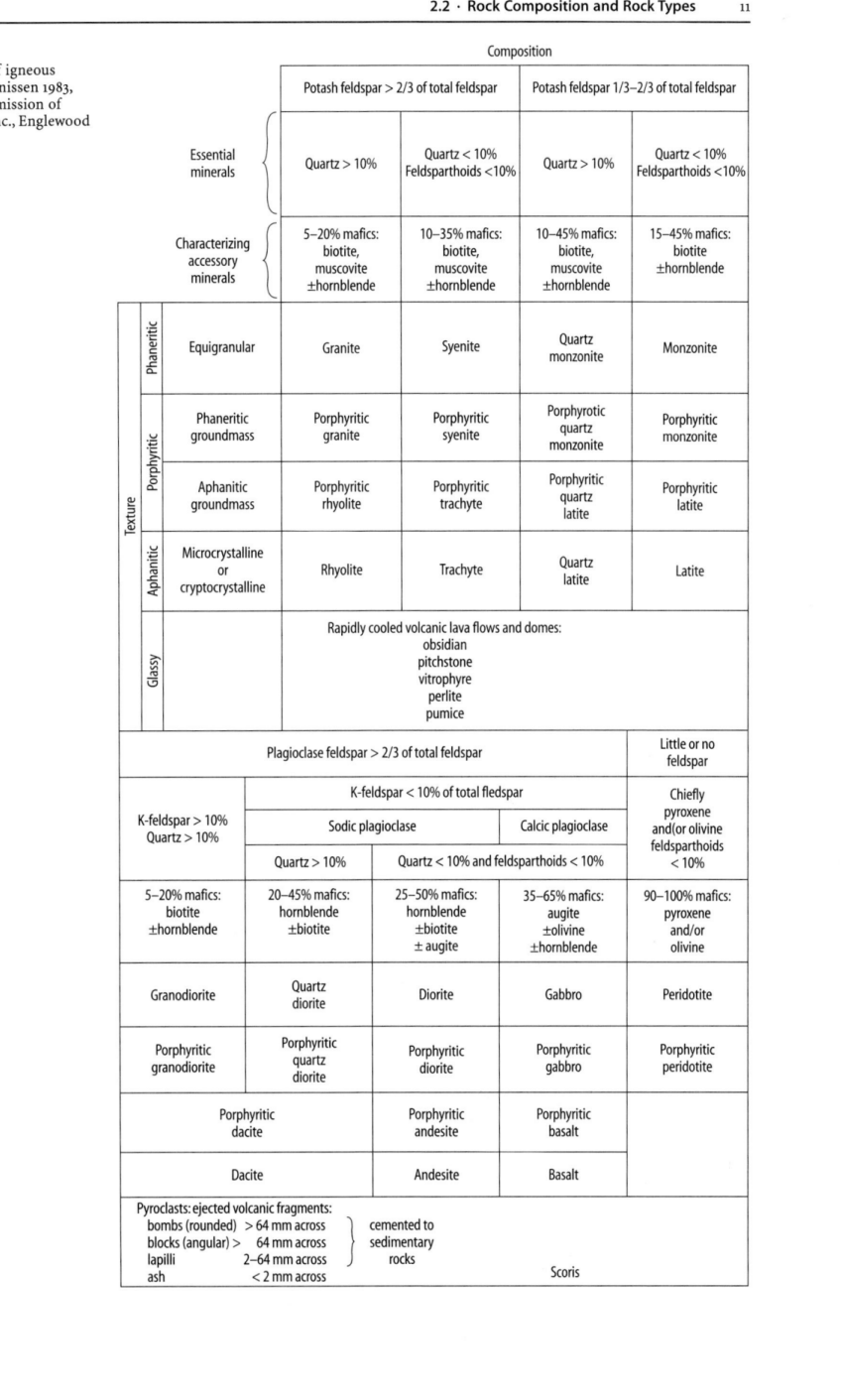

Fig. 2.1b.
Classification of igneous rocks (after Tennissen 1983, adapted by permission of Prentice Hall, Inc., Englewood Cliffs, NJ)

Composition

Texture			Potash feldspar > 2/3 of total feldspar		Potash feldspar 1/3–2/3 of total feldspar	
		Essential minerals	Quartz > 10%	Quartz < 10% Feldsparthoids <10%	Quartz > 10%	Quartz < 10% Feldsparthoids <10%
		Characterizing accessory minerals	5–20% mafics: biotite, muscovite ±hornblende	10–35% mafics: biotite, muscovite ±hornblende	10–45% mafics: biotite, muscovite ±hornblende	15–45% mafics: biotite ±hornblende
Texture	Phaneritic	Equigranular	Granite	Syenite	Quartz monzonite	Monzonite
	Porphyritic	Phaneritic groundmass	Porphyritic granite	Porphyritic syenite	Porphyrotic quartz monzonite	Porphyritic monzonite
	Porphyritic	Aphanitic groundmass	Porphyritic rhyolite	Porphyritic trachyte	Porphyritic quartz latite	Porphyritic latite
	Aphanitic	Microcrystalline or cryptocrystalline	Rhyolite	Trachyte	Quartz latite	Latite
	Glassy		Rapidly cooled volcanic lava flows and domes: obsidian, pitchstone, vitrophyre, perlite, pumice			

Plagioclase feldspar > 2/3 of total feldspar				Little or no feldspar
K-feldspar > 10% Quartz > 10%	K-feldspar < 10% of total fledspar			Chiefly pyroxene and(or olivine feldsparthoids < 10%
	Sodic plagioclase		Calcic plagioclase	
	Quartz > 10%	Quartz < 10% and feldsparthoids < 10%		
5–20% mafics: biotite ±hornblende	20–45% mafics: hornblende ±biotite	25–50% mafics: hornblende ±biotite ± augite	35–65% mafics: augite ±olivine ±hornblende	90–100% mafics: pyroxene and/or olivine
Granodiorite	Quartz diorite	Diorite	Gabbro	Peridotite
Porphyritic granodiorite	Porphyritic quartz diorite	Porphyritic diorite	Porphyritic gabbro	Porphyritic peridotite
Porphyritic dacite		Porphyritic andesite	Porphyritic basalt	
Dacite		Andesite	Basalt	
Pyroclasts: ejected volcanic fragments: bombs (rounded) > 64 mm across blocks (angular) > 64 mm across lapilli 2–64 mm across ash < 2 mm across	} cemented to sedimentary rocks		Scoris	

Table 2.1a. Classification of clastic sedimentary rocks (after Hamblin and Howard 1965, adapted by permission of Education, Inc., Upper Saddle River, NJ)

Grain size	Composition	Rock name
Coarse grained (over 2 mm in diameter)	Any rock fragments; quartz and chert predominant	Conglomerate
	Angular fragments	Breccia
Medium grained (1/16 to 2 mm in diameter)	Quartz with minor impurities	Quartz Sandstone
	Quartz with considerable clay (poorly sorted)	Graywacke
	Quartz with 25% or more feldspar	Arkose
Fine grained (less than 1/16 mm in diameter)	Quartz with mica and clay	Shale

Table 2.1.b Classification of sedimentary rocks (after Tennissen 1983, adapted by permission of Prentice Hall, Inc., Englewood Cliffs, NJ)

	Allochthonous				Autochthonous		
	Terrigenous			Pyroclastic	Residual	Organic	Chemical
	Coarse-grained	Medium-grained	Fine-grained	<4 mm and >4 mm			
Composition	Chiefly one constituent: Quartz Chert Quartzite Shale Limestone	Chiefly quartz, but also feldspar and rock chips	Chiefly clay minerals or clay-size material	Volcanic ejecta: Ash Lapilli Bombs Blocks	Organic matter Quartz Clay minerals Fe and Al oxides Amorphous silica Ca, Na, Mg compounds	Carbon: Humus and/or sapropel	Fe minerals Mn minerals PO_4 minerals Halite, gypsum, anhydrite Silica Calcite Dolomite
Rocks	Conglomerate Breccia	Sandstones: Quartz-rich sandstone Arkose Graywacke	Shale Mudstone Siltstone Carbonaceous shale	Tuff Volcanic breccia Agglomerate	Soils	Peat Lignite Coal	Ironstone Mn deposits Phosphorite Evaporites Chert
						Limestone	
							Dolostone

(b) Non-Clastic Rocks

The non-clastic rocks are formed by chemical precipitation, biological precipitation, and accumulation of organic material (Hamblin and Howard 1965; Table 2.2).

Carbonate rocks: Carbonate rocks are very common sedimentary rocks, composed predominantly of calcite and/or dolomite and constitute 10% of the exposed stratigraphic record (Pettijohn 1975; Fig. 2.2). These rocks have important economic significance because of their composition and association with energy and mineral deposits; they are used in the manufacture of cement, building stones, as concrete aggregate, as road metal, and if pulverized, as fertilizers and an agricultural dressing. They can be porous and permeable and act as reservoirs for ground water and petroleum. Carbonate rocks contain 20% of the hydrocarbons in North America and about 50% of that of the world.

Limestone is a general term for the class of rocks in which the carbonate fraction exceeds the non-carbonate constituents. It is predominantly composed of calcite or aragonite, generally of biologic origin and may contain fossils. When a rock is mainly composed of fossils or fossil fragments, it is called coquina. An abundance of organic remains may occur in carbonate rocks such as algae, mollusks, corals, echinoids, bryozoa, ostracods and foraminifera.

Limestones are polygenetic and a diverse group of rocks. Some are fragmental and the fragments have been mechanically transported, and deposited. Limestones exhibit the same textures and structures of sedimentary rock and display current bedding; or are chemical or biochemical precipitates, formed in place.

The color of carbonate rocks varies from white to black. The grain size ranges from fine to coarse. Insoluble constituents include clay, quartz, pyrite, and silicified fragments.

Table 2.2. Classification of chemical precipitate rocks (after Hamblin and Howard 1965, adapted by permission of Education, Inc., Upper Saddle River, NJ)

Chemical composition	Texture or other properties	Rock name
Calcite ($CaCO_3$)	Medium to coarse crystalline	Crystalline limestone
	Microcrystalline, dense breaks with a conchoidal fracture	Lithographic limestone
	Contains abundant fossils	Fossiliferous limestone
	Fossils and fossil fragments loosely cemented together	Coquina
	Aggregates of small concentric spheres called "oolites"	Oolitic limestone
	Bonded cave deposits	Travertine
	Shells of microscopic organisms, soft	Chalk
	Porous deposits accumulated around springs and streams	Tufa
Dolomite ($CaMg(CO_3)_2$)	Similar to crystalline limestone	Dolostone
Chalcedony (SiO_2)	Cryptocrystalline, dense	Chert, flint agate
Halite (NaCl)	Fine to coarse crystalline	Rock salt
Gypsum ($CaSO_4$)	Fine to coarse crystalline	Rock gypsum

Chalk is soft, white limestone formed by the accumulation of shells of microscopic animals. It has a similar chemical composition as limestone.

Dolostone is a term proposed for the sedimentary rock dolomite, in order to avoid confusion with the mineral of the same name.

Chemical decomposition of limestone is a naturally alkaline geochemical medium but it may be neutralized by acidic waters. The quantification of chemical decomposition of limestones carried by acid precipitation depends on many complicated factors, including the amount of precipitation and its pH, temperature, global radiation, effective catalysts, buffer capacity of the soil, soil moisture, and geological features of the saturated zone. The hydrogen ion concentration is greatly affected by climatic and meteoric influences in space and time.

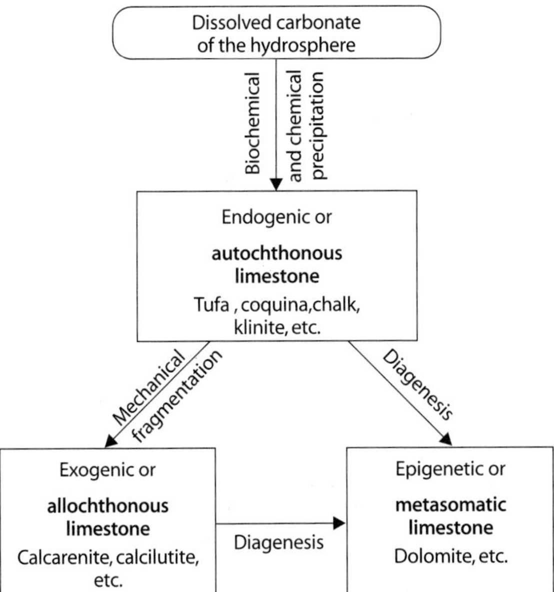
Dissolved carbonate of the hydrosphere
Biochemical and chemical precipitation
Endogenic or
autochthonous limestone
Tufa, coquina, chalk, klinite, etc.
Mechanical fragmentation
Diagenesis
Exogenic or
allochthonous limestone
Calcarenite, calcilutite, etc.
Diagenesis
Epigenetic or
metasomatic limestone
Dolomite, etc.

Fig. 2.2. Genetic classification of limestones (after Pettijohn 1975, adapted by permission of Johns Hopkins Univ., Dept. of Earth and Planetary Sciences, Baltimore, MD)

Chemical decomposition of limestone includes a large number of chemical reactions between limestone and chemical reagents liberated in various types of soil, e.g. the organic acids produced by the aerobic decay of vegetal and animal substances. The inorganic acids (carbonic, sulfuric and nitric acids) and salts resulting from the biochemical or inorganic processes of weathering in the soil also play an important role in limestone corrosion. Carbonic acid is probably the most important acid that results directly from the atmosphere (e.g. $CO_2 + H_2O \leftrightarrow H_2CO_3$) and/or formed in the root zone of soils during photogenesis. Other acids are of minor importance and may exist in the soil from a number of processes; for instance, sulfuric acid is most often a product of oxidation (inorganic or biochemical – brought about by sulfuric bacteria) of sulfides (e.g. pyrites) and hydrogen sulfide (H_2S); nitric acid in the soil originates mostly from ammonia that mainly results from organic decay. Ammonia is oxidized to acids, which are corrosive to limestone by bacteria living in the soil.

Neither nitrous nor nitric acid remains free for long in the soil. They react more or less immediately with the cations of the soil or the limestone to form nitrites or nitrates.

In rare occurrence, the hard siderite (iron carbonate) crust forming at the interface of soil and limestone cannot retard the action of iron sulfate upon the deeper limestone horizons, because it is soon dissolved by the soil solution rich in carbonic acid in the presence of water and oxygen. The ferrous carbonate is then oxidized to ferric oxide, which accumulates in the soil either as dark red hematite (Fe_2O_3) or as brown goethite ($FeO(OH)$, or sometimes expressed as $HFeO_2$) (Foster 1979; Pettijohn 1975; Gilluly 1959).

A complete image of the chemical decomposition of limestone requires the consideration of various ions of the soil solution that influence the dynamism of dissolution.

Evaporites: Evaporites precipitate from the evaporation of saline solutions. They are represented by sulfates (anhydrite, gypsum), and chlorides (mainly halite). Anhydrite generally ranges in color from white to dark gray and assumes a fine to coarse crystallinity. Gypsum frequently occurs in argillaceous strata as transparent crystals of selenite. Salt beds are normally dry and impervious to water. Because of plasticity of salt, fractures seal or close rapidly. Salt beds flow upward under sufficient load of sediments due to the contrast in density and form domes beneath the surface or form piercing diapirs when penetrating the younger beds under a continuous supply of salt or where there are pressure contrasts. The compressive strength is proportional to the confining pressure yet salt rock flows upward when the compressive strength is less than the weakest confining pressure of the overlain beds (LeRoy 1950).

Salt bodies have been of great interest to geologists due mostly to their role in the entrapment of petroleum. However, they may generally affect the quality of surrounding ground water, and controversially, the surrounding ground water greatly affects the diagenesis and dissolution of the salt (Assaad 1981).

Salt movements and salt domes: The salt's average density is 2.19 and remains constant with depth; controversy, the overburden sediments get compacted and density increases from under 2.0 for freshly deposited shale to 2.6 for shale buried under several thousands of meters. As thickness increases, the salt turns from elastic to plastic in an unstable status, tending to rise upward if the dip of the formation is at least one degree, causing the first slide (Assaad 1972). It was estimated that for a normal rock salt, the plasticity threshold might be approximately 20 kg cm^{-2} which correspond to 500 m thick of overburden. The development of salt domes usually accompanied by shearing cracks or fissures that were associated with primary peripheral sinks and by extrusion of salt through them, secondary peripheral sinks occurred and might be very promising locations for oil traps.

It is worth mentioning that the tectonic outline of areas where there are thick salt deposits, should be carefully studied to define the different types of salt structures buried deep underneath the ground for the ultimate storage or disposal of high level solidified radioactive waste as salt formations are dry, mainly impervious to water, and not associated directly with useable sources of ground-water wastes. Large spaces can be mined out and even at depths of 1 000 feet (305 m), and two thirds of the salt can be removed with only slight deformation of the support pillars and firm lining could be followed.

Carbonaceous rocks: Carbonaceous rocks are represented by three types of residue: humus, peat, and sapropel. Humus is produced within the upper part of the soil phase; peat originates from partial decay of plant material under fresh-water swamp conditions; and sapropel (high in fatty and protein substances) results from concentration of complex organic compounds, which accumulate on the bottoms of lakes, lagoons, and quiet-water embayments (LeRoy 1950).

Coal is a readily combustible rock containing more than 50% by weight and more than 70% by volume of carbonaceous material including inherent moisture, formed from compaction and induration of variously altered plant remains similar to those in peat (Jackson 1997).

(c) Miscellaneous Rock Types

Ferruginous rocks: The ferruginous sediments may be classified as carbonates (siderite), iron silicates (glauconite), ferric oxides and hydroxides (hematite, limonite) and sulfides (pyrite, marcasite).

Siderite is commonly associated with argillaceous cherty beds, concretions and lentilles (isolated mass of rock containing fossils of a fauna older than strata in which it occurs). Glauconite, which varies in color from pale green to greenish-black, constitutes an important silicate in many types of marginal marine or brackish beds (shales, sandstones, and limestones). Limonite and hematite are common oxide matrix of sedimentary clastics and occur as minor inclusions or in some cases as oolites. Pyrite and marcasite occur in some types of sedimentary rocks in varying percentages and may be found as nodules, crystal aggregates, and minor inclusions.

Manganiferous rocks: Manganese occurs in minor amounts in sedimentary rocks when the oxides, hydroxides and carbonates are the chief mineral constituents.

Phosphatic rocks: Phosphatic-bearing rocks are commonly referred to as phosphorites. Phosphatic materials are found primarily in shales and limestones. They may be of primary or secondary origin or both. Color of phosphates varies from brown to black, but it may assume lighter hues by leaching. The phosphatic material may be bedded or may occur as concentrically banded oolites and nodules. The origin of some phosphate deposits is often related to animal remains (bones and fecal remains).

Also, many phosphatic rocks originate in shelf zones as chemical precipitates from cool deep sea water, which rises and warms over the shelf (LeRoy 1950).

Structures of Sedimentary Rocks

A number of structures are unique to sedimentary rocks and are important in identifying features of an outcrop. Bedding or stratification is the property most characteristic of sedimentary rocks. It is characterized by four basic types of layers as follows: (*a*) In horizontal layers, the oldest is deposited at the bottom whereas the youngest is at the top of the bed sequence. Cross bedding indicates the direction in which the depositing currents were moving (Foster 1979; Fig. 2.3). (*b*) Graded bedding is produced when a mixture of sediments is suddenly deposited into a sedimentary basin where the large fragments sink faster than the small ones. (*c*) Ripple-marks suggest shallow water with some current action but are also known in deep water. (*d*) Mudcracks on bedding planes record periodic drying and indicate shallow water. Ripple-marks, mudcracks, and rain imprints preserved in sediment rocks, are important indicators of the environments of the past (Gilluly 1959).

2.2.2.3 *Metamorphic Rocks*

Metamorphic rocks are rocks of any type or composition that have been changed in either mineral composition or texture by any of the following: heat and pressure due to deep burial; directed pressure (stress) that fold the more or less plastic rocks and may cause deformation of these rocks, flattened or stretched pebbles or fossils; shear results when the rocks are broken and moved by directed pressure; or by chemical action of solutions where both temperature and pressure are high enough to cause a metamorphic reaction. Metamorphism leads to the deformation and recrystallization of minerals, chemical recombination, and the growth of new minerals. Certain mineral assemblages are indicative of various degrees of metamorphism e.g. chlorite, talc, and the micas form by mild metamorphism whereas garnet and hornblende develop under extremely high temperature and pressure.

Types of Metamorphism

Metamorphic rocks can be subdivided into three genetic groups, although there is gradation among them, as follows: (1) *thermal or contact metamorphic rocks* found at the margins of intrusive igneous bodies such as batholiths; (2) *dynamic metamorphic rocks* resulted from breaking and grinding; and (3) *regional metamorphic rocks* occupy large areas, deep in the crust except uplifted by tectonic movement and revealed by erosion on the surface. The rocks are generally recrystallized under stress and cause new minerals to grow in preferred orientation and may be foliated, e.g. gneiss and schist.

Classification and Identification of Metamorphic Rocks

Metamorphic rocks can be divided into two textural groups: (1) foliated – having a directional or layered aspect and (2) non-foliated-homogenous or massive rocks.

Foliated rocks are more common and may be the product of regional metamorphism. Foliation is one of the more important characteristics of dynamo-thermal metamorphism where directed stresses tend to develop various types of planar elements:

- *Schistosity* develop in intense metamorphism where mica, talc and chlorite minerals grow into visible crystals and develop this type of foliation. In origin, these minerals grow in a metamorphic environment, attain a fine-grained texture and have a foliation type of cleavage known as *slaty cleavage.*
- *Gneissic foliation* due to high-grade metamorphism, develops alternating layers of light and dark minerals that are completely rearranged.

Orthoclase and quartz are the most common light colored minerals and usually alternate with dark layers composed of hornblende and biotite.

Non-foliated-homogenous rocks are of two types: the thermal or contact metamorphic rocks. The second type develops if the newly deformed metamorphic minerals are quidimensional with no preferred orientation, e.g. monomineralic rocks, such as limestone, sandstone, and dunite when metamorphosed.

Figure 2.4 is a generalized chart showing the origin of common metamorphic rocks.

2.3 Soils and Unconsolidated Deposits

2.3.1 Soils

2.3.1.1 *Scope*

Soils are of great importance as they constitute the material that supports plant life, and so supports all terrestrial life. Soils constitute a complex interplay of weathering and biologic processes. There are many types of soils due to different prevailing factors such as climate, parent rock, and type of vegetation.

Soils rich in organic matter are preferred in agriculture, but they are unsuitable for construction purposes. Similarly, soils with high sand content are preferred for construction purposes, whereas such soils tend to be infertile and unsuitable for agriculture (Aswathanarayana 1999).

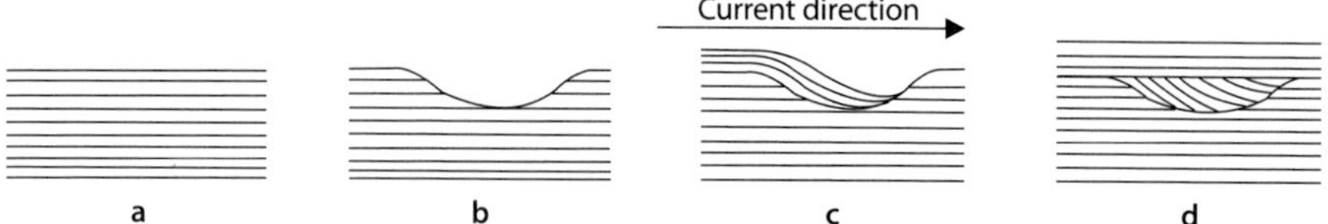
Current direction
a
b
c
d

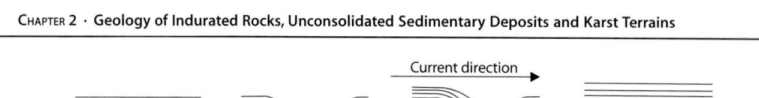

Fig. 2.3. Development of cross-beds; **a** initial deposition; **b** channel cut by current; **c** channel filled by deposition from one side; **d** normal deposition after channel is filled. Cross-beds can also be used to distinguish top and bottom (after Foster 1979, adapted by permission of Charles Merril Publishing Co., Columbus, OH)

Fig. 2.4. A generalized chart showing the origin of common metamorphic rocks (after Foster 1979, adapted by permission of Charles Merril Publishing Co., Columbus, OH)

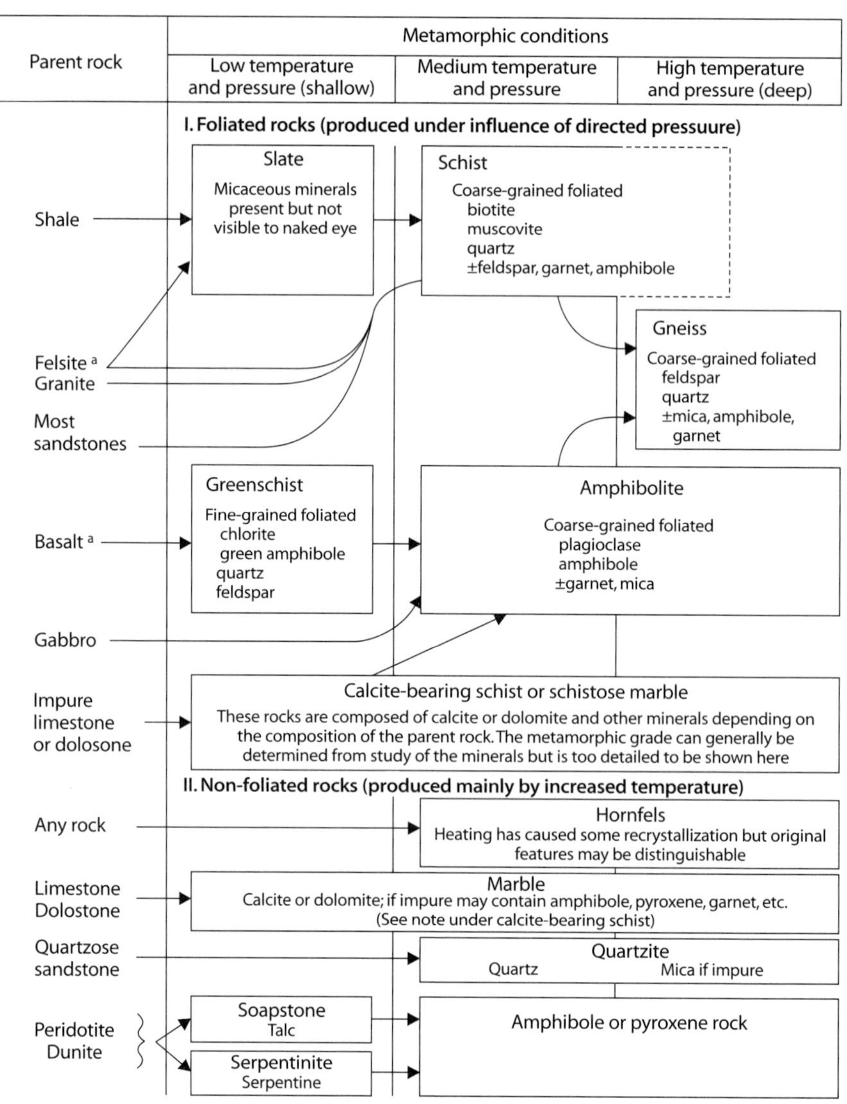
Parent rock
Metamorphic conditions
Low temperature and pressure (shallow)
Medium temperature and pressure
High temperature and pressure (deep)
I. Foliated rocks (produced under influence of directed pressuure)
Shale
Slate
Micaceous minerals present but not visible to naked eye
Schist
Coarse-grained foliated
biotite
muscovite
quartz
±feldspar, garnet, amphibole
Felsite [a]
Granite
Most sandstones
Gneiss
Coarse-grained foliated
feldspar
quartz
±mica, amphibole, garnet
Basalt [a]
Greenschist
Fine-grained foliated
chlorite
green amphibole
quartz
feldspar
Amphibolite
Coarse-grained foliated
plagioclase
amphibole
±garnet, mica
Gabbro
Impure limestone or dolosone
Calcite-bearing schist or schistose marble
These rocks are composed of calcite or dolomite and other minerals depending on the composition of the parent rock. The metamorphic grade can generally be determined from study of the minerals but is too detailed to be shown here
II. Non-foliated rocks (produced mainly by increased temperature)
Any rock
Hornfels
Heating has caused some recrystallization but original features may be distinguishable
Limestone
Dolostone
Marble
Calcite or dolomite; if impure may contain amphibole, pyroxene, garnet, etc. (See note under calcite-bearing schist)
Quartzose sandstone
Quartzite
Quartz
Mica if impure
Peridotite
Dunite
Soapstone
Talc
Serpentinite
Serpentine
Amphibole or pyroxene rock
[a] Including fragmental volcanic rocks of this composition.

2.3.1.2 *Geological Definition, Constituents and Types of Soils*

Definition: Soil is a mixture of mineral particles and organic matter of varying size and composition on the immediate surface of the earth above bedrock. For more than 50 years, the soil conservation system (SCS), part of U.S. Department of Agriculture, has been conducting periodic inventories of the Nation's soil, water, and related natural resources in USA.

Soils can be described as mature and immature. On hill slopes, erosion may prevent soils from reaching maturity and the transported soil may accumulate in valleys. Many soils that have been transported, form on surface materials and take at least a few hundreds years to develop.

Constituents of soils: Soils are classified into three zones: (*a*) the topsoil, (*b*) the subsoil, and (*c*) the partly decomposed bedrock. In forests, an additional surface organic layer may be formed at the surface.

The dark colored material, in the upper parts of many soils, is due to the presence of humus that is formed by the action of bacteria and molds on the plant material in the soil. It plays an important role in the formation and stabilization of soil aggregates, control of soil acidity, cycling of nutrient elements and detoxification of toxic substances such as heavy metals and pesticides.

Clays, which are a universal constituent of soils, can have a significant impact on land use. Wetland is a general term for marshes, swamps, and other areas.

Permanently wet and/or intermittently water-covered hydric soils, which are particularly good water filters, occur at the mouths of river valleys along low-lying coasts, and in valleys. The soil profile should be described in terms of its moisture condition, color, consistency, structure, soil type and origin (MCCSSO).

Soils contain two broad groups of minerals: primary silicate minerals, such as clay, quartz, feldspars, mica, amphibole, pyroxene and, very rarely olivine, which are directly inherited from the parent rocks, and a large number of secondary minerals which are formed in the course of soil formation.

Soil contamination: soils can be contaminated with salt as a result of natural salt seeps or leaks of salt solutions or brines and other natural causes; in areas where automobiles are concentrated or high sulfur coal is burned as a source of energy, the air becomes contaminated with acid-forming chemicals which later results in the increase of essential nutrients, such as calcium and magnesium, to leach from the root zone and decrease the growth of vegetation; mining activities including both underground and strip mining for coal, metals, and aggregates including sand and gravel, have resulted in large areas being covered with mine wastes; also, heavy metals such as cadmium, lead, and zinc at low concentrations are not toxic and are essential for proper nutrition.

Figure 2.5 shows schematically the processes of soil formation. As most trace elements come from soil and enter the life cycle either through water supply or plants, excesses or deficiencies in the trace elements may cause serious problems to animal life.

Soil types: Several types of soils are known in different States of the American soils:

1. *Prairie soils (mollisols)* the most important and productive agricultural soils in the world, e.g. the great plains of the United States such as wheatfield in Kansas, and rangeland in Nebraska;
2. *Forest soils (spodosols)* commonly form in warm to cool, humid regions with a coniferous cover and predominate in northeastern United States, such as Portland, Oregon and New England;
3. *Tropical soils (oxisols)* commonly known in Hawaii and Puerto Rico, are highly weathered, reddish or yellowish soils of humid, tropical, or subtropical regions;
4. *Organic soils (histsols)* formed in poorly drained and lowland environments in the great Lakes region and coastal eastern United States, are weathered soils, dark in color and rich in decomposed organic material;
5. *Desert soils (aridsols)*, rich in calcium carbonate, form in arid settings where irrigation water is not available, e.g. Arizona.

2.3.1.3 *Soil Classification System by Engineers (USCS)*

There are many soil classification systems that are in use by engineers and each has different particle size dimensions and terminology. Terms or soil descriptions used by geologists or soil scientists may not match the engineer's description because they are using different classification system. For geotechnical engineers (Day 2000), clay mineralogy and soil plasticity are important aspects of soil classification (Table 2.3). Table 2.4 indicates other items that should be included in the field or laboratory description of a soil (Day 2000).

In the United States, the most widely used soil classification system is the Unified Soil Classification System or the "USCS" (Day 2000; Tables 2.5 and 2.6).

2.3.1.4 *Munsell Soil Color Charts*

Munsell (1975) measured soil colors by comparison with a color chart and used seven charts, which display 196 different standard color chips arranged in three simple variables that combine to describe all colors. These variables are known in the Munsell system as hue, value, and chroma.

The hue notation of a color indicates its relation to red, yellow, green, blue, and purple; the value notation indicates its lightness; and the chroma notation indicates its strength (or departure from a neutral of the same lightness).

The colors displayed on the individual soil color charts are of constant hue, designated by a symbol in the upper right-hand corner of the card. Vertically, the colors become successively lighter from the bottom of the card to the top by visually equal steps and their value increases. Horizontally, they increase in chroma to the right and become grayer to the left. The value notation of each chip is indicated by the vertical scale in the far

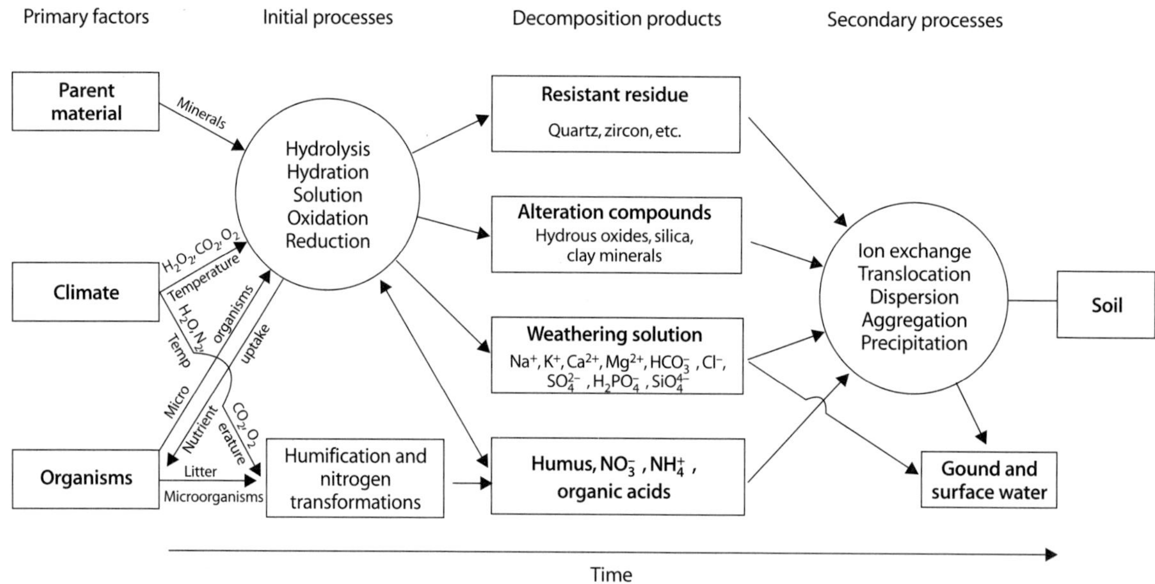

Primary factors
Initial processes
Decomposition products
Secondary processes
Parent material
Minerals
Hydrolysis
Hydration
Solution
Oxidation
Reduction
Resistant residue
Quartz, zircon, etc.
Alteration compounds
Hydrous oxides, silica, clay minerals
Ion exchange
Translocation
Dispersion
Aggregation
Precipitation
Soil
Climate
Temperature
Temp
Micro
Nutrient
organisms
uptake
Weathering solution
Organisms
Litter
Microorganisms
Humification and nitrogen transformations
Humus, NO_3^-, NH_4^+, organic acids
Gound and surface water
Time

Fig. 2.5. Processes of soil formation (after Aswathanarayana 1999; *Source*: Fitzpatrick 1993, p. 74, Longman's)

left column of the chart. The chroma notation is indicated by the horizontal scale across the bottom of the chart.

2.3.2 Unconsolidated Deposits

The following are some common unconsolidated deposits.

2.3.2.1 *Eolian Deposits*

Intermittent rainfall and running water are the main agents of erosion in most arid areas, but wind erosion is a more important agent in drier areas such as parts of North Africa than erosion caused by running water in some other countries. Dry regions form over one-quarter of the total land surface of the earth (Foster 1979).

Mechanical weathering is the process of weathering by which frost action, salt-crystal growth, absorption of water, and other physical processes break down a rock to fragments, involving no chemical change (Jackson 1997).

Deflation occurs by removal of sand- and dust-sized particles, by wind erosion that leads residual pebbles with polished facets or surfaces produced by sandblasting to two-sided *ventifact* or *dreikanter* a three-sided ventifact.

Wind transportation involves suspended load (dust) and bed load (sand). Wind deposited sediments are well sorted by size; loess is a wind deposit composed of silt; and it forms thick, sheet-like, unstratified deposits. Dunes are naturally formed accumulations of wind-blown sand and comprise different types such as barchan, transverse, parabolic, and longitudinal or "seif" depending on strength and variability of wind, amount of sand, vegetation, and other factors (Foster 1979).

Desert landscapes: A slow development of desert landscapes occur because of infrequent rain and the resulting lack of moisture, e.g. pediments are smooth, gravel-covered, concave-upward erosional surfaces cut in the bedrock of desert mountains. They are continuous with alluvial fans deposited at the mountain fronts.

2.3.2.2 *Fluvial Deposits*

Rivers are agents of erosion (by solution and abrasion), transportation, and deposition but they are the most important agents of transportation. Fluvial deposits are generated by the action of streams and rivers and are called deltas where rivers enter standing water; *alluvial fans* or plains form at the base of the mountains where erosion provides a supply of sediment and rivers flow out into broad, flat valleys; *levees* formed along banks when flood-waters spill over, reducing velocity; *terraces* form from changes in river conditions by either deposition or erosion; *braided streams* form when the sediment load is large and coarse and are characterized by many channels, separated by islands or bars; whereas *meandering streams* have a greater sinuosity and finer sediment load. *Narrow valleys* have V-shaped cross sections and are generally formed by down cutting, non-graded rivers near their headwaters; they commonly have falls, rapids, and lakes, which are temporarily features (Foster 1979).

Table 2.3. Clay mineralogy and related topics (after Day 2000, adapted by permission of McGraw-Hill Education New York, NY; hints to tables, figures, references etc. refer to the original work)

Topic	Discussion
Clay mineral structure	The amount and type of clay minerals present in a soil have a significant effect on soil engineering properties such as plasticity, swelling, shrinkage, shear strength, consolidation, and permeability. This is due in large part to their very small flat or platelike shape which enables them to attract water to their surfaces, also known as the double layer effect. The double layer is a grossly simplified interpretation of the positively charged water layer and the negatively charged surface of the clay particle itself. Two reasons for the attraction of water to the clay particle (double layer) are: 1. The dipolar structure of the water molecule which causes it to be electrostatically attracted to the surface of the clay particle; 2. The clay particles attract cations which contribute to the attraction of water by the hydration process. Ion exchange can occur in the double layer, where under certain conditions, sodium, potassium, and calcium cations can be replaced by other cations present in the water. This property is known as cation exchange capacity. In addition to the double layer, there is an "absorbed water layer" that consists of water molecules that are tightly held to the clay particle face, for example, by the process of hydrogen bonding. The presence of the very small clay particles surrounded by water helps explain their impact on the engineering properties of soil. For example, clays that have been deposited in lakes or marine environments often have a very high water content and are very compressible with a low strength because of this attracted and bonded water. Another example is desiccated clays, which have been dried, but have a strong desire for water and will swell significantly upon wetting (Chap. 12).
Plasticity	The term plasticity is applied to silts and clays and indicates an ability to be rolled and molded without breaking apart. A measure of the plasticity of a silt or clay is the plasticity index (*PI*), defined as the liquid limit (*LL*) minus the plastic limit (*PL*); see Table 3.7.
Liquidity index (*LI*)	A useful parameter is the liquidity index, defined as: $LI = (w - PL) / PI$ The liquidity index can be used to identify sensitive clays. For example, quick clays often have an in situ water content *w* that is greater than the liquid limit, and thus the liquidity index is greater than 1.0. At the other extreme are clays that have liquidity index values that are zero or even negative. These liquidity index values indicate a soil that is desiccated and could have significant expansion potential (Chap. 12). In accordance with ASTM, the Atterberg limits are performed on soil that is finer than the no. 40 sieve, but water content can be performed on soil containing larger soil particles (Table 3.3), and thus the liquidity index should be calculated only for soil that has all its particles finer than the no. 40 sieve.
Plasticity chart	Based on the Atterberg limits, the plasticity chart was developed by Casagrande (1932, 1948) and is used in the Unified Soil Classification System to classify soils. As shown in Fig. 4.1, the plasticity chart is a plot of the liquid limit (*LL*) vs. the plasticity index (*PI*). Figure 4.2 shows the location where common clay minerals plot on the plasticity chart (from Mitchell 1976 and Holtz and Kovacs 1981). Casagrande (1932) defined two basic dividing lines on the plasticity chart, as follows: 1. $LL = 50$ line: This line is used to divide silts and clays into high plasticity ($LL > 50$) and low- to medium-plasticity ($LL < 50$) categories. 2. A-line: The A-line is defined as: $PI = 0.73(LL - 20)$ where PI = plasticity index and LL = liquid limit. The A-line is used to separate clays, which plot above the A-line, from silts, which plot below the A-line. An additional line has been added to the Casagrande plasticity chart known as the U-line (see Fig. 4.1). The U-line (or upper limit line) is defined as: $PI = 0.90(LL - 8)$ The U-line is valuable because it represents the uppermost boundary of test data found thus far for natural soils. The U-line is a good check on erroneous data, and any test results that plot above the U-line should be checked. There have been other minor changes proposed for Casagrande's original plasticity chart (e.g. note the hatched zone in Fig. 4.1)
Activity	In 1953, Skempton defined the activity *A* of a clay as: $A = PI$ / clay fraction where the clay fraction = that part of the soil specimen finer than 0.002 mm, based on dry weight. Clays that are inactive are defined as those clays having an activity less than 0.75, normal activity is defined as those clays having an activity between 0.75 and 1.25, and an active clay is defined as those clays having an activity greater than 1.25. Quartz has an activity of zero, while at the other extreme is sodium montmorillonite, which can have an activity from 4 to 7. Because *PI* is determined from Atterberg limits that are performed on soil that passes the no. 40 sieve (0.425 mm), a correction is required for soils that contain a large fraction of particles coarser than the no. 40 sieve. For example, suppose a clayey gravel contains 70% gravel particles (particles coarser than no. 40 sieve), 20% silt-size particles, and 10% clay-size particles (silt and clay size particles are finer than no. 40 sieve). If the $PI = 40$ for the soil particles finer than the no. 40 sieve, then the activity for the clayey gravel would be 1.2 (i.e. 40/33.3).

2.3.2.3 *Beach Deposits*

Waves moved by wind and the earth's rotation, are agents of erosion, transportation, and deposition, and have a great deal of energy. Beach deposits, which are the most common wave-deposited features, are generated by the action of streams and waves along the coast where sediment is deposited as sand or gravel bars at headlands and across bays. In general, storms remove sand from

Table 2.3. *Continued*

Topic	Discussion
Common types of clay minerals	Clay minerals present in a soil can be identified by their X-ray diffraction patterns. This process is rather complicate, expensive, and involves special equipment which is not readily available to the geotechnical engineer. A more common approach is to use the location of clay particles as they plot on the plasticity chart (Fig. 4.2) to estimate the type of clay mineral in the soil. This approach is often inaccurate, because soil can contain more than one type of clay material. The three most common clay minerals are listed below, with their respective activity (*A*) values (from Skempton 1953 and Mitchell 1976): 1. Kaolinite ($A = 0.3$ to 0.5). The kaolin minerals are a group of clay minerals consisting of hydrous aluminum silicates. A common kaolin mineral is kaolinite, having the general formula $Al_2Si_2(OH)_4$. Kaolinite is usually formed by alteration of feldspars and other aluminum-bearing minerals. Kaolinite is usually a large clay mineral of low activity and often plots below the A-line (Fig. 4.2). Holtz and Kovacs (1981) state that kaolinite is a relatively inactive clay mineral and even though it is technically a clay, it behaves more like a silt material. Kaolinite has many industrial uses, including the production of china, medicines, and cosmetics. 2. Montmorillonite (Na-montmorillonite, $A = 4$ to 7 and Ca-montmorillonite, $A = 1.5$). A group of clay minerals that are characterized by weakly bonded layers. Each layer consists of two silica sheets with an aluminum (gibbsite) sheet in the middle. Water and exchangeable cations (Na, Ca, etc.) can enter and separate the layers, creating a very small crystal that has a strong attraction for water. Montmorillonite has the highest activity and it can have the highest water content, greatest compressibility, and lowest shear strength of all the clay minerals. As shown in Fig. 4.2, montmorillonite plots just below the U-line. Montmorillonite often forms as the result of the weathering of ferromagnesian minerals, calcic feldspars, and volcanic materials (Coduto 1994). For example, sodium montmorillonite is often formed from the weathering of volcanic ash. Other environments that are likely to form montmorillonite are alkaline conditions with a supply of magnesium ions and a lack of leaching (Coduto 1994). Such conditions are often present in semiarid and arid regions. 3. Illite ($A = 0.5$ to 1.3). This clay mineral has a structure similar to montmorillonite, but the layers are more strongly bonded together. In cation exchange capacity, in ability to absorb and retain water, and in physical characteristics such as plasticity index, illite is intermediate in activity between clays of the kaolin and montmorillonite groups. As shown in Fig. 4.2, illite often plots just above the A-line. There are many other types of clay minerals. Even within a clay mineral category, there can be different crystal components because of isomorphous substitution. This is the process where ions of approximately the same size are substituted in the crystalline framework. Also shown on Fig. 4.2 are two other less common clay minerals, chlorite and halloysite, both of which have less activity than the three clay minerals previously described. Although not very common, halloysite is an interesting clay mineral because instead of usual flat particle shape, it is tubular in shape, which can effect engineering properties in unusual ways. It has been observed that classification and compaction tests made on air-dried halloysite samples give markedly different results than tests on samples at their natural water content (Holz and Kovacs 1981).

the beach and deposit it as a bar at the edge of the surf zone, because the higher wave crests of the storm. Waves need a shallower slope to maintain the equilibrium slope on which they move the sand back and forth. Rip currents transport fine sand off-shore, especially during times when onshore winds as well as waves move surface water onshore (Foster 1979).

Beaches and sand bars, either off-shore or attached to the shore, are two main types of *wave deposits*. Generally, the size of the sediment controls the slope of the beach, with pebble beaches being steeper than sand beaches.

2.3.2.4 *Glacial Deposits*

Scope

During the last 1.8 million years, as the climate varied between arctic and temperate conditions, giant ice sheets as much as a mile (1.61 km) thick advanced and retreated across the Great Lakes region. Each advance left its mark. Boulders dragged beneath tons of glacial ice pulverized, gouged, and grooved the underlying landscape. Glaciers left behind a mixture of clay, silt, sand, and scattered gravel. When compressed by the great weight of the overlying ice, the mixture became a dense, impermeable material called glacial till. Rivers roaring from the fronts of the ice sheets cut new valleys and deposited sand and gravel that make up today's major aquifers and primary supplies for concrete. Cold, dark lakes formed where ice sheets blocked river valleys, leaving behind deposits of mud. Beneath the warm afternoon sun, floods of muddy water poured into the lakes, depositing layers of clay that are the sources for our bricks and tiles (USGS 1999).

Harsh winds blowing off the ice sheet raised clouds of sand and silt from the rivers and drying lake plains where large sand dunes are formed nearby. Glacial till, loess, and lake-bottom sediments are the sources of the fertile soils of the Nation's Corn Belt (USGS 1999).

The prosperity and resolution of land-use problems in regions where layers of sediments that blanket ancient rocky hills and valleys below farmland plains and rolling hills, depend on an understanding of the 3-D distribution and characteristics of these earth materials (American Geological Institute 2000; Fig. 2.6).

Table 2.4. Various items used to describe soil (after Day 2000, adapted by permission of McGraw-Hill Education New York, NY; hints to tables, figures, references etc. refer to the original work)

Topic	Discussion
Soil color	Usually the standard primary color (red, orange, yellow, etc.) of the soil is listed. Although not frequently used in geotechnical engineering, color charts have been developed. For example, the Munsell Soil Color Charts (1975) display 199 different standard color chips systematically arranged according to their Munsell notations, on cards carried in a loose leaf notebook. The arrangement is by the three variables that combine to describe all colors and are known in the Munsell system as hue, value, and chroma. Color can be very important in identifying different types of soil. For example the Friars formation, which is a stiff-fissured clay and is frequent cause of geotechnical problems such as landslides and expansive soil, can often be identified by its dark green color. Another example is the Sweetwater formation, which is also a stiff-fissured clay, and has a bright pink color due to the presence of montmorillonite.
Soil structure	In some cases the structure of the soil may be evident. Definition vary, but in general, the soil structure refers to both the geometric arrangement of the soil particles and the interparticle forces which may act between them (Holz and Kovacs 1981). There are many different types of soil structure, such as cluster, dispersed, flocculated, honeycomb, single-grained, and skeleton (see Appendix A for definition). In some cases, the soil structure may be visible under a magnifying glass, or in other cases the soil structure may be reasonable inferred from laboratory testing results.
Soil texture	The texture of a soil refers to the degree of fineness of the soil. For example, terms such as smooth, gritty, or sharp can be used to describe the texture of the soil when it is rubbed between the fingers.
Soil porosity	The soil description should also include the in situ condition of the soil. For example, numerous small voids may be observed in the soil, and this is referred to as pinhole porosity.
Clay consistency	For clays, the consistency (i.e. degree of firmness) should be listed. The consistency of a clay varies from "very soft" to "hard," depending on the undrained shear strength of the clay. The undrained shear strength s_u can be determined from the vane tests or the unconfined compression test (Table 3.10). Values of the undrained shear strength s_u corresponding to various degrees of consistency are as follows: – very soft: $s_u < 12$ kPa ($s_u < 12$ psf). The clay is easily penetrated several centimeters by the thumb. The clay oozes out between the fingers when squeezed in the hand. – soft: 12 kPa $\leq s_u <$ 25 kPa (250 psf $\leq s_u <$ 500 psf). The clay is easily penetrated 2 to 3 cm (1 in.) by the thumb. The clay can be molded by slight finger pressure. – medium: 25 kPa $\leq s_u <$ 50 kPa (500 psf $\leq s_u <$ 1 000 psf). The clay can be penetrated about 1 cm (0.4 in.) by the thumb with moderate effort. The clay can be molded by strong finger pressure. – stiff: 50 kPa $\leq s_u <$ 100 kPa (1 000 psf $\leq s_u <$ 2 000 psf). The clay can be indented about 0.5 cm (0.2 in.) by the thumb with great effort. – very stiff: 100 kPa $\leq s_u <$ 200 kPa (2 000 psf $\leq s_u <$ 4 000 psf). The clay cannot be intended by the thumb, but can readily indented with the thumbnail. – hard: $s_u \geq 200$ kPa ($s_u \geq 4\,000$ psf). With great difficulty, the clay can only be intended with the thumbnail.
Soil moisture condition	For sand, the density state of the soil varies from "very loose" to "very dense" (see Table 3.16). The moisture condition of the soil should also be listed. Moisture conditions vary from "dry" soil to a "saturated" soil. The degree of saturation indicates the degree to which the soil voids are filled with water (see Chap. 5). A totally dry soil will have a degree of saturation S of 0%, while a saturated soil, such as a soil below the groundwater table, will have a degree of saturation S of 100%. Typical ranges of degree of saturation vs. soil condition are as follows (Terzaghi and Peck 1967): – dry: $S =$ 0% – humid: $S =$ 1 to 25% – damp: $S =$ 26 to 50% – moist: $S =$ 51 to 75% – wet: $S =$ 76 to 99% – saturated: $S =$ 100% Especially in the arid climate of the southwestern United States, soil may be in a dry and powdery state. Often these soils are misclassified as silts, when in fact they are highly plastic clays. It is always important to add water to dry or powdery soils in order to assess their plasticity characteristics.
Additional descriptive items	Most classification systems are applicable only for soil and rock particles passing the 75 mm (3 in.) sieve. Cobbles and boulders are larger than 75 mm (3 in.), and if applicable, the words "with cobbles" or "with boulders" should be added to the soil classification. Other descriptive terminology includes the presence of rock fragments, such as "crushed shale, claystone, sandstone, siltstone, or mudstone fragments," and unusual constituents such as "shells, slag, glass fragments, and construction debris."

Definition

A glacier is a mass of moving ice. Glaciers form as a result of accumulation of snow that must be thick enough to recrystallize to ice. Glacier consist of ice crystals, air, water, and rock debris. Glaciers are much more powerful agents of erosion than rivers. Because modern day ice masses are restricted to high altitudes and polar regions, running water moves far more rock debris each year than does ice. The vast amount of debris, mainly released at the glacier front by melting, indicates the erosive power of the glaciers. The debris may be deposited in hummocky ridges or moraines, and consist of unsorted and unstratified debris deposited directly by the ice. The debris includes heterogeneously mixed boulders, sand, and silt is commonly know as till. Glacial drift

Table 2.5. Unified soil classification system (background information) (after Day 2000, adapted by permission of McGraw-Hill Education New York, NY; hints to tables, references etc. refer to the original work)

Topic	Discussion
General information	The Unified Soil Classification System is abbreviated USCS (not to be confused with the United States Customary System units which has the same abbreviation). The Unified Soil Classification System was initially developed by Casagrande (1948) and then later modified by Casagrande in 1952.
Two main groups	The Unified Soil Classification System (USCS) separates soils into two main groups: coarse-grained soils and fine-grained soils. The basis of the USCS is that the engineering behavior of coarse-grained soils is related to their grain size distributions and the engineering behavior of fine-grained soils is related to their plasticity characteristics. Table 4.4 (adapted from ASTM D 2487-93, 1998) presents a summary of the Unified Soil Classification System. As indicated in Table 4.4, the two main groups of soil are defined as follows: – Coarse-grained soils: Defined as having more than 50% (by dry mass) of soil particles retained on the no. 200 sieve. – Fine-grained soils: Defined as having 50% or more (by dry mass) of soil particles passing the no. 200 sieve. As indicated in Table 4.4, the coarse-grained soils are divided into gravel and sands. Both gravel and sands are further subdivided into four secondary groups as indicated in Table 4.4. The four secondary classifications are based on whether the soil is well graded, is poorly graded, contains silt-size particles, or contains clay-size particles. As indicated in Table 4.4, the fine-grained soils are divided into soils of low or high plasticity. The three secondary classifications are based on liquid limit (*LL*) and plasticity characteristics (*PI*).
Distribution of particle sizes	The distribution of particle sizes larger than 0.075 mm (no. 200 sieve) is determined by sieving, while the distribution of particle sizes smaller than 0.075 mm is determined by a sedimentation process (hydrometer). For the USCS, the rock fragments or soil particles vs. size are defined as follows (from largest to smallest particle size): – *Boulders*. Rocks that have an average diameter greater than 300 mm (12 in.). – *Cobbles*. Rocks that are smaller than 300 mm (12 in.) and are retained on the 75 mm (3 in.) U.S. standard sieve. – *Gravel-size particles*. Rock fragments or soil particles that will pass a 75 mm (3 in.) sieve and be retained on a no. 4 (4.75 mm) U.S. standard sieve. Gravel-size particles are subdivided into coarse gravel sizes and fine gravel sizes. – *Sand-size particles*. Soil particles that will pass a no. 4 (4.75 mm) sieve and be retained by on a no. 200 (0.075 mm) U.S. standard sieve. Sand-size particles are subdivided into coarse sand size, medium sand size, and fine sand size. – *Silt-size particles*. Fine soil particles that pass the no. 200 (0.075 mm) U.S. standard sieve and are larger than 0.002 mm – *Clay-size particles*. Fine soil particles that are smaller than 0.002 mm
Particle size vs. soil description	It is very important to distinguish the size of a soil particle and the classification of the soil. For example, a soil could have a certain fraction of particles that are of "clay size." The same soil could also be classified as "clay." But the classification of a "clay" does not necessarily mean that the majority of the soil particles are of clay size (smaller than 0.002 mm). In fact, it is not unusual for a soil to be classified as a "clay" and have larger mass of silt-size particles than clay-size particles. When reference is given to particle size, the terminology clay-size particles or silt-size particles should be used. When the reference is given to a particular soil, then the terms such as silt or clay should be used.
Coarse-grained soil coefficients	On the basis of particle sizes, the coefficients of uniformity C_u and coefficient of curvature C_c can be calculated as follows: $C_u = D_{60} / D_{10}$ $C_c = (D_{30})^1 / ((D_{10})(D_{60}))$ where D_{10} = particle size corresponding to 10% finer soil-size particles, D_{30} = particle size corresponding to 30% finer soil-size particles, and D_{60} = particle size corresponding to 60% finer soil-size particles. The coefficient of uniformity C_u and the coefficient of curvature C_c are used in the Unified Soil Classification System to determine whether a coarse-grained soil is well graded (many different particle sizes) or poorly graded (many particles of about the same size).
Group symbols	Note in column 3 of Table 4.4 that symbols (known as group symbols) are used to identify different soil types. The group symbols consist of two capital letters. The first letter indicates the following: G Gravel S Sand M Silt C Clay O Organic The second letter indicates the following: W Well graded, which indicates that a coarse-grained soil has particles of all sizes P Poorly graded, which indicates that a coarse-grained soil has particles of the same size, or the soil is skip-graded or gap-graded M Indicates a coarse-grained soil that has silt-size particles C Indicates a coarse-grained soil that has clay-size particles L Indicates a fine-grained soil of low plasticity H Indicates a fine-grained soil of high plasticity An exception is peat, where the group symbol is PT. Also note in Table 4.4 that certain soils require the use of dual symbols.

Table 2.6. Unified soil classification system (USCS) (after Day 2000, adapted by permission of McGraw-Hill Education, New York, NY; hints to figures refer to the original work)

Major divisions	Subdivisions	USCS symbols	Typical names	Laboratory classification criteria	
Coarse grained soils (more than 50% retained on no. 200 sieve)	Gravels (more than 50% of coarse fraction retained on no. 4 sieve)	GW	Well-graded gravels or gravel-sand mixtures, little or no fines	Less than 5% fines	$C_u \geq 4$ and $1 \leq C_c \leq 3$
		GP	Poorly graded gravels or gravelly sands, little or no fines	Less than 5% fines	Does not meet C_u and/or C_c criteria listed above
		GM	Silty gravels, gravel-sand-silt mixtures	More than 12% fines	Minus no. 40 soil plots below A-line
		GC	Clayey gravels, gravel-sand-clay mixtures	More than 12% fines	Minus no. 40 soil plots or or above A-line (Fig. 4.1)
	Sands (50% or more of coarse fraction passes no. 4 sieve)	SW	Well-graded sands or gravelly sands, little or no fines	Less than 5% fines	$C_u \geq 6$ and $1 \leq C_c \leq 3$
		SP	Poorly graded sands or gravelly sands, little or no fines	Less than 5% fines	Does not meet C_u and/or C_c criteria listed above
		SM	Silty sands, sand-silt mixtures	More than 12% fines	Minus no. 40 soil plots below A-line
		SC	Clayey sands, sand-clay mixtures	More than 12% fines	Minus no. 40 soil plots on or above A-line (Fig. 4.1)
Fine-grained soils (50% or more of coarse fraction passes no. 200 sieve)	Silts and clays (liquid limit less than 50)	ML	Inorganic silts, rock flour, silts of low plasticity	Inorganic soil	$PI < 4$ or plots below A-line (Fig. 4.1)
		CL	Inorganic clays of low plasticity, gravelly clays, sandy clays, etc.	Inorganic soil	$PI > 7$ and plots on or above A-line
		OL	Organic silts and organic clays of low plasticity	Organic soil	LL (oven dried) / LL (not dried) < 0.75
	Silts and clays (liquid limit 50 or more)	MH	Inorganic silts, micaceous silts, silts of high plasticity	Inorganic soil	Plots below A-line (Fig. 4.1)
		CH	Inorganic highly plastic clays, fat clays, silty clays, etc.	Inorganic soil	Plots on or above A-line (Fig. 4.1)
		OH	Organic silts and organic clays of high plasticity	Organic soil	LL (oven dried) / LL (not dried) < 0.75
Peat	Highly organic	PT	Peat and other highly organic soils	Primarily organic matter, dark in color, organic odor	

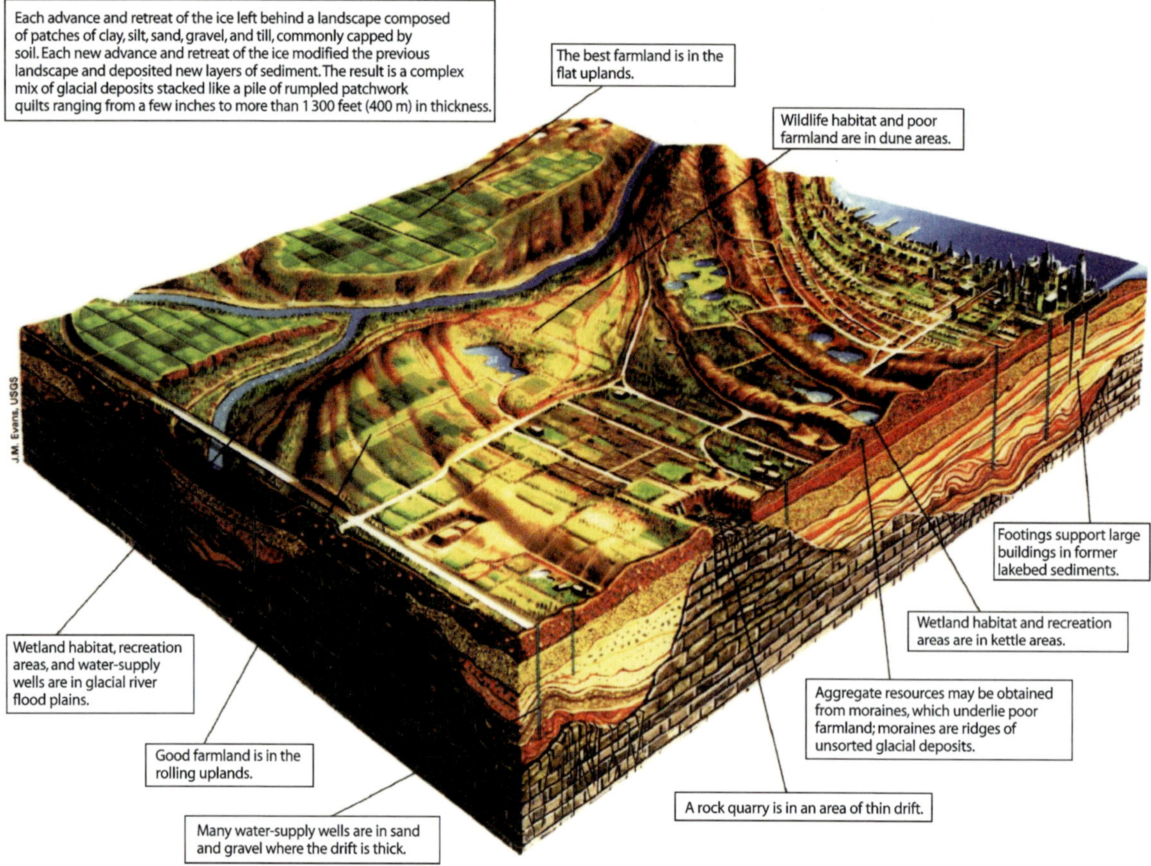
Each advance and retreat of the ice left behind a landscape composed of patches of clay, silt, sand, gravel, and till, commonly capped by soil. Each new advance and retreat of the ice modified the previous landscape and deposited new layers of sediment. The result is a complex mix of glacial deposits stacked like a pile of rumpled patchwork quilts ranging from a few inches to more than 1 300 feet (400 m) in thickness.
The best farmland is in the flat uplands.
Wildlife habitat and poor farmland are in dune areas.
J.M. Evans, USGS
Footings support large buildings in former lakebed sediments.
Wetland habitat and recreation areas are in kettle areas.
Wetland habitat, recreation areas, and water-supply wells are in glacial river flood plains.
Aggregate resources may be obtained from moraines, which underlie poor farmland; moraines are ridges of unsorted glacial deposits.
Good farmland is in the rolling uplands.
A rock quarry is in an area of thin drift.
Many water-supply wells are in sand and gravel where the drift is thick.

Fig. 2.6. Block diagram showing a generalized representation of modern surface land uses (after after American Geological Institute and National Speleological Society 2000) and their close ties to underlying deposits (reproduced with the permission of AGI)

includes all types of debris dumped by glaciers and by the streams flowing from them. Meltwater from the glaciers carries off much of the finer debris and deposits it either on the beds of the overloaded streams (glacio-fluvial deposits), in lakes (glacio-lacustrine deposits), or in seas. The moraine that marks the point of the farthest advance of the glacier is called the terminal moraine whereas those that mark stages of halt as the glacier recedes are called recessional moraines.

Glacial geologists are gradually limiting use of the term "till" to refer to 'an aggregate' whose particles were deposited by or from the direct agency of glacier ice and which, though it may have undergone subsequent glacially-induced flow, has not been significantly sorted by water or gravity movements. The term 'diamict' is frequently employed in lithofacies description to refer to unsorted, unstratified clast-sand-mud admixture regardless of depositional environment, whether glacial, paraglacial, periglacial, or non-glacial, terrestrial or aqueous.

Identification and Coding

In a lithofacies code that is increasingly employed by fluvial sedimentologists (Miall 1977, 1978) showed that the majority of fluvial deposits (including glacio-fluvial outwash deposits) are satisfactorily described using a set of 20 standard lithofacies types. Each type has been assigned code letters for convenience in logging. The codes are in two parts: the first part is a capital letter "G, S or F" which represent gravel, sand, or fines. The second part of the code consists of one or two letters, designed as mnemonics, to describe the most characteristic internal feature of the lithofacies, e.g. "Gms" for matrix-supported gravel, "Sp" for planar cross-bedded sand, etc. The principal lithofacies are listed in Table 2.7a with brief notes on their composition, structure and interpretation.

Table 2.7b (modified from Eyles et al. 1983) shows a four-part lithofacies code with the code designator "D" for diamict. Hyphens are used to indicate that diamicts display several possible combinations of internal char-

Table 2.7a. Lithofacies and sedimentary structures for fluvial and glacio-fluvial deposits (modified from Eyles et al. 1983)

Facies code	Lithofacies	Sedimentary structures	Interpretation
Gms	Massive, matrix-supported gravel	None	Debris flow deposits
Gm	Massive or crudely bedded gravel	Horizontal bedding, imbrication	Longitudinal bars, lag deposits, sieve deposites
Gt	Gravel, stratified	Trough crossbeds	Minor channel fills
Gp	Gravel, stratified	Planar crossbeds	Linguoid bars or deltaic growths from old bar remnants
St	Sand, medium to very coarse, may be pebbly	Solitary (theta) or grouped (pi) trough crossbeds	Dunes (lower flow regime)
Sp	Sand, medium to very coarse, may be pebbly	Solitary (alpha) or grouped (omikron) planar crossbeds	Linguoid, transverse bars, sand waves (lower flow regime)
Sr	Sand, very fine to coarse	Ripple marks of all types	Ripples (lower flow regime)
Sh	Sand, very fine to very coarse, may be pebbly	Horizontal lamination parting or streaming lineation	Planar bed flow (l. and u. flow regime)
Sl	Sand, fine	Low angle (10°) crossbeds	Scour fills, crevasse splays, antidunes
Se	Erosional scours with intraclasts	Crude crossbedding	Scour fills
Ss	Sand, fine to coarse, may be pebbly	Broad, shallow scours including eta cross-stratification	Scour fills
Sse, She, Spe	Sand	Analogous to Ss, Sh, Sp	Eolian deposits
Fl	Sand, silt, mud	Fine lamination, very small ripples	Overbank or waning flood deposits
Fsc	Silt, mud	Laminated to massive	Backswamp deposits
Fcf	Mud	Massive with freshwater molluscs	Backswamp pond deposits
Fm	Mud, silt	Massive, desiccation cracks	Overbank or drape deposits
Fr	Silt, mud	Rootlet traces	Seatearth
C	Coal, carbonaceous	Plants, mud films	Swamp deposits
P	Carbonate	Pedogenic features	Soil

Table 2.7b. Glacial deposits/diamict lithofacies code (modified from Eyles et al. 1983)

Diamict, D		Sands, S		Fine-grained (mud), F	
Dm:	matrix supported	Sr	rippled	Fl:	laminated
Dc:	clast supported	St:	trough cross-bedded	Fm:	massive
D-m:	massive	Sh:	horizontal lamination	F-d:	with dropstones
D-s:	stratified	Sm:	massive		
D-g:	graded	Sg:	graded		
Genetic interpretation ( )		Sd:	soft sediment deformation		
D-(r):	resedimented				
D-(c):	current reworked				
D-(s):	sheared				

acteristics. The letters "m" and "c" identify either matrix-support or clast-support, respectively. The third letter of the code refers to internal structure and distinguishes a massive unstructured organization "m" from stratified "s" and graded units "g". Massive units typically fail to show any significant internal stratification or sorting into separate size fractions. A guideline for field purposes is that a massive diamict can be regarded as a unit that shows such stratification over less than 10% of the unit thickness. Conversely a stratified diamict is one with stratification over more than 10% of unit thickness (Table 2.8). Graded units "g" are those that show distinct upward grading within, or segregation between, either clasts or matrix. The character of internal grading with regard to clast size can be depicted on the field log (Table 2.7b) by changing the size of clast symbols; matrix variation can be shown in the normal fashion by varying the width of the log column. The column width should refer to average matrix texture.

The last letters of the code emphasize certain aspects of the diamict, which are useful in environmental reconstruction and are set in parentheses to identify their genetic overtones and their use of optional extras to the main part of the objective code.

These features, which are useful with regard to glacial diamicts, relate to evidence for glacier shear or traction(s) in the form of bedding plane shears, basal grooves, consistently orientated flat-iron clasts, and shear attenuation of softer lithologies. Similar types of lithofacies codes can easily be constructed for describing fluvial and beach deposits.

Types of Glaciers

There are two main types of modern glaciers: the first is the alpine or mountain glacier that occur at all latitudes where high mountains exist; and the second is the much larger continental or icecap glacier that occur near the poles. Mountain glaciers develop in previously formed stream valleys, whose relative deepness makes them accumulation sites for snow. The glacial ice is always moving down-valley. Crevasses, or large cracks, are formed in the ice by different rates of flow in the brittle upper portion of the glacier.

The usual mountain stream valley has a V-shaped cross profile. However, in valleys from which glaciers have melted, the lower part of the profile is characterized by a U-shaped profile and the sides are steepened and the valley is flattened and straightened.

2.4 Karst Terrains

2.4.1 Definition

"Karst" is a German word, which originated from the geographical name (kras) of an area in northwestern Yugoslavia. "Kras", meaning "bare, stony ground", was derived from the Slovenian (Yugoslavian) word "Kar" (rock), as a region of Yugoslavia, and is an area characterized by bare, stony ground; underlain by some type of soluble rock (limestone, dolomite, gypsum, halite or

Table 2.8. Diagnostic criteria for recognition of common matrix-supported diamict lithofacies (modified from Eyles et al. 1983)

Facies code	Lithofacies	Description
Dmm	Matrix-supported, massive	Structureless mud/sand/pebble admixture
Dmm(r)	Dmm with evidence of resedimentation	Initially appears structureless but careful cleaning, macro sectioning, or X-ray photography reveals subtle textural variability and fine structure (e.g. silt or clay stringers with small flow noses). Stratification less than 10 percent of unit thickness.
Dmm(c)	Dmm with evidence of current reworking	Initially appears structureless but careful cleaning, macro sectioning or textural analysis reveals fine structures and textural variability produced by traction current activity (e.g. isolated ripples or ripple trains). Stratification less than 10 percent of unit thickness.
Dmm(s)	Matrix-supported, massive, sheared	Shear lamination caused by the shearing out of soft incompetent bedrock lithologies ("smudges") or slickensided bedding-plane shears resulting from subglacial shear.
Dms	Matrix-supported, stratified diamict	Obvious textural differentiation or structure with diamict. Stratification more than 10 percent of unit thickness.
Dms(r)	Dms with evidence of resedimentation	Flow noses frequently present: diamict may contain rafts of deformed silt/clay laminae and abundant silt/clay stringers and rip-up clasts. May show slight grading. Dms(r) units often have higher clast content than massive units clast clusters common. Clast fabric random or parallel to bedding. Erosion and incorporation of underlying material may be evident.
Dms(c)	Dms with evidence of current reworking	Diamict often coarse (winnowed), interbedded with sandy, silty and gravelly beds showing evidence of traction current activity (e.g. ripples, trough or planar cross-bedding). May be recorded as Dmm, St, Dms, Sr etc. according to scale of logging. Abundant sandy stringers in diamict. Units may have channelized bases.
Dmg	Matrix-supported, graded	Diamict exhibits variable vertical grading in either matrix of clast content; may grade into Dcg.
Dmg(r)	Dmg with evidence of resedimentation	Glast imbrication common

other soluble rocks; essentially devoid of surface drainage; and contains well-developed geomorphic features that were caused by solution of limestone. Karst terrains may contain a broad continuum of karst features and karst activity. Inhomogenities of the rocks play an important role in karstification that leads to subsurface drainage (Hughes et al. 1994; American Geological Institute and National Speleological Society 2000).

2.4.2 Karst and Karstification

Karst regions constitute about 25% of the land surface of the earth. Karst is a complex geological phenomenon primarily relates to carbonate rock terrains, and highly soluble rocks which have specific hydrological characteristics due to variations in development of karst features, stratigraphy, or effects of geologic structure.

Evaporites, mainly gypsum (or anhydrite) and salt, are the most soluble of common rocks. These rocks arte readily dissolved to form caves, sinkholes, disappearing streams, and other karst features commonly associated with limestone and dolomite. Evaporite-karst features can form in a matter of days, weeks, or much longer whereas carbonate-karst features take years or up to centuries to form.

Karst associated with gypsum and anhydrite rocks, is referred to as gypsum karst. Large caves are known with gypsum deposits in which the dissolutional phenomena and the hazards associated with them cause a widespread concern to environmentalists and engineering geologists. The rocks in which karst systems develop are most commonly composed of carbonate, sulfate and chloride minerals. Fissures are of primary importance as pathways for the initial; circulation in most of karst rocks. The degree and structure of fissuring in gypsum and anhydrite vary greatly from very low-fissured beds to almost brecciated rocks. This depends on many factors including particularly the age of the rock sequence, its structure, and tectonic setting, regime and the depth of occurrence (Klimchouk et al. 2000).

Karstification is an aggregate of geological processes either naturally or artificially in the earth's crust and on its surface due to chemical, physicochemical, dissolution and erosion under diverse geological and climatic conditions through time. It is expressed through the formation of openings, the destruction and alteration of the structure of the rocks, and through the creation of a particular type of ground-water circulation and a characteristic regime of drainage network and of characteristic regional topography.

The degree to which the rocks have been karstified varies greatly from place to place depending upon how much the fissures in the rock have been enlarged by the solution action of acidified rainwater and the extent to which the underground drainage system has become organized and integrated into efficient conduits for the collection, transport and ultimately discharge of recharge waters. In some areas the karstified rocks may be overlain with non-carbonate strata or unconsolidated deposits and this is termed a covered or mantled karst.

Old karstic landforms, surface and underground, which have been infilled by subsequent deposits, often have no surface expression and do not function hydrogeologically (or has lost its mass transport function). These are called paleokarsts. Paleokarsts may be reactivated if environmental conditions change. Figure 2.7 shows the hydrologic cycle in karst areas (American Geological Institute and National Speleological Society 2000).

2.4.3 Karst and Speleogenetic Processes

An international group of cave scientists summarize modern knowledge about the formation of dissolutional caves and the role of cave genetic (*speleogenetic*) processes in the development of karst aquifers.

Karst processes in carbonate rocks depend on the dissolution of limestone by water containing carbon dioxide. Carbonic acid derived from aqueous carbon dioxide acts as an aggressive agent to dissolve $CaCO_3$ which then is transported out of the karst terrain as calcium and hydrogen carbonate ions dissolved in the moving water. The maximum amount of $CaCO_3$ that can be dissolved, expressed by the maximum calcium concentration in the aggressive waters, is determined by the equilibrium chemistry of the system H_2O-CO_2-$CaCO_3$ under relevant geologic conditions, that occur in karst processes (Klimchouk et al. 2000).

2.4.4 How Important is Karst to Man's Environment?

In Yugoslavia, the home of the term "karst", 33% of the surface is karst terrain (Milanovic 1981). In the USSR, 40% of the land area consists of carbonate and other soluble rocks, and in the United States about 25% is underlain by carbonate rocks. Approximately one fifth of the earth's surface is underlain by carbonate rocks of a complex physical character that produced a diverse topographic expression by weathering under varied climatic conditions. Carbonate terrains in some areas are underlain by broad, rolling plains, whereas in others they are characterized by steep bluffs, canyons, sinks, and valleys. Owing to the variability of the solubility of limestone under different climatic and geologic conditions, man's inhabitation and development of limestone areas has often been difficult. In some areas the limestone is covered by fertile soils; in others, soils are missing. In

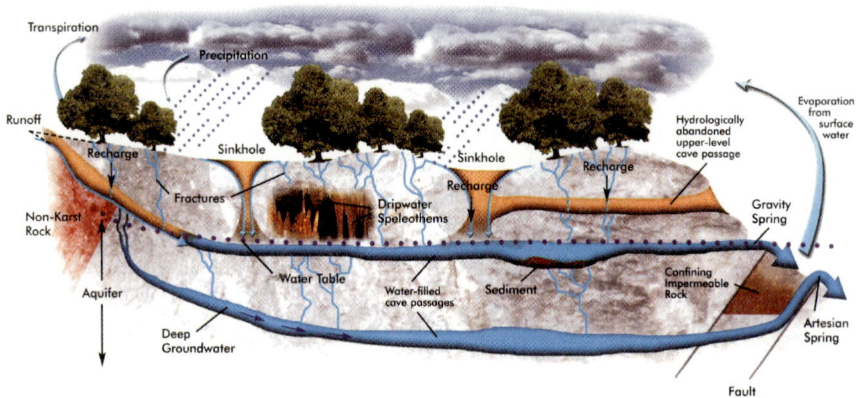
Transpiration
Precipitation
Runoff
Recharge
Sinkhole
Sinkhole
Recharge
Recharge
Hydrologically abandoned upper-level cave passage
Evaporation from surface water
Fractures
Dripwater Speleothems
Non-Karst Rock
Gravity Spring
Water Table
Confining Impermeable Rock
Aquifer
Water-filled cave passages
Sediment
Deep Groundwater
Artesian Spring
Fault

Fig. 2.7. The hydrologic cycle in karst areas (after American Geological Institute and National Speleological Society 2000; reproduced with the permission of AGI)

the midwest of the USA, a large area underlain by limestone covered a very productive, rich soil that produces large quantities of food. This area is literally "the breadbasket of the nation".

Karst areas are dynamic and environmentally sensitive. The geologic structure, solubility of the rocks involved, and the climatic conditions determine to a great degree how rapid these changes can take place. Therefore, karst investigations must consider the dynamic nature of karst.

Concurrent tectonism, and aquifer evolution, Slovenia, North Yugoslavia: Caves are natural conduits that develop within carbonate aquifers by the circulation of chemically aggressive ground water through discontinuities in the rock mass over time ranging from 10^4 to 10^6. Such particular set of discontinuities in the rock mass over time ranging.

2.4.5 Karst Features

Karst landforms are the direct result of karstification due to dissolution of soluble carbonate bedrock and subsequent physical erosion and are characterized by many areas having vertical and horizontal underground drainage. Birmingham, Alabama, Nashville, Tennessee, St. Louis, Missouri, and Guiling, China, are examples of major cities that have been built on karst terrains. A unique set of landforms is characteristic of karst, and includes some combination of the following: (1) *Karren* is a surface composed of blocks of limestone separated by narrow fissures. In calcareous districts the surface is sometimes quite bare and intersected by furrows, attaining a depth of several feet); such districts are known as *lapis*. (2) *Sinkholes* (or *dolines*) refer to areas of localized land surface subsidence, or collapse, due to karst processes. They can provide direct path for surface runoff to drain to the subsurface. A sinkhole plain in Bosnia, (ex-Yugoslavia) is a good example. (3) *Karst windows* are landforms that have features of both springs and sinkholes. They are depressions with streams flowing across their floors. (4) *Karst springs* may occur at local or regional base levels or at a point where the land surface intersects the water table. They may also occur either in valley bottoms or at sharp breaks in slope. They can also occur high, along valley sides, without obvious topographic or geologic cause.

2.4.6 Siting Landfills in Karst Terrains

Consideration of candidate sites for land disposal facilities in karst terrains is a process that requires careful screening of many potential sites, rejection of unsuitable sites, avoidance of questionable sites, and demonstration that the selected site is hydrogeologically suitable for disposal of waste.

Initial steps in the screening process typically include: (*a*) selection of a large number of candidate sites within the geographic area of interest; (*b*) ranking of the candidate sites in order of apparent suitability for disposal of wastes; (*c*) rejection of areas or sites that are obviously not suitable for disposal of wastes; and (*d*) selection of one or more of the sites for further evaluation.

Tasks, performed during screening, typically involve review of published and unpublished engineering, geologic and hydrologic literature, discussions with appropriate State or Federal personnel, study of topographic maps, interpretation of sequential aerial photographs, and verification of studies by field reconnaissance. Most of the preliminary screening can be rapidly accomplished in the office, at low cost. The stratigraphic intervals and structural anomalies, along which karst features are well developed, have typically been defined in published geologic literature and available geologic maps. That knowledge can be extended to site-specific locations through use of aerial photographs, topographic maps, and fieldwork (see Chap. 3).

See Appendix 2.A – Appearance of different sizes of sand and silt under the microscope.

References

American Geological Institute (AGI) (2000) Sustaining our soils and society. Environmental Geoscience Advisory Committee, Alexandria, Virginia (AGI Environmental Awareness series 2:40–48)

American Geological Institute and National Speleological Society (2000) Living with karst – a fragile foundation. AGI Environmental Geoscience Advisory Committee, Alexandria, Virginia, USA, pp 11–16

Assaad F (1972) Contribution to the study of the Triassic formations of the Sersou-Megress Region (High Plateau) and the Area Daia – Mzab (Saharan Platform). Arab Petroleum Congress, Sonatrach, Algiers (No. 84, B-3)

Assaad FA (1981) A further geologic study on the Triassic formations of North Central Algeria with special emphasis on Halokinesis. J Petro Geol London 4(2):163–176

Aswathanarayana U (1999) Soil resources and the environment. Science Publishers, Inc., Enfield, New Hampshire, pp 3–41

Day RW (2000) Geotechnical engineer's portable handbook. McGraw-Hill, New York

Eyles N, Eyles CH, Miall AD (1983) Lithofacies: types and vertical profile models. An alternative approach to the description and environmental interpretation of glacial diamict and diamictite sequences. Sedimentology 30:393–410

Foster RJ (1979) Physical geology. San Jose State University, Charles Merrill Publishing Company, Columbus, Ohio, pp 79–81, 84–93, 100–109

Gilluly J (1959) Principals of geology. U.S. Geological Survey, W. H. Freeman and Company, San Francisco, CA, pp 297–308

Hamblin WK, Howard HD (1965) Physical geology laboratory manual. Burgess Publishing Company, Minneapolis, pp 1, 21, 26–29, 35–37

Hughes TH, Memon BA, LaMoreaux PE (1994) Landfills in karst terrains. Bulletin of the Association of Engineering Geologists 31(2):203–208

Jackson JA (1997) Glossary of geology, 4th edn. American Geological Institute, Library of Congress Cataloging, Alexandria, Virginia

Klimchouk AB, Ford DC, Palmer AN, Dreybrodt W (2000) Speleogenesis – evolution of karst aquifers. National Speleological Society Inc., Alabama, USA, pp 1–15

Le Roy LW (1950) Subsurface geologic methods. Colorado School Of Mines, Department of Publication, Golden, Colorado, pp 71–79, 858–977

Maher JC (1964) The composite interpretive method of logging drill cuttings. Geological Survey, Oklahoma (Guidebook XIV)

Meinzer OE (1942) Physics of the earth. McGraw-Hill, New York (Part 9: Hydrology)

Miall AD (1977) A review of the braided river depositional environment. Earth Sci Rev 13:1–62 (reprinted from with permission from Elsevier)

Miall AD (ed) (1978) Lithofacies types and vertical profile models in braided rivers: a summary. In: Fluvial sedimentology. Mem Soc Petrol Geol 5:597–604

Milanovic P (1981) Karst hydrogeology (translated by Buhac JJ). Water Resources Publications, Colorado

Munsell (1975) Soil Color Charts. Macbeth Division of Klollmorgen Corporation, Baltimore, Maryland, USA (seven charts)

Pettijohn FJ (1975) Sedimentary rocks, 3rd edn. Harper and Row Publishers, New York, London, pp 316–320

Sara MN (1994) Standard handbook for solid and hazardous waste facility assessments. Lewis Publishers, an imprint of CRC Press Inc., Boca Raton, Florida, USA, pp 2.18–2.20

Tennissen AC (1983) Nature of earth materials, 2nd edn. Lamar Univ., Prentice-Hall, Inc. Englewood Cliffs, NJ, (Nature of igneous and sedimentary rocks, pp 218–225, 270–275)

USGS (1999) Sustainable growth in America's heartland – 3-D geologic maps as the foundation. The Central Great Lakes Geologic Mapping Coalition, Illinois State Geological Survey, U. S. Department of the Interior (U.S. Geological Survey Circular 1190:4–7)

Selected References

Biju-Duval B, Dercourt J, Le Pichon X (1977) From the Tethys Ocean to the Mediterranean Seas: a plate-tectonic model of the evolution of the Western Alpine System. In: Proc. of the International Symposium – Structural History of the Mediterranean basins, Split, Yugoslavia, 1976, pp 143–164

Boulton GS (1976) A genetic classification of tills and criteria for distributing tills of different origin. In: Stankowski W (ed) Till: its genesis and diagenesis. Geographia 12, UAM, Geographia Polonica, Poland

Domenico PA, Schwartz FW (1997) Physical and chemical hydrogeology, 2nd edn. John Wiley and Sons Inc., New York, pp 17–20

Klimchouk AB, Lowe D, Cooper A, Sauro U (1997) Gypsum karst of the world. International Journal of Speleology, Physical Speleology 25(3–4)

LaMoreaux PE (1991) History of karst hydrogeological studies. Proceedings of the International Conference on Environmental Changes in Karst Areas, I.G.U. – UIS-Italy, Quaderni del Dipartimento di Geografia, Universta dl Padova, 13:215–229

Trusheim F (1960) Mechanism of salt migration in Northern Germany. Bull AAPG 44(91):1519–1540

Appendix 2.A · Appearance of Different Sizes of Sand and Silt under the Microscope

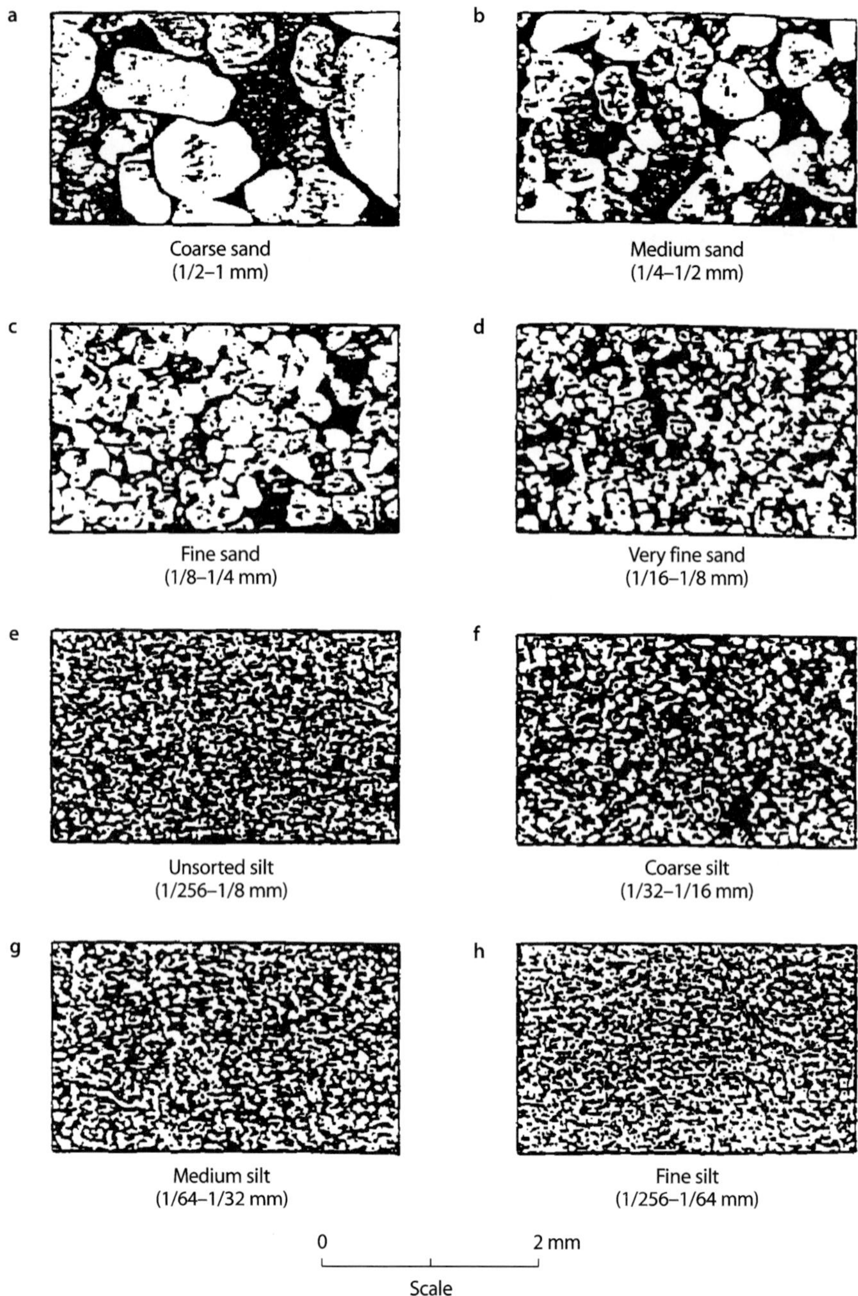
a
Coarse sand
(1/2–1 mm)
b
Medium sand
(1/4–1/2 mm)
c
Fine sand
(1/8–1/4 mm)
d
Very fine sand
(1/16–1/8 mm)
e
Unsorted silt
(1/256–1/8 mm)
f
Coarse silt
(1/32–1/16 mm)
g
Medium silt
(1/64–1/32 mm)
h
Fine silt
(1/256–1/64 mm)
0
2 mm
Scale

Fig. 2.A.1. Appearance of different sizes of sand and silt under the microscope (after Maher 1964)

Chapter 3

Topographic and Surface Geologic Maps

3.1 Topographic Maps

Topographic contour maps show the configuration of the earth's surface and are constructed by studying the variations in slopes, streams, cliffs, hilltops, etc., using stereoaerial photographs and satellite imaginary. A topographic map, which is a graphic representation of a portion of the earth's surface is constructed at a specific scale, and represents a top or surficial view of the landscape whereas a profile or cross section is constructed through certain critical points across a straight line on a map. Two types of topographic maps are usually prepared for field investigations: a regional base map and a detailed site map. The regional base map is used for location and general features and can be easily obtained from published sources and used directly for illustrative purposes. The site specific topographic map may contain 0.61 to 1.22 m contour intervals depending on the details required. U.S. Geologic Survey maps (USGS) (7.5-minute quadrangles) have contour intervals of 3 m or more. The United State Geological Surveys use geographic information systems (GIS) technology to produce highly accurate maps. GIS technology combines comprehensive database management and analytical capabilities with the ability to produce precise maps. GIS technology can produce customized maps rapidly that depict the most up-to-date information available from the database. The following review for locating features on a map is an introduction to surface mapping.

3.1.1 Longitude and Latitude

The earth's surface can be divided by a series of north-south and east-west lines to form a grid. One can refer to these lines and their subdivisions to define the position of any point on the earth's surface. The north-south lines are called lines of longitudes or meridians. They are measured in degrees, minutes and seconds. The 0° longitude or the *prime meridian* passes through Greenwich, England and is used as a reference line in mapping whereas other longitude lines are measured east and west of the Prime Meridian to the 180° line of longitude or the international date line.

The other dimension of the grid is latitude, its lines circle the globe parallel to the equator of 0° latitude and its degrees are measured north or south from 0° at the equator to 90° at the poles. The equator divides the earth into the northern and southern hemispheres (Fig. 3.1). The USGS uses the longitude-latitude grid system on all geologic and topographic maps.

Topographic maps are available from a number of sources and in a variety of scales. The USGS provides maps covering a quadrangle area bounded by lines of latitude and longitude available in 7.5' series (1:24 000), 15' series (1:62 500), 30' series (1:125 000), and 2° series (1:250 000) for most of the United States. Other countries use scales ranging from 1:10 000 to 1:1 000 000, but coverage is often incomplete. A common scale available for many areas is 1:50 000.

Table 3.1 shows sources for topographic data (Sara 1994). See Appendix 3.A – Topographic map symbols.

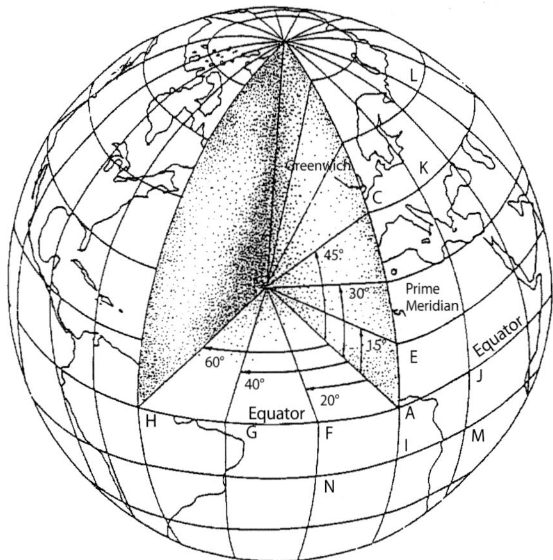

L
Greenwich
K
C
45°
30°
Prime
Meridian
15°
E
Equator
J
60°
40°
20°
Equator
H
G
F
A
M
I
N

Fig. 3.1. Diagram illustrating measurements of latitude and longitude (after Hamblin and Howard 1965, adapted by permission of Education, Inc., Upper Saddle River, NJ)

Table 3.1. Topographic data (from Sara 1994)

Source	Information obtainable	Comments
Earth Science Information Center U.S. Geological Survey 507 National Center Reston, VA 22092 Tel.: 703/860-6045 FTS 928-6045	Topographic quadrangle maps are available in several scales, most commonly 1:24 000. 1:62 500, and 1:250 000. 1:25 000 and 1:100 000-scale maps are available in limited numbers. Other scales are available for some areas.	The simplest method of selecting topographic maps is to refer to a state index map, which shows all the currently available topographic maps.
Branch of Distribution U.S. Geological Survey Map Sales Box 25286, Federal Center Denver, CO 80225 Tel.: 303/236-7477	Index and quadrangle maps for the eastern U.S. and for states west of the Mississippi River, including Alaska, Hawaii, and Louisiana.	A map should be ordered by name, series, and state. Mapping of an area is commonly available at two different scales. The quadrangle name is, in some instances, the same for both maps: where this occurs, it is especially important that the requestor specify the series designation, such as 7.5 minute (1:24 000), 15 minute (1:62 500), or two-degree (1:250 000).
Commercial map supply houses	Topographic and geologic maps	Commercial map supply houses often have full state topographic inventories that may be out of print through national distribution centers.

3.1.2 Land Office Grid System

This system involves location of an initial point of reference in a state by latitude and longitude. The latitude line for that point of reference is called the "base line" whereas the longitude line is known as the "principal meridian". From the reference point so designated, grid lines are surveyed at 9.66-kilometer intervals, at right angles to one another and enclose rectangular plots of land. The north-south lines define strips of land called ranges, numbered 1, 2, 3 etc., east and west of the principal meridian. East-west lines establish strips of land called townships numbered north and south of the base line. Each square of the grid contains 93.2 km^2 (Hamblin and Howard 1965; Fig. 3.2a–c). Any location should be designated by the township, range and section numbers, e.g. township 3S, range 2W, section 19.

3.2 Surface Geological Mapping

3.2.1 Scope

A geologic map is a map upon which geologic features of an area are recorded. It is a record of the distribution of rocks in a given area and may be a key to the determination of geologic history of an area. A book, *The Map That Changed the World,* by Simon Winchester (2001), published by Harper, describes the earliest geologic map and its evolution by William "Strata" Smith. Smith was a Welch surveyor who first noted the correlation of beds base on physical character, color, and fossil content, during his professional surveying of coalmines and canals in Great Britain. The earliest geologic map known was by a scribe of Pharaoh during the 27th dynasty who documented different rock types and water well locations.

There are many uses for a geologic map. Geologic maps are of great economic value and can be used for mapping earth materials, sand, gravel, limestone, etc. as well as for studying landslides, volcanoes, earthquakes, landforms, etc.

Geologists use geologic maps to locate areas favorable for the occurrence of fossil fuel resources, natural and industrial minerals, and development materials. They are used to identify potential geologic hazards in areas where construction is planned, e.g. for predicting foundation and slope stability problems, and for detection of sinkhole development in areas underlain by limestone or dolomite. They can also be used for selecting areas for special agricultural activities, for planning drainage and for remediation in areas of catastrophic subsidence related to karst features or landslides.

Organizations that can provide useful information about geologic mapping would include state geological surveys, USGS, and many university departments of geology, geography, and civil engineering. Other departments at universities that might provide helpful information to aid geologic mapping include biology, botany, chemistry, and agricultural science.

Vertical and horizontal control is absolutely necessary for precise geologic mapping, therefore, the Topographic Division, USGS, the U.S. Coastal and Geodetic Survey, U.S.C.O.E of Engineers, U.S. Soil Conservation

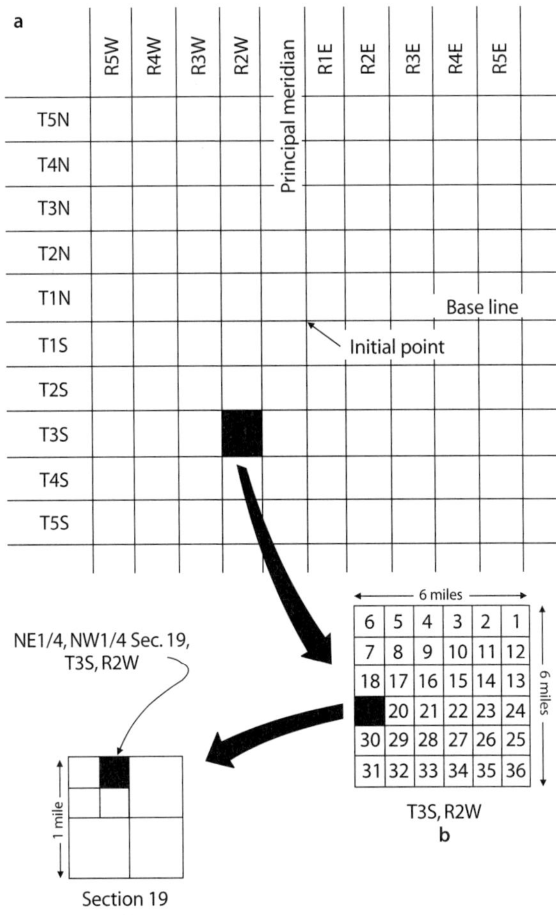
a
R5W
R4W
R3W
R2W
Principal meridian
R1E
R2E
R3E
R4E
R5E
T5N
T4N
T3N
T2N
T1N
T1S
T2S
T3S
T4S
T5S
Base line
Initial point
6 miles
6 5 4 3 2 1
7 8 9 10 11 12
18 17 16 15 14 13
20 21 22 23 24
30 29 28 27 26 25
31 32 33 34 35 36
6 miles
T3S, R2W
b
NE1/4, NW1/4 Sec. 19,
T3S, R2W
1 mile
Section 19
c

Fig. 3.2. Subdivisions of the land office grid system (after Hamblin and Howard 1965, adapted by permission of Education, upper Saddle River, NJ)

Service as well local, state and county engineering departments are sources of this information. State geological surveys and the USGS have a comprehensive Statemap cooperative program and many other cooperative studies that include geologic mapping.

Geologic maps are used to select locations for exploration borings, piezometers, the locations of production water, oil and gas wells. Table 3.2 shows the sources of geologic data (Sara 1994).

Mapping the surficial geology of a site and adjacent areas is a primary task for a geologist to define the detailed geology including soil conditions. Geologic maps contain basic information about rock types, investigated in their natural environment and in their natural relations to one another. A map that explains the surface geologic features and rock structures are implicit in their colored patterns and contour lines and symbols.

Different procedures and methods for geologic mapping are used to measure rock bodies, to plot structural measurements and to relate many kinds of data; these procedures permit interpretations of geologic features such as folds and faults and are also used to construct important projections such as cross sections (Compton 1962).

Combining topographic map features with geology is basic to the understanding of the surface outcrop pattern and for determining potential recharge/discharge patterns of the occurrence of ground water and of the exploration for minerals, oil and gas.

See Appendix 3.B – Symbols for Geologic Maps.

3.2.2 Geologic Maps in the USA

The USGS National Cooperative Geologic Mapping Program, established by Congress in 1992 and first funded in 1993, has made significant contributions to the geologic mapping program in the United States. Through its three components – Fedmap, Statemap and Edmap – the program has yielded more than 4 500 geologic maps by 2002, including digital versions of previously published maps. It has also helped geologists to develop new approaches to presenting and using digital maps (such as GIS and 3-D visualization) and to incorporate new technologies in the field and cartography. All but two states have participated in the Statemap component.

Geologic maps have direct applications. Most of the projects for Statemap have capacity for planning land uses, finding and protecting ground-water resources, finding mineral resources, making decisions about infrastructure, helping to mitigate landslide damage, siting critical facilities, monitoring coastal and stream erosion, controlling flooding, finding energy resources, lessening earthquake hazards, and controlling erosion in areas affected by wildfires (Price 2001).

Urban or suburban sprawl is a national phenomenon, and projects with Statemap and Fedmap barely keep up with the need for new maps; for example areas in and around the most rapidly expanding cities.

Fedmap projects have also focused on the geology and geologic hazards in national parks, for a sister bureau in the Department of Interior.

See 'search for references' (Sec. 14.5).

3.2.3 Geologic Maps in Canada

The Committee of Provincial Geologists (CPG 2000) is a Canadian organization of senior officials of the provincial and territorial geological surveys that have a strong service and product focus in support of the mineral industry. CPG works closely with the Federal counterpart, the Geological Survey of Canada, to capitalize on the complementary and differing mandates. Different geological surveys at different provinces carried out digital product and processing capabilities. They used GIS software to aid in map production and geological

Table 3.2. Geologic data (from Sara 1994, references cited in the table refer to the original work)

Source	Information obtainable	Comments
Geologic Indexes		
Geological Reference Sources: A Subject and Regional Bibliography of Publications and Maps in the Geological Sciences (Ward et al. 1981)	Bibliographies of geologic information for each state in the U.S. and references general maps and ground-water information for many sites	Provides a useful starting place for many site assessments. A general section outlines various bibliographic and abstracting services, indexes and catalogs, and other sources of geologic references.
A Guide to Information Sources in Mining, Minerals, and Geosciences (Kaplan 1965)	Describes more than 1 000 organizations in 142 countries. Its listings include name, address, telephone number, cable address, purpose and function, year organized, organizational structure, membership categories, and publication format. Federal and state agencies are listed for the U.S., as well as private scientific organizations, institute, and associations.	An older useful guide. Part II lists more than 600 world-wide publications and periodicals including indexing and abstracting services, bibliographies, dictionaries, handbooks, journals, source directories, and yearbooks in most fields of geosciences.
A Bibliography and Index of Geology	Includes world-wide references and contains listings by author and subject	This publication is issued monthly and cumulated annually by the American Geological Institute (AGI), and replaces separate indexes published by the U.S. Geological Survey through 1970 (North American references only) and the Geological Society of America until 1969 (references exclusive of North America only). Both publications merged in 1970 and were published by the Geological Society of America through 1978, when AGI continued its publication.
GEOREF Database	Bibliographic citations from 1961 to present	The Bibliography and Index of Geology is also part of the GEOREF computerized data maintained by AGI.
KWIC (Keyword-in-Contents) Index of Rock Mechanics Literature	Engineering geologic and geotechnical references	The KWIC index is available in two volumes at many earth science libraries (Hoek 1969; Jenkins and Brown 1979).
GEODEX Retrieval System with Matching Geotechnical Abstracts (GEODEX International, Inc., P.O. Box 279, Sonoma, California 95476)	Engineering geologic and geotechnical references	The GEODEX is a hierarchically organized system providing easy access to the geotechnical literature and can be used at many university libraries. The GEODEX system can be purchased on a subscription basis.
U.S. Federal Agencies (U.S. Geological Survey, Branch of Distribution, 604 South Pickett Street, Alexandria, Virginia 22304)	The USGS produces annually a large volume of information in many formats, including maps, reports, circulars, open-file reports, professional papers, bulletins, and many others.	To simplify the dissemination of this information, the USGS has issued a Circular (No. 777) entitled, "A Guide to Obtaining Information from the USGS" (Clarke et al. 1981). Circular 777 is updated annually and contains valuable information for anyone searching for earth sciences information.

interpretation. Catalogues of maps from geological surveys are integrated through the Canadian Geoscience Knowledge Network "CGKN" (GeoConnections 2003; e-mail: labonte@nrcan.gc.ca).

3.2.4 Digital Geological Maps

The USGS and state geological surveys are carrying out several activities in converting variable geologic data into digital geologic sets; the following are two examples from Kentucky and Hampshire Geological Surveys:

Digital geologic maps are used by Kentucky State, which is completely mapped geologically at a detailed scale (1:24 000). These maps, referred to as geologic quadrangle maps, have been used for decades to address problems associated with landslides, flooding, subsidence, ground-water supply and protection, waste disposal sites, septic systems, and other issues. During the past 5 years, the Kentucky Geological Survey (KGS) has been converting geologic quadrangle maps into digital data sets. More than 500 of the 707 geologic quadrangle maps for Kentucky have been digitized (Cobb, KGS 2002).

The digital data sets, referred to as digitally vectorized geologic quadrangles or DVGQs, allow geologic information from the DVGQs to be used together with other kinds of information – agricultural, archeological, biological, engineering, geographical, and medical – in GIS and other software. Using a GIS, people can visualize and measure relationships among the different data. The DVGQs are ideal for regional and county-level planning for:

- land and development;
- construction of roads and highways;
- management of watersheds;
- restoration of wetlands;
- mitigation of geologic hazards;
- development of oil, natural gas, coal, and mineral resources.

A free sample data is available to download at www.uky.edu/KGS/sampledvgq.

Kentucky Geological Survey, Lexington, Kentucky can be reached at website: www.uky.edu/KGS (excerpt from KGS Annual Report 2000-01)

Another state geological survey in New Hampshire collects data and perform research on the land, mineral, and water resources of the state, and disseminate the findings of such research to the public through maps, reports, and other publications. These maps like in the provinces of Canada or state surveys in the United States are widely available free or for a minimal expense. The same is true at the geological surveys of Europe or around the world. The USGS STATEMAP cooperative mapping program provides high quality surficial geology maps and as a competitive U.S. Federal program that awards matching grants to the state geological surveys representing the 50 U.S. states and territories for geological mapping projects. These maps are predominately based on U.S. topographical maps.

3.2.5 Aerial Photographic Maps

Regional studies ranging from large (hundreds of square kilometers) to small areas (hundreds of hectares) can be based on stereoscopic interpretation of aerial photographs, primarily available at two scale ranges – 1:60 000 to 1:40 000 and 1:20 000 to 1:8 000 – with the smaller scales providing an overview and the larger scales providing details. False-color infrared photographs may be obtained to locate vegetation vigor (the brighter the red, the healthier the vegetation), man-made features, high ground-water surfaces, and water bodies. Aerial photos can also provide an excellent base for plotting site features. There are many forms of remote imagery that show the site features evident on the topographic maps, as well as vegetation types, density, and image tone, and are useful for environmental as well as geologic studies.

3.2.5.1 *Uses and Techniques*

Photogeology applies to geologic studies mainly based on the examination of aerial photographs in the office.

Kinds of aerial photographs. Geologists and hydrogeologists may use three kinds of aerial photographs: (1) vertical photographs taken by a camera aimed vertically at the earth's surface are used as a base for geological mapping; (2) low oblique photographs are taken by a camera aimed at an angle to the vertical but not including the horizon; and (3) high oblique photographs are aerial photographs that show the horizon. Oblique photographs cover much larger areas and are therefore valuable in geomorphic and structural studies.

A three-dimensional or stereoscopic image of an area may be obtained by adjoining vertical photographs that overlap. Aerial photographs can be used before the field season to get an idea of the geologic features and accessibility of the area under investigation. After the fieldwork, they can be used to aid in compiling geologic and geographic data on maps. The aerial photographs normally show outcrops, rock units, and structures so clearly that boundaries of beds and other features can be drafted on these photographs (Eardley 1942).

Preparation of aerial photographs. Cameras used for vertical aerial photography are mounted in the aircraft to expose successive frames on a roll of film at a rate that gives about 60% overlap from one photograph to the next. The photographs are numbered consecutively and in order, while the aircraft is flown on as straight a flight line as possible and the photographs taken along it, comprise a flight strip. When one line has been flown to the boundaries of the area, another is started parallel to it and spaced so as to overlap the adjoining strip and each side lap is typically about 30% of each strip. When the entire area has been photographed, the contact prints are laid out so that features in the overlap areas are superimposed (Compton 1962; Fig. 3.3). A photo index of the area can then be obtained from this layout after being printed and photographed at a reduced scale.

The photograph numbers can be read from the index together with other important information such as a north arrow, the dates of photography, the number and geographic name of the project, and the approximate average scale of the photographs.

Air photography and satellite imagery are important tools for geologic mapping and are found in the following organizations, provide information and assistance:

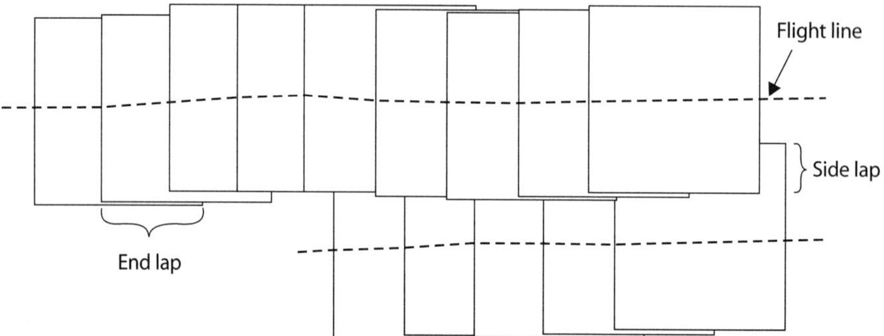
Flight line
Side lap
End lap

Fig. 3.3.
Parts of two flight strips of aerial photographs, superimposed to show characteristic overlaps (after Compton 1962)

1. U.S. Geological Survey: www.esgs.gov
2. American Geological Institute: www.agiweb.org
3. U.S. Fish and Wildlife Service: www.fws.gov
4. USDA Forest Service: www.fs.fed.us
5. National Park Service: www.aqd.nps.gov
6. Bureau of Land Management: www.blm.gov/nhp

3.2.5.2 *Uses of Stereoscope*

A stereoscope is used to obtain a stereoscopic image from two overlapping aerial photographs. The camera recorded two separate views of one object (stereo pairs) and each flight strip of a photographed area consists of a series of such pairs. An entire area can be examined stereoscopically by using one consecutive pair after another.

Two kinds of stereoscopes are known: a pocket stereoscope, which is the most simple and least expensive; and the mirror stereoscope, which is much larger and gives a view of an entire overlap area at one setting.

The pocket stereoscope consists of two magnifying lenses set in a folding metal frame. A clear stereoscopic image can be seen by setting the instrument correctly over the two photographs of a stereo pair. However, the following instructions may be considered when using the field stereoscope (Compton 1962; Fig. 3.4).

1. Set the lenses of the stereoscope so that the distance in between is the same as the pupils of the eyes.
2. Place the two photographs of a stereo pair in the same consecutive order and orientation as in their flight strip.
3. Pick a distinctive feature that lies in the overlap area near the flight line (in the center of the photograph) and place the photographs over one another so that their images coincide; then draw the pictures apart in the direction of the flight line until the two selected images are separated by about the same distance as the centers of the lenses.
4. Place the stereoscope so that one image is under the center of one lens and the axis of the stereoscope coincides with the flight line and adjust carefully the other photograph by moving it only in the direction of the flight line until the other image of the feature is under the second lens. The three-dimensional image can then be seen; if not, a slight turn of the stereoscope may be required from the supposed flight line.

3.2.5.3 *Photogeologic Features*

Photogeologic features used in photogeological interpretation, are as follows:

1. *Relief and tone* on aerial photographs are not absolute quantities for rocks. A rock that forms a positive morphological feature may be flanked by one of a country rock that forms a negative feature of different physical character. Similarly, the tone of a photograph may be affected by many factors, such as nature of rock, light conditions at time of photographing, characteristics of film, influence of filters, effects of processing, etc. The tone of the photographic image of an intrusion is related to its composition. The more basic intrusions produce the darker tones. Acid intrusive rocks are relatively light-toned and are more resistant to erosion and form positive features. Thus changes in vegetation, hydrology, geomorphology, geologic structure, as well as seep zones can be differentiated.

   Among sedimentary-bedded rocks: chalk, limestone, sandstone, quartz-schist, and quartzite tend to photograph in a light tone; whereas mudstones, shales, slates and schists in intermediate tones; and amphibolites in dark tones.

   It is possible to differentiate between beds that are steeply dipped and tightly folded with multiple intrusions and un-metamorphosed sediments lying flat or in gently folded strata without associated intrusions (NASA 2003; Berger 1994; Moore 1979).
2. *Bedding.* Aerial photographs provide evidence of bedding, which may not be available from field observations, e.g. ridges formed by resistant beds along the length of their outcrops are more clearly defined on the equivalent stereomodel than on the ground. Also,

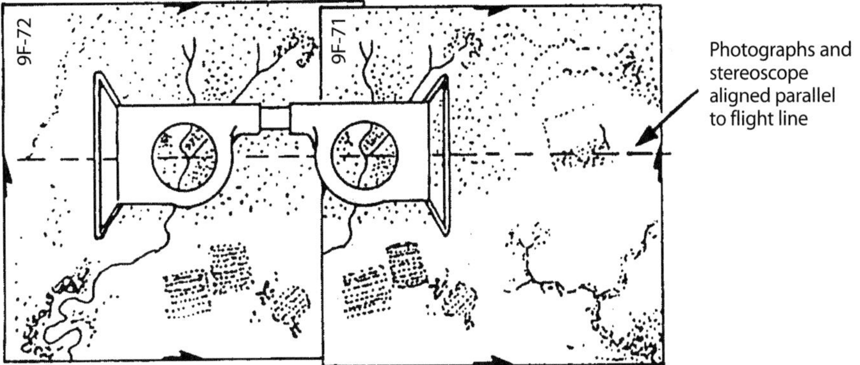
9F-72
9F-71
Photographs and stereoscope aligned parallel to flight line

Fig. 3.4. Position of pocket stereoscope relative to two photographs of a stereo pair (after Compton 1962)

beds that differ in their mineral constituents will also differ in their color and reflectivity. This difference, unless obscured by soil or vegetation cover, is represented on the stereomodel as a difference in tone.

3. *Dip slopes* provide the most reliable indication of the direction of dip available to the photogeologist. The dips are more reliably recognized on the stereomodel than in the field and accurate measurements may be defined by photogrammetric methods.
4. *Foliation* generally refers to the segregation of platy or elongate minerals into thin layers or folia, whereas schistosity refers to the parallel orientation of such minerals.
5. *Folding.* A representation of the whole fold can be seen on the stereomodel in three dimensions simultaneously; the estimation of the axial trace, position and plunge may be more reliable than similar estimations based on dips and strikes plotted on a geological map.
6. *Lineament* is any line on an aerial photograph that can represent structural control and includes any alignment of separate photographic images which may be reflected by streambeds, trees or bushes. A lineament can be defined together with drainage patterns and geomorphic trends by aerial photography (LaMoreaux and Newton 1996; LaMoreaux et al. 1989).
7. *Faulting.* A fault may be defined as a fracture along which there has been slipping of the contiguous masses against one another. Valleys and depressions are mainly caused by faults. Many fault planes become injected with magmatic or mineralizing solutions to form dykes or mineral veins. They are then likely to form positive rather than negative features. In areal photographs one can define the trace of the fault plane on the surface of the ground; unless the fault plane is vertical, its trace will be affected by relief. However, before a fault can be interpreted, there should be evidence of relative movement between different sides of the lineament.
8. *Joints* are characteristically represented on stereomodels as straight negative features. They are thus similar in photographic appearance to faults but there is no evidence of relative movement between both sides of the lineament.

3.3 Geological Surveying Methods

3.3.1 Brunton Compass

The *Brunton compass* is one of the important field instruments. It is used to measure certain parameters related to the structure of the encountered beds and the altitudes of various geologic structures. It consists of three basic instruments combined: the compass, clinometer, and hand level. When the compass is open, the compass needle rests on the pivot needle. Care should be taken to ascertain that the hinges are tight enough to avoid folding down of the lid, sighting arm and peep sights, under their own weight. The Brunton compass should never be carried open in the hand while walking over rough or rocky ground. The needle should be drained if the compass has been used in the rain (Figs. 3.5a, 3.5b; Compton 1962).

Uses of the Brunton compass:

1. *Taking bearings with the compass:* A bearing is the compass direction from one point to another. It has an undirectional sense and is taken from the compass to the point sighted when the sighting arm is aimed at the point. The white end of the needle gives the bearing directly because the E and W markings are transposed. Incorrect bearings may occur because of local deflection of the earth's magnetic field. Objects like knives, hammers and belt buckles should be kept away while reading. The same can be applied for rocks and soils rich in iron such as those containing magnetite and bodies of basalt, gabbro and ultrabasic rocks.

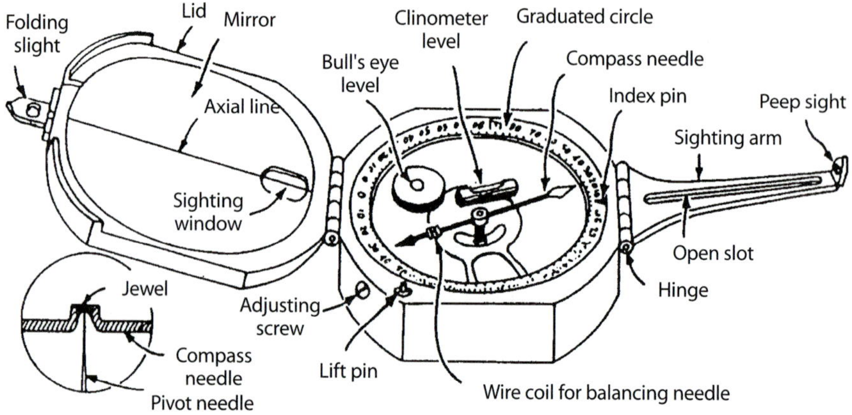
Folding
slight
Lid
Mirror
Axial line
Sighting
window
Jewel
Compass
needle
Pivot needle
Adjusting
screw
Lift pin
Bull's eye
level
Clinometer
level
Graduated circle
Compass needle
Index pin
Peep sight
Sighting arm
Open slot
Hinge
Wire coil for balancing needle

Fig. 3.5a. The Brunton compass. *Insert* at lower left shows enlarged section through needle bearing (after Compton 1962)

Fig. 3.5b. The Brunton compass

2. *Setting for magnetic declination:* The 0 point of the graduated circle of the compass can be brought to the point of the index pin by turning the adjusting screw (on the side of the case) to measure bearings from the magnetic north.
3. *Measurement of vertical angles with the clinometer:* This can be read to the nearest quarter of a degree. The instructions are summarized as follows:
   a The lid is opened for about 45°, the sighting arm is folded out with its point turned up at right angles;
   b The compass is held in a vertical plane, with the sighting arm pointing toward the right eye. The clinometer is moved by the lever (on the back of the compass box until the tube bubble is centered, as observed by the mirror. Finally, the compass is brought down then the angle is read and recorded.
4. *Defining points of the same elevations with the hand level:* The Brunton compass can be used as a hand level by setting the clinometer exactly at 0°, opening the lid 45°; extending the sighting arm with the sighting point turned up; and holding the compass as previously used when measuring vertical angles. It should be tilted slowly until the mirror image of the tube bubble is centered. If the tip of the sighting arm and the axial line of the sighting window is lined up with any point then it will be at the same elevation as the eye of the observer. A series of points of same elevations can be noted by rotating the entire instrument horizontally. The difference in elevation between two points can also be measured by standing at the lower of the two points and finding a point on the ground that is level with the eye.

MAPS

Fig. 3.6.
Completion of data

5. *Measurement of strike and dip:* The strike and dip of bedding, faults, joints and foliations can be measured with the Brunton compass. Strike is the line of intersection between a horizontal plane and the bedding plane. It can be defined by measuring the compass direction of a horizontal line on that plane. The amount of dip, on the other hand, is the slope of the bedding plane at right angles to this line. To measure the dip, the lid and the sighting arm of the compass should be opened and the compass held in the line of sight used to measure the strike. The compass is then tilted until the upper edge of the box and lid appear to lie along the bedding plane. The clinometer level is rotated until the tube bubble is centered and the dip is then recorded to the nearest degree.

3.3.2 Map-Scale Structures and Map Interpretation

Many important decisions, for locating a landfill site or for determining the location and size of an earthquake-producing fault, the occurrence of a water-bearing zone, a mineral deposit or a significant geologic feature can be based on geological maps. Because a map-scale structure is never completely sampled in three dimensions, geological maps and cross sections derived from maps are always interpretations. The interpretation may be made more accurate by careful direct structural observations For example a small outcrop of bedding attitudes can be misleading because they represent a local structure, and not a regional structure.

The primary objective of structural map making and map interpretation is to develop an internally consistent three-dimensional (3-D) picture of the structure that agrees with all the data. The basic elements of map-scale structure are the geometries of folds and faults, the shape and thickness of units, and the contact types (Groshong 1999).

Groshong (1999) discussed map-scale structures in three dimension, map interpretation (Figs. 3.7–3.24) and the orientation of planes as follows.

3.3.2.1 *Representation of a Structure in Three Dimensions*

A structure can be illustrated as a 3-D solid volume that contains numerous beds and perhaps faults, jointing or intrusions (Fig. 3.7). The most complete interpretation would be as a 3-D solid, an approach now possible with 3-D computer graphics programs.

1. Structure contour map: A structure contour map is the trace of a horizontal line on a surface (e.g. on a formation top or a fault). A structure contour map represents a topographic map of the surface of a geological horizon (Fig. 3.8). The dip direction of the surface is perpendicular to the contour lines and the dip amount is proportional to the spacing between the contours. Structure contours provide an effective method for representing the 3-D form of a surface in two dimensions. Structure contours on a faulted horizon (Fig. 3.9) are truncated at the fault.

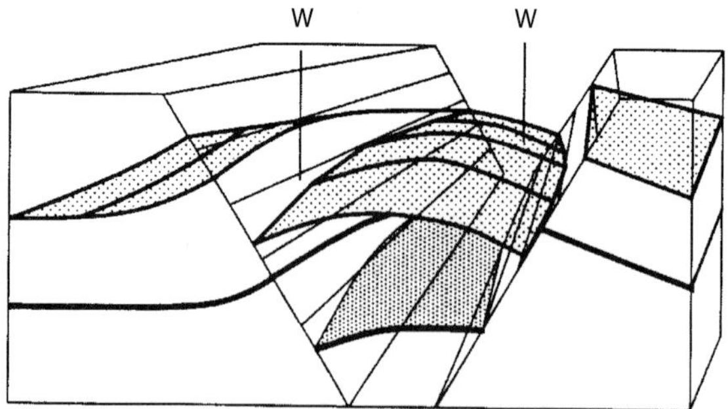
W
W

Fig. 3.7. Geometry of a structure in three dimensions. *W*: Well location where the structure is sampled

2. Triangulated irregular network (TIN): A triangulated irregular network (Fig. 3.10) is an array of points that define a surface. In a TIN, the nearest-neighbor points are connected to form triangles that form the surface (Groshong 1999). The TIN can be contoured to make a structure contour map.
3. Cross section: As a structure contour map or TIN represents the geometry of a surface in three dimensions, it is only two-dimensional because it has no thickness. A cross section of the geometry that would be seen on the surface of a slice through the volume is the simplest representation of the relationship between horizons.

3.3.2.2 *Map Units and Contact Types*

A geologic unit is a closed volume between two or more contacts, each of which is the place where two different kinds of rocks come together. The geometry of a structure is represented by the shape of the contacts between adjacent units. Dips or layering within a unit, such as in a cross-bedded sandstone, are not necessarily parallel to the contacts between map units (Groshong 1999):

1. Depositional contacts: A depositional contact is produced by the accumulation of material adjacent to the contact (Bates and Jackson 1987). Sediments, igneous or sedimentary extrusions, and air-fall igneous rocks have a depositional lower contact, which is parallel to the pre-existing surface. A conformable contact is one in which the strata are in unbroken sequence and in which the layers are formed one above the other in parallel order, representing the interrupted deposition of the same general type of material, e.g. sedimentary or volcanic (Bates and Jackson 1987). Lithologic boundaries that represent lateral facies transitions (Fig. 3.11a) were probably not horizontal to begin with. Certain sedimentary deposits drape over pre-existing topography (Fig. 3.11b) while others are deposited with primary depositional slopes (Fig. 3.11c). Contacts that dip only a few degrees might

Fig. 3.8. Structure contours; **a** lines of equal elevation on the surface of a map unit; **b** lines of equal elevation projected onto a horizontal surface to make a structure contour map

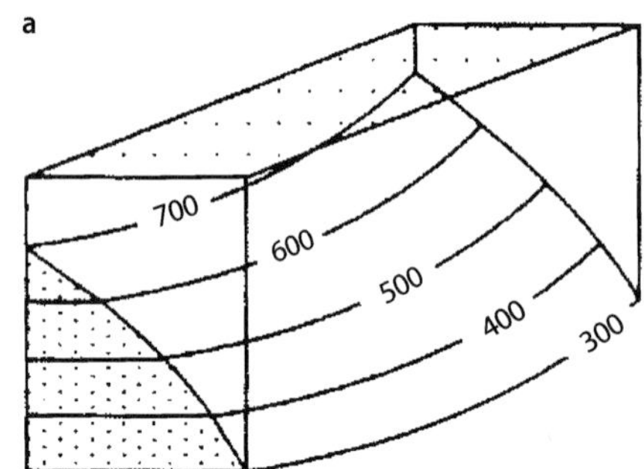
a
700
600
500
400
300

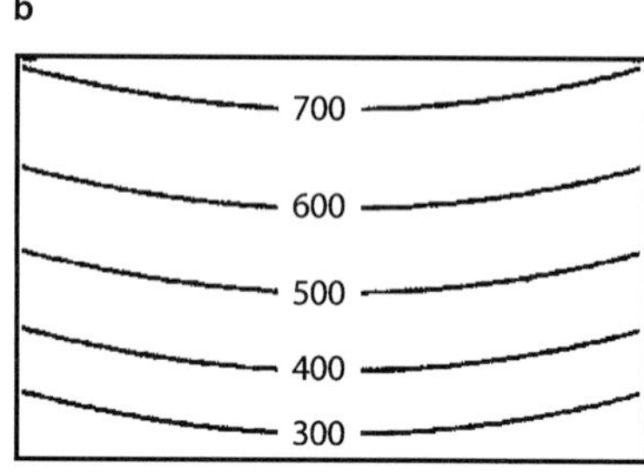
b
700
600
500
400
300

Fig. 3.9. Structure contour map of the faulted upper horizon. Contours are at 100-unit intervals, with negative elevations being below sea level. Fault gaps, where the horizon is missing are *shaded in grey*

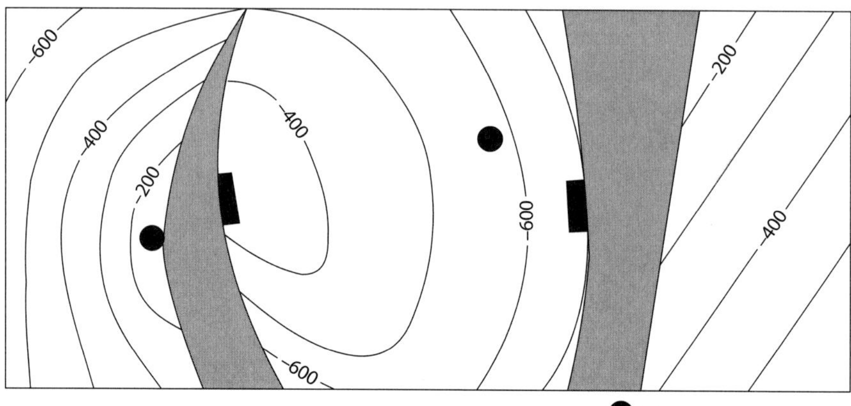
-600
-400
-200
-400
-600
-600
-200
-400
Well

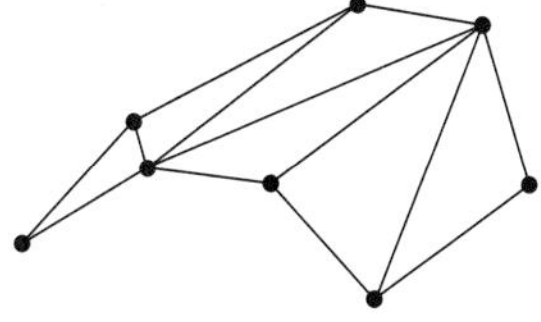

Fig. 3.10. Triangulated irregular network (TIN) of points. This could represent the map view of the points projected onto a horizontal plane or could be a perspective view of points plotted in three dimensions

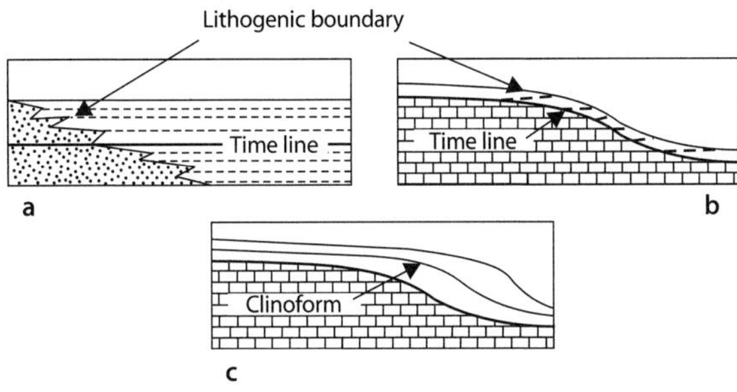

Lithogenic boundary
Time line
Time line
a
b
Clinoform
c

Fig. 3.11. Cross sections showing primary depositional lithologic contacts that are not horizontal; **a** laterally equivalent deposits of sandstone and shale; the depositional surface is a time line, not the lithologic boundary; **b** draped deposition parallel to a topographic slope; **c** Primary topography associated with clinoform deposition

be treated as originally horizontal in the interpretation of a local map area, but the depositional contact between a reef and the adjacent basin sediments may be close to vertical. Depositional contacts that had significant original topographic relief should be restored to their original depositional geometry, not to the horizontal (Fig. 3.12).

2. Unconformities: An unconformity is a surface of erosion or nondeposition that separates younger strata from older strata. An angular unconformity (Fig. 3.13a) is an unconformity with groups of rocks whose bedding planes are not parallel. A buttress unconformity (Fig. 3.13b; Bates and Jackson 1987) is a surface on which on lapping strata abut against a steep topographic scarp of regional extent. A disconformity (Fig. 3.13c) is an unconformity where the bedding planes above and below the break are essentially parallel, indicating a significant interruption in the orderly sequence of sedimentary rocks, generally by an interval of erosion (or sometimes of nondeposition), and marked by a visible and irregular or uneven erosion surface of appreciable relief. A nonconformity (Fig. 3.13d) is an unconformity developed between sedimentary rocks and older plutonic or massive metamorphic rocks that had been exposed to erosion before being covered by the overlying sediment.
3. Time-equivalent boundaries: The best map-unit boundaries for regional structural and stratigraphic interpretation are time-equivalent across the map area. Time-equivalent boundaries are normally established using fossils and/or radiometric age dates and may cross lithologic boundaries. A sequence is a conformable succession of genetically related strata bounded by unconformities and their correlative conformities (Van Wagoner et al. 1988).
4. Welds: A weld joins strata originally separated by a depleted or withdrawn unit (Jackson 1995). Welds are best known where a salt bed has been depleted by substratal dissolution or by a flow (Fig. 3.14). If the depleted unit was deposited as a part of a stratigraphically conformable sequence, the welded contact will resemble a disconformity. If the depleted unit was originally an intrusion, like a salt sill, the welded contact will return to its original stratigraphic configuration.

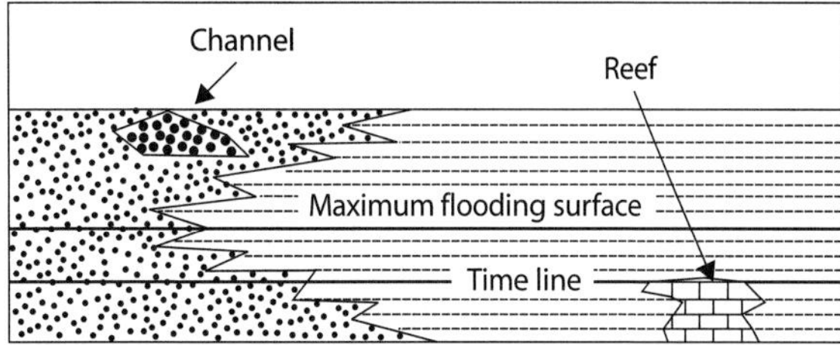

Channel
Reef
Maximum flooding surface
Time line

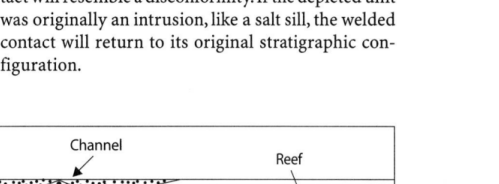

Fig. 3.12. Cross sections showing primary sedimentary facies relationships and maximum flooding surface. All time lines are horizontal in this example

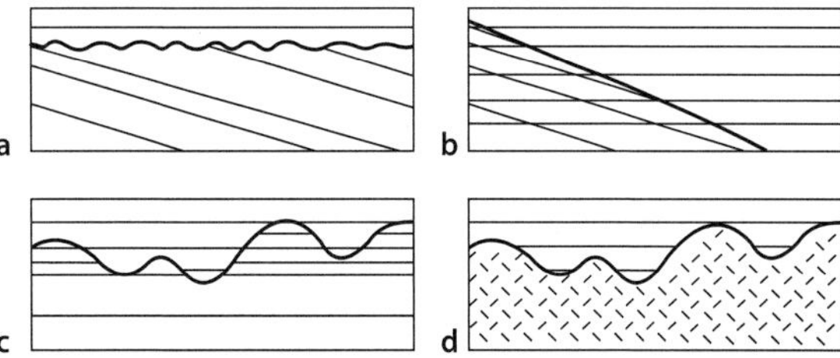

a
b
c
d

Fig. 3.13. Unconformity types; the unconformity (*heavy line*) is the contact between the older, underlying *shaded* units and the younger, overlying *unshaded* units; **a** angular unconformity; **b** buttress or onlap unconformity; **c** disconformity; **d** nonconformity. The *patterned* unit is plutonic or metamorphic rock

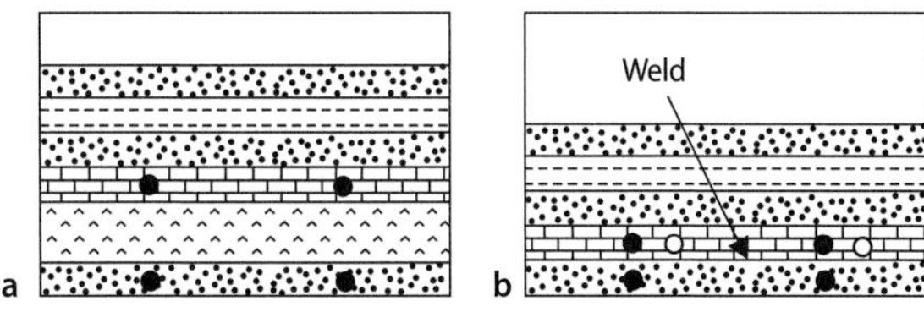

Weld
a
b

Fig. 3.14. Cross sections illustrating the formation of a welded contact. *Solid dots* are fixed material points above and below the unit, which will be depleted; **a** sequence prior to depletion; **b** sequence after depletion; *solid dots* represent the final positions of original points in a hangingwall without lateral displacement; *open circles* represent final positions of original points in a hangingwall with lateral displacement

3.3.2.3 *Thickness*

The thickness of a unit is the perpendicular distance between its bounding surfaces. The true thickness does not depend on the orientation of the bounding surfaces. If a unit has variable thickness, various alternatives might be used, such as the shortest distance between upper and lower surfaces or the distance measured perpendicular to either the upper or lower surface.

3.3.2.4 *Folds*

A fold is a bend due to deformation of the original shape of a rock surface. An antform is convex upward; an anticline is convex upward with older beds in the center. A synform is convex upward; a syncline is concave upward with younger beds in the center.

3.3.2.5 *Three-dimensional Geometry*

1. A *cylindrical fold* is defined by the locus of points generated by a straight line, called the fold axis, that is moved parallel to itself in space (Fig. 3.15a). A cylindrical fold has the shape of a portion of a cylinder. In a cylindrical fold every straight line on the folded surface is parallel to the axis. The geometry of a cylindrical fold persists unchanged along the axis as long as the axis remained straight. A *conical fold* is generated by a straight line rotated through a fixed point called the vertex (Fig. 3.15b). A conical fold changes geometry and terminates along the trend of the cone.
2. The *crest line* is the trace of the line that joins the highest points on successive cross sections through a folded surface (Figs. 3.15b, 3.16a; Dennis 1967). A trough line is the trace of the lowest elevation on cross sections through a horizon. The plunge of a cylindrical fold is parallel to the orientation of its axis or a hinge line (Fig. 3.16b). The most useful measure of a plunge of a conical fold is the orientation of its crest line or through line (Bengtson 1980).

   The complete orientation of a fold requires the specification of the orientation of both the fold and the axial surface (Fig. 3.17). In the case of a conical fold, the orientation can be specified by the orientation of the axial surface and the orientation of the crestal line on a particular horizon.

3.3.2.6 *Faults*

A fault (Fig. 3.18) is a surface or narrow zone where there has been relative displacement of the two sides parallel to the zone (Bates and Jackson 1987). A shear zone is a general term for a relatively narrow zone with sub-parallel boundaries in which shear strain is concentrated (Mitra and Marshak 1988). As the terms are usually applied, a bed, foliation trend, or other marker horizon maintain continuity across a shear but is broken and displaced across a fault. The term fault is used to include both fault and shear zones as it is difficult to distinguish between both.

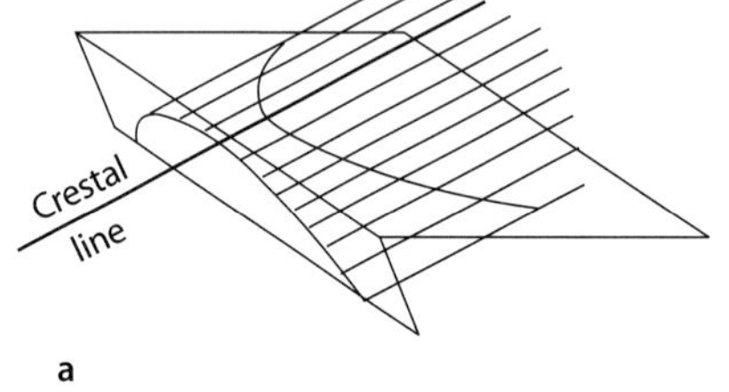
Crestal
line
a

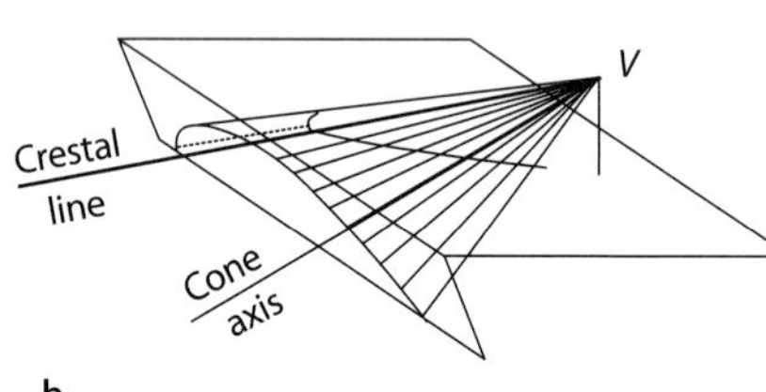
V
Crestal
line
Cone
axis
b

Fig. 3.15. Three-dimensional fold types; **a** cylindrical (all straight lines on the cylinder surface are parallel to the fold axis and to the crestal line); **b** conical (*V*: vertex of the cone; straight lines on the cone surface are not parallel to the cone axis)

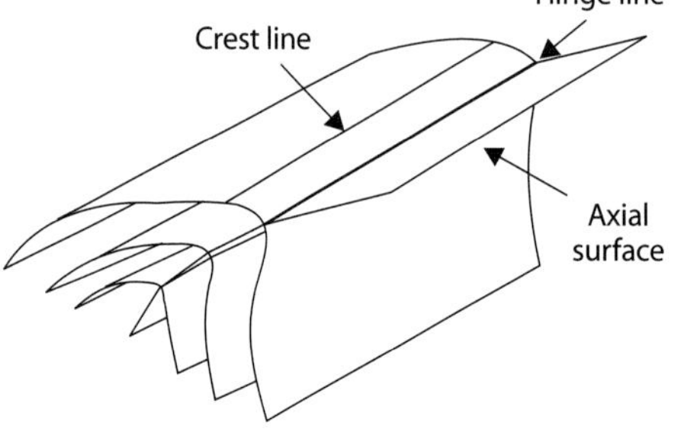
Hinge line
Crest line
Axial
surface
a

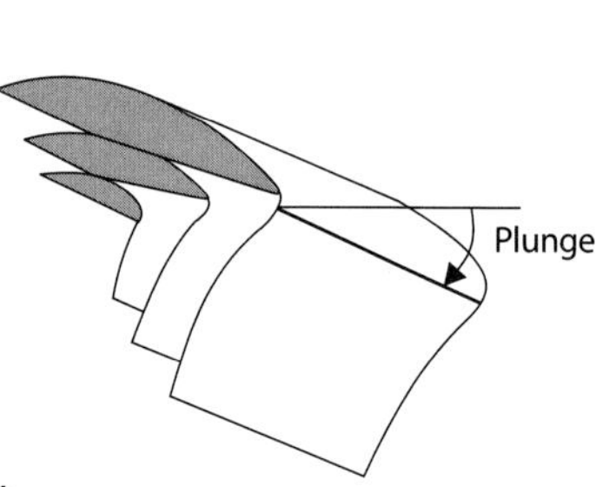
Plunge
b

Fig. 3.16. Cylindrical folds; **a** non-plunging; **b** plunging

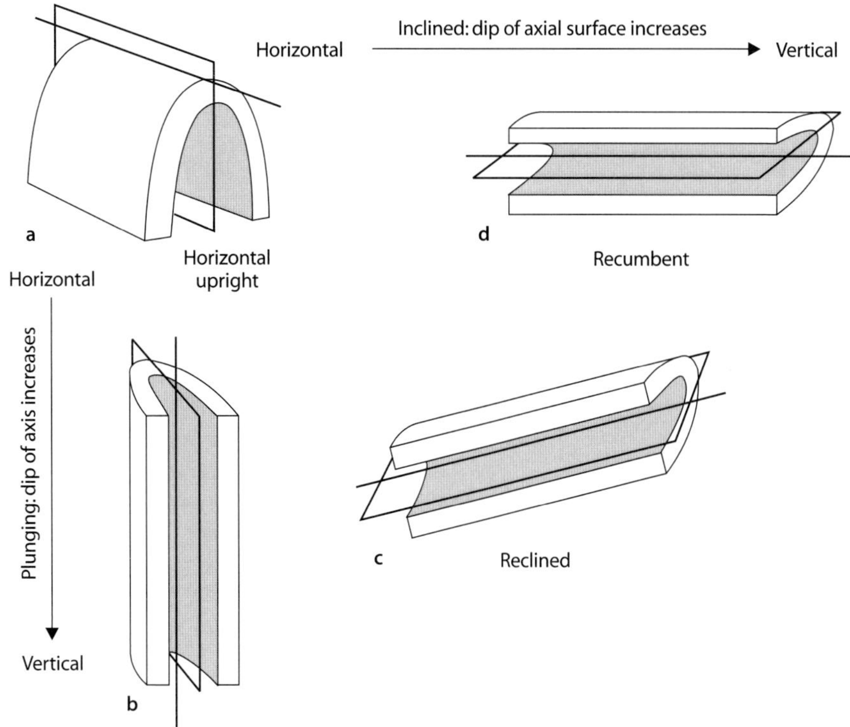
Horizontal
Inclined: dip of axial surface increases
Vertical
a
Horizontal
Horizontal upright
d
Recumbent
Plunging: dip of axis increases
Vertical
b
c
Reclined

Fig. 3.17.
Fold classification based on orientation of the axis and axial surface; **a** horizontal upright: horizontal axis and vertical axial surface; **b** vertical: vertical axis and vertical axial surface; **c** reclined: inclined axis and axial surface; **d** recumbent: horizontal axis and axial surface (after Fleuty 1964)

3.3.2.7 *Slip*

A fault slip is the relative displacement of formerly adjacent points on opposite sides of the fault, measured along the fault surface (Fig. 3.19; Dennis 1967).

A slip can be subdivided into horizontal and vertical components, the strike slip and dip slip components, respectively. A fault in which the slip direction is parallel to trace of the cut-off line of bedding can be called a trace slip fault. In horizontal beds a trace-slip fault is a strike-slip fault.

1. Separation: Fault separation is the distance between any two parts of an index plane (e.g. bed or vein) disrupted by a fault, measured in any specified direction Dennis 1967). The separation directions commonly important in mapping are parallel to fault strike, parallel to fault dip, horizontal, vertical and perpendicular to bedding.
2. *Geometrical classifications:* A fault is termed normal or reverse on the basis of the relative displacement of the hanging wall with respect to the footwall (Fig. 3.20). For a normal fault, the hanging wall is displaced down with respect to the footwall, and for a reverse fault the hanging wall is displaced up with respect to the footwall. The relative displacement may be either a slip or a separation and the use of the term should so indicate, e.g. a normal-separation fault. Using the horizontal as the plane of reference

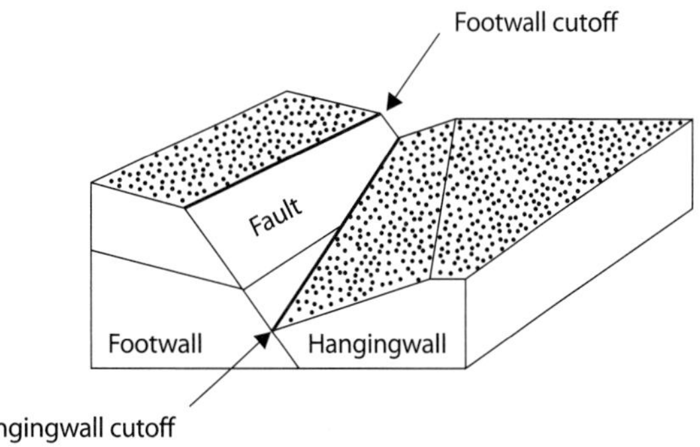
Footwall cutoff
Fault
Footwall
Hangingwall
Hangingwall cutoff

Fig. 3.18. General terminology for a surface (*patterned*) offset by a fault. *Heavy lines* are hangingwall and footwall cutoff lines

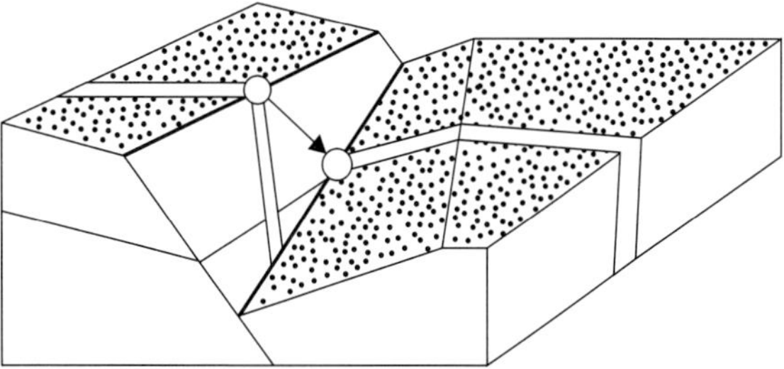

Fig. 3.19. Fault slip is the displacement of points (*open circles*) that were originally in contact across the fault. Here the correlated points represent the intersection line of a dike and a bed surface at the fault plane

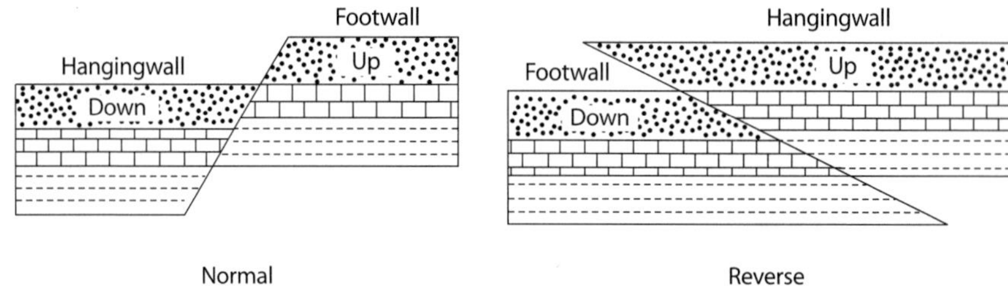
Hangingwall
Down
Footwall
Up
Normal
Footwall
Down
Hangingwall
Up
Reverse

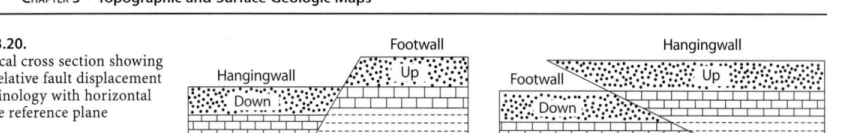

Fig. 3.20. Vertical cross section showing the relative fault displacement terminology with horizontal as the reference plane

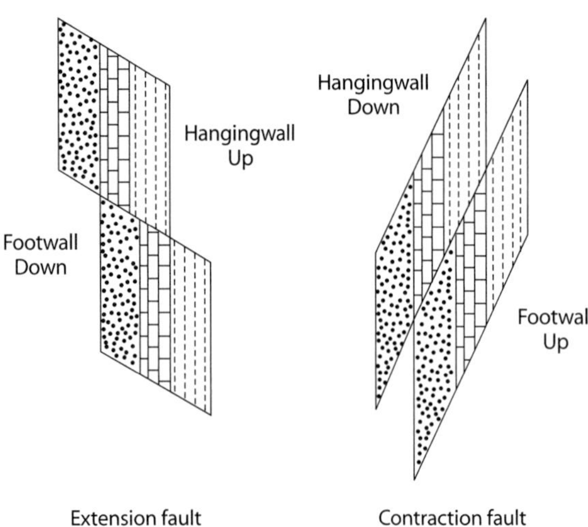
Hangingwall
Up
Footwall
Down
Extension fault
Hangingwall
Down
Footwall
Up
Contraction fault

Fig. 3.21. Vertical cross section showing the relative fault displacement terminology with bedding as the reference plane

(i.e. originally horizontal bedding), a normal-separation fault extends the cross section parallel to bedding and a reverse-separation fault shortens the cross section.

Using bedding as the frame of reference is not the same as using a horizontal plane, as illustrated in Fig. 3.21, which shows the faults from Fig. 3.20 after a 90° rotation. With bedding vertical, a reverse displacement extends the bedding while shortening a horizontal line.

3.3.3 Finding the Orientation of Planes

The basic structural measurements at a point are the orientation of lines and planes. The attitude of a plane is its orientation in three dimensions. The attitude of a plane measured by hand with a compass or given by a dipmeter log is effectively the value at a single point. Measured over such a small area, the attitude is very sensitive to small measurement errors, surface irregularities, and the presence of small-scale structures.

In gently dipping beds, the strike and dip can be determined from three points that lie at different elevations on one bedding surface. The distances and directions between the three points should be measured from a map or aerial photographs whereas the differences in elevations between them can be determined from a contour map (Groshong 1999).

Graphical three-point problem describes the determination of the attitude of a plane from three points (a, d, f) not on a straight line: a is the highest elevation; d is the lowest whereas, the intermediate elevation f occurs along the line joining a and d at point e (Fig. 3.22). The line fe is the strike line. The horizontal (map) distance from a to e is ab:

$$ab = (ac \times be) \,/\, cd \tag{3.1}$$

Plot the length ab on the map (Fig. 3.22b) and join point f and b to obtain the strike line. The dip vector lies along the perpendicular to the strike, directed from the high point to the intermediate elevation along the strike line. The dip amount is:

$$\delta = \arctan(v \,/\, h) \tag{3.2}$$

where v = the elevation difference between the highest and the lowest points and h = the horizontal (map) distance between the highest point and a strike-parallel line through d. The azimuth of the dip is measured directly from the map direction of the dip.

A typical example of a 3-point problem is seen on the map of Fig. 3.23a, which shows the elevations of three locations identified in the field as being on the same contact. These points could be elevations for an outcrop formation boundary identified in three wells.

The attitude of the contact can be calculated by drawing a line between the highest and lowest points (Fig. 3.23b); its length will be 944 m. Use Eq. 3.1 to find the distance along the line from the high point to the level of the intermediate elevation (ab = 524 m). Connect the two intermediate elevations to find the strike line. Draw a perpendicular from the strike line to the lowest point (Fig. 3.23b) and measure its length (gc = 360 m) and its azimuth in the down-dip direction (120°). Determine the dip from Eq. 3.2: d = 04°.

A dip can be converted from degrees into meters/kilometer by solving Eq. (3.2) for v and letting h be the reference length (1 000 m for m/km, respectively):

$$v = h \tan\delta \tag{3.3}$$

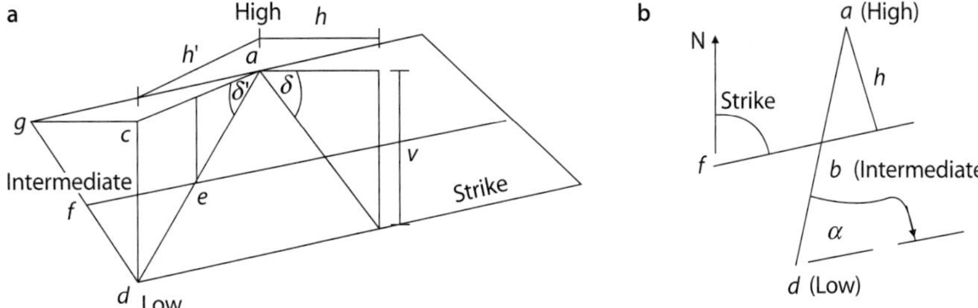
a
High
h
h'
a
δ'
δ
g
c
v
Intermediate
f
e
Strike
d
Low
b
a (High)
N
Strike
h
f
b (Intermediate)
α
d (Low)

Fig. 3.22. True dip, δ, and apparent dip, δ'; **a** perspective view; **b** map view. *N*: north. For explanation of *a–h* and *v*, see text (Sect. 3.3.3)

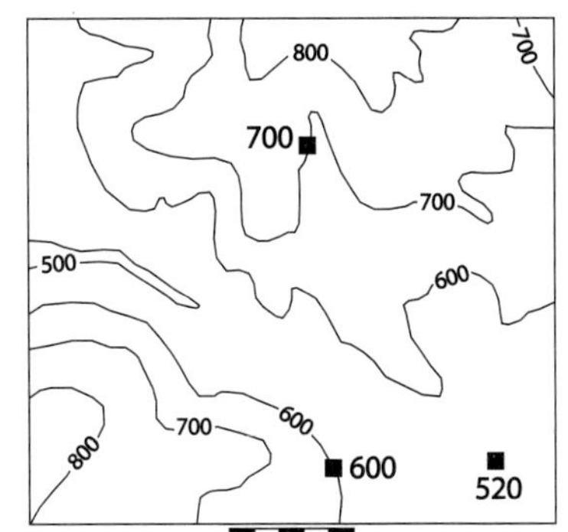
a
800
700
700
700
500
600
700
600
800
600
520

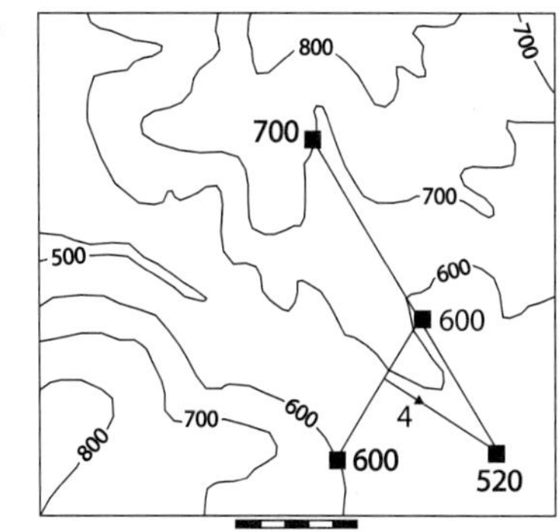
b
800
700
700
700
500
600
600
700
600
4
800
600
520

Fig. 3.23. Attitude determination from three points on a topographic map of a valley in a southeastern portion of the Blount Springs area. Elevations are in feet and the scale bar is 1000 ft; **a** three points (*solid squares*) on the Mpm-Mh contact; **b** results of 3-point attitude calculation in bold. Attitude of the contact is 04,120

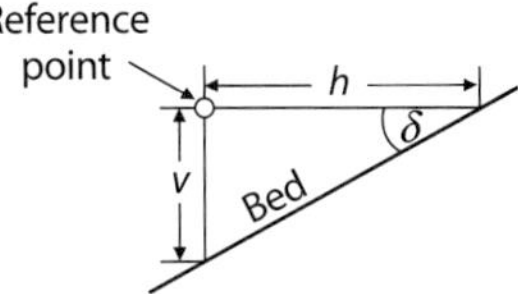
Reference
point
h
δ
v
Bed

Fig. 3.24. Distance to a point on a dipping bed, in vertical cross sections in the dip direction; vertical distance from a reference point to a dipping bed

where v = the vertical elevation change, h = reference length, and δ = dip. The same relationship can be used to determine the vertical distance from a reference point to a dipping horizon seen in a nearby outcrop (Fig. 3.24).

References

Bates RL, Jackson JA (1987) Glossary of geology, 3rd edn. American Geological Institute, Alexandria, Virginia

Bengtson CA (1980) Structural uses of tangent diagrams. Geology 8:599–602

Berger Z (1994) Satellite hydrcarbon exploration-interpretation and integration techniques. Springer-Verlag, New York, pp 66, 102–105

KGS (2002) Environmental geology. International Journal of Geosciences 42(4):439 (J. Cobb, State Geologist and Director, Kentucky Geological Survey, Lexington, Kentucky)

Committee of Provincial Geologists (2000) Provincial Geologists Journal, Canada 18:49–55

Compton RR (1962) Manual of field geology. John Wiley & Sons Inc., New York, pp 1–153

Dennis JG (1967) International tectonics dictionary. American Association of Petroleum Geologists (Mem. 7)

Eardley AJ (1942) Aerial photographs: their use and interpretation. Harper and Brothers, New York

Fleuty MJ (1964) The description of folds. Proc Geol Assoc 75:61–492

Groshong RH Jr (1999) 3-D structural geology – a practical guide to subsurface map interpretation. Springer-Verlag, Berlin, pp 1–32, 39–50

Hamblin WK, Howard JD (1965) Physical geology – laboratory manual. Burgess Publishing Company, Minneapolis, Minnesota, pp 40–50

Jackson MPA (1995) Retrospective salt tectonics. In: Jackson MPA, Roberts DG (eds) Salt tectonics: a global perspective. Am Assoc PET Geol Mem 65:1–28

LaMoreaux PE, Newton JG (1996) Catastrophic subsidence: an environmental hazard, Shelby County, Alabama. Environ Geol Water Sci 8(1/2):25–40

LaMoreaux PE, Hughes TH, Memon BA, Lineback N (1989) Hydrogeologic assessement – Figeh Spring, Damascus, Syria. Environ Geol Water Sci 13(2)73–127

Mitra G, Marshak S (1988) Description of mesoscopic structures. In: Marshak S, Mitra G (eds) Basic methods of structural geology. Prentice Hall, New Jersey, pp 213–247 (reprinted by permission of Pearson Education Inc.)

Moore GL (1979) An Introduction to satellite hydrology. USGS, EROS Data Center, Sioux Falls, South Dakota. In: Deutsch M, Wienset DR, Rango A (eds) Satellite hydrology. Proc. of 5th annual William T. Pecore Memorial, Symposium on Remote Sensing, American Water Resources Association, Minneapolis, Minnesota, pp 37, 41

NASA (2003) Remote sensing tutorial (RST). Goddard Space Flight Center, Code 420, Greenbelt, MD 20771 (CARSTADT@staac-mail.gsfc,nasa.gov)

Price GJ (2001) Geologic mapping – a state perspective. Department of Geology at the University of Maryland. In: Geotimes, Annual Highlights Issue, A review of year 2000 research, pp 28–29

Sara MN (1994) Standard handbook for solid and hazardous waste facility assessments. Lewis Publishers, an imprint of CRC Press Inc., Boca Raton, Florida, pp 3.8–13

Van Wagoner JC, Posamentier HM, Mitchum RM, Vail PR, Sarg JF, Loutit TS, Hardenbol J (1988) An overview of the fundamentals of sequence stratigraphy and key definitions. In: Wilgus CK, Hastings BS, Posamentier H, Van Wagoner J, Ross CA, Kendall CG (eds) Sea-level changes: an integrated approach. Soc Econ Paleontol Mineral Spec Publ 42:39–45

Winchester S (2001) The map that changed the world. Harper Collins Publisher Inc., New York (adapted by permission of Harper Collins Publisher Inc., New York, NY)

Selected References

Allum JAE (1960) Photogeology and regional mapping. Pergamon Press, Great Britain, pp 29–31, 38–51, 52–62

American Society of Photogrammetry (1952) Manual of photographic interpretation. Washington, DC

Compton RR (1985) Geology in the field. John Willey & Sons Inc., Canada, pp 34–46

Deutsch M, Wiesnet DR, Rango A (1981) Proceedings of the 5th annual William T. Pecora Memorial, Symposium on Remote Sensing Hydrology, American Water Resources Association (Technical Publication Series, Library of Congress, pp 1–37, 158–164)

Drury SA (1998) Images of the earth – a guide to remote sensing, 2nd edn. Oxford Science Publications

Lahee FH (1941) Field Geology, 4th edn. McGraw-Hill Book Company Inc., New York London, pp 5–17

UNESCO, WMO (1977) Hydrological maps. A contribution to the International Hydrological Decade. Studies and Reports in Hydrology, pp 29–39

Wunsch, DR, State Geologist and Director, Environmental Geology (2002) International Journal of Geosciences 42(4):439, New Hampshire Geological Survey

Appendix 3.A · Topographic Map Symbols

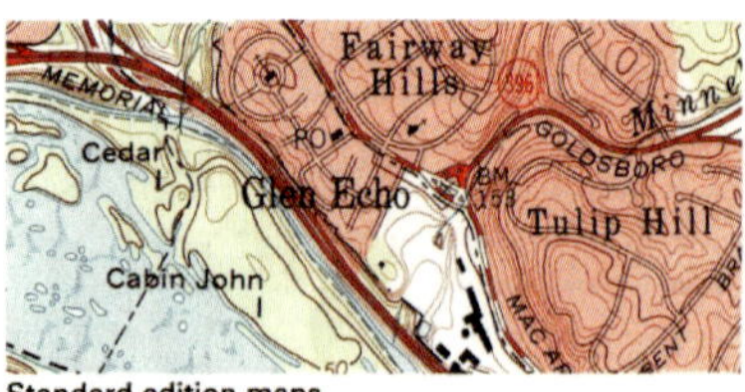

Fairway Hills
MEMORIAL
Cedar
Glen Echo
GOLDSBORO
Tulip Hill
Cabin John

Standard edition maps

Waterworks
Park
Pawnee Park
GRANT
Sewage Disposal
Community Center

New or replacement standard edition maps

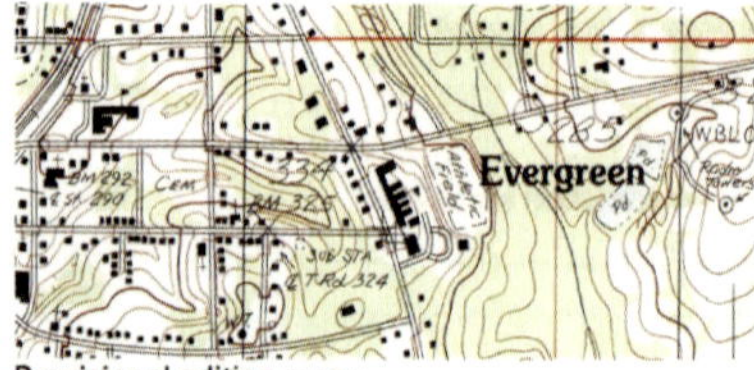

Evergreen

Provisional edition maps

Map series and quadrangles

Each map in a U. S. Geological Survey series conforms to established specifications for size, scale, content, and symbolization. Except for maps which are formatted on a County or State basis, USGS quadrangle series maps cover areas bounded by parallels of latitude and meridians of longitude.

Map scale

Map scale is the relationship between distance on a map and the corresponding distance on the ground. Scale is expressed as a ratio, such as 1:25,000, and shown graphically by bar scales marked in feet and miles or in meters and kilometers.

Standard edition maps

Standard edition topographic maps are produced at 1:20,000 scale (Puerto Rico) and 1:24,000 or 1:25,000 scale (conterminous United States and Hawaii) in either 7.5 x 7.5-or 7.5 x 15-minute format. In Alaska, standard edition maps are available at 1:63,360 scale in 7.5 x 20 to 36-minute quadrangles. Generally, distances and elevations on 1:24,000 scale maps are given in conventional units: miles and feet, and on 1:25,000-scale maps in metric units: kilometers and meters.

The shape of the Earth's surface, portrayed by contours, is the distinctive characteristic of topographic maps. Contours are imaginary lines which follow the land surface or the ocean bottom at a constant elevation above or below sea level. The contour interval is the elevation difference between adjacent contour lines. The contour interval is chosen on the basis of the map scale and on the local relief. A small contour interval is used for flat areas; larger intervals are used for mountainous terrain. In very flat areas, the contour interval may not show sufficient surface detail and supplementary contours at less than the regular interval are used.

The use of color helps to distinguish kinds of features: 0.
Black-cultural features such as roads and buildings.
Blue-hydrographic features such as lakes and rivers.
Brown-hypsographic features shown by contour lines.
Green-woodland cover, scrub, orchards, and vineyards.
Red-important roads and public land survey system.
Purple-features added from aerial photographs during map revision. The changes are not field checked.

Some quadrangles are mapped by a combination of orthophotographic images and map symbols. Orthophotographs are derived from aerial photographs by removing image displacements due to camera tilt and terrain relief variations. An orthophotoquad is a standard quadrangle format map on which an orthophotograph is combined with a grid, a few place names, and highway route numbers. An orthophotomap is a standard quadrangle format map on which a color enhanced orthophotograph is combined with the normal cartographic detail of a standard edition topographic map.

Provisional edition maps

Provisional edition maps are produced at 1:24,000 or 1:25,000 scale (1:63,360 for Alaskan 15-minute maps) in conventional or metric units and in either a 7.5 x 7.5- or 7.5 x 15-minute format. Map content generally is the same as for standard edition 1:24,000- or 1:25,000-scale quadrangle maps. However, modified symbolism and production procedures are used to speed up the completion of U. S. large-scale topographic map coverage.

The maps reflect a provisional rather than a finished appearance. For most map features and type, the original manuscripts which are prepared when the map is compiled from aerial photographs, including hand lettering, serve as the final copy for printing. Typeset lettering is applied only for features which are designated by an approved name. The number of names and descriptive labels shown on provisional maps is less than that shown on standard edition maps. For example, church, school, road, and railroad names are omitted.

Provisional edition maps are sold and distributed under the same procedures that apply to standard edition maps. At some future time, provisional maps will be updated and reissued as standard edition topographic maps.

National Mapping Program indexes

Indexes for each State, Puerto Rico, the U. S. Virgin Islands, the Pacific Islands, and Antarctica are available. Separate indexes are available for 1:100,000-scale quadrangle maps; 1:50,000- and 1:100,000-scale county maps; USGS/Defense Mapping Agency 15-minute (1:50,000-scale) maps; U. S. small scale maps (1:250,000, 1:1,000,000, 1:2,000,000 scale; State base maps; and U. S. maps); land use/land cover products; digital cartographic products; National Park maps; and orthophotoquads.

Fig. 3.A.1a. Topographic map symbols (national large scale series)

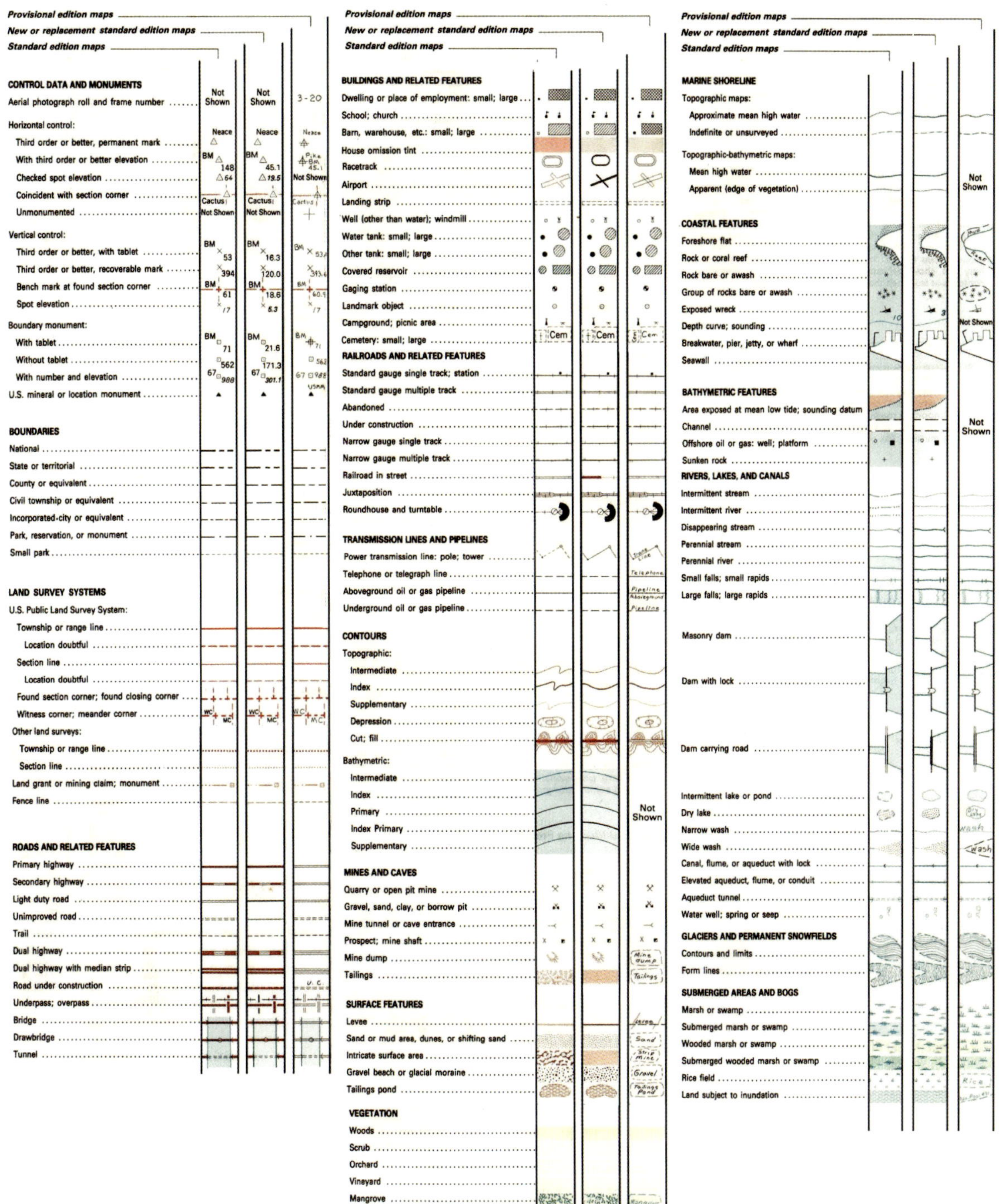
Provisional edition maps
New or replacement standard edition maps
Standard edition maps
CONTROL DATA AND MONUMENTS
Aerial photograph roll and frame number
Not Shown
Not Shown
3-20
Horizontal control:
Third order or better, permanent mark
With third order or better elevation
Checked spot elevation
Coincident with section corner
Unmonumented
Neace
BM
Cactus
Not Shown
Vertical control:
Third order or better, with tablet
Third order or better, recoverable mark
Bench mark at found section corner
Spot elevation
Boundary monument:
With tablet
Without tablet
With number and elevation
U.S. mineral or location monument
BOUNDARIES
National
State or territorial
County or equivalent
Civil township or equivalent
Incorporated city or equivalent
Park, reservation, or monument
Small park
LAND SURVEY SYSTEMS
U.S. Public Land Survey System:
Township or range line
Location doubtful
Section line
Location doubtful
Found section corner; found closing corner
Witness corner; meander corner
Other land surveys:
Township or range line
Section line
Land grant or mining claim; monument
Fence line
ROADS AND RELATED FEATURES
Primary highway
Secondary highway
Light duty road
Unimproved road
Trail
Dual highway
Dual highway with median strip
Road under construction
Underpass; overpass
Bridge
Drawbridge
Tunnel
BUILDINGS AND RELATED FEATURES
Dwelling or place of employment: small; large
School; church
Barn, warehouse, etc.: small; large
House omission tint
Racetrack
Airport
Landing strip
Well (other than water); windmill
Water tank: small; large
Other tank: small; large
Covered reservoir
Gaging station
Landmark object
Campground; picnic area
Cemetery: small; large
Cem
RAILROADS AND RELATED FEATURES
Standard gauge single track; station
Standard gauge multiple track
Abandoned
Under construction
Narrow gauge single track
Narrow gauge multiple track
Railroad in street
Juxtaposition
Roundhouse and turntable
TRANSMISSION LINES AND PIPELINES
Power transmission line: pole; tower
Telephone or telegraph line
Aboveground oil or gas pipeline
Underground oil or gas pipeline
CONTOURS
Topographic:
Intermediate
Index
Supplementary
Depression
Cut; fill
Bathymetric:
Intermediate
Index
Primary
Index Primary
Supplementary
Not Shown
MINES AND CAVES
Quarry or open pit mine
Gravel, sand, clay, or borrow pit
Mine tunnel or cave entrance
Prospect; mine shaft
Mine dump
Tailings
SURFACE FEATURES
Levee
Sand or mud area, dunes, or shifting sand
Intricate surface area
Gravel beach or glacial moraine
Tailings pond
VEGETATION
Woods
Scrub
Orchard
Vineyard
Mangrove
MARINE SHORELINE
Topographic maps:
Approximate mean high water
Indefinite or unsurveyed
Topographic-bathymetric maps:
Mean high water
Apparent (edge of vegetation)
Not Shown
COASTAL FEATURES
Foreshore flat
Rock or coral reef
Rock bare or awash
Group of rocks bare or awash
Exposed wreck
Depth curve; sounding
Breakwater, pier, jetty, or wharf
Seawall
BATHYMETRIC FEATURES
Area exposed at mean low tide; sounding datum
Channel
Offshore oil or gas: well; platform
Sunken rock
Not Shown
RIVERS, LAKES, AND CANALS
Intermittent stream
Intermittent river
Disappearing stream
Perennial stream
Perennial river
Small falls; small rapids
Large falls; large rapids
Masonry dam
Dam with lock
Dam carrying road
Intermittent lake or pond
Dry lake
Narrow wash
Wide wash
Canal, flume, or aqueduct with lock
Elevated aqueduct, flume, or conduit
Aqueduct tunnel
Water well; spring or seep
GLACIERS AND PERMANENT SNOWFIELDS
Contours and limits
Form lines
SUBMERGED AREAS AND BOGS
Marsh or swamp
Submerged marsh or swamp
Wooded marsh or swamp
Submerged wooded marsh or swamp
Rice field
Land subject to inundation

Fig. 3.A.1b. Topographic map symbols (national large scale series)

Appendix 3.B · Symbols for Geologic Maps

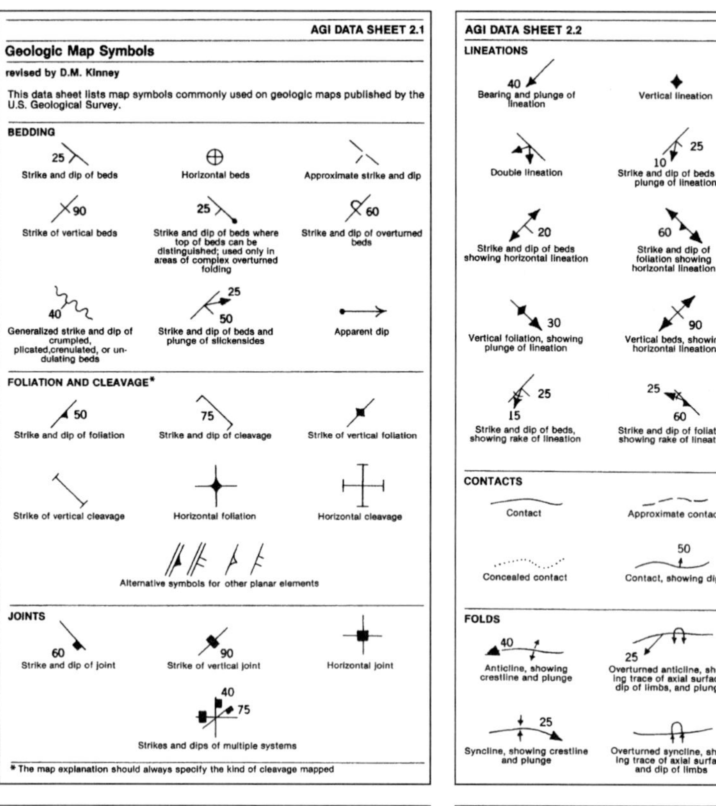

AGI DATA SHEET 2.1
Geologic Map Symbols
revised by D.M. Kinney
This data sheet lists map symbols commonly used on geologic maps published by the U.S. Geological Survey.
BEDDING
Strike and dip of beds
Horizontal beds
Approximate strike and dip
Strike of vertical beds
Strike and dip of beds where top of beds can be distinguished; used only in areas of complex overturned folding
Strike and dip of overturned beds
Generalized strike and dip of crumpled, plicated, crenulated, or undulating beds
Strike and dip of beds and plunge of slickensides
Apparent dip
FOLIATION AND CLEAVAGE*
Strike and dip of foliation
Strike and dip of cleavage
Strike of vertical foliation
Strike of vertical cleavage
Horizontal foliation
Horizontal cleavage
Alternative symbols for other planar elements
JOINTS
Strike and dip of joint
Strike of vertical joint
Horizontal joint
Strikes and dips of multiple systems
* The map explanation should always specify the kind of cleavage mapped
AGI DATA SHEET 2.2
LINEATIONS
Bearing and plunge of lineation
Vertical lineation
Horizontal lineation
Double lineation
Strike and dip of beds and plunge of lineation
Strike and dip of foliation and plunge of lineation
Strike and dip of beds showing horizontal lineation
Strike and dip of foliation showing horizontal lineation
Vertical beds, showing plunge of lineation
Vertical foliation, showing plunge of lineation
Vertical beds, showing horizontal lineation
Vertical foliation, showing horizontal lineation
Strike and dip of beds, showing rake of lineation
Strike and dip of foliation showing rake of lineation
Generalized strike of folded beds or foliation, showing plunge of fold axes
CONTACTS
Contact
Approximate contact
Inferred contact
Concealed contact
Contact, showing dip
Vertical contact
FOLDS
Anticline, showing crestline and plunge
Overturned anticline, showing trace of axial surface, dip of limbs, and plunge
Minor anticline, showing plunge
Syncline, showing crestline and plunge
Overturned syncline, showing trace of axial surface and dip of limbs
Minor syncline, showing plunge

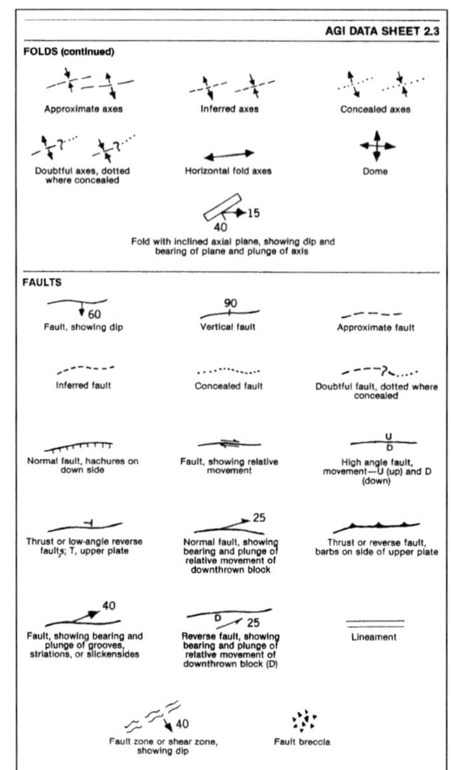

AGI DATA SHEET 2.3
FOLDS (continued)
Approximate axes
Inferred axes
Concealed axes
Doubtful axes, dotted where concealed
Horizontal fold axes
Dome
Fold with inclined axial plane, showing dip and bearing of plane and plunge of axis
FAULTS
Fault, showing dip
Vertical fault
Approximate fault
Inferred fault
Concealed fault
Doubtful fault, dotted where concealed
Normal fault, hachures on down side
Fault, showing relative movement
High angle fault, movement—U (up) and D (down)
Thrust or low-angle reverse faults; T, upper plate
Normal fault, showing bearing and plunge of relative movement of downthrown block
Thrust or reverse fault, barbs on side of upper plate
Fault, showing bearing and plunge of grooves, striations, or slickensides
Reverse fault, showing bearing and plunge of relative movement of downthrown block (D)
Lineament
Fault zone or shear zone, showing dip
Fault breccia

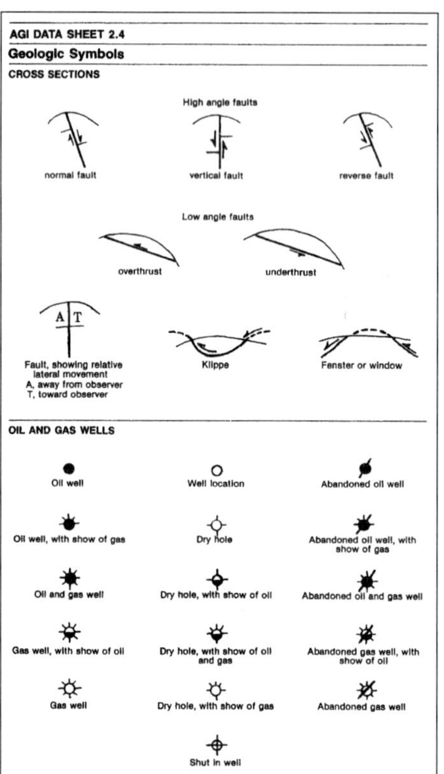

AGI DATA SHEET 2.4
Geologic Symbols
CROSS SECTIONS
High angle faults
normal fault
vertical fault
reverse fault
Low angle faults
overthrust
underthrust
Fault, showing relative lateral movement
A, away from observer
T, toward observer
Klippe
Fenster or window
OIL AND GAS WELLS
Oil well
Well location
Abandoned oil well
Oil well, with show of gas
Dry hole
Abandoned oil well, with show of gas
Oil and gas well
Dry hole, with show of oil
Abandoned oil and gas well
Gas well, with show of oil
Dry hole, with show of oil and gas
Abandoned gas well, with show of oil
Gas well
Dry hole, with show of gas
Abandoned gas well
Shut in well

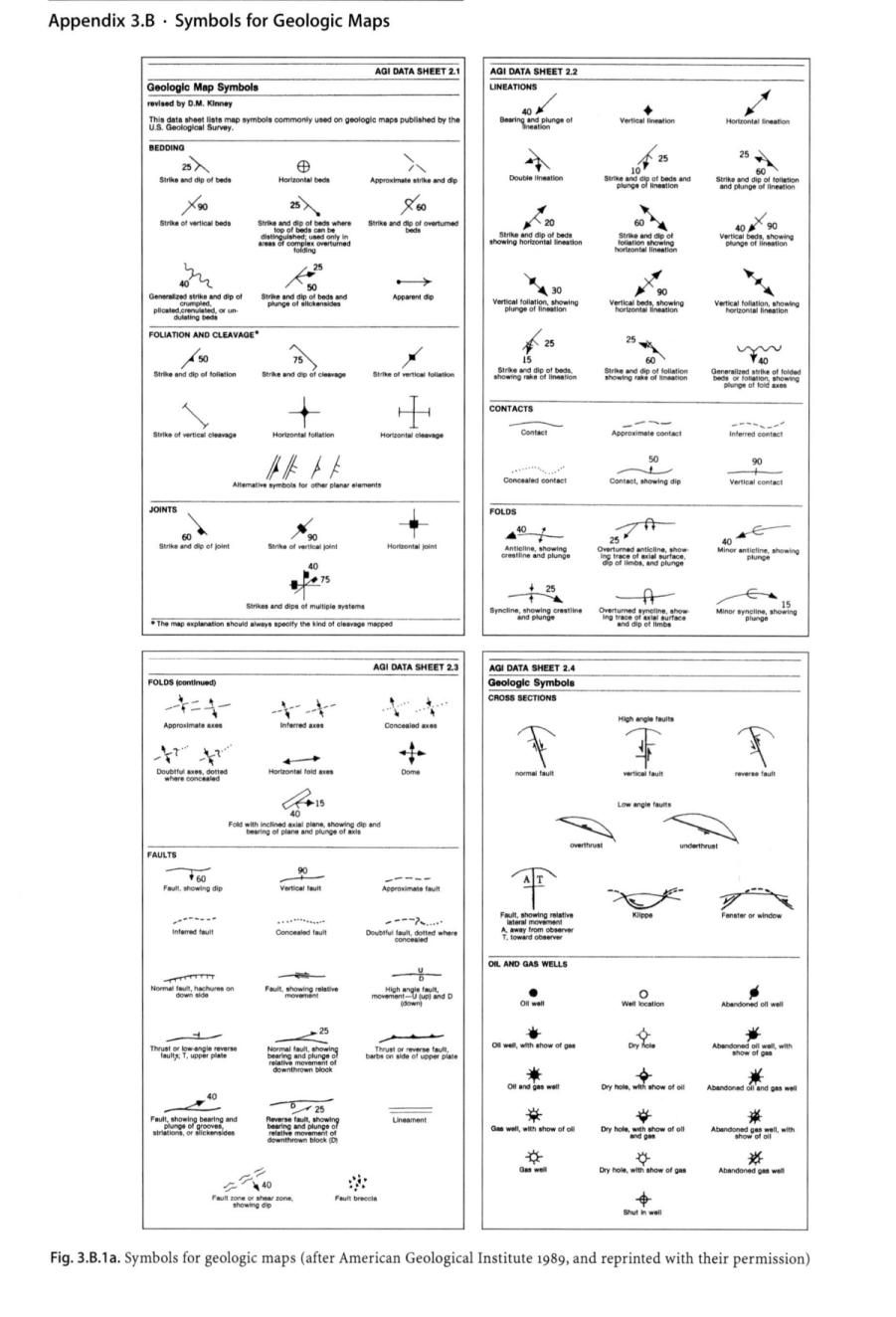

Fig. 3.B.1a. Symbols for geologic maps (after American Geological Institute 1989, and reprinted with their permission)

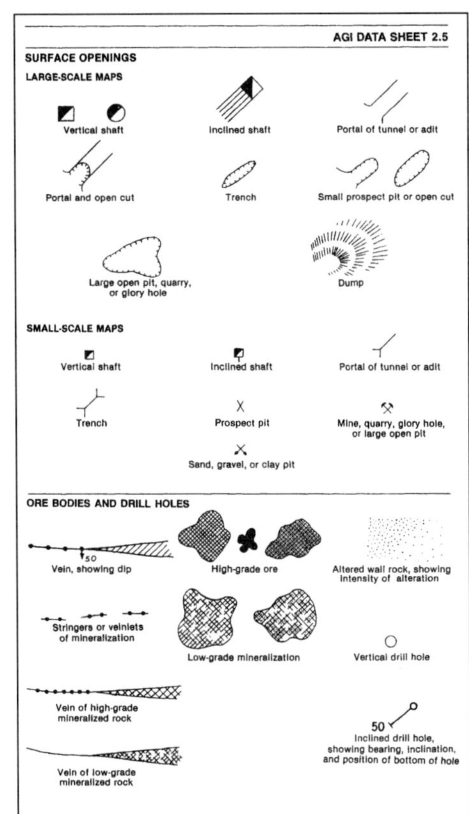
AGI DATA SHEET 2.5
SURFACE OPENINGS
LARGE-SCALE MAPS
Vertical shaft
Inclined shaft
Portal of tunnel or adit
Portal and open cut
Trench
Small prospect pit or open cut
Large open pit, quarry, or glory hole
Dump
SMALL-SCALE MAPS
Vertical shaft
Inclined shaft
Portal of tunnel or adit
Trench
Prospect pit
Mine, quarry, glory hole, or large open pit
Sand, gravel, or clay pit
ORE BODIES AND DRILL HOLES
50
Vein, showing dip
High-grade ore
Altered wall rock, showing intensity of alteration
Stringers or veinlets of mineralization
Low-grade mineralization
Vertical drill hole
Vein of high-grade mineralized rock
50
Inclined drill hole, showing bearing, inclination, and position of bottom of hole
Vein of low-grade mineralized rock

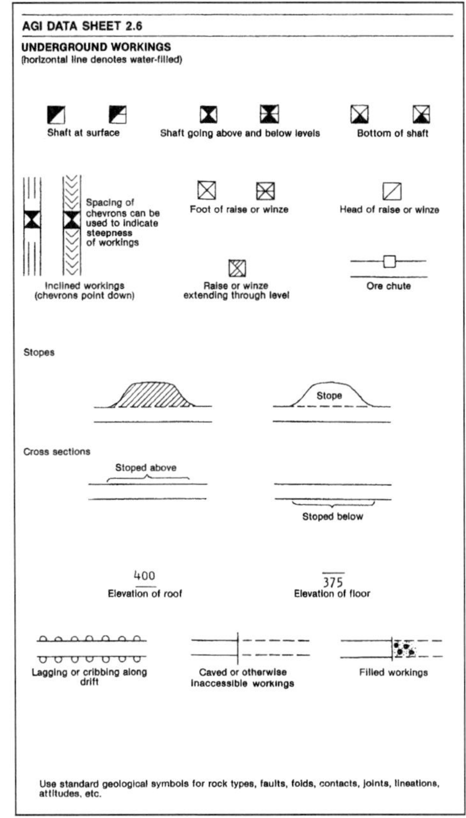
AGI DATA SHEET 2.6
UNDERGROUND WORKINGS
(horizontal line denotes water-filled)
Shaft at surface
Shaft going above and below levels
Bottom of shaft
Spacing of chevrons can be used to indicate steepness of workings
Foot of raise or winze
Head of raise or winze
Inclined workings (chevrons point down)
Raise or winze extending through level
Ore chute
Stopes
Stope
Cross sections
Stoped above
Stoped below
400
Elevation of roof
375
Elevation of floor
Lagging or cribbing along drift
Caved or otherwise inaccessible workings
Filled workings
Use standard geological symbols for rock types, faults, folds, contacts, joints, lineations, attitudes, etc.

AGI DATA SHEET 3.1

Fault Symbols

by Mason L. Hill, consulting geologist

INTRODUCTION: The following fault symbols are designed to remove the ambiguity resulting from failure of traditional symbols to distinguish between fault *slip* and fault *separation*. Where a linear geologic element is displaced, the *actual* relative movement (slip) can be determined (e.g., displaced intersection of dike and bed). Generally, however, where a tabular geologic element is displaced, only *apparent* relative movement (separation) can be determined. Thus, for example, these symbols provide for the important distinction between normal fault (only separation known) and normal slip fault (slip known). Refer to 'Dual Classification of Faults,' Mason L. Hill (1959), A.A.P.G. Bull., v. 43, p. 217–21.

GENERAL SYMBOLS

Fault trace, for maps and sections

Approximately located trace, for maps and sections

Conjectural trace, for maps and sections

Concealed map trace; conjectural (. . ? . .)

Dip direction; amount (60), approximate amount (25 ±), conjectural direction (?).

Relative slip direction; conjectural (?), slip plunge ( ), approximate plunge (25 ±).

Note: Fault trace may be distinguished from other geologic contacts by weight or color of line, or by labeling with name or symbol. Slip plunge is the vertical angle measured downward from horizontal to net slip.

SLIP SYMBOLS FOR MAPS

(Add direction and amount of dip, direction of relative slip, and slip plunge where known.)

Thrust slip fault. Sawteeth on relatively overthrust block; fault dips < 45°

Reverse slip fault. Rectangles on relatively elevated hanging wall block; fault dips > 45°. Dip direction is illustrated

65

Normal slip fault. Barbs on relatively depressed hanging wall block; fault dip and direction of relative slip are shown here

Right-lateral slip fault. Arrows show relative movement of block opposite the observer

70 35

Left-lateral slip fault. Fault dip and slip plunge are illustrated. If dip-slip and strike-slip components are nearly equal, the name reverse left-lateral slip fault is appropriate

Note: Triangles, rectangles, and barbs may be shown as appropriate and convenient along the map trace of the fault. However, none of these symbols should be used on maps unless some evidence of at least the approximate orientation of slip is obtained.

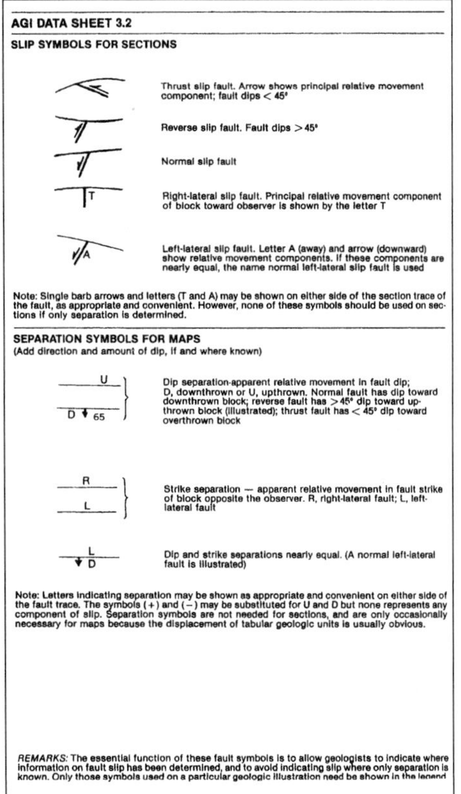
AGI DATA SHEET 3.2

SLIP SYMBOLS FOR SECTIONS

Thrust slip fault. Arrow shows principal relative movement component; fault dips < 45°

Reverse slip fault. Fault dips > 45°

Normal slip fault

T

Right-lateral slip fault. Principal relative movement component of block toward observer is shown by the letter T

A

Left-lateral slip fault. Letter A (away) and arrow (downward) show relative movement components. If these components are nearly equal, the name normal left-lateral slip fault is used

Note: Single barb arrows and letters (T and A) may be shown on either side of the section trace of the fault, as appropriate and convenient. However, none of these symbols should be used on sections if only separation is determined.

SEPARATION SYMBOLS FOR MAPS

(Add direction and amount of dip, if and where known)

U / D 65

Dip separation-apparent relative movement in fault dip; D, downthrown or U, upthrown. Normal fault has dip toward downthrown block; reverse fault has > 45° dip toward upthrown block (illustrated); thrust fault has < 45° dip toward overthrown block

R / L

Strike separation — apparent relative movement in fault strike of block opposite the observer. R, right-lateral fault; L, left-lateral fault

L / D

Dip and strike separations nearly equal. (A normal left-lateral fault is illustrated)

Note: Letters indicating separation may be shown as appropriate and convenient on either side of the fault trace. The symbols (+) and (−) may be substituted for U and D but none represents any component of slip. Separation symbols are not needed for sections, and are only occasionally necessary for maps because the displacement of tabular geologic units is usually obvious.

REMARKS: The essential function of these fault symbols is to allow geologists to indicate where information on fault slip has been determined, and to avoid indicating slip where only separation is known. Only those symbols used on a particular geologic illustration need be shown in the legend

Fig. 3.B.1b. Symbols for geologic maps (after American Geological Institute 1989, and reprinted with their permission)

Chapter 4

Surface Geophysical Exploration Methods

4.1 Introduction

Geophysical exploration methods can be used before construction to obtain information on the character of formations and on the chemical characteristics of ground water. These techniques determine density, magnetic and acoustical properties of the geologic medium. Surface geophysical methods include magnetic, gravity, seismic refraction, seismic reflection, electrical resistivity, natural potential and, ground penetrating radar. The method(s) selected will depend on the type of information needed, the nature of the subsurface materials and cultural interferences. Factors to be considered are cost, applicability, accessibility, and availability of equipment appropriate for a site.

4.2 Magnetic Survey

Magnetic surveys are primarily used to explore for oil and minerals. Magnetic exploration is based on the fact that the earth acts as a magnet. Any magnetic material placed in an external field will have magnetic poles induced upon its surface. This induced magnetization (sometimes called polarization) is in the direction of the applied field, and its strength is proportional to the strength of that field. The location of an area in relation to the magnetic poles is measured by the inclination of the earth's field or the "magnetic inclination" (USGS, U.S. Army 1998).

Susceptibility: If a homogenous external field (F_h) makes an angle (θ) with the normal to the surface of a magnetized material, the intensity of magnetization or the induced pole strength per unit area (S_i) is:

$$S_i = C_p F_h \cos\theta$$

For a field normal to the surface:

$$S_i = C_p F_h$$

where C_p = the proportionality constant, or the susceptibility.

For a vacuum and for non-magnetic substances, $C_p = 0$. Magnetic materials, which have positive susceptibility are known as paramagnetic substances and those, which have very high susceptibility are known as ferromagnetic materials. Grains of such materials tend to line up with their long dimension in the direction of the external field. All materials can be classified in one of three groups based on their magnetic behavior: diamagnetic, paramagnetic, and ferromagnetic. The material behaves paramagnetically with rise of the temperature as it becomes weakly magnetic and has a small positive susceptibility. Salts and anhydrides are designated as diamagnetic having negative susceptibility. Both paramagnetic and diamagnetic effects can only be observed in the presence of an external field (Dobrin and Savit 1988).

Sedimentary rocks are mainly non-magnetic or have very small magnetic susceptibility compared to igneous rocks. Susceptibility (or intensity of magnetization) is dimensionless. The SI system is greater by a factor of 4 than the CGS system. Figure 4.1 shows a general magnetic susceptibility for different rocks in SI units (USGS, U.S.Army 1998).

Magnetic measurements close to magnetic bodies give sharp anomalies where the anomalies are smaller, broader and smoother when these bodies are at a distance. Therefore, the distance to magnetic bodies can be determined from the sharpness of the relief of magnetic profiles. The shape of a magnetic anomaly varies with the magnetic latitude, the shape of the magnetic body, its attitude, its dimensions, its orientation with respect to magnetic north, and with the depth of the body.

In an aeromagnetic survey, a magnetometer needs to be away from distorting magnetic fields. It may be located in a tailstringer, which protrudes from the rear of the aircraft. This type of survey can be applied to a large area quickly and cheaply.

4.3 Gravimetric Survey

The variations in gravity depend upon lateral changes in the density of earth materials in the vicinity of the measuring point. Many types of rocks have characteristic ranges of densities, which may differ from those of other types that are laterally adjacent.

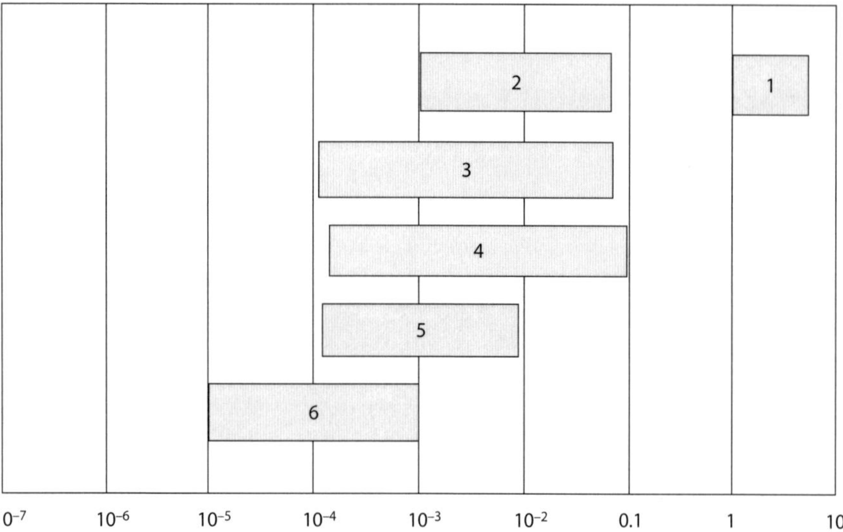

2
1
3
4
5
6
10^{-7}
10^{-6}
10^{-5}
10^{-4}
10^{-3}
10^{-2}
0.1
1
10

Fig. 4.1. General susceptibility (SI units); *1:* magnetite (Fe_3O_4), *2:* hematite (Fe_2O_3), *3:* granite, *4:* basalt, *5:* metasediment (metamorphic), *6:* shale/sandstone

Driscoll (1986) stated that the earth's gravitational attraction at a particular site is a function of the density of the surficial sediments and underlying rock units. Gravity meters can measure extremely small differences in the earth's gravitational field caused by subsurface density variations. These density variations may attribute to changes in rock type (changes in porosity or grain density), degree of saturation, fault zones and varying thicknesses of unconsolidated sediments overlying bedrock (Anderson WL 1979; Fig. 4.2a). Thus an anomaly in the earth's gravitational attraction can be related to a buried geological feature, e.g. a salt dome or other deposit, which has limited horizontal extent.

Gravity exploration is based on Newton's law of universal gravitation. It states that:

$$\text{gravitational force between two masses} = \text{universal gravitational constant} \times \frac{\text{product of masses}}{\text{distance between masses}^2}$$

In gravity exploration, differences in acceleration of gravity are measured by the use of gravity meters. The usual unit of gravity measurement is the milligal (mgal), and is defined as an acceleration of 0.001 cm s^{-2} or 0.001 dyne g^{-1}. Sometimes a gravity unit is used instead as 0.1 of a milligal (Galileo).

A gravity survey may delineate the structure of geologic materials at a site on the basis of their effect on the local gravity field. The number of readings that can be taken per day is limited by accessibility and the distance between stations, the speed at which the terrain can be traversed, and the accuracy required. As high-quality altimeters are generally only accurate to 0.6 m, gravity stations should be surveyed noticing that a 0.3 m error in estimating the surface elevation of the station will result in a reading error of approximately 0.1 milligal (Driscoll 1986).

In exploration work, any variation in gravity from that predicted from surrounding values, is referred to as a positive anomaly when higher and a negative anomaly when lower. Gravity methods are useful for large areas rapidly and inexpensively because the gravity meter is easily portable.

4.4 Microgravity and Cavity Detection

The microgravity survey technique is a powerful cavity location method. The principle of the technique is to locate areas of contrasting density in the subsurface by collecting surface measurements of the variation in the earth's gravitational field. Variations in the earth's gravitational force higher than normal, indicate underlying material of higher density while areas of lower gravity indicate areas of lower density. Because a cavity represents a mass deficiency, a small reduction in the pull of the earth's gravity is observed over the cavity, as shown in Fig. 4.2c. Although the method is simple in principle, measurement of the minute variations in the gravity field of the earth requires the use of highly sensitive instruments, strict data acquisition procedures and quality controls, as well as careful data reduction and sophisticated digital data analysis techniques to evaluate and interpret the data. The earth's normal gravity is 980 gal. Accurate gravity readings to 10 microgals are necessary to detect any voids or cavities. Multiple traverses with closely spaced gravity stations or the collection of data on a regular grid, result in improved data

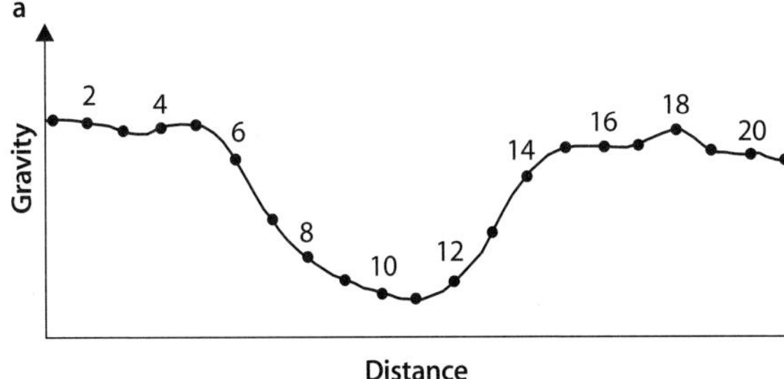
a
Gravity
2
4
6
8
10
12
14
16
18
20
Distance

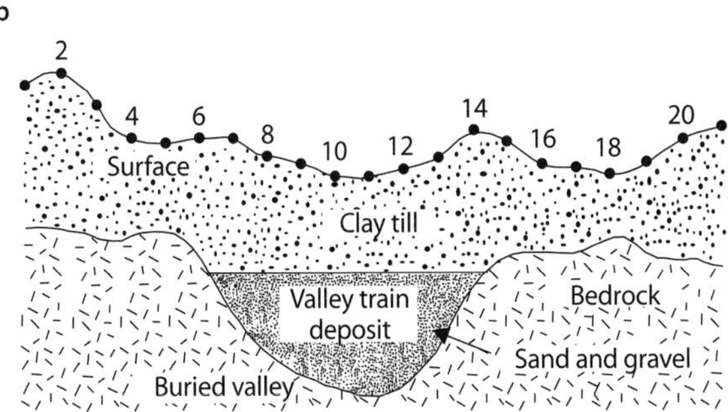
b
2
4
6
8
10
12
14
16
18
20
Surface
Clay till
Valley train deposit
Bedrock
Sand and gravel
Buried valley

Fig. 4.2a,b. Locations of buried bedrock valleys lying beneath thick sequences of unconsolidated deposits by gravitational methods; **a** results of gravity traverse bedrock profile; **b** subsurface geology (after Anderson 1979; Driscoll 1986)

accuracy that can be used to separate the cavity's effect from the geological or topographical background effects.

To detect a target using microgravity, there must be a difference in density (mass/volume) between the target and its surroundings. Cavities usually present a significant density contrast with their surroundings. Air-filled cavities offer the largest anomaly condition because of the complete absence of material in the target. Water-filled cavities, on the other hand, offer an anomaly effect of only 60% that of the same cavity containing air, and rubble or mud-filled cavities only about 40% that of air. So for an air-filled cavity, the density contrast would be typically $dr = -2.5$ g cm^{-3}; for a water-filled cavity $dr = -1.5$ g cm^{-3}; and for a rubble-filled cavity $dr = -1.0$ g cm^{-3}. Although these are large density contrasts, the targets are often of small volume (Crawford et al. 1999).

4.5 Seismic Exploration Survey

4.5.1 Definition and Discussion

The word "seismic" refers to vibrations of the earth, which includes earthquakes and the artificially created sound waves that penetrate into the earth. Sounds measured are in the frequency range of about 10–100 cycles s^{-1}. The depths investigated for a sound to travel deep into the earth and return are from about 305 km to as much as 16 km.

Seismic investigations utilize the fact that elastic waves (so called seismic waves) travel with different velocities in different rocks. By generating seismic waves at a point and observing the times of arrival of these waves at a number of other points (or stations) on the surface of the earth, it is possible to determine the velocity distribution and locate subsurface interfaces where the waves are reflected or refracted.

Seismic methods are classified into two major divisions, depending on the energy source of the seismic waves: *earthquake seismology*, and *explosion seismology*.

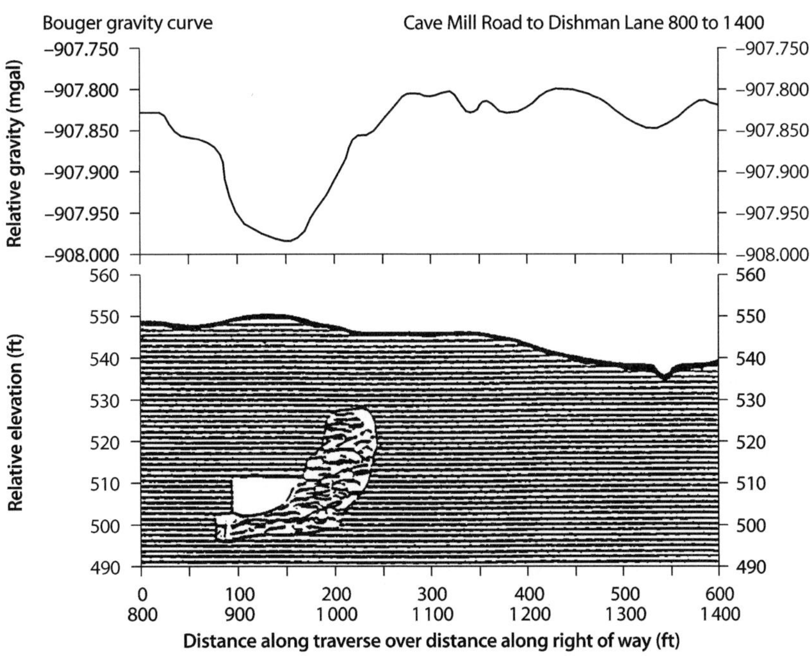
Bouger gravity curve
Cave Mill Road to Dishman Lane 800 to 1 400
Relative gravity (mgal)
-907.750
-907.800
-907.850
-907.900
-907.950
-908.000
Relative elevation (ft)
560
550
540
530
520
510
500
490
0
100
200
300
400
500
600
800
900
1 000
1 100
1 200
1 300
1 400
Distance along traverse over distance along right of way (ft)

Fig. 4.2c. Application of microgravity method to detect a cave; measurements taken at 10-foot (3-m) interval along a traverse perpendicular to the cave (after Crawford 1999)

The main contributions of earthquake seismology are information on the physical properties and structure of the earth's interior; whereas, methods of explosion seismology (reflection and refraction survey methods) are widely applied to studies of sedimentary structures, geological correlation of layered sequences and mapping of geological structures.

Geophones are motion-sensitive transducers that convert ground motion to an electrical signal whose am plitude is proportional to the velocity of the motion. For high-resolution shallow surveys, it is essential to have geophones that are designed to detect high frequencies with minimal distortion in the output signal. Single geophones are commonly used in shallow work, whereas arrays of a dozen or more geophones suitably grouped are used in conventional deeper reflection surveys.

Digital seismographs are used for recording of the electrical output from geophones, after suitable amplification and filtering (Sharma 1997).

Seismic surveys are based on the velocity distribution of artificially generated seismic waves in the ground. Seismic waves are produced by hammering on a metal plate, by dropping a heavy ball, or by using explosives. Energy from these sources is transmitted through the ground by elastic waves, which are so called because, when the waves pass a point in the rock, the particles are momentarily displaced or disturbed, but immediately return to their original position or shape after the wave passes. There are three types of waves that can be detected by geophones (detectors or seismometers), which are normally placed firmly into the ground: (1) a *compressional wave* is a type of seismic wave in which particle motion is in the same direction of the moving wave. It is also named *P-wave*, primary or longitudinal wave; (2) a *shear wave* is a type of seismic wave in which particle motion is at right angles to the direction in which the wave is moving. It is also called *S-wave*, secondary or traverse wave; (3) a *surface wave* is a type of wave that may travel along the free surface of a solid material in a vertical plane and retrograde with respect to the direct propagation or it may observed when there is a low speed layer overlying a higher speed substratum.

Compressional waves (the P-wave) are the first to arrive at the geophones, and therefore are the most useful in seismic surveys. The higher the density and elasticity of the rock unit, the faster the P-wave will be transmitted whereas in the unconsolidated or poorly consolidated material, the velocity is much less and the energy is dissipated more quickly (Table 4.1).

There are three distinct paths taken by compressional waves in the ground, direct to the ground surface, refracted and reflected. Figure 4.3a shows the three wave paths for a two-layered setting. For ground-water investigations, refracted and reflected waves are the most valuable, because they provide information about subsurface aquifer-conditions. However, recent studies show that shear waves are also very important (Driscoll 1986).

Table 4.1.
Approximate range of velocities of compressional (P) waves for representative materials found in the earth's crust

Material	Velocity[a] ($ft\ s^{-1}$)	($m\ s^{-1}$)
Weathered surface material	1 000– 2 000	305– 610
Gravel, rubble, or sand (dry)	1 500– 3 000	457– 915
Sand (wet)	2 000– 6 000	610–1 830
Clay	3 000– 9 000	915–2 740
Water (depending on temperature and salt content)	4 700– 5 500	1 430–1 680
Sea water	4 800– 5 000	1 460–1 520
Sandstone	6 000–13 000	1 830–3 960
Shale	9 000–14 000	2 740–4 270
Chalk	6 000–13 000	1 830–3 960
Limestone	7 000–20 000	2 130–6 100
Salt	14 000–17 000	4 270–5 180
Granite	15 000–19 000	4 570–5 790
Metamorphic rocks	10 000–23 000	3 050–7 010
Ice	12 050	3 670

[a] The higher values in a given range are usually obtained at depth (Jakosky 1950; Driscoll 1986).

4.5.2 Seismic Refraction/Reflection Methods

Refraction uses sound that travels along a rock layer for some distance and returns to the surface, whereas, reflection involves sound that is reflected, echoed, from a rock layer and is conducted by artificially producing a sound at or near the surface of the earth, and recording the echoes from underground. Seismic reflection can be used for regional and detailed work and used to define types of geologic structures, major changes in lithology and rock types as well as the relation between different geological features (Driscoll 1986).

4.5.2.1 *Seismic Refraction Methods*

Seismic refraction methods can use seismic waves to determine the thickness and extent of aquifer materials or where there are formation increases in density as depth increases. During a refraction survey, one should measure the time the seismic wave takes to reach one or more geophones placed at known distances from the seismic source. The depth of several geologic units can be estimated at a particular site by plotting the distance-time relationship provided each successively lower unit has a higher seismic velocity. The elapsed time and the distance traveled provides information on the type of formation (Driscoll 1986).

In a water well, geophones can be lowered into the well to successively greater depths and obtain travel times from a seismic source placed at the surface. The water table should be above the contact between the bedrock and the overlying alluvial deposits when locating the water table by the refraction method (Wallace 1970). Seismic exploration methods are generally used in conjunction with other geophysical methods and to minimize exploratory drilling costs.

4.5.2.2 *Seismic Reflection Method*

This method uses a seismic wave produced by a hammer blow or other seismic source that is reflected off the bedrock and returns directly to the geophone, as the elapsed time is recorded. Hammer stations are usually at 9.1 m or less from the geophone to maximize the reliability of the reflected wave energy. The operator strikes a hammer plate at five to ten sites that are within 9.1 m of the geophone. The seismic signals received from these sites are summed automatically by the seismograph canceling out the surface waves and other extraneous impulses or noise, which ordinarily would obscure the primary reflected wave that is then prominently displayed on a cathode ray tube (Driscoll 1986).

4.5.2.3 *Seismic Profiles*

Many interpretations of subsurface structure are based on seismic reflection profiles. Sound energy generated at or near the earth's surface is reflected by various layer boundaries in the subsurface. The time at which the reflection returns to a recorder at the surface is directly related to the depth of the reflecting horizon and the velocity of sound between the surface and the reflector. Seismic data are commonly displayed as maps or cross sections in which the vertical axis is the two-way travel time (Stone 1991; Fig. 4.3b).

The geometry of a structure that is even moderately complex displayed in travel time is likely to be signifi-

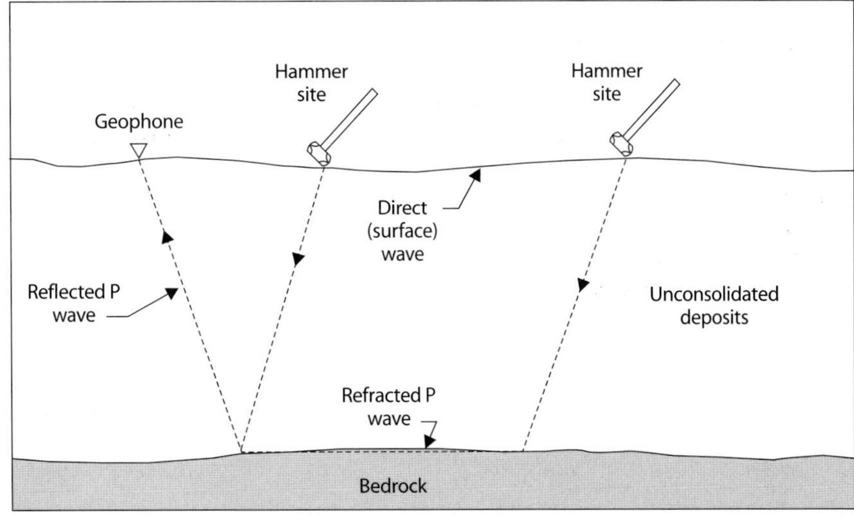
Hammer site
Hammer site
Geophone
Direct (surface) wave
Reflected P wave
Unconsolidated deposits
Refracted P wave
Bedrock

Fig. 4.3a. Waves from a seismic disturbance can travel as surface, reflected, and refracted waves. In water well exploration, analyses of refracted and reflected waves can determine the depth to bedrock at a potential drill site (after Driscoll 1986)

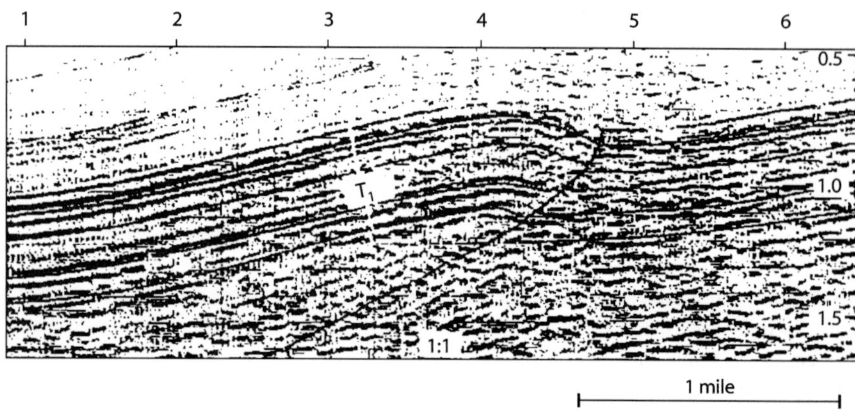
1
2
3
4
5
6
0.5
T1
1.0
1.5
1:1
1 mile

Fig. 4.3b. Time-migrated seismic profile from central Wyoming, displayed with approximatly no vertical exaggeration. The vertical scale is two-way travel time in seconds. T_1 is a unit that can be correlated across the profile (modified from Stone 1991, by Groshong 1999)

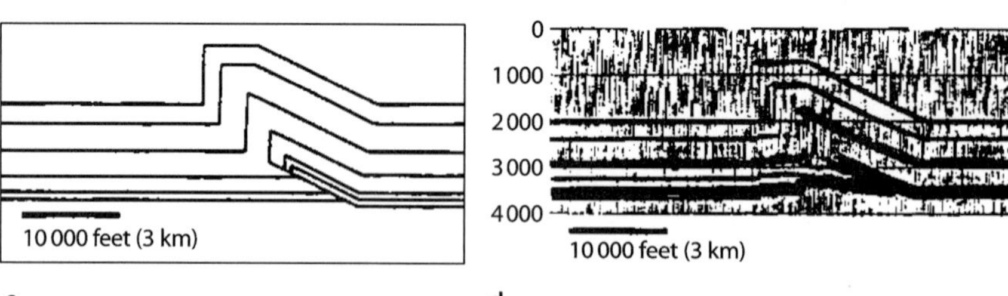
10 000 feet (3 km)
c
0
1 000
2 000
3 000
4 000
10 000 feet (3 km)
d

Fig. 4.3c,d. Seismic model of a faulted fold; **c** geometry of the model, no vertical exaggeration; **d** model time section based on normal velocity variations with lithology and depth. Vertical scale is two-way travel time in milliseconds (modified from Morse et al. 1991, after Groshong 1999)

cantly different from the true geometry of the reflecting boundaries because of the distortions introduced by steep dips and laterally and vertically varying velocities (Morse et al. 1991; Fig. 4.3c,d). The structural interpretation of seismic reflection data requires the conversion of the travel times to depth. This requires an accurate model for the velocity distribution.

4.5.3 Seismic Terms and Phenomena

4.5.3.1 *Seismic Lines*

Seismic lines are drawn on a map for seismic investigations and surveyed. Shot points along the lines are marked on the ground to indicate where sounds are to be received. At the places marked, holes are drilled and explosives placed in the holes. The explosive in the hole is detonated and the sounds from the explosion, including echoes from underground layers of rock, are recorded on a magnetic tape. The data recorded are sent to a computer designed for handling seismic data.

4.5.3.2 *Seismic Sections*

The seismic sections use the echoes to determine depths to rock layers. When this has been done from a whole set of lines, the depths to a rock layer are plotted on a map and contoured to show configuration of the layer. Seismic sections represent cross sections of the subsurface and are made up of alignments of data called traces. A trace which is a wiggle line, can be the information from one shot received by one geophone group as on a monitor record or it can be the information from a set of traces combined into one (Dobrin and Savit 1988).

4.5.3.3 *Seismic Scale*

The scale of a seismic section is shown in two different measurements. The horizontal scale is in distance and represents the length of the seismic line on the ground. The vertical scale is in time and represents the amount of time it took the sound to get down to the reflecting surface plus the time to be reflected back up. This is the reflection time, also called two-way time.

4.5.3.4 *Seismic Weathering*

Seismic investigations deal primarily with reflections. Some phenomena require either corrections, or should be attenuated to make the reflections more interpretable, e.g. the low velocity layer or the seismic weathering, refers to the material at the surface that has a considerably slower velocity of sound than slightly deeper rocks. The change in velocity is abrupt, say from 610 m s^{-1} in the weathering zone to 1 829 m s^{-1} immediately below it where the base of the weathered layer is sometimes the water table (top of ground water).

4.6 Ground Penetrating Radar Methods

4.6.1 Definition and Basic Principles

Ground-penetrating radar (GPR) produces a continuous record of subsurface sediment layers and locates reflective objects. It is a remote sensing technique that uses microwave electromagnetic energy. In GPR applications an antenna is used to transmit brief pulses of radar energy down into the ground and is housed in a protective box and pulled along the ground, usually behind a vehicle. Direct contact with the ground promotes the effective transfer of the radar waves into the ground. The antenna alternately radiates signal pulses into the ground, then receives reflected signals. Beck and Sayed (1991) explained the GPR technique as follows (Fig. 4.4).

1. The radar beam is roughly conical in shape and has an included angle from front to back of approximately 90° and a lateral angle of about 60°. Only subsurface features, which are perpendicular to some portion of the radiated signals reflect waves back to the antenna. The geometry of some curving, subsurface interfaces may cause two or more reflections to be received from different portions of a single interface.
2. When the transmitted radar waves strike an interface between layers of material with different electrical conductivities, part of the waves reflect back, and the remaining waves continue forward to the next interface. Each reflection consists of three parts in which the radar signal changes from one polarity to another and then back again. The polarity changes cause three bands to appear on the radar profile at each recorded interface. The top of the middle band represents the position of the interface, or contact between materials that have different conductivities (Beck and Sayed 1991; Fig. 4.5).
3. As reflected radar waves pass through the antenna, they cause a voltage surge. After amplification, voltage peaks that exceed a selected threshold are plotted as black bands on a strip chart by a unit called the graphic recorder which shows the subsurface profile and features of different anomalies can be identified such as soil layers, buried pipes and cavities. The lateral continuity of subsurface layers and the depth of reflective objects is graphically displayed on radar profiles in a manner far superior to cross sections constructed from drill holes. Figure 4.6 (Beck and Wilson 1988) shows a cross section of a round pipe or a cavity where a portion of the curved surface is always normal to the conical beam as the antenna approaches and passes over it. For this reason,

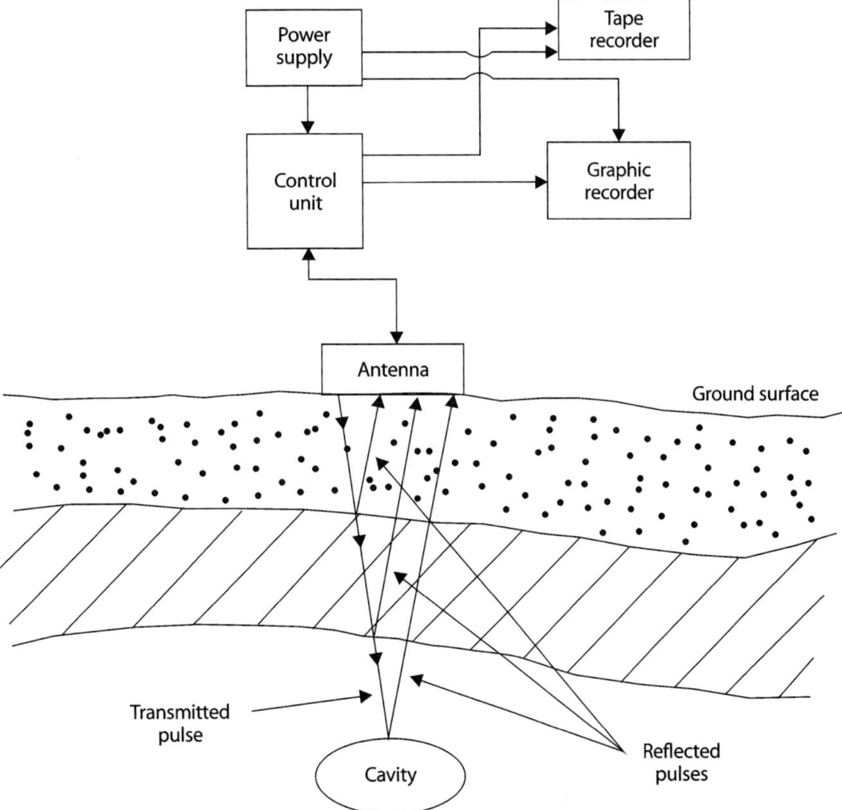
Power supply
Tape recorder
Control unit
Graphic recorder
Antenna
Ground surface
Transmitted pulse
Cavity
Reflected pulses

Fig. 4.4. Functional diagram of GPR equipment (after Beck and Sayed 1991)

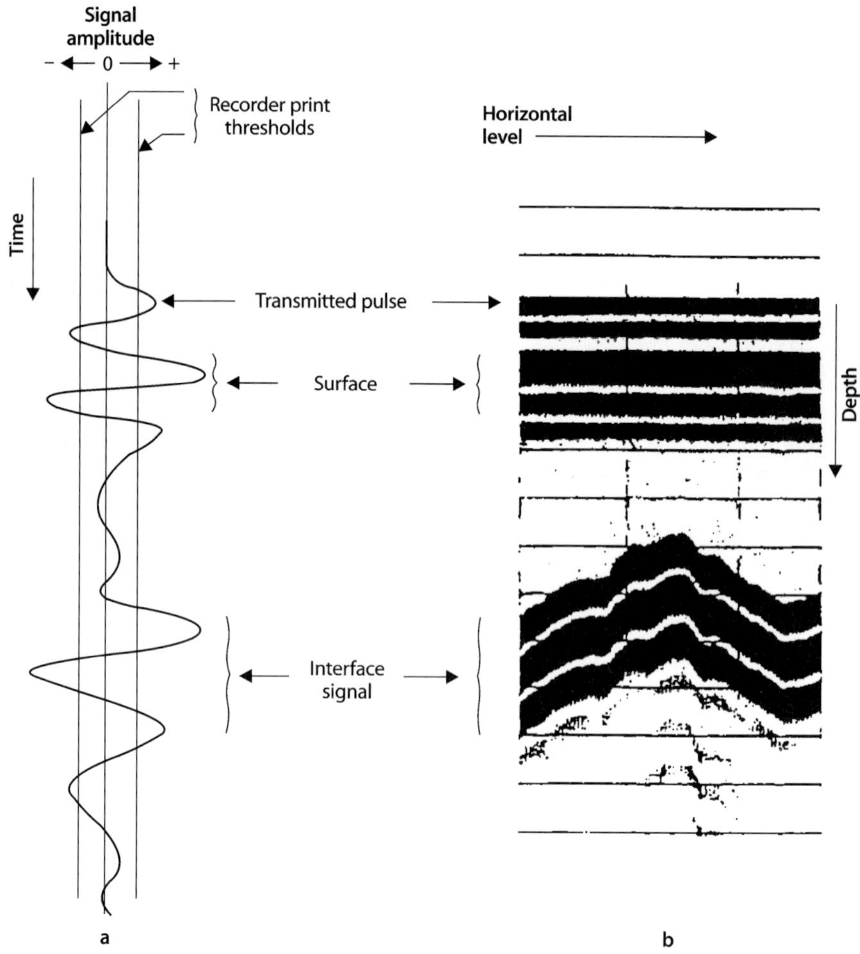

Signal amplitude
− 0 +
Recorder print thresholds
Horizontal level
Time
Transmitted pulse
Surface
Depth
Interface signal
a
b

Fig. 4.5. Components of; **a** the received radar signal and; **b** their graphic record. The second series of peaks is a reflection from the ground surface. Peaks below this are reflections of various subsurface interfaces. Because each interface causes oscillations in the reflected pulse which are gradually damped out, several bands (usually three) are printed on the recorder. This feature makes it difficult to distinguish very closely spaced interfaces (after Beck and Sayed 1991)

reflections from curved interfaces have a hyperbolic shape (Beck and Wilson 1988).

4.6.2 Methodology

Ground-penetrating radar is capable of detecting changes in materials in the ground in either solid or liquid form. Experience on hazardous waste sites, including landfills, has shown that solid waste produces a characteristic "cluttered" signature that is significantly different from the surrounding soil. Also, the presence of any liquid in the soil modifies the physical properties and produces characteristic radar signatures. There are two fundamental physical properties to which the radar responds: the electrical conductivity and the dielectric constant. Ionic liquids, which include acids, bases (caustics) and salts, increase the electrical conductivity of the host material. The rate of attenuation, or signal loss, of the radar signal as it propagates into the ground, is a direct function of the electrical conductivity. A localized increase in the electrical conductivity causes a greater loss of the signal than the surrounding earth, producing a variations in the radar response. Conversely, the non-ionic liquids, which include petroleum products, solvents, pesticides and other organic chemicals, do not alter the electrical conductivity as much as they modify the dielectric constant of the host material.

The ground-penetrating radar system provide direct images of the bedrock under a site and the soil conditions in the earth overlying the bedrock. The soil conditions can show elevated dielectric response, which may be correlated with the presence of non-ionic liquids in the soil. The soil conditions were catalogued by Stanfill and McMillan (1985b) into three categories: "highest", "moderate" or "light". This terminology has nothing to do with the concentration levels, which should be determined by the laboratory analysis of soil samples. However, the radar was exceedingly sensitive to the presence of hydrocarbons in the soil.

The GPR method produces continuous high-resolution profiles of the subsurface that are similar to those produced by continuous seismic-reflection methods. The GPR records may define the geologic framework of the aquifer system help locate hydrologic boundaries, and in some places, to interpret the aquifer lithology.

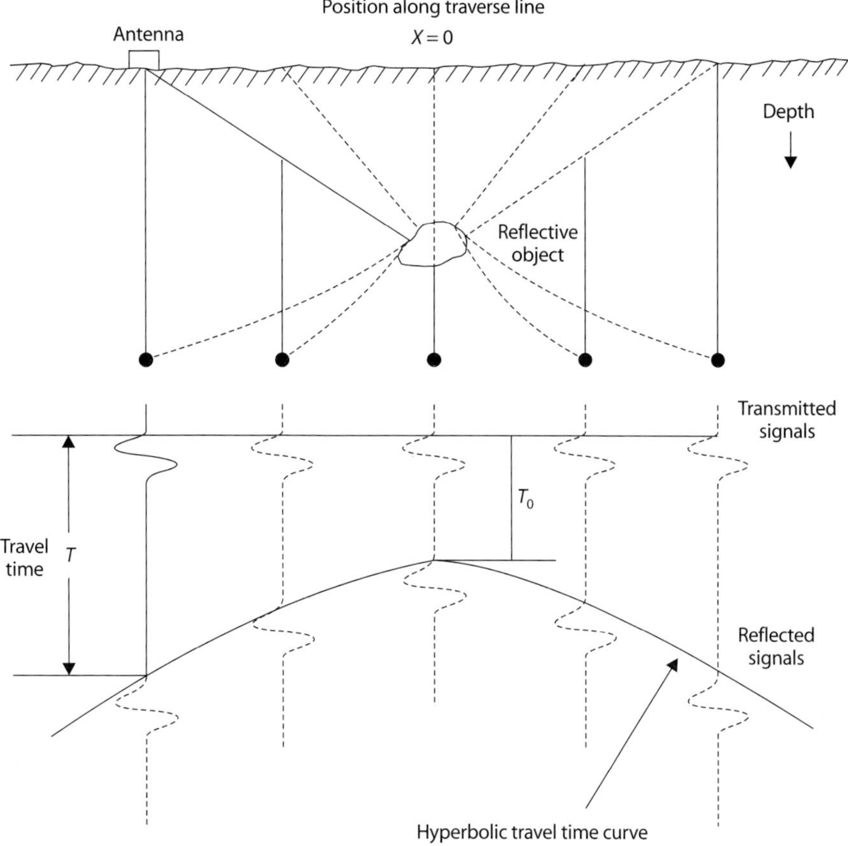
Position along traverse line
Antenna
X = 0
Depth
Reflective object
Transmitted signals
T_0
Travel time
T
Reflected signals
Hyperbolic travel time curve

Fig. 4.6.
Development of hyperbolic reflection pattern. Because the radar beam radiates out in a cone-shaped pattern, a spherical object may cause reflections from positions other than directly below the antenna. However, the graphic record will show a reflection directly below the antenna at a depth equal to the angular distance to the object. This will produce a hyperbolic reflection pattern, the peak of which corresponds to the true depth and location of the object (after Beck and Wilson 1988)

The hydrogeologic applications on-site GPR methods, include mapping the water table, mapping consecutive configuration of contamination plumes, determining moisture content in soil, investigating fractures in bedrock, and mapping thickness and distribution of sediments in lakes (Beres and Haeni 1991).

4.6.3 GPR Application

4.6.3.1 *Scope*

Electrical inhomogenities are present in most hydrogeologic settings and are determined primarily by water content, dissolved minerals, and expansive clay and heavy mineral content in the subsurface material (Wright et al. 1984; Olhöeft 1991a,b; Haeni et al. 1987). The reflected signal is amplified, transformed to the audio-frequency range, recorded, processed, and displayed. The record shows the total travel time for a signal to pass through the subsurface, reflect from an inhomogenity and return to the surface. This two-way travel time is measured in nanoseconds ($1\ \text{ns} = 10^{-9}\ \text{s}$).

Basic equations used to determine the depth to a reflector are as follows:

$$d = t\,V_\text{w} / 2 \tag{4.1}$$

and

$$V_\text{w} = c / \varepsilon^{0.5} \tag{4.2}$$

where:

- d = depth to the reflector (in meter)
- t = two-way travel time (in nanoseconds)
- c = velocity of light in free space (= 0.3 m ns^{-1})
- ε = relative dielectric permitivity (a dimensionless ratio)
- V_w = electromagnetic wave velocity (in m ns^{-1})

The relative dielectric permitivity is a measure of the capacity of a material to store a charge when an electric field is applied to it relative to the same capacity in a vacuum (Sherif 1984).

Studies show that in areas having material of low electrical conductivity, such as clay-free sand and gravel, low frequency electromagnetic waves can penetrate to depths of 30 m. In highly conductive areas, such as soils with a high percentage of clay minerals, the penetration depth of electromagnetic waves can be less than 1 m. Table 4.2a lists approximate values of conductivity and relative dielectric permitivity for selected materials (Utkinsen 1991).

Table 4.2a. Approximate values of conductivity and relative dielectric permitivity for selected materials (Beres 1991, Utkinsen 1991)

Material	Conductivity ($m\Omega m^{-1}$)	Relative dielectric permitivity
Air	0	1
Pure water	10^{-4} to 3×10^{-2}	81
Sea water	4	81
Fresh-water ice	10^{-3}	4
Sand (dry)	10^{-7} to 10^{-3}	4 to 6
Sand (saturated)	10^{-4} to 10^{-2}	30
Silt (saturated)	10^{-3} to 10^{-2}	10
Clay (saturated)	10^{-1} to 1	8 to 12
Sandstone (wet)	4.0×10^{-2}	6
Shale (wet)	10^{-1}	7
Limestone (dry)	10^{-9}	7
Limestone (wet)	2.5×10^{-2}	8
Basalt (wet)	10^{-2}	8
Granite (dry)	10^{-8}	5
Granite (wet)	10^{-3}	7

Figure 4.7 relates some reflection configuration of radar records to the stratigraphic and lithologic properties of unconsolidated aquifers in the glaciated northeast (Beres and Haeni 1991; Haeni 1988).

4.6.3.2 *Operating Parameters*

The earth is relatively transparent at radio frequencies between 10 and 1000 MHz. GPR systems operating at 120 MHz offer a good compromise between spatial resolution, which improves with higher frequency, and depth of penetration, which improves at lower frequency. At 120 MHz, a buried object 10.2 cm in diameter can be detected. The depth capability of the used model of 120 MHz antenna is best expressed in terms of electrical resistivity (the reciprocal of electrical conductivity).

At 120 MHz, the radar system achieves more than about 0.3 meter of depth per ohm-meter of resistivity. This is a significant improvement over earlier equipment when the corresponding figure was only about 40% as good.

With the current system, clays are no longer a fundamental barrier; even under the most adverse conditions, penetration of more than 3 m can be achieved. Under average conditions, penetration is normally more than 15.4 m. In sandstone formations with high resistivity, penetration as deep as 73 m has been achieved at an operating frequency of 80 MHz.

4.6.3.3 *Defining Hazardous Waste Sites*

GPR is an excellent method for gaining a better understanding of the geology of hazardous waster sites. A radar survey can establish whether or not a site has ever been excavated, determine the exact boundaries of the burials and categorize the type of buried material. It is possible to distinguish between ionic chemicals and non-ionic chemicals and to estimate their concentration levels. Chemical contamination plumes in the ground can be shown in vertical profile and then be mapped in plane view.

The ability to generate continuous subsurface profiles is important for establishing depth profiles of clay and of the underlying bedrock for inspecting the integrity of a clay liner. The locations of faults or fracture zones in rock can be observed clearly with radar. On land, the water table poses no problem; in water-filled pits, radar can be used for sub-bottom investigations. The inspection of well sites prior to drilling makes it possible to avoid buried obstacles or chemical contamination at the well site (Stanfill and McMillan 1985)

4.7 Remote Sensing and Satellite-Based Images

4.7.1 General

Remote sensing refers to specific methods used for obtaining information about earth's surface and subsurface. These methods, which sense electromagnetic (EM) radiation, have no direct contact between the sensor – carried by either an aircraft or satellite – and the object(s) being observed (Hoerig and Kuehn 2000).

The recently acquired capabilities of remote sensing have conferred important advantages on all earth sciences, including hydrology. The success of satellite data relay tests, obtained from four satellite systems (Apollo,

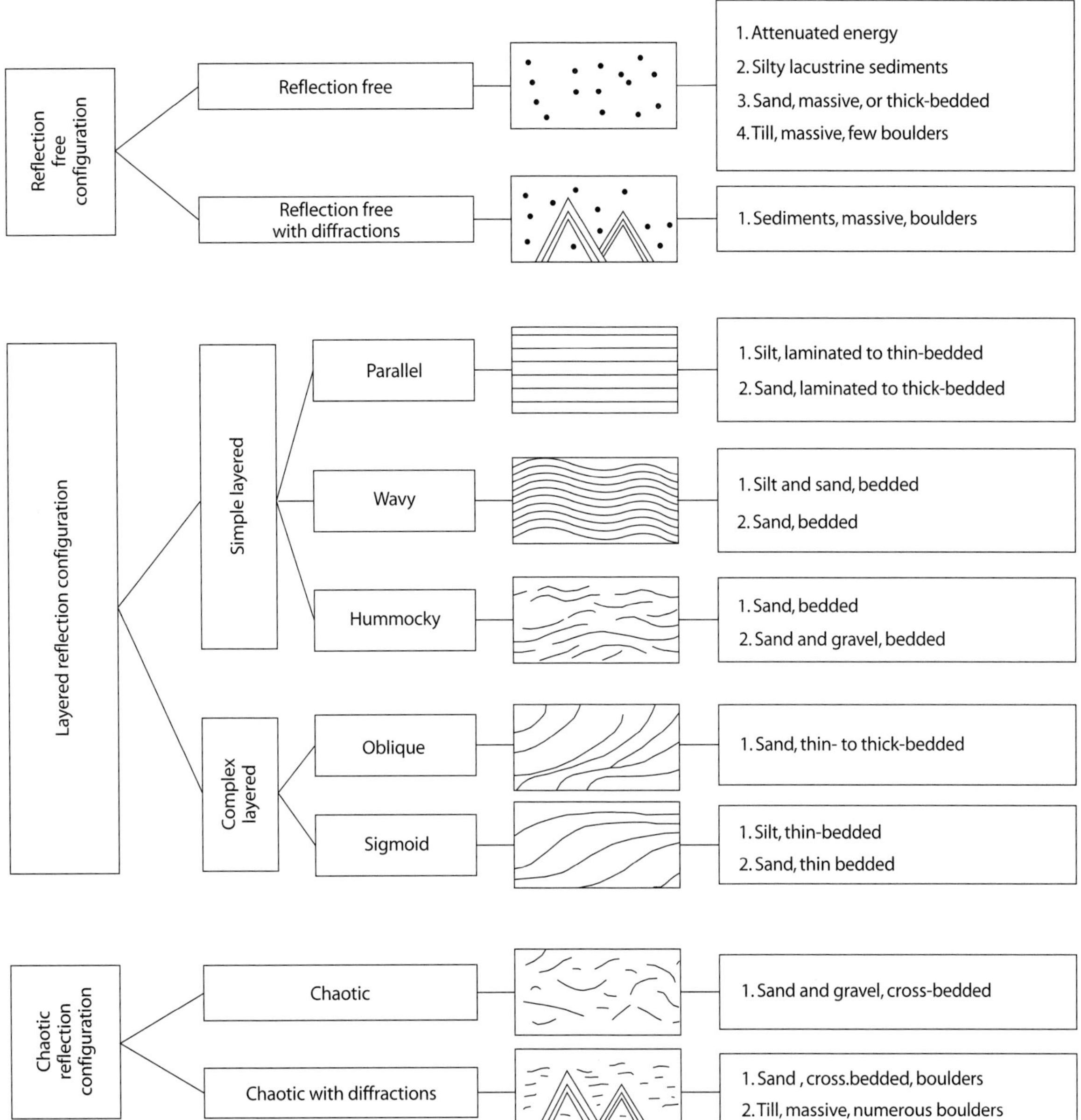
Reflection free configuration
Reflection free
1. Attenuated energy
2. Silty lacustrine sediments
3. Sand, massive, or thick-bedded
4. Till, massive, few boulders
Reflection free with diffractions
1. Sediments, massive, boulders
Layered reflection configuration
Simple layered
Parallel
1. Silt, laminated to thin-bedded
2. Sand, laminated to thick-bedded
Wavy
1. Silt and sand, bedded
2. Sand, bedded
Hummocky
1. Sand, bedded
2. Sand and gravel, bedded
Complex layered
Oblique
1. Sand, thin- to thick-bedded
Sigmoid
1. Silt, thin-bedded
2. Sand, thin bedded
Chaotic reflection configuration
Chaotic
1. Sand and gravel, cross-bedded
Chaotic with diffractions
1. Sand , cross.bedded, boulders
2. Till, massive, numerous boulders

Fig. 4.7. Chart relating the reflection configurations on the radar record to the lithologic and stratigraphic properties of sediments in the glaciated northeast (modified from Haeni 1988; Beres and Haeni 1991)

Landsat, Nimbus, and Heat Capacity Mapping Mission), has shown that a considerable savings in costs of the entire hydrologic data network can be achieved. Remote sensing can improve information on geographical distribution and availability of water resources by providing repetitive monitoring of large areas to complement conventional data sources (Calabrese and Thome 1979).

Water is a very dynamic substance with respect to form (solid, liquid, or gas) and time (tidal, diurnal, seasonal, and long term variation) and has characteristic spectral responses in the visible, near infrared, thermal infrared, and microwave ranges of the electromagnetic spectrum (Anderson DG 1979).

4.7.2 Remote Sensing and Geographic Information System (GIS)

Definitions: Remote sensing is the use of reflected and emitted electromagnetic energy such as light, heat, and radio waves to measure the physical properties of distant objects and their surroundings. The measurements, which are recorded data on a strip chart, magnetic tape, or film, can be processed, analyzed, and interpreted. The obtained information can be used to inventory resources, study the environment, solve problems, and plan future actions. Remote sensing utilizes EM radiation principally in the ultraviolet, visible light, infrared, and microwave portions of the EM spectrum. Remote sensing techniques are divided into active and passive methods. Passive methods use reflected solar radiation and radiation emitted from a surface. Active remote-sensing systems provide a source of radiation, e.g. radar (Hoerig and Kuehn 2000).

Remote sensing has two facets: the technology of acquiring data through a device which is located at a distance from the object, and analysis of that data for interpreting the physical character of the object. Both of these aspects being linked together.

Remote sensing would include microscopy, geophysics, astronomy, portrait photography and even looking at one's self in a mirror. In France and Germany, the terms "télédétection" and "Fernerkundung" are used. In this text the term remote sensing is restricted to the acquisition of information, usually in image form, above the surface of the land masses and oceans, and the atmosphere above it, by airborne or spaceborne sensors (Legg 1991).

Geographic Information System (GIS). For example, a topographic or geographic map is a collection of georeferenced data sets presented to illustrate their mutual relationships. A computerized map allows the production of specialized maps including any selected features from among a potentially very large set of data at a scale appropriate to each specific problem.

The basic principle involved in remote sensing methods is that in different wavelength ranges of the electromagnetic spectrum, each type of object reflects or emits a certain intensity of light, which is dependent upon the physical or compositional attributes of the object. Thus, using information from one or more wavelength ranges, it may be possible to differentiate between different types of objects (e.g. dry soil, vegetation area, etc.), and map their distribution on the ground.

Visible wavelengths perceived by our unaided eyes, are one of the largest atmospheric windows that covers the visible wavelengths. If there was strong atmospheric absorption in the region, now termed the "visible" portion of the spectrum, one might instead "see" in the mid-infrared or even in the thermal portion of the spectrum, therefore called the "visible wavelengths". Figure 4.8a shows spectral reflectance profiles for some representative natural surfaces (e.g. bare soil, green vegetation, and water); however, it does not show distinctive spectral differences of rocks, minerals and soils in the visible portion, just generalized differences in total brightness or albedo. Visible light is also more strongly dispersed by atmospheric haze, dust and pollutants than is radiation at infrared wavelengths (Legg 1991).

4.7.3 Preliminary Evaluation of Remote Sensing/Alabama Highways

Remote sensing considers the visible and infrared parts of the spectrum using the camera and infrared scanner to record the energy of selected wave length regions that reaches the instruments from the earth's surface in an instant of time (Newton 1976).

Locating active areas of sinkhole development along proposed highway corridors in early planning is of utmost importance. Preliminary evaluation of remote sensing data for sinkhole projects has been obtained from flights over ten areas in Alabama. Table 4.2b shows a summary of data obtained for five of these areas in preliminary evaluation.

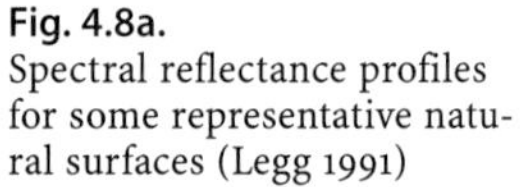

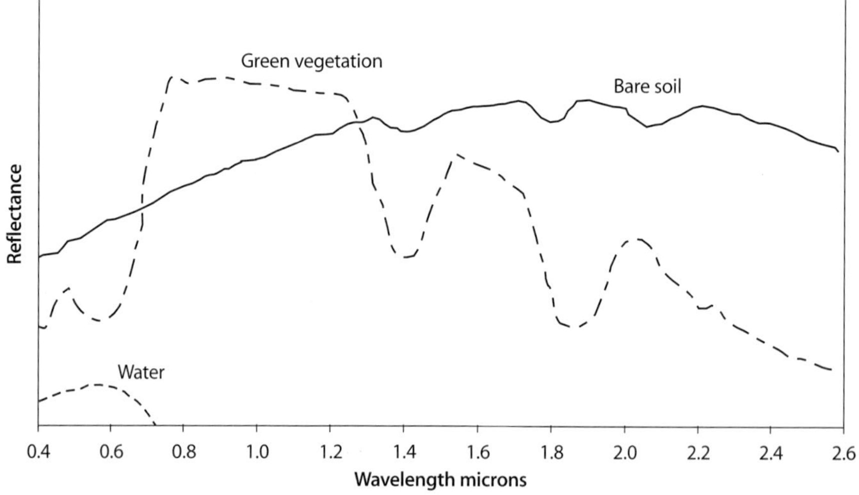
Green vegetation
Bare soil
Water
Reflectance
0.4
0.6
0.8
1.0
1.2
1.4
1.6
1.8
2.0
2.2
2.4
2.6
Wavelength microns

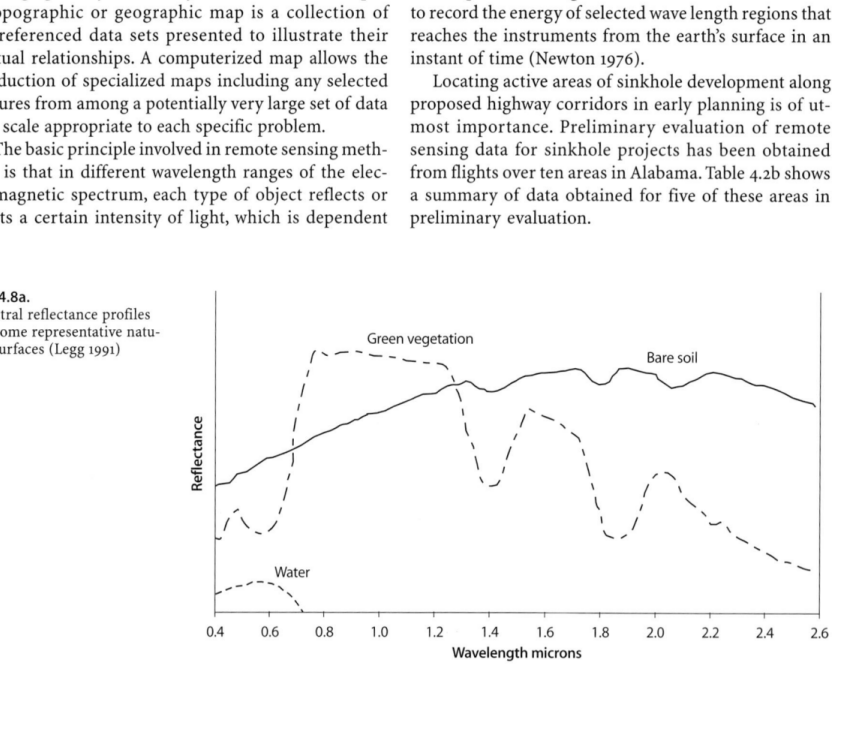

Fig. 4.8a. Spectral reflectance profiles for some representative natural surfaces (Legg 1991)

Table 4.2b. Summary of data used in preliminary evaluation (after Newton 1976)

Area	Data	Date	Filter	Nominal scale(s)	Remarks
Proposed corridor – Interstate Highway 459 near Greenwood, Jefferson County	Color Ektachrome photography (transparencies)	1/18/72	Haze	1:6 000	Excellent quality
	Color infrared photography (transparencies)	1/18/72	Wratten 15	1:6 000	Excellent quality
	Black and white infrared (contact prints)	1/18/72	Haze	1:6 000	Most photography overexposed and not interpretable
	Color Ektachrome photography (transparencies)	10/10/72	Haze	1:6 000	Partial coverage – excellent quality
	Color infrared photography (transparencies)	10/19/72	Wratten 15	1:6 000	Partial coverage – excellent quality
	Black and white infrared (contact prints)	10/10/72	Haze	1:6 000	Partial coverage – excellent quality
	Color Ektachrome photography (transparencies)	6/22/73	Haze	1:6 000	Excellent quality
	Color infrared photography (transparencies)	6/22/73	Wratten 15	1:6 000	Fair quality
	Black and white infrared (contact prints)	6/22/73	Haze	1:6 000	Excellent quality, results poor due to dry weather
	Infrared 8- to 14-micrometer imagery (day)	3/14/72	...	1:12 000	Excellent quality
	Infrared 8- to 14-micrometer imagery (night)	1/18/72	...	1:12 000	Poor weather with mist, results fair
Proposed corridor – Interstate Highway 59 in and near Bessemer, Jefferson County	Color Ektachrome photography (transparencies)	6/22/73	Haze	1:6 000	Excellent quality
	Color infrared photography (transparencies)	6/22/73	Wratten 15	1:6 000	Excellent quality
	Black and white infrared (contact prints)	6/22/73	Haze	1:6 000	Excellent quality
	Infrared 8- to 14-micrometer imagery (day)	3/14/72	...	1:12 000	Excellent quality
	Infrared 8- to 14-micrometer imagery (night)	3/14/72	...	1:12 000	Excellent quality
Interstate Highway 59, near Arkadelphia Exchange in Birmingham, Jefferson County	Color Ektachrome photography (transparencies)	6/23/73	Haze	1:6 000	Excellent quality
	Color infrared photography (transparencies)	6/23/73	Wratten 15	1:6 000	Resolution good, vigor expressed by purple hue
	Black and white infrared (contact prints)	6/23/73	Haze	1:6 000	Excellent quality
	Infrared 8- to 14-micrometer imagery (day)	3/14/72	...	1:12 000	Good quality, results poor because of intense land development
	Infrared 8- to 14-micrometer imagery (night)	3/14/72	...	1:12 000	Good quality, results poor because of intense land development
Area west of Calera, Shelby County, that trends northeastward from Alabama Highway 25 to Interstate Highway 65	Color infrared photography (transparencies)	3/12/73	Wratten 12	1:16 000	Good quality
				1:24 000	
				1:40 000	
				1:60 000	
	Black and white infrared (contact prints)	3/12/73	...	1:4 000	Excellent quality
	Color infrared photography (transparencies)	3/12/73	Wratten 12, 20 M	1:6 000	Excellent quality
West of U.S. Highway 31 between Pelham and Alabaster, Shelby County	Color infrared photography (transparencies)	3/12/73	Wratten 12	1:6 000	Excellent quality

Limited low altitude oblique photography and U.S. Department of Agriculture standard black and white serial photography used is not included.

4.7.4 Satellite Hydrology

Satellite photographs differ from aerial photographs in that the former have a lower spatial resolution and larger field of view. Aerial photographs and airborne geophysical surveying techniques helped greatly to locate the world's resources in the past. Recently the remote sensing devices mounted in high-flying aircraft and earth-orbiting satellites became an essential part of many hydrologic studies as well as for exploring the world's resources.

Remote sensing primarily records electromagnetic energy that emanates in a wave-like motion from features on the surface of the earth. This radiation is usually in a great many bands throughout most of the electromagnetic spectrum. The spectral composition of the energy emanating from a given type of features (rock type, kind of soil, species of tree, or variety of crop) depends largely on the atomic and molecular composition of the feature. Consequently, each type of feature trends to exhibit a unique "tone signature" which is the combination of brightness values seen in the series of multiband photographs (Moore 1979).

Progress on the acquisition of remote sensing data has been rapid. A large amount of progress has been made to earth and atmospheric problems. Areas of research have included development of new methods for processing, analysis, and interpretation of remote sensing data plus determination of the information content of these data. Table 4.3a shows operational uses of satellite data in hydrology (Moore 1979). Table 4.3b shows a summary information on remote sensing and surface geophysical methods (U.S. Environmental Protection Agency 1993).

4.7.5 Applications in the Field of Hydrogeology

The earth's atmosphere absorbs energy in the gamma ray, and most of the ultraviolet (UV) regions; therefore these regions are not used for remote sensing, which only records energy in the microwave, infrared, and visible regions, as the long-wave-length portion of the UV region. The major remote sensing regions (visible, infrared, and microwave) are further subdivided into bands, such as the blue, green and red bands of the visible region (Haeni 1988).

4.7.5.1 *Radar Detects Sinkholes before they Collapse*

Sinkholes are present in areas underlain by carbonate rocks. Sinkholes, depressions, are sometimes only a few meters in diameter, but others may attain major dimensions of as much as 3.2 km, with depths commonly ranging from a few to more than 10 m). The development of new collapses and the subsidence and drainage irregularities associated with their presence, pose serious problems for existing or planned highways, railroads, airports, buildings, agricultural and commercial development.

Sinkholes, as related to occurrence, are defined as "induced" and "natural". Induced sinkholes are those that can be related to man's activities, and can develop in minutes or hours after the effects of man's activities are exerted on existing geologic and hydrologic conditions, whereas, natural sinkholes may require tens, hundreds, or even thousands of years to develop. Both types of sinkholes depend on solution of the underlying bedrock but, they can be separated on the basis of their physical characteristics and environmental settings.

GPR has been applied to investigating sinkholes throughout eastern United States where the unexpectedly ground has collapsed, often with catastrophic effects, causing million of U.S. dollars in damage.

To detect unstable zones beneath a site, the GPR equipment is pulled across the ground constantly beaming radar waves into the ground and receiving back the reflections. The weak zones due to a sinkhole in an area that would cause the ground to collapse and destroy a structure built on the site can be determined.

4.7.5.2 *Image Characteristics*

Remote sensing systems detect the intensity of electromagnetic radiation that an object reflects, emits, or scatters at particular wavelength bands.

An *image* is a pictorial representation, unrelated to the wavelength, or imaging device used to produce it. Images can be described in terms of certain fundamental properties regardless of the wavelength at which the image is recorded. These properties are as follows: *scale* (ratio of the distance between two points on an image to the corresponding distance on the ground), *brightness* (the magnitude of the response produced in the eye by light), *contrast ratio* (ratio between the brightest and darkest parts of the image) and *spatial resolution* which defines the ability to distinguish between two closely spaced objects clearly and separate on an image.

Tone and texture of images are functions of the fundamental properties. Variations in brightness can be distinguished on an image as light, intermediate, or dark in tone. On aerial photographs the tone of an object is primarily determined by the ability of the object to reflect incident sunlight, although atmospheric effects and the spectral sensitivity of the film are also factors. Texture is the frequency of change and arrangement of tones on an image and can be described as fine, medium, and coarse.

A *signature* is the expression of an object on an image that enables the object to be recognized.

4.7.5.3 *Ground-Water Exploration*

NASA's ERTS (Earth Resources Technology Satellite program) has been of great use in the last decade as it can

Table 4.3a. Operational uses of satellite data in hydrology (after Moore 1979, hints to references refer to the original work)

	Application	Data sources	Remarks
Precipitation	Estimate regional precipitation from cloud area and albedo, cloud temperature, and decrease in microwave brightness temperature of ground	GOES, NOAA 5, TIROS N, and Nimbus 6 and 7; passive microwave data are available only from Nimbus	Ground radar observations generally are necessary for accurate estimates of local precipitation
Snow and ice	Snow line and snow mapping	Landsat images and digital data or meteorological satellite images and digital data	Frequent cloud cover is a serious handicap for operational use in mountainous regions
	Estimate time and rate of snow melt in plains areas from snowpack temperature and microwave brightness temperature	Thermal infrared data from HCMM, GOES, NOAA 5, TIROS N, and Nimbus 6 and 7; passive microwave data from Nimbus	Principles of this application are established, but additional research is needed in mountainous terrain, where the application is important for streamflow prediction; in plains areas, further research is needed on detection of frozen ground or flood prediction
	Map and monitor sea ice area, concentration and morphology; assess river, lake, and estuary ice conditions; glacier inventory and environmental monitoring	Landsat, HCMM, and meteorological satellite data; passive microwave data from Nimbus for sea ice	Application is important for navigation and energy budget studies
Surface water	Inventory location and area of reservoirs, lakes, and ponds larger than 1–2 ha; determine seasonal and annual changes in area; estimate changes in water volume	Landsat images and digital data	Detection and measurement accuracy is limited to 80 m satellite resolution, the occurrence of vegetated water bodies, and confusion with wet soils or terrain shadows
	Delineate drainage patterns for fluvial morphology studies	Landsat Band 7 and color composite images; Landsat RBV images	Drainage pattern and density generally are shown in more detail on Landsat images than on small scale maps
	Monitor shoreline and stream channel positions and migrations	Landsat RBV and MSS data	Monitoring capability is limited by the 30 m (RBV) or 80 m (MSS) resolution
	Regional overview of flood impact and damage	Landsat and meteorological satellite images	Satellite resolution is inadequate for hydraulic studies and detailed damage estimates, but satellite images may be used to plan other data acquisition
	Determine clear water depth by light absorption method	Landsat digital data	A few depth measurements and observations of bottom conditions are necessary
	Detect large underwater springs	Landsat RBV and Band 4 MSS images or digital data	Only a few large springs can be detected unless outflows produce water turbidity plumes
Water surface features	Detect some oil spills; inventory and monitor large areas of floating and emergent vegetation	Landsat MSS data for vegetation and some oil slicks; HCMM and meteorological satellite data for detection of large oil spills on thermal infrared imagery	Landsat spectral bands are poor for detection of oil slicks, but some oil slicks have been mapped with Landsat images
	Detect and study differences in sea state as shown by sun glint; sun elevation generally must be more than 55° above horizon	Landsat and meteorological satellite data in the visible and near infrared bands	
Physical water quality	Delineate water color and water turbidity patterns; interpret water circulation and current patterns; evaluate marine fish habitat; study fate of pollutants, biological productivity, and the sediment budgets of estuaries and coastal zones; inventory and monitor the trophic state of lakes and reservoirs; monitor reservoir filling	Landsat MSS images and digital data; Nimbus 7 data from the coastal zone color scanner	The synoptic view of satellites in obtaining optical measurements of water color and turbidity has not been fully realized and exploited
	Quantitative measurement of water turbidity including turbidity caused by plankton and colloids	Landsat and Nimbus 7 digital data; a few concurrent ground measurements generally are necessary	If various methods of solar and atmospheric data correction are proven practical, all satellite data will have value as a record of water turbidity
	Monitor thermal current patterns in large lakes, estuaries, and coastal zones; evaluate marine fish habitat	Thermal infrared imagery from HCMM, Nimbus 7, GOES, NOAA 5, and TIROS N	Digital data and a few concurrent ground measurements are necessary for quantitative results

Table 4.3a. *Continued*

	Application	Data sources	Remarks
Ground water	Detect, delineate, and interpret regional geologic structures	Landsat images and mosaics for regional structure; meteorological satellite images for continental structure	The data are widely used for this purpose; interpretations eventually should result in a better understanding of diagenetic and tectonic processes as well as the effect of these processes on ground-water occurrence and movement
	Shallow ground-water exploration by interpretation of landforms, drainage patterns and density (texture), and vegetation types and patterns	Landsat images and mosaics	Landsat images are used as a tool for ground-water exploration in most areas of the world
	Estimates of shallow ground-water salinity from salt crusts and location, type, and density of vegetation	Landsat images and digital data; some ground measurements and observations are desirable	
	Detect and inventory large ground-water seeps and shallow geothermal ground water by anomalous snow melt patterns	Landsat images and digital data	Melt patterns show the integrated result of all heat sources, including earth heat flow and the presence of ground water at shallow depth
Evapotranspiration	Estimate evapotranspiration by atmospheric model, relative biomass measurements, or relative surface albedo and temperature measurements	Atmospheric water vapor content from TIROS N; thermal data from meteorological satellites; albedo data from Landsat or meteorological satellites; relative biomass measurements from Landsat data; concurrent ground measurements are desirable to necessary	Additional research is needed to determine best approach and to improve accuracy of estimates
	Estimate moisture content of surface and near-surface soils from thermal and microwave measurements	Passive microwave data from Nimbus 7; thermal images and digital data from GOES, NOAA 5, TIROS N, and Nimbus; a few concurrent ground measurements are desirable or necessary	Additional research is needed to fully evaluate effects of vegetation and to improve accuracy of estimates
Land use/land cover	Inventory and map land cover and land use, including bare soils, cultivated cropland, center pivot irrigation systems, and wetlands; monitor environmental effects of water development and management; determine increase in water use for irrigation; estimate percent impervious area; inventory sediment source areas; locate nonpoint source pollution	Landsat images and digital data	Classification accuracy can be improved by (1) combining Landsat and topographic data – correcting Landsat radiance values for surface slope and aspect, (2) merging Landsat scenes of the same area at different times during a year – using eight bands of Landsat data for machine classification instead of four bands, (3) stratification and separate classification of spectrally similar cover types, (4) correcting Landsat data for solar and atmospheric conditions, and (5) using a combination of machine processing and manual interpretation to obtain the advantages of each procedure; considerable ground information is also needed to obtain accuracies of more than 90% for Level II (Anderson et al. 1976, p. 8) land use categories
Satellite data relay	Satellite relay of physical, chemical, and biological water data	Landsat, GOES, and commercial communications satellites	Landsat has experimental status and cannot be used for operational data relay

be applied to problems related to geology, ground water, water quality, surface mining, oil and gas exploration, and the environment (Pettyjohn 1979).

Landsat imagery, for example, is used to gather current information for resource projects conducted in under-developed areas where reconnaissance level ground-water exploration-guide maps need to be produced. The occurrence of ground water is favored by the presence of permeable rock types that influence the movement and concentration of surface and subsurface water, thus the development of soil and vegetation. These rock types and their structures, folds, and faulted zones, are identifiable on areal photography and on computer processed and enhanced landsat imagery (Zall and Russell 1979).

Of great importance is the synoptic or repetitive air photography or satellite imagery available for a site that allows the investigator to analyze what has happened in an area over time; for example, the location of an abandoned mine, tailings, railroad, or road along which spills have occurred, former burial place of barrels or waste, abandoned construction or commercial sites, or old dump areas, all of which can be studied sequentially over time.

Table 4.3b. Summary of information on remote sensing an surface geophysical methods (all rating are approximate and for general guidance only) (U.S. Environmental Protection Agency 1993)

Technique	Soils/Geology	Leachate	Buried wastes	NAPLs	Penetration depth (m)[a]	Cost[b]	Section in U.S. EPA (1993)
Airborne remote sensing and geophysics							
Visible photography+	Yes	Yes[c]	Possibly[d]	Yes[c]	Surf, only	L	1.1.1
Infrared photography+	Yes	Yes[c]	Possibly[d]	Yes[c]	Surf, only	L–M	1.1.1
Multispectral imaging	Yes	Yes[c]	No	Yes[c]	Surf, only	L	1.1.1
Ultraviolet photography	Yes	Yes[c]	No	Yes[c]	Surf, only	L	1.1.2
Thermal infrared scanning	Yes	Yes (T)	Possibly[d]	Possibly	Surf, only	M	1.1.3
Active microwave (radar)+	Yes	Possibly	No	Possibly	0.1–2	M	1.1.4
Airborne electromagnetics	Yes	Yes (C)	Yes	Possibly	0–100	M	1.1.5
Aeromagnetics	Yes	No	Yes	No	10s–100s	M	1.1.6
Surface electrical and electromagnetical methods							
Self-potential	Yes	Yes (C)	Yes	No	S ?	L	1.2.1
Electrical resistivity+	Yes	Yes (C)	Yes (M)	Possibly	S 60 (km)	L–M	1.2.2, 9.1.1
Induced polarization	Yes	Yes (C)	Yes	Possibly	S km	L–M	1.2.3
Complex resistivity	Yes	Yes (C)	Yes	Yes	S km	M–H	1.2.3
Dielectric sensors	Yes	Yes (C)	No	Possibly	S 2[e]	L–M	6.2.3
Time domain reflectometry	Yes	Yes (C)	No	Yes	S 2[e]	M–H	6.2.4
Capacitance sensors	Yes	Yes (C)	No	Possibly	S 2[e]	L–M	6.2.4
Electromagnetic induction	Yes	Yes (C)	Yes	Possibly	S 60 (200)/ c 15 (50)	L–M	1.3.1
Transient electromagnetics	Yes	Yes (C)	Yes	No	S 150 (2000+)	M–H	1.3.2
Metal detectors	No		Yes	No	C/S 0–3	L	1.3.3
VLF resistivity	Yes	Yes (C)	Yes	No	C/S 20–60	M–H	1.3.4
Magnetotellurics	Yes	Yes (C)	No	No	S 1000+	M–H	1.3.5
Surface seismic and acoustic methods							
Seismic refraction+	Yes	Yes	No	No	S 1–30 (200+)	L–M	1.4.1
Shallow seismic reflection+	Yes	No	No	No	S 10–30(2 000+)	M–H	1.4.2
Continuous seismic profiling	Yes	No	No	No	C 1–100	L–M	1.4.3
Seismic share/surface waves	Yes	No	No	No	S 2 10s–100s	M–H	1.4.4
Acoustic emission monitoring	Yes	No	No	No	S 2[e]	L	1.4.5
Sonar/fathometer	Yes	Yes	No	No	C no limit	L–H	1.4.6
Other surface geophysical methods							
Ground penetrating radar+	Yes	Yes (C)	Yes	Yes	C 1–25 (100s)	M	1.5.1
Magnetometry+	No	No	Yes (F)	No	C/S 0–20	L–M	1.5.2
Gravity	Yes	Yes	No	No	S 100s+[f]	H	1.5.3
Radiation detection	No	No	Yes (nuclear)	No	C/S near surface	L	1.5.4
Near surface geothermometry							
Soil temperature	Yes	Yes (T)	No	No	S 1–2[e]	L	1.6.1
Ground-water detection	Yes	Yes (T)	No	No	S 2[e]	L	1.6.2
Other thermal properties	Yes	No	No	No	S 1–2[e]	L–M	1.6.2

Boldface = Most commonly used methods at contaminated sites; + = covered in Superfund Field Operations Manual (U.S. EPA 1987); *(C)* = plume detected when contaminant(s) change conductivity of ground water; *(F)* = ferrous metals only; *(T)* = plume detected by temperature rather than conductivity.

[a] *S* = station measurement; *C* = continous measurement. Depths are for typical shallow applications; *()* = achievable depths.

[b] Ratings are very approximate; *L* = low; *M* = moderate; *H* = high.

[c] If leachate or NAPLs are on the ground or water surface or indirectly affect surface properties; field confirmation required.

[d] Disturbed areas that may contain buried waste can often be detected on aerial photographs.

[e] Typical maximum depth, greater depths possible, but sensor placement is more difficult and cable length must be increased.

[f] For ferrous metal detection, greater depths require larger masses of metal for detection; 100s of meters depth can be sensed when using magnetometry for mapping geologic structure.

4.7.5.4 *Characteristics of Microwave Emission*

Newton developed a technique of interpreting passive emission measurements in terms of average soil moisture over a predicted soil depth.

Soil water content is highly nonuniform with soil depth and areal coverage. The emission or scattering from a soil regime is not only affected by the relative degree of saturation of the soil in near surface soil layers, but also by the shape of the soil water profile with depth within this near surface soil zone. A single parameter soil moisture profile for estimating near surface soil water from passive microwave measurements was developed (Newton 1979).

4.7.5.5 *Aquifer Rock Identification*

Surface drainage patterns are an important key element in the identification of rock lithologies. Drainage patterns can be a qualitative indicator of rock permeability. For example, the type of drainage pattern on a terrain is a function of the amount of precipitation infiltrating into the ground vs. surface runoff. The greater number of surface drainage channels in an area can occur in the less permeable terrain where surface runoff dominates over infiltration (Fig. 4.8b; Zall and Russell 1979).

Because fractured or jointed terrain creates a controlled drainage pattern consisting of angular or straight tributary channels, their presence in a tight bedrock may indicate fractured or faulted zones containing ground water.

The drainage pattern in sandstone is widely spaced. It follows the most easily eroded joints and bedding found in sandstone bedrock. The gneissic terrain is more of angular and dendritic pattern (Fig. 4.9; Belcher 1951). Drainage patterns used in this manner is a time saving device for regional hydrogeologic mapping. The satellite image becomes a regional guide map, thus reducing the subsequent amount of aerial photographic interpretation in ground-water investigations.

The major surface drainage patterns associated with various lithologies, observable on aerial photographs, are also maple on satellite imagery. Both can be used successfully to map permeable aquifer rocks and linear features or lineaments that may be geomorphic (caused by relief) or tonal (caused by image contrast differences) (Zall and Russell 1979).

Satellite sensing has become a routine and essential part of many hydrologic studies. A geographic database that includes atmospheric and surface information for hydrologic predictions, lead to new types of hydrologic models. The information of the geographic database about an area is stored on computer for combination, comparison, and for updating purposes.

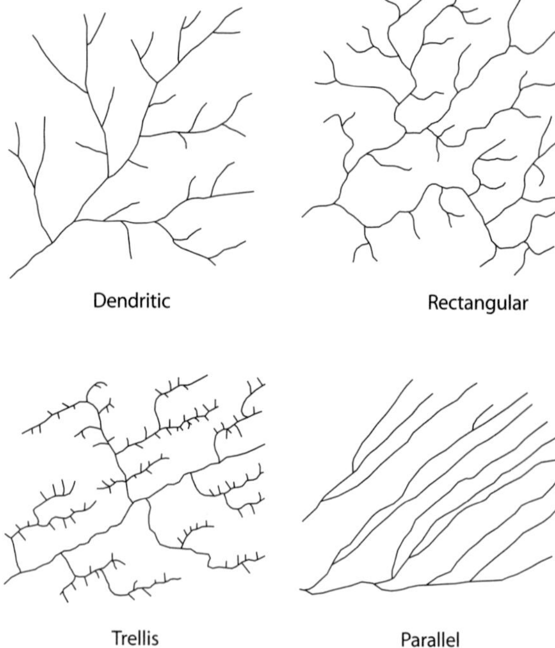
Dendritic
Rectangular
Trellis
Parallel

Fig. 4.8b. Some of the basic drainage patterns which provide structural and lithological information (Zall and Russell 1979)

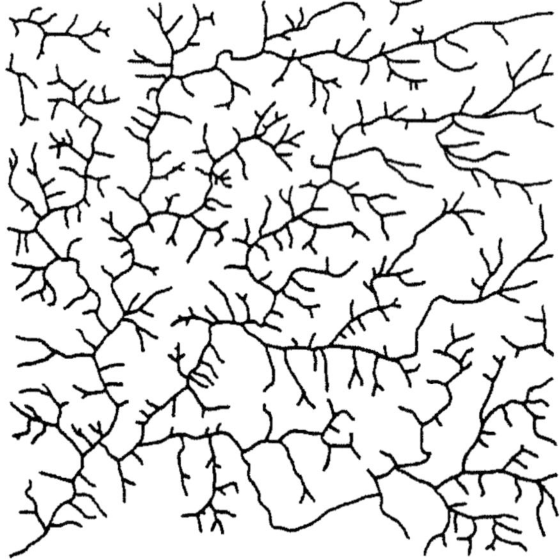

Fig. 4.9. Drainage pattern on gneiss mapped from aerial photographs (Belcher 1951)

4.8 Geophysical Investigations in Karst Areas

Karst is a characteristic terrain with distinctive hydrology and landscape arising from a combination of high rock solubility and well-developed secondary porosity; and it is often characterized by sinkholes, sinking streams, caves, and springs.

Cavities in unconsolidated deposits overlying carbonate rocks are known in areas where water table declines. The enlargement and configuration of these cavities can be variable. Figure 4.10 shows the growth and collapse of two cavities. The vertical enlargement and resulting collapse is one of the most common types; the lateral enlargement occurs where the upward enlargement encounters a bed that is able to maintain its integrity (Newton 1976).

Most carbonate areas contain solution-enlarged joints, also known as 'cutters'. These cutters are formed by dissolution of bedrock as ground water flows through fractures that may be separated by upward protruding limestone features known as 'pinnacles'. Table 4.3c shows

WTP
WTA

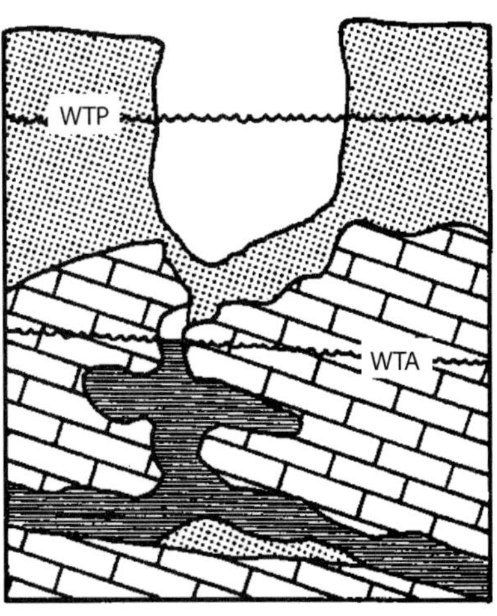
WTP
WTA

a

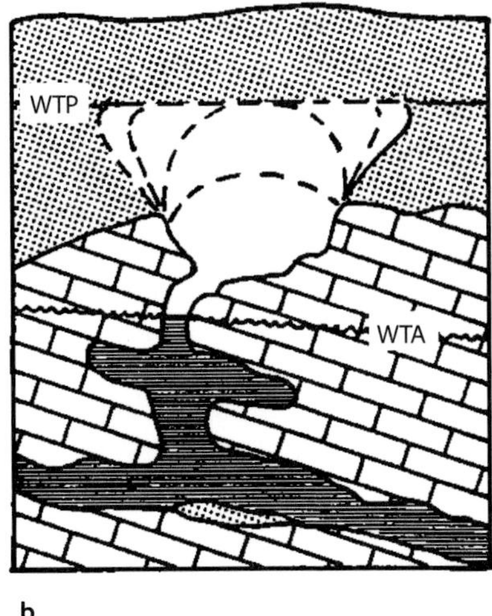
WTP
WTA

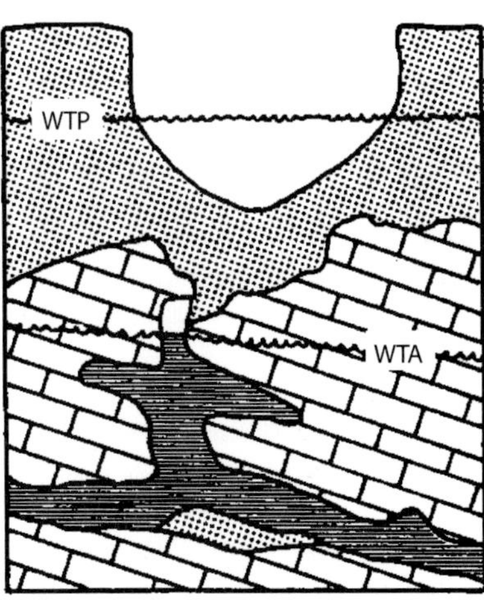
WTP
WTA

b

Boundary designating cavity growth

WTP Water table prior to decline
WTA Water table after decline

Unconsolidated deposits
Water-filled opening in limestone
Direction of water movement
Limestone

Fig. 4.10. Development of cavities in unconsolidated deposits (Newton 1976); **a** vertical enlargement and resulting collapse; **b** vertical and lateral enlargement and resulting collapse

Table 4.3c. A short list of sinkhole terminology (Fairbridge 1968; Jennings 1985; Sweeting 1972)

Term	Description
Doline	A solution depression or a sinkhole. A circular or elliptical or irregular-shaped depression in the ground surface into which surface water from the surrounding ground drains
Cutter	A solution-enlarged fissure or *slot* (a term borrowed from shallow mining of phosphate minerals in the southern U.S.)
Epikarst	The soft zone of unconsolidated residual soil immediately above the rock surface, and in the deeper slots between the solutioned pinnacles
Grike	Solution-enlarged fissure or *slot* (used in U.K.)
Karren	Local surface dissolution or surface sculpture of limestone from running water, often in the form of parallel grooves
Pinnacle	The narrow rock remaining between wide slots
Polje	An extremely wide or valley like, flat bottomed solution depression, usually with an alluvial pavement in Yugoslavia and Turkey
Pit	A more or less vertical shaft, usually a rounded stope or solution-enlarged intersectioning fissure system (see solution chimney and shaft)
Slot	A solution-enlarged steep or vertical fissure
Solution canyon	A very wide and deep slot
Solution chimney	A solution-enlarged steep fissure or pit, sometimes somewhat crooked or twisted like a cork screw
Solution shaft	A near vertical more or less cylindrical hole from solution by falling water or stope activity
Swallow hole	A sinkhole in or adjacent to a stream into which the stream flow disappears
Terrane	A variant of the word *terrain* used by geomorphologists and geologists to denote unity of geology, topography, and environment
Uvala	A complex assortment of solution depressions or sinkhole with their bottoms at different levels and sometimes depressions within depressions

a short list of sinkhole terminology (Fairbridge 1968; Jennings 1985; Sweeting 1972).

Soluble components are dissolved and removed by flowing ground water whereas, soluble residues accumulate on the sides of pinnacles and in the bottoms of cutters forming a covered karst terrain (Jennings 1985).

Sinkhole collapse is one of the main limestone features that develop in karst areas, especially where bedrock is covered by unconsolidated material. Sinkholes are likely to develop in cutter zones as a result of subterranean erosion by flowing ground water. A high-resolution geophysical technique capable of depicting the details of the bedrock surface is essential for guiding the drilling program.

Irregular distributed cutters and pinnacles have significant effects on land development. When combined with other factors, cutters constitute potential areas for sinkhole development, and pinnacles contribute to differential subsidence of the ground surface and building foundations. Because of the irregular distribution of cutters and pinnacles, it is time-consuming and expensive to define the depth to bedrock with boring data.

4.8.1 Electrical Resistivity Tomography (ERT)

Electrical resistivity tomography (ERT) is an updated version of traditional resistivity methods. Data are collected by an automated instrument (Sting 1984) and processed using numerical inversion programs (Griffiths and Baker 1993).

Measured apparent resistivity is a volume-arranged value affected by all geologic layers through which the induced electric current flows. An inversion program converts the apparent resistivity data into a model of the geology that would yield the observed distribution of apparent resistivity values. The product of the data inversion process is a two-dimensional image (a tomograph) showing a distribution of true resistivity values. The contrast between the properties of the overburden soil and the underlying rock provides the basis for applying this geophysical technique to characterize the bedrock surface and delineate the anomalous areas. However, the geophysical interpretation should be checked with ground data from exploratory boreholes.

4.8.2 Earth Resistivity Tomography Used for Investigating Karst Hazards

In geological applications, tomographic surveys normally employ a linear array of multiple electrodes on the ground surface. Computerized instrumentation automatically selects four electrodes (two current electrodes and two measurement electrodes) to be used for

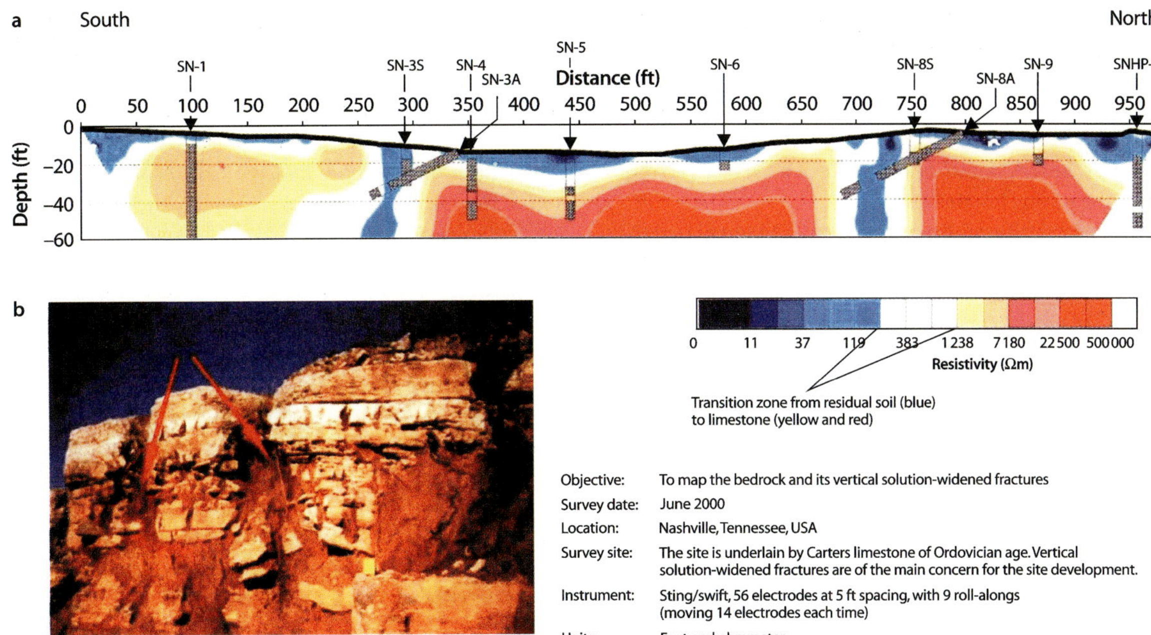
a
South
North
SN-1
SN-3S
SN-4
SN-3A
SN-5
Distance (ft)
SN-6
SN-8S
SN-8A
SN-9
SNHP-2
0 50 100 150 200 250 300 350 400 450 500 550 600 650 700 750 800 850 900 950
Depth (ft)
0
-20
-40
-60
b
0 11 37 119 383 1238 7180 22500 500000
Resistivity (Ωm)
Transition zone from residual soil (blue) to limestone (yellow and red)
Objective: To map the bedrock and its vertical solution-widened fractures
Survey date: June 2000
Location: Nashville, Tennessee, USA
Survey site: The site is underlain by Carters limestone of Ordovician age. Vertical solution-widened fractures are of the main concern for the site development.
Instrument: Sting/swift, 56 electrodes at 5 ft spacing, with 9 roll-alongs (moving 14 electrodes each time)
Units: Feet and ohmmeter

Fig. 4.11. Karst investigation; a geophysical survey using dipole-dipole resistivity in Tennessee. The purpose of the survey was to make a pre-construction evaluation of potential sinkhole hazards at the site of an electrical substation (Wanfang 1999 cited in Zhou et al. 1999); **a** electrical resistivity profile showing borehole locations and the presence of bedrock; **b** vertical solution-widened clay-filled fractures, seen at a road cut in the area

each measurement and makes it possible to collect multiple data points in a short period of time.

The current and measurement electrode pairs may be arranged in various configurations. Electrode configurations (arrays) that are commonly used by geophysicists are known by standard names: the Wenner array, the Schlumberger array, the pole-dipole array, or the dipole-dipole array. The dipole-dipole array is usually selected because it provides precise measurements, a reasonable depth of investigation, and has the greatest sensitivity to lateral resistivity boundaries. The lateral resistivity change results from the existence of fractures (either open or filled with clay) within the limestone.

Figure 4.11 shows an example of survey lines using a Sting R1 Memory Earth Resistivity Meter and the Swift Automatic Smart Electrode System. The collected data were first edited manually to remove any negative apparent values (which are theoretically impossible) and those with percent deviation greater than 2%. These collected data were then processed using the computer program RES2DINV to generate two-dimensional resistivity models of the subsurface.

Topographic irregularities on the site may introduce distortion in the tomographs that can affect interpretation of the position of the lateral boundaries. Surface elevation data along each line were incorporate in the program RES2DINV and the final cross sections were adjusted to account for the tomography.

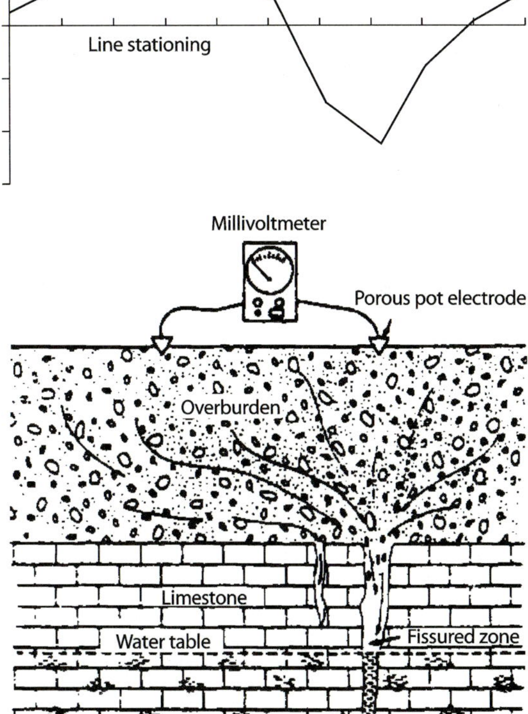
Self-potential (mV)
Line stationing
Millivoltmeter
Porous pot electrode
Overburden
Limestone
Water table
Fissured zone

Fig. 4.12. Self-potential measurements: apparatus and graph of measurement over a fissured zone of limestone illustrating negative streaming potential caused by ground-water seepage (Ogilvy and Bogoslovsky 1979)

To verify the geophysical findings, the geologic cross sections are overlaid on the geoelectrical profile. Three zones can be recognized – the overburden layer, the transitional zone, and the limestone. The transitional zone probably consists of residual clay, limestone fragments, and weathered limestone. The bedrock surface is irregular with pinnacles and cutters.

Most of the boreholes are encountered top of bed rock within the transitional zone, except SN-4 and SN-5, where the geophysical profile overestimates the depth to bedrock. This discrepancy is probably the effect of the clay-filled sinkhole. Both of the vertical low resistivity zones were confirmed by the angle drilling to be clay-filled.

The following are some of the limitations in using this method: (1) Impact of three-dimensional (3-D) geology: The tomographs are affected by features adjacent to the transects. Interpretation can be improved by using multiple intersecting transects. The use of 3-D electrical resistivity method is even more effective (Loke and Baker 1996). (2) Data quality: Electrical resistivity data are affected by various factors, such as wind, clouds, rain, nearby metallic materials, animals, and even solar flares. (3) Non-uniqueness of the modeling results: It is possible for different geological models to produce similar profiles of calculated apparent resistivity. (4) Complex geology in karst terranes: Due to complex variations within the bedrock and the unconsolidated sediments, inappropriate interpretation of the tomograph can give misleading results.

4.8.3 Natural Potential Method (NP)

The natural (electrical) potential (NP) method – also known as self potential, spontaneous potential and streaming potential (SP) – has been used to locate areas of ground-water flow in karst terrane. NP is the naturally-occurring voltage at the ground surface resulting from ambient electrical currents within the earth. Its values, measured in a similar geologic setting, are at least partly contributed by the streaming potential (Zhou et al. 1999).

Table 4.4. Geophysical data (Sara 1994; hints to sections refer to the original work)

Source	Information obtainable	Comments
U.S. Geological Survey Water Supply Papers	The most common types of data are obtained from seismic and resistivity surveys, but other types may also appear or be referenced. Water Supply Papers for an area can be by any of the computer searches or published indexes described in the first section of this paper.	The USGS also published geophysically maps of various types at relatively small scales for many areas of the U.S. Aeromagnetic maps have been completed for much of the U.S., although the flight altitude of several thousand meters and scale of 1:24 000 make these maps too general for most site specific work.
Well Log Libraries Electric Log Services P.O. Box 3150 Midland, TX 79702 Tel. 915-682-0591	Sample and electric logs for many petroleum wells can be obtained from one of several well log libraries in the U.S.	Sample logs generally extend to the surface, but geophysical logs start where the well casing ends – commonly at a depth of about 100 m. The type of geophysical logs available may include sonic velocity, radioactivity, caliper (borehole diameter), and others. The logs are indexed by survey section, and to obtain information on wells in a given area, it is necessary to compile a list of the townships, ranges, and section numbers covering the area.
Geophysical survey firms	Specific geophysical logs	Proprietary geophysical data can sometimes be obtained from private survey firms. In general, the original client must approve the exchange of information, and preference is given for academic purposes. If the information cannot be released, firms may be willing to provide references to published information they obtained before the survey, or information published as a result of the survey.
National Geophysical and Solar-Terrestrial Data Center Chief, Solid Earth Geophysics 325 Broadway Boulder, CO 80303 Tel. 303-497-6521 FTS 320-6521	NGSDC maintains a computer file of more than 136 000 earthquakes, known or suspected explosions and associated collapse phenomena coal bumps, rockbursts, quarry blasts, and other earth disturbances recorded worldwide by seismographs starting in January 1900. Historic U.S. earthquakes are included for the period starting in 1638. For U.S.$25, a search can be made for one of the following parameters: 1. Geographic area (circular or rectangular area) 2. Time period (starting 1638 for U.S.) 3. Magnitude range 4. Date 5. Time 6. Depth 7. Intensity (modified Mercalli)	Site studies for many projects now require information regarding the seismicity of the region surrounding the site. The National Geophysical and Solar-Terrestrial Data Center (NGSDC) of the National Oceanic and Atmospheric Administration (NOAA) is a focal point for dissemination of earthquake data and information for both technical and general users, except for information on recent earthquakes. (Information about recent earthquakes can be obtained by contacting the USGS.)

Table 4.5. Remote sensing (Sara 1994)

Source		Information obtainable	Comments
USGS EROS Data Center	Additional information can be found in the *publications The EROS Data Center* and *The Landsat Data User's Handbook*. To obtain these publications, request further information, place an order, contact: User Service EROS Data Center U.S. Geological Survey Sioux Falls, SD 57198 Tel. 605-594-6156 FTS 784-7151	The Earth Resources Observation Systems (EROS) program of the U.S. Department of the Interior, administered by the USGS, was established in 1966 to apply remote-sensing techniques to the inventory, monitoring, and management of natural resources. As part of this program, the EROS program provides remotely-sensed data at nominal cost to anyone in the world.	The EROS Data Center, near Sioux Falls, South Dakota, is operated by the EROS program to provide access primarily to NASA's Landsat imagery, aerial photography acquired by the U.S. Department of the Interior, and photography and multi-spectral imagery acquired by NASA from research aircraft, *Skylab*, *Apollo*, and *Gemini* spacecraft. The primary function of the Data Center are data storage and reproduction, user assistance, and training. The Data Center can provide a computer listing of all imagery on file for three geographic options: 1. Point search – all images or photographs with any portion falling over the specific point of longitude and latitude are included. 2. Area quadrilateral – any area of interest defined by four coordinates of longitude and latitude. All images or photographs with any coverage of the area are included. 3. Map specification – a point or area may be indicated on a map. (Options 1 and 2 are preferred by EROS.)
	Landsat data	Landsat satellites sensor images in four spectral bands: – Band 4 (emphasizes sediment-laden and shallow water) – Band 5 (emphasizes cultural features) – Band 6 (emphasizes vegetation, land/water boundaries, and landforms) – Band 7 (as above, with the best penetration of haze) Band 5 gives the best general-purpose view of the earth's surface; available are black and white images and false-color composites.	The Landsat satellites were designed to orbit the earth about 14 times each day at an altitude of 920 km, obtaining repetitive coverage every 18 days. The primary sensor aboard the satellites is a multi-spectral scanner that acquires parallelogram images 185 km per side in four spectral bands.
	NASA aerial photography	Photography is available in a wide variety of formats from flights at altitudes ranging from one to 18 km. Photographs generally come as 230 mm by 230 mm prints at scales of 1:60 000 or 1:120 000, and are available as black and white, color, or false-color infrared prints.	NASA aerial photography is directed at testing a variety of remote-sensing instruments and techniques in aerial flights over certain preselected test sites over the continental U.S.
	Aerial mapping photography	Aerial photographic coverage obtained by the USGS and other Federal agencies (other than the Soil Conservation Service) for mapping of the U.S. is available as 230 mm by 230 mm black and white prints which are taken at altitudes of 600 m to 12 km.	Because of the large number of individual photographs needed to show a region on the ground, photomosaic indexes are used to identify photographic coverage of a specific area. The Data Center has more than 50 000 such mosaics available for photographic selection.
U.S. Department of Agriculture	Aerial Photography Field Office U.S. Department of Agriculture P.O. Box 30010 Salt Lake City, UT 84130 Tel. 801-524-5856 FTS 588-5857	Conventional aerial photography scales of 1:20 000 to 1:40 000	Aerial photographs by the various agencies of the U.S. Department of Agriculture (Agricultural Stabilization and Conservation Service, ASCS; Soil Conservation Service, SCS; and Forest Service, USFS) cover much of the U.S.
Other sources	**Coastal Mapping Division of NOAA** An index for the collection can be obtained for free by contacting: Coastal Mapping Division National Oceanic and Atmospheric Administration 6001 Executive Boulevard Rockville, MD 20852 Tel. 301-443-8601 FTS 443-8601	The Coastal Mapping Division of NOAA maintains a file of color and black and white photographs of the tidal zone of the Atlantic, Gulf, and Pacific coasts. The scales of the photographs range from 1:20 000 to 1:60 000.	

Table 4.5. *Continued*

Source	Information obtainable	Comments
Bureau of Land Management For an index of the entire collection contact: U.S. Bureau of Land Management Larry Cunningham (SC-675) P.O. Box 25047 Denver, CO 80225-0047 Tel. 303-236-7991	The Bureau of Land Management has aerial photographic coverage of approximately 50% of its lands in 11 western states.	
National Archives and Records Service Cartographic Archives Division General Services Administration 8 Pennsylvania Avenue, N.W. Washington, DC 20408 Tel. 703-756-6700	Airphoto coverage obtained before 1942 for portions of the U.S.	This service may be important for early documentation of site activities.
Canadian airphoto coverage can be obtained from: **National Aerial Photograph Library** 615 Booth Street Ottawa, Ontario K1A 0E9 Canada Tel. 613-995-4560		
Canadian satellite imagery can be obtained from: **Canadian Centre for Remote Sensing** 2464 Sheffield Road Ottawa, Ontario K1A 0Y7 Canada Tel. 613-952-0202		
Commercial aerial photo firms For a listing of nearby firms specializing in these services, consult the yellow pages or contact: American Society of Photogrammetry 210 Little Falls Street Falls Church, VA 22046 Tel. 703-534-6617		In many instances, these firms retain negatives for photographs flown for a variety of clients and readily sell prints to any interested users.

Figure 4.12 shows apparatus and graph of measurement over a fissured zone of limestone (Ogilvy and Bogoslovsky 1979 in U.S. Environmental Protection Agency 1993).

According to the Helmoltz relationship, when water moves through a saturated capillary system by laminar flow, the NP gradient is the product of the water pressure gradient and a coupling constant (Aubert and Atangana 1996). The potential gradient is the result of the electro-filtration process, wherein the natural potential increases positively in the direction of flow. This theory has been proven by laboratory experiments in which the NP generated by the flow of water through porous material (Bogoslovsky and Ogilvy 1972).

The NP measurements can be also applied to delineate subsurface areas of localized ground-water recharge. They are made along the ground surface using the voltage-averaging mode of a multimeter with an input impedance of at least 10 MΩ.

Some of the limitations in using this method may be summarized as follows: (1) *Various sources of electrical potential:* Natural electrical potential is caused by a variety of discrete physical phenomena acting underground; e.g. streaming potential; (2) *Electrical interference:* NP data may be impacted by various sources of interference, including telluric currents; electrical resistivity variations within the ground and other factors; (3) *Averaging the topographic correction factors:* Topographic correction factors vary with time and location.

A primary geophysical investigation of a site provides one of the basic template that would apply for most initial projects. Table 4.4 defines references of potential sources of geoghysical data. Aerial photos, in stereopairs, can provide an excellent base for plotting of site features. Many forms of remote imagery show the site features evident on the topographic maps, as well as vegetation types, density, and image tone. Table 4.5 provides sources for remote-image data (Sara 1994).

References

Anderson DG (1979) Roles of satellite hydrology. In: Deutsch M, Wiesnet DR, Rango A (eds) Satellite hydrology. Proc. of the fifth annual William T. Pecora Memorial, Symposium on Remote Sensing, American Water Resources Association, Minneapolis, Minnesota, p 144

Anderson WL (1979) Michigan job uses geophysical aids. Johnson Driller's Journal, Nov/Dec, Johnson Division, UOP, St. Paul, Minnesota, (from Water and Wells, Driscoll 1986)

Aubert M, Atangana QY (1996) Self-potential method in hydrogeological exploration of volcanic areas. Ground Water 34(6): 1010–1016

Beck BF, Sayed S (1991) The sinkhole hazard in Pinellas County. A geologic summary for planning purposes. PSI/Jammal & Assoc Inc., Winter Park, Florida; Florida Sinkhole Research Institute, University of Central Florida, Orlando, FL (Report 90-91-1)

Beck BF, Wilson WL (1988) Interpretation of ground penetrating radar. Proc. of the second conference on Environmental Problem in Karst Terranes and their Solutions Conference "Profiles in Karst Terrane", Nov 16–18th, Maxwell House Hotel, Nashville, Tennessee

Belcher DJ (1951) Land form reports. Amphibious Branch, Office of Naval Research and School of Civil Engineering, Cornell University (6 volumes)

Beres M Jr, Haeni FP (1991) Application of ground penetrating radar, methods in hydrogeologic studies. Association of Ground Water Scientists and Engineers, Groundwater Journal 29(3):375–386

Bogoslovsky VA, Ogilvy AA (1972) The study of streaming potentials on fissured media models. Geophysical Prospecting 51:109–117 (in Zhou et al. 1999)

Calabrese MA, Thome PG (1979) Nasa Water Resources/Hyrdrology Remote Sensing Program in the 1980s. In: Deutsch M, Wiesnet DR, Rango A (eds) Satellite hydrology. Proc. of the fifth annual William T. Pecora Memorial, Symposium on Remote Sensing, American Water Resources Association, Minneapolis, Minnesota, p 9

Crawford NC, Lewis MA, Winter SA, Webster JA (1999) Microgravity techniques for subsurface investigations of sinkhole collapses and for detection of ground-water flow paths through karst aquifers. In: Beck BF, Petit A, Herring G (eds) Hydrogeology and engineering geology of sinkholes and karst. A.A.Balkema, Rotterdam, pp 203–218

Dobrin M B, Savit CH (1988) Introduction to geophysical prospecting. McGraw-Hill (chap 12, pp 500–501, 635–639)

Driscoll FG (1986) Groundwater and wells. Johnson Division, UOP Inc., St. Paul, Minnesota, USA, pp 168–177

Griffiths DH, Barker RD (1993) Two-dimensional resistivity imaging and modelling in areas of complex geology. J Appl Geophys 29:211–226

Groshong RH Jr (1999) 3-D structural geology – a practical guide to subsurface map interpretation. Springer-Verag, Berlin Heidelberg New York, pp 1–32, 39–50

Haeni FP (1988) Evaluation of the continuous seismic-reflection methods for determining the thickness and lithology of stratified-drift in the glaciated northeast. In: Randall AD, Johnson IA (eds) Regional aquifer systems of the United States – the northeast glacial aquifers. Am. Water Resources Association Monograph Series 11:156

Haeni FP, McKeegan DK, Capron DR (1987) Ground-penetrating radar study of the thickness and extent of sediments beneath Silver Lake, Berlin and Meriden, Connecticut. U.S. Geological Survey Water Resources Investigations 85-4108

Hoerig B, Kuehn F (2000) Remote sensing: an overview of physical fundamentals. In: Federal Institute for Geosciences and Natural Resources (BGR) Remote Sensing for site characterization-methods in environmental geology. Springer-Verag, Hannover pp 5–7

Jennings JN (1985) Karst geomorphology. Basil Blackwell, Oxford

Legg CA (1991) Remote sensing and geographic information systems: geological mapping, mineral exploration and mining. United Kingdom Overseas Development Administration, Forest Department, Colombo, Sri Lanka, pp 1–6

Loke MH, Baker RD (1996) A practical technique for 3-D resistivity surveys and data inversion. Geophysical Prospecting 44:499–523

Moore GK (1979) An introduction to satellite hydrology. In: Deutsch M, Wiesnet DR, Rango A (eds) Satellite hydrology. Proc. of the Fifth Annual William T. Pecora Memorial, Symposium on Remote Sensing, American Water Resources Association, Minneapolis, Minnesota, pp 37–41

Morse PF, Purnell GW, Medwedeff DA (1991) Seismic modeling of fault-related structures. In: Fagan SW (ed) Seismic modeling of geologic structures. Society of Exploration Geophysicists, Tulsa, Oklahoma, pp 127–152

Newton JG (1976) Early detection and correction of sinkhole problems in Alabama, with a preliminary evaluation of remote sensing applications. USGS of Alabama and U.S. Department of Transportation, Washington DC, pp 7–13, 52–54

Newton R (1979) Characteristics of microwave emission of significance to satellite remote sensing of soil water. In: Deutsch M, Wiesnet DR, Rango A (eds) Satellite hydrology. Proc. of the Fifth Annual William T. Pecora Memorial, Symposium on Remote Sensing. American Water Resources Association, Minneapolis, Minnesota, p 353

Ogilvy AA, Bogoslovsky VA (1979) Self potential measurements: apparatus and graph of measurement over a fissured zone of limestone illustrating negative streaming potential caused by ground-water seepage. In: U.S. Environmental Protection Agency (ed) Use of airborne, surface and borehole geophysical techniques at contaminated sites: a reference guide. Eastern Research Group, Center for Environmental Research Information, Cincinnati, Ohio (EPA/625/R-92/007, 1993)

Olhöeft GR (1991a) Applications and limitations of ground-penetrating radar (abs.) (1984). Society of Exploration Geophysicists, 54th Annual International Meeting, Atlanta, Georgia, Ground Water Journal, pp 147–148

Olhöeft GR (1991b) Direct detection of hydrocarbon and organic chemicals with ground-penetration radar and complex resistivity (1986). Proc. of the NWWA Conference on Petroleum Hydrocarbons and Organic Chemicals in Ground Water, Houston, Texas, Ground Water Journal, pp 1–22

Pettyjohn WA (1979) Groundwater and satellites: An overview/introduction. In: Deutsch M, Wiesnet DR, Rango A (eds) Satellite hydrology. Proc. of the Fifth Annual William T. Pecora Memorial, Symposium on Remote Sensing. American Water Resources Association, Minneapolis, Minnesota, pp 385–386

Sara MN (1994) Standard handbook for solid and hazardous waste facility assessments. Lewis Publishers, an imprint of CRC Press Inc., Boca Raton, Florida, pp 2–12, 14

Sharma PV (1997) Environmental and engineering geophysics. Cambridge University Press, New York (chap 4, pp 112–127) (reprinted by permission of Cambridge University Press)

Sherif RE (1984) Encyclopedic dictionary of exploration geophysics, 2nd edn. Society of Exploration Geophysicists, Tulsa, Oklahoma

Stanfill DF III, McMillan KS (1985a) Inspection of hazardous waste sites using ground-penetrating radar (GPR). Proc. of the National Conference on Hazardous Waste and Environmental Emergencies, Hazardous Materials Control Research Institute (H.M.C.R.I.), Cincinnati, OH, pp 244–249

Stanfill DF III; McMillan KS (1985b) Radar-mapping of gasoline and other hydrocarbons in the Ground. Proc. of the 6th National Conference on Management of Uncontrolled Hazardous Waste Sites, Hazardous Materials Control Research Institute (H.M.C.R.I.), Washington, D.C., November 1985, pp 269–274

Sting RI (1984) Instruction manual. Advanced Geosciences Inc. (Release 2.0.2)

Stone DS (1991) Analysis of scale exaggeration on seismic profiles. In: Groshong (ed) 3-D structural geology – a practical guide to subsurface map interpretation. American Associacion of Petroleum Geologists Bulletin 75(1999):1161–1177

U.S. Environmental Protection Agency (1993) Summary information on remote sensing and surface geophysical methods. In: Boulding JR (ed) Use of airborne, surface, and borehole geophysical techniques at contaminated sites, a reference guide. Eastern Research Group, Center for Environmental Research Information, Cincinnati, Ohio (EPA 625/R-92/007)

USGS, U.S. Army (1998) Earth science applications. National Training Center, Fort Irwin, California (http://wrgis.wr.usgs.gov/docs/geologic)

Utkinsen PF (1991) Application of impulse radar to civil engineering. PhD Thesis (1986), Lund University of Technology, Lund, Sweden

Wallace DE (1970) Some limitations of seismic refraction methods in geohydrological surveys of deep alluvial basins. Ground Water Journal 8(6):8–13

Wright DC, Olhöeft GR, Watts RD (1984) Ground-penetrating radar studies on Cape Cod. Proc. of the NWWA/EPA Conference on Surface and Borehole Geophysical Methods. Ground Water Investigations, San Antonio, Texas, pp 666–680

Zall L, Russell O (1979) Groundwater exploration programs in Africa. In: Deutsch M, Wiesnet DR, Rango A(eds) Satellite hydrology. Proc. of the Fifth Annual William T. Pecora Memorial, Symposium on Remote Sensing, American Water Resources Association, Minneapolis, Minnesota, pp 416–425

Zhou WF, Beck BF, Stephenson JB (1999) Application of electrical resistivity tomography and natural-potential technology to delineate potential sinkhole collapse areas in a covered karst terrane. P.E. LaMoreaux & Associates Inc., Oak Ridge, Tennessee

Selected References

Coffeen JA (1978) Seismic exploration fundamentals, seismic techniques for finding oil, 2nd edn. PennWell Publishing Company, Tulsa, Oklahoma, pp 1–6, 29–30

Haeni FP (1986) Application of continuous seismic reflection methods to hydrologic studies. Ground Water 24(1):23–31

Haeni FP, Melvin RL (1984) High-resolution continuous seismic reflection study of a stratified-drift deposit in Connecticut. Proc. of the NWWA/EPA Conference on Surface and Borehole Geophysical Methods in Ground Water Investigations, San Antonio, Texas, pp 237–256

Jakosky J (1950) Exploration geophysics. Trija Publishing Company, Los Angeles, California (from Water and Wells, Driscoll 1986)

Mooney HM (1981) Handbook of engineering geophysics, seismic, vol 1. Bison Instruments, Inc., Minneapolis, Minnesota

Sherif RE (1978) A first course in geophysical exploration and interpretation. International Human Resources Development Corporation, IHRDC Publishing, Boston, Massachusetts, pp 3–17

Part II

Subsurface Geological and Geophysical Methods

Chapter 5

Characteristics of Sedimentary Rocks – Subsurface Geological Mapping and Computer Software Data Management Systems

5.1 Introduction

Field geology seeks to describe and explain the surface features and underground structures of the lithosphere. Subsurface geology can be obtained from surface observation, vegetation trends, drainage, geophysical studies, air photographs, satellite imagery. Reading and interpretive the subsurface geology from surficial clues is like reading a mystery book. It pertains to the study of rock relationships by the use of data obtained from the surface sources as well as test drilling and underground mines, and quarries.

Geologists and hydrogeologists are concerned with subsurface geology and the main source of subsurface geologic data e.g. well samples, cores, and geophysical logs. The quality of well cuttings and cores has improved from better drilling practices, and this development has encouraged a greater emphasis on subsurface methods.

Much of this chapter deals with clastic sedimentary rocks that are disaggregated and are present as cuttings or cores and can be used for petrophysical analyses (see Chap. 13). Bedding or layering is generally present in all rocks formed as sediments.

In preparation for a subsurface study, a field geologist should equip himself with: a geologic map(s) of the region and of the site; a current topographic map of the site and surrounding area; a copy of the plans and specifications for a project; a map showing the specific locations of the proposed borings, and the coordinates, elevations, angles and bearings; a preliminary geologic column for test site and the preferred sequence of drilling and the proposed depth of each hole. Equipment, not limited to, but must include: keeping a complete and accurate record is one of the most important functions in the field; maintenance of a standard field notebook for detailed records for this work. A record that includes the description of the rock sample using a grain chart and color chart, a hand lens, binocular microscope, acid bottle, litmus paper, hardness kit, blank strip charts, will provide standard description that can become extremely valuable for litigation.

Subsurface geology involves interpretation of the stratigraphy, structure and the potential economic values of rocks below the earth's surface. These interpretations are based on information obtained from boreholes, geophysical data and projected surface information. The subsurface geologist requires a basic background in geologic structure, a broad and fundamental knowledge of rock types, a three-dimensional concept of geologic phenomena and finally, an understanding of the economics of the problem. Coordination and accurate integration of these related phases should be accomplished together with the evaluation of the rocks, their relationships, and the application of various techniques and methods that permit exact classification. Subsurface geologic interpretation demands a creative imagination and a multiple hypotheses manner of thinking (LeRoy 1950; Krumbein and Sloss 1951).

5.1.1 Test Drilling Contract

For water, minerals, energy, or environmental investigations, a private company or contractor will require a contract for drilling, sampling, or perhaps ultimately the development of a well.

In government procurement, for example, a municipal, State Geological Survey or State Engineering Division, project personnel may be assigned to monitor the contract. They are referred to as the technical officers who are the officials designated to enter into or administer contracts and make related determinations and findings. In planning test drilling and associated work to be done by a contract, the project manager determines what and where the work is needed. Generally the amount of work is initially based on the balancing of the needs and the estimated unit costs followed by revising the amount to fit the bid prices received.

5.1.2 Geologic Samples and Driller's Logs

The method and frequency of the sampling should be described and the requirements for the mud pump, commercial mud or natural clay, drilling water, and any other special items should be listed. If samples are required by other agencies, the contract should make such provisions to assure compliance. The responsibility for collecting cuttings should be clearly stated along with any required special collecting technique. A description of mud tanks or pits should be given as well as the periodicity of sampling and the cleaning of these tanks or pits. Finally, specifications must define drilling mud additive character and the disposal of drilling fluids or solids.

Driller's logs of drilling conditions, material penetrated, or drill characteristics should be called for if required and provision should be made for inspection as well as calling for additional, more correctly, or more detailed logging. It should also be stated when the log(s) will be submitted by the contractor and to whom, by name or office and address.

For example, in core sampling, the dimensions of the cores as well as the proposed depths or intervals should be listed. All depth measurements are to be referred to natural ground surface at the point where drilling began. This will be zero depth of the hole. The core sampler should state how they are prepared, stored, or preserved and who will do this work and who will furnish the containers. The top and the bottom of the core should be carefully determined and each piece of core is properly oriented as to top and bottom and placed in proper sequence in the core trough. The amount of core should then be measured and the recovery percentage entered in the field notebook (Ropp and McCoy 1979).

Core samples should be wrapped in clear plastic sheeting or bags that are plainly marked and labeled and the wrapped cores preserved in wood containers, which are to be furnished by the contractor. The containers should have six separate compartments for core samples and a hinged lid, which completely covers the container. The containers shall be plainly marked and labeled to show the identity of the hole, depth sampled, and the date.

5.2 Rock Characteristics

Rock characteristics include the megafeatures of the rocks, the color pattern, color, structure, luster, texture, and accessories (Maher 1964).

5.2.1 The Megafeatures

The megafeatures of the rocks can possibly be seen in cores, outcrops, and a few can be inferred from cuttings and electric logs. These features include weathering, induration, and bedding. *Weathering* can be detected in the cuttings and cores of some wells by the presence of leached limestone and chert fragments, variegated shale, abraded fossils and concentrations of pyrite and phosphate. The degree of induration is indicated by the terms hard, soft, tough and brittle. *Bedding* can be determined from cores and estimated fairly well from micro-resistivity curves of electric logs. The bedding classification used in describing drill cuttings, cores, and outcrop samples is as follows:

- *Fissile* – less than 0.16 cm thick
- *Platy* – 0.16 to 1.5 cm thick
- *Very thin-bedded* – 1.5 to 5.1 cm thick
- *Thin-bedded* – 5.1 to 10.2 cm thick
- *Medium-bedded* – 10.2 to 30.5 cm thick
- *Thick-bedded* – 30.5 to 91.4 cm thick
- *Massive* – more than 91.4 cm thick

5.2.2 Color Patterns

Color patterns of rock fragments are extremely important for stratigraphic analysis and may be due to primary features such as mineral composition, or microstructure of the original sediments, of secondary alteration of the rocks by weathering, leaching by ground water, recrystallization or replacement of minerals, and other metamorphic processes. Color patterns can be simply defined as staining, speckling, spotting, mottling, and banding. The color of sedimentary rocks is controlled by the grain size, the composition of the grain, and the chemical pigmentation. Colors may be primary or secondary, or both.

The *Rock Color Chart* was prepared by the Rock Color Chart Committee (1979). The *Rock Color Chart* was designed primarily for field use and it indicates the range of rock colors for all purposes as well. The form and arrangement of the chart are based on the Munsell system, the most widely accepted system of color identification in use in the USA (see Chap. 2). The rock-color standards have been accepted as the ideal system even though they have not been used in detail for commercial work. Two main reasons for the little use of the chart are: (1) A considerable time is necessary to make effective use of the color chart; (2) color details are not diagnostic in subsurface correlations and are often inconsistently determined because of different factors that may affect the eyes of the observer. The *Rock Color Chart* helps in defining some of the sediments as well as its mineral constituents, such as evaporites, carbonates, and some argillaceous sediments; White to light gray color indicates partly or total absence of bituminous and carbonaceous impurities. Iron compounds (limonite, hematite) produce yellow, tan and red hues. The presence of red feldspar in arkoses is largely responsible for reddish and pinkish coloration. Glauconite, epidote, olivine, chlorite, and ferrous iron compounds are responsible for greenish colors. It should be noted that the color of the sediment should be recorded as wet or dry as the rocks when wet invariably assume darker colors.

Colors also can be used to symbolize various lithologies and are widely used for evaluation purposes. Generally, yellow indicates sand; blue, limestone; and hues of such colors as green, red, gray and tan represent shales.

5.2.3 Rock Texture of Clastic Sediments

Rock texture refers to the size, roundness, and sorting of the individual particles (Driscoll 1986):

1. *Grain size:* The sediment-size analysis of the clastic particles (gravels, sand, silt, and clay) is classified according to the *Wentworth grade scale*, which is composed of a continuous series of size grades of particles (Krumbein and Sloss 1951; Table 5.1). The most widely used method for obtaining information on grain size distribution involves passing the clastic particles through a stacked set of 203 mm brass or stainless steel sieves which are shaken in a special vibration machine. Table 5.2 shows a sample record of the accumulated weight of material from a series of sieves where the cumulative percent retained is calculated by dividing the cumulative weight retained by the total weight of the sample. From the cumulative percent, the grain-size distribution curve shows how much of the sample material is smaller or larger than a given particle size (Fig. 5.1).

The curve in Fig. 5.2 shows that 90% of the sample consists of sand grains larger than 0.23 mm and 10% is smaller than this size. Also, the 40% sand size of the sample is 0.66 mm. In other words, 40% of the sample is coarser than 0.66 mm and 60% is finer than 0.66 mm. A logarithmic scale (semi-log charts) for the particle size may be used as it has the effect of elongating the part of the curve that represents the finer fraction, and squeezing that part of the curve representing the coarser material (Driscoll 1986).

The grain-size distribution curve: There are three essential elements to complete the description of a grain-size distribution curve: (*a*) sediment size (fineness or coarseness); (*b*) slope of the curve; and (*c*) shape of the curve. The grain-size distribution curve of the tested sample in Fig. 5.2 shows that it consists of medium and coarse sand, according to USGS classification. Applying the same system to the four curves in Figs. 5.3–5.6 gives the following descriptions:

- Class A curve – fine sand
- Class B curve – fine and very coarse sand
- Class C curve – coarse and very coarse sand
- Class D curve – coarse sand and very fine gravel

Sediment size: There are other ways to describe grain size of a sediment; e.g. the term effective size was defined as the particle size where 10% of the sand is finer and 90% is coarser. The effective size of the class A curve (Fig. 5.3) is 0.08 mm. In Fig. 5.5, the effective size of the sand is 0.25 mm; an index of fine-

Table 5.1. Grain-size classification (after Krumbein and Pettijohn 1938 cited in Driscoll 1986)

Wentworth classification	Size range (mm)
Boulder	>256
Cobble	64 to 256
Pebble[a]	4 to 64
Granule (very fine gravel)	2 to 4
Very coarse sand	1 to 2
Coarse sand	0.5 to 1
Medium sand	0.25 to 0.5
Fine sand	0.125 to 0.25
Very fine sand	0.063 to 0.125
Silt	0.004 to 0.063
Clay	<0.004

[a] The USGS has subdivided this category as follows:
Very coarse gravel 32 to 64 mm
Coarse gravel 16 to 32 mm
Medium gravel 8 to 16 mm
Fine gravel 4 to 8 mm

Table 5.2. Cumulative percent retained (after Driscoll 1986)

Size of sieve opening (mm)	Cumulative weight retained (g)	Cumulative percent retained (%)
1.17	28.4	17
0.84	45.4	28
0.58	73.7	47
0.41	110.6	70
0.30	131.4	82
0.20	150.2	94
Bottom Pan	158.8	

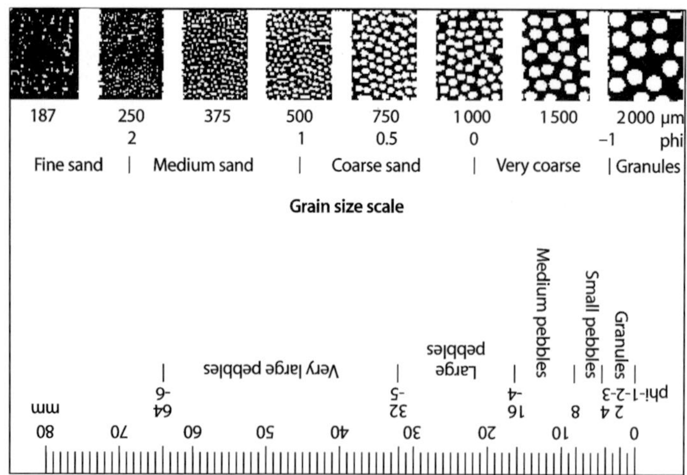
187
250
2
375
500
1
750
0.5
1 000
0
1 500
2 000 μm
−1 phi
Fine sand | Medium sand | Coarse sand | Very coarse | Granules
Grain size scale
mm 80 70 60 50 40 30 20 10 0
64 -6
Very large pebbles
32 -5
Large pebbles
16 -4
Medium pebbles
8
Small pebbles
2 4
phi-1-2-3
Granules

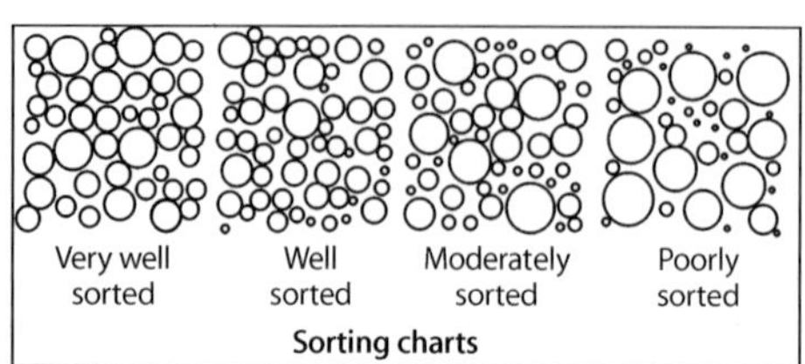
Very well sorted
Well sorted
Moderately sorted
Poorly sorted
Sorting charts

Fig. 5.1. A composite chart showing grain-size scale, percentage of area and sorting (after HRH Ltd., Aberdeen)

ness is the 50% size, which is equal to 0.56 mm in Fig. 5.2. For the class A and class B curves, the 50% size is 0.18 mm in both cases. The 50% size is considered as the average particle size for uniform (steep slope) sediments but when the general slope of the curve is flatter (class D in Fig. 5.6), the 50% size is inaccurate as an indicator of fineness or coarseness.

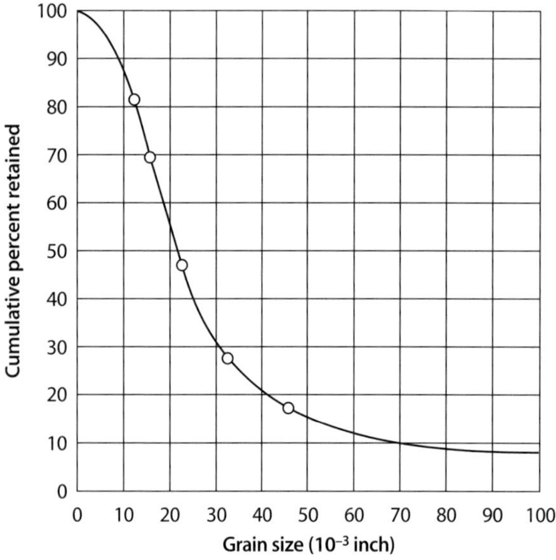
Cumulative percent retained
100
90
80
70
60
50
40
30
20
10
0
0 10 20 30 40 50 60 70 80 90 100
Grain size (10^{-3} inch)

Fig. 5.2. A graphic illustration of the grain-size distribution (after Driscoll 1986)

a *Slope of the curve:* The slope of the major portion of a grain-size distribution curve can be also described in several ways, e.g. the uniformity coefficient is defined as the 40% retained size of the sediment divided by the 90% retained size. The lower its value, the more uniform is the grading of the sample between these limits and vice versa. The uniformity coefficient is meaningful only when its value is less than 5. The uniformity coefficient for the sample in Fig. 5.2 is 2.9 (0.66 mm divided by 0.23 mm). For the class C curve (Fig. 5.5), the uniformity coefficient is 3. The uniformity coefficient is useful in describing the desired uniformity of filter-pack materials.

b *Shape of the (grain-size distribution) curve:* An "S"-shape curve is referred to most of the granular materials deposited by running water and wave action. The S-shape of the curve becomes distorted when gravel constitutes 15% or more of a mixture of sand and gravel. The curve in Fig. 5.2 and in class A (Fig. 5.3) and class C curves are typical S-shaped distributions which denote higher porosities of the given sample than those of class D curve (Fig. 5.6) that has a tail of coarse material.

2. *Roundness:* The particles may be given as "angular" (showing very little or no abrasion), "subangular" (showing some effect of wear), "subrounded" (showing considerable abrasion), and "rounded" (exhibiting conspicuous wear). Figure 5.7 shows the degree of angulation of grains (Compton 1962).

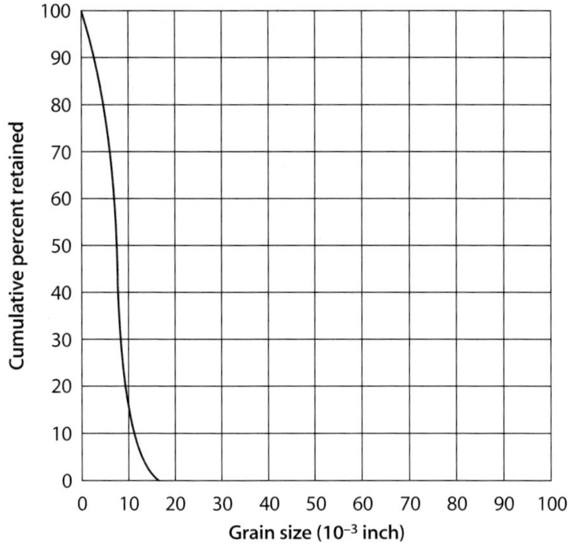
Cumulative percent retained
100
90
80
70
60
50
40
30
20
10
0
0 10 20 30 40 50 60 70 80 90 100
Grain size (10^{-3} inch)

Fig. 5.3. Class A curve for fine sand (after Driscoll 1986)

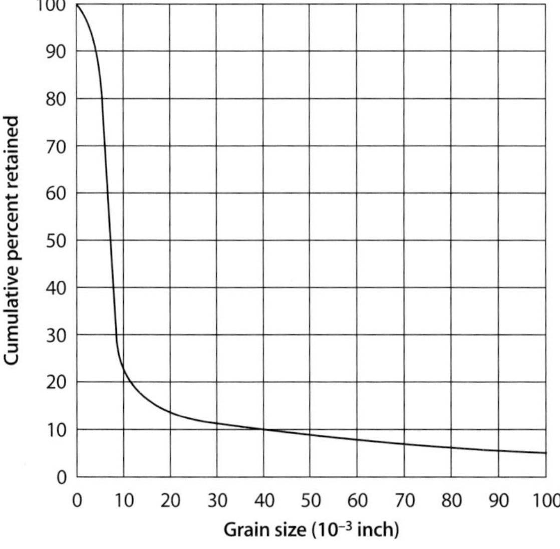
Cumulative percent retained
100
90
80
70
60
50
40
30
20
10
0
0 10 20 30 40 50 60 70 80 90 100
Grain size (10^{-3} inch)

Fig. 5.4. Class B curve for fine and very coarse sand (after Driscoll 1986)

3. *Sorting, cementation, and porosity* are all expressions related to the grain size of particles. Sorting is an expression of the range of grain size classes represented by the rock particles. It is best evaluated by determining the coefficient of sorting from sieve or other grade-size analyses.

   The following terms may be used:

- *Well-sorted* – 90% of particles concentrated in 1 or 2 size classes

Cumulative percent retained
100 90 80 70 60 50 40 30 20 10 0
0 10 20 30 40 50 60 70 80 90 100
Grain size (10^{-3} inch)

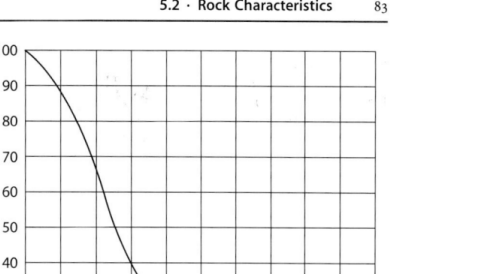

Fig. 5.5. Class C curve for coarse and very coarse sand (after Driscoll 1986)

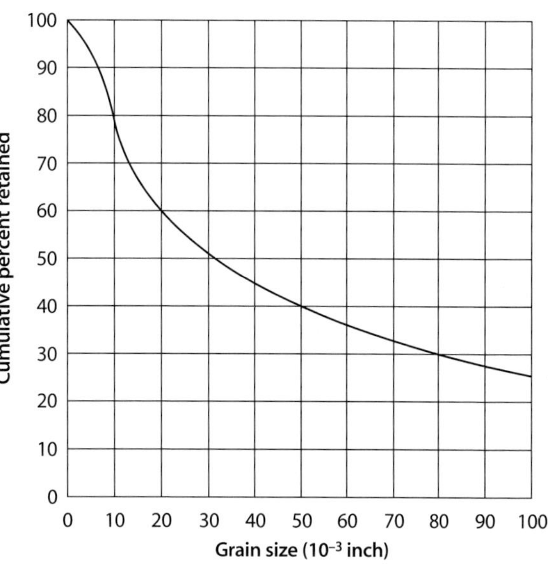
Cumulative percent retained
100
90
80
70
60
50
40
30
20
10
0
0 10 20 30 40 50 60 70 80 90 100
Grain size (10^{-3} inch)

Fig. 5.6. Class D curve for coarse sand and very fine gravel (after Driscoll 1986)

- *Medium-sorted* – 90% of particles distributed in 3 or 4 size classes
- *Poorly-sorted* – 90% of particles scattered in 5 or more size classes.

The character and composition of cementing materials of rocks are important in the interpretation of the depositional history and lithification of sediments. Sandstones or conglomerates are usually cemented with silica, calcite, dolomite, and iron oxides. Other less common cementing materials include pyrite, siderite, sul-

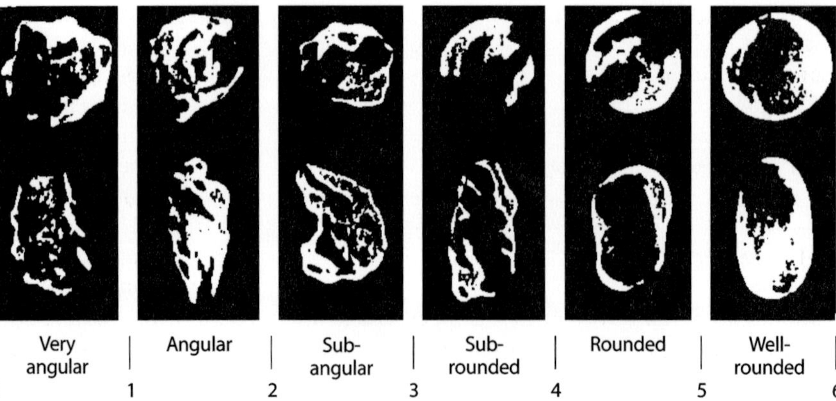
Very angular
Angular
Sub-angular
Sub-rounded
Rounded
Well-rounded
0
1
2
3
4
5
6

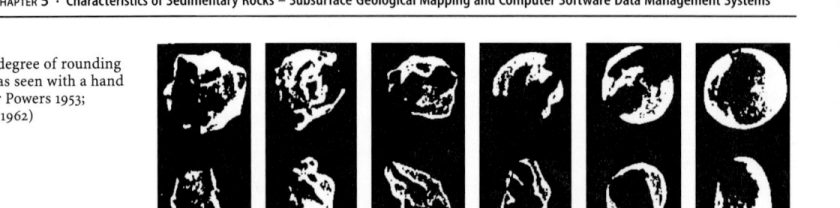

Fig. 5.7.
Terms of degree of rounding of grains as seen with a hand lens (after Powers 1953; Compton 1962)

fates, and phosphates. Clay and silt form the matrix of many sandstones and conglomerates, but these are normally described as rock constituents rather than cement.

Porosity, which is the percentage of total volume of a rock not occupied by mineral components, is directly related to sorting, cementation, size, and shape of constituent particles. Porosity can be estimated roughly from drill cuttings by comparing the rock chips with cores for which the porosity has been determined. Porosity can be described as nonporous, slightly porous, porous, and very porous. The term effective porosity refers to the amount of interconnected pore space available for fluid flow and is expressed as the ratio of interstices to total volume.

5.2.4 Rock Structure

The rock structures can be evident in drill cuttings and cores, for example: joints and fractures are significant because of their effect on the permeability of the rocks; stylolites and concretions are important in identifying certain formations.

5.2.5 Rock Luster

The luster of a rock is its appearance due to the effect of light upon it. Resinous dolomites, waxy shales and earthy limestones are examples of rocks that have distinctive lusters useful in matching rock sequences. Greasy, pearly and vitrous lusters are also known.

5.2.6 Mineral Accessories

These are particles that make up about one percent of the rock and consist of either grains or crystals. They provide significant clues as to the source mode of origin, transportation, deposition and diagenesis of the rock. Some of the common accessories are mica, siderite, limonite, carbon, and sphalerite.

5.3 Preparation of Well Logs

A sequence of studies, acquaintance of methods, and equipment and materials are handled by field hydrogeologists for preparing composite interpretative logs:

1. Name of operator and well number
2. Well location, date of start and end of drilling
3. Ground level (GL) or Kelly bushing (KB)
4. Well sample record
5. Total depth of well (TD)
6. Drilling equipment
7. Casing record
8. Geophysical well logs and drilling time log

After the log form is completed, the rock samples can be examined and described in abbreviated manner and a lithologic log is constructed with the help of one or two previously completed sample logs of nearby wells for proper correlation.

Equipment – The hand lens, color chart, sand grains chart, acid sample as well as the low-power binocular microscope are the basic tools of all sample-logging methods. Combinations of the oculars and objectives produce different magnifications. It is much preferable to use 6.3×-magnification for routine inspection because it provides a larger field of vision, requires less critical focus, transmits a greater amount of light, and causes less eye strain for the field geologist. Minute features and powdered cuttings may be examined under 18 × 27×-magnification.

Defining of different formations and adjustment of its boundaries are carried out by the help of electric and radioactive logs.

5.3.1 Types of Well Logs

The stratigraphic analysis of a sedimentary basin depends upon the type quality of well log correlations of lithologic, faunal, electric and/or radioactivity characteristics. Usually a combination of electric or radioactivity log together with lithologic data provides what is known as a composite log.

The following are the most common logs, which should be preserved by the well owner as a part of the file on each well (Maher 1964).

5.3.1.1 *Driller's Logs*

A driller's log is the record of the rock penetrated in a well through drilling. It is usually prepared by visual inspection of drill cuttings, the drilling time and the changes in fluid level along with the action of the rotary table and mud pump. The driller's logs, prepared for wells drilled by cable tool methods, are usually more reliable than those for wells drilled by rotary tools because the drilling is slower and the drill cuttings are not intermixed with mud and re-circulated with caved fragments from shallower depths.

Rock cuttings collected by the well driller are studied by the field geologist. If the well is to be screened upon completion, the well driller should retain samples of material from the principal water-bearing zones for use in selecting the slot size of screens.

5.3.1.2 *Drilling Time Logs*

A drilling time log is a record of the rate of penetration through the rocks on a rotary rig. It may be recorded directly on a log strip by a machine or plotted manually from the drilling record sheets (Maher 1964; Fig. 5.8). It is expressed as penetration (in meters) for each unit of time (in minutes or hours). The rate of penetration changes with the changes in the lithology of the formation penetrated through drilling.

A drilling time log may serve to indicate when the bit needs to be changed, when drill-stem tests should be made, and where casing and packers may be set to the best advantage. It is useful in correcting sample depths during the examination of well cuttings, especially if no electric or radioactive log is available.

5.3.1.3 *Lithologic Logs*

Lithologic logs are prepared by field geologists after examining the cuttings recovered from drilling fluids (in a normal rotary drilling process) and/or core samples recovered from core barrels. The quality of a good lithologic log is true artistry on the part of the subsurface geologist. He combines characteristics of size, shape, angularity, color, types of matrix and presence of fossils and minerals into a description that allows the interpretation of sedimentary history, structure, and potential mineral, water, or energy source trends. The descriptions provide a precise lithology and petrophysical characteristic of the aquifer zones or target area. All cuttings and core samples should be properly labeled and stored, and retained for future reference.

The character and composition of cementing materials of rocks are important in the interpretation of the depositional history and lithification of sediments. Sandstones or conglomerates are usually cemented with silica, calcite, dolomite, and iron oxides. Other less common cementing materials include pyrite, siderite, sulfates, and phosphates. Clay and silt form the matrix of many sandstones and conglomerates, but these are normally described as rock constituents rather than cement.

The preparation of cutting samples is very important for field geologists and hydrogeologists. Public sample libraries are maintained by most State Geological Surveys, whereas sample rental libraries are operated by several commercial sample laboratories. It is necessary to rewash samples that have become dusty through frequent examination or shipment from one place to another. Permission should always be obtained from the owner prior to washing borrowed or rented samples. After procuring a clean set of samples, the next step is to prepare a blank log form with the heading completed by the following data (Maher 1964).

5.3.1.4 *Porosity Related Logs*

Porosity (or primary porosity) is the percentage of total volume of voids to the total volume of a rock Primary porosity depends on the size distribution, sorting, cementation and shape of constituent particles. Porosity can be determined from a core or computed from an electric log (Focazio et al. 2002, U.S. Environmental Protection Agency 1977). The following are four related logs:

1. Caliper logs needed for quantitative analyses of the geophysical logs and for the lithologic interpretation and cement volume calculations.
2. Dipmeter logs measure the angle of dip of beds penetrated by the well and the resulted data assist in interpreting the geologic structure.
3. Deviation logs measure the degree of deviation of the borehole from the vertical.
4. Production (or injection) logs run through tubing or casing after the well is completed and are mainly used to determine the physical condition of the subsurface facilities; the production (or injection) zones; the quantity of fluid produced from (or injected into) a particular zone; and also to determine the results of well-bore stimulation treatment (U.S. Environmental Protection Agency 1977; Table 5.3).

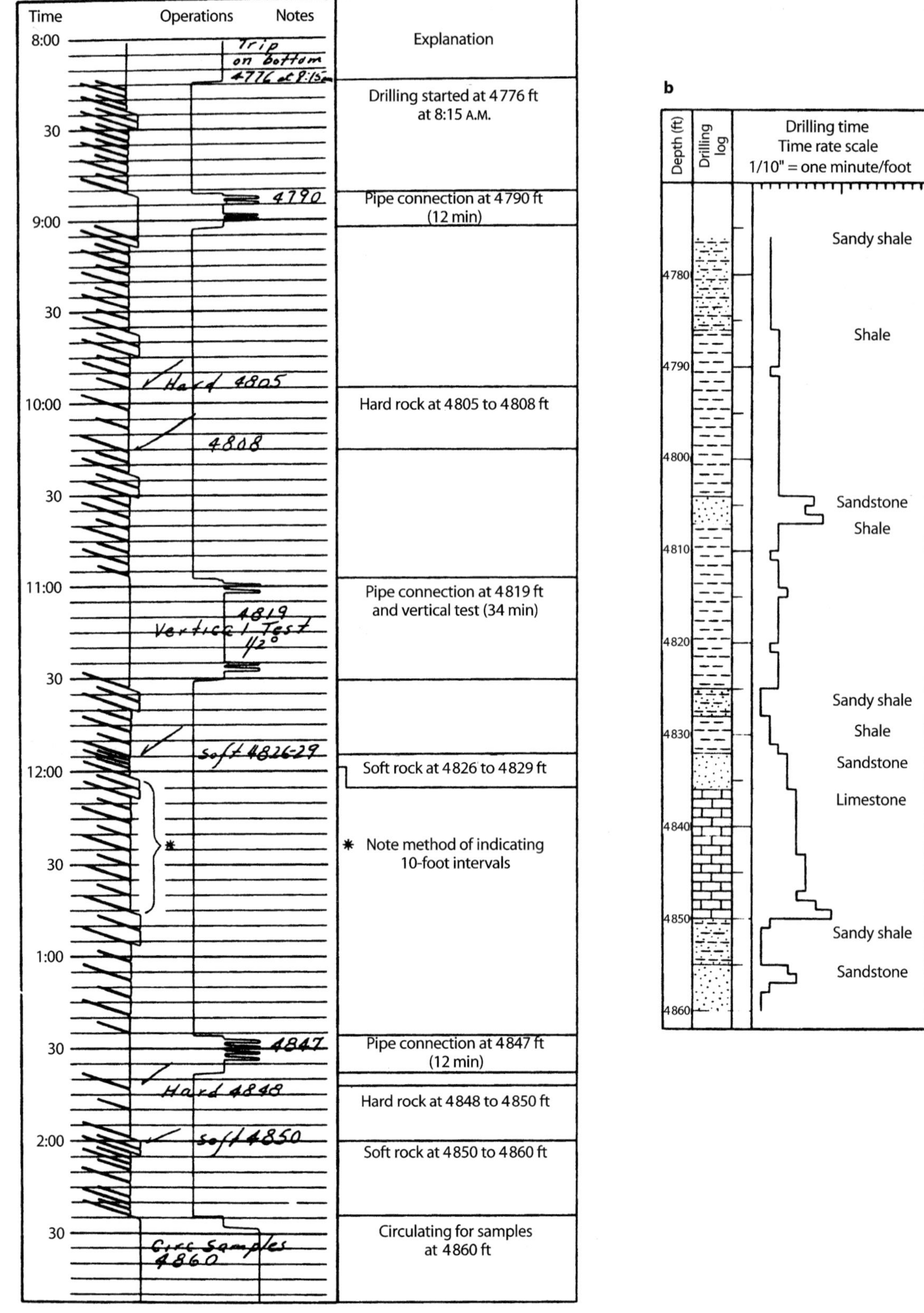
a
Time
Operations
Notes
8:00
30
9:00
30
10:00
30
11:00
30
12:00
30
1:00
30
2:00
30
Explanation
Drilling started at 4776 ft at 8:15 A.M.
Pipe connection at 4790 ft (12 min)
Hard rock at 4805 to 4808 ft
Pipe connection at 4819 ft and vertical test (34 min)
Soft rock at 4826 to 4829 ft
✱ Note method of indicating 10-foot intervals
Pipe connection at 4847 ft (12 min)
Hard rock at 4848 to 4850 ft
Soft rock at 4850 to 4860 ft
Circulating for samples at 4860 ft
b
Depth (ft)
Drilling log
Drilling time
Time rate scale
1/10" = one minute/foot
4780
4790
4800
4810
4820
4830
4840
4850
4860
Sandy shale
Shale
Sandstone
Shale
Sandy shale
Shale
Sandstone
Limestone
Sandy shale
Sandstone

Fig. 5.8. Two types of drilling-time logs for the same interval; **a** mechanically recorded drilling-time chart with driller's notes; explanation at right (adapted from Geolograph); **b** drilling-time and drillers log plotted from driller's records

It paid off!
GRUNT!
SQUEEZE

Fig. 5.9.
It paid off!?

Table 5.3.
Production-injection logs most useful in waste water injection operations (U.S. Environmental Protection Agency 1977)

Log	Function
1. Cement bond	Determine extent and effectiveness of casing cementing
2. Gamma ray	Determine lithology and presence of radioactive tracers through casing
3. Neutron	Determine lithology and porosity through casing
4. Borehole televiewer	Provide an image of casing wall or well bore
5. Casing inspection	Locate corrosion or other casing damage
6. Flowmeter	Locate zones of fluid entry or discharge and measure contribution of each zone to total injection or production
7. High resolution thermometer	Locate zones of fluid entry including zones behind casing
8. Radioactive tracer	Determine travel paths of injected fluids including behind casing
9. Fluid sampler	Recover a sample of wellbore fluids
10. Casing collar	Locate casing collars for accurate reference
11. Fluid pressure	Determine fluid pressure in borehole at any depth
12. Casing caliper	Locate casing damage

5.3.2 Downhole Methods

Scope: Comprehensive borehole evaluation is one of the most important aspects of every subsurface geological evaluation. Drill cuttings are rarely enough to provide all the information needed. Even split-spoon and other sampling methods may often fail to properly evaluate the geology and geochemistry around a borehole. For example, downhole methods at Geosphere Inc. offer a suite of downhole wireline tools, which can fill this information gap and can be found on the web site: www.mountsopris.com (E-mail: consultants@geosphereinc.com).

Downhole methods are discussed as two separate systems: borehole video and geophysical logging. These systems are housed in a climate-controlled van for easy mobilization.

A new generation borehole video system: the "Cues RVC-360 high resolution color video camera" is a fine borehole camera, which allows detailed viewing of both casing and open hole, including such subtle geologic features as formation contacts, joints, and even cross-bedding. The geophysical logging system, the "MLS Series 1500 wireline logging unit" includes a digital acquisition system, which allows virtually limitless display options whereas, the "Geonics EM-39 borehole electromagnetic logger" is especially useful in mapping the vertical extent of contaminant plumes.

- Inspection and verification of well construction
- Detailed stratigraphic evaluation
- Vertical contaminant plume definition
- Aquifer identification for setting of well screens and casing
- Fracture zone identification
- Identification of potential radium contamination zones
- Evaluation of well conditions prior to sealing and abandonment

Video inspections provide a continuous, permanent visual record of the well casing, screen, or open hole. A video camera built into a waterproof stainless steel housing is lowered into the well via a triple-armored coaxial cable. The image is transmitted back via the cable to a VHS recorder and monitor at the surface. This arrangement provides a permanent videotape recording, as well as real-time viewing, which facilitates detailed inspections of features of interest.

Field procedures for most logging programs can be simple or complex, depending on the methods chosen – location, access to the well, and the nature of the borehole. The probe is suspended from a pulley into the well, and the depth referenced to a common datum. It is then lowered to the point of refusal at the well bottom and the uphole equipment is set for depth and scales. As the sensors receive information it is sent back to the surface unit, where it is processed and plotted in analog format. The raw data are also collected digitally on a microcomputer for later processing and plotting.

5.3.3 Composite Well Logs

A composite interpretive well log can be prepared by combining the best features of lithology logs and electric logs. It is prepared by the examination of samples under the microscope with concurrent reference to the electric or radioactive log. The sample examination provides lithologic descriptions, including minute details and fossils necessary to correlate with other wells and outcrops to which the electric log adds depth corrections, establishes the bed-for-bed succession in alternating lithologies. The preparation and use of these logs are limited mostly to detailed stratigraphic research as they are very time consuming; yet for long-term projects, an update data base for subsurface geological and geophysical data, can be established for a certain area to get a computerized montage lithological log (predicted from nearby drilling well logs), a final geological composite well log, cross sections, and structural geologic maps.

5.4 Stratigraphy and Structural Geology

5.4.1 Stratigraphy

Stratigraphy is the study of the lithology, thickness, chronological sequence and correlation of beds. The lithostratigraphic column, which is a graphic representation of the rock units is the basic display of data used in stratigraphic studies. The traversed rocks can be built showing the breaks in the sequence by unconformities, faults or lack of exposures (see Appendix 5.A). Figure 5.10 is a generalized columnar section for northeast Illinois showing a variety of rock types typical of the northeast-central states (Buschbach 1972). Cross sections also display stratigraphic information, which may be constructed from the stratigraphic column of deep wells to show a typical stratigraphic sequence.

The cross sections show the structure and thickness of rock units along a selected datum plane, whereas isopach maps are used to show thickness of stratigraphic units over an area.

5.4.2 Structural Geology

Structural geology mainly deals with sedimentary, crystalline and metamorphic rocks and is related to folding, faulting, and the geographic distribution of these features which greatly affect subsurface fluid flows; the petrophysical properties of rocks; and the localization of mineral deposits and earthquakes. Sedimendary rocks may be folded into synclines (tough-like folds) or anticlines. Usually synclinal basins of a regional scale (hundreds of kilometers) are considered as particularly favorable for wastewater injection because natural wastes are denser than water. Anticlines are used for temporary underground storage of natural gas and for storage of wastes less dense than water in the injection interval.

Fractures in rocks include joints or faults. A joint is a fracture along which no movement has taken place; a

System	Series	Stage	Megagroup	Group	Formation	Graphic column	Thickness (ft)	Lithology
Ordovician	Cincinnatian	Rich.	Ottawa	Maquoketa	Neda		0–15	Shale, red, hematitic, oolitic
					Brainard		0–100	Shale, dolomitic, greenish gray
		Ma.			Ft. Atkinson		5–50	Dolomite and limestone, coarse grained, shale, green
		Ed.			Scales		90–100	Shale, dolomitic, brownish gray
	Champlanian	Trentonian		Galena	Wise Lake-Dunleith		170–210	Dolomite, buff, medium grained
					Guttenberg		0–15	Dolomite, buff, red speckled
		Blackriveran		Platteville	Nachusa		0–50	Dolomite and limestone, buff
					Grand Detour		20–40	Dolomite and limestone, gray mottling
					Mifflin		20–50	Dolomite and limestone, orange speckled
					Pecatonica		20–50	Dolomite, brown, fine grained
				Ancell	Glenwood		0–80	Sandstone and dolomite
					St. Peter		100–600	Sandstone, fine; rubble at base
	Canadian		Knox	Prairie du Chien	Shakopee		0–67	Dolomite, sandy
					New Richmond		0–35	Sandstone, dolomitic
					Oneota		190–250	Dolomite, slightly sandy; oolitic chert
					Gunter		0–15	Sandstone, dolomitic
Cambrian	Croixan	Trempealeauan			Eminence		50–150	Dolomite, sandy; oolitic chert
					Potosi		90–220	Dolomite, slightly sandy at top and base, light gray to light brown; geodic quartz
		Franconian			Franconia		50–200	Sandstone, dolomite and shale; glauconitic
					Ironton		80–130	Sandstone, medium grained, dolomitic in part
		Dresbachian			Galesville		10–100	Sandstone, fine grained
					Eau Claire		370–575	Siltstone, shale, dolomite, sandstone, glauconite
			Potsdam		Mt. Simon		1200–2900	Sandstone, fine to coarse grained

Fig. 5.10. Generalized columnar section of Cambrian and Ordovician strata in northeastern Illinois. *Black dots* indicate gas storage zones (after Buschbach 1972; U.S. Environmental Protection Agency 1977)

fault implies movement. Probably, all consolidated rocks most unconsolidated deposits contain joints, which may exert some control on water movement and chemical quality as well as serve as major conduits or pipes along which water can move and perhaps can carry contaminants. The outbreak of many waterborne diseases tied to ground-water supplies has resulted in the transmission of infectious agents through rock fractures to wells and springs.

Faults are common in mountain ranges and have resulted from either lengthening or shortening of the earth's crust. In areas covered by more recent sediments, faulting may be obscured requiring test drilling or geophysical methods for their location and definition. Movement along a fault may be horizontal, vertical, or a combination. Faults may range from millimeters to kilometers in length and with displacements of comparable magnitudes. Faults may act as barriers or as channels for fluid movement. Fractures that occur without movement are cracks or joints, which can also become important sources of porosity and permeability. The presence and nature of fractures can be determined by examining core samples obtained through drilling, by well logging and testing methods and from geophysical observations in nearby wells. Structural geologic data are displayed in maps or cross sections or as 3-dimensional fence diagrams or models. Structure contour maps which show the elevation of a particular stratigraphic horizon relative to a selected datum (MSL), provides an estimate of the approximate depth to the mapped rock unit, the direction and magnitude of dip and also may show the location of faults and folds that influence decisions concerning the location of mineral resources, oil or gas, water of the best location for a monitoring well.

5.5 Subsurface Sections and Geological Maps

Subsurface sections and geologic maps are constructed from data supplied by wells that have penetrated recognizable formations. The elevation on the datum bed needed for the preparation of the cross sections or the structure contour maps is the algebraic difference between the surface elevation of the well and the drilled depth to the datum bed. Cross sections show structural or stratigraphic variations between wells and are depicted on a surface geology map. Dips and/or strikes determined from cores can help the "subsurface geologist". Block diagrams are used to illustrate the surface and the subsurface structure of the formations and they are constructed according to principles of projection and perspectives. The use of personal computers play an important role in presenting panel diagrams as a third dimensional concept of stratigraphic relationships.

5.5.1 Isopach Maps

Isopach maps show by means of contours the variations in stratigraphic thickness of a stratum, formation, or group of formations and are based primarily upon formation thicknesses, determined from final composite well logs or subsurface exposures.

5.5.2 Facies Maps

The lithologies of stratigraphic units change in some manner from one part of a basin to another. The degree of variation and rate of change of facies may be small or large depending upon the physical conditions of the basin, the chemistry of the waters, the climate, and many other factors that determine the type of the deposited sediment. A stratigraphic unit may be a conglomerate at one locality, a sandstone or siltstone at another, and a limestone at a third. A lithofacies map shows the changes in lithology of a stratigraphic unit within a sedimentary basin and may show the different facies in either a qualitative or quantitative way.

5.6 Graphic Techniques and Representation

5.6.1 Scope

Selected and drafted illustrations are of major importance by which concepts and interpretations are displayed graphically. Lithologic, electric, and radioactive log profiles can be correlated and displayed to produce stratigraphic cross sections and 3-dimensional diagrams.

Graphics are equipped with some of the latest technical equipment that includes large format scanners, digitizing tables, color plotters, large format laminators and large format copiers, in conjunction with graphics/CAD, and photo enhancement software. Graphics are used in the design and production of illustrations, technical diagrams, detailed maps, photographs, courtroom exhibits, and physical models.

Courtroom graphics visually reinforce case themes and testimony where effective visual aids capture, focus, and reinforce juror attention and perception. In environmental and ground-water resource issues, geophysical well logs can be provided to clients in a variety of digital formats via e-mail, on diskette, or compact disc. Graphics are used in different projects of both cultural resource management services, that can be achieved by a variety of technical equipment from computer systems to GPS equipment as well as services in UST investigations that include soil and ground-water sampling and analysis, installation of monitoring wells, site assessment, remediation system design, and installation overnight and coordination.

5.6.2 Geographic Information Systems (GIS)

Geographic information has evolved as a means of assembling and analyzing diverse spatial data. Many systems have been developed, for land-use planning and natural-resource management at the urban, regional, state, and national levels of government agencies. Most systems rely on data from existing maps, or data that can be mapped readily.

Recently, environmental scientists and resource managers, have access to more data than ever. The key to coping with scientific information that was estimated to double every five years is the employment of systems that take the data, analyze it, store it, and then present it in forms that are useful (Naisbitt 1982).

Maps are a very important form of input to a geospatial data system (GDS), as well as common means to portray the results of any analysis from GIS (U.S. Presidential Executive Order No. 12906, 1994).

5.6.2.1 *Principals and Applications*

The United States Geological Survey (USGS) is responsible for gathering, analyzing and presenting information on geology, water, mineral, and energy resources, the environment and topography.

As a national earth science agency, researchers in the USGS have long been involved in the application of computers to earth science problems including digital cartography, spatial database design and GIS. Through its National Mapping Program (NMP), the USGS provides a diversity of cartographic, geographical and remotely sensed data, as well as products and information services for the United States territories and possessions. The products of the program include several series of standard topographic maps in both graphic and digital form, photo-image maps, land use and land cover maps and associated data, geographic names information, geodetic control data and remotely sensed data. The USGS continued providing the Digital Line Graph (DLG-O) data in the Optional (Native) format and the newer Spatial Data Transfer Standard (SDTS) format. These data files are for use in geographical information systems (GIS) for analysis and integration with other geospatial data (USGS 1996).

GIS in other countries: In Sweden, the national GIS-programs depend on the Geographic Data of Sweden (GSD) where the official mapping activities were focused on the production of printed maps. Sweden has a very long tradition of keeping documentation. Mapping and population registration have a long tradition in Sweden where the first work in GIS area started in 1955. In Japan, the development of GIS began in the 1930s before it was actually used formally. A new GIS for environmental change research project that began in 1990, aims to understand 100 years of environmental change in Japan since modernization in the late 19th century. An environmental database was constructed through joint efforts by geographers and researchers from other disciplines.

In Australia, the Royal Australian Army Survey Corps and the Navy Hydrographic Service are responsible for producing all hydrographic and bathometric charts for the Australian region, Papua New Guinea and large parts of the Indian, Pacific, and Southern Oceans.

The Australian Federal Government is responsible for small-scale topographic mapping (at scales of 1:100 000 and smaller across the country) as a whole. It is also responsible for mapping at all scales in the Northern Territory and in selected, more isolated parts of the continent especially when information is essential for defense needs.

Many State Geological Surveys carry extensive geologic, mineral, water, energy and environmental related projects; they are excellent source of reference to the geologist beginners work in an area.

5.6.2.2 *Available References at USGS – CD-Roms*

1. Geological Survey of Alabama (GSA 2002 Annual Report):
   - The National Coal Resources Data System (NCRDS) is comprehensive computerized database of coal information: rcarroll@ogb.gsa.tuscaloosa.al.us
   - *Alabama's abundant numerous resources*, including 16 river systems and numerous ground-water aquifers, support a vast, diversified ecosystem. In addition, the Alabama coastline supports a complex ecosystem and provides the state with significant economic benefits: dmore@ogb.gsa.tuscaloosa.al.us
   - *Geologic mapping* is used to locate areas favorable for the occurrence of fossil fuel resources, industrial minerals, and construction materials as well as to identify potential geologic hazards in areas where construction is planned: eosborne@ogb.gsa.tuscaloosa.al.us
   - *Geohazards*, such as sinkholes, earthquakes, landslides, and cracked foundations, are directly related to the nature and distribution of the rocks underlying the state. Because the distribution of these rocks were mapped and their characteristics described and the information dispensed in available maps and reports, geologists and engineers can respond to these events: draymond@ogb.gsa.tuscaloosa.al.us
2. Kentucky Geological Survey (KGS Annual Report 2000-01): Geology for environmental protection:
   a Geologic "sinks" for storing atmospheric carbon dioxide: Carbon dioxide (CO_2), a greenhouse gas, is a by-product of the combustion of fossils in coal-

fired electric power plants, industrial activities, and vehicles. Its increase is of concern to environmentalists, government agencies, and industry. A computer database, a geographic information system (GIS), and maps were built to enable to identify the amount of CO_2, available for sequestration in relation to power plants and other large CO_2 sources. These also provide information about the safety of a sequestration site, the effects of injecting CO_2 into a petroleum reservoir, and the cost to compress and transport CO_2 from an industrial site to a geologic "sink" for long-term storage: www.midcarb.org.

b Geology for energy production:
Digital Coal Atlas aids policy markers, coal companies, and planners: www.uky.edu/KGS/emsweb/rome.html.

c Geology in planning:
Digital geological maps were completed in the state of Kentucky at a detailed scale (1:24 000), known as geologic quadrangle maps, have been used to address problems associated with landslides, flooding, subsidence, ground-water supply and protection, wastedisposal sites, septic systems, and other issues: www.uky.edu/KGS/statusmap.

d Geology in hazards mitigation:
Strengthening research on earthquakes and geologic hazards by upgrading Kentucky Seismic and strong-Motion Network has been continued to expand and upgrade by the Kentucky Survey, publications: www.uky.edu/KGS/pubs/lop.htm.

5.6.3 Computer Software Data Management Systems

Structural maps, cross sections, and 3-D computer models can reveal subsurface geologic structures for an area under investigation and explain their evolution through a certain geologic period, e.g. well control and stratigraphic markers are used to construct 3-D structural model. Many software programs are used nowadays for establishing cross sections, fence or block diagrams.

Recent CD-Roms, released by U.S. Geological Survey, include:

- 2001, The Putumayo-Oriente-Maranon Province of Colombia, Ecuador, and Peru Mesozoic-Cenozoic and Paleozoic Petroleum Systems, USGS Digital Data Series DDS-63, Version 1.0 (D. K. Higley).
- 2000, USGS World Petroleum Assessment – Description and Results, USGS Digital Data Series DDS-60, Multi Disc Set, Version 1.1.
- 2001, Coalbed Methane Field Conference, USGS, May 9–10, Open-File Report 01-235, Version 1.0.
- 2002, Geology, Geochemistry, and Geophysics of Sedimentary Rock-Hosted Deposits in P.R. China, U.S. Geological Survey, Open File Report 02-131, Version 1.0 (S. G. Peters).
- 2001, A History of Phosphate Mining in Southeastern Idaho, USGS, Open-File Report 00-425, Version 1.0.
- 1999, Resources Assessment of Selected Tertiary Coal Beds and Zones in the Northern Rocky Mountains and Great Plains Region, Professional Paper 1625-A, Discs 1 and 2, Version 1.2, USGS, Rocky Mountains ands Great Plains (Fort Union Coal Assessment Team).

5.6.3.1 *General*

In the early 1990s, professional geologists and well log analysts used to apply different programs such as MSW or GTGS software (a DOS version) to manage geologic data by entering information for borehole logs. *GTGS for Windows* can be used to quickly create, edit and print geotechnical and environmental borehole logs. The graphical windows interface display the log and shows how the log looks when it is printed. *EQUIS Geology* is one of the latest product used in the environmental data management and analysis systems. Written in Visual Basic and using the Microsoft Access data base engine, EQUIS Geology offers an easy-to-use and comprehensive means of organizing geological, geotechnical, and hydrogeologic data.

During the last decade, many computer software data management systems were developed as an interpretation tool for geologists, well log analysts and engineers working with borehole data. The systems allow the user to edit and interpret borehole data on the computer screen using a mouse-pointing device. The programs in general provide functions for editing, interpretation, log calculations, cross-plotting, mapping, cross section generation, and output to printers and plotters. They also organize data on a well-by-well basis, however, with relative ease the user may select, display and correlate logs from a number of wells.

In addition to the log editing functions, the systems include mapping, GIS and geologic modeling functions that can access a common, open database storage system.

Examples of computer software systems and their benefits in subsurface geology are given below.

5.6.3.2 *Viewlog (Boring Log Editor and Cross Section-Fence Diagram Software) – Data Base*

- All data pertaining to boreholes/wells can be stored in centralized files accessible by the *Boring Log Edi-*

tor and a *Cross Section-Fence Diagram* software, or other programs such as AutoCAD.

- The *Viewlog 2.0* includes both the Borehole Log and the Cross Section Editors. The *Borehole Log Editor* includes functions for editing, display and interpretation of a wide variety of borehole measurements, including geologic description, core photos, lithology symbol columns, well construction, geophysical logs (including deviation, full-waveform sonic and BHTV), core measurements and packer tests. The *Cross Section Editor* allows interactive formation unit picking and stratigraphic interpretation in a true 3-D coordinate space. All map editor-drawing functions are available on section. Other available features are: Geologic model construction, geostatistics and variogram analysis, multiple gridding methods including fault gridding, color contouring on both plan and cross section, and file integration with the Modflow, Modpath and MT3D models.
- The *Quicklog-QuickCross/Fence Diagram software* constitutes both the QuickCross and QuickFence modules that use data already entered in Quicklog to create 2-D cross sections and 3-D fence diagrams. The diagrams may be printed directly or imported into CAD for further manipulation. There are three different cross section formats to choose from layers connected, layers filled in casing rectangles but not connected, and the casings shown with USCS text. The fence diagram features 360° rotation in 90° increments.

5.6.3.3 *Geolog and GeoSec Software (Paradigm Geophysical Co.)*

1. *Geolog well data processing and analysis* is an advanced petrophysical analysis tool; superior presentation graphics, modularity and ease of use make Geolog the industry standard for petrophysical analysis, well management and geological interpretation. The software is constructed of a number of individual modules that can be combined to meet specific requirements and can be used for a wide variety of applications, from log drafting to high-end petro-physics. Four key packages are available, namely: *GeologBasic*, *GeologSec*, *GeologFE* and *GeologGold* which combine the modules relevant to the varying needs of geologists, petrophysicsts and engineers.

   GeologBasic provides exceptional flexibility and ease of use for data loading, editing and display and the section module for producing geological cross section displays. *GeologSec* includes GeologBasic, plus the section module for producing geological cross section displays. *GelogFE,* the tool of choice for petrophysicsts, contains all GeologSec functionally and aids the Dtermin module, which provides extensive deterministic petrophysical analysis. GeologFE also enables the user to produce customized analyses routines using the Loglan programming module. *GeologGold,* the comprehensive Geolog package, offers probabilistic petrophysical functionality with the Multimin module, and borehole geophysics using Synseis. Multimin is a probabilistic modeling tool for statistically determining mineral and fluid characteristics and volumes from petrophysical data, such as logs, cores, XRD and petrographic data. *Multimin* is the solution for sophisticated optimizing petrophysics in challenging analytical environments. *Synseis* is Geolog's module for borehole geophysics and enables comprehensive processing of data in both vertical and deviated wells.
2. *GeoSec* provides the general interpreter and structural specialist with leading-edge functionality to construct comprehensive geologic cross sections and to clearly identify key geologic features and the risks associated with regional to prospect scale E&P jobs. *GeoSec2D* is the industry's leading software package for cross section construction, structural analysis, forward modeling, and structural restoration. *GeoSec3D* represents a significant step forward in the Integration of cutting-edge 3-D structural analysis and 3-D model building into the interpretation process. Built around Paradigm Shared Earth Model GeoSec3D provides geoscientists with the capability to dynamically build and validate structurally robust geologic models that accurately represent their interpretation data.

5.6.3.4 *Internet Sites/Computer Software Data Management Systems*

1. http://www.viewlog.com
2. http://www.autodesk.com
3. http://www.geosec.com
4. http://www.paradigmgeo.com

5.6.3.5 *Benefits of the Systems*

- Drilling and borehole data could be transferred directly to other applications, such as well construction diagrams or cross sections.
- Base maps and cross sections could be generated quickly and viewed on the screen of the monitor without the need for digitizing or plotting. Geologists and engineers can generate or "draft" a number of cross sections or maps without tying up Graphics while deciding which cross section to include in a report or representation. When a line of section or map selected, it could be sent to Graphics for "polishing".
- Such software systems help provide better geologic and hydrogeologic services and save much time for the staff that can be spent on other scientific aspects.

5.6.3.6 *Update Technology of Graphic System Applications, Southwest Alabama*

This section deals with oil and gas industry and geological framework of southwest Alabama combining geological and engineering data with leading-edge computer technology to characterize Gilbertown Field.

All materials were submitted by the Geological Survey of Alabama (Pashin et al. 2000), using Adobe Illustrator files (including Figs. 5.10–5.16).

General

Gilbertown Field is the oldest oil field in Alabama and produces heavy oil from naturally fractured chalk of the Cretaceous Selma Group and glauconitic sandstone of the Eutaw Formation. The field has been largely in primary recovery since 1944 and has been in danger of abandonment.

The study was designed to analyze geologic structure and reservoir heterogeneity in Gilbertown Field and adjacent areas in order to suggest ways in which oil recovery can be improved and premature abandonment can be avoided.

Structural maps, cross sections, and 3-D computer models establish that the Gilbertown fault system is part of a horst-and-graben system that is detached at the base of the Jurassic Louann Salt. Structural restoration suggests that the fault system began forming as a half graben and that the early Cretaceous was the major episode of structural growth. By the start of the late Cretaceous, however, the half graben had evolved into a symmetrical full graben.

The Eutaw Formation produces from footwall uplifts along the south side of the Gilbertown fault system. Eutaw reservoirs comprise 7 major flow units and are dominated by the low-resistivity, low-contrast pay that is difficult to characterize quantitatively. Selma chalk produces from fault-related fractures in the hanging walls of the faults. Resistivity, dipmeter, and fracture identification logs corroborate that deformation is concentrated in hanging-wall drag zones. Curvature analysis indicates that the faults contain numerous fault bends that influence fracture distribution. Clay smear and mineralization may be significant trapping mechanisms in the Eutaw Formation. The critical seal for Selma reservoirs, by contrast, is where Tertiary clay in the hanging wall is juxtaposed with poorly fractured Selma chalk in the footwall (Figs. 5.11, 5.12).

Subsurface Methods

Subsurface methods included identification and correlation of stratigraphic markers and faults in well logs, construction of cross sections and maps, development of a 3-D structural computer model of the Gilbertown area, area-balanced structural restoration, curvature analysis, and seal analysis. Petrologic methods included classification and characterization of framework composition and diagenesis in Eutaw sandstone and stable isotopic analysis of primary and antigenic carbonate in Selma chalk. Log analysis consisted of correlation of log signatures with core data and analysis of dipmeter and fracture identification logs.

More than 700 geophysical logs from the Gilbertown area were correlated to identify structurally significant stratigraphic markers and to identify faults. Markers in Jurassic through Tertiary strata were picked using resistivity and SP logs. Faults were identified, and vertical separations were quantified on the basis of missing section. Well locations, kelly bushings, depths of log picks, and vertical separations of faults were tabulated in a spreadsheet that was used to calculate the elevation of each marker and fault and the thickness of stratigraphic intervals between markers.

Structural contour maps were made showing the elevation and thickness of Jurassic through Tertiary stratigraphic units in Gilbertown Field and in adjacent areas.

Stratigraphic and structural data were used to construct a 3-D computer model of geologic structures in the Gilbertown area using GeoSec3D software. Surfaces in the model were produced by contouring or shading a triangular irregular network (TIN) of data points. Intersections of beds with faults were produced in GeoSec3D by defining new points along the triangulation network of the fault, then joining this line to the bed surface to form a seamless intersection. The computer model greatly aided our efforts to characterize structure in the Gilbertown area by enabling real-time display and rotation of any combination of fault surfaces and beds, further facilitating structural interpretations that are consistent in three dimensions. Development of cross sections, maps, and the 3-D model was an iterative process in which each step of construction led to further refinement of interpretations.

To study stratigraphy and facies variations in the Eutaw Formation, wells were correlated, and a network of stratigraphic and structural cross section was constructed using SP logs. Results of commercial core analysis and completion data were superimposed on the cross sections. Net sandstone isolith maps were then constructed for each stratigraphic interval of the Eutaw Formation using SP logs. Cores of the Eutaw Formation and Selma Group are available for 22 wells in Gilbertown Field. However, no continuous core exists. Each core was described with the aid of a binocular microscope using standard techniques, and lithologic logs were drawn for wells with samples representing a significant part of the Eutaw section.

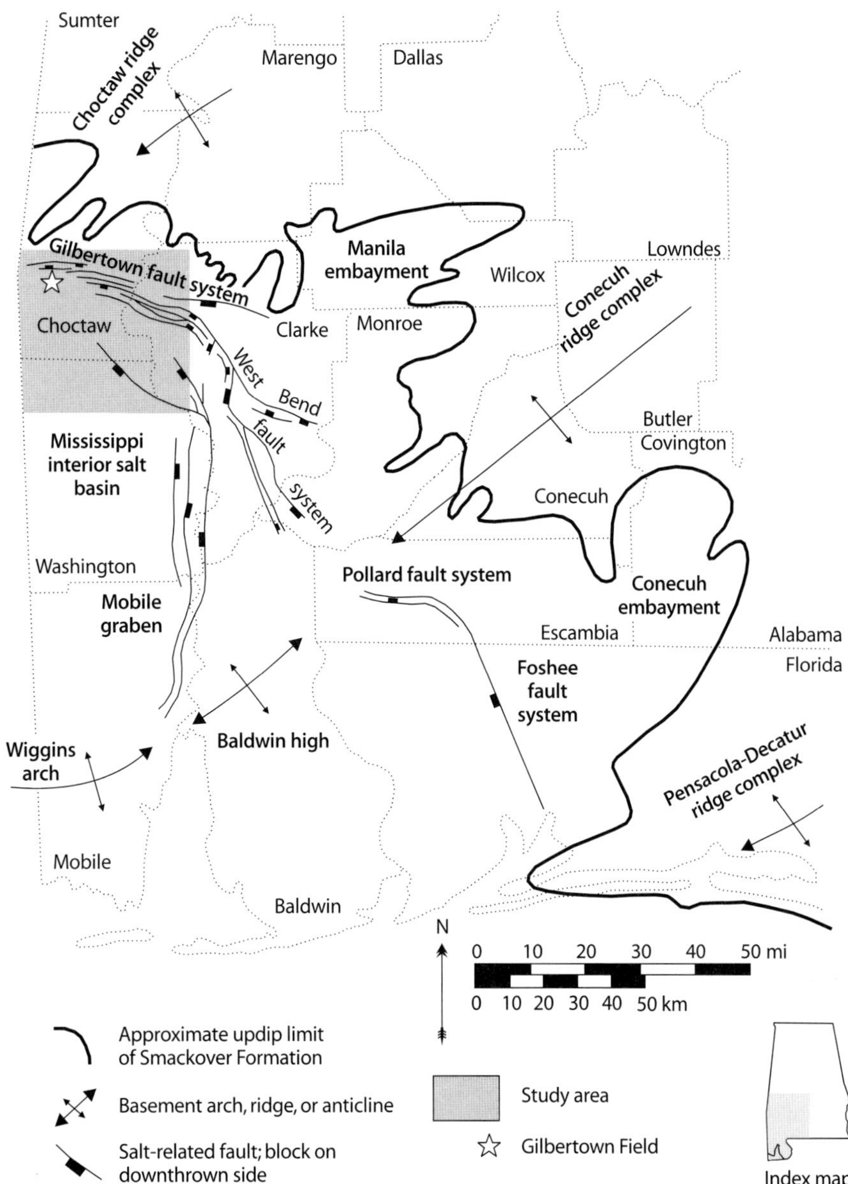
Sumter
Choctaw ridge complex
Marengo
Dallas
Gilbertown fault system
Manila embayment
Wilcox
Lowndes
Conecuh ridge complex
Choctaw
Clarke
Monroe
West Bend fault system
Butler
Covington
Mississippi interior salt basin
Conecuh
Washington
Pollard fault system
Conecuh embayment
Mobile graben
Escambia
Alabama
Florida
Foshee fault system
Baldwin high
Wiggins arch
Pensacola-Decatur ridge complex
Mobile
Baldwin
N
0 10 20 30 40 50 mi
0 10 20 30 40 50 km
Approximate updip limit of Smackover Formation
Basement arch, ridge, or anticline
Salt-related fault; block on downthrown side
Study area
Gilbertown Field
Index map

Fig. 5.11. Structural features in the Gulf Coast basin of southwest Alabama with location of study area and Gilbertown Field (modified from Mancini et al. 1991 by Pashin 2000)

Structure and Tectonics

Southwest Alabama contains a diversity of basement and salt structures (Fig. 5.11). Deep tests penetrate the Eagle Mills Formation and crystalline basement mainly northeast of the Mississippi interior salt basin and in the general area of the Wiggins arch (Horton et al. 1984; Mink et al. 1983; Guthrie and Raymond 1992). Basement structures define a series of ridges and embayments. The most conspicuous structural features in southwest Alabama are the peripheral normal faults (Figs. 5.11, 5.12). The peripheral faults mark the northeast margin of the Mississippi interior salt basin and have therefore long been considered salt structures (Murray 1961).

Numerous salt-cored anticlines are associated with extensional faulting in southwest Alabama. Most of anticlines contain concordant salt pillows in the cores, and only one salt dome within the Mobile graben can be classified as a true piercement structure (Joiner and Moore 1966)

Structure of Gilbertown Field

a *Marker beds and fault cuts:* Correlation of 725 geophysical well logs revealed numerous stratigraphic markers that could be used to characterize structure in Gilbertown Field and adjacent areas (Figs. 5.13, 5.14). Wells were drilled in search of shallow Cretaceous

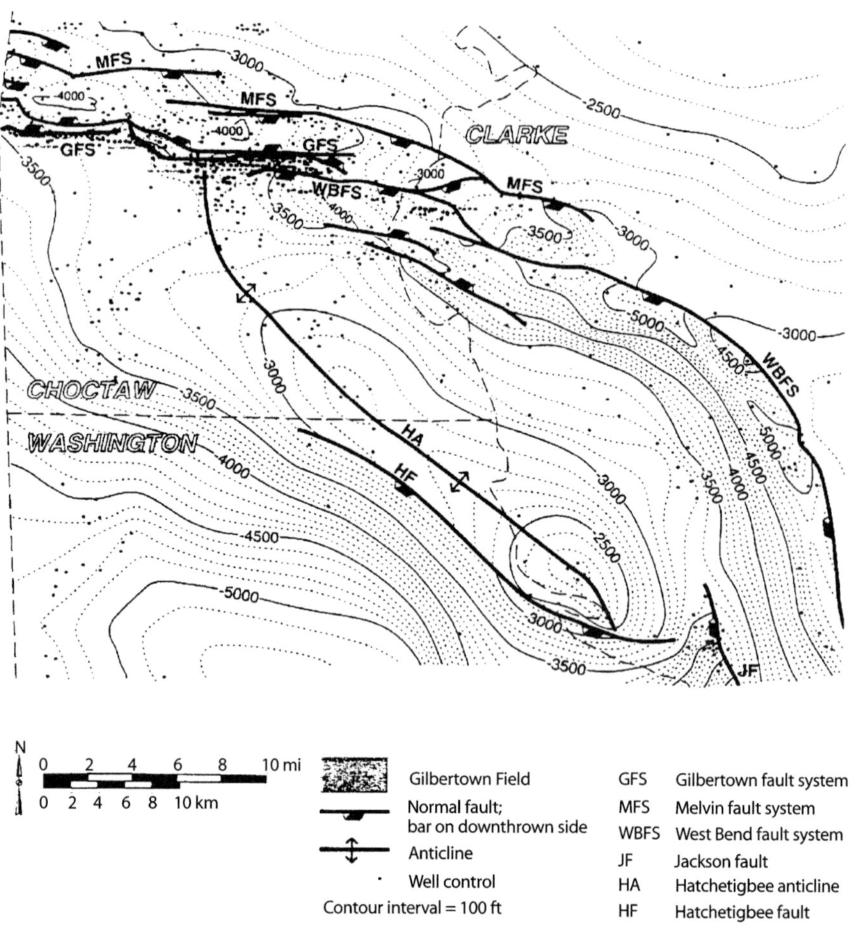
MFS
GFS
WBFS
CLARKE
CHOCTAW
WASHINGTON
HA
HF
JF
-2500
-3000
-3500
-4000
-4500
-5000
N
0 2 4 6 8 10 mi
0 2 4 6 8 10 km
Gilbertown Field
Normal fault; bar on downthrown side
Anticline
Well control
Contour interval = 100 ft
GFS Gilbertown fault system
MFS Melvin fault system
WBFS West Bend fault system
JF Jackson fault
HA Hatchetigbee anticline
HF Hatchetigbee fault

Fig. 5.12. Structural contour map of the top of the Eutaw Formation (Upper Cretaceous) showing the relationship of Gilbertown Field to the Gilbertown, Melvin, and West Bend fault systems and the Hatchetigbee anticline

and deep Jurassic reservoirs, and the stratigraphic and structural data reflect these disparate drilling targets.

The deepest stratigraphic marker that has been drilled in enough places to constrain structural cross sections is top of the Smackover Formation, which is readily identified below the basal anhydrite (Buckner Member) of the Haynesville Formation (Figs. 5.13, 5.14). Interbedded anhydrite and shale provide numerous stratigraphic markers that are useful for correlation in the Haynesville, and a widespread sandstone unit was used to divide the formation into upper and lower parts.

Lower Cretaceous strata can be subdivided crudely on the basis of shale and sandstone content. However, because of lack of markers, a significant obstacle to make structural interpretations based on well log, considering that the Lower Cretaceous is thicker than 5 000 feet (1524 m) in the Gilbertown area.

Upper Cretaceous strata, contain several regionally extensive stratigraphic markers (Figs. 5.13, 5.14). The base of Tuscaloosa Group is extremely difficult to identify in well logs, so the bottom of a massive sandstone within the lower Tuscaloosa (Mancini et al. 1987) was used as the working base of the Tuscaloosa Group. The base of the marine Tuscaloosa shale is a distinctive marker that was used to subdivide the Tuscaloosa Group into upper and lower parts.

Interbedded sandstone, shale, and marl in the Tertiary section comprise a multitude of stratigraphic units that can be correlated throughout the study area (Figs. 5.13, 5.14).

b Structure: Numerous faults comprise the Melvin, Gilbertown, and West Bend fault systems, and individual faults were labeled so they could be identified consistently (Figs. 5.15–5.17). The south-dipping Melvin fault system contains three major faults labeled MA, MB, and MC. Faults MA and MB are separated by a large relay ramp, and fault MC is a long synthetic fault that is in the hanging wall of fault MB. The north-dipping Gilbertown fault system consists of four sub-parallel faults and contains two rider blocks at the southern margin of the Gilbertown graben. The Gilbertown fault system was accordingly subdivided into West Gilbertown faults A and B (faults WGA, WGB), and East Gilbertown faults A and B (faults EGA, EGB). In the central part of Gilbertown Field the faults are linked in a structurally complex

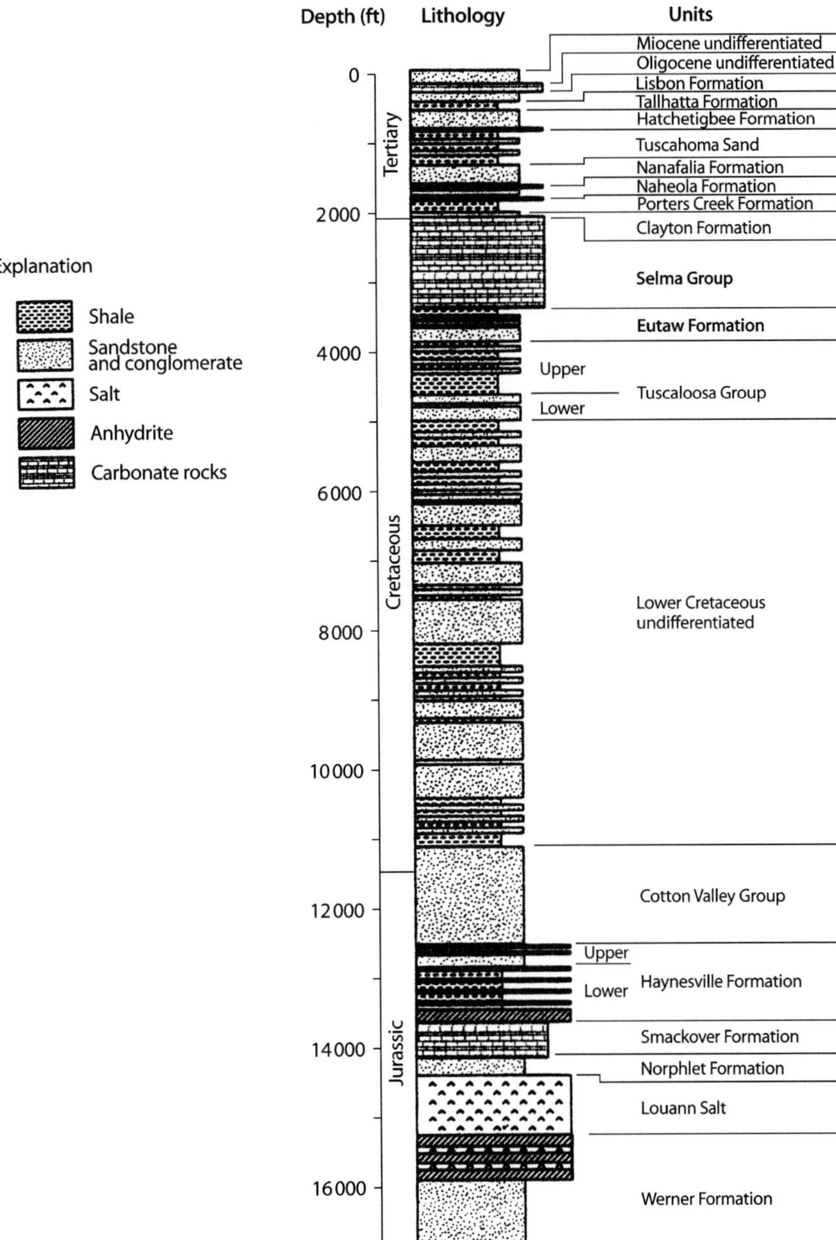
Depth (ft)
Lithology
Units
Miocene undifferentiated
Oligocene undifferentiated
Lisbon Formation
Tallhatta Formation
Hatchetigbee Formation
Tuscahoma Sand
Nanafalia Formation
Naheola Formation
Porters Creek Formation
Clayton Formation
Selma Group
Eutaw Formation
Upper
Lower
Tuscaloosa Group
Lower Cretaceous undifferentiated
Cotton Valley Group
Upper
Lower
Haynesville Formation
Smackover Formation
Norphlet Formation
Louann Salt
Werner Formation
Tertiary
Cretaceous
Jurassic
0
2000
4000
6000
8000
10000
12000
14000
16000
Explanation
Shale
Sandstone and conglomerate
Salt
Anhydrite
Carbonate rocks

Fig. 5.13. Generalized stratigraphic section showing Jurassic through Tertiary stratigraphy in Gilbertown Field and adjacent areas

relay zone. The West Bend fault (fault WB) dips southward and was mapped as a single fault.

The Gilbertown and Melvin fault systems form a full graben extending the length of the map area, whereas the Gilbertown and West Bend fault systems form a horst that is restricted to the eastern end of the map area (Figs. 5.15, 5.16). The Gilbertown graben contains most of the faults in the map area and consists of two major segments containing faults that generally strike east. The western segment comprises fault MA and the West Gilbertown faults, whereas the eastern segment contains faults MB, MC, and the east Gilbertown faults. A structurally complex relay zone is present at the intersection of the two graben segments. The relay zone marks a lateral offset of the axis of the graben and is defined by faults striking southeast and northwest. The horst is an arcuate structure in the eastern part of Gilbertown Field and is formed principally by faults EGA and WB.

5.7 Duties and Responsibilities of the Subsurface Geologist

The subsurface geologist who gets numerous and varied duties and responsibilities, should have a sense of

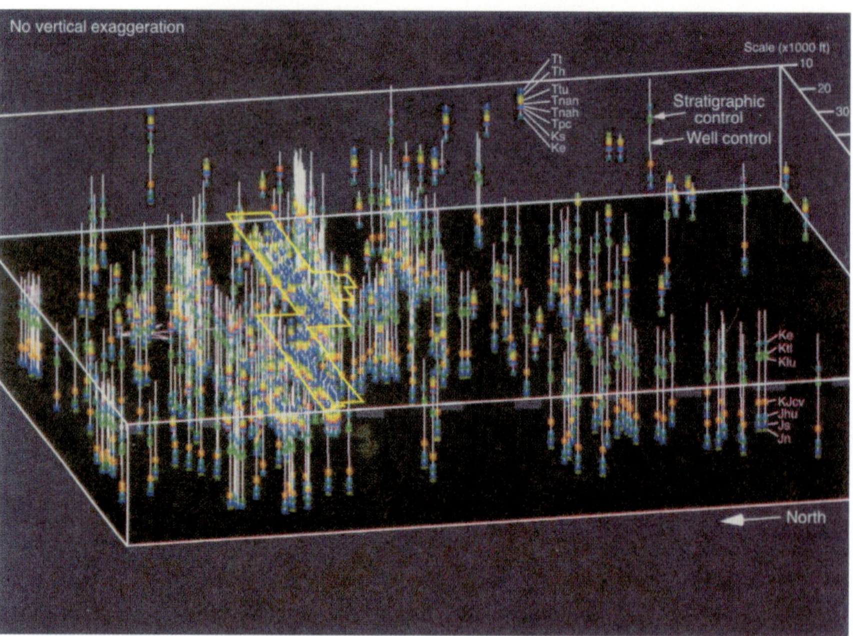
No vertical exaggeration
Scale (x1000 ft)
10
20
30
Tt
Th
Ttu
Tnan
Tnah
Tpc
Ks
Ke
Stratigraphic control
Well control
Ke
Ktl
Klu
KJcv
Jhu
Js
Jn
North

Fig. 5.14.
Well control and stratigraphic markers used to construct 3-D structural model of the Gilbertown area. Outline of Gilbertown Field shown in *yellow*

Tt	Top Tallahatta Formation	Ke	Top Eutaw Formation
Th	Top Hatchetigbee Formation	Ktl	Top Lower Tuscaloosa Group
Ttu	Top Tuscahoma Sand	Klu	Top Lower Cretaceous undifferentiated
Tnan	Top Nanafalia Formation	KJcv	Top Cotton Valley Group
Tnah	Top Naheola Formation	Jhu	Top Upper Haynesville Formation
Tpc	Top Porters Creek Formation	Js	Top Smackover Formation
Ks	Top Selma Group	Jn	Top Norphlet Formation

geologic and economic values and should cooperate fully with the field geologist, the geophysicist and all other individuals that contribute to the solution of the subsurface problems. The following are some of the main duties encountered in subsurface work.

5.7.1 Correlation of Surface to Subsurface Stratigraphic Units

Both recent and ancient deposits of the stable shelf areas are lithologically and faunally in discord with deposits of the unstable shelf. The intracratonic basin sediments and their organic elements vary widely with those accumulated under geosynclinal conditions.

5.7.2 Electrical Logging

Electrical logging successfully evaluated features of the penetrated strata. Information obtained from these logs, namely radioactive, caliper, thermal and induction logs, as well as other logs as spontaneous potential logs, is based on the characteristics of the rocks, their composition, texture and fluid content (see Chap. 7).

5.7.3 Problem/Solutions in Deep Drilling Operations

The operator and the contractor should know the magnitude of difficulties through drilling operations of sandstone-shale section, a carbonate section and/or a section containing numerous beds of saliniferous material. A rock sequence containing numerous beds of bentonite might alter an entire drilling and casing program.

Other problems may be encountered during penetration of fault surfaces, unconformities and vugulated strata in which loss of circulation of the drilling mud occurs.

5.7.4 Subsurface Data

Subsurface data may be conventionally represented by contour-type maps, which are based on structural, isopacheous, isothermal, isopermeability, isochore, lithofacies, and depth pressure information. Such maps help and improve understanding of subsurface conditions.

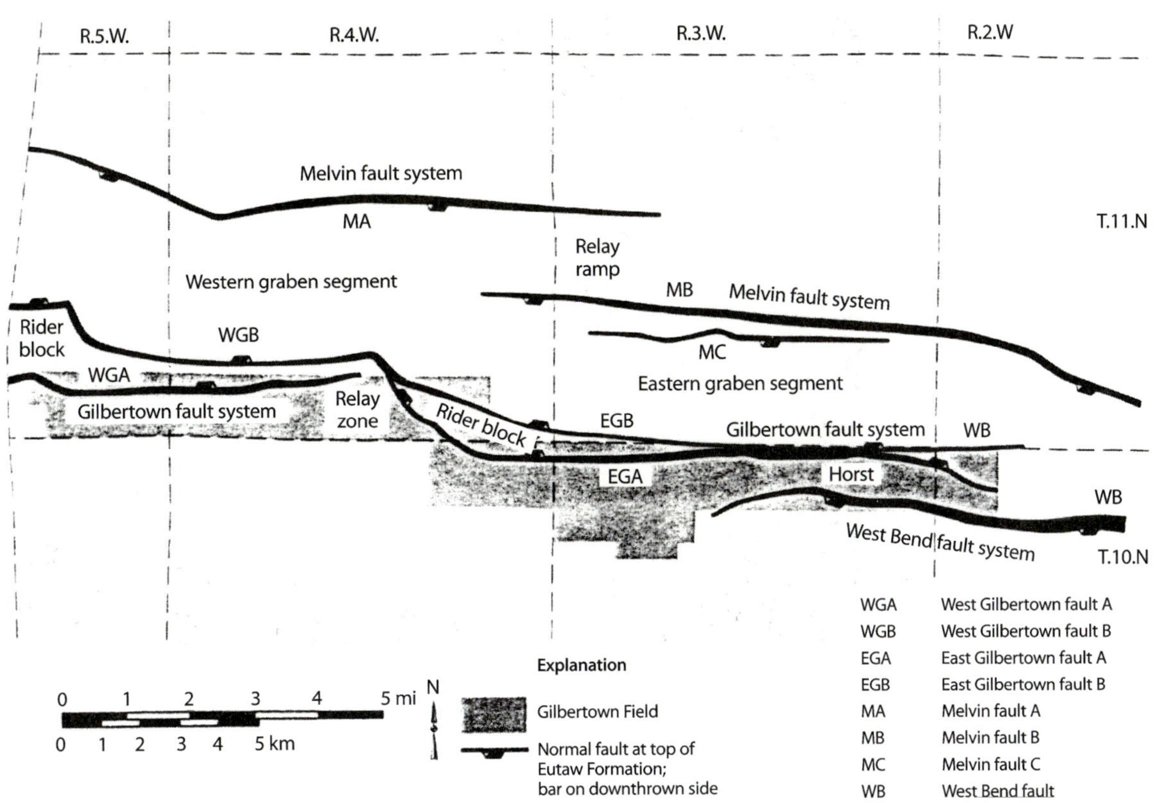

R.5.W.
R.4.W.
R.3.W.
R.2.W
Melvin fault system
MA
T.11.N
Relay ramp
Western graben segment
MB
Melvin fault system
Rider block
WGB
MC
WGA
Eastern graben segment
Gilbertown fault system
Relay zone
Rider block
EGB
Gilbertown fault system
WB
EGA
Horst
WB
West Bend fault system
T.10.N
WGA West Gilbertown fault A
WGB West Gilbertown fault B
EGA East Gilbertown fault A
EGB East Gilbertown fault B
MA Melvin fault A
MB Melvin fault B
MC Melvin fault C
WB West Bend fault
Explanation
Gilbertown Field
Normal fault at top of Eutaw Formation; bar on downthrown side
0 1 2 3 4 5 mi
0 1 2 3 4 5 km
N

Fig. 5.15. Index map showing distribution and names of major faults, Gilbertown Field and adjacent areas

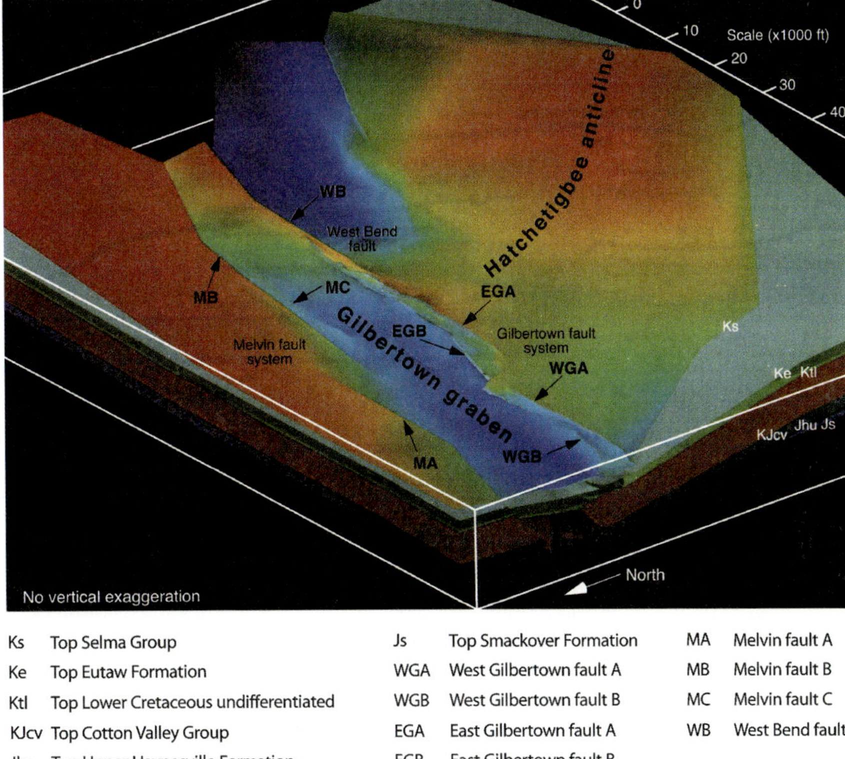

Scale (x1000 ft)
0
10
20
30
40
Hatchetigbee anticline
WB
West Bend fault
MB
MC
EGA
Gilbertown graben
EGB
Gilbertown fault system
WGA
Melvin fault system
MA
WGB
Ks
Ke Ktl
KJcv Jhu Js
North
No vertical exaggeration

Fig. 5.16. Virtual model of the Gilbertown graben constructed in GeoSec3D. The top of the uppermost unit (*Ks*) is colored by elevation, *blue* is low elevation. Fault surfaces are now shown

Ks	Top Selma Group	Js	Top Smackover Formation	MA	Melvin fault A
Ke	Top Eutaw Formation	WGA	West Gilbertown fault A	MB	Melvin fault B
Ktl	Top Lower Cretaceous undifferentiated	WGB	West Gilbertown fault B	MC	Melvin fault C
KJcv	Top Cotton Valley Group	EGA	East Gilbertown fault A	WB	West Bend fault
Jhu	Top Upper Haynesville Formation	EGB	East Gilbertown fault B		

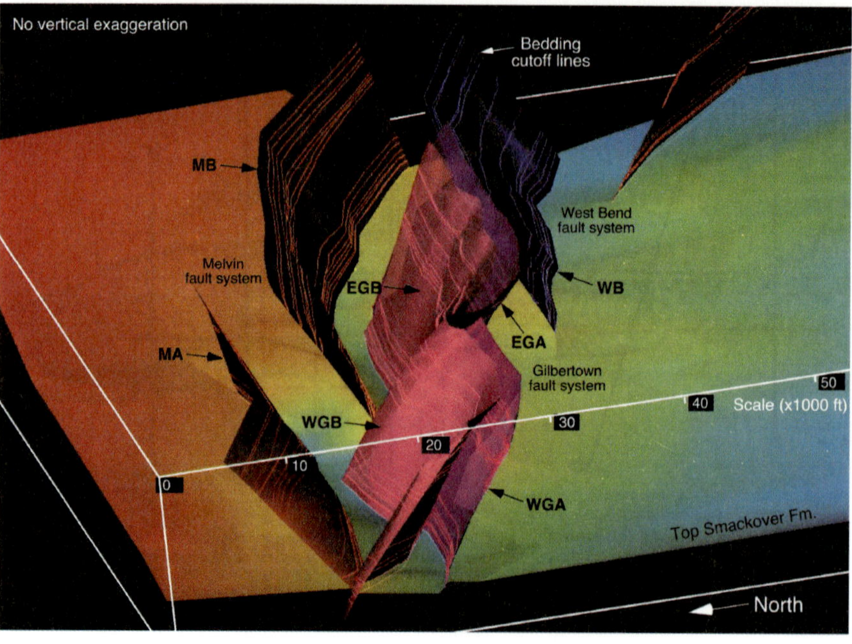

No vertical exaggeration
Bedding cutoff lines
MB
West Bend fault system
Melvin fault system
EGB
WB
EGA
MA
Gilbertown fault system
50
40
Scale (x1000 ft)
WGB
30
20
10
0
WGA
Top Smackover Fm.
North

Fig. 5.17. Virtual model of fault surfaces and bed cutoffs associated with the Gilbertown graben constructed in GeoSec3D. The top of the Smackover Formation is colored by elevation; *orange* is high elevation, *blue* is low elevation

WGA	West Gilbertown fault A	MA	Melvin fault A
WGB	West Gilbertown fault B	MB	Melvin fault B
EGA	East Gilbertown fault A	WB	West Bend fault
EGB	East Gilbertown fault B		

5.7.5 Unconformities

This deals with the extent of erosional surfaces and its relationship to adjacent strata and are easily defined by subsurface information.

References

Buschbach TC (1972) Cambrian and Ordovician stratigraphy of northeastern Illinois basin. In: Environmental Protection Series, U.S. EPA, Cincinnati, Ohio (Illinois State Geological Survey Circular 470)

Compton RR (1962) Manual of field geology. John Wiley & Sons Inc., New York, pp 1–153, 208–221, 338

Driscoll FG (1986) Sediment sieve analysis. In: Johnson Division (eds) Groundwater and wells. Minnesota (chap 12, pp 405–441)

Focazio MJ, Reilly TE, Rupert MG, Heisel DR (2002) Assessing ground-water vulnerability to contamination. USGS Circular 1224 (http://www.usgs.gov/pubs/circ/)

Guthrie GM, Raymond DE (1992) Pre-Middle Jurassic rocks beneath the Alabama Gulf Coastal Plain. Alabama Geological Survey Bulletin 150:1–155

Horton JW, Zeitz I, Neathery TL (1984) Truncation of the Appalachian Piedmont beneath the coastal plain of Alabama. Geology 12:51–55

Joiner TJ, Moore DB (1966) Structural features in South Alabama. In: Copeland CW Jr (ed) Facies changes in the Alabama Tertiary. Alabama Geological Society (Fourth Annual Field Trip Guidebook, pp 11–19)

Krumbein WC, Sloss LL (1951) Stratigraphy and sedimentation. W. H. Freeman and Co., San Francisco, California

LeRoy LW (1950) Subsurface geologic methods, 2nd edn. Colorado School of Mines, Department of Publication, Golden, Colorado, pp 71–79, 195–196, 856–977

Maher JC (1964) The composite interpretive method of logging drill cuttings. Oklahoma Geological Survey, University of Oklahoma, Norman, Oklahoma (Guide Book XIV, pp 1–8, 44–46)

Mancini EA, Mink RM, Payton JW, Bearden BL (1987) Environments of deposition and petroleum geology of Tuscaloosa Group (Upper Cretaceous), South Carton and Pollard fields, Southwestern Alabama. American Association of Petroleum Geologists Bulletin 72(103):1128–1142

Mink RM, Bearden BL, Mancini EA (1983) Regional Jurassic geologic framework of Alabama coastal waters area and adjacent federal waters area. State Oil and Gas Board of Alabama Oil and Gas Report 12:1–58

Murray GE Jr (1961) Geology of the Atlantic and Gulf Coastal Province of North America. Harper and Brothers

Naisbitt J (1982) Megatrends: ten new directions transforming our lives. Warner Books, New York

Pashin JC, Raymond DE, Alabi GG, Groshong RH Jr, Jin G (2000) Revitalizing Gilbertown oil field: characterization of fractured chalk and glauconitic sandstone reservoirs in an extensional fault system. Geological Survey of Alabama, Tuscaloosa, Alabama (Bulletin 168:1–18)

Powers MC (1953) J Sediment Petrol 23:118

Ropp JR, McCoy HJ (1979) Test drilling contract. U.S. Geological Survey, National Resources Division, Reston, Virginia, pp C1–21

Rock-Color Chart Committee (1979) Rock-color chart. Geological Society of America, Boulder, Colorado

U.S. Environmental Protection Agency (1977) 600/2-77-240 – An introduction to the technology of subsurface wastewater injection. U.S. EPA, Cincinnati, Ohio (Environmental Protection Series, pp 21–47)

USGS (1996) USGS geographic data, geography – The National Map, Sioux Falls, South Dakota (http://www.gisdatadepot.com)

U.S. Presidential Executive Order No. 12906 (1994) Geospatial information system. Federal Register 59(71):17671–17674

Selected References

Fetter CW (1988) Applied hydrogeology, 2nd edn. Merril Publishing Company, Toronto London Melborne, pp 18–30

Maguire, Goodchild MF, Rhind DW, Longman Scientific and Technical (eds) (1991) Geographical information systems – Principles and applications. John Wiley and Sons, New York

Star J, Estes J (1990) Geographic information systems – An introduction. University of California, Santa Barbara, Prentice Hall, Englewood Cliffs, New Jersey

U.S. Environmental Protection Agency (1990) Handbook – Groundwater, vol I: Groundwater and contamination. U.S. EPA, Center for Environmental Research Information, Cincinnati, Ohio (EPA/625/6-90/016a, pp 1-10)

Appendix 5.A · Lithologic Symbols for Cross and Columnar Sections

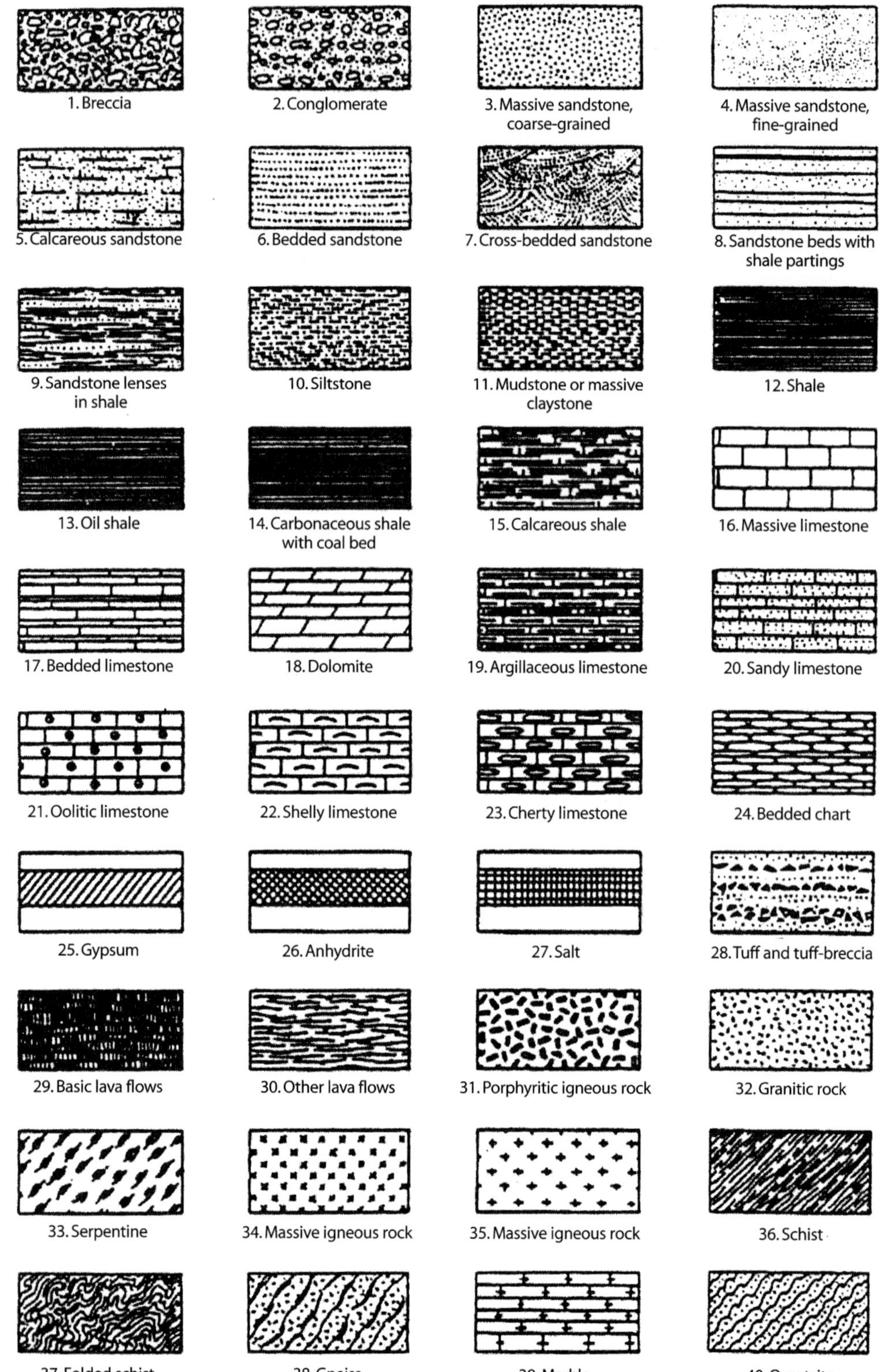

1. Breccia
2. Conglomerate
3. Massive sandstone, coarse-grained
4. Massive sandstone, fine-grained
5. Calcareous sandstone
6. Bedded sandstone
7. Cross-bedded sandstone
8. Sandstone beds with shale partings
9. Sandstone lenses in shale
10. Siltstone
11. Mudstone or massive claystone
12. Shale
13. Oil shale
14. Carbonaceous shale with coal bed
15. Calcareous shale
16. Massive limestone
17. Bedded limestone
18. Dolomite
19. Argillaceous limestone
20. Sandy limestone
21. Oolitic limestone
22. Shelly limestone
23. Cherty limestone
24. Bedded chart
25. Gypsum
26. Anhydrite
27. Salt
28. Tuff and tuff-breccia
29. Basic lava flows
30. Other lava flows
31. Porphyritic igneous rock
32. Granitic rock
33. Serpentine
34. Massive igneous rock
35. Massive igneous rock
36. Schist
37. Folded schist
38. Gneiss
39. Marble
40. Quartzite

Fig. 5.A.1. Lithologic symbols for cross and columnar sections (after Compton 1962)

Chapter 6

Drilling and Testing: Soil Samplers, Drilling Techniques, and Equipment

6.1 Introduction

Many civilizations were based on ample supplies of ground water or surface water, and many ventures have failed for lack of water. One of the earliest biblical references to ground water is the story of Moses smiting a rock with his rod and bringing forth a fountain of water. The skill shown in construction of Joseph's well at Cairo, Egypt has made it one of the best known of the ancient wells.

Drilling involves a set of processes for breaking and removing rock to produce boreholes, tunnels, and excavations. In general, the object of drilling is to reach safely a target in the subsurface, in the shortest possible time, and at the lowest possible cost. Additional constraints on sampling and evaluation may be dictated by the particular application (Geotechnical Board/Commission on Engineering and Technology Systems 1994).

The knowledge and technology needed to drill holes and to excavate tunnels and openings in rock is vital for the economic and environmental well being of all countries. Drilling is an important tool for environmental protection and remediation. Drilling is a relatively noninvasive method for investigating and removing chemical and radioactive wastes from the subsurface, and for replacing barriers in the subsurface to halt the spread of contamination. Improvements in drilling technology will continue to improve the efficiency of waste extraction and lower the cost of cleanup efforts (Bobo and Hoch 1994).

Drilling, the primary tool for extracting petroleum from the subsurface, provides a direct benefit to oil producing countries, because it leads to higher energy reserves, stable energy costs, and improved economic competitiveness. Drills are the primary tools for extracting geothermal energy (hot water and stream) from the subsurface for production of heat and electricity, as well as for exploring and producing ground water, coal, and economic ore deposits.

Wells are developed by many different types of drilling and completion techniques. Each drilling technology has capabilities that are effective in dealing with the specific geologic and hydrogeologic conditions. For example, constructing wells by jetting provides low-cost information about water levels, but severely limits the ability to collect detailed representative samples for stratigraphic information.

Drilling provides a vital operational avenue to satisfy a multitude of scientific purposes, both on the continents and in the oceans. Although drilling and exploration for resource recovery remain important purposes, the overall objectives of scientific drilling are far broader and include the following (National Research Council 1994):

- structure and chemical constitution of continental crust;
- distribution of mineral resources;
- thermal regime of the crust and crustal heat flow;
- state of stress in the earth's crust and crustal response to stress, including properties of fault zones for purpose of understanding earthquake phenomena;
- nature and age of the ocean floor with particular reference to seafloor spreading.

Development and Technology – The American Geological Institute (AGI) has coordinated the development of an interconnected national network of geographically distributed, public domain repositories of geoscience data. The objective of the National Geoscience Data Repository System (NGDRS) is to serve as a clearinghouse (AGI 2001 Annual Report).

The primary phase of the NGDRS project was performed in 1994–95 and surveyed the availability of geoscience data and the interest in preserving it. The companies surveyed indicated that they were willing to donate approximately 5 million well logs, 100 million miles of seismic data, millions of linear meters of core, and a variety of other types of scientific data. The acquisition cost of these data alone is on the order of U.S.$35 to 40 billion.

AGI has submitted the secondary phase of the NGDRS project to DOE in July 1997 and focused on establishing standards for indexing and cataloging the geoscience data and on determining the costs of transferring data from the private sector to public-sector data repositories.

6.2 Soil Sampling and Equipment

When installing test wells in consolidated formations, the reliability and overall sample quality of the drilled samples from either fluid rotary or air, water and foam systems is very similar to that of the samples obtained in unconsolidated formations.

Representative samples collected from the discharge of a rotary fluid drilled hole or those scraped from the cutting head of a drill core bit, are collected and analyzed to the best of the ability of the person supervising the operation. Great care must be taken in the collection and description of this type of sample to provide an accurate determination of the character of material being penetrated (U.S. Environmental Protection Agency 1989). A detailed description of subsurface sample is given in Chap. 5.

To evaluate the efficiency of a sampling program, the objectives must be carefully identified. It is important to define formation boundaries, and identify lenticular beds of sand and gravel in a clay matrix, to establish the proper screens (or filters) in front of aquifer intervals. Description of cuttings and core samples should be completed by the well site geologist and representative samples collected to determine grain size, porosity, permeability or physical character. Specific laboratory tests require that samples be relatively undisturbed and representative of the intervals tested. There must be sufficient quality and quantity of samples for laboratory testing. Table 6.1 demonstrates the characteristics of the sampling methods available for the drilling techniques that are most frequently employed in the installation of a test or monitoring well (Acker Drill Company Inc. 1985). Table 6.1 is arranged such that the overall reliability of the samples increases downward in the table for both unconsolidated and consolidated materials.

Sample description is as important as sample collection. It is often difficult to collect good samples of non-cohesive materials because depending on the drilling method, the fine, non-cohesive particles are frequently lost during the sampling process. Selection of drilling technique must consider the purpose of drilling and the type of lab analyses needed.

The least favorable type of sampling is the scraping of samples from the outside of the flights of solid-flight augers. This sampling method: (1) permits only discontinuous sampling; (2) does not allow identification of discrete zones; (3) does not provide samples suitable for laboratory testing; and (4) generally provides unreliable sample quality.

All-purpose sampling tools are used for visual classifications, contamination content and moisture determination (U.S. Environmental Protection Agency 1989; Acker 1974; Acker Drill Company Inc. 1985).

SQUIRT!
TEST WELL
GROUND WATER IN USA

Fig. 6.1. No way

6.2.1 Split-Barrel Samplers

Split-barrel sampling techniques were developed to meet the requirements of foundation engineering. The split-barrel sampler help to collect 46 cm samples at 1.5 m intervals as the borehole is advanced. It is furnished with spacer and sample retainers (U.S. Environmental Protection Agency 1989; Mobile Drilling Company 1988; Fig. 6.2). It is attached to the end of the drill rods and lowered to the bottom of the borehole where it rests on top of fresh undisturbed sediment. To obtain valid samples, the bottom of the borehole must be clean. A good sampling program can only be conducted in a stabilized borehole.

The procedure for collecting split-spoon samples and the standard dimensions for samplers are described in ASTM D1586 (American Society for Testing and Materials 1984). A split-barrel sampler is of standard dimensions and is driven by a 63.5 kg weight dropped through a 76 cm interval.

The split-spoon sampler provides an indication of the compaction/density of the soils being sampled. Require-

Table 6.1. Characteristics of common formation-sampling methods (after Acker Drill Company 1985)

Type of formation	Sample collection method	Sample quality	Potential for continuous sample collection	Samples suitable for lab tests	Discrete zones identifiable	Increasing reliability
Unconsolidated	Solid core auger	Poor	No	No	No	↓
	Ditch (direct rotary)	Poor	Yes	No	No	
	Air rotary with casing driver	Fair	Yes	No	Yes	
	Dual-wall reverse circulation rotary	Good	Yes	No	Yes	
	Piston samplers	Good	No	Yes	Yes	
	Split spoon and thin-wall samplers	Good	Yes	Yes	Yes	
	Special samplers (Denison, Vicksburg)	Good	Yes	Yes	Yes	
	Cores	Good	Yes	Yes	Yes	
Consolidated	Ditch (rotary)	Poor	Yes	No	No	↓
	Surface (dry air)	Poor	Yes	No	Yes	
	Surface (water/foam)	Fair	Yes	No	Yes	
	Cores (wireline or conventional)	Good	Yes	Yes	Yes	

ments of sampling vary from continuous sampling, one sample each 1.5 m, one sample each 3.1 m, or one sample wash change in lithology, etc. When only 45.7 cm intervals are sampled out of every 1.5 m penetrated, drilling characteristics (i.e. rate of penetration, vibrations, stability, etc.) of the sediment being penetrated are also used to infer characteristics of unsampled material. "Continuous" samples can also be taken with the split-barrel method by augering, or drilling to the bottom of the previously-sampled interval. Continuous sampling is time consuming, but is a way to obtain good samples of unconsolidated sediments (U.S. Environmental Protection Agency 1989).

The Standard Penetration Test (SPT) provides a measure of the resistance of the soil to penetration through the blow count "*N*". The SPT has been used widely for preliminary exploration, and many useful correlations have been established between the blow count, *N*, and soil properties, foundation performance, and susceptibility to liquefaction.

Table 6.2 shows the penetration characteristics of a variety of unconsolidated materials. The samples collected by split-spoon sampler are considered to be "disturbed" samples. They are, therefore, unsuitable for certain laboratory tests, such as permeability (Acker 1974).

6.2.2 Thin-Wall or "Shelby Tube" Samplers

Work performed by Hvorslev (1949) and others has shown that if relatively undisturbed samples are to be obtained, it is necessary that the thickness of the wall of the sampling tube should be less than 2.5% of the total outside diameter of the sampling tube. Because the split-barrel sampler must be driven to collect samples, the wall thickness of the sampler must be structurally sufficient to withstand the driving forces. Therefore, the wall thickness of a split barrel sampler is too great for the collection of undisturbed samples.

The standard practice for collecting thin-wall samples, commonly referred to as Shelby tube samples, requires placing a thin-wall sampling tube at the end of the drill rods. The sampler and rods are lowered to the bottom of the borehole just as with the split-spoon sampler. Instead of driving the sampler into the ground, the weight of the drill rig is placed on the sampler and it is

Table 6.2. Standard penetration test correlation chart (after Acker 1974)

Soil type	Designation	Blows (foot)[a]
Sand and silt	Loose	0–10
	Medium	11–30
	Dense	31–50
	Very dense	≥50
Clay	Very soft	≤2
	Soft	3–5
	Medium	6–15
	Stiff	16–25
	Hard	≥25

[a] Assumes: (*a*) 2-inch outside diameter by 13/8-inch diameter sampler; (*b*) 140-pound hammer falling through 30 inches.

Fig. 6.2.
Diagram of a split-barrel sampler and sample retainers (Mobile Drilling Company 1988)

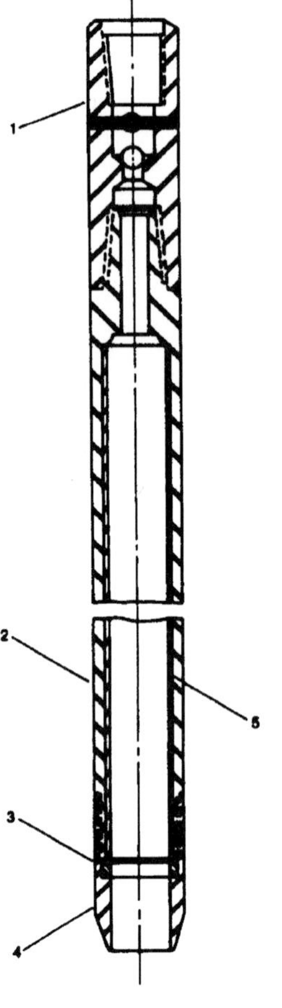
1
2
5
3
4

(Fast Thread Version)

Mobile's LYNAC® Sampler is an improved version of the industry standard split barrel sampler. It includes a shoe, barrel and head with "fast threads" to speed assembly and disassembly. Optional MOBILOK™, tapered threads (AWML) expedite attaching the sampler to driving tools. Normally driven by a 140 lb. Safety Hammer, an In-Hole Sampling Hammer or Mobile's SPT Automatic Hammer. The sampler barrel has a stepped-joint design to facilitate reassembly of the barrel and a heat-treated shoe to better withstand severe driving conditions. In addition, a ball check valve prevents wash-out during removal from the hole and the shoe design accommodates a Flap Valve or Spring Retainer. Recommended for all Standard Penetration Test procedures. Furnished with a spacer, order sample retainers separately. Sizes are identified by sampler O.D.

Description	Lb/Kg	Part No.
1'6" (457mm), AW Rod	14 (6.4)	67039-12
2'0" (610mm), AW Rod	17 (7.7)	67039-17
1'6" (457mm), AWML Rod	14 (6.4)	67039-02
2'0" (610mm), AWML Rod	17 (17.7)	67039-07

SAMPLER ASSEMBLY: ASTM (SHARP) SHOE

Description	Lb/Kg	Part No.
1'6" (457mm), AW Rod	14 (6.4)	67039-11
2'0" (610mm), AW Rod	17 (7.7)	67039-16
1'6" (457mm), AWML Rod	14 (6.4)	67039-01
2'0" (610mm), AWML Rod	17 (7.7)	67039-06

COMPONENT PARTS

Ref	Description	Lb/Kg	Part No.
1	Head Assembly, AW Rod Box	4 (1.8)	67024-06
1	Head Assembly, AWML Rod Box	4 (1.8)	67024-05
2	Split Barrel: 1'6" (457mm), Set of 2	9 (4.1)	67025-16
2	Split Barrel: 2'0" (610mm), Set of 2	10 (4.5)	67025-17
3	Spacer (for use w/o retainer or flap valve)	*	190006-01
3a	Basket Retainer, Heavy Duty, Steel	*	002417
3b	Basket Retainer, Light Duty, Plastic	*	190176
3c	Spring Retainer, Light Duty, Steel (006746 req'd)	*	005420
3d	Adapter Ring (for use with 005420)	*	006746
3e	Flap Valve, Heavy Duty, Steel	*	002421
4	Blunt Shoe	1 (.5)	190071-05
4	Sharp Shoe	1 (.5)	190071-06
5	Plastic Liner, 1'6" (457mm)	*	190138-04
5	Plastic Liner, 2'0" (610mm)	*	190138-05

3a
3c
3e
3b
3d
SAMPLE RETAINERS

pressed into place. This sampling procedure is described in detail in ASTM D1587 (American Society for Testing and Materials 1983; Mobile Drilling Company 1988; Fig. 6.3).

The thin walls of the sampler present a serious limitation on obtaining undisturbed samples in compact sediments. A thin-wall sampler may not have sufficient strength to penetrate these materials. A standard 5.1 cm inside diameter, thin-wall sampler will frequently collapse without satisfactorily collecting a sample in soils with "N"-values of 30 or greater (see Chap. 13).

6.2.3 Specialized Soil Samplers

Many special-function samplers have been developed for specific use. These include: (1) strong thin-wall samplers that collect "undisturbed" samples; (2) large-diameter samplers that collect coarse sand and gravel for gradation analyses; and (3) piston samplers that collect samples in heaving sands. Two good examples of the reinforced-type design are the Vicksburg sampler and the Dennison sampler, as shown in Figs. 6.4a and 6.4b (American Society for Testing and Materials 1984). Both samplers were developed by the United States Army Corps of Engineers. The Vicksburg sampler is a 12.8 cm inside diameter by 13.3 cm outside diameter sampler that qualifies as a thin-wall sampler but is structurally much stronger than a Shelby tube. The Dennison sampler is a double-tube core design with a thin inner tube that qualifies as a thin-wall sampler. The outer tube permits penetration in extremely cemented deposits, or unconsolidated materials while the inner tube collects a thin-

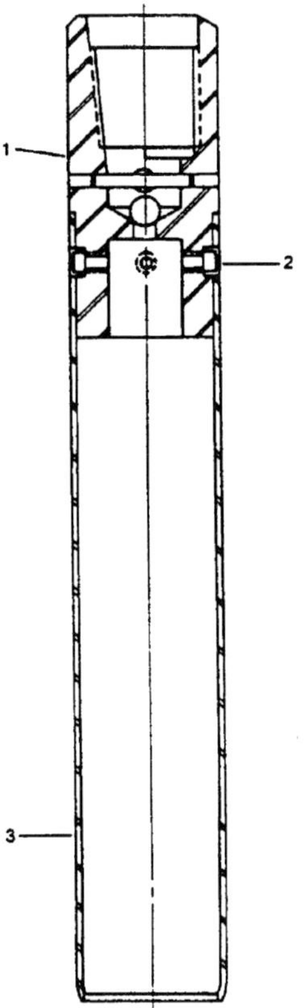
1
2
3

Fig. 6.3.
Diagram of a shelby tube sampler (after Mobile Drilling Company 1988; Acker Drill Company 1985)

"SHELBY" TUBE SAMPLER

This sampler is the simplest and probably most widely used of the "insitu" quality samplers. It consists of a head section which contains a check valve and drill rod box connector and a thin wall sample tube. The tube is loosely attached to the head by means of four socket head capscrews which are turned "in", or clockwise, to remove the tube. During the sampling operation, the tube moves slightly upward to bear against a shoulder which is machined into the head section thus assuring absolutely uniform force application to the tube. "Shelby" samplers are furnished complete with ball valve for positive vacuum control. Sampler should be forced down under steady pressure. Standard tube length is 2'6" (762 mm). Heads are available with both standard and MOBILOK™ (AWML & NWML) thread designs. **Sizes are identified by sampler O.D.**

SAMPLER ASSEMBLY

Description	Lb/Kg	Part No.
2" (51mm) x 2'6" (762mm), AW Rod Box	9 (4.1)	67010-07
2" (51mm) x 3'0" (914mm), AW Box	10 (4.5)	67010-08
2" (51mm) x 2'6" (762mm), AWML Box	9 (4.1)	67010-01
2" (51mm) x 3'0" (914mm), AWML Box	10 (4.5)	67010-02
3" (76mm) x 2'6" (762mm), AW Box	11 (5)	67013-07
3" (76mm) x 3'0" (914mm), AW Box	13 (5.9)	67013-08
3" (76mm) x 2'6" (762mm), AWML Box	11 (5)	67013-01
3" (76mm) x 3'0" (914mm), AWML Box	13 (5.9)	67013-02
3" (76mm) x 2'6" (762mm), NW Box	17 (7.7)	67013-19
3" (76mm) x 3'0" (914mm), NW Box	18 (8.2)	67013-20
3" (76mm) x 2'6" (762mm), NWML Box	17 (7.7)	67013-13
3" (76mm) x 3'0" (914mm), NWML Box	18 (8.2)	67013-14

COMPONENT PARTS: 2" (51mm) O.D.

Ref	Description	Lb/Kg	Part No.
1	Head, AW Rod Box (with Ball & Roll Pin)	6 (2.7)	67026-06
1	Head: AWML Rod Box (with Ball & Roll Pin)	6 (2.7)	67026-05
2	Screw (4 required)	*	006404
3	Tube: 2'6" (762mm), Steel	3 (1.4)	190044-01
3	Tube: 3'0" (914mm), Steel	4 (1.8)	190044-02
	Cap, Plastic	*	006425

COMPONENT PARTS: 3" (76mm) O.D.

Ref	Description	Lb/Kg	Part No.
1	Head, AW Rod Box (with Ball & Roll Pin)(Requires 4 screws)	9 (4.1)	67026-02
1	Head, AWML Rod Box (with Ball & Roll Pin)(Requires 4 screws)	9 (4.1)	67026-01
1	Head, NW Rod Box (with Ball & Roll Pin)(Requires 4 screws)	12 (5.4)	67026-04
1	Head, NWML Rod Box (with Ball & Roll Pin)(Requires 4 screws)	12 (5.4)	67026-03
2	Screw (4 required)	*	006405
3	Tube, 2'6" (762mm), Steel	5 (2.3)	190047-01
3	Tube, 3'0" (914mm), Steel	6 (2.7)	190047-02
	Cap, Plastic 3" (76mm)	*	005227

wall sample (U.S. Environmental Protection Agency 1989).

Examples of piston samplers include the internal-sleeve piston sampler developed by Zapico et al. (1987) and the wireline piston sampler described by Leach et al. (1988; Figs. 6.5 and 6.6). Both samplers have been designed to be used with a hinged "clam-shell" device on the cutting head of a hollow-stem auger (Fig. 6.7). The clam-shell has been used for the following reasons: (1) improve upon a non-retrievable knock-out plug technique; (2) simplify sample retrieval; and (3) increase the reliability of the sampling procedure in heaving sands. The Zapico et al. (1987) device requires the use of water or drilling mud for hydrostatic control while the Leach et al. (1988) device permits the collection of the sample without the introduction of external fluid.

The limitation of using this technique is that only one sample per each split spoon run can be collected because the clam-shell device will not close after the sampler is inserted through the opening. This means that although sample reliability is good, the cost per sample is high.

In split-barrel and thin-wall sampling, a portion of the sample may be lost during the sampling process. To be noted in the sample description is the percent recovery, or the length of sample actually recovered divided by the total length of the sample. A "basket" or a "retainer" is placed inside the split-barrel sampler to help retain fine sands and to prevent the sample from falling into the borehole as the sample is removed.

A check valve can be installed above the sample to relieve hydrostatic pressure during sample collection, and to prevent backflow and consequent washing during withdrawal of the sampler.

Except for loss of sample during collection, it is possible to collect continuous samples with conventional

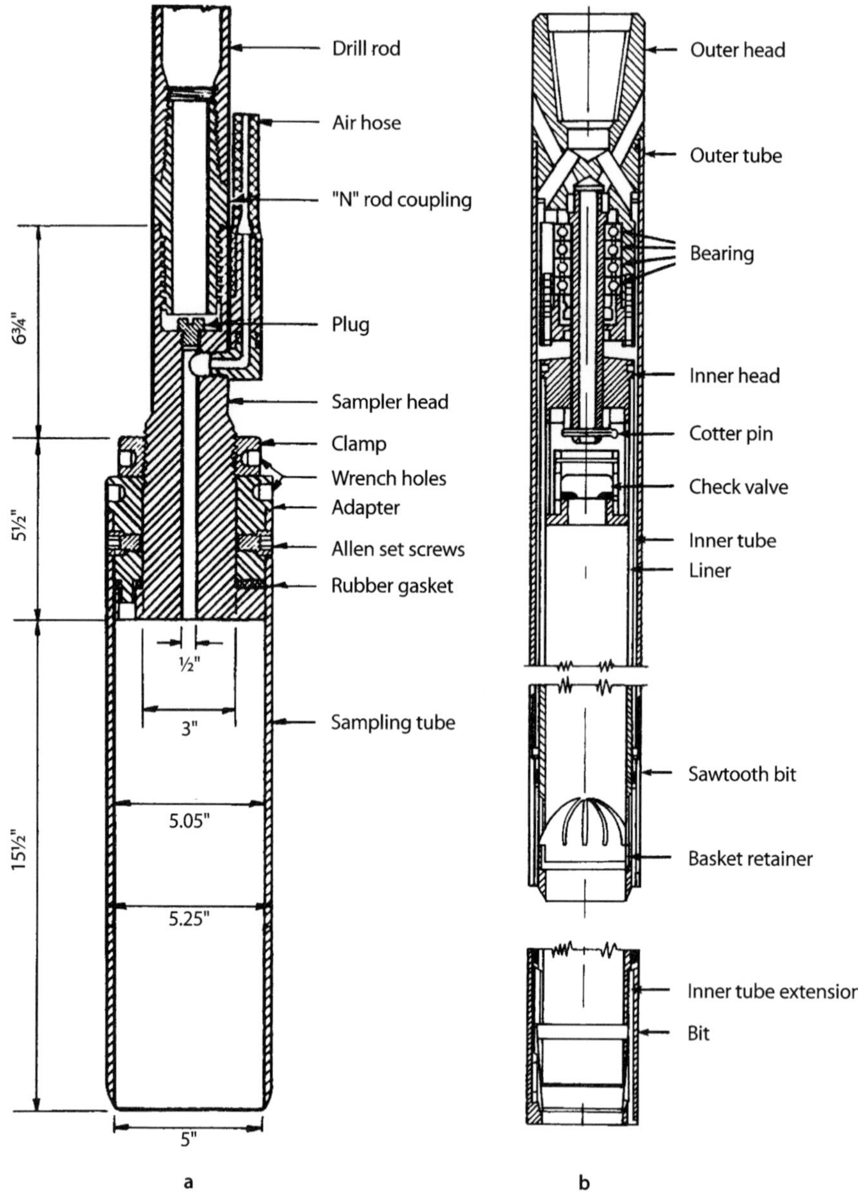
Drill rod
Air hose
"N" rod coupling
Plug
Sampler head
Clamp
Wrench holes
Adapter
Allen set screws
Rubber gasket
Sampling tube
6¾"
5½"
15½"
½"
3"
5.05"
5.25"
5"
a
Outer head
Outer tube
Bearing
Inner head
Cotter pin
Check valve
Inner tube
Liner
Sawtooth bit
Basket retainer
Inner tube extension
Bit
b

Fig. 6.4.
Two types of special soil samplers; **a** Vicksburg sampler (Krynine and Judd 1957); **b** Dennison sampler (Acker 1985)

split-spoon or thin-wall techniques as follows: (1) collecting a sample; (2) removing the sampler from the borehole; (3) drilling the sampled interval; (4) reinserting the sampler; and (5) repeating the process. This effort is time consuming and relatively expensive, and it becomes increasingly expensive to remove and reinsert the sampler and rods when the depths exceed 30.5 m (U.S. Environmental Protection Agency 1989).

Continuous samplers have been developed to increase efficiency of sampling, an example of such a system is shown in Fig. 6.8 (Central Mine Equipment Company 1987). A continuous sample is collected by attaching a 1.5 m thin-wall tube in advance of the cutting head of the hollow-stem auger. The tube is held in place by a specially-designed latching mechanism that permits the sample-tube to be retracted by wireline when full and replaced with a new tube. A ball-bearing fitting in the latching mechanism permits the auger flights to be rotated without rotation of the sampling tube. Therefore, the sampling tube is forced downward into the ground as the augers are rotated.

Mobile Drill's, Over-Shot, Wireline, Continuous-sampling System (Mobile Drilling Company 1988) has been recognized as the leading method for obtaining continuous samples while drilling in cohesive soils. The method is used for identifying unconsolidated sediment, environmental sampling, water well monitoring or retrieving high quality samples of unsaturated sand and gravel. This innovative system operates much more efficiently

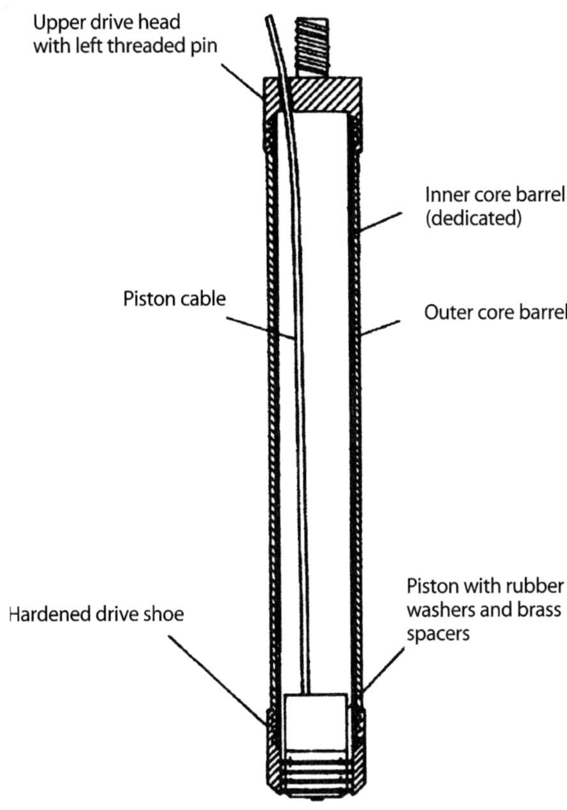
Upper drive head
with left threaded pin
Inner core barrel
(dedicated)
Piston cable
Outer core barrel
Piston with rubber
washers and brass
spacers
Hardened drive shoe

Fig. 6.5. Internal sleeve wireline piston sampler (Zapico et al. 1987)

and faster than basic samplers where the rods must be tripped in and out for retrieval of the sample barrel.

The hollow-stem augers are drilled in the normal way with the sample barrel being held in place by drill rods attached to a bearing in the drive cap. Samples are then retrieved by tripping the drill rods out of the hole (Mobile Drilling Company 1988; Fig. 6.10).

6.2.4 Core Samplers

Cores are collected to fully characterize both unconsolidated sediment and bedrock. Coring can be conducted by using either a single-tube or a double-tube core barrel (Mobile Drilling Company 1988; Fig. 6.11a,b). In coring, a carbide or diamond-tipped bit is attached to the lower end of the core barrel. As the bit cuts deeper, the sample moves up into the core tube.

In the single-wall tube, drilling fluid circulates downward around the core that has been cut, flows between the core and the core barrel and exits through the bit. The drilling fluid then circulates up the annular space and is discharged at the land surface. Because the drilling fluid is directly in contact with the core, poorly cemented or soft material is frequently eroded and the core may be partially or totally destroyed. This problem exists where material is friable, erodable, soluble, or highly fractured. In such types of materials, very little core may be recovered. A double-wall core barrel may be used under these circumstances. In this method the drilling fluid is circulated between the two walls of the core barrel and does not directly contact the core. The core moves into the inner tube, where it is protected. Therefore, a double-wall core barrel may provide better cores of poorly-consolidated materials (U.S. Environmental Protection Agency 1989).

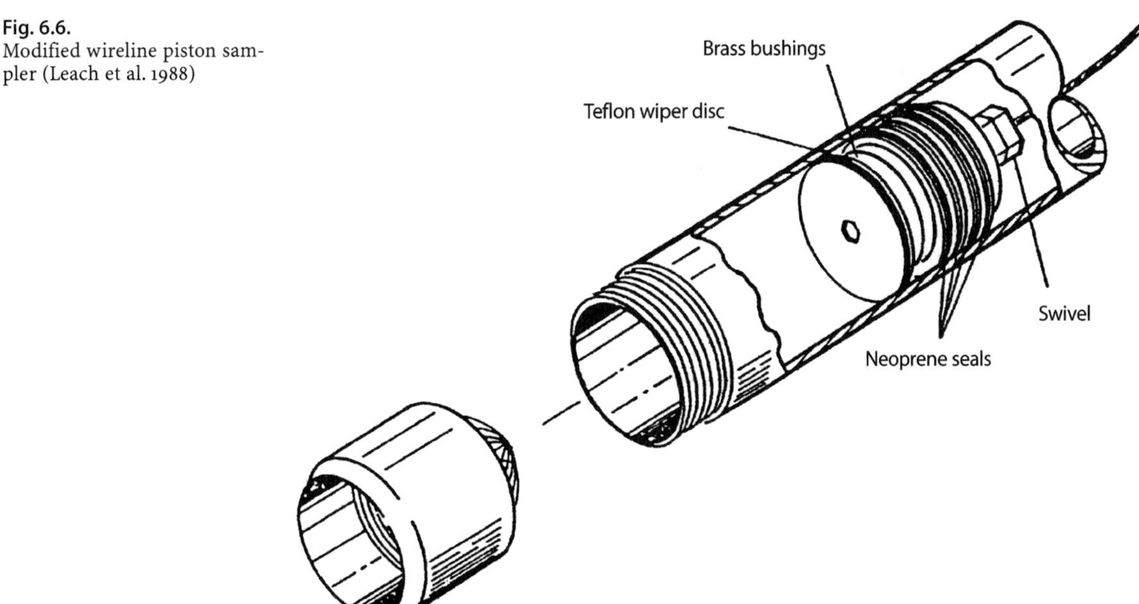
Brass bushings
Teflon wiper disc
Swivel
Neoprene seals

Fig. 6.6. Modified wireline piston sampler (Leach et al. 1988)

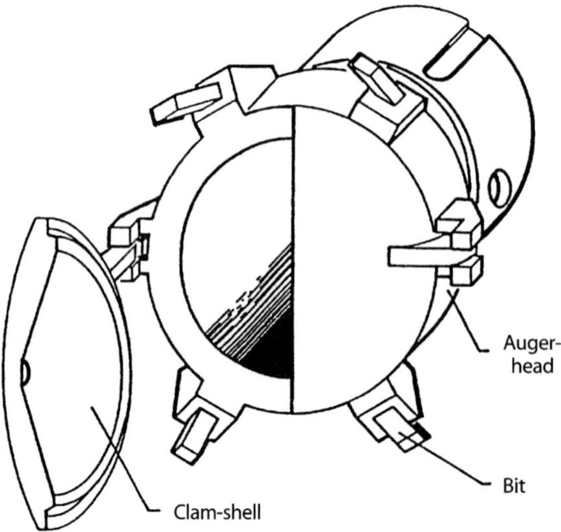
Auger-
head
Bit
Clam-shell

Fig. 6.7. Clam-shell fitted auger head (Leach et al. 1988)

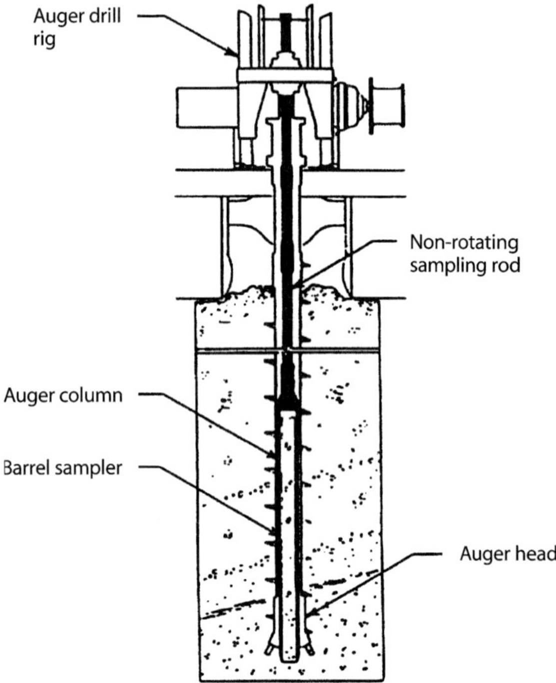
Auger drill
rig
Non-rotating
sampling rod
Auger column
Barrel sampler
Auger head

Fig. 6.8. Diagram of a continuous sampling tube system (after Central Mine Equipment Company 1987)

6.3 Drilling Methods and Equipment for Installation of Test Wells

The surest way to learn the character of the formations beneath the earth's surface is to drill through them, obtain samples while drilling, and record a log of the bore-

"Just Missed It"
!?
TEST
WELL

Fig. 6.9. My test well is dry!

hole. Well logging consists of recording characteristic properties of the various strata in terms of depth.

There are many methods for drilling, each method has advantages related to ease of construction, cost factors, character of formations to be penetrated, well diameter and depth, sanitary protection, and intended use of the well itself.

The following section contains a description of common methods of well construction together with a discussion of the applications and limitations of each technique.

6.3.1 Hand Augers

Hand augers or power augers may be used to install shallow monitoring wells (0 to 4.6 m in depth) with casing diameters of 2.54 cm or less. A typical hand auger (Mobile Drilling Company 1988; U.S. Environmental Protection Agency 1989; Fig. 6.12) cuts a hole that ranges from 7.6 to 22.9 cm in diameter. The auger is advanced by hand-turning the bit into the soil until the auger is filled. The auger is then removed from the hole and the sample is removed from the auger. Motorized units that require one or two operators are available.

The borehole cannot be advanced in certain conditions below the water table because the borehole would collapse. It is often possible to stabilize the borehole

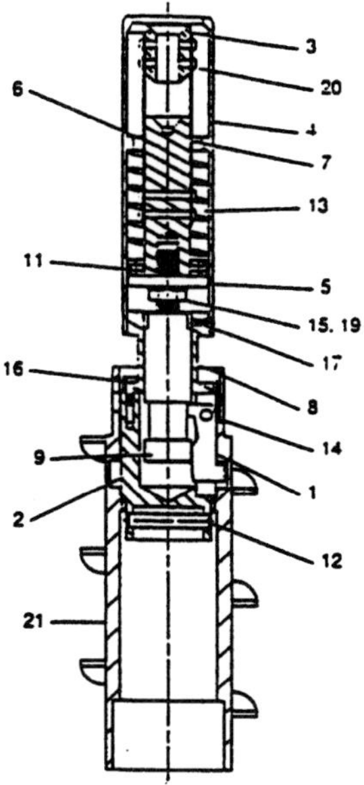

3
20
6
4
7
13
11
5
15, 19
16
17
8
9
14
1
2
12
21

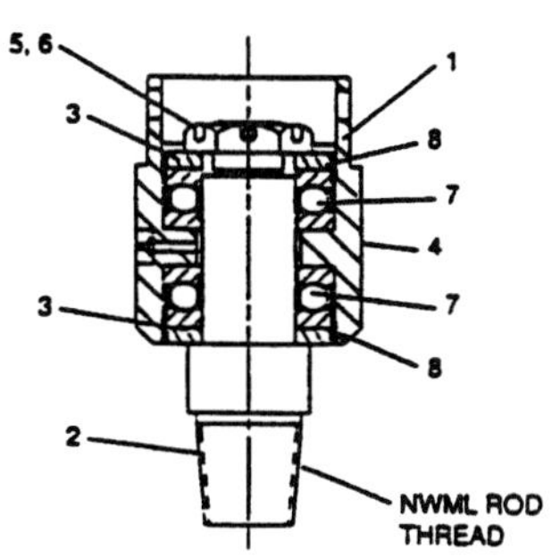

5, 6
1
3
8
7
4
3
7
8
2
NWML ROD
THREAD

6-⅝" (168 mm) TRI-LOK
OVERSHOT WIRELINE SYSTEM

6-⅝" (168mm) OVERSHOT WIRELINE ASSEMBLY..67029-10
Includes latch assembly, bearing assembly, overshot retriever, pilot bit assembly and accessories.

LATCH ASSEMBLY 6-⅝" (168mm) 67020-08

Ref.	Description	Lb/Kg	Part No.
1	Latch (6-⅝") (168mm)	3(1.4)	190009-02
2	Latch Body (6-⅝") (168mm)	23(10.4)	190110
3	Latch Spear	2(.9)	190118-01
4	Spring Housing	1(.5)	190134
5	Washer	1(.5)	190157
6	Overshot Bar	8(3.6)	190125
7	Spring	*	190128
8	Guide	17(7.7)	190181
9	Latch Plunger	15(6.8)	190182
11	Spacer	*	210032-61
12	Ball Pin	1(.5)	210033-54
13	Compression Spring	2(.9)	212160-05
14	Roll Pin	*	3068-0244
15	Lockwasher	*	3126-0016
16	Hex Socket Head Capscrew	*	3130-0063
17	Hex Socket Head Capscrew	*	3133-0007
19	Hex Jam Nut	*	3204-0016
20	Button Head Capscrew	*	3559-0003
21	Latch Housing	86(39.0)	190108

BEARING ASSEMBLY 6-⅝" (168mm) 67020-04

Ref.	Description	Lb/Kg	Part No.
1	Bearing Carrier	13(5.9)	190111
2	Bearing Shaft	9(4.1)	190114
3	Washer	*	190121
4	Grease Fitting	*	3129-0001
5	Cotter Pin	*	3194-0086
6	Shaft Nut	*	3230-0009
7	Ball Thrust Bearing	*	3535-0003
8	O-Ring	*	3538-0238

Fig. 6.10. A mobile drill's overshot wireline continuous sampling system (Mobile Drilling Company 1988)

below the water table by adding water, with or without drilling mud or other additives. The auger may then be advanced a few feet into a shallow aquifer. Another option to overcome borehole collapse below the water table is to drive a wellpoint into the augered hole and thereby advance the wellpoint below the water table. The wellpoint can provide access for measurement of water levels and for water-quality samples.

Better samples may sometimes be obtained by reducing the hole size one or more times while augering to the desired depth. As the borehole size decreases, the amount of energy required to turn the auger is also reduced. Because the head of the auger is removable, the borehole diameter can be reduced by using smaller diameter auger heads. Shaft extensions are usually added in 0.91 to 1.21 m increments. Where necessary, short sections of lightweight casing can be installed to prevent material from caving into the borehole. A more complete list of the applications and limitations of hand augers are given in Table 6.3.

6.3.2 Driven Wells

Driven wells consist of a wellpoint (screen with a solid pointed end) attached to the bottom of a casing (Fig. 6.13). Wellpoints and casings are usually 3.2 to 5.1 cm in diameter and are made of steel. The connection between the wellpoint and the casing is made either by welding or using drive couplings. Drive couplings are specially designed to withstand the force of the blows used to drive the casing. However, when the casing fails during installation, it usually fails at a coupling. When constructing a well, a drive cap is placed on top of the uppermost section of casing, and the screen and casing are driven into the ground. New sections of drive casing are usually attached in 1.2 to 1.5 m sections as the well is driven deeper. Crude stratigraphic information can be obtained by recording the number of blows per foot of penetration as the wellpoint is driven (U.S. Environmental Protection Agency 1989; Mobile Drilling Company 1988).

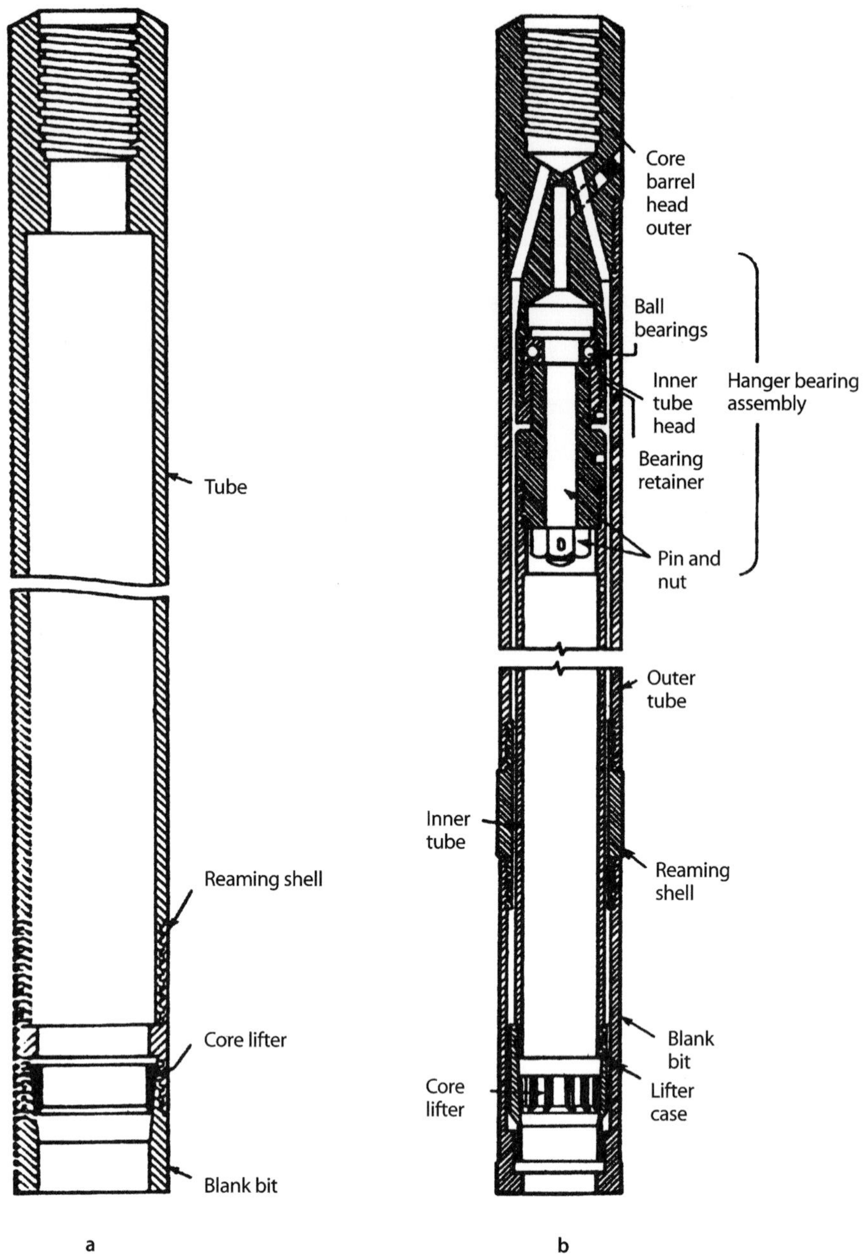
Tube
Reaming shell
Core lifter
Blank bit
a
Core barrel head outer
Ball bearings
Inner tube head
Hanger bearing assembly
Bearing retainer
Pin and nut
Outer tube
Inner tube
Reaming shell
Blank bit
Core lifter
Lifter case
b

Fig. 6.11. Diagram of two types of core barrels; **a** single-tube; **b** double-tube (Mobile Drilling Company 1988)

Wellpoints can either be driven by hand or with heavy drive-heads mounted on a tripod, stiff-leg derrick, or similar hoisting device. When driven by hand, a weighted drive sleeve such as that used to install fence posts can be used. Depths up to 9.1 m can be achieved by hand-driven in sands or sand and gravel containing thin clay. Wellpoints can be driven to depths of 15.2 m or more using hammers up to 453.6 kg in weight. Driving wellpoints through dense silts and clays and/or boulder silts and clays is extremely difficult or impossible. In the coarser materials, penetration can be terminated by the presence of a boulder. Additionally, if the wellpoint is not strong, it may be damaged or destroyed by driving in dense soils or by encountering boulders. The screen openings in the wellpoint can become plugged when driving the wellpoint through silts and/or clays. The screen may be very difficult to clean or to reopen during development, particularly if the screen is placed in a zone of low permeability.

Driven wells may be installed using a technique similar to that used in cable tool drilling, to minimize difficulties in penetration and clogging of the screen. A 10 cm casing (with only a drive shoe and no wellpoint) can be driven to the targeted depth. As the casing is driven, the inside of the casing can be cleaned by use of a bailer. With the casing still in the borehole, a wellpoint attached

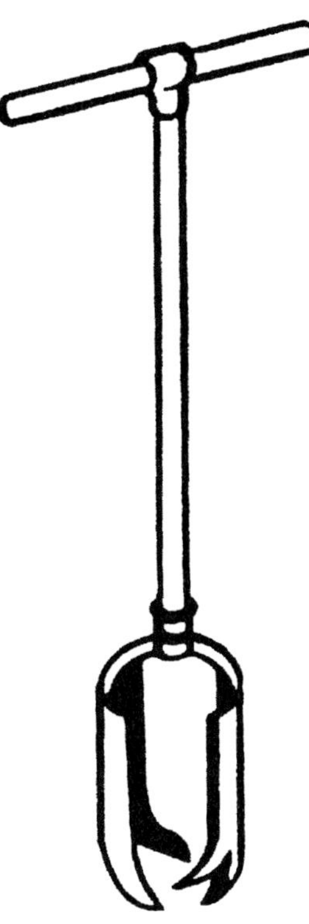

Fig. 6.12.
Diagram of a hand auger

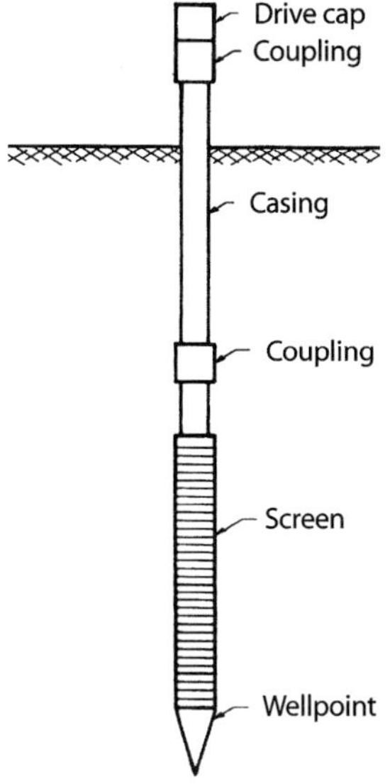
Drive cap
Coupling
Casing
Coupling
Screen
Wellpoint

Fig. 6.13.
Diagram of a wellpoint

to an inner string of casing is lowered into the borehole and the outer casing is removed. As the casing is removed, the well must be properly sealed and grouted.

A second option to complete the well with the casing still in the borehole is to power a wellpoint with a packer at the top to the bottom of the casing. The casing can then be pulled back to expose the screen. The original casing could then remain in the borehole to complete the well. Either of these completion techniques permit the installation of thermoplastic or fluoropolymer, or steel as the screen material (Table 6.4).

6.3.3 Jet Percussion

In the jet-percussion drilling method, a wedge-shaped drill bit is attached to the lower end of the drill pipe (Speedstar Division of Koehring Company 1983; Fig. 6.14). Water is pumped down the drill pipe under pressure and discharges through ports on each side of the drill bit. The bit is alternately raised and dropped to loosen unconsolidated materials or to break up rock at the bottom of the borehole. Concomitantly, the drill pipe is rotated by hand, at the surface, to cut a round and straight hole. The drilling fluid flows over the bit and up the annular space between the drill pipe and the borehole wall. The drilling fluid lubricates the bit, carries cuttings to the surface and deposits the cuttings in a settling pit. The fluid is then re-circulated down the drill pipe.

In unconsolidated material, a casing is advanced by a drive-block as the borehole is deepened. If the casing is positioned near the bottom of the borehole, good samples can be obtained as the cuttings are circulated to the surface and stratigraphic variations can be identified. Where the borehole is stable, the well can be drilled without simultaneously driving the casing.

After the casing has been advanced to the desired depth, a well intake can be installed by lowering through the casing. The casing is then pulled-back to expose the well intake. Casing diameters of 10 cm or less can be installed

Table 6.3.
Applications and limitations of hand augers (U.S. Environmental Protection Agency 1989)

Applications	Limitations
Shallow soils investigations	Limited to very shallow depths
Soils samples	Unable to penetrate extremely dense or rocky soil
Water-bearing zone identification	Borehole stability difficult to maintain
Piezometer, lysimeter and small-diameter monitoring well installation	Labor intensive
Labor intensive, therefore applicable when labor is inexpensive	
No casing material restrictions	

Table 6.4.
Applications and limitations of driven wells (U.S. Environmental Protection Agency 1989)

Applications	Limitations
Water-level monitoring in shallow formations	Depth limited to approximately 50 feet (15.24 m) (except in sandy material)
Water samples can be collected	Small diameter casing
Dewatering	No soil samples
Water supply	Steel casing interferes with some chemical analysis
Low cost encourages multiple sampling points	Lack of stratigraphic detail creates uncertainty regarding screened zones and/or cross contamination
	Cannot penetrate dense and/or some dry materials
	No annular space for completion procedures

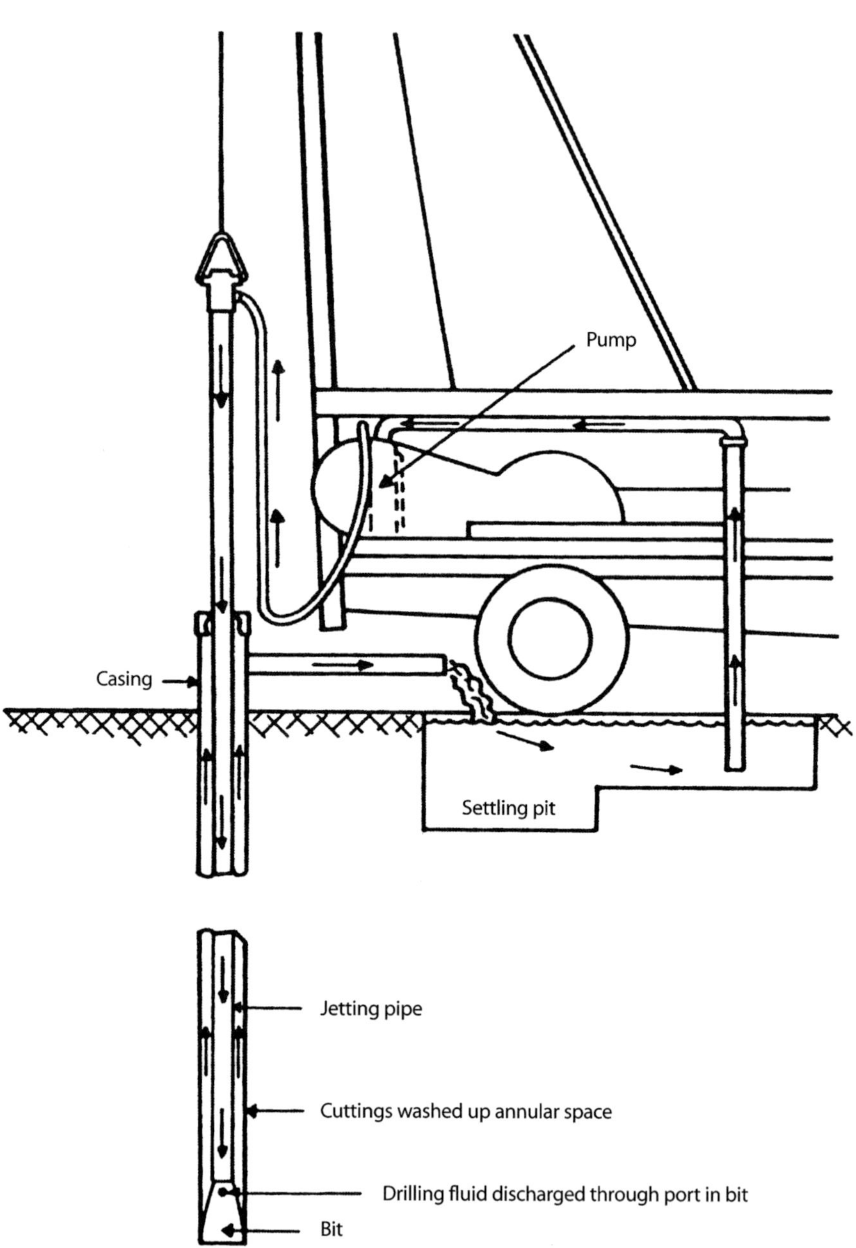
Pump
Casing
Settling pit
Jetting pipe
Cuttings washed up annular space
Drilling fluid discharged through port in bit
Bit

Fig. 6.14.
Diagram of a jet percussion drilling (after Speedstar Division of Koehring Company 1983)

by jet percussion. Depths of wells are typically less than 45 m, although much greater depths have been attained. This method is most effective in drilling unconsolidated sands (U.S. Environmental Protection Agency 1989).

6.3.4 Solid-Flight Augers

Solid-flight augers (i.e. solid-stem, solid-core or continuous flight augers) are typically used in multiple sections to provide continuous flighting. The lowermost part of the flight is provided with a cutter head that is approximately 5.1 cm larger in diameter than the flighting of the augers (Fig. 6.15). As the cutting head is advanced into the earth, the cuttings are circulated upward to the surface by moving along the continuous flighting.

The augers are rotated by a rotary drive head at the surface and forced downward by a hydraulic pull-down or feed device. The individual flights are typically 1.5 m long and are connected by a variety of pin, box and key-lock combinations and devices. Available auger diameters typically range from 15.2 to 35.6 cm in outside diameter. Many of the drilling rigs used for installation of test well in stable unconsolidated material can reach depths of approximately 21.3 m with 35.6 cm augers, and approximately 45.7 m with 15.2 cm augers.

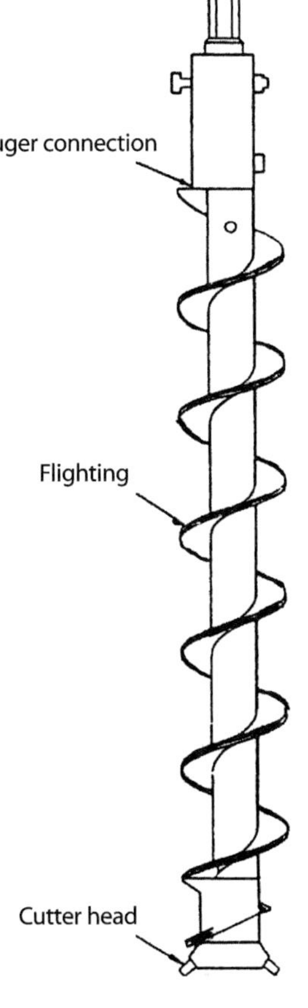
Auger connection
Flighting
Cutter head

Fig. 6.15. Diagram of a solid-flight auger (after Central Mine Equipment Company 1987)

In stable soils, cuttings can be collected at the surface as the material is rotated up the auger flights. The sample being rotated to the surface is rarely bypassed, and rarely falls back into the borehole along the annular opening and may not reach the surface until thoroughly mixed with other materials. However, samples are completely disturbed and there is a delay time in getting returns to the surface, so one must pay attention to the "drill chatter" and talk to the driller. Except under rare or shallow conditions, solid-stem augers should not be used as a method for installation of wells.

Expertise needed in identifying first appearance of material in cuttings and "log time" for the most accurate results from logging. This requires close coordination between geologist and driller.

Samples may also be collected by carefully drilling to the desired depth, stopping auger rotation, and removing the augers from the borehole. In a relatively stable unit, samples will be retained on the auger flights as the augers are removed from the borehole. The inner material is typically more representative of the subsurface materials at the drilled depths and may be exposed by scraping the outer material away from the sample on the augers. Because the borehole often caves after the saturated zone is reached, samples collected below the water table are less reliable.

Because the core of augers is solid steel, the only way to collect "undisturbed" split-spoon or thin-wall samples is to remove the entire string of augers from the borehole, insert the sampler on the end of the drill rod, and put the entire string back into the borehole. This sampling process becomes very tedious and expensive as the borehole gets deeper because the complete string of augers must be removed and reinserted each time a sample is taken. Sampling subsequent to auger removal is only possible if the walls of the borehole are sufficiently stable to prevent collapse during sampling. Boreholes may not be stable after even a moderately-thin saturated zone has been penetrated.

The casing and well intake are also difficult to install after a saturated zone has been penetrated. In this situation, it is sometimes possible to auger to the top of a saturated zone, remove the solid augers and then install a monitoring well by either driving, jetting or bailing a well intake into position (Table 6.5).

6.3.5 Hollow-Stem Augers

The hollow-stem auger is used to advance and case the hole simultaneously. It may be used with or without a plug assembly depending on the job requirements. When a plug is used for the purpose of keeping soil from entering the mouth of the lead auger, it is held in place by center (drill) rod.

Table 6.5. Applications and limitations of solid-flight augers (U.S. Environmental Protection Agency 1989)

Applications	Limitations
Shallow soils investigations	Unacceptable soil samples unless split-spoon or thin-wall samples are taken
Soil samples	Soil sample data limited to areas and depths where stable soils are predominant
Vadose zone monitoring wells (lysimeters)	Unable to install monitoring wells in most unconsolidated aquifers because of borehole caving upon auger removal
Monitoring wells in saturated, stable soils	Depth capability decreases as diameter of auger increases
Identification of depth to bedrock	Monitoring well diameter limited by auger diameter
Fast and mobile	

Hollow-stem augers are rotated dry and often to depths of 91.4 m. Many special applications can be carried out in addition to full range soil sampling. Piezometer and wellpoint placement, slope indicator placement, water wells, ground-water monitoring wells, diamond drilling, anchor bolt placement as well as grouting and blast hole loading are some of the jobs that hollow-stem augers facilitate.

Similar to solid-flight augers, hollow-stem auger drilling is accomplished using a series of interconnected auger flights with a cutting head at the lowermost end. As the augers are rotated and pressed downward, the cuttings are rotated up the continuous flighting.

Unlike the solid-flight augers, the center core of the auger is open in the hollow-stem flights (Central Mine Equipment Company 1987; Fig. 6.16a). Thus, as the augers are rotated and pressed into the ground, the augers act as casing and stabilize the borehole. Small-diameter drill rods and samplers can then be passed through the hollow center of the augers for sampling. The casing and well intake also can be installed without borehole collapse (U.S. Environmental Protection Agency 1989).

Hollow-stem augers and cutterheads: A wide range of cutterheads for hollow-stem augers are available to suit any type of material being drilled. The blade-type cutterhead can be used with steel or carbide insert cutter-blades designed to perform better in less demanding materials. Innovative design, state of the art engineering and manufacturing processes make Foremost Drills the recognized industry leader in hollow-stem augers and related accessories (Central Mine Equipment Company 1987; Fig. 6.16b).

In general, to collect the samples through hollow-stem augers, the augers can be drilled to desired depth with a "knock-out" plug installed; then punched out for sampling; drilled with the central rod and bit in place; removed for sampling split-spoon, or thin-wall; or drilled with a 1.5 to 3.1 m core barrel in the central hole for continuous sampling.

If the jetting action is carried to the bottom of the augers, the material immediately below the augers will be disturbed. Next, either a split-spoon (ASTM 1586) or thin-wall (ASTM 1587) sampler is placed on the lower end of the drill rods and lowered to the bottom of the borehole. The split-spoon sampler can then be driven to collect a disturbed sample or the thin-wall sampler can be pressed to collect an "undisturbed" sample from the strata immediately below the cutting head of the auger. Samples can either be taken continuously or at selected intervals.

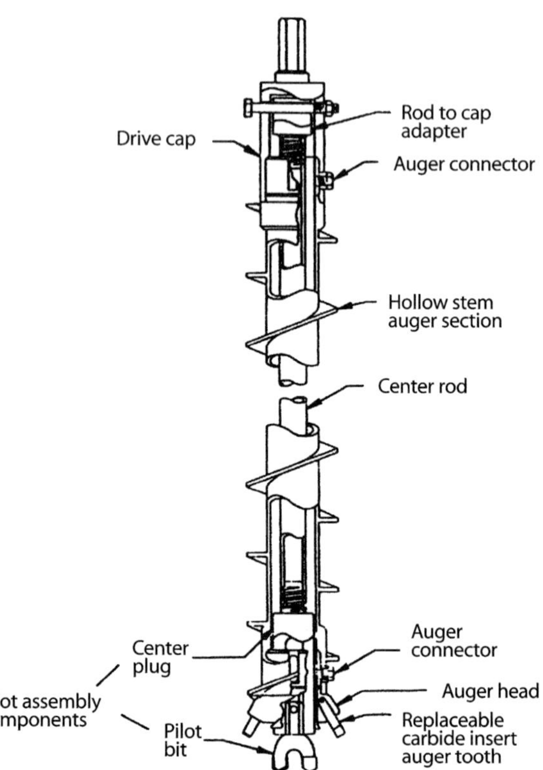
Drive cap
Rod to cap adapter
Auger connector
Hollow stem auger section
Center rod
Center plug
Auger connector
Auger head
Pilot assembly components
Pilot bit
Replaceable carbide insert auger tooth

Fig. 6.16a. Typical components of a hollow-stem auger (after Central Mine Equipment Company 1987)

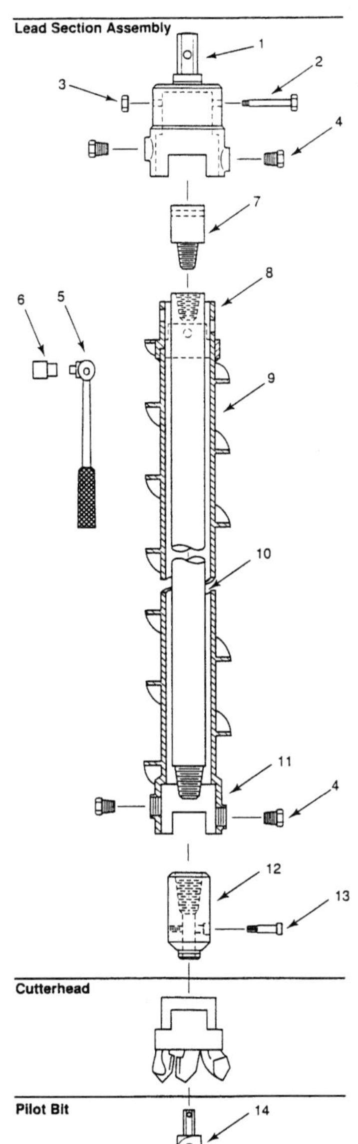
Lead Section Assembly
1
2
3
4
7
8
6
5
9
10
11
4
12
13
Cutterhead
Pilot Bit
14

Fig. 6.16b.
Lite-flite hollow stem auger and cutterhead (Mobile Drilling Company 1988); a new version of hollow stem augers by Central Mine Equipment Company (1987)

2-1/4″ (57mm) LITE-FLITE™ AUGER

LITE-FLITE augers are designed to fill the need for a lightweight, low cost hollow stem auger for use with lightweight drilling rigs having a maximum torque output of not more than 750 lbs.-ft. (103.72 kg-meters) . LITE-FLITE's 2-1/4″ (57mm) I.D. will allow monitor well placement and standard penetration testing with 2″ (51mm) tools and equipment to a maximum of 75′ (22.9m). **Sizes are identified by hollow stem auger I.D.** Order a lead section and the following as needed: Cutterhead, pilot bit, extra auger sections and center rods.

LEAD SECTION ASSEMBLY: 4-3/8″ (111mm) O.D.

Description	Lb/Kg	Part No.
2′6″ (762mm), 13/16″ (21mm) Hex, AWML Rod	38 (17.2)	61023-01
2′6″ (762mm), 13/16″ (21mm) Hex, EW Rod	35 (15.9)	61023-04
5′0″ (1.5m), 1-1/8″ (29mm) Hex, AW Rod	62 (28.1)	61021-05
2′6″ (762mm), 1-1/8″ (29mm) Hex, AWML Rod	39 (17.7)	61023-02
5′0″ (1.5m), 1-1/8″ (29mm) Hex, AWML Rod	62 (28.1)	61021-06
2′6″ (762mm), 1-1/8″ (29mm) Hex, EW Rod	35 (15.9)	61023-05
5′0″ (1.5m), 1-1/8″ (29mm) Hex, EW Rod	60 (27.2)	61021-04

COMPONENT PARTS

Ref	Description	Lb/Kg	Part No.
1	Drive Cap 13/16″ (21mm) Hex	6 (2.7)	150404
1	Drive Cap 1-1/8″ (29mm) Hex	6 (2.7)	150399
2	Rod Bolt	*	3100-0128
3	Hex Nut	*	3122-0012
4	Lock Bolt Without Hard Facing	*	217135
4	Lock Bolt With Hard Facing	*	150383
5	Handle, 1/2″ (13mm) Sq Drive Flex x 18″ (457mm)	*	3781-0009
6	Socket, 15/16″ (24mm) Hex	*	3782-0013
7	Adapter: EW Rod to Drive Cap	1 (.5)	150402
7	Adapter: AW Rod to Drive Cap	2 (.9)	150310
7	Adapter: AWML Rod to Drive Cap	2 (.9)	150311
8	Pin Coupling (Repair Only)	3 (1.4)	150384
9	Auger Section: 2′6″ (762mm)	17 (7.7)	150414
9	Auger Section: 5′0″ (1.5m)	32 (14.5)	150386
10	Center Rod: 5′0″ (1.5m), AW	22 (10.0)	001605
10	Center Rod: 2′6″ (762mm), AWML	7 (3.2)	150416
10	Center Rod: 5′0″ (1.5m), AWML	15 (6.8)	006276
10	Center Rod: 2′6″ (762mm), EW	7 (3.2)	001753
10	Center Rod: 5′0″ (1.5m), EW	15 (6.8)	001604
11	Box Coupling (Repair Only)	3 (1.4)	150385
12	Plug: 13/16″ (21mm) Hex Socket to EW Box	4 (1.8)	180448-01
12	Plug: 13/16″ (21mm) Hex Socket to AW Box	4 (1.8)	180448-02
12	Plug: 13/16″ (21mm) Hex Socket to AWML Box	4 (1.8)	180448-03
13	Plug Bolt	*	3130-0062
14	Pilot Bit: 13/16″ (21mm) Hex	1 (.5)	004981

Cutterhead—see page 3-18.

With the augers acting as casing and with access to the bottom of the borehole through the hollow-stem, it is possible to drill below the top of the saturated zone. When the saturated zone is penetrated, finely-ground material and water may mix to form a mud that coats the borehole wall. This "mud plaster" may seal water-bearing zones and minimize inter-zonal cross connection. This sealing is uncontrolled and unpredictable because it depends on: (1) the quality of the silt/clay seal; (2) the differential hydrostatic pressure between the zones; and (3) the transmissivity of the zones. Therefore, the seal developed during augering cannot be relied upon to prevent cross contamination. One other potential source of cross contamination is through leakage into or out of the augers at the flighting joints. This leakage can be minimized by installing o-ring seals at the joints connecting the flights.

To prevent intrusion of material while drilling, hollow-stem auger boreholes can be drilled with a center plug that is installed at the bottom of the drill rods and inserted during drilling. A small drag bit may also be added to prevent intrusion into the hollow-stem. When drilling into an aquifer that is under low to moderate confining pressure, the sand and gravel of the aquifer frequently "heave" upward into the hollow stem. This heaving occurs because the pressure in the aquifer is greater than the atmospheric pressure in the borehole. If a center plug is used during drilling, heave frequently occurs as the rods are pulled back and the bottom of the borehole is opened. This problem may be increased by the suction created as the center plug and drill rods are removed.

When heaving occurs, the bottom portion of the hollow stem fills with sediment, and the auger must be cleaned out before formation samples can be collected. However, the act of cleaning out the auger can result in further heaving, thus compounding the problem. Furthermore, as the sand and gravel heave upward into the hollow stem, the materials immediately below the auger are no longer naturally compacted or stratified. The sediments moving into the hollow stem are disaggregated by the upward-flowing water. It is obvious that once heaving has occurred, it is impossible to obtain a representative or undisturbed sample at that depth (U.S. Environmental Protection Agency 1989).

Four common strategies that can be used to decrease heaving problems are:

1. adding water into the hollow stem in an attempt to maintain sufficient positive head inside the augers to offset the hydrostatic pressure of the saturated zone;
2. adding drilling mud additives (weight and viscosity control) to the water inside the hollow stem to improve the ability of the fluid to counteract the hydrostatic pressure of the saturated zone;
3. either screening the lower auger section or screening the lowermost portion of the drill rods both above and below the center plug, in such a manner that water is allowed to enter the auger. This arrangement equalizes the hydraulic pressure, but prevents the saturated materials from entering the augers.
4. drilling with a pilot bit, knock-out plug or winged clam to physically prevent the sediment from entering the hollow stem.

The most common field procedure is to add water to the hollow stem. However, this method is frequently unsuccessful because it is difficult to maintain enough water in the auger to equalize the hydraulic pressure as the inner drill rods are raised during sampling. Adding drilling mud may lessen the heaving problem, but volume replacement of mud, displayed by removal of drilling rods, must be fast enough to maintain a positive head on the saturated zone. Additionally, additives to the drilling mud may not be desirable where there are questions about the water quality of samples from a well. A third option, screening the lowermost auger flight, serves two purposes: (1) the hydrostatic pressure can equalize with minimal disturbance of the sediment; and (2) water-quality samples and small-scale pumping tests can be performed on individual zones within an aquifer or on separate aquifers as the units are encountered. Wire-wound screened augers were developed particularly for this purpose and are commercially available (U.S. Environmental Protection Agency 1989; Fig. 6.17).

By using a pilot bit, knock-out plug or winged clam, heaving is physically prevented until these devices are removed for sampling. In essence, the hollow stem functions as a solid stem auger while the devices are in place. However, after these devices are dislodged during sampling, problems with heaving may still need to be overcome by using an alternative strategy.

Hollow-stem augers are typically limited to drilling in unconsolidated materials. However, if the cutting head of the auger is equipped with carbide-tipped cutting teeth, it is possible to drill a short distance into the top of weathered bedrock. The augers can then be used as temporary surface casing to shut off water flow that may occur at the soil/rock interface. The seal by the augers may not be complete; therefore, this practice is not recommended where cross contamination is a concern. The rock beneath the casing can then be drilled with a small-diameter tricone bit or can be cored.

The most widely-available hollow-stem augers are 15.9 cm outside diameter auger flights with a 8.3 cm inside-diameter hollow-stems. The equipment most frequently available to power the augers can reach depths of 45.7 to 53.3 m in clayey/silty/sandy soils. Much greater depths have been attained, but they cannot be predictably reached in most settings. A 30.5 cm outside diameter auger with a 15.2 cm diameter hollow stem is becoming increasingly available, but the depth limit for

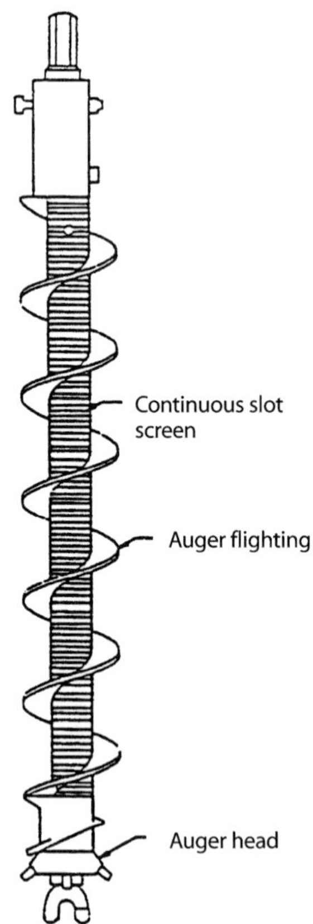
Continuous slot screen
Auger flighting
Auger head

Fig. 6.17.
Diagram of a screened auger

"What is that, Mr. Geologist?"
DRILL RIG
TEST DRILLING
(TEST)

Fig. 6.18.
Test drilling

this size auger is usually 15.2 to 22.9 m. Because of the availability and relative ease of sample collection, hollow-stem augering techniques are used for installation of the overwhelming majority of monitoring wells in the United States (Table 6.6).

6.3.6 Mud-Rotary Drilling

6.3.6.1 *Drilling fluids*

Properly mixed drilling fluid serves several functions in mud-rotary drilling. The mud: (1) cools and lubricates the bit; (2) stabilizes the borehole wall; (3) prevents the inflow of formation fluids; and (4) minimizes cross-contamination between aquifers. To perform these functions, the drilling fluid tends to infiltrate permeable zones and may interact chemically with the subsurface water. The chemical interaction can interfere with the specific function of a test well and prevent collection of a sample that is representative of the in-situ groundwater quality. This is why the mud must be removed during the development process.

Samples can be obtained directly from the stream of circulated fluid by placing a sample-collecting device in the discharge flow before it enters the settling pit. However, the quality of the samples obtained from the circulated fluid are generally not satisfactory for characterization of the subsurface materials, nor for the design of monitoring wells.

Table 6.6.
Applications and limitations of hollow-stem augers (U.S. Environmental Protection Agency 1989)

Applications	Limitations
All types of soil investigations	Difficulty in preserving sample integrity in heaving formations
Permits good soil sampling with split-spoon or thin-wall samplers	Formation invasion by water or drilling mud if used to control heaving
Water-quality sampling	Possible cross contamination of aquifers where annular space not positively controlled by water or drilling mud or surface casing
Monitoring well installation in all unconsolidated formations	Limited diameter of augers limits casing size
Can serve as temporary casing for coring rock	Smearing of clays may seal off aquifer to be monitored
Can be used in stable formations to set surface casing (example: drill 12-inch borehole; remove augers; set 8-inch casing; drill 7¼-inch borehole with 3¼-inch ID augers to rock; core rock with 3-inch tools; install 1-inch piezometer; pull augers)	

In rotary drilling, the drilling fluid is pumped down the drill rods and through a bit that is attached at the lower end of the drill rods. The fluid circulates back to the surface by moving up the annular space between the drill rods and the wall of the borehole. At the surface, the fluid discharges through a pipe or ditch and enters into a segregated or baffled sedimentation tank, pond or pit. The settling pit overflows into a suction pit where a pump re-circulates the fluid back through the drill rods (National Water Well Association of Australia 1984; Fig. 6.19).

During drilling, the drill stem is rotated at the surface by either top head or rotary table drives. Down pressure is attained either by pull-down devices or drill collars. Pull-down devices transfer weight of the drilling rig to the bit; drill collars add weight directly to the drill stem. When drill collars are used, the rig holds back the excess weight to control the weight on the bit. Most rigs for installation monitoring wells use the pull-down technique because the wells are relatively shallow.

Mud-rotary drilling is also an effective means of drilling and/or coring consolidated rock. Where overburden

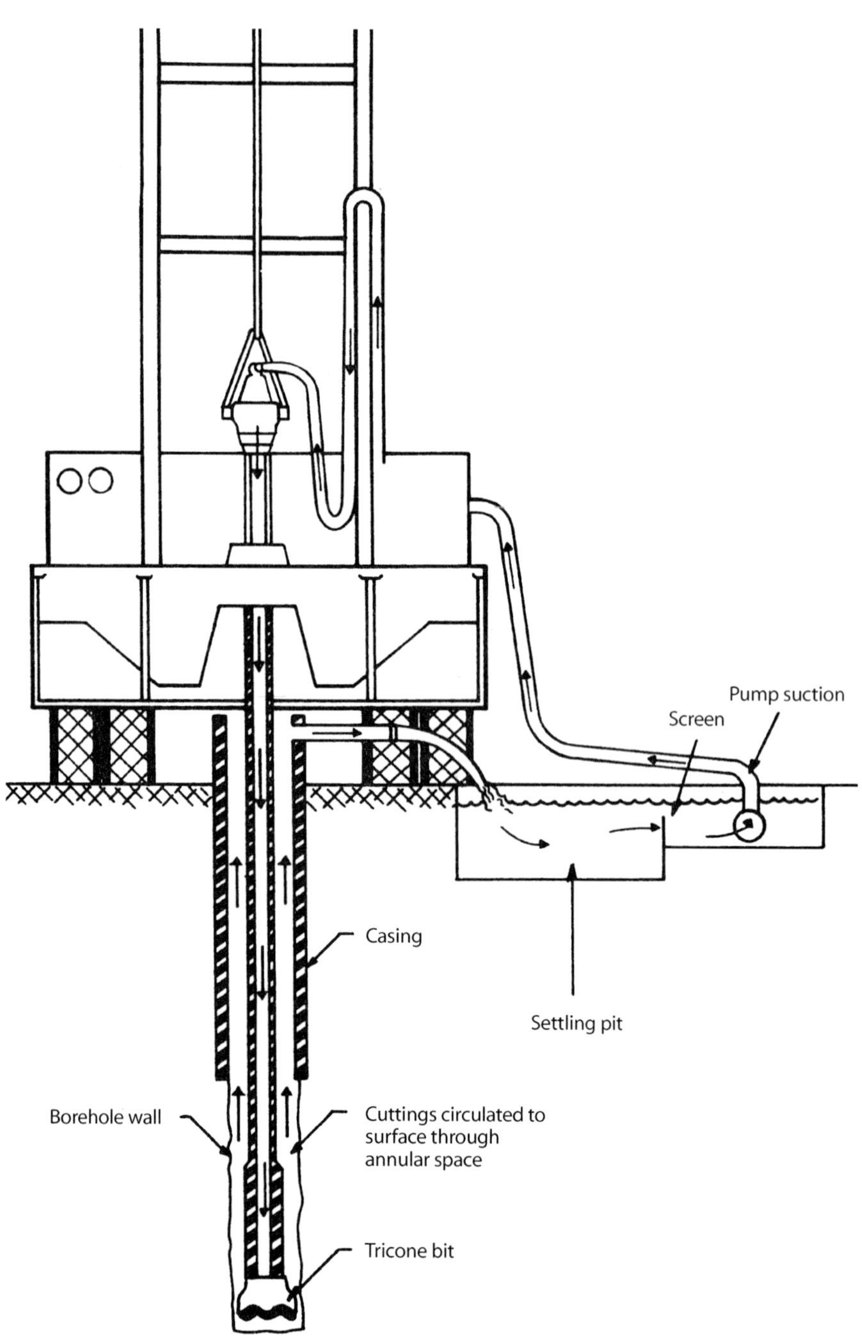
Pump suction
Screen
Casing
Settling pit
Borehole wall
Cuttings circulated to surface through annular space
Tricone bit

Fig. 6.19. Diagram of a rotary circulation system (National Water Well Association of Australia 1984)

is present, an oversized borehole can be drilled into rock and surface casing installed and grouted in place. After the grout sets, drilling can proceed using a tricone bit (Mobile Drilling Company 1988; Fig. 6.20a).

Teeth and insert cuttings elements come in varying shapes, sizes, and grades of tungsten carbide. The variety of cutting elements allows drillers to tailor products and address specific drilling conditions encountered (Fig. 6.20b). The S series bits have widely spaced, long, tapered teeth with broad, axial crests for the bottom hole action necessary to achieve high penetration rates. They are applied for softer geologic materials clays, shales, soft sandstones, and soft limestones. M series bits are designed with shorter, stronger teeth to withdraw the weight required for units of medium hardness, such as limestones, sandstones, and dolomites. H series bits have a heavy-gauge bevel and short, closely spaced teeth to withstand loads and heavy impacts. They are applied for hard shales, limestones, sandstones, and dolomites (Mobile Drilling Company 1988).

Samples can be collected either from the circulated fluid or by a core barrel that is inserted into the borehole.

The maximum diameter of the boreholes used for installation of test well is typically 30.5 cm. Unconsolidated deposits are sometimes drilled with drag- or fishtail-type bits, and consolidated units such as sandstone and shale are drilled with tricone bits. Where surface casing is installed, nominal 20.3 cm casing is typically used, and a 19.37 or 20 cm borehole is continued below the casing. In unconsolidated units, these diameters permit a maximum 10.2 cm diameter monitoring well to be installed, filter-packed and sealed in the open borehole. In consolidated units, a 11.75 cm outside diameter casing can be used in a 19.37 cm borehole because there are relatively few stability problems in the walls of boreholes in consolidated rock. The smaller annular space is usu-

Fig. 6.20a. Steel tricone bits (Mobile Drilling Company 1988)

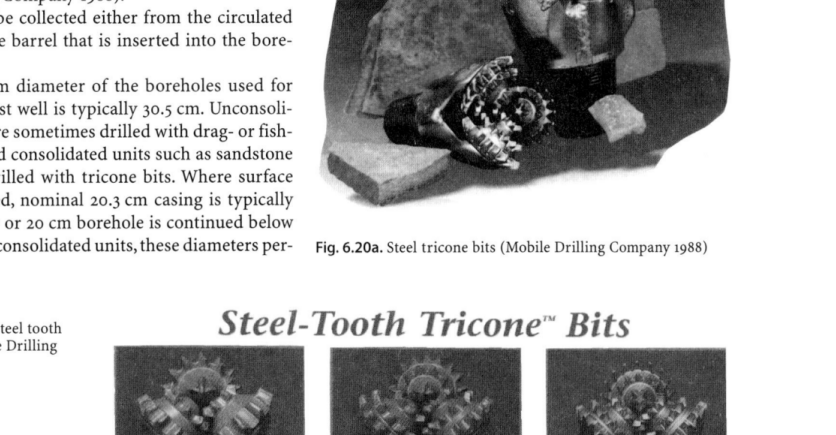

Fig. 6.20b. Different series of steel tooth tricone bits (Mobile Drilling Company 1988)

Steel-Tooth Tricone™ Bits

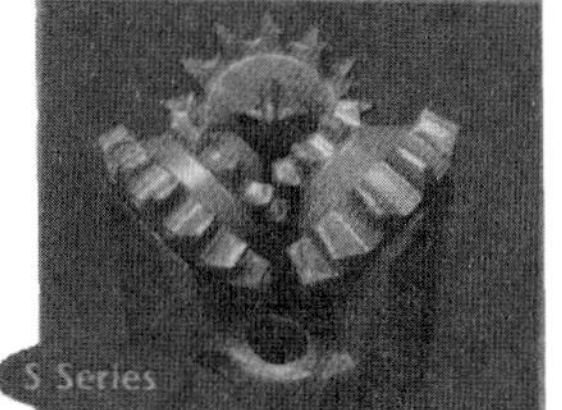
S Series

The S series has widely spaced, long, tapered teeth with broad, axial crests for the bottom-hole action necessary to achieve high penetration rates. Inter-fitted rows of teeth prevent formation packing and facilitate the cleaning action. The gauge bevel is hardfaced for wear resistance. Tungsten carbide hardfacing on the other critical areas of the S series cutting structure provides superior abrasive wear resistance and allows the teeth to self-sharpen.

Applications: Softer formations such as clays, shales, soft sandstones, and soft limestones.
Available in Rotablast and regular models.

Suggested Operating Parameters:
Weight on Bit - 1,000 to 3,000 lb per inch of diameter
RPM - 70 to 120 rpm.
IADC range - 111-142

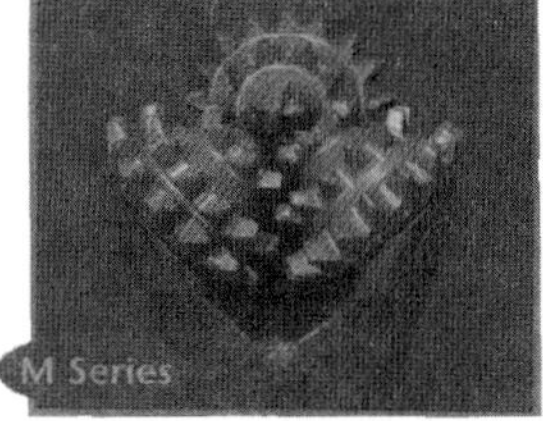
M Series

M series bits are designed with shorter, stronger teeth to withstand the weight required for these formations. The M series shirttail is overlaid with tungsten carbide hardfacing for abrasive wear resistance.

Applications: Medium formations, such as limestones, sandstones, and dolomites.

Suggested Operating Parameters:
Weight on Bit - 1,000 to 5,000 lb per inch of diameter
RPM - 60 tp 100 rpm
IADC code range - 211-242

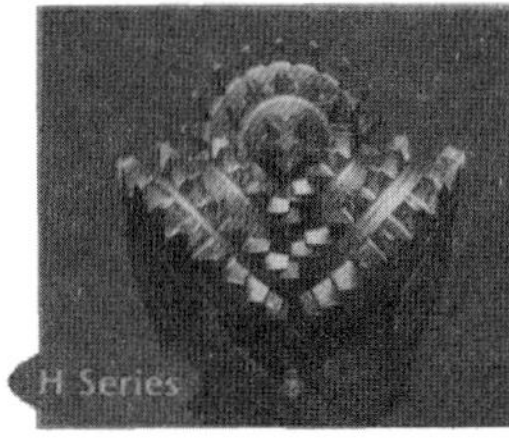
H Series

H series bits have a heavy-gauge bevel and short, closely spaced teeth to withstand heavier impact loads. Tungsten carbide hardfacing on the shirttail offers superior wear resistance. The H series has proven successful in drilling operations in which excessive gauge wear must be avoided.

Applications: Hard shale formations, limestones, sandstones, and dolomite formations.

Suggested Operating Parameters:
Weight on Bit - 4,000 to 7,000 lb per inch of diameter
RPM - 60 to 80 rpm.
IADC code range - 311-342.

ally sufficient to permit placement of filter pack, bentonite seal and grout by use of a tremie pipe (Table 6.7).

6.3.6.2 *Characteristics of Drilling Fluid*

The principal properties of water-based drilling fluids are (Driscoll 1986)

- density (weight),
- viscosity,
- yield point,
- gel strength,
- fluid-loss-control effectiveness, and
- lubricity (lubrication capacity).

Well construction uses only the simplest drilling fluid water and water added as a drilling fluid should be the best quality of water that is available. The chemical and bacteriological quality of this water must be determined by laboratory analyses in order to identify potential interference with substances being monitored (Petroleum Extension Service 1980).

When only "clean" water is circulated in the borehole, the water can pick up clay and silt that form a natural drilling mud. During this process, both the weight and viscosity of the drilling fluid increases. The degree of change in these properties depends on the nature of the geologic units being penetrated. It is possible to attain a maximum weight of approximately 1.32 kg l^{-1} when drilling in natural clays. The same, maximum weight can also be achieved by adding natural clays or bentonite to the water to make a drilling mud in locations where the geologic units do not naturally have these minerals.

Where additional weight is needed to maintain stability of the borehole, heavier additives are required. Barite (barium sulfate) is the most common material used for weight control of drilling muds. Pure barite has specific gravity of 4.25; the specific gravity of typical clay additives approximates 2.65. Figure 6.21 shows the range of drilling fluid densities that can be obtained by using a variety of different drilling additives (Driscoll 1986).

When the weight of the drilling fluid or the hydrostatic pressure in the borehole exceeds that of the aquifer, there is a loss of fluid from the borehole into the permeable zones. As fluid moves from the borehole into the lower pressure zones, fine particulate matter that has been incorporated during the drilling operation, plus any solids that have been added to the drilling fluid, can be deposited in the pore space of the zone being infiltrated. As a consequence, a "filter cake" is formed on the wall of the borehole. Where bentonitic drilling mud is being used, the filter cake can be impermeable and quite tough.

Another important property of a drilling fluid is viscosity. Viscosity is the resistance offered to flow. In combination with the velocity of the circulated fluid, viscosity controls the ability of the fluid to remove cuttings from the borehole. In test wells where water is the primary drilling fluid, the viscosity is the result of the interaction of water with the particulate matter that is drilled. Viscosity is also affected by the interaction of water with the clays that are sometimes added during the drilling process. Sodium montmorillonite (sodium bentonite) is the constituent most often added to increase viscosity.

Viscosity has no relationship to density. In the field, viscosity is measured by the time required for a known quantity of fluid to flow through an orifice of special

Table 6.7.
Applications and limitations of direct mud rotary drilling (U.S. Environmental Protection Agency 1989)

Applications	Limitations
Rapid drilling of clay, silt and reasonably compacted sand and gravel	Difficult to remove drilling mud and wall cake from outer perimeter of filter pack during development
Allows split-spoon and thin-wall sampling in unconsolidated materials	Bentonite or other drilling fluid additives may influence quality of ground-water samples
Allows core sampling in consolidated rock	Circulated (ditch) samples poor for monitoring well screen selection
Drilling rigs widely available	Split-spoon and thin-wall samplers are expensive and of questionable cost effectiveness at depths greater than 150 feet (45 m)
Abundant and flexible range of tool sizes and depth capabilities	Wireline coring techniques for sampling both unconsolidated and consolidated formations often not available locally
Very sophisticated drilling and mud programs available	Difficult to identify aquifers
Geophysical borehole logs	Drilling fluid invasion of permeable zones may compromise validity of subsequent test well samples

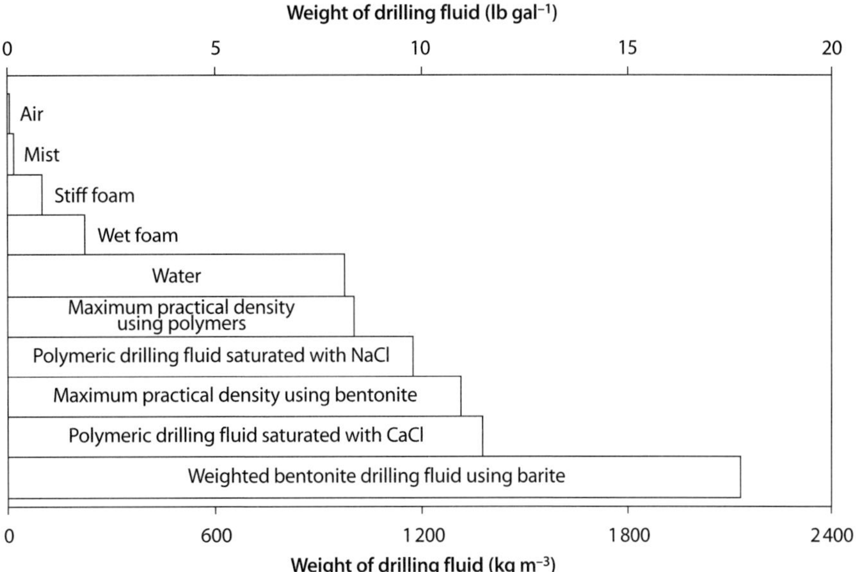
Weight of drilling fluid (lb gal^{-1})
0
5
10
15
20
Air
Mist
Stiff foam
Wet foam
Water
Maximum practical density using polymers
Polymeric drilling fluid saturated with NaCl
Maximum practical density using bentonite
Polymeric drilling fluid saturated with CaCl
Weighted bentonite drilling fluid using barite
0
600
1200
1800
2400
Weight of drilling fluid (kg m^{-3})

Fig. 6.21. Practical drilling fluid densities (Driscoll 1986)

dimensions. The instrument used for this measurement is called a marsh funnel. The relative viscosity of the drilling mud is described as the marsh funnel viscosity and measured in seconds. Table 6.8 presents the approximate marsh funnel viscosities required for drilling in typical unconsolidated materials. These typical values are based on the assumption that the pump circulating the drilling mud provides an adequate uphole velocity to clean cuttings from the borehole at these viscosities. For comparison, the marsh funnel viscosity of clear water at 70 °F (21.1 °C) is 26 seconds (Driscoll 1986).

Clays, including llite, chlorite, kaolinite and mixed-layer clay, have a relatively low capability to expand when saturated. The reason that sodium montmorillonite is so effective in increasing viscosity is because of its crystalline layered structure, its bonding characteristics, and the ease of hydration of the clay layers (NB: The smectite clays, including montmorillonite add "interlayer" water in the layers that contain sodium which has a weak bond with the Al-silicate layers.). Figure 6.22 (Petroleum Extension Service 1980) demonstrates the variation in the viscosity-building characteristics of a variety of clays. Wyoming bentonite (a natural sodium-rich montmorillonite) is shown at the extreme left. The effects of the type of water mixed with sodium bentonite is indicated by Fig. 6.23 that shows the variation in viscosity that results from using soft water in preparation of drilling mud (Driscoll 1986). Sodium montmorillonite is most commonly used as the viscosity-building clay. However, the calcium and magnesium ions in hard water, replace sodium cations in the montmorillonite structure. As a consequence, a much lower viscosity is obtained for a given quantity of solids added. Replacement of sodium cations is similar to the process that occurs in the subsurface when bentonitic materials are left as mudcake in the well. This process can have a profound influence on the quality of the ground-water samples collected from the test well.

Table 6.8. Approximate marsh funnel viscosities required for drilling in typical types of unconsolidated materials (Driscoll 1986)

Material drilled	Appropriate marsh funnel viscosity (seconds)
Fine sand	35–45
Medium sand	45–55
Coarse sand	55–65
Gravel	65–75
Coarse gravel	75–85

Yield point and gel strength are two additional properties that are considered in evaluating the characteristics of drilling mud. Yield point is a measure of the amount of pressure, after a shut down, that must be exerted by the pump upon restarting to cause the drilling fluid to start to flow. Gel strength is a measure of capability of the drilling fluid to maintain suspension of particulate matter in the mud column when the pump is shut down. There is a close relationship between viscosity, yield point, and gel strength. In monitoring well installation these properties are rarely controlled because the control of these properties requires the addition of additives that can impact the quality of the water produced by the completed well. They are important, however, in evaluating the reliability of samples taken from the mud stream. Where drilling fluid quality is uncontrolled, ditch samples are generally unreliable.

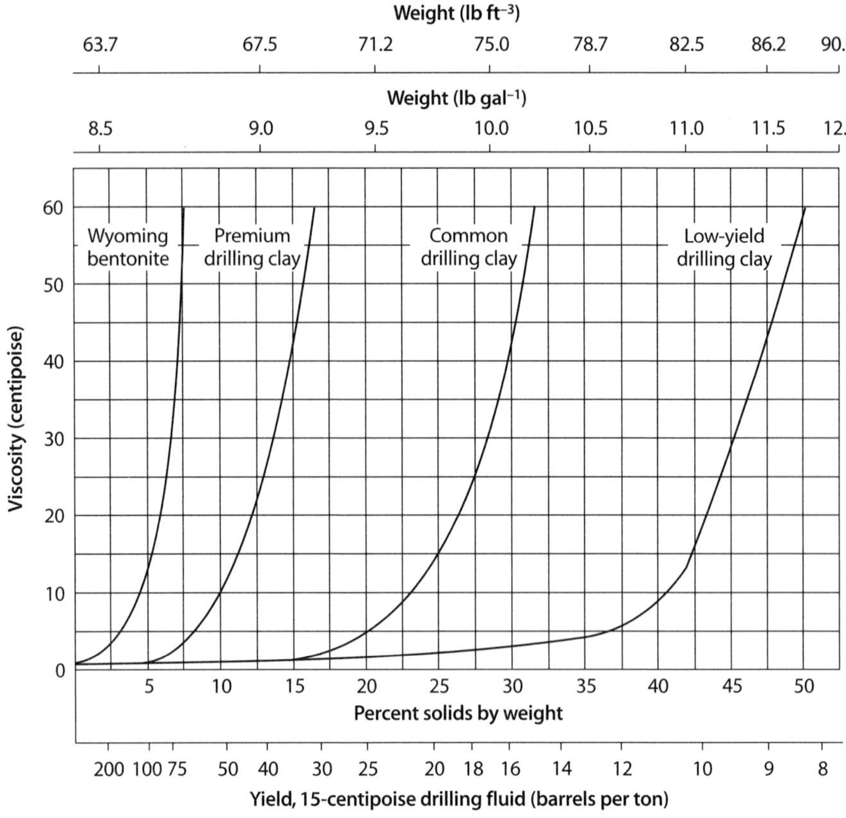
Weight (lb ft^{-3})
63.7 67.5 71.2 75.0 78.7 82.5 86.2 90.0
Weight (lb gal^{-1})
8.5 9.0 9.5 10.0 10.5 11.0 11.5 12.0
Wyoming bentonite
Premium drilling clay
Common drilling clay
Low-yield drilling clay
Viscosity (centipoise)
0 10 20 30 40 50 60
5 10 15 20 25 30 35 40 45 50
Percent solids by weight
200 100 75 50 40 30 25 20 18 16 14 12 10 9 8
Yield, 15-centipoise drilling fluid (barrels per ton)

Fig. 6.22. Viscosity-building characteristics of drilling clays (Petroleum Extension Service 1980)

6.3.6.3 *Influence of Drilling Fluid on the Construction of Monitoring Well*

Construction of a monitoring well can be limited to the use of simple water-based drilling fluids. This limitation is important so as not to influence the ground-water quality in the area of the well. Even when water-based fluids are used, many problems are created or exacerbated by the use of drilling fluids. These problems include: (1) fluid infiltration/flushing of the intended monitoring zone; (2) difficulties in well development (particularly where an artificial filter-pack has been installed); and (3) chemical, biological and physical reactivity of the drilling fluid with the indigenous fluids in the ground (U.S. Environmental Protection Agency 1975; Driscoll 1986).

As drilling fluid is circulated in the borehole during drilling operations, it can escape into the units being penetrated. Infiltration is more pronounced in the more permeable zones. As the permeable zones are of primary interest in the monitoring effort, the most "damage" can be inflicted on the zone of greatest concern. For example the chemistry of the water in the formation reacts with the infiltrate, then subsequent samples taken from this zone will not accurately reflect the conditions that are intended to be monitored. Every attempt should be made to remove drilling fluids from the targeted monitoring zone during the well-development process. This is accomplished by removing in sufficient quantities of formation water to recover all the infiltrate that may have penetrated into the unit.

6.3.6.4 *Mud-based Applications*

It is desirable to install test wells using the cleanest drilling water that is available. When drilling using either cable tool or hollow-stem augering techniques, it is sometimes necessary to add water to the borehole to continue drilling. The addition of water may be required to: (1) stabilize the borehole, (2) improve the cutting action of the bit, or (3) enable the driller to remove the cuttings from the borehole. With drive-and-bail and hollow-stem auger techniques, it may be necessary to add water to the borehole to minimize heaving of the unit upward into the casing or hollow stem. (U.S. Environmental Protection Agency 1989; Driscoll 1986).

When drilling mud is added during either cable tool drilling or hollow-stem augering, the effectiveness of the drilling fluid is enhanced by the addition of bentonite to the drilling mud. The bentonite is added to the borehole for stabilization of the subsurface units. When either clean water or clean water plus additives are added

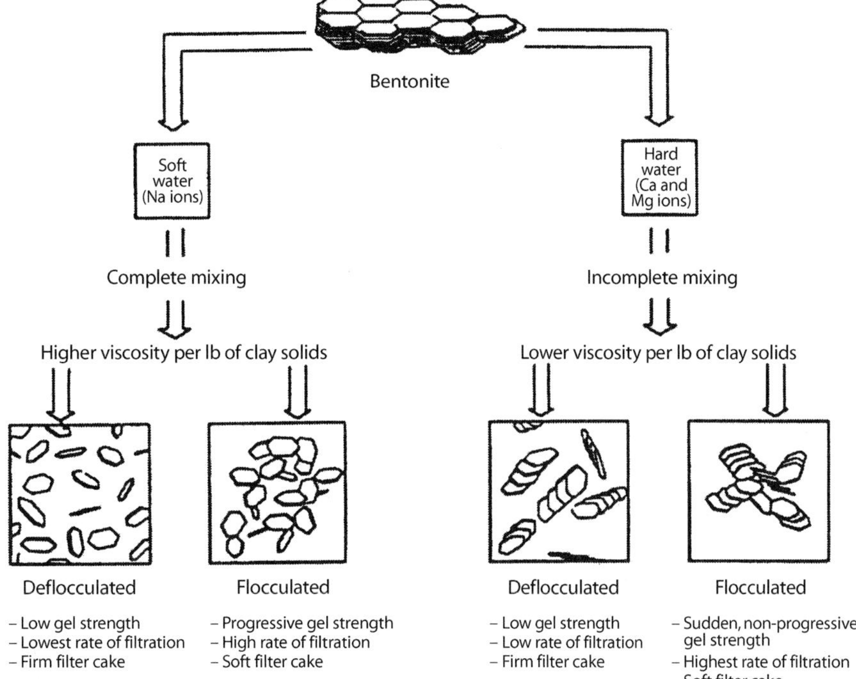
Bentonite
Soft water (Na ions)
Hard water (Ca and Mg ions)
Complete mixing
Incomplete mixing
Higher viscosity per lb of clay solids
Lower viscosity per lb of clay solids
Deflocculated
Flocculated
Deflocculated
Flocculated
- Low gel strength
- Lowest rate of filtration
- Firm filter cake
- Progressive gel strength
- High rate of filtration
- Soft filter cake
- Low gel strength
- Low rate of filtration
- Firm filter cake
- Sudden, non-progressive gel strength
- Highest rate of filtration
- Soft filter cake

Fig. 6.23. Schematic of the behavior of clay particles when mixed into water (Driscoll 1986)

to the borehole, the problems of flushing, potential contamination, and water-quality modification are the same as when using fluid rotary drilling. For these reasons, it is suggested that addition of drilling mud additives and/or even clean water be avoided when using cable tool or hollow-stem augers if at all possible.

6.3.6.5 *Air-based Drilling Fluids*

A variety of air-based drilling fluids are available (Driscoll 1986):

- air alone
- air mist
- air plus a small amount of water/perhaps a small amount of surfactant
- air foam
- stable foam – air plus surfactant
- stiff foam – air, surfactant plus polymer or bentonite
- aerated mud/water base – drilling fluid plus air

When a well is drilled using additives other than dry air, flushing, potential contamination and modification of water-quality are all of concern. Even with the use of dry air, there is the possibility that modification of the chemical environment may occur near the borehole due to changes in the oxidation/reduction potential induced by aeration. This may cause stripping of volatile organics from geologic material and ground water in the vicinity of the borehole. With time, stripping will diminish and disappear, but the time necessary for this to occur varies with the hydrogeologic conditions.

Where dry air is being used, a filter must be placed in the discharge line to remove lubricating oil. This particular variety of dry-air drilling has the potential to contaminate the subsurface with lubricating oil (U.S. Environmental Protection Agency 1989; Driscoll 1986).

Wells can be installed in bedrock using air as the circulation medium and employing roller-cone bits. Air can also be used successfully in unconsolidated material when applied in conjunction with a casing hammer or a dual-wall casing technique. For effective drilling, the air supply must be sufficient to lift the cuttings from the bottom of the borehole, up through the annular space and to the discharge point at the surface.

6.3.7 Air-Rotary Drilling

Air-rotary drilling is similar to mud rotary with the exception that the circulation medium is air instead of water or drilling mud. Air is compressed and circulated down through the drill rods and up the open hole. The rotary drill bit is attached to the lower end of the drill pipe, and the drill bit is advanced as in direct mud rotary drilling. As the bit cuts into the unit, cuttings are immediately removed from the bottom of the borehole and transported to the surface by the air that is circulating down through the drill pipe and up the annular space. The circulating air also cools the bit. When no water enters the borehole from the unit, penetration and sampling may be enhanced by adding small quantities of water and/or a foaming surfactant. Foam effectively removes the cuttings and lubricates and cools the bit. However, the drilling foam is not chemically inert and may react with the ground water. Even if the foam is removed during the development process, one may question whether a representative sample can be collected.

The diameter of the roller-cone or tricone bit used in air rotary drilling is limited to approximately 30.5 cm, although larger bits are available. For the down-the-hole hammer, the practical limitation is 20.3 cm nominal diameter. There is no significant depth limitation for monitoring well construction with the air rotary technique, with the possible exception of compressor capacity limits in deep holes with high water tables and back pressure.

Samples can be collected as the air discharges cuttings at the surface. When the penetrated unit is dry, the rock is pulverized by the bit, and samples are typically very fine-grained. This "dust" which represents the penetrated unit is difficult to evaluate in terms of its physical properties and characteristics. However, the size of the fragments that are discharged at the surface can be much larger when small quantities of water are encountered during drilling or when water and surfactant are added to the borehole to assist in the drilling process. The larger fragments provide excellent quality samples for interpretation. Because the borehole is cleaned continuously and all of the cuttings are discharged, there is minimal opportunity for re-circulation; and there is minimal contamination of the cuttings by previously drilled zones.

When drilling through relatively dry sediment, thick water-bearing zones can easily be observed as drilling proceeds. However, thin water-bearing zones are not identifiable, because either the pressure of the air in the borehole exceeds the hydraulic pressure of the water-bearing zone; or the combination and quantity of dust and air discharged is sufficient to remove the small amount of moisture from the thin water-bearing zone. Where thin zones are anticipated, the samples must be carefully evaluated and drilling must be slowed to reduce absorption of the water by the dust. It may be desirable to frequently stop drilling to allow ground water to enter the open borehole. Identification of both thin and thick water-bearing zones is extremely important because this information can assist in the placement of well intakes and/or in the selection of isolated zones for packer tests.

Air-rotary drilling is typically limited to drilling in consolidated rock because of borehole instability in unconsolidated material. In air-rotary drilling, no casing is used nor drilling fluid added to support the borehole walls. The borehole is held open by stability of the rock and/or the air pressure used during drilling. In unconsolidated materials, there is the tendency for the borehole to collapse during drilling. Therefore, air-rotary drilling in unconsolidated units is unreliable and poses a risk for equipment. Where sufficient thicknesses of unconsolidated deposits overlie a consolidated unit that will be drilled by air rotary techniques, surface casing through the unconsolidated material is installed by an alternative technique. Drilling can then be accomplished using air with either a roller-cone bit or down-the-hole hammer (Ingersoll-Rand 1976, 1985, 1988).

Boreholes drilled by air rotary methods are typically installed as open-hole completions. Because the borehole is uncased, the potential exists for cross-connection between water-bearing zones within the borehole. Further, the re-circulated air effectively cleans cuttings from the borehole walls so that the borehole is usually not coated with a mud cake, such as occurs with mud rotary drilling or with augering techniques. This cleaner borehole wall increases the potential for cross connection, but increases the effectiveness of well completion and development.

The air introduced during drilling may strip volatile organic compounds from the samples taken during drilling, and from the ground water in the vicinity of the borehole. The time of recovery from the effects of air-stripping will diminish and disappear with time and vary with the hydrogeologic conditions. The importance of these factors should be evaluated before choosing the air-rotary drilling technique.

A summary of applications and limitations of air rotary drilling is found in Table 6.9.

6.3.8 Air Rotary With Casing Driver

This method is an adaptation of air-rotary drilling that uses a casing-driving technique in concert with air (or mud) rotary drilling. The addition of a casing driver makes it possible to use air rotary drilling techniques in unconsolidated material. The casing driver is installed in the mast of a top-head-drive air-rotary drilling rig. The casing can then be driven as the drill bit is advanced (Aardvark Corporation 1977; Fig. 6.24).

The normal drilling procedure is to extend the drill bit 15.2 to 30.5 cm ahead of the casing. The distance that the drill bit can be extended beyond the casing is primarily a function of the stability of the borehole wall. It is also possible to drive the casing ahead of the bit. This procedure can be performed in unconsolidated sediments where caving and an oversize borehole are of concern. After the casing has been driven approximately 30.5 cm, the drill bit is used to clean the material from inside the casing. This technique also minimizes air or mud contact with the strata (Driscoll 1986).

In air-rotary drilling through unconsolidated material and into consolidated bed rock, the casing is advanced simultaneously with the drill bit. Drilling can

Table 6.9. Applications and limitations of air-rotary drilling (U.S. Environmental Protection Agency 1989)

Applications	Limitations
Rapid drilling of semi-consolidated and consolidated rock	Surface casing frequently required to protect top of hole
Good quality/reliable formation samples (particularly if small quantities of water and surfactant are used)	Drilling restricted to semi- consolidated and consolidated formations
Equipment generally available	Samples reliable but occur as small particles that are difficult to interpret
Allows easy and quick identification of lithologic changes	Drying effect of air may mask lower yield water producing zones
Allows identification of most water-bearing zones	Air stream requires contaminant filtration
Allows estimation of yields in strong water-producing zones with short "down time"	Air may modify chemical or biological conditions; recovery time is uncertain

proceed by the standard air rotary technique when the casing has been driven into the top of the bedrock. The air rotary in combination with a casing driver is particularly efficient where drilling through heterogeneous glacial deposits. The sand-gravel-silt-boulder-type materials that commonly occur in glaciated regions. The sandy and/or gravelly, unstable zones are supported by the casing while the boulder zones and tills are rapidly penetrated by the rotary bit. The potential for inter-aquifer cross-contamination is minimized, because all zones within the glacial deposits are cased as the borehole is advanced.

The protective casing also permits the collection of reliable samples because the entire hole is cased, except for the interval of active drilling. An additional advantage of the drill-through casing driver is that the same equipment can be used to list the casing and expose the well intake, after the casing and a well intake have been installed in the borehole.

As with the direct air-rotary method, water in aquifer zones that have low hydrostatic pressure may be inhibited from entering the borehole by the air pressure exerted by the drilling process. Additionally, the dust created as the rock is pulverized and can serve to seal off water bearing zones, and may not be identified (Table 6.10).

6.3.9 Dual-Wall Reverse Circulation

In dual-wall reverse-circulation rotary drilling the circulating fluid is pumped down between the outer casing and the inner drill pipe, out through the drill bit, and up the inside of the drill pipe (Fig. 6.25). Water or air is the circulation fluid used in the dual-wall reverse-circulation method. The inner pipe (drill pipe) rotates the bit, and the outer pipe acts as casing. Similar to method of the air rotary with a casing driver, the outer pipe stabilizes the borehole, minimizes cross-contamination of cuttings, and minimizes cross-contamination between water bearing zones within the borehole.

The dual-wall reverse-circulation rotary method is one of the techniques available for obtaining representative and continuous formation samples while drilling. If the drill bit is a roller-cone, the drill bit is only a few inches ahead of the double-wall pipe. The samples circulated to the surface are representative of a very short section of the subsurface unit. When drilling with air, a representative sample of a thin zone can be obtained from the material and/or the water-bearing zone. Water samples can only be obtained where the sediment has sufficient hydrostatic pressure to overcome the air pressure and dust dehydration/sealing effects (Driscoll 1986).

Unconsolidated materials can be penetrated quite readily with the dual-wall reverse-circulation method. Sediments that contain boulders or coarse gravelly materials are difficult to drill, and can be penetrated relatively easily with this technique. The increased efficiency is due to the ability to maximize the energy at the bottom of the borehole while the dual-wall system eliminates problems with lost circulation and/or borehole stability.

An in-line filter must be used to remove oil or other impurities from the air-stream when drilling with air and a tricone bit. However, oil is required in the air-stream to lubricate the hammer when using a down-the-hole hammer method. If oil or other introduced contaminants are of concern, the use of a down-the-hole hammer may not be advisable.

When the borehole has been advanced to the desired depth, the well can be installed by either inserting a small-diameter casing and well intake through an open-mouth bit (Driscoll 1986), or by removing the outer casing prior to installation of the monitoring well and installing the monitoring well in the open borehole. When installing a casing through the bit, the maximum diameter casing that can be installed is approximately 10.2 cm.

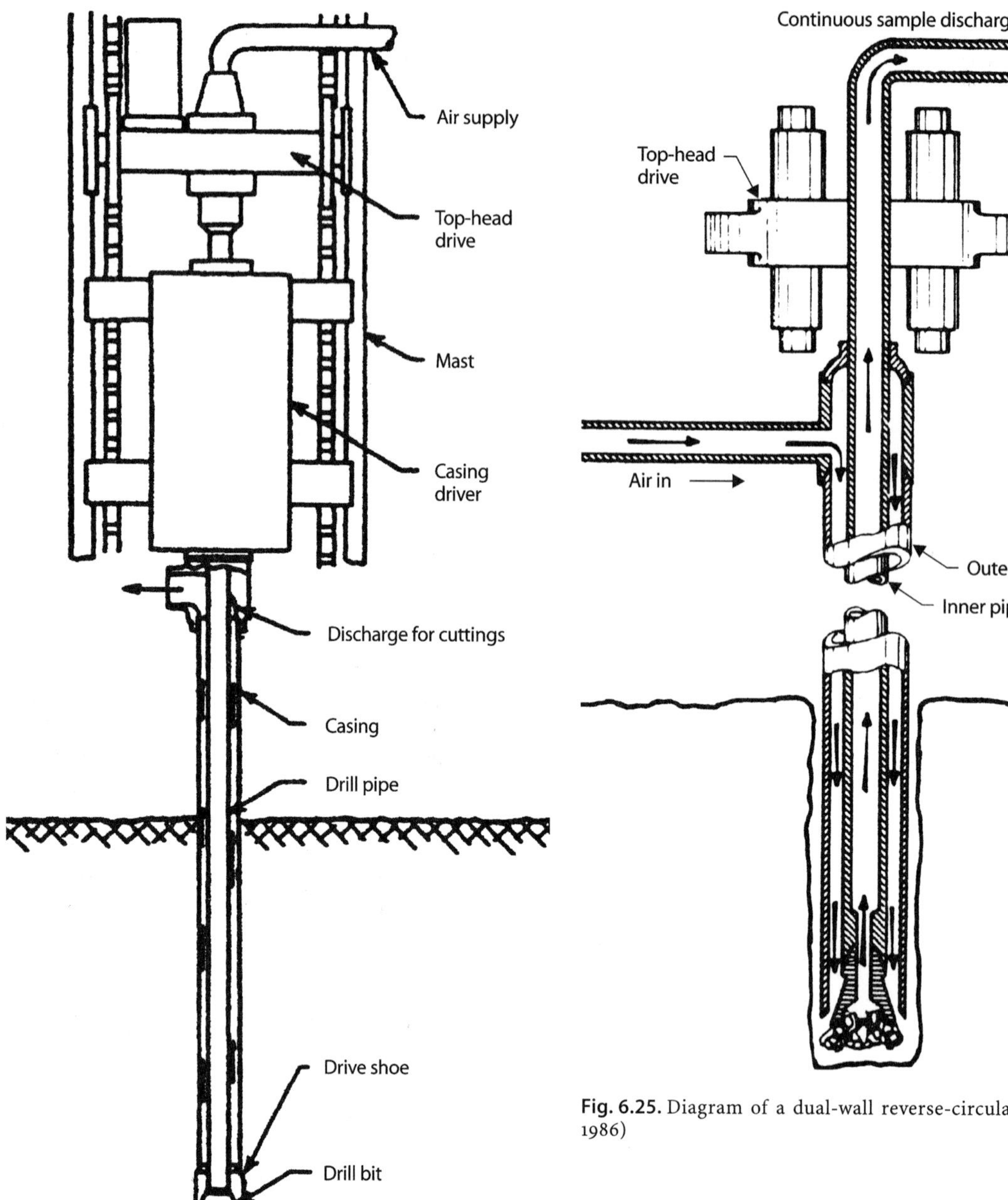
Air supply
Top-head drive
Mast
Casing driver
Discharge for cuttings
Casing
Drill pipe
Drive shoe
Drill bit
Continuous sample discharge
Top-head drive
Air in
Outer pipe
Inner pipe

Fig. 6.24. Diagram of a drill-through casing driver (Aardvark Corporation 1977)

Fig. 6.25. Diagram of a dual-wall reverse-circulation (Driscoll 1986)

This is controlled by the 25.4 cm maximum borehole size that available with existing drill pipe and a maximum diameter of the bit. The borehole must be stable to permit completion in an open-hole (Table 6.11).

6.3.10 Cable Tool Drilling Method (Cable Tool Percussion)

Cable tool drilling is the oldest drilling technology. Prior to development of the mud rotary technique, cable tools were the standard technology used for almost all forms of drilling, salt water, water mineral oil and gas construction.

The cable tool percussion method carries out the drilling operation by lifting and dropping regularly a heavy string of drilling tools in the borehole. The drill bit breaks or crushes hard rock into small fragments and loosens the material if working in soft, unconsolidated rocks. The reciprocating action of the tools mixes the crushed or loosened particles with water to form a slurry or sludge. The resulting slurry is removed at intervals from the borehole by means of a sand pump or bailer.

A full string of drilling tools consists of four items: the drill bit, drill stem, drilling jars, and rope socket. The drill stem gives additional weight to the bit and the ef-

Table 6.10.
Applications and limitations of air rotary with casing driver drilling (U.S. Environmental Protection Agency 1989)

Applications	Limitations
Rapid drilling unconsolidated sands, silts and clays	Thin, low pressure water-bearing zones easily overlooked if drilling not stopped at appropriate places to observe whether or not water levels are recovering
Drilling in alluvial material (including boulder formations)	Samples pulverized as in all rotary drilling
Casing supports borehole thereby maintaining borehole integrity and minimizing inter-aquifer cross contamination	Air may modify chemical or biological conditions; recovery time is uncertain
Eliminates circulation problems common with direct mud rotary method	
Good formation samples	
Minimal formation damage as casing pulled back (smearing of clays and silts can be anticipated)	

Table 6.11.
Applications and limitations of dual-wall reverse-circulation rotary drilling (U.S. Environmental Protection Agency 1989)

Applications	Limitations
Very rapid drilling through both unconsolidated and consolidated formations	Limited borehole size that limits diameter of monitoring wells
Allows continuous sampling in all types of formations	In unstable formations, well diameters are limited to approximately 4 inches (10.2 cm)
Very good representative samples can be obtained with minimal risk of contamina tion of sample and/or water-bearing zone	Equipment availability more common in the southwest
In stable formations, wells with diameters as large as 6 inches (15.2 cm) can be installed in open hole completions	Air may modify chemical or biological conditions; recovery time is uncertain
	Unable to install filter pack unless completed open hole

fect of its added length helps to maintain a straight hole when drilling in hard rock. The jars consist of a pair of linked steel bars and are used to jar the tools loose when the bit is apt to stick or become wedged. The rope socket connects the string of tools to the cable. In addition, its weight supplies part of the energy of the upward blows by the jars when their use becomes necessary. The elements of the tool string are screwed together with threaded tool joints of standard API designs and dimensions.

When drilling in hard rock or sediment, the bit pounds a hole into the rock and the cuttings are periodically excavated from the borehole by removing the drill bit and inserting a bailer. The bailer is a bucket made from sections of thin-wall pipe with a valve on bottom that is actuated by the weight of the bailer. The valve may be either of a flat pattern or a ball-and-tongue pattern called a dart valve. A bail handle at the top of this tool provides the means of suspending it from a cable referred to as the sand line (Fig. 6.26; Bollenbach 1975).

The bailer is fed into the borehole on a separate line. The bailer will not function unless there is sufficient water in the borehole to slurry the mixture of cuttings in water. If enough water is present, the bailer picks up the cuttings through the valve on the bottom of the bailer and is hoisted to the surface. The cuttings are discharged from either the top or bottom of the bailer, and a sample of the cuttings can be collected. If the cuttings are not removed from the borehole, the bit constantly re-drills the same material, and the drilling effort becomes very inefficient (Buckeye Drill Company/Bucyrus Erie Company 1982).

When drilling unconsolidated deposits comprised primarily of sand silt and clay, the drilling action is very similar to that described previously. Water must be added to the borehole if the material encountered during drilling does not produce a sufficient quantity of water to slurry the mud and silt. If the borehole is not stable or causes caving, casing can be driven as the bit advances to maintain the wall of the borehole.

When drilling unconsolidated deposits comprised primarily of water-bearing sands and gravels, an alternate and more effective drilling technique is available for cable tool operations. In the "drive and bail" technique, casing is driven into unconsolidated material approximately 0.9 to 1.5 m, and the bailer is used to bail the cuttings from within the casing.

These cuttings provide excellent samples because the casing serves, in effect, as a large thin-wall sampler. Although the sample is "disturbed", the sample is representative because the bailer has the capability of picking up all sizes of rock particles.

When drilling by the drive and bail technique, "heaving" of material from the bottom of the casing upward may present a problem. When heaving occurs, samples are not representative of the material penetrated by the casing. Instead, samples represent a mixture of materials from the zone immediately beneath the drill pipe. Heaving occurs when the hydrostatic pressure on the outside of the casing exceeds the pressure on the inside of the casing. The heaving is exacerbated by the action of the drill bit and by the action of the bailer that is used to take the samples. If the bailer is lifted or "spudded" rapidly, suction can develop that can pull the material up into the casing. This problem is particularly prevalent when the drill advances from a dense material into relatively unconsolidated sand and gravel that is under a great hydrostatic pressure.

Several techniques have been developed to offset the problem of heaving. These techniques include:

- maintaining the casing full of water as it is driven and as the well is bailed. The column of water in the casing creates a higher hydrostatic head within the casing than is present in the surrounding material;
- maintaining a "plug" inside the casing when the samples are taken with the bailer. The plug is created by collecting samples with the bailer between 0.31 and 0.9 m above the bottom of the casing. The plug in the bottom of the "borehole" offsets heaving when the pressure differential is low;
- overdriving the casing through the zone that has the tendency to heave;
- adding drilling mud to the borehole until the weight of the mud and slurred material in the casing exceed the hydrostatic pressure of the heaving zone. This option is the least desirable because it adds drilling mud to the borehole and decreases efficiency of the drill bit.

If it is necessary to maintain a slurry in the casing to control heaving, it is still possible to collect both disturbed and undisturbed samples from beneath the casing by inserting smaller-diameter drill rods and samplers inside the casing at selected intervals. Sample descriptions of these samples become a "real art" as well as knowing the expected stratigraphic sequence and identifying first appearances of material being drilled through.

Cable tool drilling has become less prevalent in the last 25 years because the rate of penetration is slower than either rotary techniques in hard consolidated rock, or augering techniques in unconsolidated material. Because cable tool drilling is much slower, it is generally more expensive. Cable tool drilling is still important in monitoring well applications because of the versatility of the method. Cable tool rigs can be used to drill both the hardest and the softest geologic units. Cable tool rigs can drill boreholes with a diameter suitable to fulfill the needs of a monitoring well network. There is no significant depth limitation for the installation of monitoring wells.

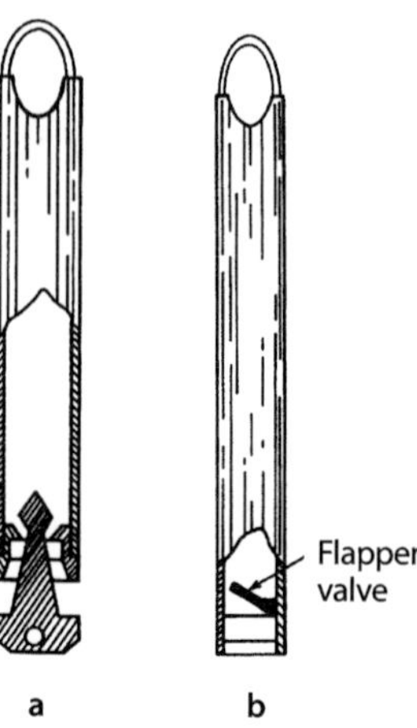
Flapper valve
a
b

Fig. 6.26. Diagrams of two types of bailers; **a** dart valve; **b** flat bottom (U.S. Environmental Protection Agency 1989)

When comparing cable tool to other drilling technologies, cable tool drilling may be the desired method. In a carefully drilled cable tool borehole, thin individual zones and changes in lithology are more easily identified than with alternative technologies. For example, smearing along sidewalls in unconsolidated sediment is generally less severe and the well cake is thinner than with hollow-stem augering. Therefore, the prospect of a successful completion in a thin water-bearing zone is generally enhanced.

6.3.11 Other Drilling Methods

Two other drilling techniques that are commonly available to install monitoring wells are: (1) bucket auger, and (2) reverse circulation rotary. Bucket augers are primarily used for large-diameter borings for foundations and footings for buildings. Reverse-circulation rotary is used primarily for the installation of large-diameter, deep, water wells.

While either of these technologies can be used for installation of monitoring wells, the diameters of the boreholes and the size of the required equipment normally preclude them from such applications. Unless an extraordinarily large diameter well is being installed, the size of the zone disturbed by the large diameter hole excavated by either of these techniques, severely compromises the data acquisition process carried out in sampling of monitoring wells. While either of these techniques have possible application for installation of monitoring wells, they are not considered to be valid for application.

6.4 Drilling Rigs and Drilling Tools

Spiral drill collars – In deep-hole drilling or drilling in deviated or directional holes, spiral drilling collars are designed to minimize the risk of the collar sticking in the hole by reducing the surface area, which comes in contact with the hole wall. Three spiral grooves run the length of the collar to within 61 cm of each end, allowing adequate room for tongs and for re-threading, should the need arise.

The following are some drilling tools and drilling rigs that are used to meet today's drilling requirements in the USA:

OMSCO Drill Pipe – OMSCO Drill Pipe and Tool Joints are manufactured from steel and according to standard API specifications of tool jointed drill pipes and API grades and upsets.

All OMSCO Tool Joints are completely thread gauged and magnetic particle inspected, shot blasted, phoscoated (anti-galling treatment), and hardness tested (Fig. 6.27).

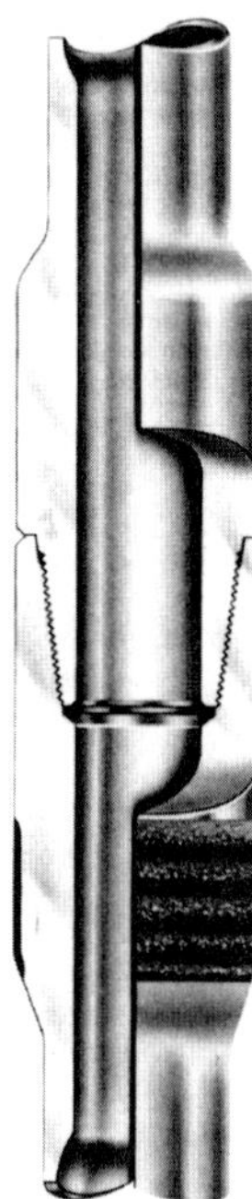

Fig. 6.27. OMSCO drill pipe

Drills:

1. *Mobile Drill/Model B-31* controls drilling operations because of compact, field proven, and its versatile design (Mobile Drilling Company 1988; Fig. 6.28).
2. *Model B-24 Surveyor* is a hydraulic model designed and tested on remote sites. It is a versatile low-maintenance full-range exploration rig that meets the worldwide demand for drilling in areas normally inaccessible to conventional machines. It is very adequate for soils and rock investigation, mineral exploration, piezometer installation, aggregate exploration, test coring permafrost, seismic and cathodic work, percolation test holes, shallow water wells, asphalt/coring seabed sampling (Mobile Drilling Company 1988; Fig. 6.29).
3. *Barber DR series drill* is the dual rotary series (DR) that utilizes a lower rotary table to rotate and drive casing through unconsolidated overburden such as gravel, sand, and boulders. The top rotary head simultaneously handles a drill string equipped with a down hole hammer, drag bit or rolling cone bit to drill inside or ahead through the casing.

   A patented carbide studded shoe welded on the bottom casing to cut its way through suspended boulders and into bedrock with no requirement for under reaming.
4. *Cyclone Top-Head Drive rigs* are ideal for dual-tube drilling (or double-wall pipe system) as they can be adapted to accept the dual-tube system, easily and at little expense. The dual-tube drill pipe consists of two tubes, one within the other, as shown in Fig. 6.30. The hole cleaning air or fluid is forced down the annulus. Between the inner and outer pipes to the drill bit, where it sweeps the cuttings back up through the center tube at high velocity (Ingersoll-Rand 1988). The Cyclone Top-Head Drive rigs are useful for obtaining uncontaminated and continuous sampling, faster penetration and lower operating costs as well as straighter holes (Mobile Drilling Company 1988; Fig. 6.30).

6.5 Design and Completion of Wells

6.5.1 Design Planning of Wells

The first step in planning a well is to get enough geologic and engineering information for the well site and for any previously constructed wells in the area. The well designer should know the anticipated, maximum total-depth; the lithologic sequence to be penetrated; the approximate location of the well; and the thickness and lithology of aquifers and confining intervals. The well designer should also have information regarding the bit records, drilling mud records, casing and cementing programs, and the driller's logs and drilling time-logs from other holes drilled in the area. Records of previous wells drilled in the area should be carefully studied, to include

Model B-31
68" (1730 mm) feed cylinder
Gasoline or Diesel Engine
Vehicle PTO Power
centralized
adjustable
control panel
5-speed forward/reverse
transmission
vane type
hydraulic
motor
hollow spindle
rotary table
LIFELINE® safety
power shut-off
MOBILE
DRILL®
Mobile custom body
LIFELINE® safety
power shut-off
90° universal auger coupling
with quick change adaptor
manual stabilizing
jacks
(Hydraulic optional)

Fig. 6.28.
Model B-31

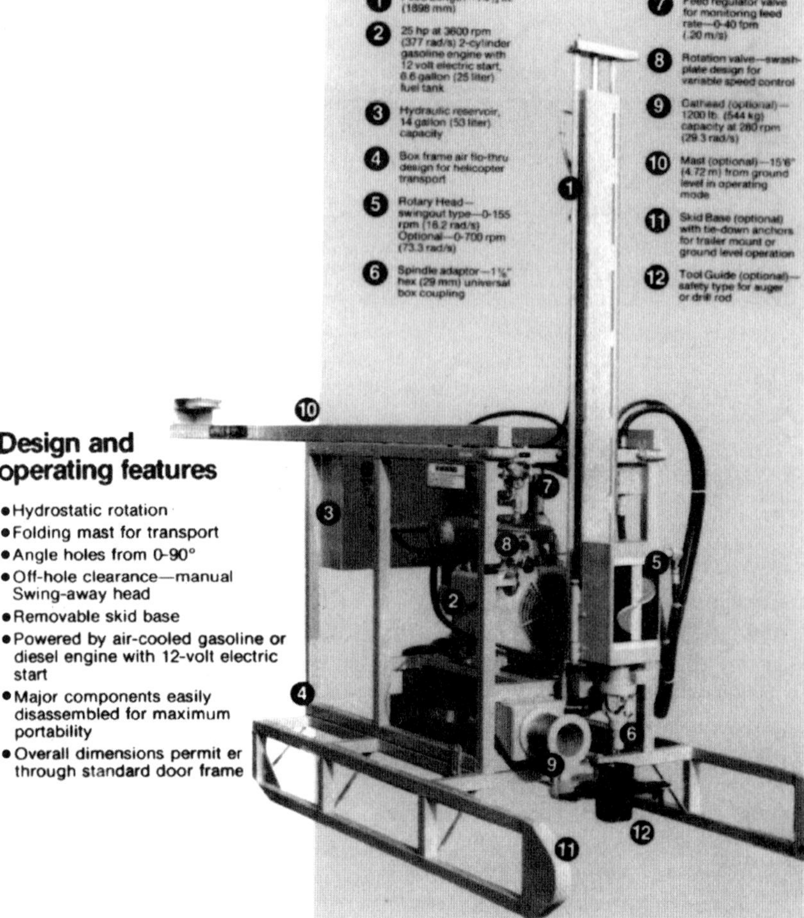
1 Feed Length—74¾ in. (1898 mm)
2 25 hp at 3600 rpm (377 rad/s) 2-cylinder gasoline engine with 12 volt electric start, 6.6 gallon (25 liter) fuel tank
3 Hydraulic reservoir, 14 gallon (53 liter) capacity
4 Box frame air flo-thru design for helicopter transport
5 Rotary Head—swingout type—0-155 rpm (16.2 rad/s) Optional—0-700 rpm (73.3 rad/s)
6 Spindle adaptor—1⅛" hex (29 mm) universal box coupling
7 Feed regulator valve for monitoring feed rate—0-40 fpm (.20 m/s)
8 Rotation valve—swash-plate design for variable speed control
9 Cathead (optional)—1200 lb. (544 kg) capacity at 280 rpm (29.3 rad/s)
10 Mast (optional)—15'6" (4.72 m) from ground level in operating mode
11 Skid Base (optional) with tie-down anchors for trailer mount or ground level operation
12 Tool Guide (optional)—safety type for auger or drill rod
Design and operating features
• Hydrostatic rotation
• Folding mast for transport
• Angle holes from 0-90°
• Off-hole clearance—manual Swing-away head
• Removable skid base
• Powered by air-cooled gasoline or diesel engine with 12-volt electric start
• Major components easily disassembled for maximum portability
• Overall dimensions permit er through standard door frame

Fig. 6.29.
Model B-24 surveyor

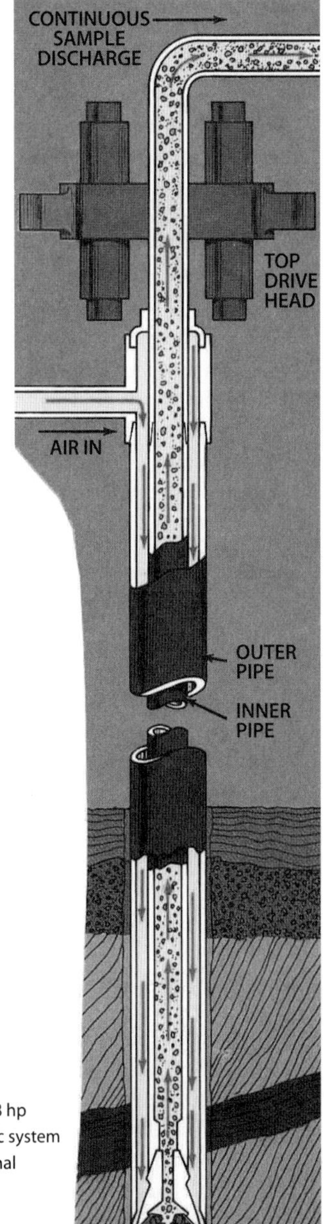
CONTINUOUS SAMPLE DISCHARGE
TOP DRIVE HEAD
AIR IN
OUTER PIPE
INNER PIPE

Fig. 6.30.
Cyclone top-head

- High capacity air compressor – 825 cfm @ 350 psi with clutch
- Maneuverable, diesel powered, tandem rear axle truck
- Rugged, single reduction, top head drive – 80 500 in., lbs, torque, 118 hp
- Reliable, fuel efficient deck engine powers compressor and hydraulic system
- Multipurpose drilling can be equipped with a great variety of optional accessories
- Compact design is light weight and highly mobile
- Load sensing open loop hydraulic system for ease of operation and fuel savings

information about zones of lost circulation, zones of abnormal hole enlargements, and zones in which deviation of the hole occurred; drill-pipe lost or stuck in the hole.

6.5.2 Well Completion

6.5.2.1 *Scope*

It is important to plan for the proper method of bottom-hole completion. In general, the methods for well completion can be categorized according to the competence of the units in which these wells are completed. Competent rock types include limestones, dolomites, and consolidated sandstones that will stand unsupported in a borehole. Incompetent units include unconsolidated sands and gravels, which cave readily into the borehole if not artificially supported. Of course, there are intermediate cases of geologic materials that require different treatment during planning of a well.

Most of the wells are completed mainly by one of the following three methods:

1. Open-hole completions are commonly used in wells penetrating hard rocks, where all of the unit is water bearing, or used to receive wastewater. Casing and screen are not subjected to potential corrosive action of the formation water or of injected waste.
2. Screen and gravel-pack are used for wells in areas where partially consolidated or unconsolidated sands are the producing aquifers, or the injection intervals selected to receive wastewater (Fig. 6.31a).
3. Fully cased and cemented wells can be installed in either competent or somewhat incompetent geologic interval. The production casing or the injection casing is installed through the full depth of the well, and selected intervals are then opened by perforating the casing and cemented zones using a series of solid projectiles or small shaped explosive charges (Fig. 6.31b).

Most wastewater injection wells are constructed with screened injection tubing inside a long string of casing and with a packer set between the tubing and the casing near the bottom of the casing (Fig. 6.31c).

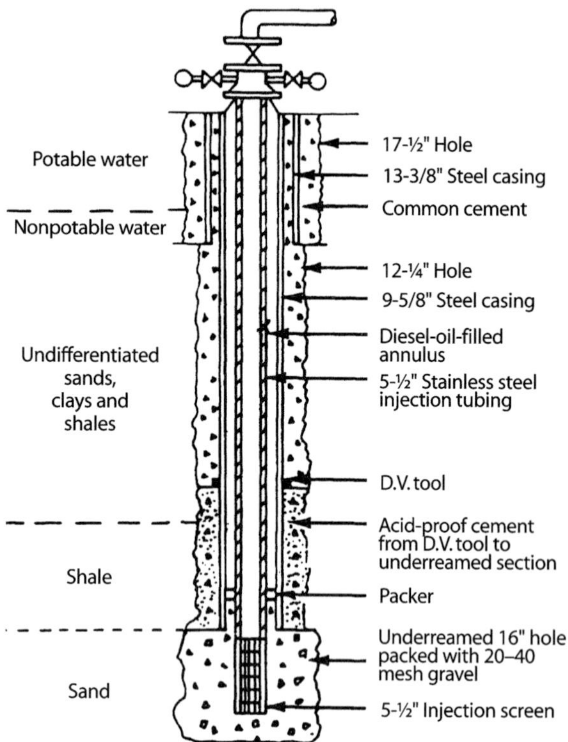
Potable water
Nonpotable water
Undifferentiated sands, clays and shales
Shale
Sand
17-½" Hole
13-3/8" Steel casing
Common cement
12-¼" Hole
9-5/8" Steel casing
Diesel-oil-filled annulus
5-½" Stainless steel injection tubing
D.V. tool
Acid-proof cement from D.V. tool to underreamed section
Packer
Underreamed 16" hole packed with 20–40 mesh gravel
5-½" Injection screen

Fig. 6.31a. Example of bottom-hole completion by screen and gravel-pack method (Barlow 1972; U.S. Environmental Protection Agency 1977)

6.5.2.2 *Well Completion in Limestone Aquifers*

Most water wells completed in limestone, produce from secondary porosity along fracture zones or bedding planes, and result in some drilling problems; e.g. loss of circulation of the drilling fluid during penetration of fractured limestones may result in problems in setting casing or in completing the hole to the desired depth after setting casing. One of the techniques to overcome loss of circulation is to re-circulate drill cuttings and plug the limestone before drilling reached the water producing zones. Another successful technique to plug lost circulation zones is to cement some sections of the hole prior to cementing setting.

In general, screens in limestones are only used as stabilizers and to keep collapse breccia from damaging the pump. Well completion in limestone, slotted black iron pipe is most commonly used as a screen, unless corrosive conditions in the water warrant some other type of material (Alsay-Pippin Corporation 1980).

Waste injection wells both chemical and effluent waste injection wells completed in limestone formations are generally constructed in the same manner as any other well with a few exceptions due to U.S. EPA regulations.

6.5.2.3 *Well Completion in Granular Aquifers*

Water wells completed in unconsolidated materials are screened wells that fall into two categories: naturally developed and gravel-packed wells. In a naturally developed well used for municipal or industrial applications, small slot openings in the screen are used, and the well is much more subject to failure through the ef-

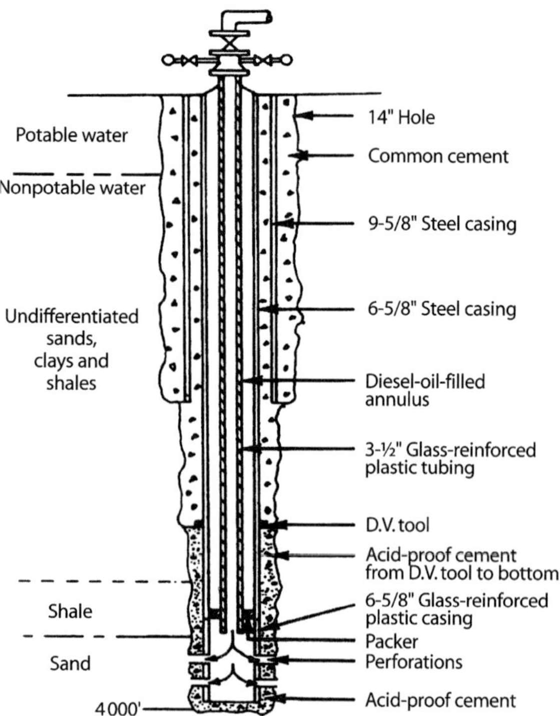
Potable water
Nonpotable water
Undifferentiated sands, clays and shales
Shale
Sand
4000'
14" Hole
Common cement
9-5/8" Steel casing
6-5/8" Steel casing
Diesel-oil-filled annulus
3-½" Glass-reinforced plastic tubing
D.V. tool
Acid-proof cement from D.V. tool to bottom
6-5/8" Glass-reinforced plastic casing
Packer
Perforations
Acid-proof cement

Fig. 6.31b. Example of bottom-hole completion by fully cased and perforated methods method (Barlow 1972; U.S. Environmental Protection Agency 1977)

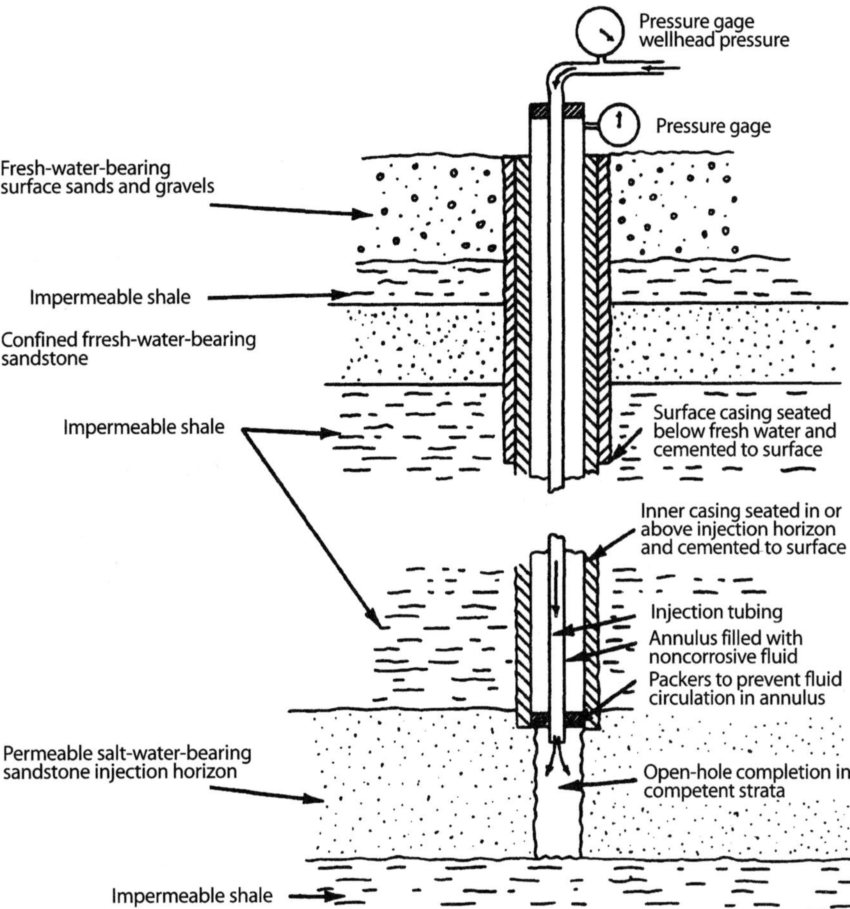
Pressure gage
wellhead pressure
Pressure gage
Fresh-water-bearing
surface sands and gravels
Impermeable shale
Confined frresh-water-bearing
sandstone
Impermeable shale
Surface casing seated
below fresh water and
cemented to surface
Inner casing seated in or
above injection horizon
and cemented to surface
Injection tubing
Annulus filled with
noncorrosive fluid
Packers to prevent fluid
circulation in annulus
Permeable salt-water-bearing
sandstone injection horizon
Open-hole completion in
competent strata
Impermeable shale

Fig. 6.31c. Schematic diagram of an industrial waste injection well completed in competent sandstone (modified after Warner 1985; U.S. Environmental Protection Agency 1977)

fects of iron bacteria or incrustation than the gravel packed construction. The naturally developed well is constructed as follows: (*a*) drill a pilot hole to determine depths of casing and screen; (*b*) describe the lithology of samples; (*c*) run electric logs to define the boundaries of beds; (*d*) ream hole, set and cement casing; (*e*) drill out bottom and set screen; and (*f*) develop and test pump. After these steps are completed, the casing is set and cemented in place, the hole is then drilled below the casing and the screen is lowered into place for development.

In gravel pack completions, testing for gravel pack wells is carried out in the same manner. A naturally developed wells installation of a gravel pack well requires a high degree of sophistication on the part of a tool pusher and drilling crew. In the gravel wall well, selection of gravel size must be integrated with the formation analysis and with the screen selection.

The under-reamed gravel pack well is an attempt to correct problems with sanding in some gravel pack wells caused from a lack of knowledge and tools for installation of gravel pack wells.

Figure 6.32 shows a schematic cross section of typical under-reamed gravel packed well (Alsay-Pippin Corporation 1980).

Screened Injection Wells: The construction of injection wells completed in unconsolidated sediments is basically the same as that of a water well except that it may be deeper, constructed of more corrosion resistant materials and a highly sophisticated cementing program is used and may include an Epseal Slurry (an epoxy cement mixture) at the bottom of the final casing string. The injection tubing in this type of well is of fibercast or some similar type of corrosion resistant material.

At the bottom of the injection tubing, a packer is installed (such as a Baker AD-1) and a screen and riser pipe are set in place and proceedings carried out as outlined above for a water well. The injection tubing is lowered into place and slipped into the top of the screen riser pipe. The packer is locked into place so that the installation can be completed according to U.S. EPA regulations.

6.6 Procedures and Problems in Industrial Drilling

The following are some actual procedures and problems involved in industrial drilling activity which might face a consultant hydrogeologist in the field while carrying

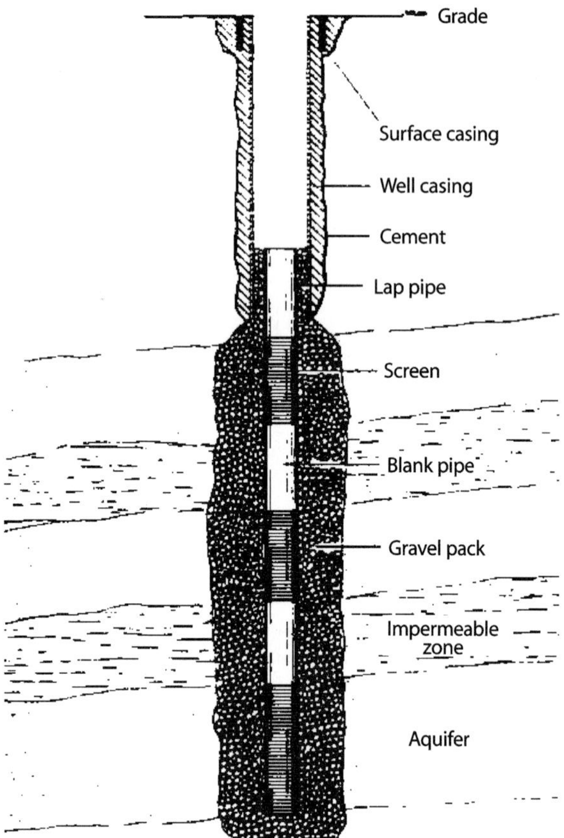
Grade
Surface casing
Well casing
Cement
Lap pipe
Screen
Blank pipe
Gravel pack
Impermeable zone
Aquifer

Fig. 6.32. A graphic cross section of typical under-reamed gravel packed well (Alsay-Pippen Corporation 1980)

out a municipal or industrial water well or injection well (Alsay-Pippin Corporation 1980)

6.6.1 Scope

A consultant geologist or hydrogeologist who is called upon to write specifications for, or involved in, a municipal or industrial water well or injection well, has to deal with the actual construction procedures and problems during the drilling activity. As cable tool drilling may be required as a method for industrial applications, specifically in boulder zones, breccias, and some glacial diamicts. The following information is a discussion of standard rotary type drilling equipment and techniques.

6.6.2 Drilling Fluid Systems

The consultant always recognizes the importance of drilling fluids while completing a well. The Baroid Company annually conducts seminars in drilling fluid systems for water-well drillers. A set of specifications are required for any mud program and includes: adequate pits or tanks so that a minimum of sand or other materials are circulated through the drilling fluid system; awareness of the use of a marsh funnel viscometer and mud scale by the driller; driller's review with the consultant the mud program prior to beginning construction as well as submitting the daily report on mud weight and viscosity together with any additives used for weight control, chemical treatment, and development, etc.

Bentonite or clay base materials are commonly used as drilling fluids with other types of drilling fluid additives such as polymer muds used in the water well industry and can be furnished by the mud supply companies. Polymer additive has the property of returning from a viscous fluid to the consistency of water as a result of enzyme action within a short period of time (less than a week) depending on temperatures and other conditions. Residual bacteria which might contaminate a well during development or pumping process is very hard to eliminate and usually many state health departments reject a well which contains such residual bacteria.

6.6.3 Straight Hole Techniques

Rotary drilling may encounter the problem of drilling a crooked hole thus creating difficulties in setting casing or screens. This problem is common in the water well industry more than in the oil industry as the latter is usually running a stiff bottom hole assembly very close to the diameter of casing to be installed. The industrial driller of an industrial well is normally dealing with larger casing diameters, which do not have the flexibility of small diameter casings.

Drilling of a pilot hole in advance of the larger diameter hole is commonly done to avoid problems and to provide reliable subsurface information by taking samples, running logs and other procedures that serve in planning and aligning the larger diameter hole.

A standard rule of thumb for rotary drilling has been to run with "compression on the collars and tension on the drill pipe". It is experienced that one of the most important tools possessed by any driller in maintaining a straight hole is the weight indicator. Knowing the weight of stiff bottom hole assembly, bits, collars, stabilizers, and transition collar, the driller can help prevent deviation of the hole by careful attention to the weight indicator.

Many tools are available on the market to aid the consultant and the driller in checking hole alignment. The use of inclinometers has become widespread and is generally an accepted practice in the drilling industry. One of the first companies that manufactured, sold and rented inclinometers is the Totco Company so that today many people refer to all inclinometers utilized inside the drill pipe as a "Totco".

Common practice is to require that hold deviation should not exceed three degrees.

6.6.4 Setting Casing

If a pilot hole program and straight hole drilling techniques have been carried out properly, there should generally be no problem with the casing program. Except for very shallow casing strings, casing cementing programs are best left to drilling companies such as Halliburton or Dow Well.

Generally, some type of guide for the casing or shoe should be placed on the end of any string of casing to be set in a rotary drilled hole together with centralizers which are normally made of some type of plate steel welded to the casing and can be provided by cementing companies.

After the long or critical string of casing has been set and cemented in an industrial well, a cement bond log or temperature log it should be run to indicate if the annulus between the casing and cement if new mill coated pipe has been used in the installation.

6.6.5 Cementing

Casing cementing is best left to the major cementing companies, the consultant should be aware of a few procedures that need to be observed prior to and during cementing operations. The industrial drilling contractors or consultants should be aware not to accomplish casing cementing by dumping cement into the casing then attempting to put on a header and pressurize behind it. Also, the practice of utilizing some type of plug to follow the cement to the bottom of the casing is not acceptable even on some small diameter well installations. A general accepted practice is to run a tremie line through some type of packer or Braden head assembly to within a few meters of the bottom of the well casing knowing that there are a number of commercial type packers available on the market.

A good supply to water for clearing the pump and tremie lines is a must. Also, it is a good idea to have a properly operating pressure gauge on the grout line so that remedial actions can be taken if the pressure begins to approach bursting strength of the pipe.

6.6.6 Fishing Operations

Fishing operation is the most dreaded aspect of any drilling program. Every driller faces sooner or later the problem of loosing tools or other steel debris in the hole. In the oil industry, fishing specialists are available but in the water well and industrial drilling industry, the drilling contractor develops many of his own tools and techniques, e.g. taper taps, overshots, and junk baskets.

Once a "fish" is downhole it must be recovered. In the event the pipe cannot be recovered or if there is collapsed casing downhole that cannot be otherwise pulled, milling operations can be considered. Junk downhole must be securely cemented in place prior to continued drilling. The case of limestone or dolomite formations acid treatment can sometimes be considered. In other formations, chemical treatment, such as Baroid's "Torq-trim" or other types of additives may be useful.

6.6.7 Geoprobe Systems

In the last few years, drilling and related equipments were designed to operate more efficiently, compact, mobile and easy to use. The first GeoProbe Series 8-machine was specifically designed to perform soil sampling. Recently, Geoprobe System develops, designs, manufactures, and distributes Geoprobe machines and tools for environmental and geotechnical subsurface investigations. Geoprobe is a hydraulically powered machine that utilize both static force percussion to advance sampling and logging tools into the subsurface. It has made many types and styles of probe units. An example is the 2002 Model 6610DT-drilling machine, used for a variety of projects. It can switch from direct push to augering in very few minutes. It is a wireless remote control or by two hydraulic levers, each lever controlling the forward and backward movement of either the right or left side track respectively. Other tools were designed for soil gas sampling.

6.7 Field Notes, Safety and Precautions

6.7.1 Check List for Drilling and Well Development Work

1. Prior to performing fieldwork, the following information should be recorded in the field book(s):
   a Name of drilling company
   b Names of driller and assistant driller(s)
   c Type and model of rig
   d Date and time of arrival on site
   e Unusual weather conditions (note: drill rigs are very susceptible to lightening strikes)
2. The following information should be recorded in the field book(s) during the drilling operations:
   a Name and number of well (according to location map)

b Time operations begin and description of activity (e.g. decontamination, setting up, drilling with hollow stem, etc.)
c Name of each person (worker) on site and their task
d Name of each visitor to the site, time of arrival and departure and reason (if any) to visit the site
e Time and interval of each type of soil sample with description of the method used, and TIP reading (sample of description should include type of material, color, grain size, percent of recovery, etc.)
f Downtime (time began/ended) and reason and/or standby time (time began/ended) and reason, name of driller and assistant driller(s) present during such times.
g Time and depth at which ground water is encountered, where applicable, and final depth to ground water.
h Complete Chain-of-Custody forms, place sample in sample bottle, and send sample to laboratory for analysis if TIP reading is greater than 50 ppm.

3. During coring operations, the following information should be recorded in the field book(s) and/or the following activities should be performed:
a Name and number of well
b Date and time operations begin and description of activity
c Name of each person (worker) on site and their task
d Name of each visitor to the site, time of arrival and departure, and reason (if any) to visit the site
e Coring interval and description of core
f Record of any cavities
g Percentage of recovery
h TIP reading if taken
i Time and depth at which ground water is encountered and final depth of ground-water level
j Loss of circulation and/or loss of water and quantity
k In the field, store core in core boxes (provided by driller); mark intervals and boxes with well name and number, project number and date
l Photograph each core
m If required, complete Chain-of-Custody forms, place sample in sample bottle and send sample to the laboratory for analysis if TIP reading is greater than 50 ppm

4. During drilling of bedrock, the following information should be recorded in the field book(s) and/or the following activities should\be performed:
a All personnel present (names, time of arrival, time of departure)
b Rig type and model number – drilling string, rock bit, etc.
c Procedure decontamination if required, should be recorded
d Date and time of start of drilling
e Depth at various times and rate of penetration
f Obtain and label sample of cuttings and record a description of the samples in field book, especially at any change (texture, color, etc.) and depth
g Depth at which water is encountered
h Cavities and their interval
i Where required, TIP reading of cuttings. In the event this reading is greater than 50 ppm, take a sample, label it, and send it to a laboratory for analysis. Always adhere to chain-of-custody procedures.

5. During the installation of casing, the following information should be recorded in the field book(s) and/or the following activities should be performed:
a Total depth of bore hole where the casing will be installed
b Length of each segment of casing and total length of the entire string
c Description (including times) of grouting operation and quantities of materials used (Bentonite, cement, water)
d Obtain samples of materials used
e Photo document all activities
f Description in detail of protective casing and concrete pad at wellhead
g Mark a measuring point on the casing and mark the well number on both the casing and the protective casing

6. During well development, the following information should be recorded in the field book(s) and/or the following activities should be performed:
a Name and number of well
b Name of all personnel present
c Total depth of well before development
d Type and number of pump and pump setting
e Static water level before installation of pump
f Date, time and rate at start of pumping
g Collect a sample of the first discharge and measure temperature, SC, pH, and Eh. Describe color, odor, solid material (if present), and record volume pumped thus far.
h In monitoring wells, collect a sample after three well volumes have been pumped and record the above parameters and description. Repeat procedure at regular intervals until the water becomes clear and parameters are stable. Record times at every sampling.
i In monitoring wells, collect samples to be sent to the laboratory at the end of development (after consultation with a certified laboratory) with proper Chain-of-Custody forms and documentation of sampling in field book(s)
j Record time of pump off
k Record water level at time of pump off
l Measure recovery as far as possible

m Measure total depth after development
n Photo document activities

6.7.2 Electrocution on the Drilling Rig

Electricity is the most useful power controlled by man; ground-water professionals can be in great danger when proper precautions are not taken. The most frequent cause of job-related deaths in the ground-water industry is electrocution, caused by contacting overhead power lines while raising the drink of a drilling rig. Drilling can be performed in a safe manner, when working in the vicinity of overhead power lines; if planning and management includes strict safety precautions; such as the following (National Ground Water Association 2001):

- Consider electric power always to live by as well as a dangerous factor.
- Always maintain safe electric wires.
- Never locate a well under or near overhead wires.
- The local power company should be called upon for checking the security of the electric system
- Insulate all of the handles that are used to operate the rig.
- The drill operator should be aware from a probable high power line touching the rig.
- Stop and survey the entire area-up and down, left and right before setting up the rig mast.

6.7.3 Safety on the Rig "Hard Hats and Safety Shoes"

"Safety on the Rig" is described in the *Manual of Recommended Safe Operating Procedures and Guidelines for Water Well Contractors and Pump Installers*, which was prepared by the Safety Committee of the National Water Well Association (1980).

Safety rules and practices are mandatory in the drilling business. The importance of protective measures on and around drilling rigs cannot be overstated.

Drilling crews must know how to work safely on a rig to protect themselves and the expensive equipment they operate.

The Harvard Business School published a survey of studies made of the relationship of sales and losses. Among other facts, it revealed that U.S.$25 worth of product must be processed and sold for every U.S. dollar spent on accidents. For every U.S.$1 000 accident, U.S.$25 000 worth of product must be earmarked to pay the loss. Also, customers want to hire contractors who have good safety records because this generally means a good and safe drilling job.

It is well known that in drilling operations, the driller is responsible for his own crew. This supervision, including safety instructions, extends on to all management personnel. In practicing safety, one must continually think of others as well as oneself.

6.7.4 Checklist for a Drilling Site

Prior to initiation of drilling activities, on-site personnel should carefully observe the area and the conditions of the site and rig. Develop a conversation/report with your driller and review precautions for safety/accident prevention.

Prior to and during any drilling activity, the following should be checked or verified:

1. The location of search above for electrical wires
2. The location check for underground cables or pipes
3. Proper blocking under hydraulic jacks
4. Fire extinguisher
5. First aid kit
6. List of phone numbers
7. Location and route to the nearest hospital (doctor)
8. Assure employees to have proper protective clothing (boots, gloves, hard hat, face shield, glasses, respirator)
9. Install barricades (around mud pits) and location
10. Assure clean location
11. Assure proper lighting
12. Clothing – tight, not loose fitting
13. Welding – do not stare at burning or welding
14. Stay away from moving rig and associated vehicles
15. Rain gear, warm clothes, cool clothes
16. Drinking water
17. Protection from elements (heater, umbrella)
18. Hoses on ground, section hose, water line
19. Equipment on rig:
    a Elevators
    b Service line hook and safety latch
    c Swivels
    d Cable conditions (frayed, spliced, clamped)
    e Rod rack
    f Break out tongs
    g Protective covers (fan and drive belt, mud pump)
    h Operational gauges
    i Hoisting plugs
    j Safety chain on Kelly hose

See the following appendices:

- Appendix 6.A – Drilling forms (four forms)
- Appendix 6.B – Guide to water well drilling rigs (four forms)
- Appendix 6.C – Well inventory forms (two forms)

References

Aardvark Corporation (1977) Production literature. Aardvark Corporation, Puyallup, Washington

Acker WL (1974) Basic procedures for soil sampling and core drilling. Acker Drill Company Inc., Scranton, Pennsylvania

Acker Drill Company (1985) Soil sampling tools catalog. Acker Drill Company Inc., Scranton, Pennsylvania

Alsay-Pippin Corporation (ed) (1980) Handbook of industrial drilling procedures and techniques. Alsay-Pippin Corporation, P.O. Box 6650, Lake Worth, Fl. 33461, pp1–12, 33–36

American Society for Testing and Materials (1983) Standard practice for thin-wall tube sampling of soils. 1986 Annual Book of American Society for Testing and Materials Standards, Philadelphia, Pennsylvania (D1587, pp 305–307)

American Society for Testing and Materials (1984) Standard method for penetration test and split barrel sampling of soils. 1986 Annual Book of American Society for Testing and Materials Standard, Philadelphia, Pennsylvania (D1586, pp 298–303)

Barlow AC (1972) Basic development – well design in underground waste management and environmental implications. Cook TD (ed) American Assoc. Petroleum Geologists, Tulsa, Oklahoma (Memoir 18, pp 72–76)

Bobo RA, Hoch RS (1994) Keys to successful competitive drilling – part 5-A. World Oil 145(4):91–98

Bollenbach WM Jr (1975) Ground water and wells – a reference book for the water-well industry, 4th edn. Johnson Division UOP Inc., St. Paul Minnesota, pp 99–144

Buckeye Drill Company/Bucyrus Erie Company (1982) Buckeye drill operation manual. Buckeye Drill Company, Zanesville, Ohio

Central Mine Equipment Company (1987) Catalog of product literature. Central Mine Equipment Company, St. Louis, Missouri

Driscoll FG (1986) Groundwater and wells. Johnson Division, St. Paul, Minnesota

Geotechnical Board/Commission on Engineering and Technical Systems (1994) Drilling and excavation technologies for the future. Committee on Advanced Drilling Technologies. National Research Council, National Academies Press, Washington, DC, pp 7–30

Hvorslev MJ (1949) Subsurface exploration and sampling of soils for civil engineering purposes. United States Army Corps of Engineers, Waterways Experiment Station, Vicksburg, Mississippi

Ingersoll-Rand (1976) The water well drilling equipment selection guide. Ingersoll-Rand, Washington, New Jersey

Ingersoll-Rand (1985) Drilling technology. Ingersoll-Rand Rotary Drill Division, Garland, Texas

Ingersoll-Rand (1988) Catalogue. Ingersoll-Rotary Drill Division, Garland, Texas

Krynine DP, Judd WR (1957) Principles of engineering geology and geotechnics. McGraw-Hill, New York, New York

Leach LE, Beck FP, Wilson JT, Kampbell DH (1988) Aseptic subsurface sampling techniques for hollow-stem auger drilling. Proceedings of the Second National Outdoor Action Conference on Aquifer Restoration, Ground-Water Monitoring and Geophysical Methods. National Water Well Association, Dublin, Ohio (vol I, pp 31–51)

Mobile Drilling Company (1988) Auger tools and accessories, Model B-24 Surveyor, Model B-31. Catalog 182. Mobile Drilling Company, Indianapolis, Indiana

National Ground Water Association (NGWA)(2001) Tailgate talk, electrocution on the drilling rig, third quarter. Safety Health News (http://www.ngwa.org, tel. (800) 551-7379)

National Research Council (1994) Drilling and excavation technologies for the future. Committee on Advanced Drilling Technologies, Commission on Geosciences, Environment and Resources, NRC. National Academies Press, Washington, D.C. (pp 7–30, phrases)

National Water Well Association (NWWA) (1980) Manual of recommended safe operating procedures and guidelines for water well contractors and pump installers. Safety Committee of the National Water Well Association, Heiss HW Jr (ed), Worthington, Ohio, pp 4–24

National Water Well Association of Australia (1984) Drillers training and reference manual. National Water Well Association of Australia, St. Ives, South Wales

Petroleum Extension Service (1980) Principles of drilling fluid control. Petroleum Extension Service, University of Texas, Austin

Speedstar Division of Koehring Company (1983) Well drilling manual. National Water Well Association, Dublin, Ohio

U.S. Environmental Protection Agency (1975) Manual of water well construction practices. U.S. Environmental Protection Agency, Office of Water Supply (EPA-570-9-75-001)

U.S. Environmental Protection Agency (1977) An introduction to the technology of subsurface wastewater injection. U.S. EPA, Cincinnati, Ohio (Environmental Protection Series, 600/2-77-240, pp 234–246)

U.S. Environmental Protection Agency (1989) Handbook of suggested practices for the design and installation of ground-water monitoring wells (600/4-89/034). Cooperative Agreement CR-812350-01. Environmental Monitoring Systems Laboratory, Office of Research and Development, Las Vegas, Nevada, National Water Well Association, pp 71–144 (section 4)

Zapico MM, Vales S, Cherry JA (1987) A wireline piston core barrel for sampling cohensionless sand and gravel below the water table. Ground Water Monitoring Review 7(3):74–82

Selected References

American Geographic Institute (AGI) (2001) Annual report in GeoRef Information System. Alexandria, Virginia (E-mail: agi@agiweb.org, pp 9–11,)

Bollenbach WM Jr (1974) Ground water and wells – a reference book for the water-well industry. Johnson Division, Universal Oil Products Co., Saint Paul, Minnesota 55165 (chap 11, pp 209–248)

Layne-Western Company Inc. (1983) Water geological and mineral exploration utilizing dual-wall reverse circulation. Product literature. Layne-Western Company Inc., Mission, Kansas, 8 pp

National Research Council (1979) Continental scientific drilling program. U.S. Geodynamics Committee, Geophysical Research Board, NRC. National Academy Press, Washington, D.C.

National Research Council (1989) The adequacy of environmental information for outer continental shelf oil and gas decisions. Florida and California Commission on Geosciences, Environment and Resources, NRC. National Academy Press, Washington, D.C.

Appendix 6.A · Drilling Forms

DAILY DRILLING SUMMARY

CONTRACTOR ______________ DATE ______________ SHIFT ______________

SITE NAME ______________ LOCATION ______________

BOREHOLE NUMBER(S) THIS DATE ______________

DRILL TIME LOG: Explain all down and standby time—who authorized—unusual circumstances, etc.

CATEGORY	TOTAL HOURS	A.M. 6	7	8	9	10	11	12 P.M.	1	2	3	4	5	6	7	8	9	10	11	12 A.M.	1	2	3	4	5	6
MOB/DEMOB																										
DRILLING																										
WELL CONST.																										
MOVE/DECON																										
TESTING																										
STANDBY																										
DOWN TIME																										
OTHER																										

REMARKS

EXPENDABLES: Itemize quantity, size, etc.

ITEM	QUANTITY	PART NO.

BOREHOLE NO.	FROM FEET	TO FEET	FOOTAGE DRILLED FEET	PIPE & CASING IN HOLE SIZE	FEET	BITS/CASING SHOES, ETC. SIZE	NUMBER	ON	OFF	FEET

PERSONNEL TIME LOG:

POSITION	NAME	HOURS
GEOLOGIST		
DRILLER		
HELPER		

COMMENTS

GEOLOGIST	CONSULTANT REPRESENTATIVE
DRILLER	CONTRACTOR REPRESENTATIVE

Fig. 6.A.1. Daily drilling summary

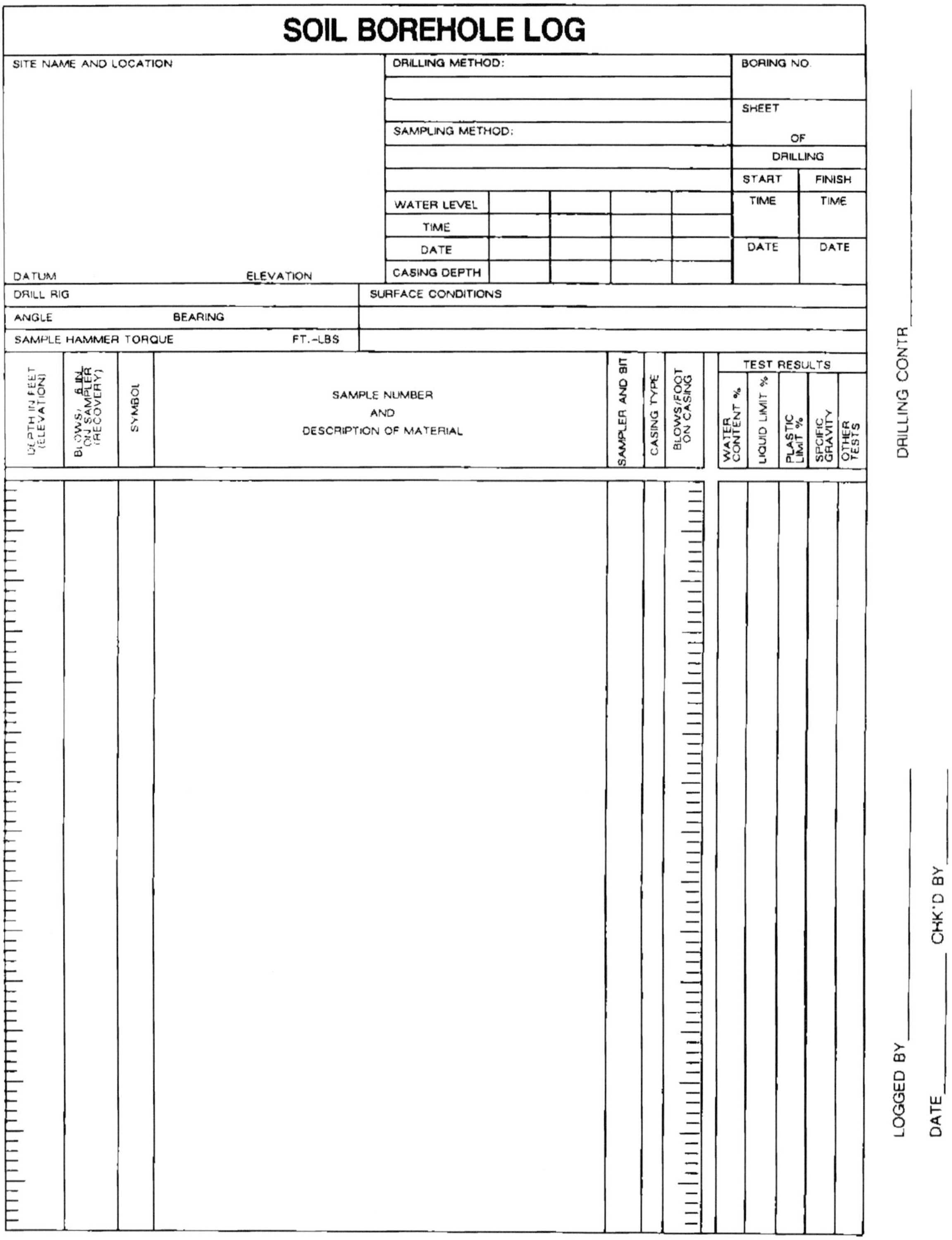

SOIL BOREHOLE LOG

SITE NAME AND LOCATION	DRILLING METHOD:	BORING NO.
	SAMPLING METHOD:	SHEET OF
		DRILLING: START / FINISH
	WATER LEVEL / TIME / DATE	TIME / TIME
DATUM ELEVATION	CASING DEPTH	DATE / DATE

DRILL RIG	SURFACE CONDITIONS
ANGLE BEARING	
SAMPLE HAMMER TORQUE FT.-LBS	

DEPTH IN FEET (ELEVATION)	BLOWS/6 IN. ON SAMPLER (RECOVERY)	SYMBOL	SAMPLE NUMBER AND DESCRIPTION OF MATERIAL	SAMPLER AND BIT	CASING TYPE	BLOWS/FOOT ON CASING	TEST RESULTS: WATER CONTENT %	LIQUID LIMIT %	PLASTIC LIMIT %	SPECIFIC GRAVITY	OTHER TESTS

DRILLING CONTR. ________

LOGGED BY ________ CHK'D BY ________

DATE ________

Fig. 6.A.2. Soil borehole log

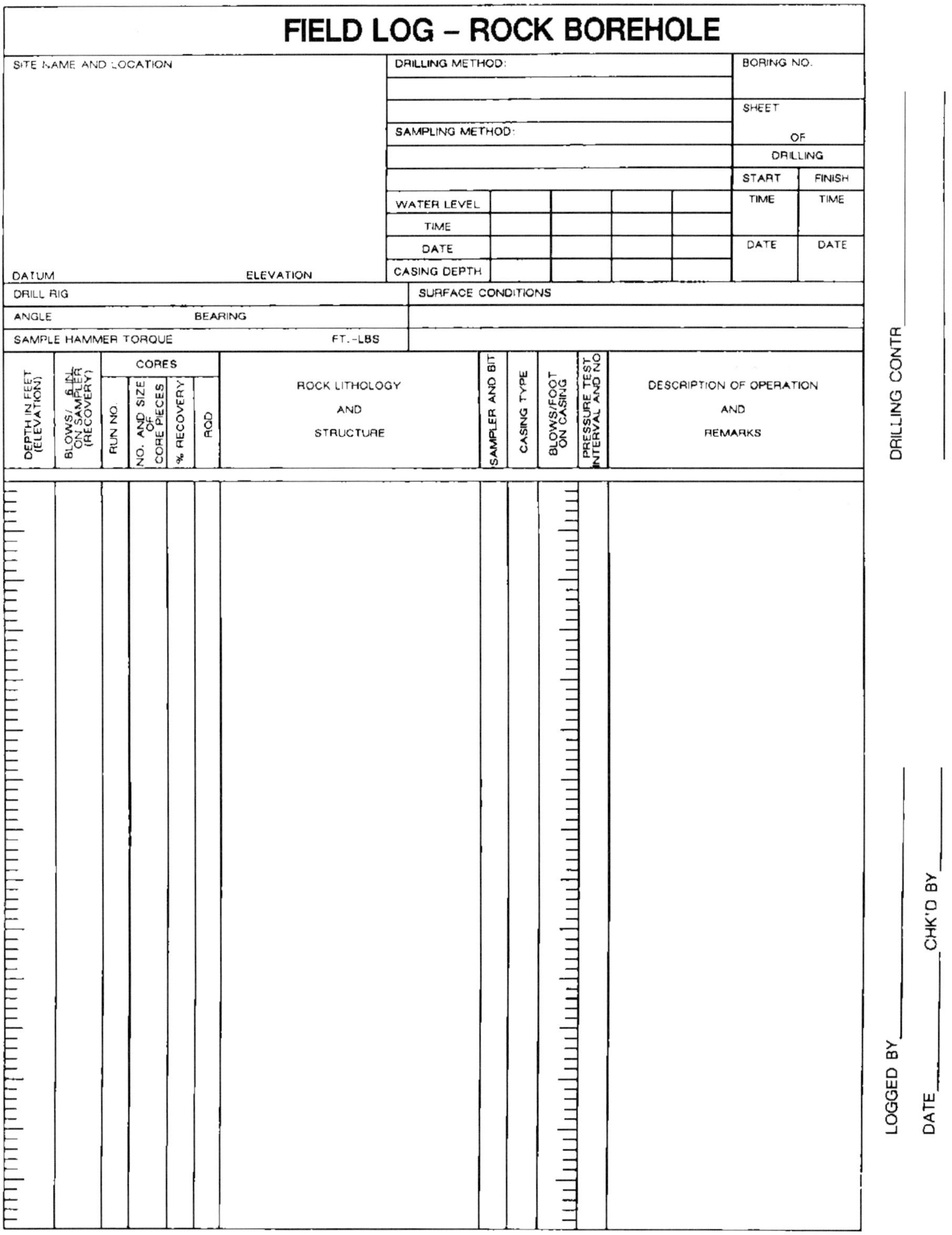

FIELD LOG – ROCK BOREHOLE

SITE NAME AND LOCATION

DRILLING METHOD:

BORING NO.

SHEET

OF

SAMPLING METHOD:

DRILLING

START	FINISH
TIME	TIME
DATE	DATE

WATER LEVEL				
TIME				
DATE				
CASING DEPTH				

DATUM ELEVATION

DRILL RIG

SURFACE CONDITIONS

ANGLE BEARING

SAMPLE HAMMER TORQUE FT.-LBS

DEPTH IN FEET (ELEVATION)	BLOWS/ 6 IN. ON SAMPLER (RECOVERY)	CORES: RUN NO.	CORES: NO. AND SIZE OF CORE PIECES	CORES: % RECOVERY	CORES: RQD	ROCK LITHOLOGY AND STRUCTURE	SAMPLER AND BIT	CASING TYPE	BLOWS/FOOT ON CASING	PRESSURE TEST INTERVAL AND NO	DESCRIPTION OF OPERATION AND REMARKS

DRILLING CONTR

LOGGED BY

CHK'D BY

DATE

Fig. 6.A.3. Field log – rock borehole

Well No. ____________

Boring No. X-Ref: ____________

MONITOR WELL CONSTRUCTION SUMMARY

Survey Coords: ____________ Elevation Ground Level ____________

____________ Top of Casing ____________

Drilling Summary:

Total Depth ____________
Borehole Diameter ____________
Casing Stick-up Height: ____________
Driller ____________
Rig ____________
Bit(s) ____________
Drilling Fluid ____________
Protective Casing ____________

Construction Time Log:

Task	Start Date	Start Time	Finish Date	Finish Time
Drilling				
Geophys. Logging:				
Casing:				
Filter Placement:				
Cementing:				
Development:				

Well Design & Specifications

Basis: Geologic Log ____ Geophysical Log ____
Casing String (s): C = Casing S = Screen.

Depth	String(s)	Elevation
___ - ___		___ - ___
___ - ___		___ - ___
___ - ___		___ - ___
___ - ___		___ - ___
___ - ___		___ - ___

Casing: C1 ____________

C2 ____________

Screen: S1 ____________

S2 ____________

Filter Pack: ____________

Grout Seal: ____________

Bentonite Seal: ____________

Well Development:

Stabilization Test Data:

Time	pH	Spec. Cond.	Temp (C)

Recovery Data:

Q=

S_o =

% RECOVERY 100 80 60 40 20 0

20 40 60 80 100

TIME ( )

Comments: ____________

SITE NAME ____________ LOCATION ____________

WC

SUPERVISED BY ____________ DATE ____________

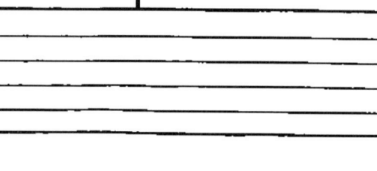

Fig. 6.A.4. Monitor well construction summary

Appendix 6.B · Guide to U.S. Water Well Drilling Rigs

Company name and address	Drilling method	Transport mount	Powered by:			Drill with:				Pullback capacity (in kilos):			
			Truck engine	Deck engine	Both	Air	Foam	Mud	Other	Up to 13608	13609–27216	27217–34020	34021 a. above
Acker Drill Co. Inc. P.O. Box 830 Scranton, PA 18501 PH: (717) 586-2061 Telex: 831-815 Fax: (717) 586-2659 U.S. contact: Stan T. Gordon	Auger	Truck			●			●		●	●		
		Trailer		●				●		●	●		
		Skid		●						●	●		
		Other											
	Bucket	Truck											
		Trailer											
		Skid											
		Other											
	Cable tool (Percussion)	Truck											
		Trailer											
		Skid											
		Other											
	Reverse circulation	Truck			●			●		●	●		
		Trailer		●				●		●	●		
		Skid		●			●	●		●	●		
		Other											
	Table drive rotary	Truck											
		Trailer											
		Skid											
		Other											
	Top drive rotary	Truck			●	●	●	●		●			
		Trailer		●		●	●	●		●			
		Skid		●	●	●	●		●				
		Other											
Ardco Industries P.O. Box 451960 Houston, TX 77245-1960 PH: (713) 433-6751 Telex: 775-017 ARDCOGEMCO HOU Fax: (713) 433-5655 U.S. contact: Garth Cook Int. contact: Garth Cook	Auger	Truck	●		●	●	●	●	●	●	●	●	
		Trailer	●		●	●	●	●	●	●	●	●	
		Skid	●		●	●	●	●	●	●	●	●	
		Other	●		●	●	●	●	●	●	●	●	
	Bucket	Truck											
		Trailer											
		Skid											
		Other											
	Cable tool (Percussion)	Truck											
		Trailer											
		Skid											
		Other											
	Reverse circulation	Truck	●			●	●	●				●	
		Trailer	●			●	●	●				●	
		Skid	●			●	●	●				●	
		Other	●			●	●	●				●	
	Table drive rotary	Truck			●	●	●	●			●	●	
		Trailer			●	●	●	●			●	●	
		Skid			●	●	●	●			●	●	
		Other			●	●	●	●			●	●	
	Top drive rotary	Truck			●	●	●	●	●	●	●		
		Trailer			●	●	●	●	●	●	●		
		Skid			●	●	●	●	●	●	●		
		Other			●	●	●	●					
Central Mine Equipment Co. 6200 North Broadway St. Louis, MO 63147	Auger	Truck		●					●				
		Trailer		●					●				
		Skid		●					●				
		Other		●					●				
	Bucket	Truck											
		Trailer											
		Skid											
		Other											
	Cable tool (Percussion)	Truck											
		Trailer											
		Skid											
		Other											
	Reverse circulation	Truck											
		Trailer											
		Skid											
		Other											
	Table drive rotary	Truck											
		Trailer											
		Skid											
		Other											
	Top drive rotary	Truck											
		Trailer											
		Skid											
		Other											

Fig. 6.B.1. Guide to U.S. water well drilling rigs

Company name and address	Drilling method	Transport mount	Powered by:			Drill with:				Pullback capacity (in kilos):			
			Truck engine	Deck engine	Both	Air	Foam	Mud	Other	Up to 13608	13609–27216	27217–34020	34021 a. above
Diedrich Drill Inc. 1719 State St. P.O. Box 1670 LaPorte, IN 46350	Auger	Truck		•		•	•	•	•	•	•		
		Trailer		•		•	•	•	•	•	•		
		Skid		•		•	•	•	•	•	•		
		Other			•	•	•	•	•	•	•		
	Bucket	Truck											
		Trailer											
		Skid											
		Other											
	Cable tool (Percussion)	Truck											
		Trailer											
		Skid											
		Other											
	Reverse circulation	Truck											
		Trailer											
		Skid											
		Other											
	Table drive rotary	Truck											
		Trailer											
		Skid											
		Other											
	Top drive rotary	Truck											
		Trailer											
		Skid											
		Other											
George E. Failing Co. 2215 S. Van Buren Enid, OK 73702 PH: (405) 234-4141 Telex: 796524 GEFCO ENID Fax: (405) 233-6807 U.S. contact: Jeff Smith Int. contact: Jeff Smith	Auger	Truck			•					•			
		Trailer		•						•			
		Skid		•						•			
		Other	•	•	•	•	•	•		•	•		
	Bucket	Truck											
		Trailer											
		Skid											
		Other											
	Cable tool (Percussion)	Truck											
		Trailer											
		Skid											
		Other											
	Reverse circulation	Truck			•	•	•	•			•		
		Trailer		•		•	•	•			•		
		Skid		•		•	•	•			•		
		Other											
	Table drive rotary	Truck			•	•	•	•					•
		Trailer		•		•	•	•					•
		Skid		•		•	•	•					•
		Other											
	Top drive rotary	Truck			•	•	•	•					•
		Trailer		•		•	•	•					•
		Skid		•		•	•	•					•
		Other											
Ingersoil-Rand Co. Rotary Drill Division 2100 N. First St. Garland, TX 75046	Auger	Truck	•	•		•	•	•	•	•	•		
		Trailer											
		Skid											
		Other											
	Bucket	Truck											
		Trailer											
		Skid											
		Other											
	Cable tool (Percussion)	Truck											
		Trailer											
		Skid											
		Other											
	Reverse circulation	Truck											
		Trailer											
		Skid											
		Other											
	Table drive rotary	Truck											
		Trailer											
		Skid											
		Other											
	Top drive rotary	Truck	•	•		•	•	•	•	•	•	•	•
		Trailer		•		•	•	•	•	•	•	•	•
		Skid		•		•	•	•	•	•	•	•	•
		Other											

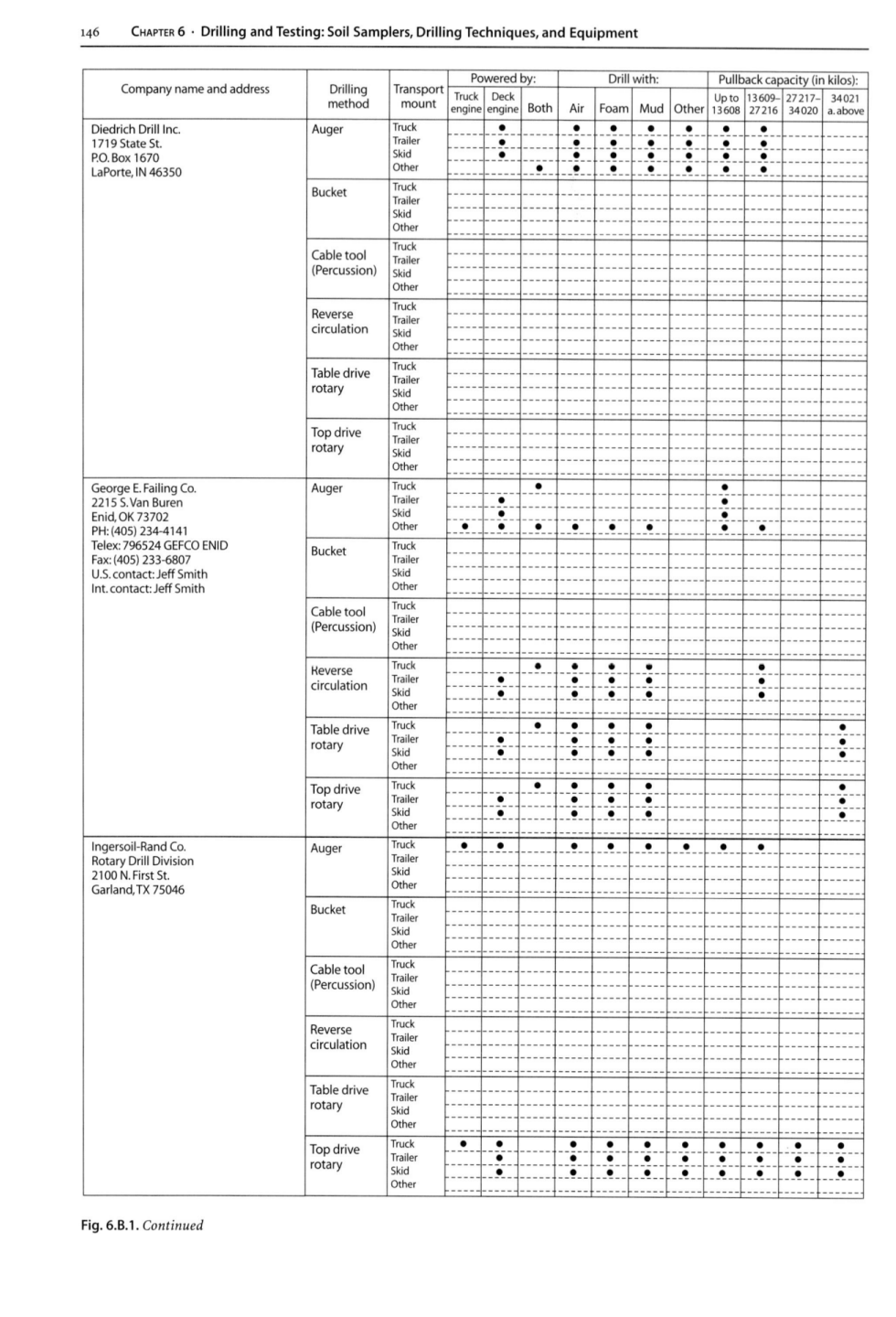

Fig. 6.B.1. *Continued*

Company name and address	Drilling method	Transport mount	Powered by:			Drill with:				Pullback capacity (in kilos):			
			Truck engine	Deck engine	Both	Air	Foam	Mud	Other	Up to 13608	13609–27216	27217–34020	34021 a. above
Mobile Drill Co., Inc. 3807 Madison Ave. Indianapolis, IN 46227 PH: (317) 787-6371 Telex: 240003 MODRL Fax: (317) 784-5661 Toll free: (800) 428-4475 or (800) 7-MODRIL Contact: Charles W. Saunders West Coast Supply Center 5636 Corporate Ave. Unit 4 Cypress, CA 90630 PH: (714) 827-6460 Fax: (714) 827-9471 Toll free: (800) 447-3745	Auger	Truck			•			•	•	•			
		Trailer		•				•	•	•			
		Skid		•				•	•	•			
		Other			•			•	•	•			
	Bucket	Truck											
		Trailer											
		Skid											
		Other											
	Cable tool (Percussion)	Truck											
		Trailer											
		Skid											
		Other											
	Reverse circulation	Truck			•	•	•	•		•			
		Trailer											
		Skid											
		Other											
	Table drive rotary	Truck											
		Trailer											
		Skid											
		Other											
	Top drive rotary	Truck			•	•	•	•	•	•			
		Trailer		•		•	•	•	•	•			
		Skid											
		Other			•	•	•	•	•	•			
NITCO Drilling Products Div. 1100A Regal Row Austin, TX 78748	Auger	Truck			•					•	•		
		Trailer		•						•			
		Skid											
		Other			•						•		
	Bucket	Truck											
		Trailer											
		Skid											
		Other											
	Cable tool (Percussion)	Truck											
		Trailer											
		Skid											
		Other											
	Reverse circulation	Truck											
		Trailer											
		Skid											
		Other											
	Table drive rotary	Truck											
		Trailer											
		Skid											
		Other											
	Top drive rotary	Truck			•	•	•	•		•	•	•	•
		Trailer		•		•	•	•		•			
		Skid											
		Other			•	•	•	•			•		
PortaDrill Part of Ingersoil-Rand Co. P.O. Box 39-P Denver, CO 80239 PH: (303) 371-3711 Telex: 45830 Fax: (303) 355-3432 U.S. contact: Henry A. Winter Jr. or Joe Obermayr Int. contact: Henry A. Winter	Auger	Truck											
		Trailer											
		Skid											
		Other											
	Bucket	Truck											
		Trailer											
		Skid											
		Other											
	Cable tool (Percussion)	Truck											
		Trailer											
		Skid											
		Other											
	Reverse circulation	Truck	•			•			•		•		
		Trailer	•	•		•			•		•		
		Skid											
		Other											
	Table drive rotary	Truck	•		•							•	
		Trailer											
		Skid											
		Other											
	Top drive rotary	Truck											
		Trailer											
		Skid											
		Other											

Fig. 6.B.1. *Continued*

Company name and address	Drilling method	Transport mount	Powered by:			Drill with:				Pullback capacity (in kilos):			
			Truck engine	Deck engine	Both	Air	Foam	Mud	Other	Up to 13608	13609–27216	27217–34020	34021 a. above
Tamrock Drilltech P.O. Box 338 Alachua, FL 32615 PH: (904) 462-4100 Fax: (904) 462-3247	Auger	Truck											
		Trailer											
		Skid											
		Other											
	Bucket	Truck											
		Trailer											
		Skid											
		Other											
	Cable tool (Percussion)	Truck											
		Trailer											
		Skid											
		Other											
	Reverse circulation	Truck											
		Trailer											
		Skid											
		Other											
	Table drive rotary	Truck											
		Trailer											
		Skid											
		Other											
	Top drive rotary	Truck		•		•	•	•	DTH	•	•	•	•
		Trailer											
		Skid								•	•	•	
		Other											
Walker-Neer Corp. P.O. Box 2490 Wichita Falls, TX 76307 PH: (817) 723-0711 Telex: 734411 Fax: (817) 761-2804 U.S. contact: Dale Matthews Int. contact: C. A. Willis	Auger	Truck											
		Trailer											
		Skid											
		Other											
	Bucket	Truck		•					•		•		
		Trailer		•					•		•		•
		Skid											
		Other											
	Cable tool (Percussion)	Truck		•					•	•	•		
		Trailer		•					•	•	•	•	•
		Skid		•					•	•	•	•	
		Other											
	Reverse circulation	Truck											
		Trailer											
		Skid											
		Other											
	Table drive rotary	Truck		•				•		•	•		
		Trailer		•		•		•		•	•	•	•
		Skid		•		•		•		•	•	•	
		Other											
	Top drive rotary	Truck											
		Trailer											
		Skid											
		Other											
Wellmaster Pipe and Supply Inc. 62 Goshen St. P.O. Box 456 Tillsonburg, Ontario, Canada N4G 4J1 PH: (519) 688-0500 Telex: 064-73538 Fax: (519) 688-0563 U.S. contact: James McKenzie Int. contact: James McKenzie	Auger	Truck											
		Trailer											
		Skid											
		Other											
	Bucket	Truck											
		Trailer											
		Skid											
		Other											
	Cable tool (Percussion)	Truck		•									•
		Trailer		•									•
		Skid		•									•
		Other											
	Reverse circulation	Truck											
		Trailer											
		Skid											
		Other											
	Table drive rotary	Truck											
		Trailer											
		Skid											
		Other											
	Top drive rotary	Truck											
		Trailer											
		Skid											
		Other											

Fig. 6.B.1. *Continued*

Appendix 6.C · Well Inventory Forms

Well identification ______________________

State ________ County ________ Topo map ________

____ 1/4 ____ 1/4 Section ________ Township ________ N/S, Range ________ E/W

Latitude ________ Longitude ________

Owner/Tenant (name) ________________ Phone no. ________

Address ______________________

Driller ________________ Date drilled ________

Topographic setting ______________________

Use of water: Domestic ____ Irrigation ____ Industrial ____ Stock ____

Unused ____ Other ________________

Use of well: Industrial ____ Observation ____ Test ____ Monitor ____

Other ______________________

Well description: Drilled ____ Dug ____ Spring ____

Elevation MP ________ (MSL)

Description MP ______________________

Elevation LS ________ (MSL) Data source ________

Casing type ________ Diameter ________ Depth ________

Screen type ________ Diameter ________ Depth ________

Formation ________________ Lithology ________________

Water retrieval method ______________________

Description of sampling "port" closest to well head ______________________

Potential sampling method ______________________

Quality of water (color, odor, etc.) ______________________

Any previous sampling (who/where?) ______________________

Land use

1. Domestic

Septic tanks and field lines:

When installed? ______________________

Any problems? ______________________

Any problems w/ neighbors? ______________________

Location? (add to sketch) ______________________

Fig. 6.C.1. Well inventary form

Land use

2. Agricultural

Fertilizer use: What? ____
When? ____
How much? ____

Pesticide: What? ____
When? ____
How much? ____

Herbicide: What? ____
When? ____
How much? ____

Animal pens: What animals? ____

3. Industrial wells:

Production wells: Location? ____
When/How long? ____

Injection wells: Location? (sketch) ____
When/How long? ____

Brine pits: Location? ____
Size? ____
When/How long? ____
Use? ____

Specific conductance ____

Temperature ____ pH ____

Logs available ____

Water level (below MP)	Water level (MSL)	Date	Measured by
____	____	____	____
____	____	____	____

Comments: ____

Accessible for future monitoring: ____

Accessible for geophysical logging: ____

Site sketch:

Recorded by ____ Date ____

Fig. 6.C.1. *Continued*

Chapter 7

Geophysical Well Logging Methods and Interpretations

Only basic concepts and practical guide lines are intended for this chapter on geophysical well logging. The literature is large on the subject and some select references are given for those needing more detailed information.

7.1 Geophysical Well Logging

Geophysical logs are used for recording the geophysical properties of the penetrated formation and their fluid contents. The geophysical properties measure the electrical resistivity, conductivity, the ability to transmit and reflect sonic energy, natural radioactivity, hydrogen ion content, temperature, density, etc. They are then interpreted in terms of lithology, porosity, and fluid content (U.S. Environmental Protection Agency 1977; Table 7.1).

7.2 Basics of Well Log Interpretations

Several texts, manuals and guidebooks discuss different geophysical log methods to define the productive and non-productive reservoirs in the petroleum business but less attention was given to the application of geophysical methods on the ground-water reservoirs. It is necessary to present the basic concepts of well log interpretations and factors affecting logging measurements (LeRoy 1950).

Asquith and Gibson (1982) discussed different examples of well log analysis and its quantitative interpretations. Explanations of the related illustrations mainly belong to Schlumberger (1972) and Dresser Industries Inc. (1975) are given in Appendix 7.B.

7.2.1 Basic Concepts

The parameters of log interpretations are determined by electrical, nuclear or sonic logs (acoustic). Rock properties that affect logging measurements are porosity, permeability, water saturation and resistivity and are explained as follows (Schlumberger 1974):

1. *Porosity* (ϕ) is defined as the percentage of voids to the total volume of rock and is represented by the formula:

$$\text{Porosity}\,(\phi) = \frac{\text{Volume of pores}}{\text{Total volume of rock}}$$

Table 7.1. Geophysical well logging methods and practical applications (U.S. Environmental Protection Agency 1977; modified after Jennings and Timur 1973)

	Method	Property	Application
1	Spontaneous potential (SP) log	Electrochemical and electrokinitic potentials	Formation water resistivity (R_w); shaliness (sand or shale)
2	Non-focused electric log	Resistivity	Water and gas/oil saturation; porosity of water zones; R_w in zones of known porosity; formation resistivity (R_t); resistivity of invaded zone (R_i)
3	Focused and non-focused micro-resistivity logs	Resistivity	Resistivity of the flushed zone (R_{xo}); porosity; bed thickness
4	Sonic log	Travel time of sound	Rock permeability
5	Caliper log	Diameter of borehole	Without casing
6	Gamma Ray	Natural radioactivity	Lithology (shales and sands)
7	Gamma-gamma	Bulk density	Porosity, lithology
8	Neutron-gamma	Hydrogen content	Porosity with the aid of hydrogen content

The effective porosity is defined as the amount of void space that is interconnected and can transmit fluids.

2. *Permeability* ($\bar{k}$) is the property of the rock to transmit fluids and is controlled by the size of the connecting passages between pores, and is measured in darcies or millidarcies.
3. *Water saturation* (S_w) is the percentage of pore volume in a rock which is occupied by formation water and is represented by the formula:

$$S_w = \frac{\text{Formation water occupying pores}}{\text{Total pore space in the rock}}$$

4. *Resistivity* (R) is the rock property that resists the flow of electric current. Resistivity is the measurement of resistance (in Ωm), whereas conductivity is the reciprocal of resistivity and is measured in mΩm^{-1}:

$$R = \frac{rA}{L} \tag{7.1}$$

where:
R = resistivity (Ωm)
r = resistance (Ω)
A = cross sectional area of measured substance (m^2)
L = length of substance being measured (m)

7.2.2 Borehole Parameters

Certain terms and symbols (Fig. 7.1) are used in well log interpretations and may be given as follows:

1. *Borehole diameter* (d_h) is the outside diameter of the drill bit and describes the borehole size of the well. The actual borehole size may be larger than the bit diameter due to collapse of shale or poorly cemented porous rocks or may be smaller due to build up of mud cake on porous and permeable formation. The size of the borehole is measured by a caliper log.
2. *Drilling Mud* (R_m) is a circulating fluid having a special viscosity and density to help remove cuttings from the well bore, lubricate and cool the drill bit, and keep the hydrostatic pressure in the mud column greater than the formation pressure. This difference in pressure prevents blow out and forces some of the drilling fluid to invade porous and permeable formations.
3. *Mud filtrate* (R_{mf}) is the fluid of the drilling mud that filters into the formation during invasion whereas its solid particles of the clay minerals are trapped on the side of the borehole and form the mud cake (R_{mc}).
4. *Invaded zone* (R_{xo}, R_i) consists of both the flushed zone (R_{xo}) and a transition or annulus (R_i) zone. The flushed zone occurs close to the borehole where the mud filtrate has almost completely flushed out the formation fluids. It extends only a few inches from the well bore and is part of the invaded zone. It is completely cleared of its formation water (R_w) by mud filtrate (R_{mf}) when the invasion is deep or moderate. The transition zone is the zone where the formation's fluids and mud filtrate are mixed and occur between the flushed zone (R_{xo}) and the uninvaded zone (R_w). The depth of invasion of the mud filtrate into the invaded zone is referred to as the diameter of invasion (d_i and d_j) and depends on the permeability of the mud cake and not upon the porosity of the rock. The solid particles in the drilling muds coalesce and form an impermeable mud cake that prohibits any further invasion.
5. *Uninvaded zone* (R_w) is beyond the invaded zone where the pores are only saturated with formation fluid.

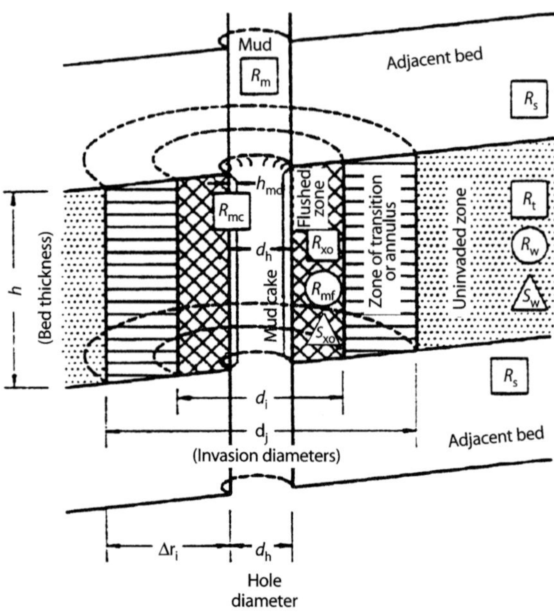
Resistivity of the zone
Resistivity of the water in the zone
Water saturation in the zone
Mud
R_m
Adjacent bed
R_s
h_{mc}
R_{mc}
Flushed zone
R_{xo}
d_h
R_{mf}
S_{xo}
Mud cake
Zone of transition or annulus
Uninvaded zone
R_t
R_w
S_w
h
(Bed thickness)
d_i
d_j
(Invasion diameters)
R_s
Adjacent bed
Δr_j
d_h
Hole diameter

Fig. 7.1. A diagram shows the invasion of fluids through the surrounding rock; the cylindrical nature of the invasion is also shown by *dashed lines* (after Asquith and Gibson 1982)

7.2.3 Formation Temperature (T_f)

Formation temperature is important in log analysis because the resistivities of the drilling mud (R_m), the mud filtrate (R_{mf}), and the formation water (R_w) vary within temperature. The formation temperatures can be calculated by defining the slope or temperature gradient from the following equation (Schlumberger 1974; Wylie and Rose 1950):

$$m = \frac{y - c}{x} \tag{7.2}$$

where:
m = temperature gradient
y = bottom hole temperature (BHT)
c = surface temperature
x = total depth (TD)

Knowing the value of the temperature gradient, the formation temperature (T_f) can be given from the following equation:

$$y = mx + c \tag{7.3}$$

where:
y = formation temperature
x = formation depth (m)
c = surface temperature

The resistivity values (R_{mf} and R_m) which are usually recorded on a log's header of each well, can be corrected together with R_w to formation temperature by applying Arp's formula:

$$R_{T_f} = R_{Temp}(Temp + 6.77) \,/\, (T_f + 6.77) \tag{7.4}$$

where:
R_{T_f} = resistivity at formation temperature
R_{Temp} = resistivity at a temperature other than the formation temperature (measured in the lab at room temperature)
$Temp$ = temperature at which resistivity is measured
T_f = formation temperature

The resistivity of a formation water (R_w) can be obtained by analysis of water samples from a drill stem test, a water producing well or from a catalog of water resistivity values.

7.2.4 Specific Log Types

Specific log types such as SP, resistivity, porosity, and gamma ray logs are discussed in the text of *Basic Well Log Analysis for Geologists* by Asquith and Gibson (1982). Formulas are considered in this section for computer programming whereas explanation of the different figures given below are provided in Appendix 7.B (Schlumberger 1972, 1974).

7.2.4.1 *The Spontaneous Potential Log (SP)*

One of the earliest logs developed and has continued to be used in well log interpretation. It is a record of direct current (DC) voltage differences between the naturally occurring potential of a moveable electrode running down the well borehole and that of a fixed electrode located at the surface and is measured in millivolts.

The SP log is only used with conductive (salt water based) drilling muds and it is influenced by parameters affecting the bore hole environment. It is used to detect permeable beds, determine formation water resistivity (R_w) and the volume of shale in permeable beds. The SP response of shale is relatively constant and follows a straight line called a shale baseline whereas, permeable zones are indicated by a deflection of the SP curve from the shale baseline (Fig. 7.2). The presence of shale in a permeable formation reduces the SP deflection.

In water-bearing zones, the amount of the Sp reduction is proportional to the amount of shale in the formation. Also, the magnitude of the Sp deflection is due to the difference in resistivity between mud filtrate (R_{mf}) and formation water (R_w) and not to the amount of permeability.

7.2.4.2 *The Resistivity Log (R)*

An electric log can be used to determine resistivity, porosity and specific permeable zones. Because the reservoir rock's matrix is non-conductive, the ability of rock to transmit a current is mainly a function of water in the pores.

The resistivity log can be used to determine a formation's water saturation (S_w) by applying the Archie equation (Archie 1942):

$$S_w = \frac{(FR_w)^{1/n}}{R_t} \tag{7.5}$$

where:
S_w = water saturation
F = formation factor
R_w = resistivity of formation water
R_t = true formation resistivity as measured by a deep reading resistivity log
n = saturation exponent (~2.0)

The formation factor may be calculated from the following formula:

$$F = \frac{a}{\phi^m} \tag{7.6}$$

where:

a = tortuosity factor, "tortuosity is a function of the complexity of the path, the fluid must travel through the rock"

m = cementation exponent

ϕ = formation porosity

The ability of rock to transmit an electrical current is almost entirely the result of the water in the pore space because the minerals that make up the grains in the matrix are non-conductive. The formation's resistivity close to the borehole (R_{xo} or R_i) are used to determine porosity in a water-bearing zone and can be related to shallow resistivity (R_{xo}) by the following equations:

$$S_{xo} = \frac{\sqrt{FR_{mf}}}{S_{xo}^2} \tag{7.7}$$

(S_{xo} = 1.0 (100%) in water bearing zones)
Therefore:

$$F = \frac{R_{xo}}{R_{mf}} S_{xo}^2$$

and

$$\frac{a}{\phi^m} = \frac{R_{xo}}{R_{mf}} S_{xo}^2$$

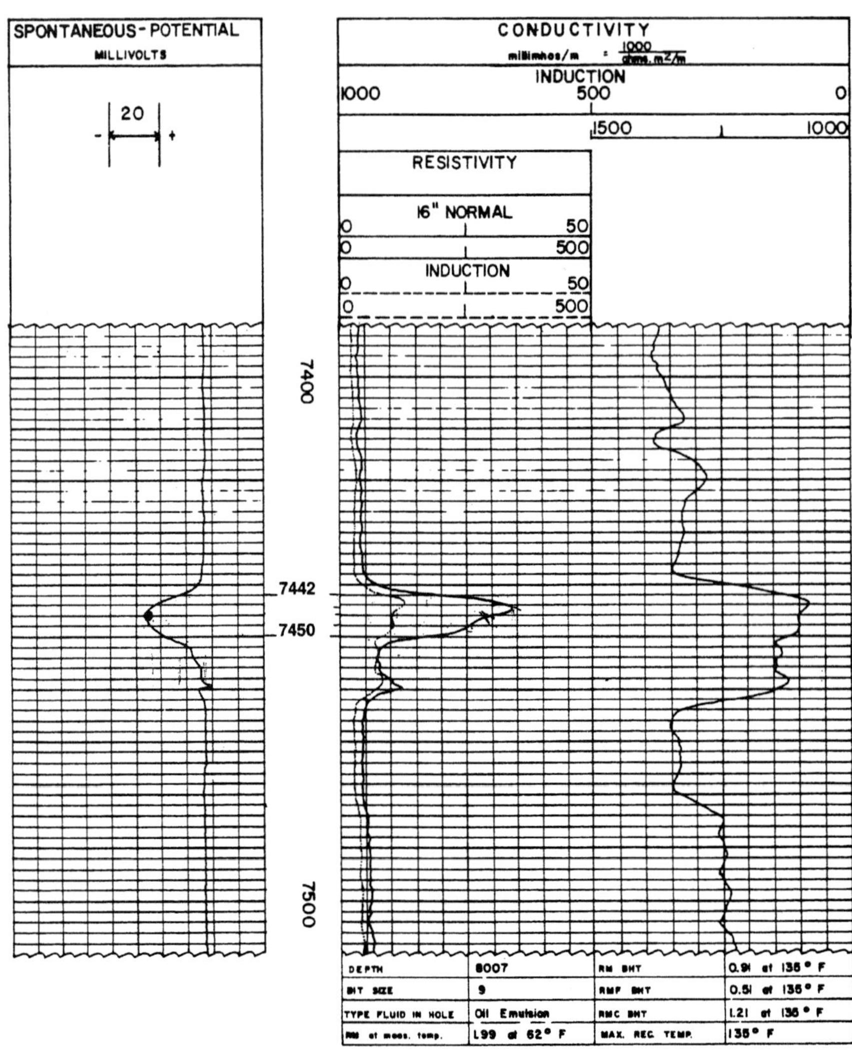
SPONTANEOUS-POTENTIAL
MILLIVOLTS
20
CONDUCTIVITY
millimhos/m
INDUCTION
1000
500
0
1500
1000
RESISTIVITY
16" NORMAL
0
50
0
500
INDUCTION
0
50
0
500
7400
7442
7450
7500
DEPTH
8007
BIT SIZE
9
TYPE FLUID IN HOLE
Oil Emulsion
RM BHT
0.91 at 136° F
RMF BHT
0.51 at 136° F
RMC BHT
1.21 at 136° F
MAX. REC. TEMP.
136° F

Fig. 7.2. Spontaneous potential log (after Asquith and Gibson 1982)

Solve for porosity:

$$\phi = \left(\frac{a \dfrac{R_{mf}}{R_{xo}}}{S_{xo}^2} \right)^{1/m} \tag{7.8}$$

where:

ϕ = formation porosity
R_{mf} = resistivity of mud filtrate at formation temperature
S_{xo} = water saturation of the flushed zone
R_{xo} = resistivity of the flushed zone from microlaterolog, laterolog 8 or microspherically focused log values
a = constant (a = 1.0 for carbonate, 0.62 for unconsolidated sands, 0.81 for consolidated sands)
m = constant (m = 2.0 for consolidated sands and carbonates, 2.15 for unconsolidated sands)

There are two basic types of logs which measure formation resistivity, namely the induction and electrode logs.

1. The *induction electric log* is used in fresh-water drilling mud ($R_{mf} > 3R_w$) and produces three curves: SP, short normal and induction. These three curves can be obtained simultaneously during the logging of the well.

   The short normal curve (in Track 2 of Fig. 7.3) measures shallow resistivity of the invaded zone (R_i) and can be compared with the resistivity of the uninvaded zone (R_w). Invasion is detected by the separation between the short normal and the induction curves, indicating a permeable formation. The short normal tool has an electrode spacing of 40–64 cm and it can record a reliable value for resistivity from a bed of 1.22 m in thickness. The induction curve on the Induction Electric Log is shown in Track 2 of Fig. 7.3. The induction derived conductivity curve is shown in Track 3 and it determines more

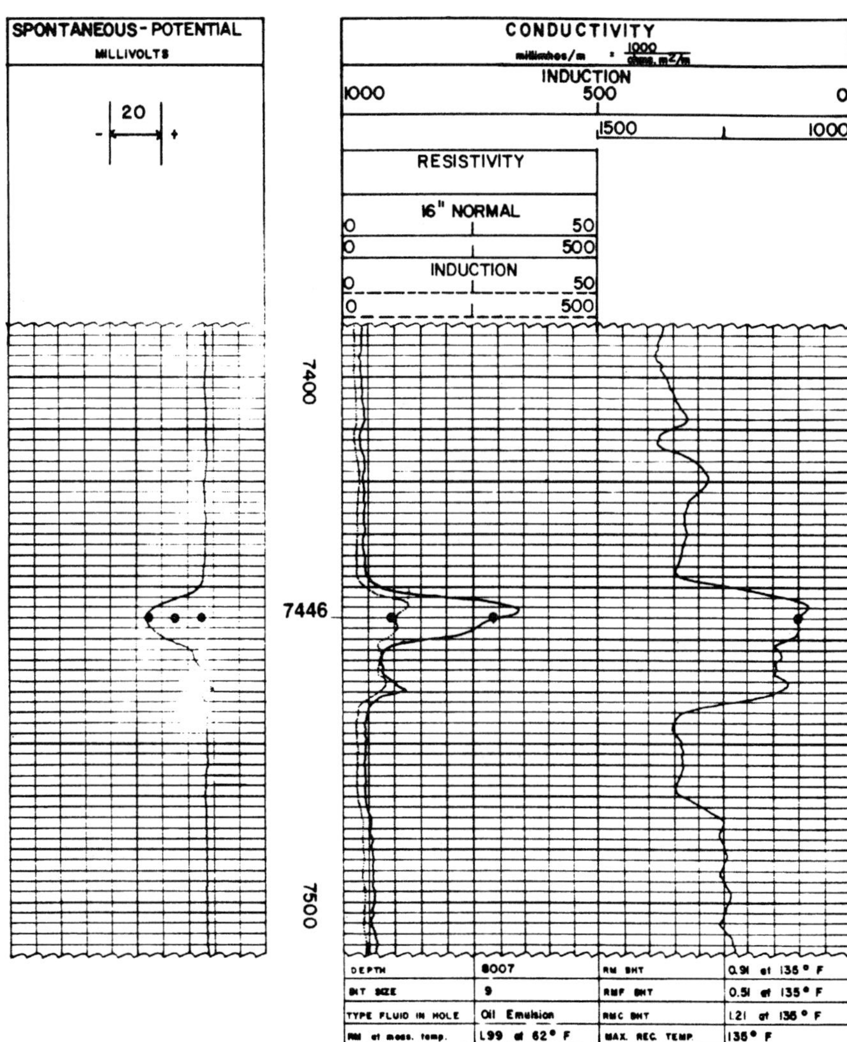
SPONTANEOUS - POTENTIAL
MILLIVOLTS
20
CONDUCTIVITY
millimhos/m = 1000 / ohms. m²/m
INDUCTION
1000
500
0
1500
1000
RESISTIVITY
16" NORMAL
0
50
0
500
INDUCTION
0
50
0
500
7400
7446
7500
DEPTH
8007
RM BHT
0.91 at 135° F
BIT SIZE
9
RMF BHT
0.51 at 135° F
TYPE FLUID IN HOLE
Oil Emulsion
RMC BHT
1.21 at 135° F
RM at meas. temp.
1.99 at 62° F
MAX. REC. TEMP.
135° F

Fig. 7.3.
Induction electric log (after Asquith and Gibson 1982)

accurately the R_w value of low resistivity formations. The induction log can be run in air-, oil-, or foam-filled boreholes because it does not require the transmission of electricity through drilling fluid. A modern induction log is called the dual induction focused log curves (Fig. 7.4) and consists of a deep-reading inductive device ($R_{IIM} = R_w$); a medium-reading induction device ($R_{ILM} = R_i$); and a shallow reading focused laterolog (R_{xo}), which is similar to the short normal and may be either LL-8 or SFL. The dual induction focused log is used in formations that are deeply invaded by mud filtrate.

2. *Electrode logs* are used with salt-saturated drilling muds ($R_{mf} = R_w$)3: laterolog, micro laterolog, microlog, proximity log and spherically focused logs are examples of electrode resistivity tools.

   The laterolog is designed to measure true formation resistivity (R_w) in bore holes filled with saltwater muds ($R_{mf} = R_w$).

   The microlog (ML) is a pad type resistivity device that primarily detects the mud cake by two resistivity measurements; the micro normal which investigates 7–10 cm into the formation (R_{xo}) and the micro-inverse which investigates 2–5 cm and measures the resistivity of the mud cake (R_{mc}). The detection of the mud cake by the ML indicates that invasion has occurred and the formation is permeable. Permeable zones show up as positive separation when the micro normal curves read higher resistivity than the micro inverse curves. Shale zones show negative separatism or no separation. The ML does not work well in saltwater-based drilling muds ($R_{mf} = R_w$) because the mud cake may not be strong enough to keep the pad away from the formation, and hence, positive separation cannot occur.

   The micro laterolog (MLL) and the proximity log (PL) are designed to measure the resistivity of the flushed zone (R_{xo}). The MLL should run only with saltwater-based drilling mud because it is strongly influenced by mudcake thicknesses greater than 2/3 cm.

   The following resistivity logs are normally used for qualitative analysis of formations in deep water

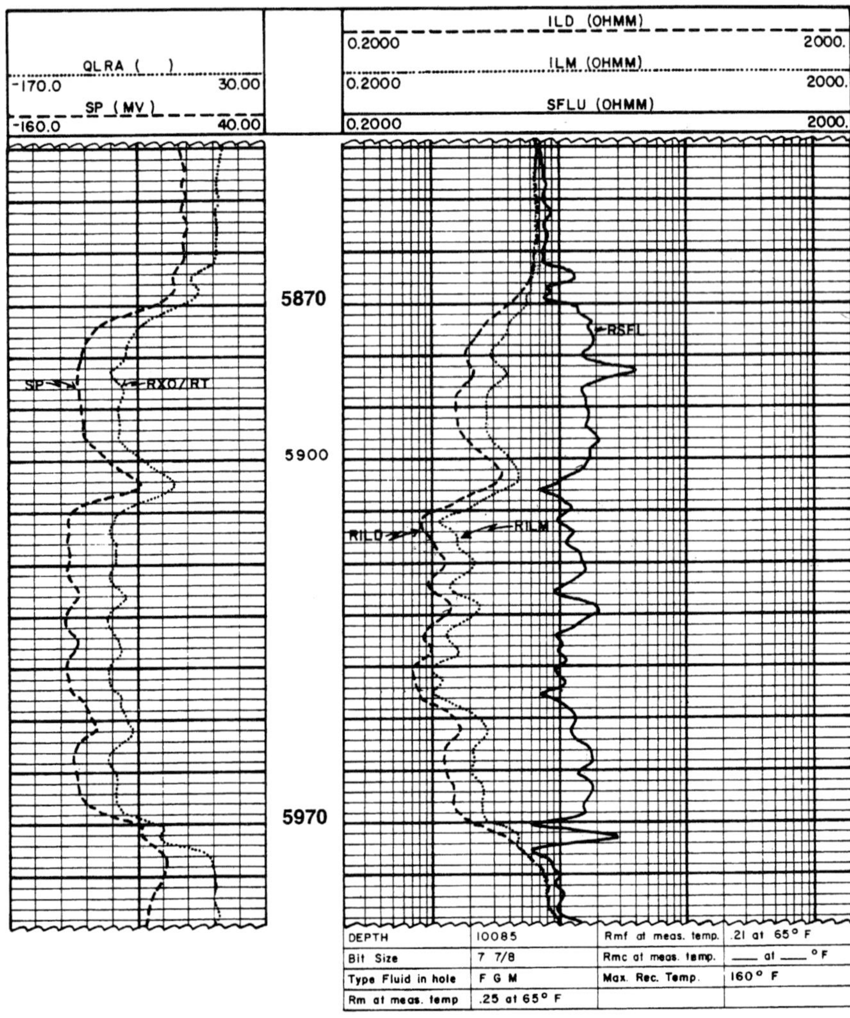
QLRA ( )
-170.0
30.00
SP (MV)
-160.0
40.00
ILD (OHMM)
0.2000
2000.
ILM (OHMM)
0.2000
2000.
SFLU (OHMM)
0.2000
2000.
5870
5900
5970
SP
RXO/RT
RSFL
RILD
RILM
DEPTH
10085
Rmf at meas. temp.
.21 at 65° F
Bit Size
7 7/8
Rmc at meas. temp.
at °F
Type Fluid in hole
F G M
Max. Rec. Temp.
160° F
Rm at meas. temp
.25 at 65° F

Fig. 7.4. Dual induction focused log through a water-bearing zone, the drilling mud is freshwater based (after Asquith and Gibson 1982)

wells, namely the dual laterolog (LLD)/microspherically focused log (MSFL), micrstill/SP log, and proximity log/micro log and caliper (Figs. 7.5, 7.6 and 7.7).

3. *Porosity logs* include sonic log, density log and neutron log. The sonic log records matrix porosity whereas the nuclear logs (density or neutron) determine the total porosity.
   a The *sonic log* can determine porosity in consolidated sandstones and carbonates with intergranular porosity or intercrystalline porosity. It measures interval transit time (Δt) in microseconds per foot (see Fig. 7.8). The interval transit time (Δt), which is the reciprocal of the velocity of a compressional sound wave traveling one foot of formation per second, depends on both lithology and porosity. Therefore, a formation matrix velocity must be known to derive sonic porosity by the following formula (Table 7.2):

$$\phi_{\text{sonic}} = \frac{\Delta t_{\text{log}} - \Delta t_{\text{ma}}}{\Delta t_{\text{f}} - \Delta t_{\text{ma}}} \tag{7.9}$$

where:

ϕ_{sonic} = sonic derived porosity (for consolidated sandstone and carbonates with intergranular porosity
Δt_{ma} = interval transit time of the matrix
Δt_{log} = interval transit time of formation
Δt_{f} = interval transit time of the fluid in the well bore (fresh mud = 189; salt mud = 185)

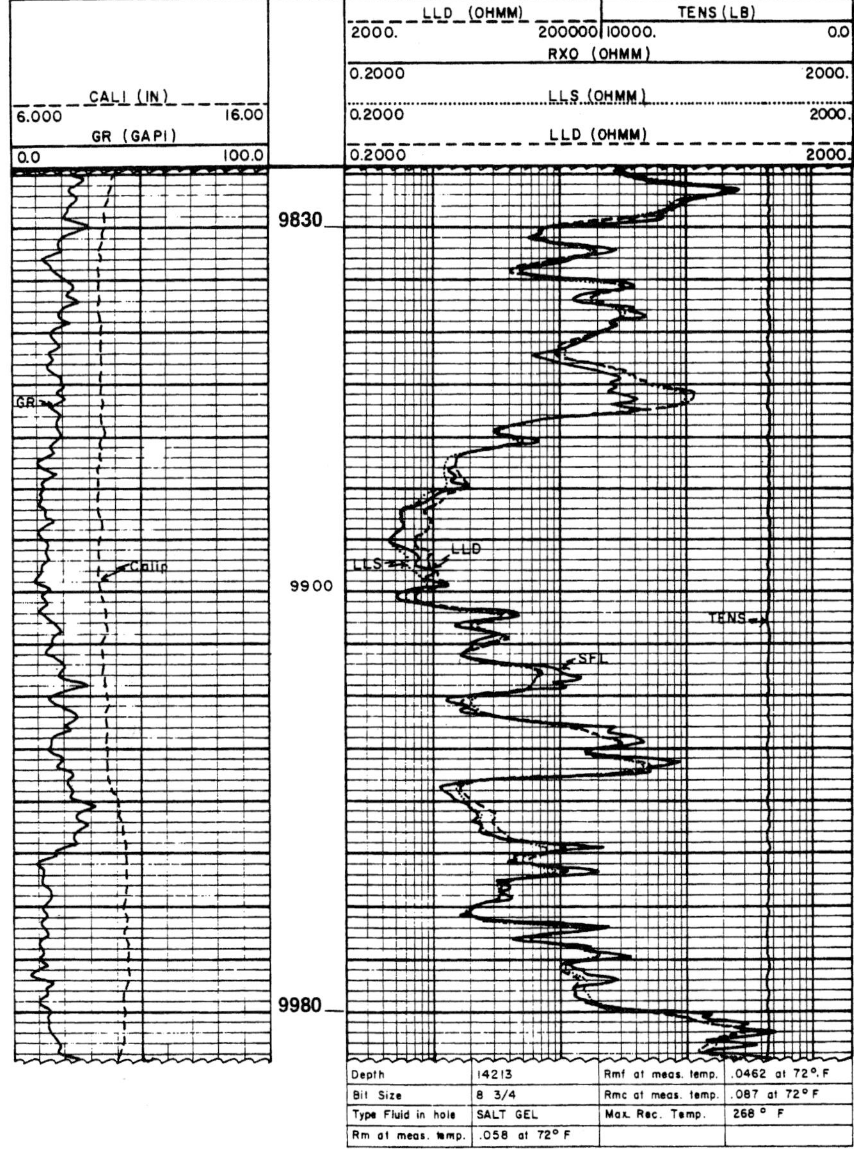
CALI (IN)
6.000
16.00
GR (GAPI)
0.0
100.0
LLD (OHMM)
2000.
200000
TENS (LB)
10000.
0.0
RXO (OHMM)
0.2000
2000.
LLS (OHMM)
0.2000
2000.
LLD (OHMM)
0.2000
2000.
9830
GR
Calip
LLS
LLD
9900
TENS
SFL
9980
Depth
14213
Rmf at meas. temp.
.0462 at 72°F
Bit Size
8 3/4
Rmc at meas. temp.
.087 at 72°F
Type Fluid in hole
SALT GEL
Max. Rec. Temp.
268 ° F
Rm at meas. temp.
.058 at 72° F

Fig. 7.5. Dual laterolog micro-spherically focused log through a water-bearing zone, the drilling mud is saltwater based (after Asquith and Gibson 1982)

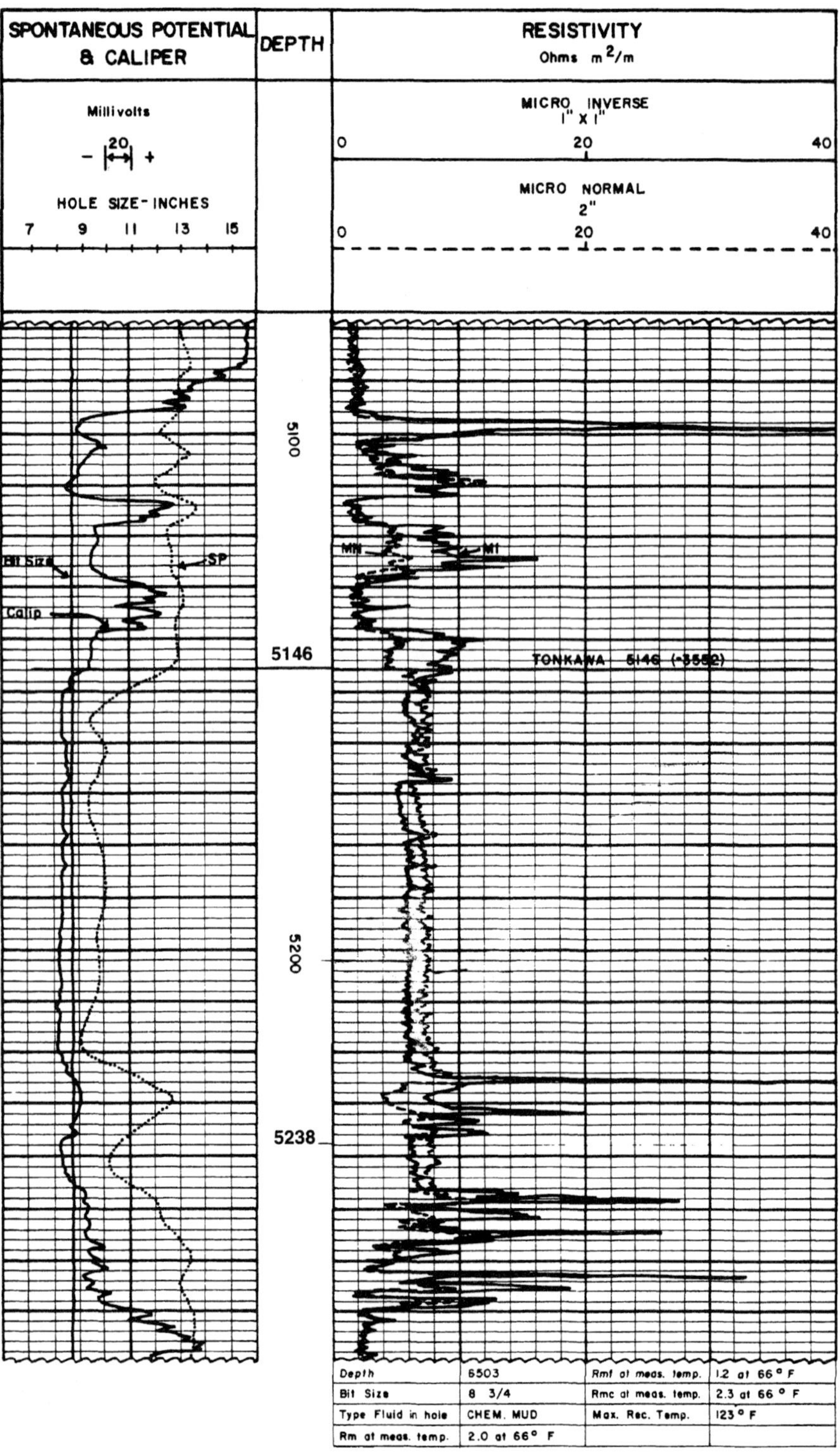

SPONTANEOUS POTENTIAL & CALIPER
DEPTH
RESISTIVITY
Ohms m²/m
Millivolts
- 20 +
HOLE SIZE - INCHES
7 9 11 13 15
MICRO INVERSE
1" x 1"
0 20 40
MICRO NORMAL
2"
0 20 40
5100
Bit Size
SP
Calip
5146
TONKAWA 5146 (-3552)
MN
MI
5200
5238
Depth 6503
Bit Size 8 3/4
Type Fluid in hole CHEM. MUD
Rm at meas. temp. 2.0 at 66° F
Rmf at meas. temp. 1.2 at 66° F
Rmc at meas. temp. 2.3 at 66° F
Max. Rec. Temp. 123° F

Fig. 7.6. Microlog with spontaneous potential log and caliper (after Asquith and Gibson 1982)

b *Density log* measures electron density of a formation and it assists to identify evaporite minerals and evaluate shaly sand reservoirs and complex lithologies. The density logging device consists of a gamma ray source that emits gamma rays into the formation. These gamma rays collide with electrons in the formation; the collisions result in a loss of energy from the gamma ray particle. Accordingly, electron density can be related to bulk density (ρ_b) of a formation in g cm^{-3}. The bulk density curve is recorded in Tracks 2 and 3 (Fig. 7.9).

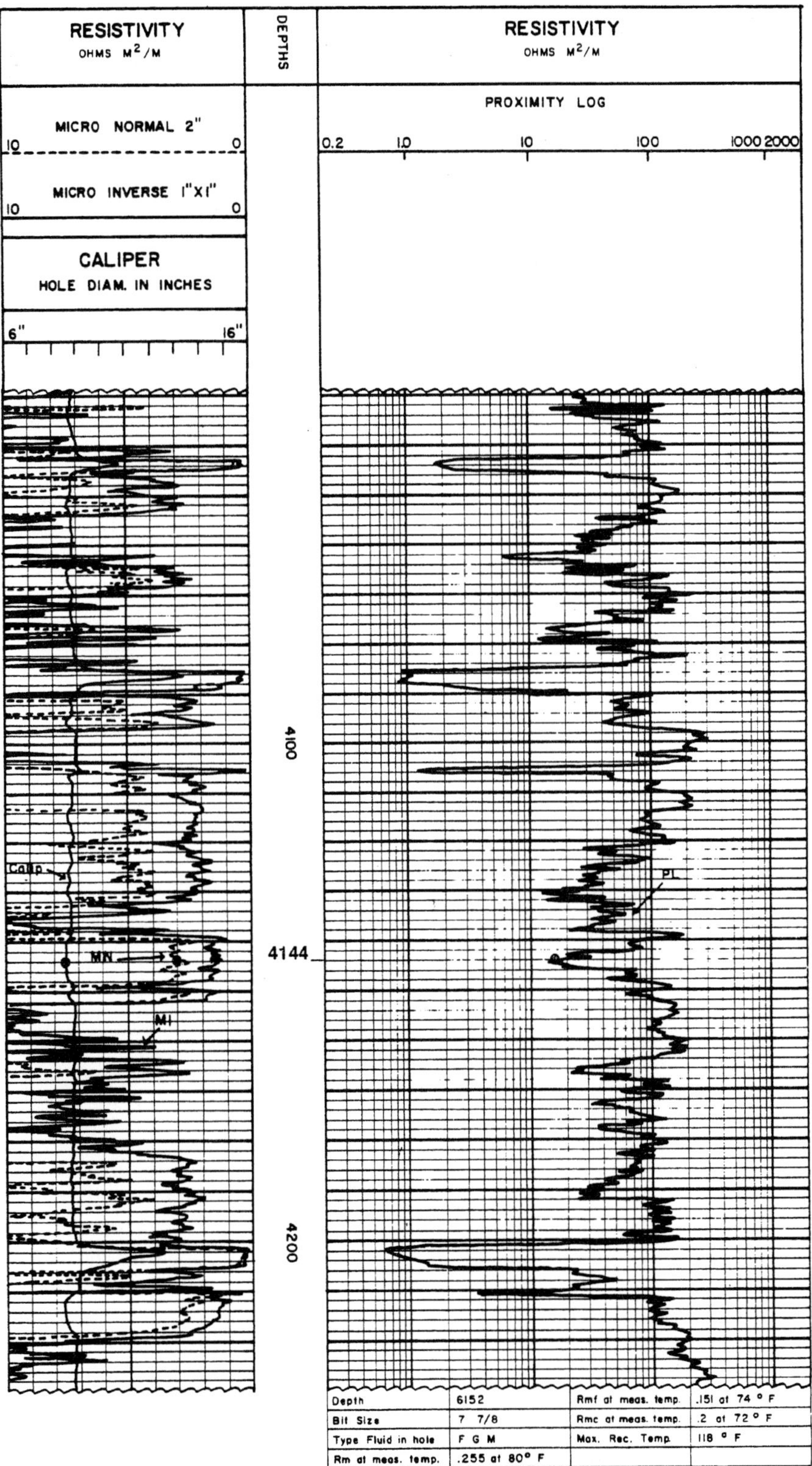
RESISTIVITY
OHMS M²/M
MICRO NORMAL 2"
10 0
MICRO INVERSE 1"X1"
10 0
CALIPER
HOLE DIAM. IN INCHES
6" 16"
Calip
MN
MI
DEPTHS
4100
4144
4200
RESISTIVITY
OHMS M²/M
PROXIMITY LOG
0.2 1.0 10 100 1000 2000
PL
Depth 6152
Bit Size 7 7/8
Type Fluid in hole F G M
Rm at meas. temp. .255 at 80° F
Rmf at meas. temp. .151 at 74 ° F
Rmc at meas. temp. .2 at 72 ° F
Max. Rec. Temp. 118 ° F

Fig. 7.7. Proximity log with a micro log and caliper (after Asquith and Gibson 1982)

Formation bulk density (ρ_b) is a function of matrix density, porosity, and density of the fluid in the pores (salt mud or fresh mud). To determine density porosity, by calculation, the matrix density (Table 7.3) and type of fluid in the borehole must be known.

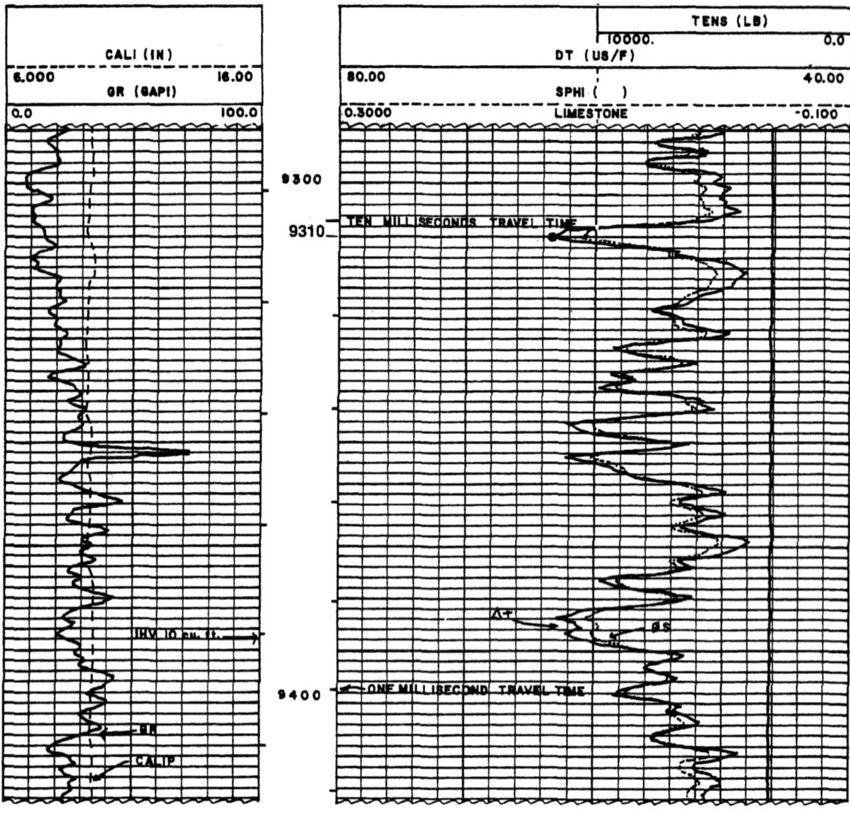

CALI (IN)
6.000
16.00
GR (GAPI)
0.0
100.0
9300
9310
9400
GR
CALIP
TENS (LB)
10000.
0.0
DT (US/F)
80.00
40.00
SPHI ( )
0.3000
LIMESTONE
-0.100
TEN MILLISECONDS TRAVEL TIME
ONE MILLISECOND TRAVEL TIME

Fig. 7.8.
A sonic log with gamma ray and caliper (after Asquith and Gibson 1982)

Table 7.2.
Sonic velocities and interval transit times for different matrices used in the Sonic Porosity Formula (after Schlumberger 1972)

	V_{ma} (ft s^{-1})	Δt_{ma} (μs ft^{-1})
Sandstone	18000 to 19500	55.5 to 51.0
Limestone	21000 to 23000	47.6
Dolomite	23000 to 26000	43.5
Anhydrite	20000	50.0
Salt	15000	67.0
Casing (iron)	17500	57.0

c *Neutron logs* are porosity logs that measure the hydrogen ion concentration in a formation. In clean formations (i.e. shale free) where the porosity is filled with water, the neutron log measures liquid-filled porosity. Neutrons which are created from a chemical source in the neutron logging tools, collide with the nuclei of the formation material resulting in the loss of some of its energy. Maximum energy loss occurs when the neutron collides with a hydrogen atom because both the hydrogen atom and the neutron have almost equal mass. Therefore, the maximum amount of energy loss is a function of a formation's hydrogen concentration.

d *Combination neutron-density log* consists of neutron and density curves recorded in Tracks 2 and 3 and are normally recorded in limestone porosity units with each division equal to either two percent or three percent porosity (Fig. 7.10).

True porosity can be obtained by: (1) reading apparent limestone porosities from the neutron and density curves, and (2) using the root mean square formula for calculating neutron-density porosity as follows:

$$\phi_{N\text{-}D} = \sqrt{\frac{\phi_N^2 + \phi_D^2}{2}} \quad (7.10)$$

where:

$\phi_{N\text{-}D}$ = neutron-density porosity
ϕ_N = neutron-porosity (limestone units)
ϕ_D = density porosity (limestone units)

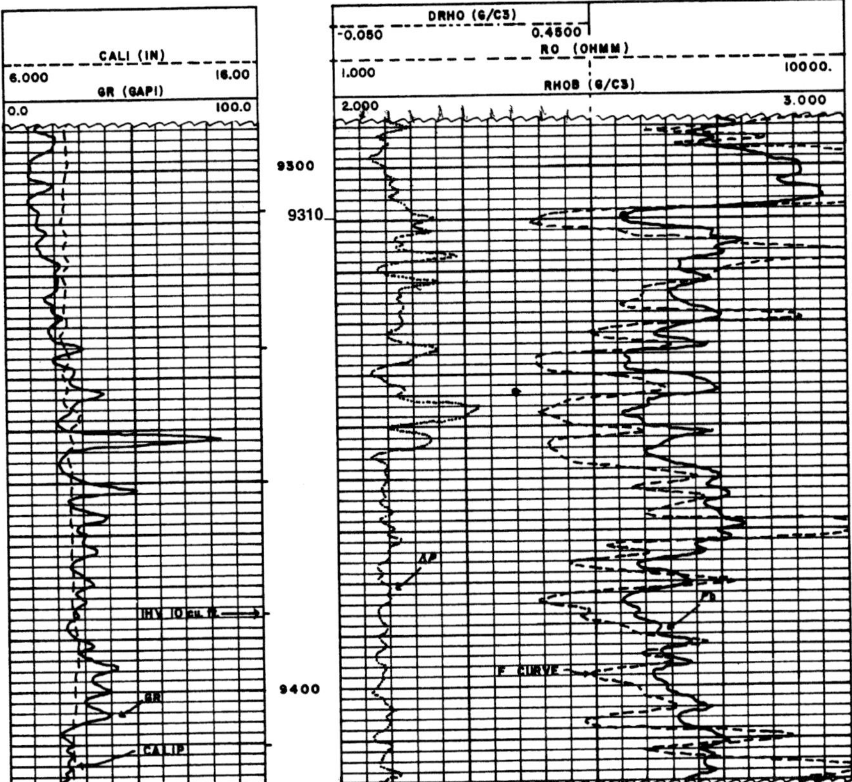

CALI (IN)
6.000
16.00
GR (GAPI)
0.0
100.0
9300
9310
9400
GR
CALIP
DRHO (G/C3)
-0.050
0.4500
RO (OHMM)
1.000
10000.
RHOB (G/C3)
2.000
3.000
F CURVE

Fig. 7.9. A bulk density log with gamma ray log, caliper and formation factor curve (after Asquith and Gibson 1982)

4. *Gamma ray logs* measure natural radioactivity in formations and can be used for identifying lithologies and for correlating zones. Shale-free sandstones and carbonates have low concentrations of radioactive material and therefore give low gamma ray readings. As shale content increases, the gamma ray log response increases because of the concentration of radioactive material in shale. However, potassium-feldspar, micas, glauconite, or uranium-rich waters produce a high gamma ray response in clean or shale-free sandstones and in this case a "spectralog" can be run in addition to the gamma ray log as it breaks the natural radioactivity of a formation into the different types of radioactive material such as potassium, thorium and uranium.

Table 7.3. Matrix densities of common lithologies used in the Density Porosity Formula (after Schlumberger 1972)

	ρ_{ma} (g cm^{-3})
Sandstone	2.648
Limestone	2.710
Dolomite	2.876
Anhydrite	2.977
Salt	2.032

Volume of shale calculation: Because of the radioactivity of the shale, the gamma raylog can be used to calculate volume of shale in porous reservoirs by first determining the gamma ray index as follows:

$$I_{GR} = \frac{GR_{\log} - GR_{\min}}{GR_{\max} - GR_{\min}} \tag{7.11}$$

where:

I_{GR} = Gamma ray index
GR_{Log} = Gamma ray reading of formation
GR_{min} = Minimum gamma ray (clear sand or carbonate)
GR_{max} = Maximum gamma ray (shale)

(Some log analysts resist the use of Eq. 7.11 to gas bearing formations and use instead: $\phi_{N\text{-}D} = (\phi_N + \phi_D) / 2$ in oil or water bearing formations.)

The volume of shale is also calculated mathematically from the gamma ray index (I_{GR}) by the following *Dresser Atlas* (Dresser Industries Inc. 1979) formula:

- For consolidated/older rocks:

$$V_{sh} = 0.33(2^{(2 \times I_{GR})} - 1.0) \tag{7.12}$$

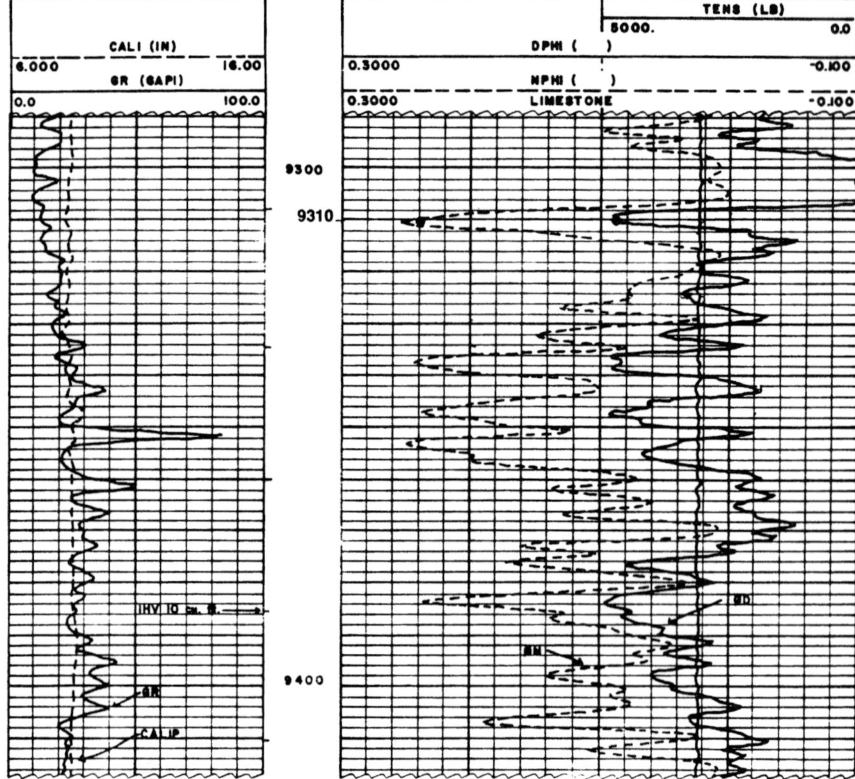
CALI (IN)
6.000
16.00
GR (GAPI)
0.0
100.0
9300
9310
9400
GR
CALIP
TENS (LB)
5000.
0.0
DPHI ( )
0.3000
-0.100
NPHI ( )
0.3000
LIMESTONE
-0.100
SD
SH

Fig. 7.10.
A combination neutron-density log with gamma ray log and caliper (after Asquith and Gibson 1982)

- For unconsolidated/Tertiary rocks:

$$V_{sh} = 0.083(2^{(3.7\times I_{GR})} - 1.0) \tag{7.13}$$

where:
V_{sh} = volume of shale
I_{GR} = gamma ray index

7.2.5 Log Interpretation and Applications

7.2.5.1 *Micro-resistivity Logs*

Complete interpretation of electric logs can be made empirically by comparing an electric log a sample log from the same well (Maher 1964). Figure 7.11 shows certain generalizations of this interpretation by a hypothetical electric log. The curves representing highly resistive rocks in this figure include limestone, dolomite, anhydrite, or quartzite. The numbers below refer to some general examples to aid the field geologist interpret electric logs:

1. Shale is indicated when the micro-resistivity curves have little or no separation and all curves show low readings. The shale baseline of the spontaneous potential curve (SP) may drift gently with depth and may shift abruptly between marine and continental sediments, but it remains relatively constant in shale or clay beds of the same origin.
2. Sandstone containing fresh water is indicated by the separation of the micro-resistivity curves, the large deflections of all resistivity curves to the right, and a moderate deflection of the SP curve to either the left or right away from the shale baseline.
3. Sandstone containing salt water is indicated by the separation of the micro-resistivity curves, the moderate deflection of the short normal curve to the right, the slight deflection of the long normal curve, the left deflection of the lateral curve, and the large deflection of the SP curve to the left.
4. Sandstone containing oil or gas is indicated by the separation of the micro-resistivity curves, the large deflections of all resistivity curves to the right and the large deflection of the self-potential curve to the left.
5. Sandstone containing oil or gas and salt water is indicated by the separation of the micro-resistivity curves, the large deflection of the short and long normal curves at the top and their gradual recession toward the bottom of the left deflection of the lateral curve in the lower part.
6. Sandy shale containing salt water is indicated by the lack of separation of the micro-resistivity curves ex-

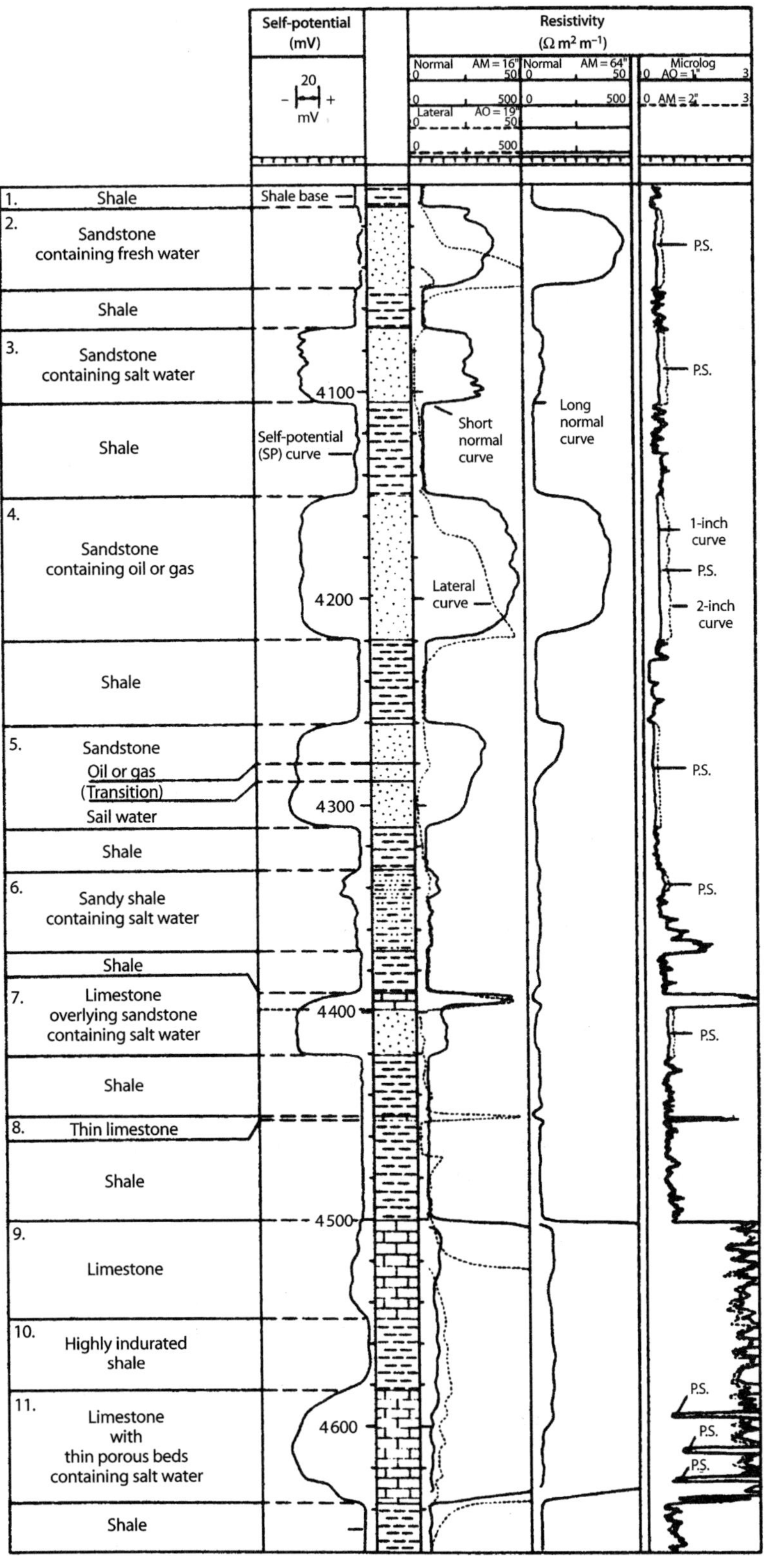
Self-potential (mV)
20
mV
Resistivity (Ω m² m⁻¹)
Normal AM = 16"
Normal AM = 64"
Lateral AO = 19"
Microlog AO = 1"
AM = 2"
1. Shale
Shale base
2. Sandstone containing fresh water
Shale
3. Sandstone containing salt water
4100
Shale
Self-potential (SP) curve
Short normal curve
Long normal curve
4. Sandstone containing oil or gas
4200
Lateral curve
1-inch curve
2-inch curve
P.S.
Shale
5. Sandstone
Oil or gas
(Transition)
Sail water
4300
Shale
6. Sandy shale containing salt water
Shale
7. Limestone overlying sandstone containing salt water
4400
Shale
8. Thin limestone
Shale
4500
9. Limestone
10. Highly indurated shale
11. Limestone with thin porous beds containing salt water
4600
Shale

Fig. 7.11. Electric log curves and their characteristic expression of common lithologies, fluids, and gas. Numbers on column indicate depth in feet. *AM* and *AO* refer to electrical circuits employed in obtaining the respective resistivity curves (adapted from unpublished diagrams of C. K. Ruddick, Schlumberger Well Surveying Corporation, Tusla, OK, USA)

cept at the top where mud has invaded a slightly permeable part, and the slight deflections of the resistivity and SP curves.

7. Limestone overlying sandstone containing salt water is indicated by the combination of lateral and self potential curves. The limestone causes pronounced

deflections and near coincidence of the two micro-resistivity curves and similar deflections of the short normal and lateral curves, as well as by the rounded slope of the self-potential curve.
8. Thin limestone is indicated by the pronounced and nearly coincident deflections of the micro-resistivity curves, the small reverse deflections of the short and long normal curves, the pronounced deflection of the lateral curve, and the lack of deflection of the self-potential curve.
9. Limestone is indicated by the pronounced deflections of the micro-resistivity and resistivity curves, and the small rounded deflection of the SP curve.
10. Highly indurated shale is indicated by the pronounced deflections of the micro-resistivity and resistivity curves, and the lack of deflection of the SP curve.
11. Limestone with thin beds containing salt water is indicated by the alternating high and low resistivities recorded by the micro-resistivity curves, the undulating character of the short normal and lateral curves, and the rounded slope of the top and base of the self-potential curve. The abrupt slope changes in the middle of the self-potential curve are indicative of porous beds, and the positive separation of the micro-resistivity curves where low resistivities are recorded opposite these beds, suggests appreciable permeability.

7.2.5.2 *Radioactivity Logs*

Maher (1964) outlined the empirical interpretation of radioactivity logs and described their usefulness in the detailed examination of drill cuttings.

The main operational variables that affect a radioactivity log are casing, hole size, and fluid level. Although radioactivity logs can be made effectively through one or more strings of casing, a shift of both the gamma-ray and neutron curves may occur at the end of each string of casing. Shifts in the neutron curve generally occur wherever the diameter of the hole has been changed and at the level of fluid in the hole.

The gamma-ray curve may be interpreted in terms of lithology and the neutron curve may be used to locate porous zones and to estimate percentage of porosity. These interpretations are made by comparisons of the curve values on the individual logs. Gamma-ray curves expressing low values suggest anhydrite, salt, limestone, dolomite, or sandstone; those of medium value suggest shaly limestone, calcareous shale, shaly sandstone, sandy shale, shaly dolomite, or dolomitic shale; and those of high value suggest shale (including siltstone), bentonite, volcanic ash, and granite (Wylie and Rose 1950).

General interpretations are discussed below by Maher (1964), are illustrated in Fig. 7.12 and by a hypothetical radioactivity log. The numbers below refer to the examples presented in this illustration:

1. Shale is usually indicated by high gamma-ray-curve values and low neutron-curve values. Black organic shale has a maximum value of gamma ray curve. Shale has a minimum response on the neutron curve because of its high porosity and consequent large content of interstitial water.
2. Anhydrite usually produces a low gamma ray curve value, lower than that of limestone, dolomite, or sandstone, and a high neutron curve value, which indicates little fluid content and little porosity.
3. Alternating beds of anhydrite and salt are suggested by a succession of similar but unequal values in the high range of gamma ray and neutron curves. The salt beds are generally separable from the anhydrite beds because of their slightly higher gamma ray curve values and slightly lower neutron curve values. Pure salt beds may record gamma ray curve values less than those for anhydrite but generally salt beds are not pure.
4. Sandstone produces a low value for the gamma-ray curve and a low to medium value for the neutron curve. Porous limestone or dolomite may create a similar response and may not be distinguished with certainty from sandstone without sample information.
5. Thin-bedded sandstone and shale produce an alternating succession of high and medium values on the gamma ray curve and alternating unequal low values on the neutron curve. Porous limestone, dolomite, and shale produce similar curves.
6. Shaly sandstone is suggested by medium gamma-ray-curve values and medium to low neutron curve values. Shaly limestone or dolomite may produce similar curve characteristics.
7. Limestone and dolomite are generally indicated by low gamma ray curve values and high neutron curve values.
8. Interbedded limestone and shale produce alternating unequal low to medium gamma-ray-curve values and irregular high neutron-curve values. Interbedded dolomite and shale produce similar curves.
9. Shaly limestone, like shaly sandstone or dolomite, is suggested by medium gamma ray curve values and medium to low neutron-curve values.
10. Shale generally produces high to extremely high values on the gamma-ray curve and low values on the neutron curve. Volcanic ash or bentonite in any shale usually causes a similar response.
11. Limestone with porous beds in middle is suggested by low gamma ray curve values and neutron curve values ranging from high to low. Dolomite with a zone of porosity produces a similar response, although the neutron curve values are slightly lower in intensity.
12. Alternating beds of limestone and dolomite are suggested by the succession of low but unequal gamma ray curve values and alternating high and medium values of the neutron curve. Porous dolomite is indicated by the low neutron-curve value of the lower part of the unit.

Fig. 7.12. Radioactivity-log curves and their characteristic expression of common lithologies (adapted from Lane-Wells 1964)

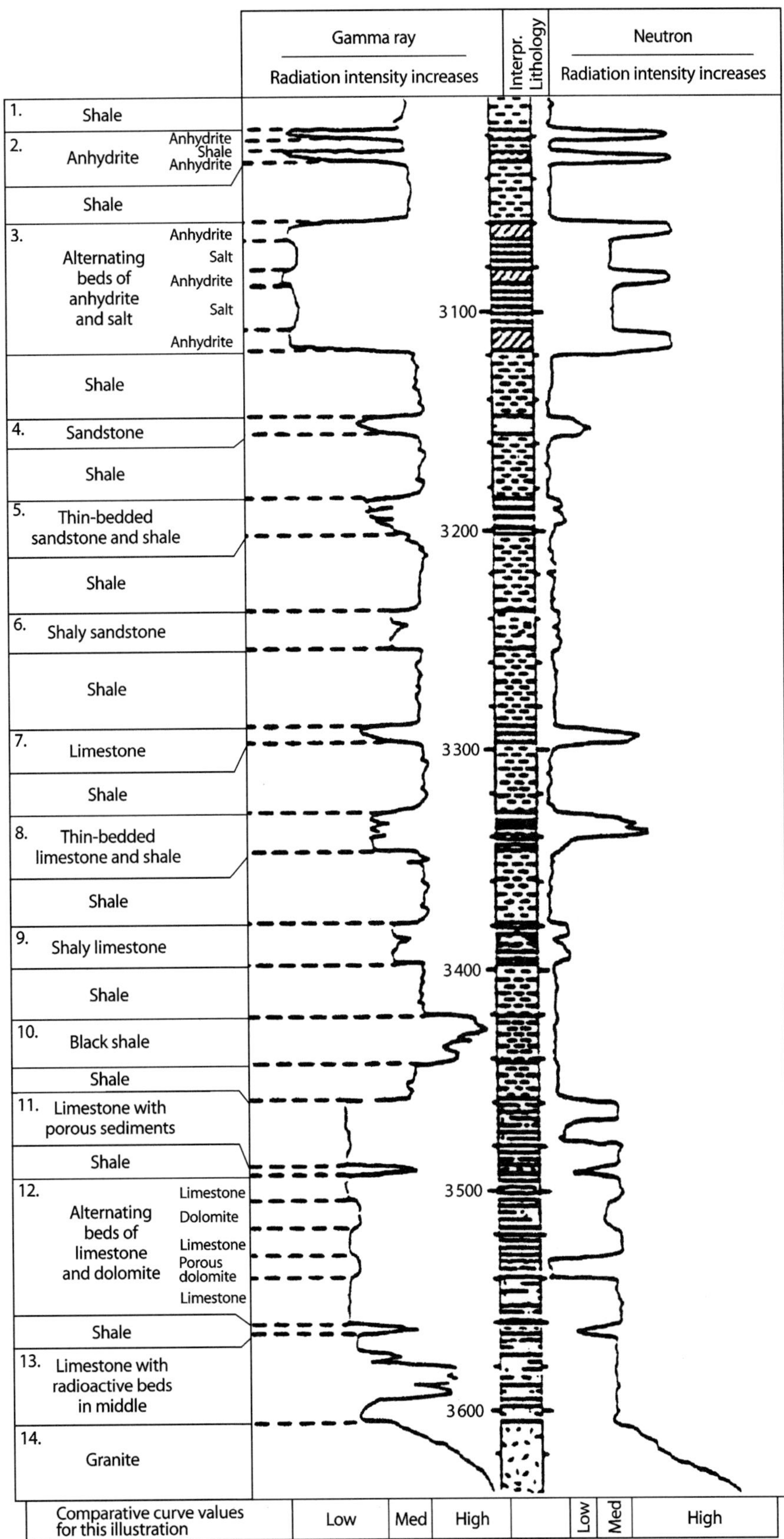
Gamma ray
Radiation intensity increases
Interpr. Lithology
Neutron
Radiation intensity increases
1. Shale
2. Anhydrite
Anhydrite
Shale
Anhydrite
Shale
3. Alternating beds of anhydrite and salt
Anhydrite
Salt
Anhydrite
Salt
Anhydrite
Shale
4. Sandstone
Shale
5. Thin-bedded sandstone and shale
Shale
6. Shaly sandstone
Shale
7. Limestone
Shale
8. Thin-bedded limestone and shale
Shale
9. Shaly limestone
Shale
10. Black shale
Shale
11. Limestone with porous sediments
Shale
12. Alternating beds of limestone and dolomite
Limestone
Dolomite
Limestone
Porous dolomite
Limestone
Shale
13. Limestone with radioactive beds in middle
14. Granite
3100
3200
3300
3400
3500
3600
Comparative curve values for this illustration
Low
Med
High
Low
Med
High

Table 7.4. Summary of borehole log applications (after Day 2000)

Required information	Potential logging techniques
Lithology, Stratigraphy Formation Properties	
General lithology and stratigraphic correlation	Electric (SP, single-point resistance, normal and focused resistivity, dipmeter, IP, cross-well AC voltage); EM (induction, dielectric); all nuclear (open or cased holes); caliper logs made in open holes, borehole television
Bed thickness	Single-point resistance, focused resistivity (thin beds), gamma, gamma-gamma, neutron, acoustic velocity
Cavity detection	Caliper, acoustic televiewer, cross-hole radar, cross-hole seismic
Sedimentary structure orientation	Dipmeter, borehole television, acoustic televiewer
Large geologic structures	Gravity, surface-borehole/cross-hole seismic, cross-hole radar
Total porosity/bulk density	Calibrated dielectric, sonic logs in open holes; cross-hole radar; calibrated neutron, neutron lifetime, gamma-gamma logs, computer-assisted tomography (CAT) in open or cased holes; nuclear magnetic resonance, induced polarization, cross-hole seismic
Effective porosity	Calibrated long-normal and focused resistivity or induction logs
Clay or shale content	Gamma log, induction log, IP log
Relative sand-shale content	Gamma, SP log
Grain size/pore size distribution	*Grain size*: possible relation to formation factor derived from electric, induction or gamma logs; *pore size distribution*: nuclear magnetic resonance; *soil macroporosity*: computerized axial tomography (CAT)
Compressible/stress-strain properties	Acoustic waveform, uphole/downhole seismic, cross-hole seismic
Geochemistry	Neutron activation log, spectral-gamma log
Aquifer properties	
Location of water level or saturated zones	Electric, induction, acoustic velocity, temperature or fluid conductivity in open hole or inside casing; neutron or gamma-gamma logs in open hole or outside casing
Moisture content	Calibrated neutron logs, gamma-gamma logs, nuclear magnetic resonance, computerized axial tomography (CAT)
Permeability/hydraulic conductivity	No direct measurement by logging; may be related to porosity, single borehole tracer methods (injectivity), 2-wave sonic amplitude, temperature, nuclear magnetic resonance; estimation may be possible using vertical seismic profiling
Secondary permeability-fractures, solution openings	Caliper, temperature, flowmeters (mechanical, thermal, EM), sonic, acoustic waveform/televiewer, borehole television logs, SP resistance, induction logs, cross-well AC voltage, surface-borehole CSAMT, vertical seismic profiling, cross-hole seismic
Specific yield of unconfined aquifers	Calibrated neutron logs during pumping
Ground-water flow and direction	
Infiltration	Temperature logs, time-interval neutron logs under special circumstances or radioactive tracers
Direction, velocity, and path of ground-water flow	Thermal flowmeter single-well tracer techniques – point dilution and single-well pulse; multiwell tracer techniques
Source and movement of water in a well	Infectivity profile mechanical, thermal, EM flowmeters; tracer logging during pumping or injection; temperature logs

Table 7.4. *Continued*

Required information	Potential logging techniques
Borehole fluid characterization	
Water quality/salinity	Calibrated fluid conductivity and temperature; SP log, single-point resistance, normal/multielectrode resistivity, neutron lifetime
Water chemistry	Dissolved oxygen, Eh, pH probes; specific ion electrodes
Pore fluid chemistry	Induced polarization log, neutron activation (if matrix effects can be accounted for)
Mudcake detection	Microresistivity, caliper, acoustic televiewer
Contaminant characterization	
Conductive plumes	Induction log, resistivity, surface-borehole CSAMT
Contaminant chemistry	Specific ion electrodes, fiber optic chemical sensors
Hydrocarbon detection	Dielectric log, IP log
Radioactive contaminants	Spectral gamma log
Dispersion, dilution, and movement of waste	Fluid conductivity and temperature logs, gamma logs for some radioactive wastes, fluid sampler
Buried object detection	Geophysical diffraction tomography
Borehole/casing characterization	
Determining construction of existing wells, diameter and position of casing, perforations, screens	Gamma-gamma, caliper, collar, and perforation locator, borehole television
Guide to screen setting	All logs providing data on the lithology, water-bearing characteristics, and correlation and thickness of aquifers
Borehole deviation	Deviation log, dipmeter, single-shot probe, dolly and cage tests
Cementing/gravel pack	Caliper, temperature, gamma-gamma; acoustic waveform for cement bond; noise/Sonan log
Casing corrosion/integrity	Borehole television/photography, under some conditions caliper or collar locator
Casing detection/logging	Casing collar locator, borehole television/photography; various electric, nuclear and acoustic logs
Casing leaks and/or plugged screen	Tracer and flowmeters
Behind casing flow	Neutron activation and neutron lifetime logs

13. Limestone, with radioactive beds in the middle, is suggested by low gamma ray curve values at the top and base. High gamma ray curve deviations are recorded by sandstone containing radioactive minerals.
14. Granite and highly radioactive igneous rocks are generally indicated by extremely high gamma ray curve and neutron curve values.

Maher (1964) discussed the use of radioactivity logs in stratigraphic studies as they are particularly valuable in locating zones of porosity in formations, estimating porosity, and in making local correlation's where the stratigraphic section is well known. They are also useful in regional structural studies wherever a thin radioactive bed extends over a considerable area. As with electric logs, however, they cannot be used to establish detailed regional correlation in relatively unexplored regions nor can they be used to interpret lithologic details. Radioactivity logs are also valuable in regional studies for accurately determining the tops and bottoms of formations.

Table 7.4 presents a summary of borehole log applications.

Table 7.5 shows general texts on borehole geophysical logging and interpretations.

Appendix 7.A presents electric log interpretations.

Appendix 7.B contents quantitative interpratations of specific geophysical well logs.

Table 7.5. General tests on borehole geophysical logging and interpretation (Day 2000; for references listed in the table see Day 2000)

Reference	Description
Asquith and Gibson (1982)	Text on basic well log analysis for geologists
Birdwell Division (1973)	Company that used to be in business of providing well logging services. 1973 guide on geophysical well log interpretation including SP, resistivity, gamma, gamma-gamma, neutron, fluid conductivity, temperature, and 3-D velocity. Hamilton and Myung (1979) provide summary information on major geophysical logging techniques
Doveton (1986)	Text of log analysis for interpretation of subsurface geology with emphasis on computer models
Dresser Atlas (1974, 1975, 1976, 1982)	Various publications by a company that used to be in the business of providing logging services: Log review (1974) covers induction, resistivity, acoustic velocity, gamma-gamma, neutron-gamma, diplog, neutron lifetime. Log interpretation fundamentals (1975) and charts (1979). Also, a home study course on well logging and interpretation (1982)
Ellis (1987)	Text on well logging resistivity, SP, induction, gamma, neutron, acoustic
Foster and Beaumont (1990)	2-volume collection of reprints of papers on formation evaluation: (I) log evaluation, (II) log interpretation. Oriented toward petroleum applications
Hearst and Nelson (1985)	Text on well logging for physical properties
Helander (1983)	Text covering SP, resistivity, acoustic, and radioactivity logging and interpretation
Hilchie (1982a)	Text on log interpretation oriented toward geologists and engineers: resistivity, SP, induction, acoustic, gamma, density, neutron, combined porosity, and focused resistivity logs
Hilchie (1982b)	Text on advanced well log interpretation
Labo (1987)	Text covering density, gravimetric, acoustic, seismic, and dipmeter logs
LeRoy et al. (1987)	Edited volume with several chapters devoted to geophysical logging methods
Lynch (1962)	Text on formation evaluation
Nelson (1985)	Text covering use of downhole methods for characterization of fractured rock
Pirson (1963, 1983)	1963 handbook on well log analysis and 1983 text on geologic well log interpretation
Rider (1986)	Text on geological interpretation of logs: caliper, temperature, SP, resistivity, induction, gamma, spectral gamma, sonic/acoustic velocity, density
Schlumberger (1989a,b, 1991)	Latest edition of Schlumberger Educational Services publications on log interpretation principles and applications covering uncased holes (1989a), cased holes (1989b), and log interpretation charts (1991). See citations for methods covered. Earlier publications include Schlumberger (1972, 1974)
Scott and Tibbets (1974)	Bureau of Mines information circular reviewing well log techniques for mineral deposit evaluation
Serra (1984a,b)	Volume 1: acquisition of well log data; Volume 2: log interpretation. See citation for methods covered
SPWLA (1978a,b, 1990)	Series of reprint volumes containing papers on acoustic logging (1978a), gamma, neutron and density logging (1978b), and borehole imaging (1990)
Tearpocke and Bischke (1991)	Text on subsurface geological mapping using a variety of sources of information, including geophysical data
Tittman (1986)	Well logging text covering electrical, nuclear, and sonic methods
Wyllie (1963)	Text on fundamentals of well log interpretation. See citation for methods covered

References

Archie GE (1942) The electrical resistivity log as an aid in determining some reservoir characteristics. J Petrol Technol 5:54–62

Asquith GB, Gibson CR (1982) Basic well log analysis for geologists. Am. Assoc. of Petroleum Geologists, Tulsa, Oklahoma, pp 1–103

Day RW (2000) Geotechnical engineer's portable handbook. McGraw-Hill, New York

Dresser Industries Inc. (1975, 1979) Dresser atlas – log interpretation fundamentals and charts. Houston, Texas

Jenning HY, Timur A (1973) Significant contributions in formation evaluation and well testing. J Petroleum Technology 25:79–88

Lane-Wells (1964) Manual – radioactivity well logging. In: Maher JC (ed) The composite interpretive method of logging drill cuttings, 2nd edn. Oklahoma Geological Survey, University of Oklahoma, Norman (Guide Book XIV, pp 10–14)

LeRoy LW (1950) Subsurface geologic methods, 2nd edn. Colorado School of Mines, Department of Publication, Golden, Colorado, pp 71–79, 195–196, 856–977

Maher JC (1964) The composite interpretative method of logging drill cuttings. Oklahoma Geological Survey, University of Oklahoma, Norman (Guide Book XIV, pp 24–30)

Schlumberger (1972) Log interpretation manual/principles, vol I. Schlumberger Well Series Inc., Ridgefield. In: Asquith GB, Gibson CR (1982) Basic well log analysis for geologists. The American Association of Petroleum Geologists, Tulsa, Oklahoma, USA (Methods in exploration series)

Schlumberger (1974) Log interpretation manual/applications, vol II. Schlumberger Well Series Inc., Ridgefield. In: Asquith GB, Gibson CR (1982) Basic well log analysis for geologists. The American Association of Petroleum Geologists, Tulsa, Oklahoma, USA (Methods in exploration series)

U.S. Environmental Protection Agency (1977) An introduction to the technology of subsurface waste injection. U.S. EPA, Cincinnati, Ohio (600/2-77-240, 1977, pp 73–88)

Wylie MRJ, Rose WD (1950) Some theoretical considerations related to the quantitative evaluations of electric log data. J Petroleum Technology 189:105–110

Appendix 7.A · Electric Log Interpretations

7.A.1 Calculation of Formation Temperature

The formation temperature is estimated (Asquith and Gibson 1982) by depending on the theory of the linear regression equation for determining the geothermal gradient or slope (m) as follows (Schlumberger 1974; Archie 1942):

$$y = (mx) + c \quad \text{or} \quad m = (y - c) / x$$

where
- y = temperature (bottom hole temperature BHT or formation temperature T_f)
- c = constant – e.g. the surface temperature (T_{surf} = 70 °F or 21 °C)
- x = depth (total depth TD or formation depth FD)

Solve for m and then for the formation temperature T_f as follows:
Therefore:

$$m = \frac{BHT - T_{surf}}{TD} \text{ (°F/100ft)}$$

Also:

$$T_f = (m \times FD) + T_{surf}$$

Then the resistivities of the different fluids (R_m, R_{mf}, or R_w) can be corrected to formation temperature as follows.
Resistivity at formation temperature

$$R_w T_f = R_{w,\,surf}(T_{surf} + 6.77) / (T_f + 6.77)$$

N.B.: $R_{w,\,surf}$ and T_{surf} are usually given in the log's header and $R_{w,\,surf}$ can be also determined from DST or SP curve.

7.A.2 Porosity Logs

There are three types of porosity logs: sonic, density and neutron logs as follows (Schlumberger 1974).

7.A.2.1 *Sonic Log*

The *sonic log* is a porosity log that measures the interval transit time (Δt) of a compressional sound wave through one foot of formation. The unit of measure is microseconds per foot (μs ft^{-1}). Interval transit time is related to formation porosity. Matrix porosity can be obtained from sonic log which does not consider the fracture secondary porosity (vugs or fractures). Sonic log uses Wylie and Rose equation (1950).

$$\phi_{SN} = \frac{\Delta t_{log} - \Delta t_{ma}}{\Delta t_{fluid} - \Delta t_{ma}}$$

(for consolidated sandstone, and carbonates with intergranular porosity), where:
- ϕ_{SN} = sonic derived porosity
- Δt_{ma} = interval transit time of the matrix (Table 7.A1)
- Δt_{log} = interval transit time of formation
- Δt_{fluid} = interval transit time of the fluid in the well bore (fresh mud = 189; salt mud = 185).

N.B.: In unconsolidated sands, an empirical compaction factor (Cp) should be determined by multiplying the sonic derived porosity by 1/Cp:

$$Cp = (\Delta t_{sh} \times 0.01C)$$

where:
- Δt_{sh} = interval transit time for adjacent shale
- C = constant; normally = 1.0

7.A.2.2 *Density Log*

The *formation density log* is a porosity log that measures the *electron density* of a formation that is related to the formation's bulk density (ρ_b) in g cm^{-3}. Bulk density, in turn, can be related to formation porosity in g cm^{-3}.

It can assist to identify evaporite minerals, and evaluate shaly sand reservoirs. The formula for calculating density porosity is:

$$\phi_{DEN} = \frac{\rho_{ma} - \rho_b}{\rho_{ma} - \rho_{fl}}$$

where
- ϕ_{DEN} = density derived porosity
- ρ_{ma} = matrix density (for sandstone = 2.648; limestone = 2.710; dolomite = 2.876; anhyrite = 2.977; salt = 2.032)
- ρ_b = formation bulk density
- ρ_{fl} = fluid density (1.1 salt mud, and 1.0 fresh mud).

7.A.2.3 *Neutron Log*

The *neutron log* is a porosity log that measures the hydrogen ion concentration in a formation. In shale-free formations where porosity is filled with water, the neutron log measures water-filled porosity.

7.A.2.4 *Combination Neutron-Density Log*

The combination neutron-density log is a combination porosity log. It is used to define lithology. It can be determined by the following equation:

$$\phi_{N\text{-}D} = \sqrt{\frac{\phi_N^2 + \phi_D^2}{2}}$$

where

$\phi_{N\text{-}D}$ = neutron-density porosity
ϕ_N = neutron porosity (limestone units)
ϕ_D = density porosity (limestone units)

7.A.3 Archie Equation (S_w and S_{xo})

Water saturation of the uninvaded zone is calculated by the Archie (1942) formula:

$$S_W = \left(\frac{a}{\phi^m}\frac{R_W}{R_t}\right)^{1/n}$$

where:

S_w = water saturation of the uninvaded zone (Archie method)
R_w = resistivity of formation at formation temperature
R_t = true resistivity of formation (i.e. R_{Ild} or R_{LLd} corrected for invasion)
ϕ = porosity
a = tortosity factor (Table 7.A2)
m = cementation exponent (Table 7.A2)
n = saturation exponent which is normally equal to 2.0

Water saturation of a formation's flushed zone (S_{xo}) can be evaluated as follows:

$$S_{xo} = \left(\frac{aR_{mf}}{\phi^m R_{xo}}\right)^{1/n}$$

Table 7.A.1. Sonic velocities and interval transit times for different matrices. These constants are used in the sonic porosity formula (after Schlumberger 1972)

	V_{ma} (ft s^{-1})	Δt_{ma} (μs ft^{-1})	Δt_{ma} commonly used (μs ft^{-1})
Sandstone	18 000 to 19 500	55.5 to 51.0	55.5 to 51.0
Limestone	21 000 to 23 000	47.6 to 43.5	47.6
Dolomite	23 000 to 26 000	43.5 to 38.5	43.5
Anhydrite	20 000	50.0	50.0
Salt	15 000	66.7	67.0
Casing (iron)	17 500	57.0	57.0

Table 7.A.2. Different coefficients and exponents used to calculate formation factor (*F*) (modified after Asquith and Gibson 1982; hints to references refer to the original work)

$F = a/\phi^m$	General relationship, where: a = tortuosity factor m = cementation exponent ϕ = porosity
$F = 1/\phi^2$	For carbonates
$F = 0.81/\phi^2$	For consolidated sandstones
$F = 0.62/\phi^{2.15}$	Humble formula for unconsolidated sands
$F = 1.45/\phi^{1.54}$	For average sands (after Carothers 1958)
$F = 1.65/\phi^{1.33}$	For shaly sands (after Carothers 1958)
$F = 1.45/\phi^{1.70}$	For calcareous sands (after Carothers 1958)
$F = 0.85/\phi^{2.14}$	For carbonates (after Carothers 1958)
$F = 2.45/\phi^{1.08}$	For Pliocene sands, Southern California (after Carothers and Porter 1970)
$F = 1\text{–}97/\phi^{1.29}$	For Miocene sands, Texas-Louisiana Gulf Coast (after Carothers and Porter 1970)
$F = 1.0/\phi^{(2.05-\phi)}$	For clean granular formations (after Sethi 1979)

Table 7.A.3. Fundamental equations of well log interpretation (after Asquith and Gibson 1982)

Porosity:	
Sonic log	$\phi_{SN} = (\Delta t_{log} - \Delta t_{ma}) / (\Delta t_{fluid} - \Delta t_{ma})$
Density log	$\phi_{DEN} = (\rho_{ma} - \rho_b) / (\rho_{ma} - \rho_{fl})$
Neutron-density log	$\phi_{N\text{-}D} = \sqrt{((\phi_N^2 - \phi_D^2) / 2)}$
Formation factor:	
$F = m / \phi^m$	General
$F = 1.0 / \phi^2$	Carbonates
$F = 0.81 / \phi^2$	Consolidated sandstones
$F = 0.62 / \phi^{2.15}$	Uncosolidated sands
Formation water resistivity:	
$SSP = -K \times \log (R_{mf} / R_w)$	
$R_w = R_0 / F$	
Water saturations:	
$S_w^{n*} = F \times (R_w / R_t)$	Water saturation uninvaded zone
$S_{xo}^{n*} = F \times (R_{mf} / R_{xo})$	Water saturation flushed zone
$S_{wr} = (R_{xo} / R_t)^{0.625} / (R_{mf} / R_w)$	Water saturation uninvaded ratio method

n^* = saturation exponent which varies from 1.8 to 2.5 but most often equals 2.0.

where:

S_{xo} = water saturation of the flushed zone
R_{mf} = resistivity of the mud filtrate at formation temperature
R_{xo} = shallow resistivity from laterolog 8, microspherically focused log*, or microlaterolog*

Water saturation of the flushed zone (S_{xo}) can be used as an indicator of hydrocarbon moveability, which is not of our interest.

Table 7.A.3 shows fundamental equations of well log interpretation.

Appendix 7.B · Quantitative Interpretation of Specific Geophysical Well Logs

The following are the quantitative interpretation of specific geophysical well logs given in Figs. 7.2–7.10:

Fig. 7.2 – Spontaneous Potential Log Curve

The left track of the log shows the spontaneous potential (SP) log. It is equal to −40 mV (measured from the shale base line) at a depth of 7446 feet (2270 m).

- Bed thickness = 8 ft; 7442–7450 ft (2.44 m; 2268.32–2270.76 m)
- Resistivity short normal (R_J) = 28 Ωm
- Formation depth = 7446 ft (2270 m)

Fig. 7.3 – Induction Electric Log Curves

The middle log track contains two resistivity curves:

- The first curve measures shallow resistivity (R_J, 16" – short normal electrode log represented by solid line) and it shows a value of 28 Ωm at the sample depth of 7446 ft (counted as ±6 increments)
- The second curve measures deep resistivity (R_w, an induction log represented by *dotted line*) and it shows a value of 10 Ωm (or 2 increments) at the above sample depth.
- The log track on the far right contains a conductivity curve measured by the induction log which actually measures conductivity from which resistivity can be derived (as the reciprocal of the conductivity). The conductivity increases from right to left in increments of 50 mΩm^{-1}. At a depth of 7446 m, Track 3 shows a value of 100 mΩm^{-1} and as resistivity = 1000 / conductivity, then resistivity = 10 mΩm at the above depth.

Fig. 7.4 – Dual Induction Focused Log Curves

When freshwater based drilling muds invade a water-bearing zone ($R_{xo} > R_I > R_w$). The three curves on the right side of the log show higher resistivity values as distances increase to the right as follows:

- Log curve R_{ILD} – Deep induction log resistivity curves measure the formation resistivity of the uninvaded zone (R_w). At the water bearing interval = 5 870–5 970 ft (1 789–1 820 m), the "ILD" curve shows a low resistivity as R_w is much less than the R_{mf}.

- Log curve R_{ILM} – Medium induction log resistivity curves measure the resistivity of the invaded zone (R_J) which is intermediate resistivity because of the mixture of formation water (R_w) and mud filtrate (R_{mf}).
- Log curve R_{SFL} – Spherically focused log resistivity curves measure the resistivity of the flushed zone (R_{xo}) which is high because of the high resistivity of the mud filtrate (R_{mf}).

Fig. 7.5 – Dual Laterolog – Microspherically Focused Log Curves

Saltwater-based drilling muds invade a water bearing zone (low R_{mf} and low R_w), the three curves on the right side of the log show resistivity values to be higher as distance increases to the right as follows:

- Log Curve LLD – Deep laterolog resistivity curves measure formation resistivity. At the water-bearing interval 9 830–9 980, the LLD curve read low resistivity because of the formation water (R_w).
- Log Curve LLS – Shallow laterolog resistivity curves measure the resistivity in the invaded zone (R_J) which is low because R_{mf} is approximately equal to R_w.
- Log Curve MSFL – Microspherically focused log resistivity curves measure the resistivity of the flushed zone (R_{xo}) which is also low because the saltwater mud filtrate has low resistivity.

Fig. 7.6 – Microlog with Spontaneous Potential Log and Caliper

At the water-bearing zone interval at depth 5 146–5 238 ft (1569–1597 m), the log shows permeability in two ways: Positive separation between the micro-normal and micro-inverse logs in Tracks 2 and 3 and decreased borehole size due to mudcake detected by caliper log in Track 1.

The caliper shows a borehole diameter more than 11 inches (27.9 cm) just above the water-bearing zone, but the hole size decreases to about 8.5 inches (21.6 cm) within the zone (*solid line* in Track 1), thus indicating the presence of mudcake and a permeable zone.

The positive separation between the micro-normal and micro-inverse log (of about 2 Ωm) is indicated where the resistivity value of the micro-normal log (*dashed line*) is greater than the resistivity value for the micro-inverse log (*solid line*).

Fig. 7.7 – Proximity Log with Microlog and Caliper

The proximity log reads the resistivity of the flushed zone (R_{xo}), the microlog determines the permeable zone and the caliper log determines the size of the borehole.

Track 1 depicts both a microlog and a caliper log. At the sample depth of 4 144 ft (1 263 m), the micro-normal (*dashed line*) shows higher resistivity than micro-inverse (*solid line*); both increases from right to left. Micro-inverse has a value of about 1.5 and micro-normal has a value of about 3.0. This positive separation indicates a permeable zone. The caliper log indicates a borehole about 9 inches (22.86 cm) in diameter because of the presence of a mudcake.

Tracks 2 and 3 show the proximity log that measures the resistivity of the flushed zone (R_{xo}). It needs a proximity value of 18 Ωm at the sample depth 4 144 ft (1 263 m) on the logarithmic scale.

Fig. 7.8 – Sonic Log with Gamma Ray Log and Caliper

Track 1 includes the gamma ray and caliper curves. The gamma ray scale (*solid line*) reads from 0 to 100 API gamma ray units, increasing from left to right in increments of 10 units. The caliper scale (*dashed line*) ranges from 6 to 16 inches (15.24–40.64 cm), from left to right in one-inch (2.54 cm) increments.

Tracks 2 and 3 show both the interval transit line (Δt) scale (*solid line*) and the porosity (*dashed line*) scale. Sonic log interval transit time (Δt) ranges from 40–80 μsec ft^{-1} (131.23–262.46 μsec m^{-1}) on the scale, whereas the sonic porosity measurement (limestone matrix) ranges from –10% to +30% porosity increasing from right to left and is shown by the dashed line. At the sample depth of 9 310 ft (2 838 m) a sonic log interval transit time (Δt) value is of 63 μsec ft^{-1} (206.7 μsec m^{-1}).

Fig. 7.9 – A Bulk Density Log with a Gamma Ray Log Caliper and Formation Factor Curve (F)

Track 1 includes both the gamma ray and caliper logs. The gamma ray values range from 0–100 API gamma ray units, and the caliper measures the borehole size from 6–16 inches (15.24–40.64 cm).

Tracks 2 and 3 record the bulk density curve (ρ_b) correction curve ($\Delta\rho$) and formation factor curve (F).

The bulk density (P_b) scale (*solid line*) ranges in value from 2.0 to 3.0 g cm^{-3}. The density log connection curve (P_{cr}) ranges in value from –0.05 to +0.45 g cm^{-3} in increments of 0.05 g cm^{-3} (only uses the left half of the log track). The formation factor curve (F) ranges in value from 1 to 10 000. The sample depth (9 310 ft/2 838 m) shows a bulk density (P_b) of 2.56 g cm^{-3}.

Fig. 7.10 – A Combination Neutron-Density Log with Gamma Ray Log and Caliper

Track 1 contains both gamma ray and caliper curves scales previously explained.

Tracks 2 and 3 include both neutron porosity (ϕ_N) and density porosity (ϕ_D) curves, ranging from −10 to +30% and is measured in limestone porosity units. On this log, the density porosity (ϕ_{DEN}) is represented by a *solid line* and the neutron porosity (ϕ_N) is represented by a *dashed line.*

At the sample depth 9 310 ft (2 838 m), the neutron porosity value (ϕ_N) is 24% and the density porosity value (ϕ_{DEN}) is 9%.

Part III

Ground-Water Hydrology, Ground-Water Contamination and Waste Management

Chapter 8

Ground-Water Hydrology, Hydrogeologic Methods, and Hydrogeologic Data Acquisition

8.1 Introduction

Ground water is one of most valuable natural resources and includes about 14% of all fresh water on the earth. It is the source of about 40% of the water used for all purposes exclusive of hydroelectric generation and water for cooling electric power plants.

Ground-water hydrology and hydrogeology deals with the occurrence, storage, movement, quality and quantity of water beneath the earth's surface. It involves the application of the physical, chemical, biological, and mathematical sciences (Meinzer 1942).

A few significant concept mark the development of hydrogeology in the last century, mainly its expansion beyond the search for water resources and increasing interest in qualitative and quantitative methodology. Advances made in understanding and mathematically describing the storage and movement of water beneath the land surface have accelerated over the past several decades (Hornberger 1993).

Water beneath the land surface occurs in two different zones, the upper zone, the vadose zone or the unsaturated zone, extends from the land surface to the water table and contains water and air. A lower zone beneath the water table is ground water or water in the phreatic water zone (saturated zone), in which all interconnected openings are full of water. Recharge of the saturated zone occurs by percolation of water from the land surface through the unsaturated zone into the saturated zone. The hydrostatic pressure at the top of the water table or saturated zone is one atmosphere (101 325 Pa) (Fig. 8.1).

The vadose zone (also called the zone of aeration) is divided into three parts: the zone of soil water on the top (a maximum depth of a meter or two), the intermediate zone, and the capillary zone (or capillary fringe), which varies in thickness according to the void size and physical character of the geologic units. For example, it can be 3 m thick in a clay material or a few cm wide in coarse sand.

At the water table, the pressure head is zero (i.e. equal to the atmospheric pressure). The atmospheric pressure increases below the water table and decreases above the water table. Thus the pressure head is negative in the vadose zone, which is sometimes referred to as soil tension or suction (Heath 1987).

The hydrological cycle – Water is a continually moving around through, and above the Earth as water vapor, liquid water, and ice; it is continually changing its form and continually being recycled all around the globe between

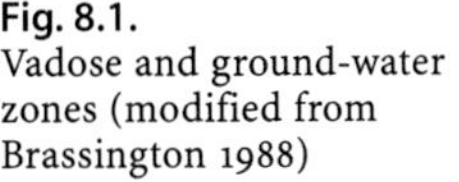

Fig. 8.1. Vadose and ground-water zones (modified from Brassington 1988)

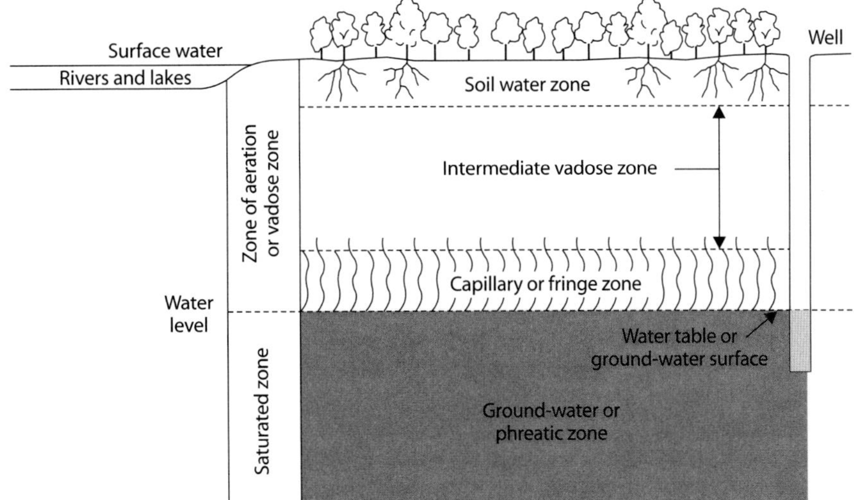
Surface water
Rivers and lakes
Well
Soil water zone
Intermediate vadose zone
Zone of aeration or vadose zone
Capillary or fringe zone
Water level
Water table or ground-water surface
Saturated zone
Ground-water or phreatic zone

the continents, the oceans, and the atmosphere; is is entirely possible that the water you drink for lunch was once used by 'Mama Alosaurus' to give her baby a bath (USGS 1984).

About 97% of the world's water is found in the oceans; 77% of the remaining portion of three percent "that is not in the ocean" is locked up in glaciers and icecaps, mainly in Greenland and Antarctica, and in saline inland seas; 22% of this portion of Earth's water is ground water. Accordingly, we can notice that rivers make up less than 4/10 of one percent of this remaining water (USGS 1984, http://ga.water.usgs.gov/edu/earthwherewater.html).

The term *hydrologic cycle* refers to the continuous movement of water above, on, and below the surface of the earth. In the hydrologic cycle, water evaporates from the oceans, lakes, bogs, streams and enters the atmosphere. This evaporated moisture is lifted and carried into the air until it condenses as rainfall or snow. Precipitation may run off the ground surface into streams to oceans penetrate into the ground, or absorbed by plants through transpiration. Surface runoff returns back to the atmosphere through evaporation and transpiration. The remaining water percolates downward as ground water and later may flow out as a spring or seep into streams. Surface runoff then flows to streams and oceans, or evaporates into the atmosphere to complete the hydrologic cycle (NASA GSFC 2003, http://earthobservatoiry.nasa.gov/Library/water/water_2.html).

The hydrologic cycle comprises various processes of evaporation, precipitation, interception, transpiration, infiltration, percolation, storage and runoff as shown in a graphic presentation of the hydrologic cycle (Fig. 8.2, Heath 1987).

Subsurface flow systems – The water-bearing rocks are described according to their capacity to retain and/or transmit water. The subsurface flow systems are classified into the following three categories:

- An *aquifer* is defined as a saturated permeable geologic unit, which is a part of a formation or group of formations that can transmit significant quantities of water to wells and springs under ordinary hydraulic gradients. A confined aquifer is one that is interlayered between relatively impervious beds. An unconfined aquifer is generally near land surface where the water table occurs at shallow depths below land. A water table map or hydraulic head of an aquifer shown by a potentiometric surface map will indicate the direction of the ground-water flow. A perched unconfined aquifer is a saturated lens underlain by a relatively impermeable layer and occurs above the regional water table.
- An *aquiclude* is a rock capable of absorbing water slowly, but will not transmit ground water rapidly enough to supply a well or a spring with a significant amount of water.

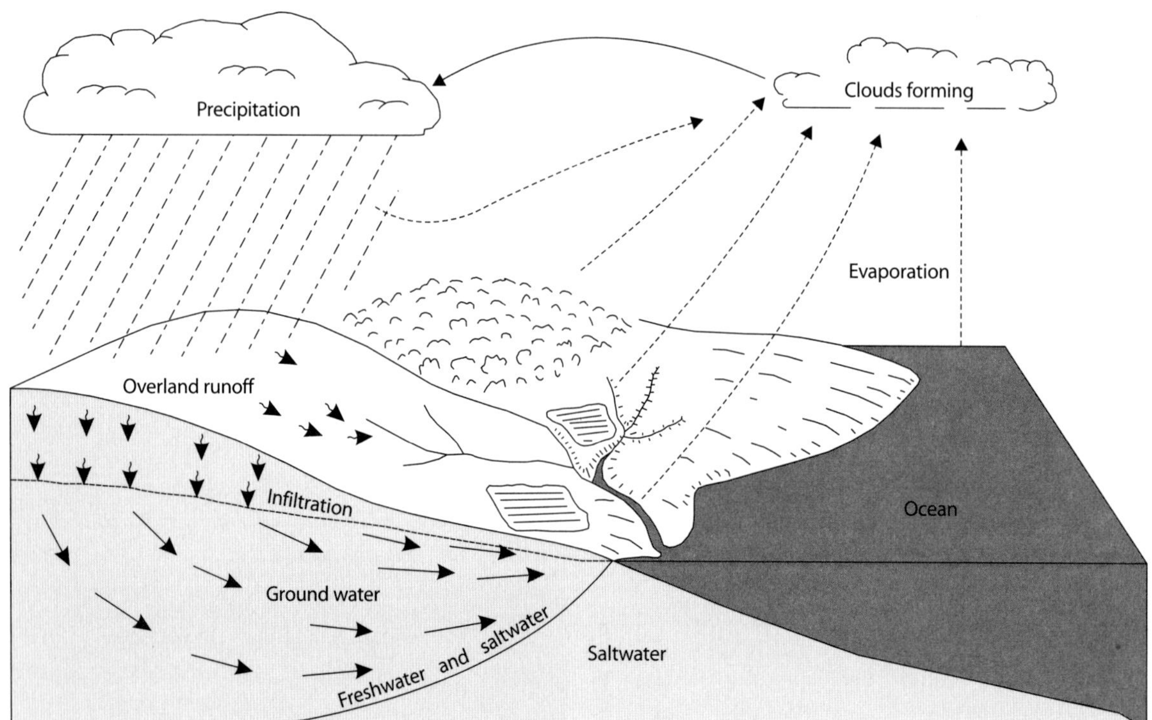
Precipitation
Clouds forming
Evaporation
Overland runoff
Infiltration
Ocean
Ground water
Saltwater
Freshwater and saltwater

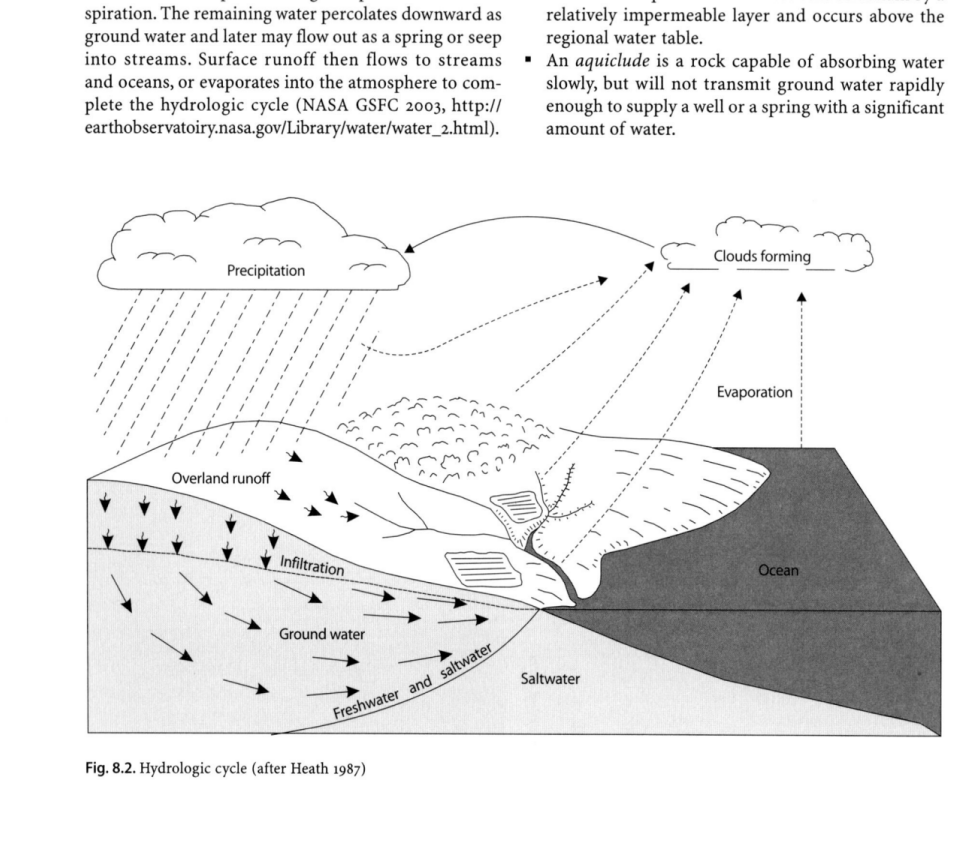

Fig. 8.2. Hydrologic cycle (after Heath 1987)

- An *aquitard* is a leaky confining bed that does not readily yield water to wells or springs. It may serve as a storage unit for ground water. Very few aquifers are completely uniform and may contain both aquiclude and aquitard materials that play an important role in controlling the movement of water.

8.2 Ground-Water Hydrology

8.2.1 Hydraulic Properties of Granular Aquifers

Geological features such as lithology, petrology and structure have a great influence on the hydraulic properties of granular aquifers. There are several physical properties of the fluid and the porous media that may describe the hydraulic aspects of saturated ground-water flow. They are summarized as follows.

Porosity: The amount of water that a rock can hold depends upon the porosity, which is basically a rock quality dependent on the grain size and degree of roundness, the degree of sorting, the extent of chemical solution and cementation and the amount of fracturing. Quantitatively, it is the ratio of the aggregate volume of voids in a rock or soil to its total volume (U.S. Environmental Protection Agency 1977):

$$\text{Porosity}\ \phi = \frac{V_V}{V_t}\ (\%) \tag{8.1}$$

where:

ϕ = porosity (in percent)
V_v = volume of voids
V_t = total volume of rock sample

Total porosity is a measure of all void space, whereas the effective porosity considers only the volume of the interconnected voids available to fluids flowing through the rock. The effective porosity better defines the hydraulic properties of the rock unit. Primary porosity includes original intergranular or intercrystalline pores, whereas secondary porosity results from fractures, solution channels, cavities or space (particularly in karst), and/or through recrystallization processes and dolomitization.

Porosities in sedimentary rocks vary from over 35% in newly deposited sands to less than 5% in lithified sandstones. Dense limestones and dolomites may have almost no porosity.

Porosity and specific yield: The porosity does not provide a direct measure of the amount of water that will drain out of the aquifer. Specific yield is the ratio (in percent) of the volume of water, which after being saturated, will yield by gravity to its own volume while, in case of the specific retention (surface tension forces on individual grains), it will retain against the pull of gravity to its own volume. As shown in Fig. 8.3, the specific retention decreases rapidly with increasing grain size until it remains roughly around 6% for coarse sands and much less for larger sized sediments. Specific yield is at a maximum in medium grained sands because porosity decreases with well-graded (poorly sorted) and coarser sediments. Very well sorted coarse-grained sediments, significantly reduces the specific retention (Brassington 1988).

The relationship between porosity and specific yield differs in solid rocks from that in unconsolidated sediments because the effect of cementation and compaction in solid rock reduces specific yield while fracturing increases it. Table 8.1 shows approximate porosity and specific yield values for different rock materials.

Compressibility: The increase or decrease in the grain-to-grain pressures within the matrix of an aquifer re-

Table 8.1. Approximate porosity and specific yield for different rock materials (adapted from Water Supply Papers 1662-D and 1839-D by permission of the U.S. Geological Survey; after Brassington 1988)

Material	Porosity (%)	Specific yield (%)
Coarse gravel	28	23
Medium gravel	32	24
Fine gravel	34	25
Coarse sand	39	27
Medium sand	39	28
Fine sand	43	23
Silt	46	8
Clay	42	3
Fine-grained sandstone	33	21
Med-grained sandstone	37	27
Limestone	30	14
Dolomite	26	
Dune sand	45	38
Loess	49	18
Peat	92	44
Schist	38	26
Siltstone	35	12
Till (mainly silt)	34	6
Till (mainly sand)	31	16
Till (mainly gravel)	–	16
Tuff	41	21
Basalt	17	–
Gabbro (weathered)	43	–
Granite (weathered)	45	–
Shale	6	–

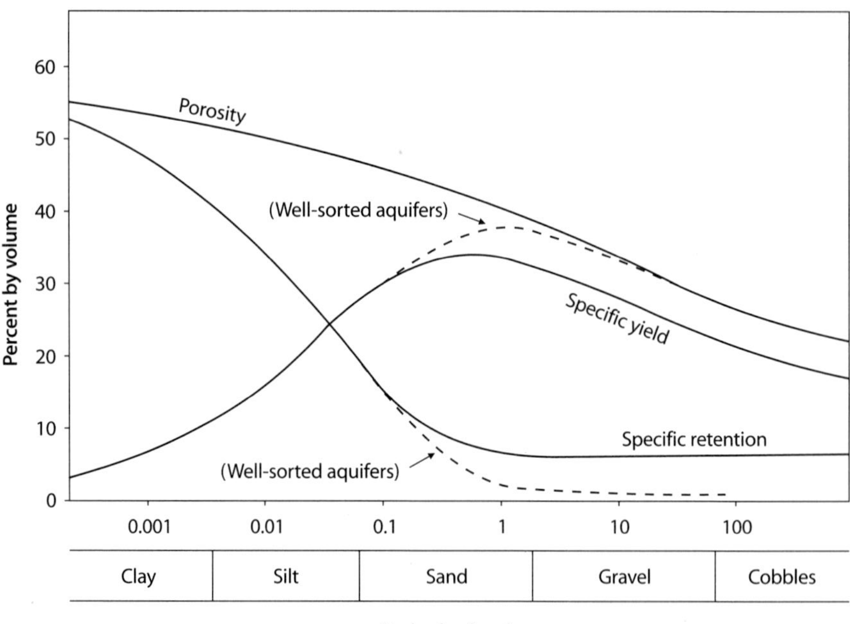

60
50
40
30
20
10
0
Percent by volume
Porosity
(Well-sorted aquifers)
Specific yield
Specific retention
(Well-sorted aquifers)
0.001
0.01
0.1
1
10
100
Clay
Silt
Sand
Gravel
Cobbles
Grain size (mm)

Fig. 8.3. The relationship between porosity, specific yield, specific retention and grain size for unconsolidated sediments only; the lines on this graph are best-fit curves drawn through scattered points (after Brassington 1988)

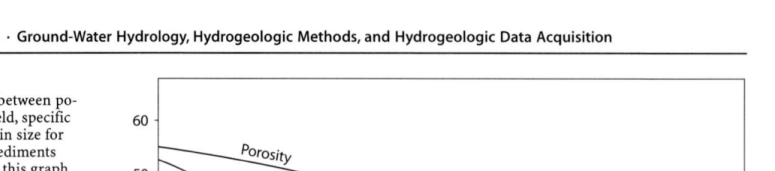

sults in compression or expansion that lead to volumetric changes; however, according to fluid mass laws, no change in fluid pressure can occur by loss (or gain) of water. The total compressibility of an aquifer formation (c) that encompasses both the aquifer (elastic medium α) and the contained fluids (β), ranges from 5×10^{-6} to 10×10^{-6} psi^{-1} (703 to 1 406 kg cm^{-2}) as compared with the compressibility of water alone of about 3×10^{-6} psi^{-1} (2 344 kg cm^{-2}) (Amax et al. 1960). Compressibility and the coefficient of storage are combined with each other as a function of the aquifer thickness.

The water compressibility should be considered if a confined ground-water reservoir is used to take up liquid wastes. The formation water is then compressed instead of being displaced, but care must be taken to avoid any hydro-fracturing in the aquifers and the overburden. Quantitatively, compressibility of an aquifer is defined as (U.S. Environmental Protection Agency 1977; Ward 1975):

$$\alpha = \frac{-\delta V}{V \delta p} \,(\text{psi}^{-1}) \tag{8.2}$$

where:

α = compressibility of an aquifer
δV = differential volume V
δp = differential pressure p

Storativity (S): The storativity or storage coefficient is defined as the volume of water that an aquifer releases from or takes into storage per unit surface area of the aquifer per unit change in the hydraulic head.

The storage coefficient S is quantitatively expressed as follows:

$$S = \phi \gamma b \left(\beta + \frac{\alpha}{\phi} \right) \tag{8.3}$$

where:

$\gamma = \varrho g$ = specific weight of water per unit area or hydrostatic pressure per foot of aquifer thickness
b = aquifer thickness
β = compressibility of water (constant)

Values of S are dimensionless and normally range from 5×10^{-5} to 5×10^{-3} for confined aquifers. Porosity and storativity are interrelated physical parameters, which are attributed to the capacity of an aquifer.

Darcy's law: Much of the quantitative study of ground-water flow is based on the results of experiments carried out in 1856 by Henry Darcy, a French hydraulic engineer who investigated the flow of water in horizontal beds of sand to be used for water filtration. Darcy's law can be performed with water flowing at a rate Q through a cylinder of cross-sectional area A packed with sand and having piezometers of a distance l apart, as shown in Fig. 8.4.

Darcy's law stated that the flow rate through porous media is proportional to the head loss and inversely proportional to the length of the flow path. The head loss, which is defined as the potential energy loss within the sand cylinder due to frictional resistance dissipated as

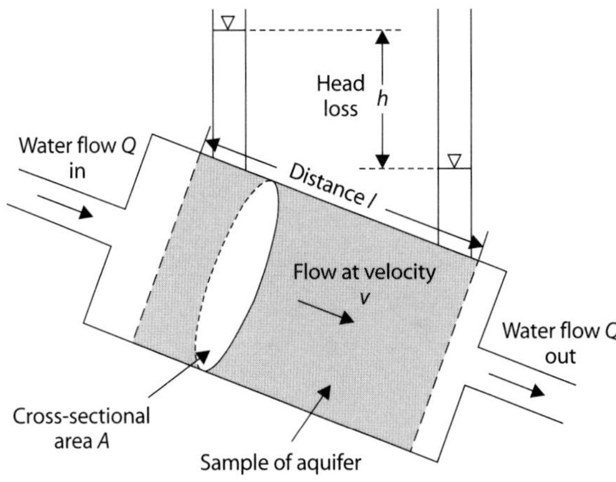
Head
loss
h
Water flow Q
in
Distance l
Flow at velocity
v
Water flow Q
out
Cross-sectional
area A
Sample of aquifer

Fig. 8.4. Application of Darcy's law in discharge calculation. The velocity (v) of water flowing through a porous medium is equal to the hydraulic gradient (h/l), times a constant (K), which is called permeability. For a porous medium, the value of permeability varies according to the fluid involved, and water permeability is called hydraulic conductivity. As the amount of flow (Q) is determined by the velocity (v), and the cross-sectional area of the sample (A), Darcy's law can be used to calculate discharge (after Brassington 1988)

heat energy, is independent of the inclination of the cylinder (Ward 1975).

The slope of the water table is called the hydraulic gradient and is a dimensionless ratio of the fluid head loss h to distance length l of porous medium through which flow occurs. Darcy's law relates the velocity of ground-water flow v to the hydraulic gradient $\delta h/\delta l$. The following equation states Darcy's law in its simplest form, that the flow velocity v equals the product of the constant K and the hydraulic gradient (Brassington 1988, 1998):

$$v = \frac{Q}{A} = -K\frac{\delta h}{\delta l} \tag{8.4}$$

where Q is the discharge or the flow rate, v is the Darcy velocity or specific discharge. The negative sign indicates that the flow of water is in the direction of decreasing head. Because velocity in laminar flow is proportional to the first power of the hydraulic gradient (Poiseuille's law), it is reasonable to apply Darcy's law to laminar flow in porous media.

For flow in pipes or in rock fractures (as in karst terrains), the Reynolds number, which expresses the dimensionless ratio of inertial to viscous forces, serves as a criterion to distinguish between laminar and turbulent flow. Reynolds number has been used to establish the limit of flows described by Darcy's law corresponding to the value where the linear relationship is no longer valid and it is expressed as:

$$N_R = \frac{PvD}{\mu} \tag{8.5}$$

where P is the fluid density, D the diameter (of a pipe), and μ the dynamic viscosity of the fluid. Experiments show that Darcy's law is valid for $N_R < 1$

For fully developed turbulence the head loss varies approximately with the second power of the velocity rather than linearly.

Intrinsic permeability: The permeability of a rock or soil is a rock parameter that defines its ability to transmit fluid under applied potential gradient, and is independent of fluid properties. To avoid confusion with hydraulic conductivity, which includes the properties of ground water, an intrinsic permeability ($\bar{k}$) may be expressed as follows:

$$\bar{k} = \frac{K\mu}{Pg} \tag{8.6}$$

where g is acceleration of gravity.

Combining Eqs. 8.4 and 8.5 yields:

$$\bar{k} = \frac{\mu v}{Pg\frac{\delta h}{\delta l}} \tag{8.7}$$

$$\bar{k} = \frac{Q\mu}{APg\frac{\delta h}{\delta l}} \tag{8.8}$$

which has units:

$$\bar{k} = -\frac{(\text{kg m}^{-1}\text{s}^{-1})(\text{m s}^{-1})}{(\text{kg m}^{-3})(\text{m s}^{-2})(\text{m m}^{-1})} = \text{m}^2 \tag{8.9}$$

Intrinsic permeability possesses units of area. Because values of $\bar{k}$ in Eq. 8.8 are so small, the U.S. Geological Survey expresses $\bar{k}$ in square micrometers $(\mu\text{m})^2 = 10^{-12}\ \text{m}^2$.

Because permeability depends on the grain size, the smaller the grain size, the larger will be the surface area exposed to the flowing fluid. Because the frictional resistance of the surface area lowers the flow rate, the smaller the grain size, the lower the permeability. (See Chap. 13 – Application of a Permeability Test).

Relative permeability and the vadose zone: The pressure head which is negative in the vadose zone, also characterized by a term known as relative permeability, is the result of capillary and adsorptive forces acting on the soil matrix. The capillary potential or the soil suction is a negative pressure and can be measured in unsaturated soils by tensiometers in units of bars, or centibars (1 bar = 1 atmosphere). As a soil becomes wet, the capillary potential increases from a very low (negative value) to zero value (i.e. saturated). The soil suction can range from 0, which means the soil is saturated, to as high as 600 bar, as found in some extremely dry soils (Sara 1994).

Permeability and specific yield: The permeability of a rock is closely related to specific yield. Aquifers that have a high specific yield tend to be more permeable whereas less permeable rocks usually have lower specific yields. Unconsolidated sediments tend to be significantly more permeable than their consolidated counterparts because cementation reduces the overall void space in the rock and minimizes the interconnection between pore spaces (Brassington 1988). The permeability of consolidated rocks (igneous, metamorphic and sedimentary) is increased by jointing, fracturing and/or by solutions that affect indurated rocks and is termed secondary permeability. Intergranular or primary permeability, a feature of unconsolidated deposits and weathered rocks, occurs in most sedimentary rocks and weathered igneous rocks that also have a high porosity (Brassington 1988; Table 8.2).

Hydraulic conductivity (K) is used for practical work in ground-water hydrology, where water is the prevailing fluid. A medium has a unit hydraulic conductivity if it will transmit in unit time a unit volume of ground water at the prevailing kinematic viscosity (equal to dynamic viscosity/fluid density) through a cross section of unit area, measured at right angles to the direction of flow, under a unit hydraulic gradient. The units are:

$$K = -\frac{v}{\delta h / \delta l} = -\frac{\mathrm{m\,day^{-1}}}{\mathrm{m\,m^{-1}}} = \mathrm{m\,day^{-1}} \qquad (8.10)$$

indicating that hydraulic conductivity has units of velocity.

As mentioned above, Q is the flow rate through porous medium ($\mathrm{m^3\,d^{-1}}$). K is the volume of water that will flow through a unit cross sectional area of aquifers in unit time under a unit hydraulic gradient and at a specified temperature. Darcy's law can be expressed in terms of the volume of water flowing through an aquifer, rather than its velocity as follows:

$$Q = -AK\frac{\delta h}{\delta l} \qquad (8.11)$$

Hydraulic conductivity and the vadose zone: Because of the variations in soil moisture, the hydraulic conductivity of unsaturated materials may vary, even in a homogenous lithology. In vadose zone flow systems, the movement of pore liquids occurs through fine-grained soils rather than coarse-grained materials. Pore liquids in unsaturated flow will not readily move from a fine-grained to a coarse-grained material (the Richard's principal), because the contact will act as a boundary, and fluids will build up, or mound, before entering the coarse-grained material (if they enter at all) (Sara 1994).

Transmissivity: The term transmissivity (T) is widely used in ground-water hydraulics. It is defined as the rate at which water of prevailing kinematic viscosity is transmitted through a unit width of aquifer under a unit hydraulic gradient. It follows that

$$T = Kb = (\mathrm{m\,day^{-1}})(\mathrm{m}) = \mathrm{m^2\,day^{-1}} \qquad (8.12)$$

where b is saturated thickness of the aquifer.

Hydraulic conductivity and the yield of a well: The hydraulic properties of aquifers are obtained to identify geologic materials with the highest yields (e.g. glacial outwash) for citing new wells or looking for

Table 8.2. Classification of rock types in terms of permeability (after Brassington 1988)

Type of permeability	Sedimentary		Igneous and metamorphic	Volcanic	
	Unconsoildated	Consolidated		Consolidated	Unconsolidated
Intergranular	Gravelly sand, clayey sand, sandy clay		Weathered zone of granite-gneiss	Weathered zone of basalt	Volcanic ejecta, blocks, fragments and ash
Intergranular and secondary	Breccia, conglomerate, sandstone, slate	Zoogenic limestone, oolitic limestone, calcareous grit		Volcanic tuff, volcanic breccia, pumice	
Secondary	Limestone, dolomite, dolomitic limestone		Granite, gneiss, gabbro, quartzite, diorite, schist, mica-schist	Basalt, andesite, rhyolite	

a suitable location for a waste disposal site with geologic beds having a very low hydraulic conductivity and low permeability (e.g. glacial clay, volcanic tufa, etc.; Brassington 1988; Table 8.3a).

When a well is pumped, the water level around the well falls and forms a cone of depression (Brassington 1988; Fig. 8.5). The shape and extent of the cone of depression depends on the rate of pumping, the length of the pumping time, and the hydraulic characteristics of the aquifer. The amount that the water table has been lowered is called the drawdown. One of the many formulae, which relate these parameters, is the equilibrium well equation:

$$Q = \frac{K(H^2 - h^2)}{C\log(R/r)} \tag{8.13}$$

where:

K = the hydraulic conductivity
Q = the pumping rate ($m^3 d^{-1}$)
H = the thickness of saturated aquifer penetrated by the well (m)
h = the height of water in the well (m)
r = the radius of the well (m)
R = the radius of the cone of depression (m)
C = a constant with a value of 0.733

If the hydraulic conductivity is known, this equation can be used to estimate the yield of a well at various

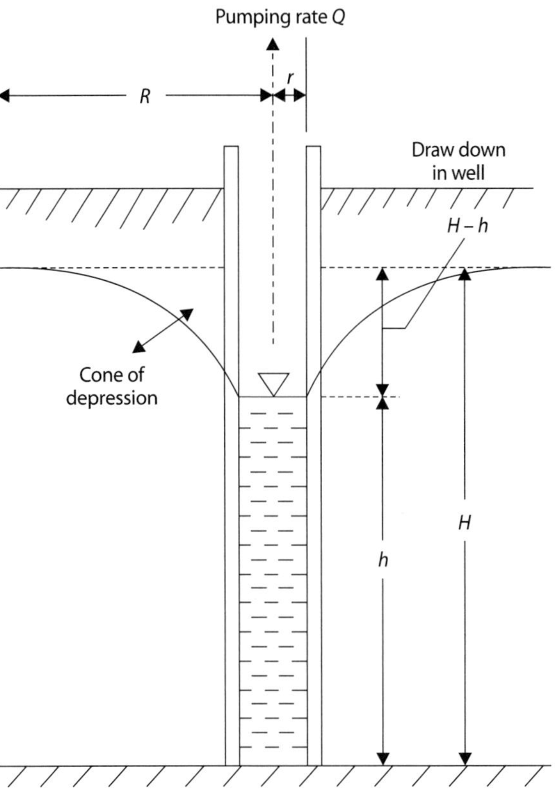
Pumping rate Q
R
r
Draw down
in well
H – h
Cone of
depression
H
h

Fig. 8.5. The water table is drawn down into a cone of depression around a pumped well. Q, R, r, H and h are used in the equilibrium well equation (see text) for the determination of the hydraulic conductivity of the aquifer (after Brassington 1988)

Table 8.3a. An example for defining aquifers of different hydraulic properties (after Brassington 1988)

	Grain size sorting, etc.	Estimated hydraulic conductivity (m d^{-1})	Estimated specific yield (%)	Type of permeability	Notes
Main aquifer					
1. Glacial sands and gravels	Medium/course sands and fine gravel with some cobbles	$10–10^2$	25	Primary	Grain-size analysis
2. Triassic sandstone	Fine/medium sets well cemented in parts	1–10	15	Primary and bedding fissures	Confined by till in part
3. Carboniferous limestone	Massive, dense rock	10^2	15	Secondary via fissures	Some evididence of karst development
Poor aquifers					
1. Alluvium	Mainly silt and thin sands	10	5	Intergranular	
2. Granite	Weathering ca. 1–2 m deep	10	5	Secondary via fissures	Joint sets mapped
Non-aquifers					
1. Glacial clay	Mainly clay, some silt	10^6	<5	Primary	Till and varved clays
2. Carboniferous mudstone	Clay/silts	10^4	<1	Secondary in weathered rock	

stabilized amounts of drawdown. It can also be used to calculate the hydraulic conductivity if the stabilized drawdown and pumping rates are measured.

8.2.2 Aquifer Testing

8.2.2.1 *Drill Stem Testing (DST)*

Drill stem test used in petroleum engineering is the equivalent of the recovery test. It shows the productive capacity of an aquifer in a well when still full of drilling mud. The testing tool attached to the drill pipe is lowered into an open hole and placed opposite the aquifer to be tested. The testing tool is isolated by an expandable packer or packers. The hydrostatic pressure of the mud column inside the hole is always greater than the formation pressure of the production zone to be tested. The basic drill-stem test tool assembly is normally attached to the lower part of the string of the drill pipe and consists of the following (U.S. Environmental Protection Agency 1977; Edwards and Winn 1974; Kilpatrick 1954):

1. A rubber packer(s) expanded against the hole to separate the annular sections above and below the encountered zone.
2. A tester valve to control mudflow into the drill pipe during entry into the hole and to allow formation fluids to enter during the test.
3. An equalizing or bypass valve to allow pressure equalization across packer(s) after completion of the flow test.
4. Pressure recording equipment for obtaining quantitative results during the period of pressure building (shut in pressure, SIP) following the period in which the formation fluids are allowed to flow.

Figure 8.6 illustrates the procedure for testing the bottom section of a borehole and it may be summarized in the following steps:

a While running in the hole, the test valve is closed, the bypass is opened and the packer(s) is collapsed, allowing the displaced mud to rise as shown by the arrows.

b The packer(s) is then set (compressed and expanded) after the pipe reaches the bottom. This isolates the lower zone from the rest of the open hole. Then the bypass is closed as the tester valve is opened allowing the formation fluid at the isolated section to enter the nearby empty drill pipe, which is exposed to the low pressure. The flowing formation pressure can then be measured during the flow period.

c The closed-in pressure valve (CIPV) is shut while the tester valve remains open, and the formation pressure is then allowed to build back up in a dual closed-in pressure test, the flow period and closed in-period are repeated by the use of the dual closed-in pressure valve (DCIPV).

d After the final closed-in period, the tester valve is then closed to trap any fluid above it, and the bypass valve is opened to equalize the pressure across the packer.

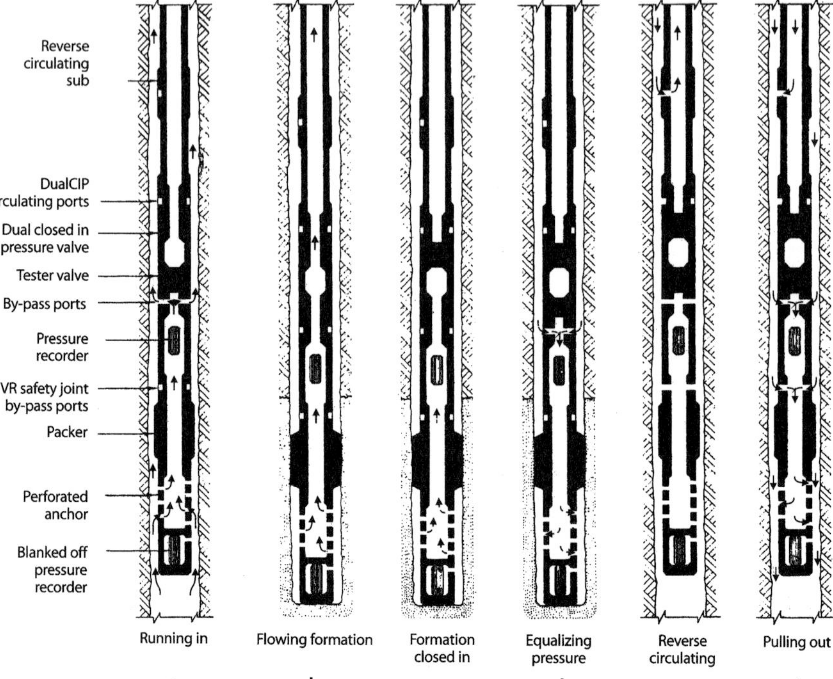
Reverse circulating sub
DualCIP circulating ports
Dual closed in pressure valve
Tester valve
By-pass ports
Pressure recorder
VR safety joint by-pass ports
Packer
Perforated anchor
Blanked off pressure recorder
Running in
Flowing formation
Formation closed in
Equalizing pressure
Reverse circulating
Pulling out
a
b
c
d
e
f

Fig. 8.6. Fluid passage diagram for a conventional open-hole, single-packer, drill-stem test (Edwards and Winn 1974; U.S. Environmental Protection Agency 1977)

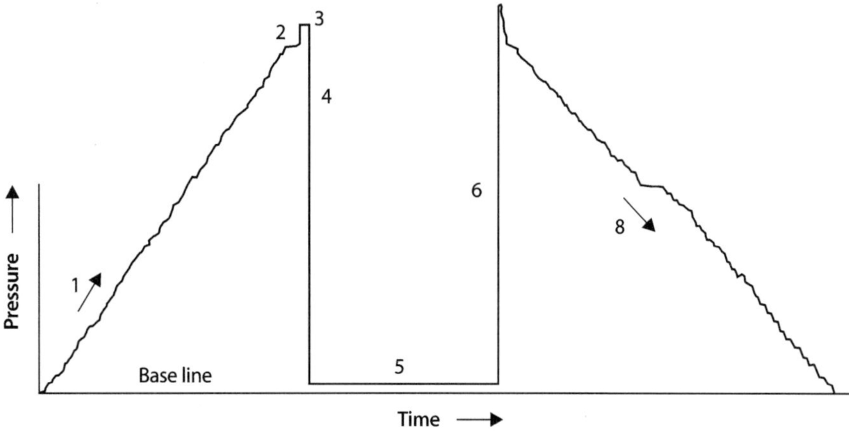
Pressure
Time
Base line
1
2
3
4
5
6
8

Fig. 8.7. Sequence of events during a drill-stem test when no fluids were produced (after Kilpatrick 1954; U.S. Environmental Protection Agency 1977); *1*: running in hole; *2*: hydrostatic pressure (weight of mud column); *3*: squeeze created by setting packer; *4*: opened tester, releasing pressure below packer; *5*: flow period, test zone open to atmosphere; *6*: closed tester and equalizing hydrostatic pressure below packer; *7*: pulled packer loose; *8*: pulling out of hole

e The setting weight is taken off and the packer(s) is pulled free. The fluid in the drill pipe is circulated out to the surface.

f The reverse circulating step may be bypassed and the pipe pulled from the hole until the tested formation fluid section reaches the surface. The fluid content of each successive pipe section is examined when it is removed.

There are hundreds of case studies. The DST can be interpreted in charts. Tests through perforations are sometimes required to retest an aquifer zone after casing has been emplaced.

Figure 8.7 is a schematic DST pressure record during a drill stem test where no fluids are produced.

SWISHHHHHH

Fig. 8.8. Just missed it

8.2.2.2 *Swabbing*

Swabbing lifts fluid from the borehole through the drill pipe, casing, or tubing by a swab that falls freely downward through the pipe. A volume of fluid above the swab is then drawn out as it is raised. Swabbing can be continued until all drilling mud is drawn from the pipe, thus allowing sampling of a formation water. Swabbing is preferable to DST where unconsolidated formations cause testing to be difficult. It can also be used in conjunction with DST to increase the volume of the obtained fluid (U.S. Environmental Protection Agency 1977).

8.2.2.3 *Specific Capacity*

Well capacity or discharge per unit time, is often used as a measure of well yield. The accepted general standard of strength of one well vs. another is the unit drawdown.

The drawdown observed in a pumping well is composed of two parts: (1) drawdown due to laminar flow of water in the aquifer towards the well, referred to as formation loss and calculated with the well flow equations and, (2) drawdown resulting from the turbulent flow of water in the immediate vicinity of the well casing. Specific capacity is a simple preliminary pumping test commonly known as a driller's test for determining the specific capacity of a well. It is an index of well productivity and is obtained by dividing the rate of discharge by the total drawdown. After stabilization of water level during a constant pumping rate, specific capacity is expressed as liters per minute per meter of drawdown ($l\ min^{-1}\ m^{-1}$ dd or $m^3\ min^{-1}\ m^{-1}$). The pumping well can be pumped at a series of rates, depending on its believed potential yield.

For example if a well is pumped at a set rate, e.g. 200 $m^3\ min^{-1}$, and the drawdown stabilized at that rate is equal to 20 m; then the "specific capacity" is 10 $m^3\ min^{-1}\ m^{-1}$. Results from a specific capacity test can be used to determine an approximation of the productivity of the well and the appropriate pumping rate and pump size for a detailed test. Specific capacity is not a detailed hydrologic analysis of the water-bearing characteristics or the efficiency of the well construction (Fig. 8.9).

Well logging techniques combined with measurements of flow velocity in the borehole, can provide information on the discharge-drawdown characteristics of aquifers penetrated by a well. The information is most conveniently presented in a graph showing aquifer discharges as functions of the water level in the well at a particular time.

To determine the discharge-drawdown characteristics, a well is pumped at a steady rate for a length of time. While the well is being pumped, measurements are made of drawdown and of the discharge rates. Discharge rates and drawdowns are recorded as functions of time, and their values for any given time during the test are obtained by interpolation. The procedure can be repeated for several different rates of total well discharge.

8.2.2.4 *Pumping Test for Confined or Unconfined Aquifers*

The development of the non-equilibrium formula by Theis (1935) for the non-steady flow of ground-water levels enabled hydrologists for the first time to predict future changes in ground-water levels, resulting from pumping or recharging of wells and was a major advance in the field of ground-water hydraulics. Subsequently, general modifications or adjustments applicable to the earlier methods were followed.

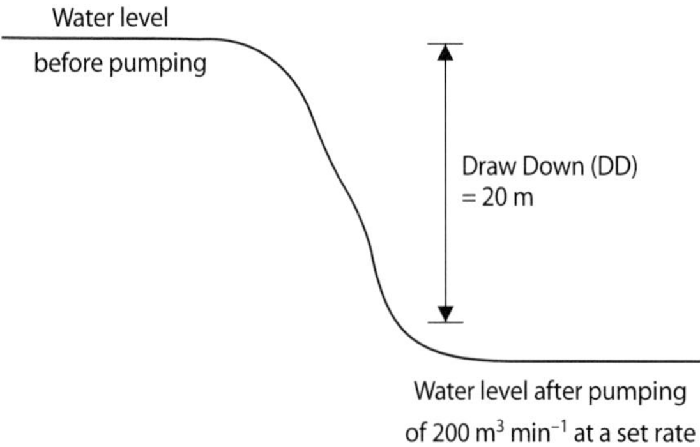
Water level
before pumping
Draw Down (DD)
= 20 m
Water level after pumping
of 200 m³ min⁻¹ at a set rate

Fig. 8.9. An explanatory diagram for specific capacity calculation (Sp Cap = 10 $m^3\ min^{-1}\ m^{-1}$)

When water is pumped from a borehole, at first the water level is drawn down more or less rapidly depending on the recharge and then the rate of decline of the water level gradually slows down until a stable pumping level is achieved. The amount of drawdown is largely controlled by four factors:

1. The aquifer characteristics;
2. The recharge condition;
3. The rate of pumping;
4. The length of time since pumping started.

Figure 8.10a shows the components of drawdown in a pumping well. The presence of a seepage face indicates that the water level in the borehole is drawn down to a much lower level than that in the surrounding aquifer. The water level in the aquifer is drawn down below the regional water level to form a cone of depression. When the pump is turned off, the water level in the borehole recovers. The recovery rate decreases with time as ground water flows in to fill up the cone of depression (Fig. 8.10b). Full recovery to the regional water level may take several days, weeks or even months (Brassington 1988).

8.2.2.5 *Slug Testing (for Determining Hydraulic Conductivity of Confined and Unconfined Aquifers)*

The pressure recovery in a borehole after withdrawal of a known volume of water (slug), or the pressure decline after injection of a known volume of water (slug), is termed the slug test. The analysis of water level vs. time in a single borehole in response to a slug injection or withdrawal has been pioneered by Hvorslev (1951) and Cooper et al. (1967).

The Bouwer and Rice slug test presented in 1976, was modified by Bouwer in 1989 to measure the hydraulic conductivity (K) of aquifers around boreholes (production, monitoring, or test wells) from the rate of rise of the water level in a well after a certain volume or "slug" of water is suddenly removed from the well; or from the subsequent rate of fall of the water level in the well by adding a slug of water. The slug test method is simpler and quicker than the pumping test because it uses a single well and no pumping or observation wells are used (Bouwer and Rice 1976; Bouwer 1989).

Uses and limitations: Instantaneous lowering of the water level in a well can be achieved by quickly removing a certain volume or slug of water with a bailer. It can also be achieved by partially or completely submerging

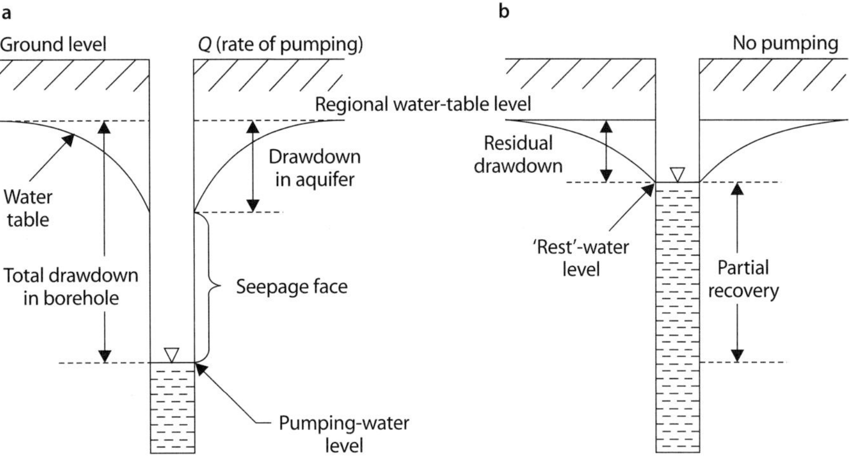
a
Ground level
Q (rate of pumping)
Water table
Drawdown in aquifer
Total drawdown in borehole
Seepage face
Pumping-water level
Regional water-table level
b
No pumping
Residual drawdown
'Rest'-water level
Partial recovery

Fig. 8.10. Drawdown and recovery of water levels in a pumping well; **a** the amount that the eater level is drawn down below the regional water table is the sum of the drawdown in the aquifer and the height of the seepage face; the value of both components will vary with different pumping rates; **b** after pumping is stopped, the seepage face quickly disappears, but recovery within the aquifer takes a long time (after Brassington 1988)

an object in the water, letting the water level reach equilibrium, and then quickly removing the object. If the aquifer is very permeable, the water level in the well may rise rapidly. Such rapid rises can be measured with pressure transducers and fast-response strip chart recorders or X-Y plotters.

Slug tests may be conducted in isolated portions of the aquifer to determine the vertical distribution of the hydraulic conductivity.

While originally developed for unconfined aquifers, the Bouwer and Rice (1976) method can be used for confined or stratified aquifers if the top of the screen or perforated section is some distance below the upper confining layer.

The geometry and symbols of a slug test (Bouwer 1989) can be summarized as follows:

When the water level in the well is at distance, y, lower than the static ground-water table around the well, the rate of flow of ground water (Q) is calculated with the Thiem equation as:

$$Q = 2\pi K L_e \frac{y}{\ln(R_e / r_w)} \quad (\mathrm{m^3\,h^{-1}}) \tag{8.14}$$

where:

- Q = the rate of flow into the well (length^3/time);
- L_e = length of screened, perforated, or otherwise open section of well;
- y = vertical difference between water level inside well and static water table outside well;
- R_e = effective radial distance over which y is dissipated; and
- r_w = radial distance of undisturbed portion of a quifer from centerline.

The rate of rise $\delta y/\delta t$ of the water level in the well after the water level has been quickly lowered some distance is:

$$\frac{\delta y}{\delta t} = -\frac{Q}{\pi r_c^2} \tag{8.15}$$

where r_c is the radius of the casing or other section of the well where the rise of the water level is measured. If the water level rises in the screened or open section of the well with a gravel pack around it, the thickness and porosity of the gravel envelope should be taken into account when calculating the equivalent value of r_c for the rising water level.

8.2.3 Hydraulic Testing and Characteristics of Aquifers

8.2.3.1 *Scope*

Hydraulic testing is a description of the field tests and testing procedures required to obtain certain hydraulic properties, pressure measurements, or indirect determinations of ground-water velocity in different rocks. It primarily dealt with pumping tests designed for aquifers that need for water supply and recently, dealt with low-permeability rocks or rocks with a fracture-type permeability due largely to concerns of hazardous waste migration and nuclear waste burial (Domenico and Schwartz 1990).

8.2.3.2 *Prototype Geologic Models*

Domenico and Schwartz (1990) discussed some specific or prototype geologic environment on which every hydrologic model is employed in hydraulic testing assuming that a typical confined aquifer of large areal extent is isotropic and homogenous, overlain by a confining layer over which there is a water table. There are three variations of this type of prototype model that can be summarized as follows:

1. *The nonleaky response and leaky response:* (*a*) The nonleaky response: A confining layer that is impermeable and contains an incompressible fluid within an incompressible matrix. All water removed from the aquifer will come from storage within the aquifer, and the water-level change (drawdown) vs. time response at some observation point will be exponential (plotted as a straight line on semilogarithmic paper). (*b*) The leaky response: The confining layer has some finite permeability but still contains an incompressible fluid within an incompressible matrix. It may be possible to invoke the transfer of water across the confining layer. The time-drawdown observation will reflect this additional water source with an upward inflection at some point in time.
2. *Leakage across a confining layer:* If pumping is near a stream or a lake and surface water is brought into aquifer due to established hydraulic gradients, leakage also occured the same as that across a confined layer that caused the upward inflection.
3. *Leakage with storage in the confining layer:* This version is for a permeable confining layer with a finite specific storage. The confining layer can contribute water to the aquifer, resulting in an upward inflection.

Another geologic prototype is the aquifer that is considered homogenous but anisotropic e.g. the aquifer is horizontal and one of the principal directions of the hydraulic conductivity tensor is vertical (parallel to the well). Variations of this model include situations where the principal directions of the hydraulic conductivity tensor are neither vertical nor horizontal. Two- and three-anisotropic models may be useful in the analysis of fractured rock.

8.2.3.3 *Conventional Hydraulic Test Procedures*

Conventional hydraulic test procedures are most commonly used in formations moderately high permeability for determining the transmissive and storage properties of aquifers. Theis (1935) discussed those tests that required one pumping well and one or more observation wells (or piezometers) in which it was possible to measure the response to pumping. He applied a mathematical expression for removal of heat at a constant rate from a homogenous, infinite slab as a useful analogy for study of ground-water flow to a pumping well and is known as the "*Theis nonequilibrium pumping test method*". It is assumed that the slab is initially at some uniform temperature. An infinitesimal rod of lower temperature parallel to the "*z*"-axis is then allowed to draw off the heat. In mathematical terminology, the rod represents a continuous line sink. By analogy, the infinite, homogenous slab is replaced by an extensive, homogenous aquifer, and the rod by a well of infinitesimal diameter and the rate of pumping is analogous to the rate of heat withdrawal, and water-level change at any distance from the pumping well is a function of the pumping rate, the properties of the aquifer, and time.

8.2.3.4 *Hydraulic Characteristics of Aquifers*

Partial penetration aquifers – A well is referred to as partially penetrating when the screened or open section of the well casing does not coincide with the full thickness of the aquifer it penetrates. Under such conditions the flow toward the pumping well (or observation point) will be three dimensional because of vertical flow components.

Superposition aquifers – The Theis nonequilibrium equation represents a solution to the diffusion equation for a prescribed set of boundary and initial conditions. The pumping test procedure is relatively straightforward where a transient response to a steady pumping rate is observed over a limited period of time (~24 hours) at some known distance from the pumping well. Given the transmissive and storage properties as determined over this short pumping period, it is possible to predict the water level at later times and at other distances in response to any steady pumping rate "*Q*", assuming that the storativity and transmissivity do not change with time whereas, the postulated time of pumping "*t*", the distance "*r*", and the pumping rate "*Q*" may be taken as variables.

Bounded aquifers – Geologic boundaries limit the extent of real aquifers and serve to distort the calculated cones of depression forming around pumping wells. The method of images, which plays an important role in the mathematical theory of electricity and is employed in the solution of some geophysical problems, aids in the evaluation of the influence of aquifer boundaries on well flow. This theory as described by Ferris (1951), permits treatment of the aquifer limited in one or more directions. However, the additional assumption of straight-line boundaries has been added to give aquifers of rather simple geometric form; e.g. if formation "*A*" is bounded by a relatively impermeable formation "*B*" and the boundary between the two located at a variable distance "*r*" from a pumping well, then no flow can occur from "*B*" toward the pumping well and the boundary is a no-flow (barrier) boundary. The effect of a barrier boundary is to increase the drawdown in a well. On the other hand, if the aquifer is bounded by a stream that provides recharge to the aquifer, the effect is to decrease the drawdown in a well. A zero-drawdown (constant head) boundary can be simulated by an imaginary well, located as earlier, with the exception that the imaginary well must recharge water at the same rate as the pumping well.

8.2.4 Pumping Test Plan

8.2.4.1 *Scope*

An outline for a quantitative test that will produce aquifer characteristics sufficient for hydrogeologic site characterization, with the supporting hydrogeologic characteristics must include the determination of transmissibility, storage, and leakage by one of a number of quantitative test methods. The numbers needed for a determination of size, shape, and movement of a contaminant plume can be determined, and data will be available for analysis by a number of models.

A final word of caution; good results from a quantitative test evaluation requires a calibration of the test results as well as a final consideration of the detailed geologic conditions of the site.

Example: A 72-hour pumping test and a 48-hour recovery test should be performed to obtain information on the following:

- The hydraulic relationship (if any) between aquifers penetrated and can be determined
- The areal extent of the impact of pumping (cone of influence)
- Hydraulic characteristics, transmissivity (T), hydraulic conductivity (K), storage coefficient (S) and leakance (L), if applicable

The pumping well is PMW-4C. Wells PMW-4A and PMW-4B will be monitored throughout the test period. Prior to the initiation of pumping test a specific capacity test will be run. A period of pre-monitoring will also be carried out. Water levels in all wells installed for the Phase II assessment will be monitored during the testing period, on a regular basis (see location map, Fig. 8.11).

Well construction details: Well completion details are summarized on Table 8.3b. The pumping well (PMW-4C) and monitoring well (PMW-4B) have been completed in the Citronelle aquifer. Monitoring well PMW-4A has been completed in the Miocene aquifer.

Wellhead set-up: A submersible pump will be set at a depth of 35.65 m below surface level, approximately 3.05 m from the bottom of the well. A flow meter will be set at the wellhead to monitor and record the flow rate. All water will be discharged into a frac tank before being discharged at a distance of 90–120 m down gradient from the wellhead.

Monitoring network: Wells PMW-4B and PMW-4A will be monitored throughout the period of pre-monitoring, pumping and recovery. Water levels in the Phase II monitoring wells will be checked periodically throughout the test period also.

Instrumentation: In-situ data loggers will be used to record water level changes in the pumping well PMW-4C and monitoring wells PMW-4A and PMW-4B. The data loggers will be programmed to record water levels on a logarithmic frequency for the first 100 minutes of the test and on a linear frequency of 5 to 10 minutes for the remainder of the pumping phase of the test. At the start of the recovery phase the data loggers will be programmed to record water levels on a logarithmic frequency for the first 100 minutes of the test and on a linear frequency of 5 to 10 minutes for the remainder of the recovery phase. Data will be downloaded from the data loggers daily. The data loggers will be calibrated with manual measurements at the start of the test. Manual measurements will be made at the three-instrumented wells for continued calibration and data back up on the attached data sheet (Appendix 8.C, Fig. 8.C.1).

Water quality: Field parameters will be taken hourly during the test period and will include, temperature, pH,

Table 8.3b. Well construction

Well no.	Depth	Stick up	Total depth	Screened interval	Drilling/construction[a]		Water level	Date	Diameter
	(ft. BLS)	(ft.)	(ft. BTOC)	(ft. BLS)	Start date	Completion	ft. (BTOC)		(inches)
PMW-1	64.00	2.50	66.50	34.00–64.00	9/17/01	9/25/01	43.69	10/03/01	4
PMW-2	305.62	2.50	308.12	245.39–304.72	7/31/01	8/28/01	166.35	10/03/01	4
PMW-3	405.58	2.50	408.08	345.39–404.72	8/14/01	9/13/01	161.99	10/03/01	4
PMW-4A	360.00	2.50	362.50	320.00–360.00	7/10/01	8/09/01	162.58	10/02/01	4
PMW-4B	125.46	2.50	127.96	45.39–124.72	9/26/01	10/01/01	49.32	10/02/01	4
PMW-4C	125.43	2.50	127.93	50.37–124.89	9/17/01	9/26/01	54.72	10/02/01	6
PMW-5	100.00	2.50	102.50	60.32–99.72	9/11/01	9/13/01	33.21	10/03/01	4
PMW-6	90.00	2.50	92.50	40.28–89.61	9/04/01	9/07/01	64.83	10/03/01	4
PMW-7	100.00	2.50	102.50	59.39–99.72	9/25/01	10/01/01	77.39	10/02/01	4

[a] Including well development.

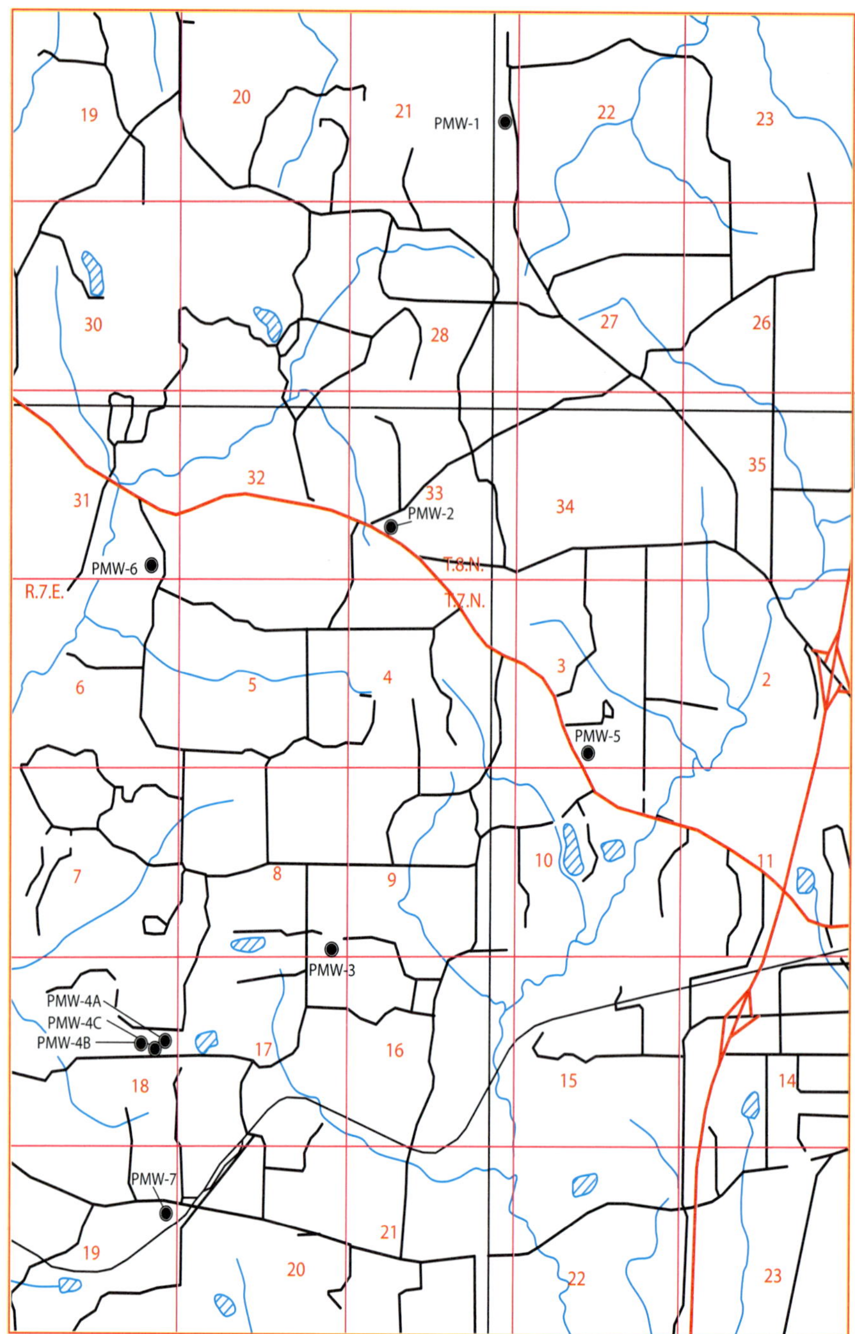

19
20
21
PMW-1
22
23
30
28
27
26
31
32
33
PMW-2
34
35
PMW-6
R.7.E.
T.8.N.
T.7.N.
6
5
4
3
2
PMW-5
7
8
9
10
11
PMW-3
PMW-4A
PMW-4C
PMW-4B
17
16
15
14
18
PMW-7
19
20
21
22
23

Fig. 8.11. A location map of monitoring and pumping wells

Eh, specific conductance, and turbidity. Color and odor will also be recorded. A field water quality form is attached (Appendix 8.C, Fig. 8.C.2). At the beginning, middle and end of the pumping period the pumping well will be sampled for the Phase II full suite of parameters.

Meteorological data: A rain gauge and microbarograph will be installed on-site prior to pre-test monitoring to produce continuous records of precipitation and atmospheric pressure. These instruments will be inspected periodically to ensure their proper operation.

Record keeping: Each well (pumping and monitoring) will have a designated pumping test form booklet on which manual water levels, measured discharge rates, and other data will be recorded. A pumping test form is attached (Appendix 8.C, Fig. 8.C.1). Data from the electronic data recorders will be cross-checked with manual measurements at a minimum of every hour during the pumping test. Discharge rates will also be checked frequently during the test and will be adjusted if necessary to keep the rate constant. All adjustments made will be noted. The shift leader or other personnel as appropriate will record general site operations and activities in the site field book.

Personnel: The drilling company will install and maintain the pump, wellhead assembly, frac tank and discharge equipment throughout the period of the test. Hydrogeologists or engineering staff will supervise a 24-hour presence on site, in three one-man shifts during the pumping phase of the test. During pre-monitoring and recovery, personnel will be on-site during the day only.

Equipment: New version of equipment and software programs are used for getting computerized results out of the pumping tests, e.g. *Hermit 3000 environmental data logger* is an example of equipment used to measure and record parameters such as level, pressure, temperature, conductivity, and pH using standard in-situ transducers. Special care is required in ground-shipping as Hermit 3000 uses lithium batteries which the Department of Transportation considers a hazardous material.

Data analysis: The data will be analyzed in a number of different ways. An example of one analysis method that will be used is as follows. The water-level data will be tabulated as time-drawdown and time-recovery data and plotted separately on double logarithmic graphic paper at the same scale as that of the type curve or curves, with time on the abscissa and drawdown or recovery on the ordinate. The log-log graphs of time-drawdown and time-recovery will be separately superimposed, keeping the coordinate axis of the two graphs parallel and matched to the nonleaky artesian type curve. During the first few minutes of the test, some deviation of field data from the type curve is expected due to fluctuations in the pumping rates. An arbitrary point, designated as the match point, will be selected, representing the matched portion of the field data curve with the theoretical type curve. Match point coordinates $W(u)$, $W(u,r/B)$ $1/u$, s, and t, will be determined and will be shown on the time-drawdown and time-recovery plots. Match point coordinates will be substituted into the following Eqs. 8.16 and 8.17 to determine the transmissivity and coefficient of storage of the aquifer:

$$T = \frac{114.6\,QW(u)}{s} \tag{8.16}$$

or

$$T = \frac{114.6\,QW(u,r/B)}{s} \tag{8.17}$$

$$u = \frac{1.87r^2S}{Tt} \tag{8.18}$$

where

T = coefficient of transmissivity ($\mathrm{l\,d^{-1}\,m^{-1}}$)
Q = discharge ($\mathrm{l\,min^{-1}}$)
$W(u)$ = well function for nonleaky artesian aquifer
$W(u,r/B)$ = well function for leaky artesian aquifer
s = drawdown (m)
s' = recovery (m)
S = coefficient of storage (dimensionless)
t = time in days after pumping started
t' = time in days after pumping terminated
R = distance in feet from pumped well to observation point

Site safety: A standard site safety plan is attached and includes details about the nearest hospital etc. (see Appendix 8.C, Attachments 8.C.1–8.C.3).

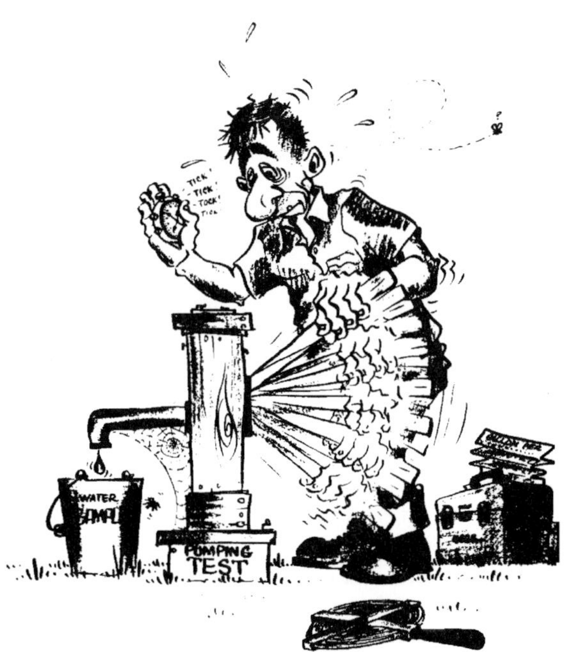
WATER
PUMPING
TEST

Fig. 8.12. Detailed pumping test underway

8.2.5 Well and Pump Renovation

When a well and/or pump unit has ceased to function or has declined in capacity, which might occur at any time, a consultant needs to either write specifications or negotiate a remedy with the contractor.

If the pump runs, but does not produce its rated capacity, or perhaps does not pump water at all, the drawdown in the well should be first checked to determine whether the problem is with the pump or with the well. If the drawdown is less than it should be or perhaps nonexistent, the pump should be pulled to determine causes of mechanical problems. If after testing the pump, well drawdown seems to be excessive or it is pumping sand and measures to renovate the well seem obvious, then a downhole TV camera can locate the problem.

A renovation technique for an old well is the use of acid for water well treatment e.g. muriatic acid (at least 20% solution), which is simply hydrochloric acid containing impurities (mainly sulfuric acid).

As a rule, the quantity of acid to be utilized in a limestone well should be at least three times the volume of the producing zone of the borehole to be treated. In the case of a gravel pack well, care should be taken to introduce an amount not greater than the volume of the gravel pack surrounding the screen and result in contaminating the formation with the acid and produce undesirable secondary precipitation.

Generally, enough fresh water should be pumped behind the acid load to displace it from the borehole from all of the tubing and acid pumping lines. Also, the length of time between acidizing and beginning redevelopment of a well should generally not exceed one hour to avoid neutralization processes.

Iron bacteria is a cause of well failure in some areas as they deteriorate well screens and iron wastes also create problems with plugging up the gravel pack around the well screens. Chlorine shock treatment, along with acidizing, has proven to be effective in dislodging the iron bacteria residue so that it can be cleaned from the well by ordinary development techniques (Alsay-Pippin Corporation 1980).

8.3 Ground-Water Models

Ground-water models are embodiments of scientific hypotheses. They can not be proven or validated until tested. Model testing and evaluation lead to improved models and a better understanding of site characteristics from the geology, hydrology and chemistry point of view.

Only after detailed data are available and calibration is completed, a model can be considered as a usable product. Models can be valuable tools for analyzing ground-water systems. However, their predicted accuracy is limited.

The use of the word model has many meanings to many people; a model is a representation of a real system or process. There are several types of ground-water models: (1) A *conceptual model* is a hypothesis for how a system or process operates. The idea can be expressed quantitatively as a mathematical model or may be qualitative. Mathematical models are expressions that contain mathematical variables, parameters, and constants that replace objects, forces, and events (Krumbein and Graybill 1965). (2) A *deterministic ground-water model* is based on a balance of the various fluxes of different quantities such as: conservation of mass, momentum, and energy. Originally, the description of the governing process was the result of great individual insight coupled with experimentation, e.g. Darcy's law. Deterministic ground-water models generally require the solution of partial differential equations. (3) *Analytical models* require that the parameters and boundaries be highly idealized as exact solutions can often be obtained analytically. (4) *Numerical models* relax the idealized conditions of analytical models and are therefore more realistic and flexible; however, numerical methods provide only approximate solutions. Numerical methods yield approximate solutions to the governing equation (or equations); they require discretization of space and time. (5) A *generic model* is considered when a numerical algorithm is implemented in a computer code to solve one or more partial differential equations. When the parameters (such as hydraulic conductivity and storativity), boundary conditions, and grid dimensions of the generic model are specified to represent a particular geographical area, the resulting computer program is a site-specific model. If the user of a model is unaware or ignores the details of the numerical method, including the derivative approximations, the scale of discretization, and the matrix solution techniques, significant errors can be introduced and remain undetected.

When a numerical algorithm is implanted in a computer code to solve one or more partial differential equations, the resulting computer code can be considered a generic model. When the parameters (such as hydraulic conductivity and storativity), boundary conditions, and grid dimensions of the generic model are specified to represent a particular geographical area, the resulting computer program is a site-specific model. If the user of a model is unaware of or ignores the details of the numerical method, including the derivative approximations, the scale of discretization, and the matrix solution techniques, significant errors can be intro-duced and remain undetected (Konikow and Bredehoeft 1992).

8.4 Hydrogeologic Methods and Equipment

8.4.1 Field Investigation

Within the last decade, a substantial number of ground-water investigations have been conducted. Many of these have been centered at specific contaminated sites in response to Federal legislation concerned with sources of drinking water, threats to human health and the environment posed by toxic and hazardous waste, and restoration of contaminated aquifers. In general, most of the sites consist of only several hectares or a few square km, but a number of reconnaissance studies have focused on thousands of square km.

In most cases the cost of these investigations has been excessively high, due in large measure to the expense of analytical services. The most disconcerting feature of many of these investigations is that their results were found to be inadequate, and additional work and expense were required. It must be understood that a data base will almost always be inadequate to some and its resolution will eventually be dictated by time, common sense, and budgetary constraints. Although these constraints will always be present to one degree or another, it is imperative that the most reliable and applicable information be collected commensurate with the available resources (Brassington 1988).

Detailed hydrological and geological information is essential for water resource development. A proper understanding of the local ground-water system, based on adequate field observations, or the hydrogeologic characterization of the site are needed to assess development and management of ground water from wells and springs, dewatering a quarry or mines or the location of a safe hazardous waste disposal site, landfills, septic tanks or other activities that may pollute ground water. There are several phases to such studies and the order in which they are carried out is as follows:

1. *Desk study:* A primary step includes: (*a*) collection and examination of published topographic and hydrologic information for an area to identify the potential of an aquifer and define its physical character, lithologic and aerial extent, boundary conditions, water quality; and (*b*) an examination of topographic maps for possible use for geologic mapping, well inventory, and general accessibility.
2. *Reconnaissance study:* A reconnaissance study of the area requires site-specific evaluation, walking over the area, choosing access for geological test drilling, and determining the need for geological mapping to define geological features as well as seepage and spring lines. A reconnaissance survey can help in locating wells for future observation, geophysics, logging or water sampling, and getting acquainted with the people of the area.
3. *Detailed study and data evaluation:* Geographic, geologic, and hydrologic data should be collected and recorded; e.g. when a well or spring is located, its position and elevation should be noted and its flow or yield as well as its conductivity and temperature should be measured. When a well is found, its depth and water level should be measured and recorded, showing whether the well is being pumped. The locations of sinkholes and other geological features should also be recorded.
4. *Monitoring program:* A monitoring program should be initiated as early as possible by measuring and recording data on a regular basis. The data should include the flow of springs and streams, the water level in wells, and the quantity of water pumped from them. The amount of rainfall, evaporation measurements, and chemical analyses of water samples from springs and wells are also needed to provide data on the quality and quantity of water flowing into or out of the ground-water system, and to measure impacts related to the problems or issues being studied.

Figure 8.13 shows a progressive chart to examine different geological and environmental hydrogeological factors that effect the suitability of a site for waste disposal (Sara 1994).

8.4.2 Ground-Water Measurements

A field hydrogeologist will need tools to remove the cover from the top of a well before taking a water level reading or a water sample. Other tools may be needed to remove equipment that impedes the measurement or collection of hydrologic data. On-site readings require the use of sensitive probes such as a thermometer or conductivity meter.

A flow meter measures stream flow velocity or microbarographs, rain gauges may also be needed to provide information on all segments of the hydrologic cycle.

8.4.2.1 *Water Level Devices*

Measurements may be carried out with a number of different devices and procedures. Water level measurements should include (1) identification of the well by number and location; (2) location and elevation of reference point; (3) elevation of ground surface; (4) date of measurement; (5) measured depth to water or the bottom of the hole, if dry; (6) computed elevation of the water table or piezometer surface; (7) for piezometers, the aquifer or other zone represented by the reading; and (8) a note

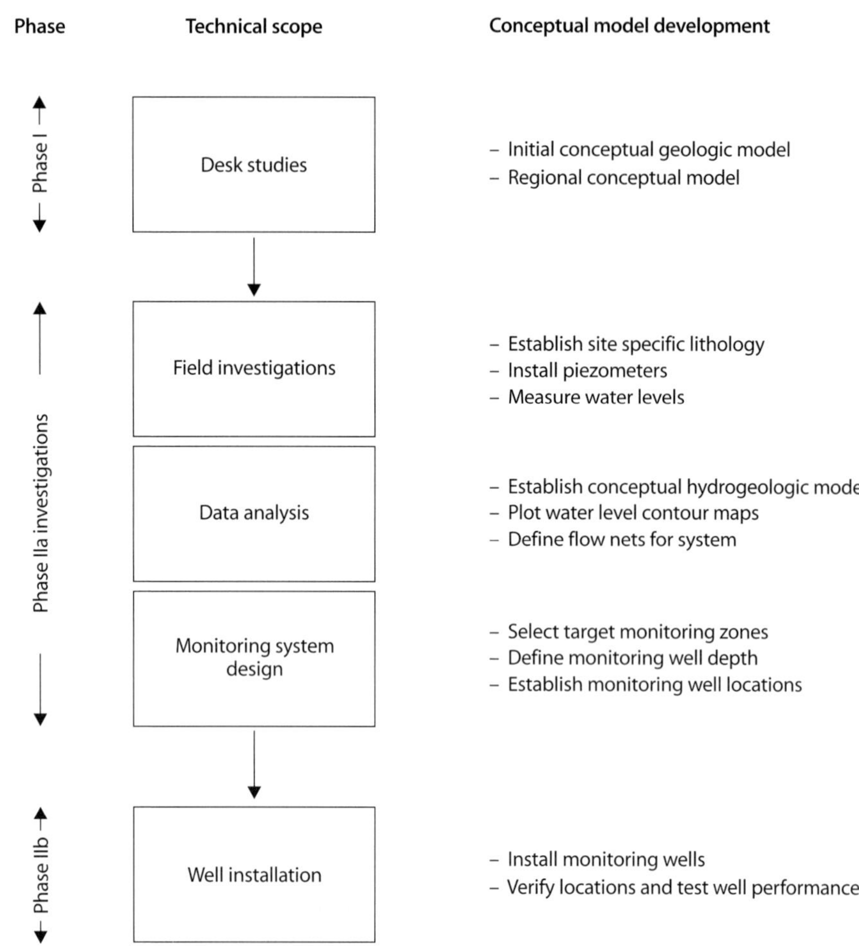
Phase
Technical scope
Conceptual model development
Phase I
Desk studies
- Initial conceptual geologic model
- Regional conceptual model
Phase IIa investigations
Field investigations
- Establish site specific lithology
- Install piezometers
- Measure water levels
Data analysis
- Establish conceptual hydrogeologic model
- Plot water level contour maps
- Define flow nets for system
Monitoring system design
- Select target monitoring zones
- Define monitoring well depth
- Establish monitoring well locations
Phase IIb
Well installation
- Install monitoring wells
- Verify locations and test well performance

Fig. 8.13. A progressive chart showing site characterization (after Sara 1994)

on the status of the well whether it is pumped recently when measured, or a nearby well was pumping during the measurement. The following are common devices used for measuring water levels:

a *Chalked steel-tape:* The device is the most common device for measuring static water levels and has a weight attached on the lower end. It is a simple water level measurement using a tape and coating it with chalk over an interval that includes the water level (carpenter's blue chalk). This is followed by lowering the tape down the well; then lift it up and read the interval depth to the top of the wet area of the tape. Then subtract the top wetted surface from "held level".

b *Electric sounders:* There are a number of commercial models available. Some electric sounders use a single-wire line and probe, and rely on grounding to complete the circuit; others use a two-wire line and double contacts on he electrode. Most sounders are powered with flashlight batteries and the closing of the circuit by immersion in water is registered on a milliammeter. Electric sounders are generally more suitable than other devices for measuring the depth to water in wells that are being pumped (USGS 1977)

Figure 8.14 is a water level indicator showing a water level measurement obtained by using a length of twin conductor cables, graduated in meters or feet and wrapped on a pool with a pair of electrodes attached to the end. The electrodes are lowered into the well until they come into contact with the water surface at which time, a circuit is closed which activates either a light or a buzzer (Brassington 1988).

The following precautions must be taken to obtain a precise water level reading when using the water level indicator:

1. The indicator should be tested before lowering it down the borehole by exposing the inner electrode and completing the circuit by immersing the end in water. If the lamp or buzzer does not work, the batteries (and bulb) should be checked and the cable inspected for breaks.
2. Select a water level indicator with a cable long enough to measure the deepest water level in the investigation area, keep in mind that pumping water levels in abstraction boreholes are much

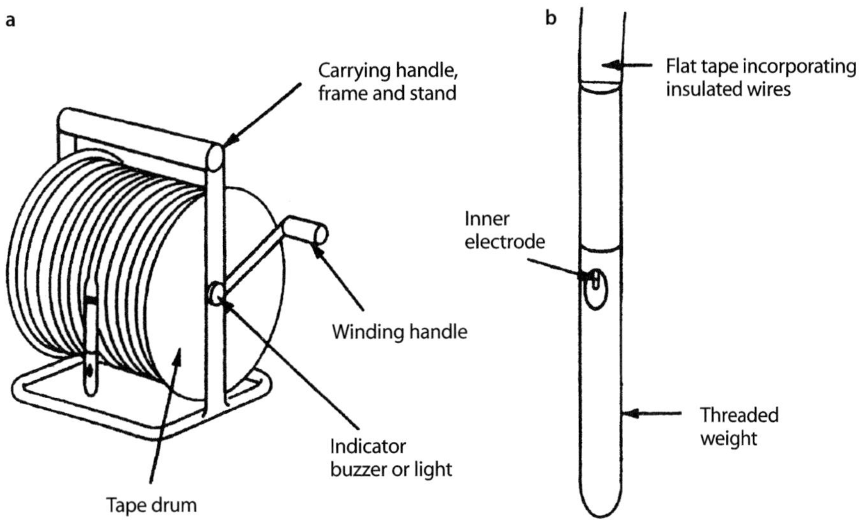
a
b
Carrying handle, frame and stand
Flat tape incorporating insulated wires
Inner electrode
Winding handle
Threaded weight
Indicator buzzer or light
Tape drum

Fig. 8.14. A water level indicator used with 6 batteries (1.5 V each), housed in the drum spindle, which also contains the electronic circuitry. The probe is made of stainless steel or brass and acts as an electrode, with a second inner electrode (after Brassington 1988); **a** general assembly; **b** detail of probe

deeper than those of the observation wells in the surrounding areas and can have rapidly fluctuating water levels.

3. While using the water level indicator, the measurements are taken by lowering the probe down the borehole until it makes contact with the water surface. This step should be repeated several times to enable "feeling" the water surface.
4. Selection of measuring point (MP) is carried out by placing the tape against a fixed datum point such as the top of the casing and then read the water level to the nearest centimeter or inch. Mark the measuring point (MP) and report its location in the well inventory form.

c *Water-level recorders:*

1. A water-level recorder is used to obtain a continuous record of ground-water levels. A simple float operating recorder has a paper chart on a revolving drum, and a clockwork mechanism for the time. A well-known type of the floating operating recorders use a horizontal drum (Fig. 8.15), properly geared to allow it to function through large changes of water level, such as during a pumping test. The chart on the recorder can be selected for different time periods and must be changed within the specified time period to avoid the loss of the record.
2. The mechanism of the horizontal drum recorder includes a float, which has a steel tape attached to it and passes over a pulley and has a counterweight attached to the other end. As water levels change, the float responds, moving the pulley, which is attached through a system of gears to a horizontal chart drum. A pen moves horizontally across the chart, driven at a steady rate by the clockwork-mechanism and changes in water level are thus recorded by the pen's trace. The scale of the graph can be changed by selecting the appropriate gears to alter both the time scale and the vertical scale as required.
3. More sophisticated electronic equipment is also available for recording water levels using a pressure-sensing transducer. The transducer measures pressure created by submergence in the water. A data logger records the pressure at predetermined time intervals. Fluctuations in the water level are seen as variations in pressure on the transducer. This information is converted directly into water level data, which records information in a special format that can be read by a computer.

In most hydrogeological studies, ground-water level data show seasonal fluctuations in response to recharge or due pumping. Aquifers that are in hydraulic contact with a river will fluctuate in response to changes in river level. Also, as there is a balance between the hydrostatic pressure in the aquifer and the barometric pressure, significant fluctuations in wells in confined aquifers might be produced if influenced by changes in river level.

8.4.4.2 *Water Samplers*

A water sample from a borehole with no pump on it, is obtained by lowering a depth sampler to a predetermined level, which is then activated to obtain a sample for chemical analysis. Care should be taken when using the mechanical messenger type of sampler at shallow depths (Fig. 8.16).

Bottles that are used to collect water samples from wells and/or springs vary in size and composition based on the parameters to be measured. The following requirements are necessary when preparing the samples for transport back to the laboratory (Brassington 1988):

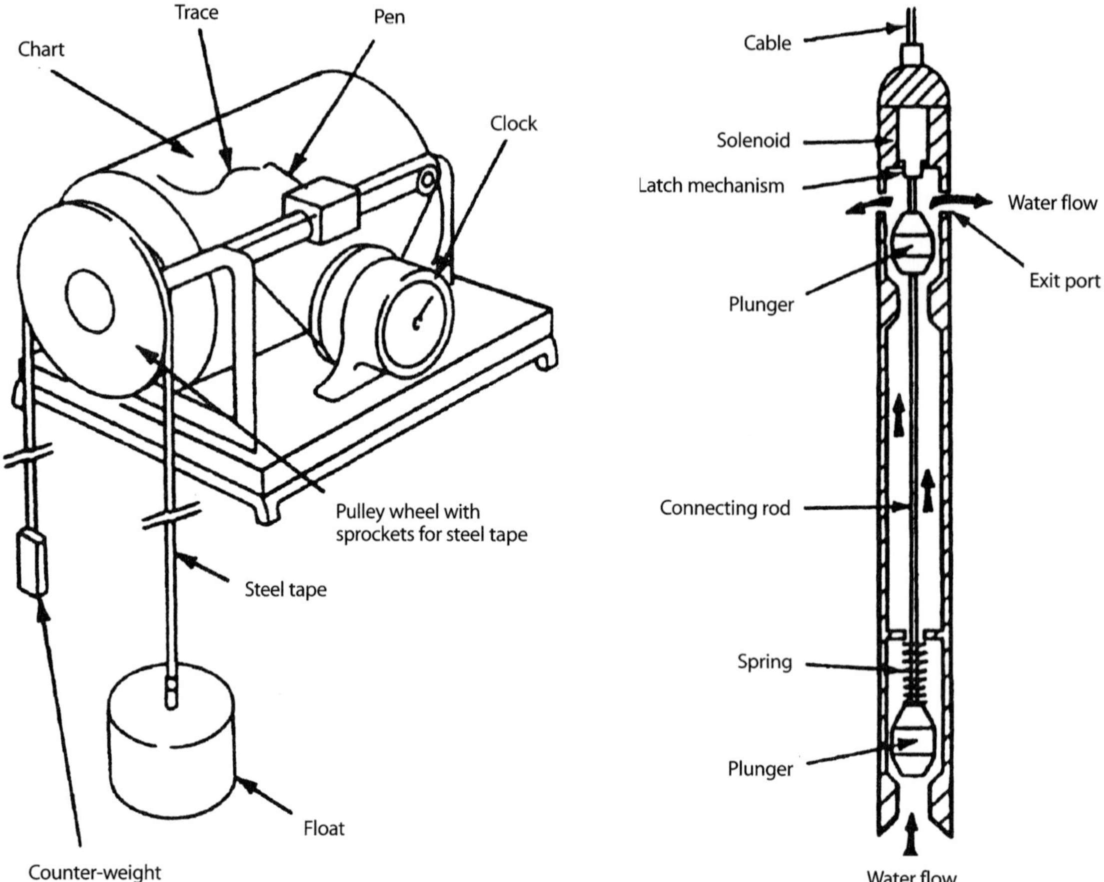
Trace
Pen
Chart
Clock
Pulley wheel with sprockets for steel tape
Steel tape
Float
Counter-weight
Cable
Solenoid
Latch mechanism
Water flow
Exit port
Plunger
Connecting rod
Spring
Plunger
Water flow

Fig. 8.15. Horizontal drum recorder; the drum revolves in response to changes in water level, while the pen is driven by a clock. The instrument is enclosed by a metal cover (after Brassington 1988)

Fig. 8.16. A depth sampler consists of a stainless steel tube, open at each end, which can be closed by spring-loaded bungs and has a capacity of one liter. Water continuously flows through the instrument as it is lowered down the borehole, so that when it stops it contains water from that particular depth. The plunger-like valves are closed either electrically (as in the diagram), or by dropping a weight attached to the cable. Electrically operated samplers are usually lowered on the cable, which carries the electrical charge. Mechanical samplers are lowered on a small-diameter (2–4 mm) steel-wire cable. The valve mechanism is activated by a "messenger" weight, which is clamped to the cable and allowed to free-fall to the sampler (after Brassington 1988)

a A general description of the appearance of the sample (clean or cloudy, etc.) is recorded along with the sampler's name and other parameters, usually measured in the field, such as: pH, temperature, specific conductance and time.
b Labeling of the bottles is important to identify the borehole and/or well, and the depth from which the sample was taken. All information on the label of each bottle should be recorded in the field notebook together with any measured parameters at the site. Pumped samples obtained from water wells or monitoring wells can provide valuable information on quality of water. To avoid contamination, samples should be collected from the discharge pipe, close to the wellhead and not from the storage tank.

In Germany, before ground-water sampling, nearly 1.5 times (U.S. EPA and most of the United States required three well volumes) of the volume of the well content is pumped while continuously measuring the electrical conductivity (in Siemens) until consistence of this parameter is reached. For sampling of dissolved heavy metals in ground water or seepage water, membrane filtration of 0.45 μm is used (Sanders 1998).

(See Appendix 8.D – Ground-water sampling, analytical procedures, and decontamination equipment.)

8.4.3 Surface Hydrogeological Phenomena, and Discussion of Surface Components of the Hydrological Cycle

8.4.3.1 *General*

Water is essential to life. It is a part of the physiological process of nutrition and waste removal from cells of all living things. Aquatic ecosystems, such as wetlands, streams, and lakes, are especially sensitive to changes in water quality and quantity. Aquatic ecosystems receive sediment, nutrients, and toxic substances that are produced or used within their watershed. As a result, an aquatic ecosystem is indicative of the conditions of the terrestrial habitat in its watershed. Drainage basins or watersheds are the basic physical feature contributing water streams, and they have many different shapes and sizes (see Chap. 4)

8.4.3.2 *Definitions*

Because surface water hydrology is interrelated to the environmental hydrogeology, it is important to define some of the prevailing hydrogeological phenomena as follows:

a *Watershed* is the drainage basin of a watercourse, which is the entire area contributing to the runoff and sustaining part or all of the main stream and its tributaries. *Catchment* is another term synonymous to watershed or drainage basin. However, any of these terms may be used to denote the area where the surface runoff travels over the ground surface and through channels to reach the basin outlet.

b *Runoff* is that part of precipitation, as well as any flow contributions, which appears in surface streams of either perennial or intermittent form and can be measured at several locations within a drainage basin. This is the flow collected from all or part of a drainage basin or watershed, and it appears at an outlet of the basin. According to the source from which the flow is derived, runoff may consist of surface runoff, interflow, and ground-water discharge. The surface runoff is that part of runoff which flows over the ground surface and through streams to reach the catchment outlet. The part of surface runoff that flows over the land surface toward stream channels is called overland flow. After the flow enters the stream, it joins with other components of flow to form total runoff, which is called stream flow.

The interflow, also known as subsurface flow, subsurface storm flow, or storm seepage, is that part of precipitation which infiltrates the soil surface and moves laterally through the upper soil horizons toward the streams as ephemeral, shallow, perched ground water above the main ground-water level.

The ground-water runoff, or ground-water flow, is that part of the runoff due to deep percolation of the infiltrated water which has passed into the ground and become, ground water, and been discharged into the stream.

The base flow is defined as the sustained runoff. It is composed of ground-water runoff and delayed subsurface runoff. However, the base flow is completely excluded in arid zones, since ground water may percolate deeply inside the ground and not discharge to the stream channels.

During a runoff-producing storm, the total precipitation may be considered to consist of precipitation excess and abstractions. The precipitation excess is that part of the total precipitation that contributes directly to the surface runoff. When the precipitation is rainfall, the precipitation excess is known as rainfall excess. The abstractions are that part of precipitation that does not contribute to surface runoff, such as interception, evaporation, transpiration, depression storage, and filtration (Soliman et al. 1998).

The part of precipitation that contributes entirely to the direct runoff may be called the effective precipitation, or effective rainfall if only rainfall is involved. Figure 8.17 demonstrates a flow chart identifying the various items from the total precipitation to the total runoff.

8.4.3.3 *Flow Measurements of Rainfall, Springs and Streams*

a *General:* Measurements of the components of the hydrological cycle other than ground water may be provided from rain gauges or stream flow gauging stations. This type of information is needed; for example, in Southwest Florida to meet the Department of Environmental Regulations (DER), the State of Florida has developed regulations to be applied to the development of ground water. These regulations require strict adherence to defining the impact on the surface water, the shallow surficial aquifer, and the deeper intermediate and Floridan aquifers.

Regulations require the Development of a Regional Impact Statement (DRI). Extensive pumping tests, surface water and ground-water studies, monitoring for discharge, water levels, and quality of water are required to identify these impacts. "The 5-3-1 criteria" which requires that a determination be made to show that there will not be more than a 5-foot (1.53 m) average decline in water level in the Floridan aquifer at the boundary of the property under investigation, not more than 3-foot (91.4 cm) decline in the surficial aquifer at the boundary, and no more than a 1-foot (30.5 cm) decline in the nearest water body (pond, lake, etc). In addition, surface water flow in streams of the area must not be decreased more than 5% unless a variance to the rule is obtained.

Surface water flow is effected by differences in soils, geology, vegetation cover, attitude, elevation, and precipitation intensities for the various surface water basins within the tract. Each year, streams recede

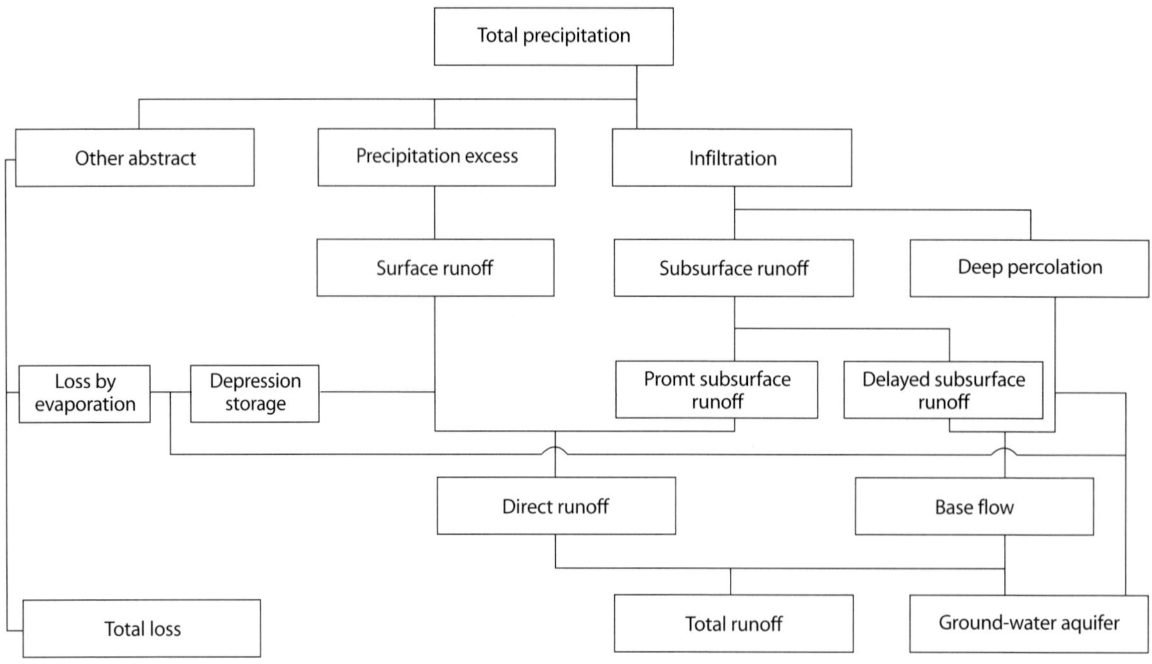
Total precipitation
Other abstract
Precipitation excess
Infiltration
Surface runoff
Subsurface runoff
Deep percolation
Loss by evaporation
Depression storage
Promt subsurface runoff
Delayed subsurface runoff
Direct runoff
Base flow
Total loss
Total runoff
Ground-water aquifer

Fig. 8.17. Various items from total precipitation to total runoff (Soliman 1998)

to low flows in certain seasons, therefore a seasonal distribution of average monthly flow must be determined. The annual minimum instantaneous flow or daily flow is subject to alterations by transient, natural, or man-made causes and therefore the lowest 7-day average flow each year. It is used as the reference period for low flows. In the USA, the yearly minimum 7-day low flows are determined from data collected by the U.S. Geological Survey at gauging stations strategically located over each state. These long-term gauging station records provide the 7-day minimum flows.

b *Precipitation:* In most parts of the world, precipitation is measured by a network of rain gauges operated by national and local government agencies. Extra gauges may be needed nearby a study area to examine local variations in precipitation, especially in areas of high relief. Daily precipitation is measured continuously and reported as daily accumulation of precipitation (in millimeters); the volume of rainfall is recorded as trace (tr.) when it is less than 0.1 mm, and as "Nil" if there is no rain (or snow, hail, etc.).

Precautions should be taken in siting a rain gauge as it should not be sheltered by trees or buildings or be exposed to strong winds that blow raindrops out of the mouth of the gauge.

A "standard" daily rain gauge is used by the British Meteorological Office. The instrument is set into the ground to prevent it from being knocked over and to keep the collected rain cool, thereby reducing evaporation losses in warm weather. Measurements are taken at the same time each morning. A special measuring cylinder is used to measure the rainfall to 0.01 mm. Snowfall is recorded as an equivalent depth of rain in millimeters of water and it can be measured by collecting a representative depth of snow in a cylinder, carefully melting in room temperature and then measuring the volume of water produced. Figure 8.18 shows an example of recording rainfall field data (Brassington 1988).

The determination of infiltration – the downward entry of water into a soil (or sediment) – is receiving increasing attention in hydrologic studies because of the need of more quantitative data on all phases of the hydrologic cycle.

The zone controlling the rate of infiltration is usually the least permeable zone. Many other factors affect infiltration rate – the sediment (soil) structure, the condition of the sediment surface, the distribution of soil moisture or the head of applied water, the depth to ground water, the chemical quality and the turbidity of the applied water, the temperature of the water and the sediments, and the type of equipment or method used.

c *Evaporation:* Evaporation measurements are quite important in certain regions of USA as well as in Africa because of hot weather. The British standard evaporation tank (Fig. 8.19a) and the U.S. Class-A evaporation pan (Fig. 8.19b) are normally used. The former is 0.56 m^2 and 1.55 cm deep and is set into the

Station name: Antioch		Month: August			Year: 1992
Enter amount of measured at 9:00 local time against **YESTERDAY's** date					
Date	mm	Enter time of measurement if not close to 9:00 GMT and notes on significant weather	Date	mm	Enter time of measurement if not close to 9:00 GMT and notes on significant weather
1	2.0		16	1.1	
2	Trace		17	5.7	Hail
3	1.7	Snow	18	0.6	
4	Trace		19	1.0	
5	3.3		20	2.4	Snow
6	7.1	Rain/snow	21	–	
7	7.0	Snow	22	5.4	Sleet in A.M.
8	–	Thaw midday	23	4.3	Snow before dawn
9	–		24	10.6	Heavy shower late A.M.
10	–		25		
11	–		26		Sleet in afternoon
12	Trace		27	8.0	(Acc. total)
13	Trace		28	0.1	
14	0.5		29	0.6	
15	0.3		30	–	
			31	4.3	
Observer:			Total	66.0	

Fig. 8.18. An example to record rainfall field data. No reading were taken for the 25th and 26th; instead the rainfall for these days has been included with the readings of the 27th as an accumulated total (after Brassington 1988)

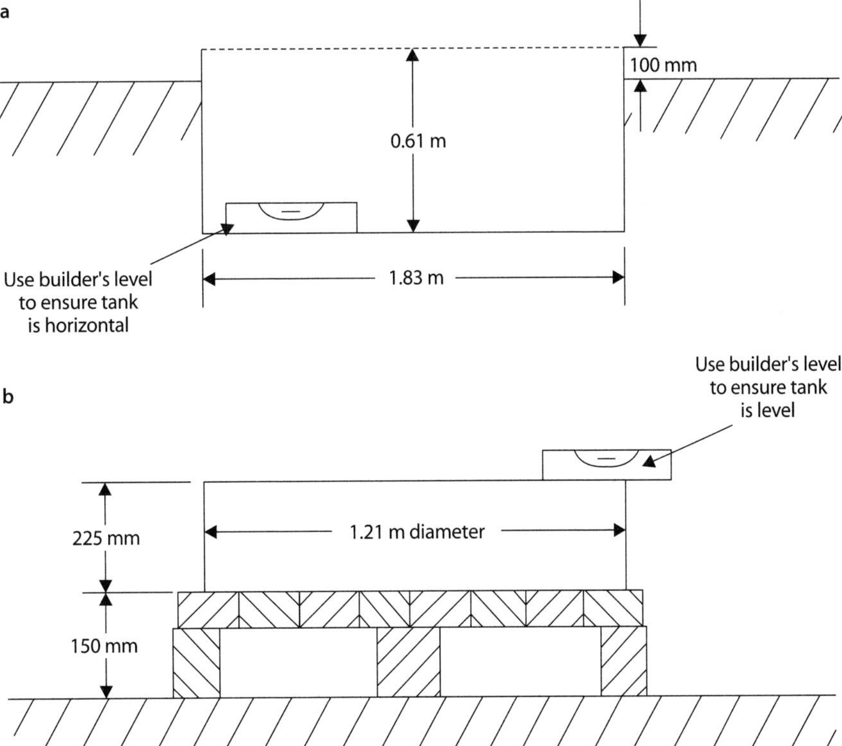
a
100 mm
0.61 m
Use builder's level to ensure tank is horizontal
1.83 m
b
Use builder's level to ensure tank is level
225 mm
1.21 m diameter
150 mm

Fig. 8.19. Two types of evaporation tank; **a** the British standard tank; **b** the U.S. Class-A pan (after Brassington 1988)

ground with the rim 100 mm above ground level. The latter is circular with a diameter of 1.21 m and is a 22.5 mm deep. It is set 150 mm above the ground on a wooden platform so that air can circulate around it. In both cases, the tanks are filled with water and the water level is maintained. Figure 8.19 shows an example of daily record of evaporation losses. Table 8.4 shows that rainfall is attributed to the previous day and the difference in tank-water levels is used to calculate the evaporation losses. For example, there was no rain on August 1 and evaporation was then directly calculated. When rain has fallen then the raise in tank level should be subtracted from it to calculate the evaporation as follows

1. The decrease in water level from August 1 to August 2 due to evaporation was 0.5 mm.
2. Rise of tank level from August 4 to August 5 = 5.8 mm
3. Rainfall on August 4 was 8.1 mm; evaporation was therefore 2.3 mm.

Other formula for evapo-transpiration (both evaporation and transpiration) include:

$$ET + S = P - (RSS + RH) \tag{8.19}$$

where ET = evapo-transpiration; S = underground storage; P = precipitation; RS = surface runoff; RSS = subsurface runoff; RH = hypodermic runoff / interflow.

d *Springs:* The flow of springs and some small streams may be measured by using a bucket or a "jug" and stopwatch method. This may be carried out by placing a jug with a known capacity of one liter or using a bigger container such as a 10-liter bucket, if the spring fills the jug in less than five seconds. If the 10-liter bucket fills rapidly then a simple thin plate weir can be used (LaMoreaux and Tanner 2001).

For a small stream, certain modifications may be necessary as shown in Fig. 8.20. The flow should be diverted through a short length of pipe. A sufficient gap below the end of the pipe is required to insert the jug or bucket and stand it upright. This can be achieved by building a small dam of stones and clay or concrete through which the pipe projects for at least 200 mm.

It is important to start the stopwatch at the same instant when the first drop of water falls into the bucket, and it should be stopped when it is filled and the mark is reached. The bucket should be all the time in the upright position. This measurement is repeated at least three times and the average is taken as the correct flow. Care should be taken when dealing with drinking water supplies to avoid any contamination.

e *Streamflow measurement:* The flows of streams and rivers are calculated from measurements of water velocities and the channel cross sectional area or by installing a weir or flume. The flow records can also be obtained from the local water authority or similar organization that measures river flow.

Thin-plate weirs are often used for streamflow measurements. They work by restricting the size of the stream channel. This causes the water to pond on the upstream side before passing over the weir. The rate of the water flow over the weir depends on the height of water it on the upstream side.

Two types of thin-plate weir are known, a V-notch weir and a rectangular weir. The weir should have a lip between 1 and 2 mm. The downstream face should slope away from the lip at an angle of at least 60° in a V-notch weir. In the case of rectangular weirs, this angle must be at least 45°. Flows of up to 60 or 70 liters per second can be measured with a V-notch weir. Higher flows can be measured with a rectangular weir of appropriate width. Figure 8.21 shows three types of V-notch weir, each with a slightly different shaped notch.

A straight section of channel, at least 3 m long, should be upstream from the weir; because weirs work by controlling the level of the water surface on the upstream side, the flow of water over a weir is related to the depth of water above the weir crest. The flow can then be obtained from the appropriate tables. Also in flowmeter measurements, it is well known that the flow velocity in m s^{-1} is calculated by dividing Q ($m^3 s^{-1}$) by the area (m^2) of the weir (Brassington 1988).

Table 8.4. Daily readings of rainfall and water levels in evaporation tank (after Brassington 1988)

August	Observations made at 09:00 local time		Daily records	
	Rainfall (mm)	Evaporation tank water level (mm)	Rainfall (mm)	Evaporation (mm)
1	1.2	23.6	–	1.5
2	–	22.1	10.2	0.7
3	10.2	31.6	–	1.8
4	–	29.8	8.1	2.3
5	8.1	35.6	–	1.6
6	–	34.0	0.4	2.0
7	0.4	32.4	[a]	[a]

[a] Values not included.

f *National Streamflow Information Program (NSIP):* Nationally, USGS surface-water data describe stream levels, streamflow (discharge), reservoir and lake levels, surface-water quality, and rainfall. The data are collected by automatic recorders and manual measurements at field installations across the nation. The NSIP was recommended to produce information for multiple uses and consist of the following components: (1) A nationwide system of Federal-interest stream-gaging stations for measuring streamflow and related environmental variables (precipitation, temperature) reliably and continuously in time; (2) a program for intensive data collection in response to major floods and droughts; (3) a program for periodic assessments and interpretation of streamflow data to better define its statistical characteristics and trends; (4) a system for real-time streamflow information delivery to customers that includes data processing, quality assurance, archival, and access; (5) a program of techniques development and research (USGS News 2002: http://water.usgs.gov; http://water.usgs.gov/ogw/programs.html/).

g *USGS Water-Quality Programs* mainly deal with three key components that are critical for successful water-resource management, including (1) long-term monitoring, (2) resource assessment, and (3) research.

USGS long-term data collection is needed to (1) distinguish long-term trends from short-term fluctuations and natural fluctuations from effects of human activities; (2) evaluate how environmental controls and strategies are working; and (3) choose the most cost-effective resource strategies for the future.

USGS resource assessment addresses the many complexities of contaminant occurrence and transport, which vary seasonably and among watersheds because of differences in land use and chemical applications, land-management practices, degree of watershed development, and natural factors, such as soils, geology, hydrology, and other natural factors.

USGS research identifies emerging contaminants (such as pesticide degradates, hormones, steroids, and pharmaceuticals); provides new information and innovative study approaches for addressing contami-

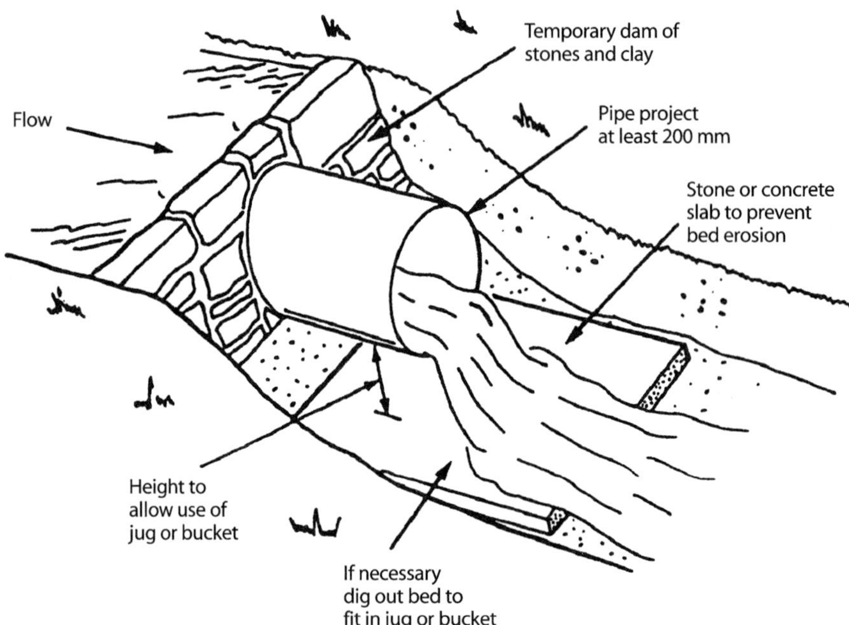
Temporary dam of
stones and clay
Flow
Pipe project
at least 200 mm
Stone or concrete
slab to prevent
bed erosion
Height to
allow use of
jug or bucket
If necessary
dig out bed to
fit in jug or bucket

Fig. 8.20.
Measurement of a spring flow by installing a temporary dam and directing the flow through a pipe (after Brassington 1988)

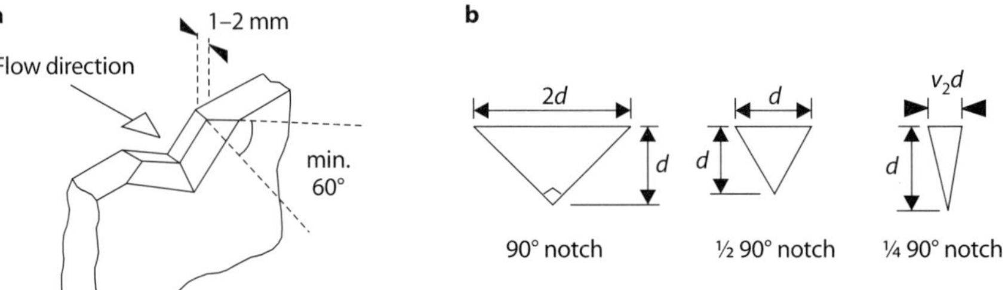
a
1–2 mm
Flow direction
min.
60°
b
2d
d
d
d
½d
d
90° notch
½ 90° notch
¼ 90° notch

Fig. 8.21.
A V-notch weir used for accurate measurements of the flow of streams. The general arrangements shown in (**a**) apply to the three types of V-notches shown in (**b**) (after Brassington 1988)

nation issues; and develops methodology for cost-effective hydrologic assessment (USGS; News 2002) (http://water.usgs.gov/nawqa; http://water.usgs.gov/pubs/FS/fs-076-02).

8.5 Acquisition of Hydrogeologic Data

The regulations for landfill and hazardous sites were promulgated by the U.S. EPA, CFR 40 Federal and State regulatory agencies. Those regulations were considered by many countries all over the world.

State and Federal regulations have established restrictions for location of hazardous waste and municipal, solid waste landfills. Regulations require owners/operators to demonstrate that the hydrogeology has been completely characterized at proposed landfills, and that locations for monitoring wells have been properly selected. Owners/operators are also required to demonstrate that engineering measures have been incorporated in the design of the municipal solid waste landfills, so that the site is not subject to destabilized events, as a result of location in unstable areas, such as karst terrains (Sara 1994).

Table 8.5a includes a list of generic categories of information that should be considered during evaluation of potential sites for land disposal. It also includes broader categories, an understanding of which is necessary during the preliminary screening of sites and provides a basis for formulation of a conceptual hydro-geologic model as described by Sara (1994), of sites selected for further studies.

8.5.1 Site Assessments

Preliminary investigations are first needed to provide later a comprehensive overview of available information concerning a site. Many factors influence the applicability of a site for use as a landfill: rainfall, runoff, and public concern. However, the specific geologic and hydrogeologic conditions that have the most critical effects on the proposed waste disposal facility should be evaluated (Hughes et al. 1994). Many errors and misinterpretations in geologic data can occur when poorly placed exploration boreholes contact stratigraphic materials that are structurally complex. Any site assessment project where significant field data gathering is required should be conducted in a phased approach. Phase I would consist of primarily a literature and field reconnaissance that would set the stage for later intensive Phase II field data gathering. Phase I investigations can be conducted for new sites, either greenfield or acquisitions, expansions to currently operating sites, evaluations of associative risk of a site or as a first step in a superfund remedial investigation/feasibility study (RI/FS).

A preliminary investigation should always summarize the available literature and provide as complete a picture as possible of the site, including facility operations and the basic geologic and hydrogeologic environment.

The planning, field assessment, design, and construction of any waste disposal facility require both regional information for planning and detailed site-specific data. General site information can be gathered by using the sources listed in Table 8.5b (Sara 1994).

Vadose zone evaluations are especially important for land disposal facilities where thick unsaturated deposits separate the facility from aquifer units.

8.5.2 Surface-Water Hydrology

The purpose of surface water hydrology studies is to describe the drainage systems, flow characteristics, water quality of the streams and water bodies, and to aid in determining the ground water/surface water relationships. The typical Phase II scope of work for surface water studies includes site reconnaissance by a combined hydrology/geology team, a stream gaging program, and various engineering analyses of hydrologic and stream flow characteristics for a 12-month minimum time period with careful long-term extrapolation.

The base line data for surface water hydrology should be developed to describe drainage systems, flow characteristics, and water quality of the site area. An important use of this information is to assist in determining ground water/surface water relationships at the site.

Periodic discharge measurements normally are made at selected stream sites using a standardized price and standard U.S. Geological Survey techniques. Measurement of total suspended solids within a given drainage basin provides a basis for calculating the erosion rates. Monitoring points established to evaluate the rate and volume of erosion, during the baseline period, will provide information to assist in design of effective site or cell-closure reclamation plans (Sara 1994).

The 100-year flood plain is normally a zone excluded from the disposal of solid waste. Equally important is the protection of wetlands and control of runoff from waste disposal areas into surface water bodies. Data on the 100-year flood plain, wetlands, stream flow and runoff, water quality, and water use may be obtained by review of the most recent U.S. Geological Survey, Army Corps of Engineers, or the Federal Insurance Administration (FIA). Tables 8.6 and 8.7 (Sara 1994) provide data sources for the required information.

Table 8.5a.
Generic categories for evaluation of potential sites for land disposal (after Hughes et al. 1994)

Stratigraphy
(Regional and local)
- Stratigraphic column
- Thickness of each carbonate
  - Unit
- Thickness of non-carbonate
  - Interbeds
- Type of bedding
  - Thin
  - Medium
  - Thick
- Purity of east carbonate unit
  - Limestone or dolomite
    - Pure
    - Sandy
    - Silty
    - Clayey
    - Siliceous
    - Interbeds

Overburden
(Soils and sub-soils)
- Distribution
- Origin
  - Transported
    - Glacial
    - Alluvial
    - Colluvial
  - Residual
  - Other
- Characteristics and variability
  - Thickness
  - Physical properties
  - Hydrologic properties

Hydrology
- Surface water
  - Discharge
    - Variability
      - Seasonal
      - Gaining
      - Losing
- Ground water
  - Diffuse flow
  - Conduit flow
  - Fissure flow
  - Recharge
  - Storage
  - Discharge
- Fluctuation of water levels
- Relationships of surface water
  - and ground-water flow

Geologic structure
(Regional and local)
- Nearly horizontal bedding
- Tilted beds
  - Homoclines
  - Monoclines
- Folded beds
  - Anticlines
  - Synclines
  - Monoclines
  - Domes
  - Basins
  - Other
- Fractures
  - Lineaments
  - Locations
  - Relationships with
    - Geomorphic features
    - Karst features
    - Stratigraphy
    - Structural features
- Joint system
  - Joint sets
    - Orientation
    - Spacing
    - Continuity
    - Open
    - Closed
    - Filled
- Faults
  - Orientation
  - Frequency
  - Continuity
  - Type
    - Normal
    - Reverse
    - Thrust
    - Other
  - Age of faults
    - Holocene
    - Pre-Holocene

Activities of man
- Construction
  - Excavation
  - Blasting
  - Vibration
  - Loading
    - Fill
    - Buildings
  - Changes in drainage
  - Dams and lakes
- Withdrawal of ground water
  - Wells
  - Dewatering
  - Irrigation

Geomorphology
(Regional and local)
- Relief sopes
- Density of drainage network
- Characteristics of streams
  - Drainage pattern(s)
    - Dendritic
    - Trellis
    - Rectangular
    - Other
  - Perennial
  - Intermittent
- Terraces
- Springs and/or seeps
- Lakes and ponds
- Flood plains and wetlands
- Karst features (active and historic)
  - Karst plains
  - Poljes
  - Dry valleys, blind valleys, sinking creeks
  - Depressions and general subsidence
  - Subsidence cones, in overburden
  - Sinkholes
  - Roof collapse
  - Uvalas
  - Caverns, caves and cavities
  - Rise pits
  - Swallow holes
  - Estavelles
  - Karren
  - Other
- Paleo-karst

Climate
- Precipitation (rain and snow)
  - Seasonal
  - Annual
  - Long-Term
- Evapo-transpiration
- Vegetation

8.5.3 Preliminary Conceptual Model of a Site

A prime importance for use of a site for a waste disposal is the hydrogeologic conditions, which should be incorporated into a conceptual model. Figure 8.22 (LaMoreaux et al. 1999; Sara 1994) illustrate examples of the effects of geology on the movement of leachate from a waste disposal site in cross section views.

8.5.4 Basic Data Checklist

The potential effects of disposal at the site includes identification of fatal flaws and establishes the need for additional information to be secured during site reconnaissance.

Before conducting the site reconnaissance, the information presented on the basic data checklist (LaMoreaux

Table 8.5b. Basic data sources (after Sara 1994)

Source	Information obtainable	Comments
Libraries	Earth science bibliographic indices	Many of the types of information discussed below can be obtained from libraries. Excellent library facilities are available at the U.S. Geological Survey offices (USGS) in Reston, VA; Denver, CO; and Menlo Park, CA. Local university libraries can contain good collections of earth science and related information and typically are depositories for federal documents. In addition, local public libraries normally have information on the physical and historical characteristics of the surrounding area.
Computer literature searches	Bibliographic indices	Perhaps one of the most useful and cost effective developments in bibliographic indexes has been the increased availability of computerized reference searches. Online computer searches save significant time and money by giving rapid retrieval of citations of all listed articles on a given subject and eliminate manual searching of annual cumulated indexes. A search is done by use of keywords, author names, or title words, and can be delimited by ranges of dates or a given number of the most recent or oldest references. The average search requires about 15 minutes of online searching and cost about U.S.$50 for computer time and offline printing of citations and abstracts.
SDI services	Stored bibliographic searches	An extremely useful feature of computerized information retrieval systems is the selective dissemination of information (SDI) service. SDI is a procedure for storing search profiles and providing updates of an original computer search. The engineer should consult SDI services for topics of relevance to the proposed project.
State and federal projects	Site specific assessment data for dams, harbors, river basin impoundments, and federal highways	Project reports contain data on all eight categories considered, as well as analysis, construction drawings, and references. These reports can generally be obtained most easily by contacting the responsible agency. Surface water and geological foundation conditions such as fracture orientation, permeability, faulting, rippability, and weathered profiles are particularly well covered in these investigations.
Univestity sources	Engineering and geology theses	College and university geology theses, in most instances, are well-documented studies dealing with specific areas, generally prepared under the guidance of faculty members having expertise in the subject under investigation. Most theses are not published.
Comprehensive Dissertation Index	Doctoral dissertations	Citation began in 1861 and include almost every doctoral dissertation accepted in North America thereafter. The index is available at larger library reference desks and is organized into 32 subject volumes and 5 author volumes. Specific titles are located through title keywords or author names. Ph.D. dissertations from all U.S. universities.
AGI directory of Geoscience Department	Faculty members	Regular updates of faculty, specialties, and telephone date.
DATRIX II University Microfilms International 300 North Zeeb Road; Ann Arbor, MI 48106, USA; Tel. 800-521-3042; 313-761-4700 (in Alaska, Hawaii, and Michigan)	Dissertations and masters thesis	Using title keywords, a bibliography of relevant theses can be compiled and mailed to the user within one week. In addition, the DATRIX Alert system can automatically provide new bibliographic citations as they become available.
United States Geology: A dissertation bibliography by State	Ph.D. dissertation or master thesis	Free index from University Microfilms International. Some universities do not submit dissertations to University Microfilms for reproduction or abstracting, however, and the dissertations from these schools do not appear in the United States Geology Index. Citations for dissertations not abstracted must be located through DATRIX II or Comprehensive Dissetation Index.
Dissertation Abstracts International, vol. B – science and engineering, a monthly publication of University Microfilms International	Extended abstracts of dissertations from more than 400 U.S. and Canadian universities	Once the citation for a specific dissertation has been obtained from Comprehensive Dissertation Index or from DATRIX II, the abstract can be scanned to determine whether it is relevant to the project at hand. Since some universities do not participate, some theses indexed in the two sources listed above must be obtained directly from the author or the university at which the research was completed. Abstracts of masters theses available from University Microfilms are summarized in 150-word abstracts in Masters Abstracts and are also indexed by author and title keywords. Both Dissertation Abstracts International and Masters Abstracts are available at many university libraries. A hard (paper) or microform (microfilm or microfiche) copy of any dissertation or thesis abstracted can be purchased from University Microfilms.
Local, state, and regional agencies	Soils, land use, flood plains, ground water, aerial photographs	Local, state, and regional agencies. Local county, town, and city planning boards commonly provide data on general physical characteristics of areas within their jurisdiction. Many states maintain a department of the environment or natural resources. While the primary function of these agencies is not geological in nature, these organizations commonly have extensive information related to geology, remote sensing, and water.

Table 8.5. *Continued*

Source	Information obtainable	Comments
Knowledgeable individuals	Historic information, past site owners and practices	Time can be saved in the initial stages of a data search by contacting knowledgeable individuals for references and an overview of an area, as well as for specific problems and details that may be unpublished. People to contact include university professors; and persons from relevant state and federal agencies such as state geological surveys, the USGS, or the Army Corps of Engineers; corporate, regional, and district operations staff that have experience within the area. Local well drillers, consulting engineers, and architects.

Table 8.6. Hydrologic data (after Sara 1994; hints to references refer to the original work)

Source	Information obtainable	Comments
Water Publications of State Agencies (Giefer and Todd 1972, 1976)	This books list state agencies involved with research related to water and also lists all publications of these agencies. In general, hydrologic data can be classified into four primary categories: stream discharge, stream water quality, ground-water level, and ground-water quality	The trend for the past decade has been to compile such basic data in computerized data banks, and a number of such information systems are now available for private and public users. Many data now collected by federal and state water-related agencies are available through computer files, but most data collected by private consultants, local and county agencies, and well drilling contractors remain with the organization that gathered them.
Local Assistance Center of the National Water Data Exchange NAWDEX U.S. Geological Survey 421 National Center Reston, VA 22092 Tel.: 703-648-4000	NAWDEX identifies organizations that collect water data, offices within these obtained, alternate sources from which an organization's data may be obtained, the geographic areas in which an organization collects data, and the types of data collected. Information has been compiled for more than 600 organizations, and information on other organizations is added continually. More than 300 000 data collection sites are indexed.	NAWDEX, which began operation in 1976 is administered by the U.S. Geological Survey organizations from which the data may be consists of a computer directory system which locates sources of needed water data. The system helps to link data users to data collectors. For example, the NAWDEX Master Water Data Index can identify the sites at which water data are available in a geographic area, and the Water Data Sources Directory can then identify the names and addresses of organizations from which the data may be obtained. In addition, listings and summary counts of data, references to other water data systems, and bibliographic data services are available.
Published water-supply studies and data	Stream discharge, ground-water level, and water quality data have been obtained during short-term, site-specific studies, and these data are typically available only in published or unpublished site reports. Data related to lakes, reservoirs, and wetlands are commonly found only in such reports.	Although significant progress has been made in computerizing surface- and ground-water data, the majority remains available only through published and unpublished reports
Catalog of Information on Water Data	The reference consists of four parts: Part A: Stream flow and stage Part B: Quality of surface water Part C: Quality of ground water Part D: Aerial investigations and miscellaneous activities	Bibliographic publication indexes USGS sampling and measurement sites throughout the U.S.
Geologic and Water-Supply Reports and Maps (available for each state)		This publication lists references for each USGS division for each state or district; the listing, however, is by report number, requiring a scan of the entire list for information on a particular area.
Water Resources Investigations (by state) Office of Water Data U.S. Geological Survey 417 National Center 12201 Sunrise Valley Drive Reston, VA 22092 Additional assistance can be obtained by contacting: Hydrologic Information Unit; U.S. Geological Survey; 420 National Center; 12201 Sunrise Valley Drive Reston, VA 22092	Listed are all agencies cooperating with the USGS in collecting water data, information on obtaining further information, and a selected list of references by both the USGS and cooperating agencies.	This booklet describes the projects and related publications for all current USGS work in a state or group of states. Also available is a useful summary folder with the same title that depicts hydrologic data stations and hydrologic investigations in a district as of the date of publication.
Federal flood insurance studies	To meet the provisions of the *National Flood Insurance Act* of 1968, the USGS, with funding by the Federal Insurance Administration, has mapped the 100-year floodplain of most municipal areas at a scale of 1:24 000	Floodplain maps can be obtained free from the nearest district office of the USGS and commonly from other agencies, such as the relevant city, town, or county planning office, or the Federal Insurance Administration. In some areas more detailed "flood insurance studies" have been completed for the Federal Emergency Management Agency; these maps include 100-year and 500-year floodplain maps. The complete studies are available at the nearest USGS office, the relevant city, town, or county planning office or the Federal Emergency Management Agency.

Table 8.7. Climatic data (after Sara 1994; references refer to the original work)

Source	Information obtainable	Comments
National Climatic Center (NCC) Federal Building Asheville, NC 28801 Tel.: 704-259-0682	Readily available are data from the monthly publication *Climatological Data*, which reports temperature and precipitation statistics for all monitoring stations in a given state or region. An annual summary is also available.	The National Climatic Center (NCC) collects and catalogs nearly all U.S. weather records. Climatic data (which are essential for construction planning, environmental assessments, and conducting surface and ground-water modeling) can be obtained from the NCC.
	In addition to collecting basic data, NCC provides the following services:	NCC can provide data on file in hard (paper) copy, in microfiche, or on magnetic tape.
	1. Supply of publications, reference manuals, catalog of holdings, and data report atlases 2. Data and map reproduction in various forms 3. Analysis and preparation of statistical summaries 4. Evaluation of data records for specific analytical requirements 5. Library search for bibliographic references, abstracts, and documents 6. Referral to organizations holding requested information 7. Provision of general atmospheric sciences information	For general summary statistics and maps, the publication *Climates of the States – NOAA Narrative Summaries, Tables, and Maps for Each State* by Gale Research Company (1980) is helpful.

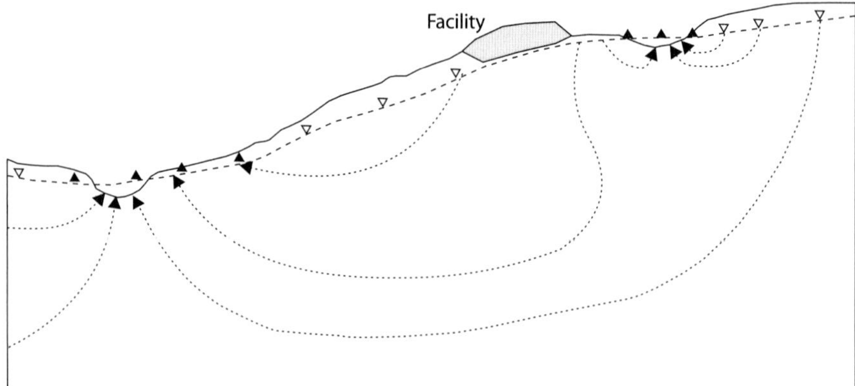
Facility

Fig. 8.22. Simple conceptual model – cross section flow (after Sara 1994)

et al. 1999; Sara 1994; Table 8.8), should be reviewed to assure that the data compiled are as complete as possible. The responsible engineer or geologist should then visit the site to substantiate preliminary conclusion based on the information compiled during the research and to obtain necessary additional site information.

8.5.5 Greenfield Siting

Landfill siting studies are historically controversial because of potential conflicts with diverse public values. People may recognize the need for solid waste management, but are frequently not willing to bear the burden of "other people's trash". Other public interests may be concerned about increased user costs while still others support waste reduction, processing, or recycling technologies as an alternative to landfill siting disposal. Because of high public sensitivity to landfill siting and the potential for conflicting public interests, a responsive public involvement program is critical to a successful landfill siting of a sanitary landfill that requires sound technical studies (Sara 1994; Fig. 8.23).

Land disposal is a sociopolitical process that should accommodate local and regional concerns. Table 8.9 gives greenfield siting criteria for successful siting of a sanitary landfill.

See Search for References: Sec. 14.5.

8.6 Karst Aquifers and Cave Patterns

Cave patterns are controlled by a hierarchy of hydrogeologic factors. The location and overall trend of a

Table 8.8.
Phase I basic data check list (after Sara 1994)

A. Maps and cross section
  1. Planimetric
  2. Topographic
  3. Geologic
    a Structure
    b Stratigraphy
    c Lithology
  4. Hydrologic
    a Location of wells, observation holes, and springs
    b Ground-water table and piezometric contours
    c Depth to water
    d Quality of water
    e Recharge, discharge, and contributing areas
  5. Vegetative cover
  6. Soils
  7. Aerial photographs

B. Data on wells, observation holes, and springs
  1. Location, depth, diameter, types of wells, and logs
  2. Static and pumping water level, hydrographs, yield, specific capacity, quality of water
  3. Present and projected ground-water development and use
  4. Corrosion, incrustation, well interference, and similar operation and maintenance problems
  5. Location, type, geologic setting, and hydrographs of springs
  6. Observation well networks
  7. Water sampling sites

C. Aquifer data
  1. Type, such as unconfined, artesian, or perched
  2. Thickness, depths, and formational designation
  3. Boundaries
  4. Transmissivity, storativity, and permeability
  5. Specific retention
  6. Discharge and recharge
  7. Ground and surface water relationships
  8. Aquifer models

D. Climatic data
  1. Precipitation
  2. Temperature
  3. Evapotranspiration
  4. Wind velocities, directions, and intensities

E. Surface water
  1. Use
  2. Quality and standards
  3. Runoff distribution, reservoir capacities, inflow and outflow data
  4. Return flows, section gain or loss
  5. Recording stations

F. Ecological studies
  1. Endangered species
  2. Threatened species
  3. Critical habitat

Source: U.S. Department of the Interior

cave depends on the distribution of discharge and recharge points within the karst aquifers. The hydrogeologic setting of a karst aquifer is the most significant factor in determining the cave patterns within it.

Any geologic setting that allows the movement of aggressive ground water through soluble rock will favor the origin of caves and related surface features. Cave origin is enhanced where runoff from large catchments

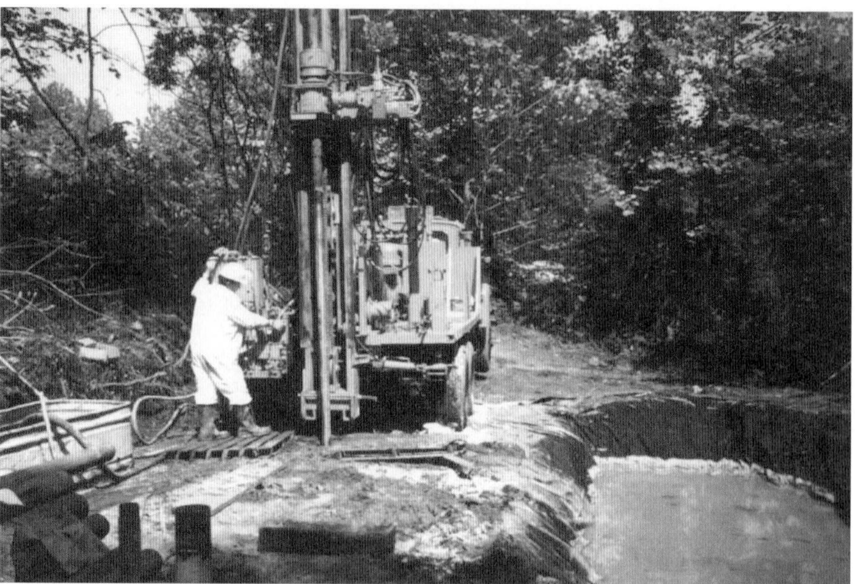

Fig. 8.23. A Monitoring well installation in a landfill (Sara 1994)

is concentrated into a few small areas of ground-water recharge. Caves are thus most abundant in soluble rocks that lie beneath perched stream valleys or glacial cirques, or which border areas of exposed insoluble rocks. Convex topography is less favorable, because runoff is divergent and infiltration tends to be dispersed (Palmer 2000).

8.7 Hydrological Mapping Techniques

The United Nations Educational, Scientific and Cultural Organization (UNESCO) along with the International Hydrological Decade (IHD) started its *Studies and Reports in Hydrology* series in the mid 1960s and ended in 1974 but the national activities continued the series to present the data collected and the main results of hydrological studies undertaken within the framework of the decade and the new International Hydrological Program, as well as to provide information on the hydrological research techniques used (UNESCO, WMO 1977).

Studies and reports carried out by UNESCO, WMO (1977) discussed the growing need for the international exchange and use of hydrological information, which makes it imperative to establish degrees of compatibility and standardization in the preparation of hydrological maps. This need is evident, for example, in the program to compile and update information from many nations to improve understanding of the world water balance – one of the major objectives of the use of the International Hydrological Decade (IHD). Standardization will be even more necessary to the plans for monitoring global environmental changes and for plotting the resulting information global projections.

Maps including hydrological maps, have reflected local needs, capabilities, standards and traditions. Hydrological maps are commonly used to represent large amounts of information about the water regimes of the surface and near surface of the earth because they display the information in its spatial relationships and in relationship to the configuration of the land itself. The preparation of hydrological maps depend in several aspects on the examination of the hydrological cycle as follows: (1) *Residence time* is the length if time during which an increment of water remains in one identifiable element of the hydrological cycle; (2) *Spatial geometry* of water bodies is a factor in preparing hydrological maps, e.g. surface water is quickly concentrated in channels which, except for special engineering studies are rarely shown to have more than a lineal dimension. In contrast, ground water may extend over large areas through considerable thickness; (3) *Climate* differ around the globe, and the hydrological cycle has many variations as well. The mapping techniques differ greatly in cold regions where the hydrological cycle involves three phases of water, from that of the warmer areas where the hydrological cycle involves only two.

There are many ways for classifying hydrological maps. Classifications of maps on the basis of purpose, reliability, scale, and data geometry are useful in providing auxiliary means for analyzing all types of hydrological maps.

8.8 Classification of Hydrological Maps

Classification of data is a standard first step in the process of scientific analysis and synthesis. Classification

Table 8.9. Greenfield siting criteria (after Sara 1994)

	Criterion	Phase I: Site identification	Phase II: Site evaluation
1	Estimated service life	Try to delineate a site of areas sufficient to provide a long service life and adequate buffer area	Compare acreage of alternative sites
2	Traffic	Locate site as close to a highway as reasonable given other criteria	Compare potential traffic impacts on existing roads (landfill traffic as % of existing ADT)
3	Ground-water protection		
	a Depth	Choose areas with deeper ground water	Compare average depth
	b Quality	Choose areas with poorer quality water	Compare quality indices
	c Domestic users down-gradient	NA at this phase; land use avoidance will minimize potential impact down-gradient	Determine and compare the number of domestic users within 1 mile (1.6 km)
4	Noise	Choose areas far from existing residences in quiet areas, or in already noisier areas	Measure ambient noise levels, calculate and compare impact indices
5	Visual	Choose area that is visually screened, can readily be screened, or is not near sensitive features	Calculate and compare indices of potential visual impact, evaluate effectiveness screening or other alternatives
6	Existing land use	Choose sites as far from existing residences; review Subtitle D Airport Restrictions	Calculate and compare the number of residences within 1 mile (1.6 km) (or a greater distance if there is no difference at that one)
7	Future land use	Identify boundaries of proposed developments on the site or (if nearby; available) choose sites as far as possible from proposed developments	Discuss prospects for other developments and general plan categories; determine and calculate indices of future land use impacts; compare sites
8	Timeliness of size acquisition	Identify locations of private, state and federal lands; choose some sites of each land type to ensure site availability if acquisition problems arise with any given area	Map land parcel boundaries; based on discussions with land management agencies, estimate months necessary to acquire; compare sites; calculate, for each site, annualized
9	Costs	NA in this phase	The variety of siting areas identified will ensure variation in costs of land acquisition, site develop-haul costs, the most significant cost development, off-site development, variable. General debt service and haul costs, supplied in Phase II to specific sites. Studies during this phase will establish volumes, locations, and unit costs.
10	Cultural resources	Avoid known historic or archaeological districts (required for project sites on or near on state or federal land)	NA, assuming avoidance of known sites or candidate landfill sites; if some cultural sites are nearby, however, may want to rate probabilities of cultural resources by landfill site; no matter what the results of this phase, a detailed reconnaissance of the selected site will be require for acquisition of state or federal lands
11	Biological resources	Avoid rare, endangered or sensitive biological species	NA, assuming avoidance of sensitive biological resources in Phase I
12	Economic impacts	NA in this phase	Avoidance of existing or proposed land uses will tend to minimize potential impacts; based on existing, proposed and projected land uses, and on recent land values, characterize sites by relative property value impacts
13	Geologic hazards	Review Subtitle D Restrictions on Locations	Detailed geologic review of the potential site(s)
14	Meteorology	NA in this phase	Identify prevailing wind direction(s) and frequencies; identify sites with existing or future residential developments within 2 miles (3.2 km)

provides guides to the types of map best suited to particular purposes.

Hydrological maps can be classified in many ways, and no one classification is satisfactory for all purposes. Several systems of classification were examined and a matrix was developed that has been useful in analyzing the extent to which individual sources of hydrological maps are adequately portraying the full scope of the hydrological cycle and the local, regional, and national water resources they purport to represent.

Classifications of maps on the basis of purpose, reliability, scale, and data geometry are useful in providing

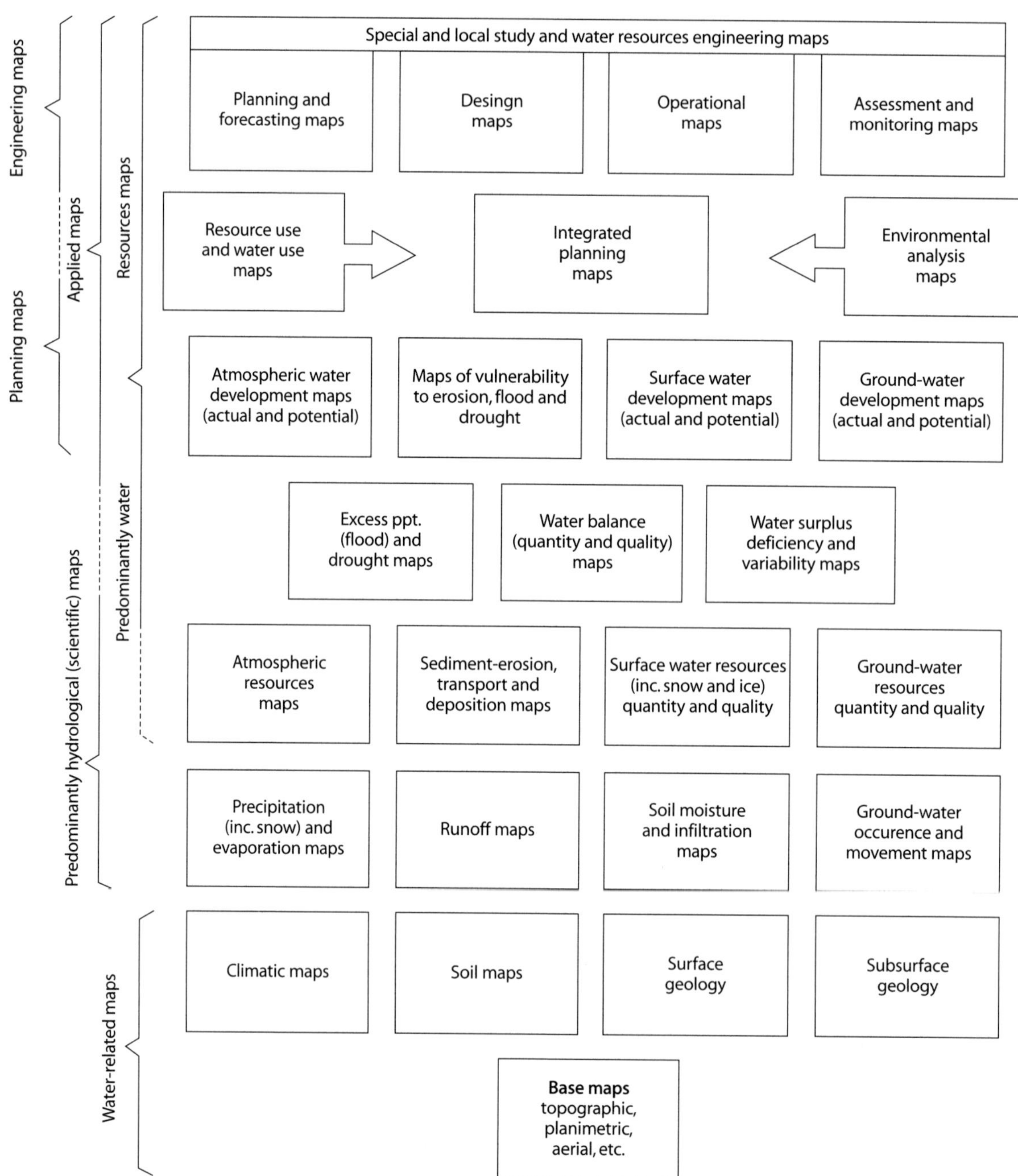
Engineering maps
Planning maps
Applied maps
Resources maps
Predominantly hydrological (scientific) maps
Predominantly water
Water-related maps
Special and local study and water resources engineering maps
Planning and forecasting maps
Desingn maps
Operational maps
Assessment and monitoring maps
Resource use and water use maps
Integrated planning maps
Environmental analysis maps
Atmospheric water development maps (actual and potential)
Maps of vulnerability to erosion, flood and drought
Surface water development maps (actual and potential)
Ground-water development maps (actual and potential)
Excess ppt. (flood) and drought maps
Water balance (quantity and quality) maps
Water surplus deficiency and variability maps
Atmospheric resources maps
Sediment-erosion, transport and deposition maps
Surface water resources (inc. snow and ice) quantity and quality
Ground-water resources quantity and quality
Precipitation (inc. snow) and evaporation maps
Runoff maps
Soil moisture and infiltration maps
Ground-water occurence and movement maps
Climatic maps
Soil maps
Surface geology
Subsurface geology
Base maps
topographic, planimetric, aerial, etc.

Fig. 8.24. Experimental hierarchy of hydrological, water-resources and related maps (after UNESCO, WMO 1977)

auxiliary means for analyzing all types of hydrological maps; one possible hierarch of hydrological maps classified as to purpose is shown in Fig. 8.24 (UNESCO, WMO, 1977).

See Sec. 14.5 (Search of References).

References

Alsay-Pippin Corporation (1980) Handbook of industrial drilling procedures and techniques. Lake Worth, Florida

Amax JW, Bass DM, Whiting RL (1960) Petroleum reservoir engineering. McGraw-Hill, New York (in U.S. Environmental Protection Agency 1977)

Bouwer H (1989) The Bouwer and Rice slug test. An update. Groundwater Magazine 27(3):304–309

Bouwer H, Rice RC (1976) A slug test for determining hydraulic conductivity of unconfined aquifer with completely or partially penetrating wells. Water Resources Res 12(3):423–426

Brassington R (1988) Field hydrogeology. Geological Society of London, John Wiley & Sons Inc., New York (Professional Handbook Series, pp 9–11, 16–20, 49–62, 77–78, 93–107)

Cooper HH, Bredehoeft JD, Papadopulos IS (1967) Response of a finite diameter well to an instantaneous charge of water. Water Resources Res 3:263–269
Domenico PA, Schwartz FW (1990) Physical and chemical hydrogeology – hydraulic testing: models, methods, and applications. John Wiley & Sons Inc., New York (chap 5, p 142–144, 181) (reprinted by permission of John Wiley & Sons Ltd.)
Edwards AG, Winn RH (1974) A summary of modern tools and techniques used in drill stem testing. Presented at the dedication of the U.S. East-West Trade Center, Tulsa, Oklahoma (U.S. Environmental Protection Agency 600/2.77-240, 1977)
Ferris JG (1951) Ground water. In: Wister CO, Brater EF (eds) Hydrology. John Wiley & Sons, New York
Heath RC (1987) Basic ground water hydrology. USGS, U.S. Government Printing Office, Denver, Colorado (Geological Survey Water-Supply Paper 2220, pp 1–6)
Hornberger GM (1993) Hydrologic science: keeping pace with changing values and perceptions. National Academy Press, Washington DC
Hughes TH, Memon BA, LaMoreaux PE (1994) Landfills in karst terrains. Bulletin of the Association of Engineering Geologists 31(2):203–208
Hvorslev MJ (1951) Time lag and soil permeability in ground-water observations. Waterways Experiment Station, Corps of Engineers, U.S. Army, Vicksburg, Mississippi (Tech Report, District Section, Bulletin 36)
Kilpatrick FA (1954) Formation testing, the petroleum engineer. In: USEPA (ed) An introduction to the technology of subsurface wastewater injection. USEPA, Cincinnati, Ohio (U.S. Environmental Protection Agency, 600/2-77-240, pp 90–91, 1977)
Konikow LF, Bredehoeft JD (1992) Ground-water models cannot be validated. U.S. Geological Survey, USA (Advances in Water Resources 15:75–83)
Krumbein WC, Graybill SA (1965) An introduction to statistical models in geology. McGraw Hill Book Company, New York
LaMoreaux PE, Tanner J (2001) Springs and bottled waters of the world – ancient history, source, occurrence, quality, and use. Springer-Verlag, Berlin
Meinzer OE (1942) Physics of the earth. Part 9 – Hydrology. McGrasw-Hill, New York
NASA GSFC (2003) The wate rcycle – a multi phase journey (http://earthobsevatoiry.nasa.gov/Library/Water/water_2.html)
Sanders L (1998) A manual of field hydrogeology. Prentice Hall, Upper Saddle River, New Jersey
Sara MN (1994) Standard handbook for solid hazardous waste facility assessments. Lewis Publishers, an imprint of CRC Press, Boca Rotan, Florida, pp 2.1–2.13, 2.20–2.22, 2.30–2.35, 3.1–3.4
Soliman MM, LaMoreaux PE, Memon B, Assaad F, LaMoreaux JW (1998) Environmental hydrogeology. Lewis Publishers, CRC, Boca Rotan, Florida, pp 41–43
Palmer AN (2000) Hydrologic control of cave pattern in speleogenesis – evolution of karst aquifers. National Speleological Society Inc., Huntsville, AL 35810, USA, pp 77–79
Theis CV (1935) The relation between the lowering of the piezometric and rate and duration of discharge of a well using ground-water storage. American Geophysical Union, Transactions of the 16th Meeting, v2, pp 519–524
UNESCO, WMO (1977) Hydrological maps – studies and reports in hydrology – a contribution to the International Hydrological Decade.
U.S. Environmental Protection Agency (1977) An introduction to the technology of subsurface waste-water injection. U.S. EPA, Cincinnati, Ohio (Environmental Protection Series, 600/2-77-240, pp 71–73, 90–91)
USGS (1977) Ground water manual – a water resources technical publication. U.S. Department of the Interior, Bureau of Reclamation, USA, pp 195–200
USGS (1984) Water resources – Earth's water distribution (http://ga.water.usgs.gov/edu/earthwherewater.html)
Ward RC (1975) Principles of hydrology. McGraw-Hill Publishing Company Limited, Great Britain, pp 4–6

Selected References

American Geological Institute (AGI) (2002) Water. Environ. Awareness series; in print
Barlow AC (1972) Basic disposal well design in underground waste management and environmental implications. In: Cook TD (ed) American Association of Petroleum Geologists, Tulsa, Oklahoma, (Memoir 18, pp 72–76)
Brassington R (1998) Field hydrogeology. John Wiley & Sons Ltd., Chichester, England, pp 66–85, 120–131
Brown RH (1953) Selected procedures for analyzing aquifer test data. J Am Wat Works Ass 45(8):844–866
Cooper HH Jr, Jacob CE (1946) A generalized graphical method for evaluating formation constants and summarizing well-field history. Transactions of the American Geophysical Union 27(IV):526–534
Dawson KJ, Istok JD (1991) Aquifer testing – design and analysis of pumping and slug tests. Department of Civil Engineering, Oregon State University
Deming D (2002) Introduction to hydrogeology. University of Oklahoma, Library of Congress Cataloging-in-publication Data, McGraw Hill, Boston, MA (chap 1, pp 1–18)
Domenico PA, Schwartz FW (1997) Physical and chemical hydrogeology – hydraulic testing: models, methods, and applications, 2nd edn. John Wiley & Sons. Inc., New York (chap 6, pp 103–105, 115–116, 118–120)
Ferris JG, Knowles, DB, Brown RH, Stallman RW (1962) Theory of aquifer tests. U.S. Geological Survey Water-Supply Paper 1536-E
Freeze RA, Cherry JA (1979) Ground water. Prentice Hall Inc., Englewwo Cliffs, New Jersey, pp 45–61, 152–163
LaMoreaux PE, Hughes TH, Memon BA, Lineback N (1999) Hydrogeological assessment – Figeh Spring, Damascus, Syria. Envon Geol Water Soc 13(2):73–127
Lohman SW (1972) Ground water hydraulics. U.S. Geological Survey Professional Paper 708
Todd DK (1980) Ground water hydrology, 2nd edn. University of California, Berkeley and David Keith Todd Consulting Engineers, Inc., John Wiley & Sons Inc., New York, pp 64–70
Walton WC (1970) Ground water reservoir evaluation. McGraw-Hill Series. In: Water Resources and Environmental Engineering, pp 3–5
Warner DL (1965) Deep well injection of liquid waste. U.S. Dept. of Health Education and Welfare, Public Health Service (Publication no. 99, WP-21)
World Health Organization (WHO) (1993) Guideline drinking-water quality, 2nd edn, vol 1: recommendations. Geneva, Switzerland

Appendix 8.A · Selected Photos of Field Instruments

The following figures were taken for some instruments normally used by field hydrogeologists.

Fig. 8.A.1. Type KL OTT electric contact gauge is used for the instantaneous measurement of water levels making use of the conductivity of the water. It works with four batteries (1.5 V each) by which at normal use, the gauge works longer than 12 months

Fig. 8.A.2. The Hermit 1000 C environmental data logger measures a variety of hydrologic parameters such as water level, pressure, temperature, conductivity and pH value using In-Situ transducers; collects time-drawdown data from constant-rate or stepped-rate pump tests, including the recovery phase; perform long term monitoring of aquifers, lakes, streams or reservoirs; display and report all measured parameters in their selected units (see the Operator's Manual of Hermit 1000 C by In-Situ Inc. 1992)

MICROBAROGRAPH

Fig. 8.A.3. A microbarograph is used to register and record atmospheric or barometric pressure. This instrument is designed to maintain its precision through the varied conditions

Fig. 8.A.4. YSJ Models 33 and 33 MSC-T meters are potable, battery powered, transistorized instruments designed to accurately measure salinity, conductivity and temperature. They use a probe consisting of a rugged, plastic conductivity cell and a precision YSI thermistor temperature sensor combined in a simple unit

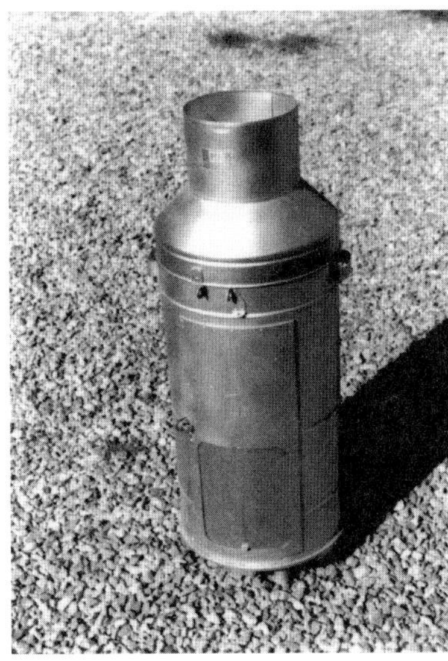

Fig. 8.A.5. The universal recording rain gauge uses a weighing mechanism which converts the weight of the rainfall caught by a circular, horizontal opening at the top of the gauge into the curvillinear movement of a recording pen which makes an inked trace on a rectangular paper

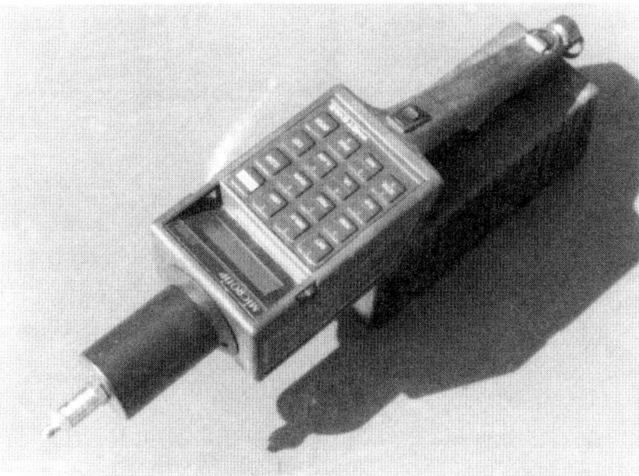

Fig. 8.A.6. MicroTip is the intelligent hand held analyzer for toxic gases and vapors; it incorporates advanced microprocessor technology for real time digital or graphic assessment of toxic gases and vapors. An ultraviolet light source is used to ionize the molecules of chemical substances in a gaseous or vaporous state. Also, data logging capability is built-in and provides automatic storage of date, time, concentration, and event/location together with direct downloading of stored data to an external computer or printer

Appendix 8.B · A Site or Facility Characterization Using Electromagnetic Radiography (EMR)

A. G. Finci · D. F. Stanfill III · L. Whitmill · M. Kraft

Abstract

Site restoration must address what lies buried below the surface of the ground. Direct images of low-level contamination, as well as pipes, utilities, foundations and geologic structures, can be obtained with Electromagnetic Radiography (EMR). The quality of the information far exceeds what can be generated by any other method.

8.B.1 Introduction

EMR evolved from field experiments conducted on hazardous waste sites using an electromagnetic impulse system operating in the 30 to 480 MHz spectrum.[1] The technology traces back to earlier work with customized, high-performance ground-penetrating radar (GPR) equipment (Stanfill and McMillan 1985a,b). The focus of EMR development has been on detecting and imaging low-level chemical contamination in the ground. This capability stems from the excitation of discrete energy bands at the molecular level. Detection thresholds in the parts-per-billion range (μg kg^{-1}) have been achieved, making EMR an increasingly important technology for site assessment. Field operations are currently providing 100% volumetric inspection of several acres per day, at depths up to 50 feet (15.3 m) or more.

8.B.2 History

The origin of EMR traces back to a field survey of a hazardous waste site in Solvay, NY, in September 1991. The site contained many different chemicals, both organic and inorganic, as well as mercury and other metals, that were widely distributed over several acres. The instrumentation used for the electromagnetic survey was derived from a custom-designed, high-performance GPR system that had been modified to detect chemical contamination in the ground. Upon completion of the field survey and post-survey analysis of the recorded data, it was discovered that specific chemicals, or suites of chemicals, were producing unique responses within the 30–480 MHz operating range of the instrument.

Based on thousands of man-hours of commercial experience in using this proprietary instrument on hundreds of hazardous waste sites dating back to 1979 (Picillo Property, Coventry, Rhode Island Superfund site), it had long been suspected that specific chemicals were producing unique responses, thus holding the potential for the eventual "fingerprinting" and identifica-

[1] Electromagnetic Radiography (EMR) is a trademark of Detection Sciences Inc.

tion of specific chemicals. Whereas most surveys performed in the commercial sector had tended to focus on the detection of a single chemical such as TCE, the Solvay project provided the first experimental evidence that specific groups of chemicals were producing unique electromagnetic responses.

It was further suspected that the unique responses of chemicals were a result to the excitation of discrete energy bands at the molecular level. It can be shown that neither electrical conductivity nor differences in the dielectric constant (the fundamental physics of GPR) could be responsible for the field results obtained with various chemicals under widely varying site conditions. The EMR response of any specific chemical, such as nitroglycerine (NG), was found to be independent of the host material. The turning point from purely empirical observations came on October 7, 1997, with the proposal of theoretical models to explain the experimental results. Mission Research Corporation, along with team members Detection Sciences, Inc. and the Sandia National Laboratories, is currently working on DOE STTR Contract DE-FG03-99ER86095, "EMR for Front End Operations," to achieve better understanding of the physics underlying EMR.

At present, field surveys are carried out to detect low-level chemical contamination in the ground using purely empirical (non-analytical) methods. By directly imaging chemical contamination in the ground, the lateral and vertical distribution of the contamination, as well as the migration patterns, can be observed. Generic behavior of chemicals, such as observing vertical migration columns, or horizontal stratification can be used to identify dense, non-aqueous phase liquids (DNAPLs) vs. light, non-aqueous phase liquids (LNAPLs). EMR also responds to concentration levels. The locations of "hot spots" can be pinpointed with an accuracy of ±1 foot (30.48 cm).

8.B.3 Field Deployment

Figure 8.B.1 shows a typical set up for performing a field survey. The antenna is towed behind a vehicle that carries the EMR controls, supplies and recording equipment. All data is permanently recorded on a 20-bit MiniDisc (MD) recorder. To insure the quality of the MD recordings, a thermal scanning chart recorder is tied to the output of the MD recorder. The 9-inch chart recorder provides real-time, "quick look" capability to view the vertical profile being generated along the survey line. A "fifth-wheel" odometer automatically logs distance traveled along the survey line. In difficult or soft terrain, an all-terrain vehicle (ATV) is used to tow the antenna. Where vehicle access is not feasible, the antenna can be manually pulled over the ground.

8.B.4 DNAPLs

EMR provides direct images of DNAPLs. A pair of vertical migration columns of TCE is shown in Fig. 8.B.2. The site, which consists of alluvial clay, is located in the vicinity of Shreveport, Louisiana. An existing recovery well located only 14 feet (4.3 m) from the vertical column (on the right) was yielding less than a half gallon a day. A new boring was placed directly within the vertical column, and levels in the thousands of ppm were measured at this new location. A recovery well was installed within this vertical column. The yield increased to several gallons a day (1 gallon = 3.7854 l).

Close examination of the vertical migration columns reveals some interesting behavior. First, there is no evidence of contamination in the upper layers of soil, indi-

Fig. 8.B.1.
120 MHz antenna being towed by a van, with the odometer wheel logging the distance

cating that the vertical column was not formed as a result of a surface spill. Second, there appears to be some retardation taking place starting around the 24-foot level (7.32 m), as evidenced by the increased concentration levels at this depth (the darker, more intense banding indicates higher concentrations). This behavior implies the beginning of a confining or semi-confining layer at this depth. This finding is consistent with the boring information developed by the environmental engineering company who was responsible for site clean up.

Another interesting behavior revealed by the EMR data is the hydraulic "drag," or lateral pulling of the vertical column that is taking place in response to the hydrology of the site. The contaminant is being pulled sideways to the right, taking on the appearance of "streamers" flowing from the vertical column. This lateral movement is spoiling what would otherwise be a sheer, vertical edge that would be more typical of the vertical movements of DNAPLs.

The EMR survey also solved some existing site "mysteries" relating to the distribution and behavior of the TCE. A subsurface "ridge" was found to be cutting the site into two separate flow regimes, and an ancient stream channel was found that had not previously been detected with borings. Both of these turned out to be controlling features. Modeling can only go so far, and can be no better than the baseline assumptions. In the end, nothing beats direct observation for determining DNAPL behavior.

Another example of the vertical migration of a DNAPL is shown by Fig. 8.B.3. Here, again, the contaminant is TCE. The concentration levels are in the low ppm range. On this site, which is in Princeton, Illinois, the TCE is also stratified, reflecting differing degrees of retardation, and therefore differences in permeability with depth. Within the vertical column formed by the TCE, however, the permeabilities are significantly higher than the surrounding, clayey soil, as evidenced by the lack of contaminant in the surrounding soil. There is also a distinct "graininess" within the column compared to the relatively featureless appearance of the surrounding soil. This graininess also signifies higher permeability, as explained in the following paragraphs.

8.B.5 Infiltration Zones

The vertical pathways by which DNAPLs migrate are often associated with infiltration zones. Infiltration zones come about because rainwater does not percolate uniformly into the ground. Over geologic time, preferential paths develop for the infiltration of surface water. These pathways are characterized by the loss of fine-grained material (fines) that result in decreased den-

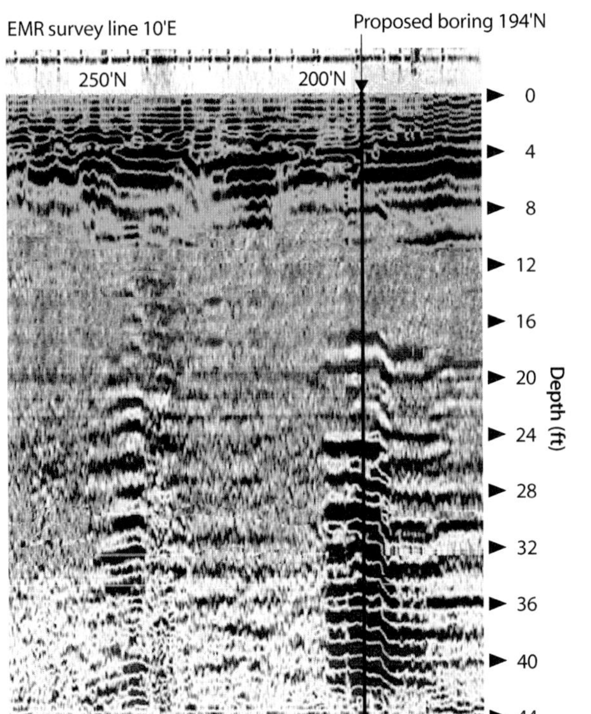
EMR survey line 10'E
Proposed boring 194'N
250'N
200'N
0
4
8
12
16
20
24
28
32
36
40
44
Depth (ft)

Fig. 8.B.2. Vertical migration of TCE in infiltration zone, Shreveport, LA, USA

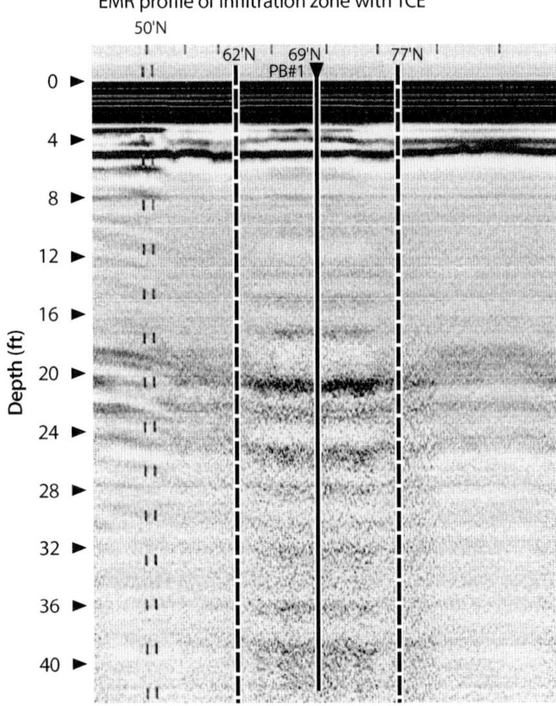
EMR profile of infiltration zone with TCE
50'N
62'N
69'N
77'N
PB#1
0
4
8
12
16
20
24
28
32
36
40
Depth (ft)

Fig. 8.B.3. Vertical migration of TCE in infiltration zone, Princeton, IL, USA sity, higher porosity and increased permeability. The fact that the fines have been washed out of the infiltration zone implies the existence of an underlying aquifer. The fines cannot simply disappear; they must be transported somewhere. The transport mechanism is the underlying aquifer, which acts as a horizontal "conveyor belt" to carry away the fines. Unfortunately, this means that infiltration zones necessarily communicate with an aquifer.

DNAPLs spilled on the surface of the ground will migrate vertically, including migrating vertically down through a water table (called "sinkers"), until they reach an impermeable or semi-impermeable barrier such as clay or bedrock. In response to the hydrology of the site, the DNAPL will then migrate laterally on top of the confining or semi-confining layer until it encounters an infiltration zone. At this point, the infiltration zone tends to act as a collection point, or sump, allowing the DNAPL to resume its vertical migration, most likely all the way down to an underlying aquifer. There is increasing awareness in the environmental research community about this type of behavior, often called "fingers" or "fingering." We prefer using the term "infiltration zones" to more accurately reflect the geologic conditions leading to this type of behavior.

8.B.6 Clay

Despite its bad reputation for limiting penetration, clay is surprisingly amenable to investigation. Its uniformity makes it a better environment for detecting low-level contaminants than a more chaotic environment, such as glacial till. The ability to detect contaminants in clay is further abetted by several processes. First, it is believed that solvents such as TCE tend to displace water in the clay. With less water, the clay becomes less electrically conductive (less ionization), which is the root cause of the lack of penetration. (Attenuation of the signal is a direct function of electrical conductivity; conversely, penetration is a direct function of resistivity, which is the inverse of conductivity.) The presence of a non-ionic, non-electrically conductive liquid contaminant in the clay also serves to reduce the electrical conductivity. Solvents, as well as other chemicals, also tend to alter the chemistry of the clay itself in ways that are often beneficial to penetration. The net result is that the clay becomes much more transparent when non-ionic contaminants are present.

Other processes provide favorable environments in clay. Residual clays (as opposed to deposited clays) are formed over geologic time from the underlying bedrock. All of the faults, fracture and contacts present in the original rock are preserved in the residual clay. These faults and fractures tend to permit "piping," providing a pathway for the infiltration of surface water. Weathering and oxidation change the local chemistry of the clay, as well as its physical properties. All of these processes tend to make piping zones in the clay more transparent and less electrically conductive than they would otherwise be, even without the presence of non-ionic contaminants.

These processes facilitate the inspection of clay for contamination, particularly contaminants in the form of non-ionic DNAPLs. Conversely, in areas where electromagnetic penetration is difficult (very high electrical conductivity), chemical penetration is also difficult. It has been found that the electromagnetic transparency is an index of permeability. Conversely, electromagnetic opacity provides an indication of the relative impermeability of the clay. As a Figure of Merit, the penetration depth of EMR currently runs about 4 feet (1.22 m) per ohm-meter of resistivity. This can be stretched to about 8 feet (2.44) per ohm-meter with signal processing. Typical clays run around 6 to 8 Ωm of resistivity, providing about 50 feet (15.24 m) of penetration, exclusive of any beneficial effects to be gained from the presence of non-ionic chemicals in the clay. Because these relationships are non-linear, this Figure of Merit is useful only for resistivities in the single digit range (expressed in ohm-meters).

8.B.7 Mercury

A project is currently in progress at the DOE Idaho National Engineering and Environmental Laboratory (INEEL), Lockheed contract K99-181398, to demonstrate the ability of EMR to detect mercury in the ground. Two small but distinct vertical migration columns, typical of DNAPL behavior, were observed and shown in Fig. 8.B.4. Circumstantial evidence suggests that this anomaly is mercury, but conventional borings and laboratory testing of the soil samples are needed to confirm the EMR results. (Official test results were not available in time for this paper.)

8.B.8 LNAPLs

The principal manifestation of an LNAPL is a signature that is horizontally stratified. The characteristic horizontal stratification of an LNAPL provides a strong means of distinguishing an LNAPL from a DNAPL, because a DNAPL's distinctive characteristic signature tends to be sharply defined vertical migration columns.

Horizontal stratification comes about as a result of two mechanisms. The first is the layering of the soil, or soil horizons, where the layers have different lateral permeabilities. If a stratum that is more permeable lies above another stratum that is less permeable, the tendency of an LNAPL is to flow horizontally within the

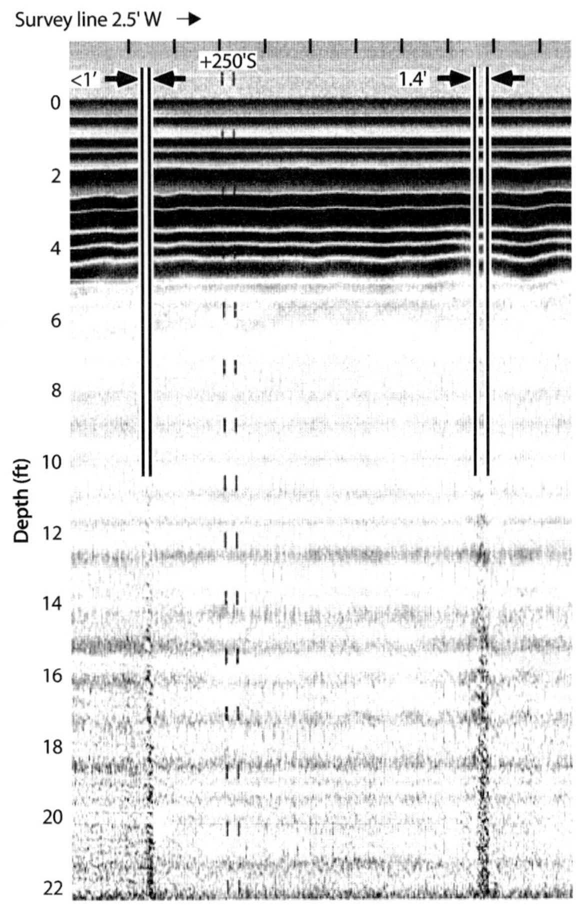
Survey line 2.5' W
<1'
+250'S
1.4'
Depth (ft)
0
2
4
6
8
10
12
14
16
18
20
22

Fig. 8.B.4. Two small, but distinct vertical (mercury) migration columns, typical of DNAPL behavior, were observed

more permeable stratum, particularly in response to the hydrology of the site. (Such lateral flow, or horizontal migration of a plume, makes it possible to observe the hydrology of a site.) The lateral migration process can be further influenced by soil composition. Silicatious material tends to be hydrophilic. It is much more difficult for oil to displace water in silicatious material than it is, for example, in calcareous materials that tend to be hydrophobic. Thus, the horizontal stratification of LNAPLs can be brought about not only because of differences in horizontal permeability, but also because of differences in the moisture retention properties of the different stratum and the relative ease that the contaminant can replace the water. The extreme case of stratification occurs when the LNAPL comes in direct contact with the water table and floats directly above the water as an "inverted bubble," producing a visible depression in the water table. Under these conditions, the LNAPL becomes what is known as "free product," which is amenable to extraction by pumping. The absence of an inverted bubble indicates that the product cannot be removed by pumping.

8.B.9 Topological Lows

In the past, topological lows were always a logical place to drill in search for DNAPLs. With EMR, it is not only possible to locate the topological lows, it is also possible to tell whether chemicals have collected in the low spot. Consequently, there is no point in drilling if chemicals are not seen to be present. The exception is in cases where the confining layer may be so deep as to be out of range of EMR. The existence and location of a topological low, however, can still be inferred by the trends in the upper soils above the confining layer, and drilling can be carried out "right on target" to determine if chemicals are present or not.

8.B.10 "Hot Spots"

EMR is unsurpassed for pinpointing the location of "hot spots" having higher concentrations of chemicals, particularly in relatively small locations such as infiltration zones that may be only a few feet across. With experience in using the instrument, it is possible to provide rough order-of-magnitude estimates of concentration levels. Saturated and near-saturated conditions produce their own unique signature, as do concentrations in the thousands and hundreds of ppm, and low ppm to upper ppb range. Thus, it is possible to specify optimum locations for drilling or product recovery and to avoid wasting drill holes in areas where no contamination is present. The exception is the drilling of control borings in sterile areas to show that the EMR system is capable of making such distinctions. In one such case at a site in Kaoshuing, Taiwan, at a location where EMR detected the presence of NG in a waste runoff ditch, the concentration of NG as measured by laboratory analysis of soil samples was 400 ppm. A control boring was located in the same ditch only 5 feet (1.52 m) away (up gradient), where EMR did not detect any NG. The control soil sample, measured in the same laboratory, proved to have no detectable level of NG.

8.B.11 Dissolved Phase

It was long known that liquid phase contaminants trapped in the pore spaces of the soil (vadose zone) are easily observed, and their lateral and vertical extent could be established within ±1 foot (30.48 cm). The dissolved phase, however, was another matter. The concern was that the high dielectric constant of water (relative dielectric ε_r 80) would mask any subtle effects of low-level contaminants having solubilities of less than 0.1%. The breakthrough came in 1993 with an aniline spill on Interstate 70 in Alabama. Aniline has a solubility of 4%, so it was thought that the aniline might be detected in the ground water. The dissolved phase did, in fact, prove to be visible. This was followed by other investigations where the dissolved phase was also detected. Later that year, at Newark Air Force Base, Ohio, the investigation concerned CFC-113 (Freon 113) under a reinforced concrete floor in a clean room area. Typical of DNAPL behavior, the CFC-113 was found to have formed a distinct vertical migration column under the floor. Slant drilling from outside the building showed the vertical migration column to have a concentration level of 31 ppm. About 50 feet (15.24 m) away, the shallow ground water under the reinforced concrete slab was seen to have two distinct layers of contamination at depths of about 3 and 5 feet (0.91 and 1.52 m). The upper layer appeared to have a somewhat lower concentration than the lower layer. Laboratory measurements showed the upper layer to have a concentration of 1.3 ppm and the lower layer 2.7 ppm. Since that time, it has been determined that there are no EMR distinctions between the dissolved phase and the liquid phase in the vadose zone. Both can be detected with equal facility, because the EMR response appears to be independent of the properties of the host material and does not depend on differentiation of properties.

8.B.12 Faults, Fractures and Geologic Units

The technology has proven to be an excellent fault locator. Faults and fracture zones show up vividly in the record. By running successive, parallel lines, a fracture trace analysis can be generated, even in residual clays where the underlying bedrock may not be visible. The fracture trace analysis shows the strike of faults and their complementary sets, but does not establish the dip. This is because the radiation travels within a fault and reflects back to the antenna, but there is no way to establish the angle of reflection. Working strictly in the time domain, the only thing that is certain is that a reflection must travel back along the same path that it came or it will not reflect back to the antenna. The path can be anywhere within the beam angle of the system. Usually, the "bright spot" emanates directly under the antenna, but there is nothing to prevent radiation from going off at some angle other than straight down and returning along that same path. For this reason, the dip of a fault cannot be accurately determined.

Fractures are another matter. The observation of a fracture zone almost always occurs directly under the antenna. Otherwise, the radiation will reflect off in some other direction, and will not be seen by the antenna. EMR makes it possible to determine if the fracture zone contains chemical contamination or not.

Geologic units, such as clay or sand lenses, peat, confining layers, infiltration zones and ancient river beds, can be directly imaged, and their influence on a site can be assessed. Often unsuspected features, such as infiltration zones and ancient stream beds, are found to be the controlling feature(s) on a site, such as Shreveport, LA, where localized vertical infiltration zones were found, as well as a Pleistocene stream bed that was directly responsible for transporting the TCE offsite into neighboring property.

8.B.13 Use of Borings

Digging holes or using exploration borings to find what is in the ground can only bring partial answers at best. There is always the question of what may lie hidden between borings. Experience has shown that DNAPLs tend to migrate in sharply defined vertical columns. An upgradient test boring placed only 1 or 2 feet (0.3 or 0.6 m) outside a vertical column may give little or no indication of the high concentration levels within the column. Although borings are well suited for gathering soil samples for laboratory analysis, borings are poorly suited for providing a complete, comprehensive assessment of site conditions. If borings are spaced relatively far apart, they will likely fail to locate "hot spots" and other controlling features. Closer spacing leads to prohibitive costs, and may still fail to pinpoint specific, localized conditions. EMR completely eliminates the need for exploratory borings, and can determine the optimum placement for the handful of borings needed to obtain soil samples to quantify the EMR.

8.B.14 Conclusions

EMR is a valuable tool for site assessment, particularly when it involves chemical detection. It produces far more information at lower cost than any other method of site assessment. Moreover, it is possible to provide 100% volumetric inspection at a cost-per-acre that is significantly less than the test borings that it replaces, even when the borings are widely spaced. Quite simply, there is nothing to beat the direct imaging and visualization of contaminants to know what is taking place on a site, and EMR provides the means for doing exactly that.

References

Stanfill DF III, McMillan KS (1985a) Inspection of hazardous waste sites using ground-penetrating radar (GPR). Hazardous Materials Control Research Institute (H.M.C.R.I.), Cincinnati, OH (Proc. National Conference on Hazardous Waste and Environmental Emergencies, May 1985, pp 244–249)

Stanfill DF III, McMillan KS (1985b) Radar-mapping of gasoline and other hydrocarbons in the ground. Hazardous Materials Control Research Institute (H.M.C.R.I.), Washington, D.C. (Proc. 6th National Conference on Management of Uncontrolled Hazardous Waste Sites, November, 1985, pp 269–274)

Appendix 8.C · Pumping Test Plan

Attachment 8.C.1 Pumping Test/Recovery Data Sheet

Pumping Test/Recovery Data Sheet

Project no. ________________ Date of test ________________

Area of study ________________ Location ________________

Observed by ________________ Sheet no. ________________

Pumped well no. (PW) ________________ Observation well no. (OW) ________________

Owner of well ________________ Well inventory sheet no. ________________

Depth of well ________________

Initial depth to water ________________ Final depth to water ________________

Distance of OW from PW (r) ________________ ft or m (3.2808 feet = 1 meter)

Drawdown/recovery ________________________ (1 inch = 2.54 cm)

Date	Time	Time since pumping started or stopped	Depth to water level below measuring point		Calculated drawdown or recovery	Pitot reading	Totalizer/ discharge rate *Q*	XD reading/ remarks	By
		(min)	(m)	(ft)	(ft)		(gpm)		

Fig. 8.C.1. Pumping test/recovery data sheet

Attachment 8.C.2 Field Water Quality Parameters

Field Water Quality Parameters

Location: Well:

Date	Time	T (°C)	SC (µS)	pH	Eh (mV)	Color	Odor	By	Remarks

Fig. 8.C.2. Field water quality parameters

Attachment 8.C.3 General Safety Plan

8.C.3.1 *Introduction*

Procedures are prescribed to follow and forms to complete for work at sites where hazardous substances may be or have been documented to exist, and a site safety plan must be prepared (or reviewed) by a qualified safety person for each project involving hazardous substances. In addition, a *general field operations safety plan* (plan) is required to be completed for general, non-hazardous substance, project fieldwork. The plan covers safety considerations and requirements, emergency situation instructions, and standard operating guidelines and procedures required to maintain safe working conditions at such sites (subsurface investigations at petroleum sites, drilling projects, construction projects).

8.C.3.2 *Minimum Requirements*

Minimum requirements for the site safety plan include:

- Evaluate the risks associated with the site and with each operation to be conducted.
- Identify key personnel and alternates responsible for site safety and response operations.
- Address any personal protective equipment to be worn by personnel during various site operations.
- Implement control procedures to prevent access to the site by unauthorized personnel.
- Designate any specific work areas and/or areas where only authorized personnel will be allowed access.
- Establish site emergency procedures. For example, escape routes, signals for evacuating work parties, emergency communications (internal and external), procedures for fire and/or explosion, etc.
- Determine and document location of the nearest medical facility and medical life squad unit for emergency medical care.
- Implement a program for monitoring safety conditions, including environmental sampling, if required.
- Train personnel for any non-routine site activities.

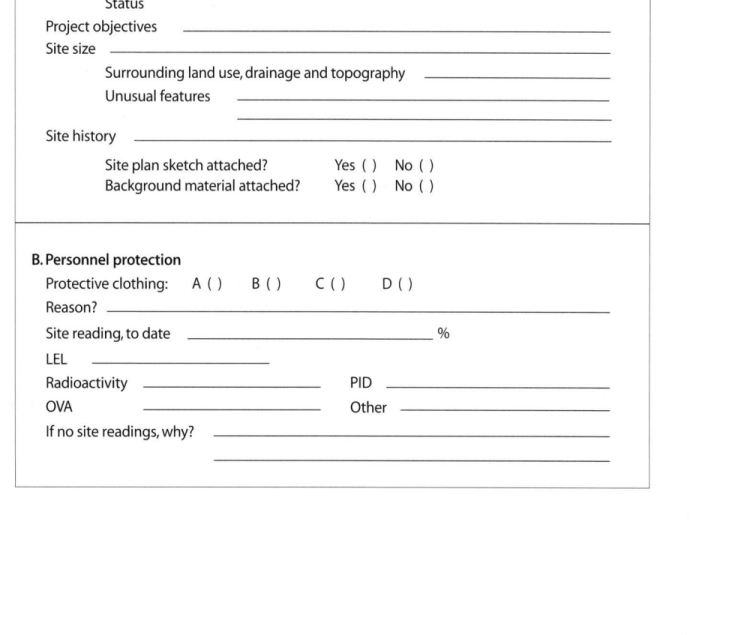

Fig. 8.C.3.
General safety plan

Date ____________ Project no. ____________

Project manager/VP-in charge ____________

A. Site description

Location ____________

Type: UST ( ) Industrial ( ) Mine/quarry ( ) Private property ( )

Other ____________

Status

Project objectives ____________

Site size ____________

Surrounding land use, drainage and topography ____________

Unusual features ____________

Site history ____________

Site plan sketch attached? Yes ( ) No ( )

Background material attached? Yes ( ) No ( )

B. Personnel protection

Protective clothing: A ( ) B ( ) C ( ) D ( )

Reason? ____________

Site reading, to date ____________ %

LEL ____________

Radioactivity ____________ PID ____________

OVA ____________ Other ____________

If no site readings, why? ____________

Fig. 8.C.3.
Continued

Respirator protective equipment:

SCBA ______

Full face or half face respirator ______
Dust mask ______

Protective clothing/equipment:
"Steel toe boots" ______ ______
"Disposable gloves" ______ ______

Field monitoring equipment and materials:
"First aid kits in each vehicle" ______ ______
______ ______ ______

C. Decontamination procedures

Describe methods and location(s) at site:
"See sampling and analysis plan for decontamination of equipment used"

______
______
______

General information

Project team members: ______ ______
______ ______

Site safety coordinator: ______ ______

D. Emergency information

First aid instruction (see "first aid kits")

______
______

Sources of help

Fire Department
Name ______ Town ______
Telephone ______

Police Department
Name Sheriff Town ______
Telephone ______
Name Police Dept. Town ______
Telephone ______

Ambulance/Rescue
Name call hospital or Police Town ______
Telephone ______

Hospital
Name ______ Town ______
Telephone ______

E. Poison information

Name ______ Town ______
Telephone ______

Site telephone
Name vehicle cell phones Town ______
Telephone ______

Emergency telephone numbers
Contact ______ Telephone ______
Contact ______ Telephone ______
Contact ______ Telephone ______
Contact ______ Telephone ______
Contact ______ Telephone ______

Fig. 8.C.3.
Continued

F. Subcontractor information

"This plan does not address hazards specific to subcontractor's work (e.g. drill rigg safety as it applies to the operation of the rig). Subcontractors are responsible for health and safety procedures and plans specific to their work."

Company name/Contact ______________________
Telephone/cell ______________________

Company name/Contact ______________________
Telephone/cell ______________________

Company name/Contact ______________________
Telephone/cell ______________________

G. General physical (safety) hazards and controls

Hazard	Engineering or administrative controls	Tasks[a]				
		1				
Protruding objects	Flag visible objects	X				
Vehicle traffic	Provide traffic controls	X				
Stairways, ladders, and scaffolds	Generally required where there is break in elevation of 19 inches (48 cm) or more, keep access ways clear	NA				
Elevated work areas/falls	Provide guardrail, safety net, floor covers, body harness, where applicable	NA				
Snakes and insects	Wear protective clothing, apply topical ointments, seek medical attention, if poisonous	X				
Poisonous vegetation	Avoid contact, wear protective clothing, wash area with soap and water, apply topical ointments	X				
Heat stress	Increase fluids intake, increase rest or break periods, work in shaded areas, if heat exhaustion or heat stroke symptons occur – seek medical attention	X				
Cold stress	Wear appropriate clothing, monitor wind chill, limit exposure time	X				
Flying debris/objects	Provide shielding and PPE, maintain distance	NA				
Noise >85 dBA	Noise protection and monitoring	X				
Steep terrain/unstable surface	Brace and shore equipment, provide signage	NA				
Electrical shock	Do not tamper with electrical wiring unless qualified	X				
Suspended loads	Work not permitted under suspended loads	NA				
Moving vehicles	Back-up alarms required for heavy equipment, observe traffic conditions carefully	X				
Overhead electrical wires	Equipment (e.g. drill rig) to remain at least 15 feet (4.5 m) from overhead power line	NA				
Buried utilities, drums, tanks	Locate prior to digging or drilling and mark locations	NA				
Slip, trip, and fall hazards back injury	Provide slip resistant surfaces, signage, barriers use proper lifting techniques or provide mechanical lifting aids	X				
Confined space entry	Must be evaluated by qualified person	NA				
Site location	Do not work alone, mobile phone	X				

[a] 1 – Aquifer testing and water-level monitoring.

Fig. 8.C.3.
Continued

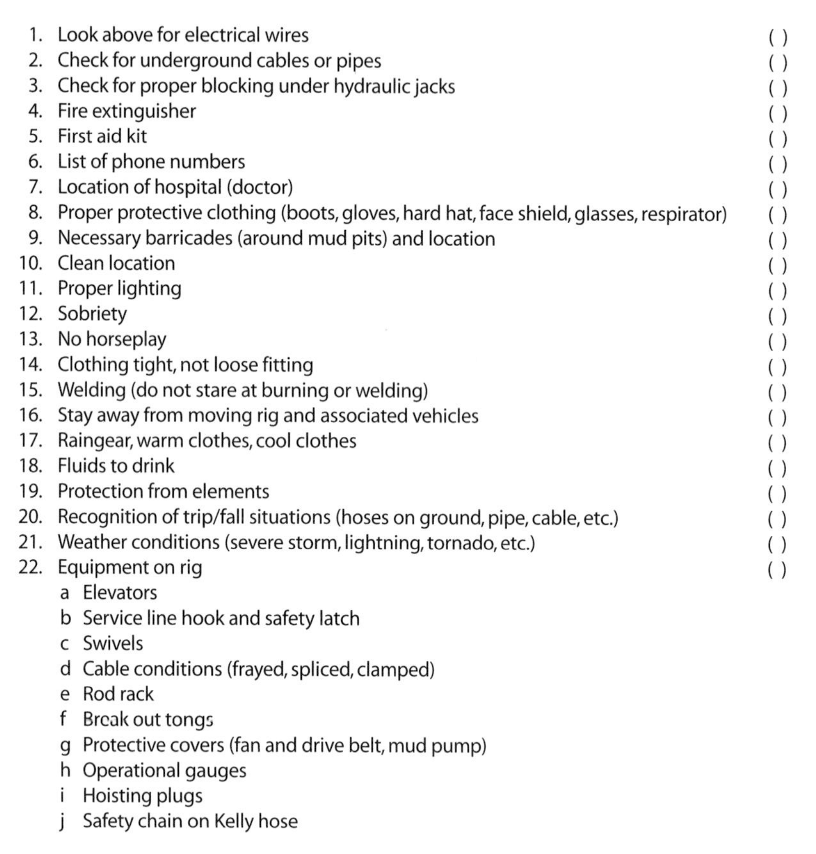

H. Safety checklist

Prior to initiation of activities on-site personnel should take a few minutes to carefully observe the area and conditions of the site and equipment. Develop a conversation/rapport report with your driller and review safety/accident prevention precautions.

Prior to and during any activity, the following minimum requirements should be checked:

1. Look above for electrical wires ( )
2. Check for underground cables or pipes ( )
3. Check for proper blocking under hydraulic jacks ( )
4. Fire extinguisher ( )
5. First aid kit ( )
6. List of phone numbers ( )
7. Location of hospital (doctor) ( )
8. Proper protective clothing (boots, gloves, hard hat, face shield, glasses, respirator) ( )
9. Necessary barricades (around mud pits) and location ( )
10. Clean location ( )
11. Proper lighting ( )
12. Sobriety ( )
13. No horseplay ( )
14. Clothing tight, not loose fitting ( )
15. Welding (do not stare at burning or welding) ( )
16. Stay away from moving rig and associated vehicles ( )
17. Raingear, warm clothes, cool clothes ( )
18. Fluids to drink ( )
19. Protection from elements ( )
20. Recognition of trip/fall situations (hoses on ground, pipe, cable, etc.) ( )
21. Weather conditions (severe storm, lightning, tornado, etc.) ( )
22. Equipment on rig ( )
    - a Elevators
    - b Service line hook and safety latch
    - c Swivels
    - d Cable conditions (frayed, spliced, clamped)
    - e Rod rack
    - f Break out tongs
    - g Protective covers (fan and drive belt, mud pump)
    - h Operational gauges
    - i Hoisting plugs
    - j Safety chain on Kelly hose

Appendix 8.D · Ground-Water Sampling, Analytical Procedures, and Decontamination of Equipment

8.D.1 Scope

Every site evaluation because of the complexity of climate, topography, and geology will be different. A geoscientist must recognize this important fact as a basis for planning a geologic investigation, test drilling, geophysical studies, photogeological analysis, and subsequently, a water sampling program that may include samples of rainfall, vegetation, surficial material, surface water (springs, lakes, streams) and samples from wells or springs. The extent of sampling and duration, the constituent analytical work requirements must consider all of the above parameters related to the purpose of the project. What problem or problems the geoscientist faces in execution of work must be addressed.

8.D.2 Introduction

The objectives of the *sampling and analysis plan* (plan) are to describe the methods to be used to collect and analyze ground-water samples for the comprehensive sampling effort. This plan has been developed based as adapted from industry accepted or mandated protocols. The various procedures and plans have been reviewed and approved for other project specific work by the Alabama Department of Environmental Management (ADEM), Mississippi Department of Environmental

Quality (MDEQ), Tennessee Department of Environmental Protection (TDEP), Florida Department of Environmental Protection (FDEP), and U.S. Environmental Protection Agency (U.S. EPA) Region IV, and others. The development, as described herein, have been significantly based on SW846, U.S. EPA Region IV Environmental Compliance Branch Standard Operating Procedures and Quality Assurance Manual, and Florida Standard Operating Procedures.

8.D.3 Ground-Water Sampling

The importance of proper sampling techniques and sample handling cannot be overemphasized. Precautions must be taken to ensure that the sample is representative and to ensure that the sample is neither altered nor contaminated by sampling and handling procedures. Water samples will be analyzed for selected volatile organic materials, metals, and conventional parameters as described in Sec. 8.D.4.

8.D.3.1 *Measurement of Water Level and Total Depth Well*

In addition, the depth to the bottom of the well will be measured by lowering the water-level indicator or other measuring tape into the well until slack. The point at which the tape goes slack will be confirmed by slightly raising and lowering the measuring device. The total depth will be measured from the same measuring point used to obtain the water level.

In wells with pumps this depth measurement may represent the top of a submersible pump or some submerged part of other types of pumps, however, near the bottom of the well.

The two measurements will be used in determining the volume of water in the well-bore and calculating the volume of water to be purged from each well.

After measurement of the water level and depth of a well the tape and probe will be decontaminated as described in Sec. 8.D.6.

8.D.3.2 *Well Purging*

To obtain a representative sample of the ground water, it must be understood that the composition of the water within the well casing and in close proximity to the well is generally not representative of the overall ground-water quality at the sampling site. The well is pumped until it is thoroughly flushed of standing water and typical, according to standard protocols, a total of 3 well bore volumes. The sample will then be representative of water contained in the aquifer.

Purging will be accomplished using pumps currently in the wells, or a portable submersible pump or by bailing. The volume of water purged and the purge rate will be recorded in the field book.

8.D.3.3 *Collection of Ground-Water Samples*

Ground-water samples will be collected from the discharge point closest to the well where wells are equipped with operating pumps. Wells with no pumps will be sampled with disposable bailers after the well is purged by bailing or by using a portable submersible pump operated by generator. Care will be taken to prevent contact of any discharge line or apparatus with the sample container or other external items. The following procedures will be used to prevent surface contaminants from entering the well and contacting the ground-water samples:

- Field personnel will wear new disposable gloves while sampling each well;
- When bailing or the portable pump are employed, new plastic sheeting will be placed around each well for a distance of at least 3 feet (91 cm) in all directions.

Field measurements of the following parameters will be made at the time of sample collection on a portion of each water sample, and recorded in field log books and the chain-of-custody form.

- pH
- Specific conductance
- Temperature

Because of the magnitude of samples to be collected, identification labels for the various sample containers required have been prepared prior to actual sampling. An identification label has been affixed to each appropriate sample container (Table 8.D.1). Information completed, using waterproof ink includes:

- Site location
- Preservation method
- Analysis to be completed

The following well-specific information will be added to the labels, at the time of sample collection, prior to filling the sample containers and with the container top in-place:

- Sample point identification
- Collection date
- Collection time
- Collector's identification

Sample containers will be placed in an ice chest that has been pre-cooled to about 4 °C. The temperature of the samples will be maintained by packing ice around the sample containers.

8.D.3.4 *Field Instrument Calibration*

All field metering equipment (including pH, specific conductance, temperature, etc.) will be calibrated in accordance with manufacturers' instructions and standard operating procedures. Calibration will be completed prior to use of equipment each day, unless manufacturers' instructions or other circumstances indicate that more frequent calibration is necessary. A record of all calibration procedures will be maintained in the field log book.

8.D.4 Analytical Procedures and Sampling Requirements

Information on sampling and analytical requirements, including container types and sizes, preservatives, and holding times, is provided in Table 8.D.1. The analytes are given as follows:

- *Full suite*: BETX, chloride, barium, lead, sodium, total dissolved solids, mercury, strontium, radium 226/228, nitrate, ammonia, total coliforms, and sulfate
- *Short list*: chloride, sodium, total dissolved solids, sulfate, and barium

Parameters added to the full suite of parameters and subsequently approved by the panel:

Table 8.D.1. Analytical methods, sample containerization, and assigned laboratories for completion of analysis of ground-water samples

Full suite parameters	Short list parameters	Analyte	Analytical method	Method detection limit	Sampling container and volume	Holding time	Preservative	LAB	QA/QC LAB Duplicates
+		Benzene	EPA 602	0.01 ppb	40 ml vials	14 days	HCl/ice	LAB A	LAB D
+		Toluene	EPA 602	0.01 ppb	40 ml vials	14 days	HCl/ice	LAB A	LAB D
+		Ethylbenzene	EPA 602	0.01 ppb	40 ml vials	14 days	HCl/ice	LAB A	LAB D
+		Xylene	EPA 602	0.02 ppb	40 ml vials	14 days	HCl/ice	LAB A	LAB D
+	+	Chloride	EPA 325.2	1.0 mg l^{-1}	16 oz plastic	28 days	None/ice	LAB A	LAB D
+	+	Sulfate	EPA 375.4	1 mg l^{-1}	16 oz plastic	14 days	None/ice	LAB A	LAB D
+	+	Total dissolved solids	EPA 160.1	1.0 mg l^{-1}	16 oz plastic	7 days	None/ice	LAB A	LAB D
+		Arsenic	EPA 206.2	0.001 mg l^{-1}	16 oz plastic	6 months	HNO_3	LAB A	LAB D
+		Cadmium	EPA 200.7	0.005 mg l^{-1}	16 oz plastic	6 months	HNO_3	LAB A	LAB D
+		Chromium	EPA 200.7	0.04 mg l^{-1}	16 oz plastic	6 months	HNO_3	LAB A	LAB D
+		Selenium	EPA 270.2	0.002 mg l^{-1}	16 oz plastic	6 months	HNO_3	LAB A	LAB D
+	+	Barium	EPA 200.7	0.1 mg l^{-1}	16 oz plastic	6 months	HNO_3	LAB A	LAB D
+		Lead	EPA 239.2	0.001 mg l^{-1}	16 oz plastic	6 months	HNO_3	LAB A	LAB D
+	+	Sodium	EPA 200.7	0.01 mg l^{-1}	16 oz plastic	6 months	HNO_3	LAB A	LAB D
+		Mercury	EPA 245.1	0.0001 mg l^{-1}	16 oz plastic	28 days	HNO_3	LAB A	LAB D
+		Strontium (elemental)	EPA 200.7	0.1 mg l^{-1}	16 oz plastic	6 months	HNO_3	LAB A	LAB D
+		Dissolved metals	Per analyte		8 oz plastic	24 hours	None/ice	LAB A	LAB D
+		Nitrate/nitrite	EPA 353.2	0.05 mg l^{-1}	8 oz plastic	28 days	H_2SO_4	LAB A	LAB D
+		Ammonia	EPA 350.1	0.01 mg l^{-1}	8 oz plastic	28 days	H_2SO_4	LAB A	LAB D
+		Total coliforms	Colilert	Present/not	8 oz sterilyzed	24 hours	Sodium thiosulfate	LAB B	LAB D
+		Radium-226	EPA 903.0		2 gals (8 l)	6 months	None/ice	LAB C	LAB D
+		Radium-228	EPA 904.0		2 gals (8 l)	6 months	None/ice	LAB C	LAB D
+	+	Strontium	EiChroM Sr-01		2 gals (8 l)	6 months	None/ice	LAB C	LAB D

- arsenic
- cadmium
- chromium
- selenium
- dissolved metals (cadmium, chromium, selenium, arsenic, barium, lead, mercury, sodium)

The specific analytes to be tested for ground-water samples from specific wells have been approved by the panel.

8.D.4.1 *Quality Assurance/Quality Control; Field QA/QC*

Field personnel will maintain a bound log book to document field activities. Information entered in the log book will include:

- Date
- Project name and number
- Project address and site identification number
- Events (i.e. description of operations)
- Time of initiation and completion of each event
- Name(s) of field personnel and pertinent visitor(s) or observers
- General weather conditions
- Data obtained in field (pH/specific conductance readings, water-level measurements, etc.)
- Record of calibration of field instruments

8.D.4.2 *QA/QC Samples*

All samples will be collected and analyzed using standard quality assurance/quality control (QA/QC) protocol, in accordance with standard practices. Laboratory QA/QC protocol include sample check-in and tracking, routine maintenance and calibration of instruments, and use of proper analytical methods and reporting.

- *Field blank*
  Trip blanks will be prepared by pouring distilled water into appropriate sample containers. The bottles will be filled at the time of preparation and assemblage of sample containers prior to mobilization. One trip blank will be included in each shipping container (ice chest) and analyzed for the selected volatile organic compounds.
- *Duplicate samples*
  A duplicate ground-water samples will be collected for approximately one out of every twenty samples, in accordance with the panel's workplan. The duplicate samples will be analyzed by the designated QA/QC laboratory, EDL. The duplicate samples will be collected using the same methods and equipment used for collection of the investigatory sample. The samples will be preserved, sealed, labeled, transported to the laboratory, and independently analyzed for the same parameters as the investigatory sample from that well.

8.D.4.3 *General QA/QC of Laboratory Procedures*

- *Replicates*
  One replicate sample is analyzed per set of samples, with a minimum of one replicate per 10 samples.
- *Spiked samples*
  One spiked sample is analyzed per set of samples, with a minimum of one spike per 10 samples. When tests are conducted for analytes that are not usually present, such as pesticides in drinking water, two replicate spikes are used for measuring precision.
- *Reagents*
  Reagents may be one or a combination of the following: "ACS" grade, analytical grade, pesticide grade, or a grade specified in an analytical method. Some chemical reagents alter slowly because of chemical or biological changes. For these chemical reagents, the practical life is indicated on the container label or stated in the analytical method. Outdated reagents shall not be used in any analysis. With every set of samples, deionized water, or an appropriate solvent, is analyzed to determine if the reagents contain any interfering substances all reagents (containers) should be shelf dated upon receipt.
- *Calibration standards*
  Calibration standards are used to verify the accuracy of the calibration curve and at least one calibration standard is analyzed with each set of samples.
- *Calibration curve*
  Curves are generated to determine and document the linear working-range for each analyte for a particular method or instrument. New curves are generated when new reagents are prepared, or when there is a modification, repair or replacement of the detector.
- *Precision*
  Precision is based on the results of replicate analyses and is expressed in terms of standard deviation (*SD*). Upper and lower control limits are established by values from 20 or more replicate pairs. Precision must be within 3.27 relative standard deviation (*RSD*) for the data to be acceptable.
- *Accuracy*
  Accuracy is a measure of the difference between the mean of 20 determinations, which were used to establish the upper and lower control limits, and the known amount of chemical added to a sample. Accuracy is expressed as percent recovery of the amount of chemical added to the sample.

- *Surrogate standards*
- *Quality control charts for precision*
  Surrogate standards are either deuterated analogs of priority pollutants or compounds that have similar chemical characteristics to the analytes of interest but do not interfere with their analysis. Samples are spiked with a surrogate spiking solution. Recovery of the surrogate is used to determine accuracy of the analytical procedure.

8.D.4.4 *Specific Routine Procedures Used to Assess; Data Precision, Accuracy, and Completeness*

Two types of QC charts for precision and accuracy are used to assess the internal QA. Charts are constructed for each analytical instrument, analytical procedure (method), and matrices.

When most samples have measurable levels of the constituent being determined, analysis of duplicate samples is effective for assessing precision. Standard deviation (*SD*) is obtained from the average range of duplicate analyses. Construct the central line and warning and control limits.

$$CV = SD \,/\, Mean$$

$$RSD = CV \times 100\%$$

where:
SD = standard deviation
CV = coefficient of variance
RSD= relative standard deviation

- *Range control charts*
  The average value for the range (R) is calculated from K sets of duplicate measurements:

  $$R = (R_1 + R_2 + \ldots + R_k) = K.$$

  As many duplicate measurement as feasible, at least 15 or more, are made to calculate R.
- *Quality control charts for accuracy*
  Recovery of spike samples, spike blanks or surrogate samples are being used to calculate the percent recovery depending on the stage at which the spike or surrogate is added, information on the efficiency, stability and variability of recovery can be evaluated.
  Mean % recovery (x) is used to calculate standard deviation (*SD*).
  Control charts are constructed accordingly.
- *Completeness*
  Completeness is a measure of the amount of valid data obtained from a measurement system compared to the amount that was expected to be obtained under correct normal conditions.
  Completeness is calculated by the following equation:

  $$100 \times \frac{\text{Data generated} - \text{Unusable data}}{\text{Expected data}}$$
  $$= \%\,\text{completeness}$$

8.D.4.5 *Corrective Action for Unacceptable Quality Control Data*

When results from spiked samples and replicate samples are outside the statistical control limits, or if values of either or both of these samples are on the same side of their respective mean value for seven successive analyses, the system is considered out-of-control. When an out-of-control situation occurs, the analyses will stop until the problem is resolved and its solution documented. All analyses since the last in-control point must be repeated.

The following is the basic method to identify and correct out-of-control data.

- *Out-of-control precision data*
  When the difference between replicates is outside the control limits, each step of the method is examined to determine the source of the error. Causes leading to poor precision can be, but are not limited to: measuring errors, contaminated glassware, improper mixing, plugged flow cell, erratic flow of solvents or gases, loss of sample, or the incorrect recording of data. After the source of the error is corrected, a control sample is analyzed and any needed recalibration is performed.
- *Out-of-control accuracy data*
  When the value for the spiked sample is outside the control limits, a control sample is analyzed to see if the problem is with the equipment or the sample. If the analysis of the control sample is acceptable, then the sample preparation must be examined. Standard addition or a modified sample preparation technique may be required if the error is not found in the concentration of, or volume of, the spiking solution.
  If the analysis of the control sample is not acceptable, then the system is either recalibrated, parts replaced, or a service technician is called in order to produce an acceptable control sample analysis.
- *Out-of-control by trend development*
  As the analytical system "ages," changes occur in the concentration of standards and reagents. Changes also occur in light sources, electrodes, columns, and other replaceable items. These changes slowly produce a deviation from the calculated means for precision and accuracy. When seven successive analyses result in values on the same side of the mean, the system is

out-of-control. Changes are then made, such as making new standards, cleaning the detector or flow cell, and recalibration. Any samples analyzed since the last in-control point will be reanalyzed. In most cases, trend development is the least likely causes of out-of-control data because of the practice of using reagents, standards and controls within their dated shelf lives and performing routine maintenance on laboratory instruments.

- *Initiating corrective action*
The analyst and/or the supervisor initiate corrective action. The quality control supervisor will approve any action after the reanalysis confirms a problem. The problem and its solution must be documented. If the problem is sample related, the laboratory supervisor will notify the field operators so that a new sampling schedule can be implemented allowing for the additional time for analyzing each sample with modifications.

Corrective action will also be initiated after receiving unacceptable results from QA activities including, but not limited to: performance and systems audits, inter-laboratory comparison studies, performance and certification tests, and other evaluations required by Federal, local or private agencies.

8.D.5 Sample Custody

8.D.5.1 *Field Custody Procedures*

1. To simplify the chain-of-custody record as few people as possible will handle the samples or other physical evidence.
2. The field investigator is personally responsible for the care and custody of the samples collected until they are properly transferred to another person or facility.
3. Labels or tags will be affixed to sample containers prior to or at the time of sampling and filled out with waterproof ink, at the time of collection, with the following minimum information:
   - Sample identification
   - Name of collector
   - Data and time of collection
4. All information pertinent to performance of a field survey or sampling will be recorded in a logbook. The book will be bound, preferably with consecutively numbered pages. At a minimum, entries in the log book will include the following:
   - Purpose of sampling (surveillance, contract number)
   - Location of sampling point
   - Name and address of field contact
   - Type of sample (sludge, wastewater, ground water, surface water)
   - Suspected waste composition, including concentrations
   - Producer of waste and address, if different than location
   - Type of process (if known) producing waste
   - Number and volume of sample taken
   - Description of sampling point and sampling methodology
   - Date and time of collection
   - Collector's sample identification number(s)
   - Sample distribution and how transported (name of laboratory, UPS, Federal Express)
   - References such as maps or photographs of the sampling site
   - Field observations
   - Any field measurements made (water level, pH, temperature, conductivity, etc.)
   - Signatures of personnel responsible for observations

8.D.5.2 *Chain-of-Custody Forms*

To establish the documentation necessary to trace sample possession from the time of collection, a chain-of-custody form will be completed and will accompany every sample.

The record will contain the following minimum information.

- Sample number
- Signature of collector
- Data and time of collection
- Place and address of collection
- Sample type
- Preservatives
- Analysis requested
- Signature of persons involved in the chain of possession (Field Collector, Courier, Laboratory Personnel)
- Inclusive dates of possession

8.D.5.3 *Transfer of Custody and Shipment*

1. Packaging requirements for shipment of samples is dependent on the nature of the sample (type of sample, contaminants, and preservatives) and the mode of transportation.
2. A chain-of-custody form will accompany all samples. When transferring the possession of samples, the individuals receiving the samples will sign, date, and note the time that they received the samples on the form.
3. Samples will be properly packaged for shipment and delivered or shipped to the contract laboratory for analysis. Shipping containers will be secured by us-

ing nylon strapping tape and custody seal. The strapping tape will be placed on the container so that all joints of the tape are secured by the seal (the seal will be placed under the joint and wrapped over the top of it). Thus the tape cannot be removed without breaking the seal or cutting the tape. The seal will be signed, dated, and the time recorded by the field investigator.

4. Whenever samples are split with a facility, State regulatory agency, or other government agency, the facility, State regulatory agency, or other government agency representative will sign the appropriate chain-of-custody record for these samples.
5. All samples shipped will be accompanied by the chain-of-custody form(s). The original and one copy of the form will be placed in a plastic bag inside the secured shipping container. The field investigator or project leader will retain one copy of the chain-of-custody form. The original of the chain-of-custody form will be transmitted to the field investigator or project leader after the laboratory accepts the samples.
6. If sent by mail, the package will be registered with return receipt requested. If sent by common carrier, a bill of lading or air bill shall be used. Receipts from post office, copies of bills of lading and air bills will be retained as part of the documentation of the chain-of-custody.

8.D.5.4 *Laboratory Custody Procedures*

1. *Sample delivery to the laboratory*
   The sample will be delivered to the laboratory for analysis as soon as practicable so that the tests are completed within appropriate holding times. The sample must be accompanied by the chain-of-custody record and by a request-sheet for sample analysis. The sample must be delivered to the person in the laboratory authorized to receive samples (often referred to as the sample custodian).
2. *Receipt and logging of samples*
   - In the laboratory, a custodian is assigned to receive the samples. After signing for receipt of chain-of-custody for a sample, the custodian will inspect the condition of the sample and the sample seal, reconcile the information on the sample label and seal against that on the chain-of-custody record, assign a laboratory number, log in the sample in the laboratory log book, and store the sample in a secured sample storage room or cabinet until assigned to an analyst for analysis.
   - The sample custodian will inspect the sample for any leakage from the container. A leaky container containing multiphase sample will not be accepted for analysis. This sample is no longer a representative sample. If the sample is contained in a plastic bottle and the container walls indicate that the sample is under pressure or releasing gases, the sample should be treated with caution because it may be explosive or release volatiles. The custodian will examine whether the sample seal is intact or broken. Any discrepancies between the information on the sample label and seal and the information on the chain-of-custody record and the sample analysis request sheet shall be resolved before the sample is assigned for analysis. This effort will require communication with the sample collector. Results of the inspection shall be documented on the sample analysis request sheet and on the laboratory sample logbook.
   - Incoming samples usually carry the inspector's or collector's identification numbers. To further identify these samples, the laboratory will assign its own identification numbers. Each sample should be marked with the assigned laboratory number. This number is correspondingly recorded on a laboratory sample logbook along with the information describing the sample. The information is copied from the sample analysis request sheet and cross-checked against that on the sample label.
3. *Assignment of sample for analysis*
   - In most cases, the laboratory supervisor assigns the sample for analysis. The supervisor will review the information on the sample analysis request sheet. The technician assigned to analysis shall record in the laboratory notebook the identifying information about the sample, the date of receipt, and other pertinent information. This record will also include the subsequent testing data and calculations. The sample may be split with other laboratories in order to obtain all the necessary analytical information. In such cases, the chain-of-custody procedures must be employed at the other laboratory and while the sample is being transported to the other laboratory.
   - After the sample has been received in the laboratory, the supervisor or assignee is responsible for its care and custody. He will be prepared to testify that the sample was in his possession or secured in the laboratory at all times from the moment it was received from the custodian until the analyses were performed.

8.D.6 Decontamination of Equipment

Standard decontamination protocol for equipment will consist of:

- Step 1: If needed, scrub equipment thoroughly with soft-bristle brushes in a phosphate-free detergent solution (i.e. Alconox or Liquinox) to remove and sediment or debris.
- Step 2: Rinse equipment with distilled water by spraying until dripping.
- Step 3: Rinse equipment with isopropanol by spraying until dripping.
- Step 4: Rinse equipment with solution of Clorox and distilled water.
- Step 5: Rinse equipment with distilled water by spraying until dripping.
- Step 6: Place equipment on plastic or aluminum foil and allow to air-dry for 5 to 10 minutes.
- Step 7: Wrap equipment in plastic or aluminum foil for handling and/or storage until next use.

Some equipment, such as the portable pump, will be submersed or submersed and operated in each of the fluids to complete the decontamination process. After decontamination, equipment will be handled only with new disposable gloves. Equipment that is not to be used immediately after decontamination will be allowed to dry and placed in a case or plastic bag.

Selected References

Driscoll FG (ed) (1986) Ground water and wells, 2nd edn. Johnson Division, St. Paul, MN

Florida Department of Environmental Regulation (1992) Standard operating procedures

Meinzer OE (1942) Physics of the earth, part 9: hydrology. McGraw-Hill, New York

P. E. LaMoreaux and Associates Inc. (2000) Comprehensive quality assurance plan. Tuscaloosa, Alabama

U.S. Environmental Protection Agency (1996) Environmental compliance branch standard operating procedures and quality assurance manual. Washington, D.C.

U.S. Environmental Protection Agency (2002) SW-846 test methods for evaluating solid wastes, physical/chemical methods. Washington, D.C. (current on-line version)

Chapter 9

Ground-Water Monitoring Wells, Contamination, and Waste Management

9.1 Ground-Water Flow in Granular and Fractured Rocks

9.1.1 Scope

Ground water in granular aquifers, fractured aquifers, and in karst systems, moves in response to hydraulic gradients from points of recharge to points of discharge. The horizontal gradient of the ground-water surface, the general shape of the water table, and the general direction of movement can be determined from a water-level contour or potentiometric map. The contours generally are based on the National Geodetic Vertical Datum (NGVD). However, in remote areas it is sometimes necessary to establish a temporary bench mark (TBM) and base line. The general direction of ground-water movement can be estimated by drawing flow lines perpendicular to the water-level contours. Results from tracer test studies can be used to support the interpretation of the direction of ground-water movement as shown by the water-level contour map.

9.1.2 Determination of the Direction and Rates of Ground-Water Flow in Granular Aquifers

Water-table or potentiometric-surface maps, are used to estimate the direction and rate of ground-water flow and contaminant movement in granular aquifers and with adequate knowledge of the geology for sites underlain by fractured or karstified rocks.. Such estimates are more complicated in fractured-rock and karst aquifers where the assumption of two-dimensional flow is generally not valid and flows are anisotropic at site-specific scales.

Flow rates are directly determined from the results of aquifer-scale or site-scale tracer tests which are a valuable tool for characterization of fractured-rock and karst aquifers.

Many new techniques have evolved during the later part of the 20th century that are used to describe more precisely the physical character of the geologic systems so that quantitative methods could be applied to granular and fractured and soluble rocks. The techniques include sequential satellite imagery, air photography, air and ground remote sensing (resistivity, sonic, radar), sophistication of chemical analyses (from part per million to part per ton), and computer recording, storage, evaluation, and recovery of data, and computer graphic techniques. With this more detailed knowledge of the geologic system, more meaningful results can be obtained from pumping tests on granular and karst aquifers. However, no quantitative study in fractured rock or karst can be accomplished without a detailed study and knowledge of the geology including stratigraphy, structure, and depositional environment.

9.1.3 State-of-the-Art For Modeling Two-Phase Flow in Fractured Rocks

In fractured rocks, the interconnected discontinuities are considered to be the main passages for fluid flow, with the solid rock blocks considered to be impermeable. Therefore, in the field, one of two approaches might be followed when dealing with the flow of fluids in fractured rock: continuum or discontinuum (or discrete) (Bear 1993).

The *hydrogeological continuum model* assumes that the aquifer approximates a porous medium at some working scale "equivalent porous-medium model." In other words, the continuum model assumes that the fractured mass is hydraulically equivalent to a porous medium and Darcy's law can then be applied without involving new theories.

The continuum model has been used to simulate non-aqueous-phase liquid (NAPL) migration from landfill sites in fractured dolomite rock; and also has been used to apply the theory of flow through fractured rock and homogenous, anisotropic, porous media to determine when a fractured rock behaves as a continuum (Zhou et al. 1997).

The *hydrogeological discrete fracture model* assumes that the majority of the ground water moves through discrete fractures or conduits and that the hydraulic properties of the matrix portion of the aquifer are unimportant. The discrete representation of the fractures has been used to describe single-phase flow, solute transport, and two-phase flow. Unlike the continuum approach, the discrete fracture approach emphasizes the effect of the geometry of fractures on fracture flow.

The *dual porosity model* of ground-water flow lies between that of the continuum and discrete models. The model is a more complex conceptualization of two-phase flow in fractured media because it requires distinguishing between the porosity rock matrix and the fracture porosity.

The design of a ground-water monitoring system must be based on empirical data from the site to be monitored, and a hydrogeologic investigation must be conducted to determine which model applies to the site of interest. The release of non-aqueous phase liquids (NAPLs) to the subsurface has resulted in numerous problems of ground-water contamination in fractured rock and the potential for ground-water contamination by NAPLs is high due to their widespread use and physicochemical properties as contaminants. Although knowledge concerning the behavior of NAPL migration in ground water in fractured rock is essential for both evaluation of ground-water contamination and aquifer remediation (Bear 1993).

The mathematical modeling of fluid flow must be specifically related to the scale of interest. In the vicinity of a contamination source, the main focus should be on two-phase flow within a single, well-defined fracture and on the mass transfer process from the fracture to the matrix blocks that bound it. For large-scale problems (in terms of spatial dimensions), the dual porosity approach may be used. In the latter conceptual model, the fractured porous medium domain is represented by two distinct, but interacting, subsystems: one consisting of the network of fractures, and the other of the porous blocks.

Although the developed models have the potential to provide useful predictions of fluid flow, further effort must be made to develop geophysical, tracer, and pumping test techniques, both individually and as combined tools, to obtain a reasonable body of information and to calibrate the models.

9.1.4 Transport by Concentration Gradients – Definitions

The transport of solutes dissolved in ground water is known as *mass* or *solute transport*. A *molecular diffusion* is a process where a solute in water moves from an area of greater concentration toward an area of less concentration. A *mechanical dispersion* is the mixing along the flow path of ground water containing a solute that moves at a different velocity from without a solute (Fetter 1999). *Degradation* is the general lowering of the surface of the land by erosive process and removal of solutes and their transportation by flowing ground water. *Sorption* is a general term including absorption and adsorption.

9.2 Development of Ground-Water Monitoring Wells

9.2.1 Geologic and Hydrogeologic Conditions of a Site

The geologic and hydrogeologic conditions at a site control the occurrence, movement and storage of ground water and the transport of the contaminants in the subsurface. These conditions in turn will significantly influence the design and construction used to install a monitoring well.

Because the occurrence of ground water is closely related to topographic and geologic conditions, areas with similar rock composition and structure are grouped into ground-water regions. Heath (1984) developed a classification system that divides the United States into ground-water regions based on the occurrence and availability of ground water. Additional factors that should be considered are the petrophysical attributes, the mineral composition, and the hydraulic characteristics of each aquifer in each region.

One must select and understand the characteristics of the target monitoring zone before designing and installing ground-water monitoring wells (ASTM 1995a). Ground-water monitoring wells can be installed to detect the presence or absence of a contaminant, and/or collect representative data about ground-water quality as well as illustrate depth to ground water, ground-water gradient and movement.

Development of a conceptual hydrogeologic model that identifies potential flow paths and the target monitoring zone(s), must be accomplished prior to the design and installation of a monitoring well. It can be accomplished in two phases: (1) an initial reconnaissance study to identify and locate those stratigraphic or structural zones with the greatest potential to transmit ground water into, within and from the project area; and (2) a field investigation to refine the preliminary conceptual hydrogeologic model and to define and characterize the flow paths influenced by the existing porosity, hydraulic conductivity, stratigraphy, lithology, and structure of each hydraulic unit. Hydrogeologic characterization may require collection, study, and interpretation of representative soil and/or rock samples from surface geologic mapping, test drilling, and, where applicable, application of surface and subsurface geophysical methods. Also required is the determination of ground-water flow direction by measuring the vertical and horizontal hydraulic gradient within each flow path.

A series of hydrogeologic cross sections should be developed to refine the conceptual model. The cross sections and/or fence diagrams will demonstrate three-dimensional (3-D) correlation of geological materials and allow comparison with geophysical logs. Subsurface, geologic cross sections, and geophysical well logs are tools for defining the stratigraphy and the structural geology of an area. A sequence of studies, as well as acquaintance with methods, equipment and materials is discussed in detail in Chaps. 5 and 7.

9.2.2 Development of Ground-Water Monitoring Wells in Granular Aquifers (ASTM D-5521-94)

The design of a ground-water monitoring system must be based on empirical data from the site to be monitored and a hydrogeological investigation must be conducted to determine the hydrogeologic model that applies to the site of interest. Chapter 6 includes discussion of monitoring well installation, well design, and methods of completion (ASTM 1994).

Screened wells are installed for the purpose of obtaining representative ground-water quality samples from granular aquifers. A primary filter pack or gravel pack, which consists of a granular material that has a known chemical composition and a properly size and gradation of grains, is installed in the annulus between the screen and the borehole wall. The grain size and gradation of the filter are selected to stabilize the hydraulic unit adjacent to the screen and permit the finest soil grains to enter the screen only during development. Table 9.1 shows recommended filter pack characteristics for common screen slot sizes, and Fig. 9.1 shows a design for a single-cased monitoring well. The developed and screened monitoring wells should yield relatively sediment-free water samples from a granular aquifer whose grain size ranges from gravels to silty sands (ASTM 1995a).

Methods for designing and completing wells were discussed in Sec. 6.5 (of Chap. 6).

Monitoring wells should be developed by surging or other methods to assure that the well can yield water. Well development is directed toward modifying adjacent materials to remove fine-grained materials from the vicinity of the bore hole formation and filter pack, to stabilize the artificial filter pack and materials adjacent to the well screen, and to retrieve lost drilling fluid that may alter the quality and quantity of ground water in the vicinity of the well.

9.2.3 Development of Ground-Water Monitoring Wells in Karst and Fractured Rock Aquifers (ASTM D-5717-95)

The hydrogeologic characteristics of ground-water monitoring systems in karst and fractured-rock aquifers are significantly different from those of porous media. Table 9.2 lists aquifer characteristics and provides a comparison of the qualitative differences between granular, fractured-rock, and karst aquifers (ASTM 1995b). In karst aquifers, most flow of water occurs through one or more of the following structures: joints, faults, bedding planes, pores, cavities, conduits, and caves. The installation of a filter pack can become difficult or may not be possible in karst or highly fractured bedrock.

9.2.4 Record-Keeping (U.S. EPA/4-89)

The goals of a monitoring well program must ensure accurate characterization of the subsurface hydro-geology and representative water-quality samples, and require a record-keeping process to document construction, installation, sampling and maintenance phases as well as a plan for proper location of a monitoring well

Table 9.1. Recommended (achievable) filter pack characteristics for common screen slot sizes (after ASTM D-5092)

Size of screen opening (mm (in.))	Slot no.	Sand pack mesh size name(s)	1% passing size (D-1) (mm)	Effective size (D-10) (mm)	30% passing size (D-30) (mm)	Range of uniformity coefficient	Roundness scale
0.125 (0.005)	5[a]	100	0.09 to 0.12	0.14 to 0.17	0.17 to 0.21	1.3 to 2.0	2 to 5
0.250 (0.010)	10	20 to 40	0.25 to 0.35	0.40 to 0.50	0.50 to 0.60	1.1 to 1.6	3 to 5
0.500 (0.020)	20	10 to 20	0.70 to 0.90	1.00 to 1.20	1.20 to 1.50	1.1 to 1.6	3 to 6
0.750 (0.030)	30	10 to 20	0.70 to 0.90	1.00 to 1.20	1.20 to 1.50	1.1 to 1.6	3 to 6
1.000 (0.040)	40	8 to 12	1.20 to 1.40	1.60 to 1.80	1.70 to 2.00	1.1 to 1.6	4 to 6
1.500 (0.060)	60	6 to 9	1.50 to 1.80	2.30 to 2.80	2.50 to 3.00	1.1 to 1.7	4 to 6
2.000 (0.080)	80	4 to 8	2.00 to 2.40	2.40 to 3.00	2.60 to 3.10	1.1 to 1.7	4 to 6

[a] A 5-slot (0.152 mm) opening is not currently available in slotted PVC but is available in Vee wire PVC and stainless; 6-slot opening may be substituted in these cases.

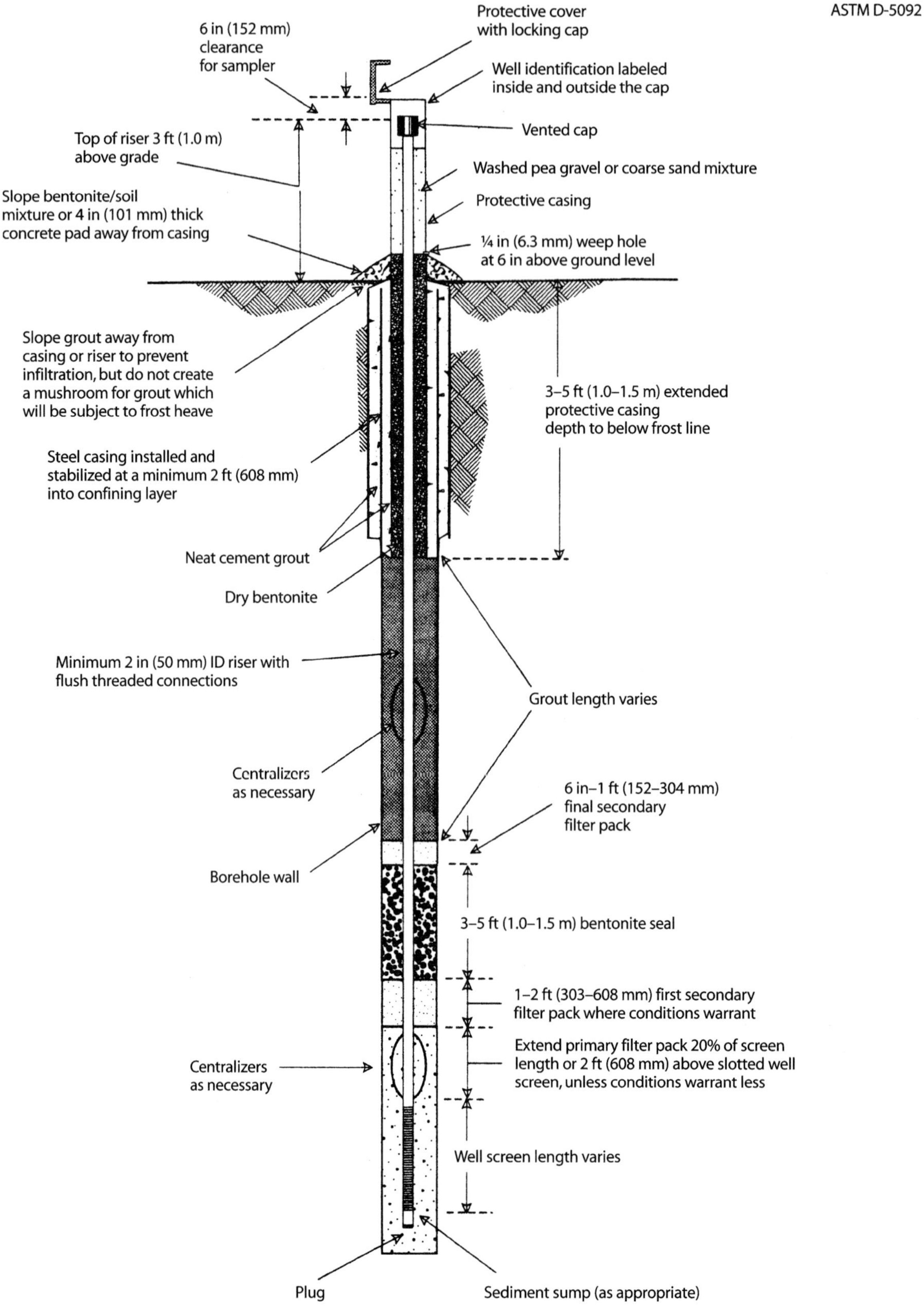

ASTM D-5092

Protective cover
with locking cap

6 in (152 mm)
clearance
for sampler

Well identification labeled
inside and outside the cap

Vented cap

Top of riser 3 ft (1.0 m)
above grade

Washed pea gravel or coarse sand mixture

Protective casing

Slope bentonite/soil
mixture or 4 in (101 mm) thick
concrete pad away from casing

¼ in (6.3 mm) weep hole
at 6 in above ground level

Slope grout away from
casing or riser to prevent
infiltration, but do not create
a mushroom for grout which
will be subject to frost heave

3–5 ft (1.0–1.5 m) extended
protective casing
depth to below frost line

Steel casing installed and
stabilized at a minimum 2 ft (608 mm)
into confining layer

Neat cement grout

Dry bentonite

Minimum 2 in (50 mm) ID riser with
flush threaded connections

Grout length varies

Centralizers
as necessary

6 in–1 ft (152–304 mm)
final secondary
filter pack

Borehole wall

3–5 ft (1.0–1.5 m) bentonite seal

1–2 ft (303–608 mm) first secondary
filter pack where conditions warrant

Extend primary filter pack 20% of screen
length or 2 ft (608 mm) above slotted well
screen, unless conditions warrant less

Centralizers
as necessary

Well screen length varies

Plug

Sediment sump (as appropriate)

Fig. 9.1. Monitoring well design – single-cased well (ASTM D-5092)

Table 9.2. Comparison of granular, fractured-rock, and karst aquifers (after ASTM D-5717-95)

Aquifer characteristics	Aquifer type		
	Granular	Fractured rock	Karst
Effective porosity	Mostly primary through intergranular pores	Mostly secondary through joints, fractures, and bedding plane partings	Mostly tertiary (secondary modified by dissolution): through pores, bedding planes, fractures, conduits, and caves
Isotropy	More isotropic	Possibly anisotropic	Highly anisotropic
Homogeneity	More homogenous	Less homogenous	Non-homogenous
Flow	Slow, laminar	Possibly rapid and possibly turbulent	Likely rapid and likely turbulent
Flow predictions	Darcy's law usually applies	Darcy's law may not apply	Darcy's law rarely applies
Storage	Within saturated zone	Within saturated zone	Within both saturated zone and epikarst
Recharge	Dispersed	Primarily dispersed, with some point recharge	Ranges from almost completely dispersed to almost completely point recharge
Temporal head variation	Minimal variation	Moderate variation	Moderate to extreme variation
Temporal water chemistry variation	Minimal variation	Minimal to moderate variation	Moderate to extreme variation

network both horizontally and vertically. Also, records should include a complete history of actions related to each well such as dates and notation of sample collection; physical observations about the well; and date, method and materials used for abandonment, as well as notations about suspected problems with the well.

Installation of ground-water monitoring wells requires decontamination of the drilling and sampling equipment as a quality-control measure. The decontamination process comprises neutralizing, washing, and rinsing equipment that comes in contact with material or ground water that is known or is suspected of being contaminated (Aller et al. 1989).

9.3 Types of Waste Disposal Facilities and Waste Characteristics

9.3.1 Types of Waste Disposal Facilities (U.S. EPA 600/4-89)

A monitoring program should be designed to evaluate whether ground water is being contaminated from a point or non-point source of waste. Geologic and hydrologic characteristics of the site must be described in detail to accomplish this objective. The following are the most prominent types of waste disposal facilities (Aller et al. 1989):

a A *landfill* is a waste unit where solid waste is typically disposed of, by spreading, compacting and covering the waste. Wastes which are disposed of in landfills are classified as either hazardous or non-hazardous, and they are usually emplaced and described in one of three settings: (1) on or above the natural ground surface where surface topography is more or less flat, (2) in valleys, ravines or other depressions, or (3) in trenches excavated into the subsurface.

b *Land-treatment facility* involves the application of waste liquids and sludges onto the ground surface to allow for biological or chemical degradation of the waste, or for the beneficial use of nutrients contained in the waste. Land-treatment operations commonly involve spray irrigation or land spreading of sludges on agricultural, forested, or reclaimed land.

c *Surface impoundments or lagoons* used for storage, treatment, and/or disposal of both hazardous and non-hazardous liquid wastes can be constructed either in natural depressions or excavations and are typically used to settle suspended solids.

d *Underground storage tanks* are used to store hazardous and non-hazardous waste, industrial liquids, and raw materials (ex. fuel oils). Both steel and fiberglass tanks are used to store petroleum products and other products including: solvents, acids, and technical grade chemicals.

e *Radioactive waste disposal sites* include nuclear fuel and other radioactive wastes. The disposal methods for radioactive wastes depend on the radiation levels and the waste characteristics. Low-level radioactive wastes are usually disposed in shallow burial sites. High-level radioactive wastes may be reprocessed or stored in specially constructed facilities.

9.3.2 Waste Characteristics

The physical and chemical characteristics of the waste(s) present at a site should be carefully considered together with site hydrogeology when designing a monitoring program. Two physical properties affect transport and fate of a compound in the subsurface: the relative solubility and density of the contaminant. Contaminants can be classified into the following categories that subsequently influence design of monitoring wells (Aller et al. 1989):

a *Primarily miscible/soluble contaminants* exhibit densities greater than, less than or equal to water. The contaminant moves in the same direction and with the same velocity as ground water where the density of the contaminant closely approximates that of water. Figure 9.2 illustrates the migration of a high-density miscible contaminant that sinks vertically through the aquifer and accumulates on top of the lower permeability boundary (Kovski 1989). The contaminant then moves in response to gravity and follows the topography of the lower permeability boundary, possibly in opposition to the direction of regional ground-water flow. Figure 9.3 illustrates the migration of a low density, soluble contaminant that accumulates at the top of the water table. Dissolution and dispersion of the contaminant occurs as the accumulated contaminant migrates with the ground water.

b *Relatively immiscible/insoluble contaminants* where immiscible compounds in both the saturated and unsaturated zones, exist as either free liquids or as dissolved constituents depending on the relative solubility of the contaminant. The relative density of the contaminant affects the occurrence and movement of the contaminant in the subsurface and must be considered when locating monitoring wells and when the interval(s) to be screened in the aquifer. Figure 9.4 illustrates the migration of a low-density, immiscible contaminant that moves downward through the vadose zone and accumulates at the top of the water table and/or within the capillary fringe. A residual amount of fluid is retained in the vadose zone in response to surficial and interstitial forces (Kovski 1989; Yaniga and Warburton 1984). Monitoring wells designed to detect or assess low-density immiscible contaminants should be screened in the upper part of the aquifer. Usually the screen should span the vadose zone and the upper portion of the aquifer to allow the floating contaminant to enter the well.

High-density immiscible fluids are called dense, non-aqueous phase liquids (DNAPLs), which include most halogenated hydrocarbons and other aliphatic compounds. Figure 9.5 illustrates the movement of DNAPLs in the subsurface and is primarily controlled by capillary forces and density in the unsaturated zone (Villaume 1985). Both residual contaminant and the contaminant plume may continue to contribute dissolved constituents to the ground water for an extended period of time. Thus, a vapor plume from the contaminant source may also form and migrate in the vadose zone. These plumes can often be detected through soil gas sampling techniques.

Pumping or injection wells in an area of monitoring wells can affect ground-water flow direction and velocity and/or can influence ground-water quality. The presence of a well or a group of wells will provide evidence of the cone of depression that can greatly affect the flow of ground water or the rate of migration of the contaminant plume. Other factors such as storm sewers, surface runoff catchments, sanitary sewers, buried underground cables, underground pipelines or other subsurface disturbances must be considered to determine any potential impacts to the monitoring program.

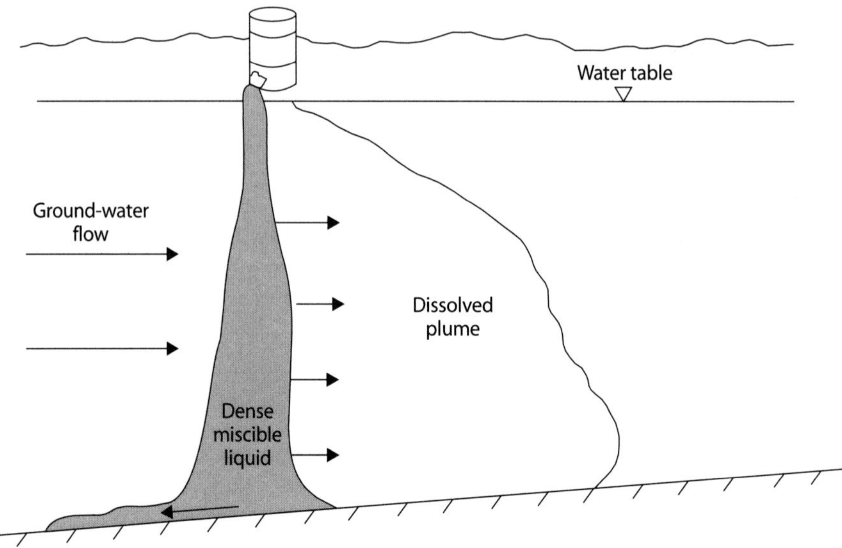
Water table
Ground-water flow
Dissolved plume
Dense miscible liquid

Fig. 9.2. Migration of a high density, miscible contaminant in the subsurface (U.S. Environmental Protection Agency 1989)

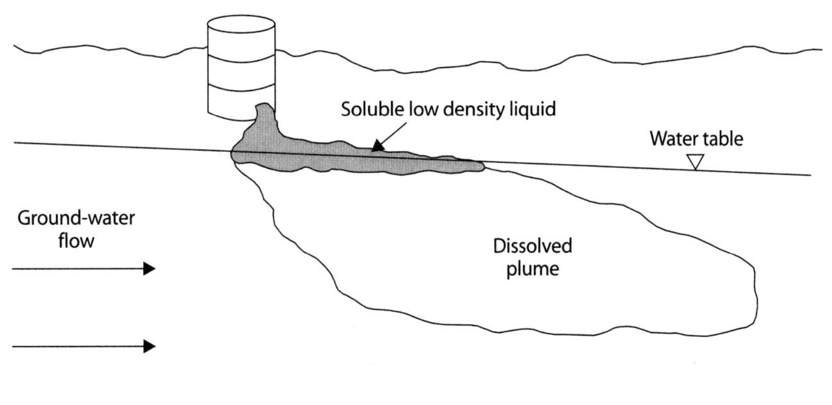

Soluble low density liquid
Water table
Ground-water flow
Dissolved plume

Fig. 9.3.
Migration of a low density, soluble contaminant in the subsurface (U.S. Environmental Protection Agency 1989)

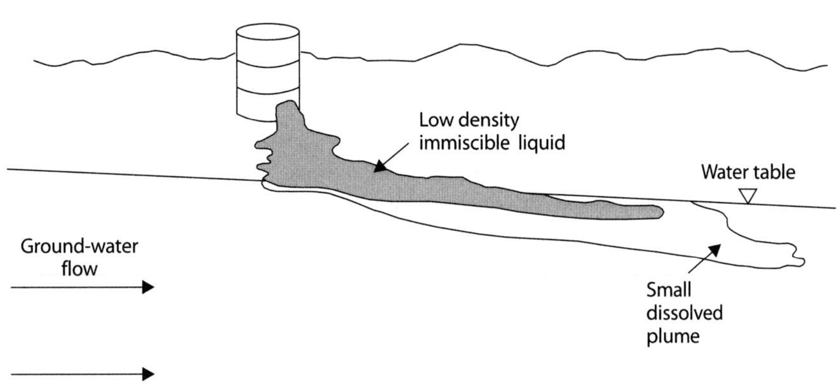

Low density immiscible liquid
Water table
Ground-water flow
Small dissolved plume

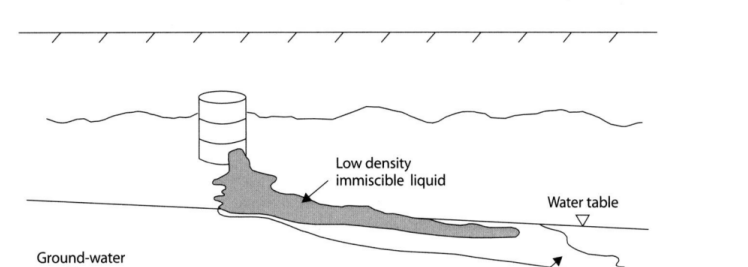

Fig. 9.4.
Migration of a low density, immiscible contaminant in the subsurface (U.S. Environmental Protection Agency 1989)

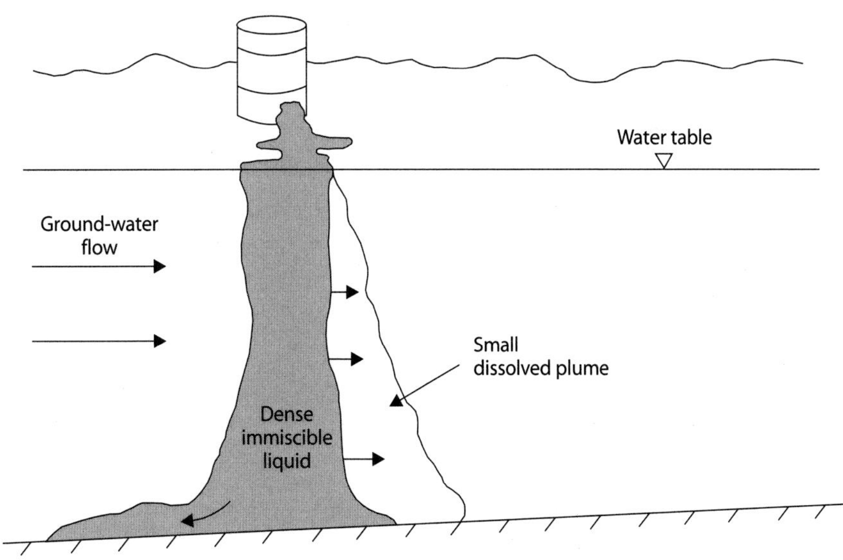

Water table
Ground-water flow
Small dissolved plume
Dense immiscible liquid

Fig. 9.5.
Migration of a dense, non-aqueous phase liquid (DNAPL) in the subsurface (U.S. Environmental Protection Agency 1989)

9.3.3 Seepage of Water at the Edges of Waste Disposal Sites

Anomalous plant growths, discoloration of the soil, or visibly wet areas at the edge of a landfill may indicate seepage of water from the landfill and potential ground-water contamination at a site. Water that seeps from a landfill can be highly contaminated, and once leachate is identified from a landfill, further action is needed to characterize the leachate and curtail its movement.

Gas seepage can also occur around a landfill. Gases can have an odor, can flare, but are rarely explosive. Gas monitoring and venting should be a part of any landfill construction monitoring and maintenance program.

As previously described, remote-sensing techniques are divided into active and passive methods. Passive methods use reflected solar radiation and radiation emitted from a surface. Interaction of electromagnetic radiation with the earth's surface provides information about the reflecting or absorbing surface. A map derived from the interpretation of aerial photographs and other remote sensing data is influenced by subjective factors that depend on the correctness of interpretations of remote-sensing data in the field. For example, signs of water leachate were detected near an edge of an abandoned disposal site that was transformed into a park in Berlin, Germany (Kuehn and Hoerig 2000).

9.4 Sources of Pollution and Ground-Water Contamination

9.4.1 Air Pollution and Its Effects on Surface Water Resources

Soil and unconsolidated sediment are useful materials that are present on the earth's surface yet, some environmental concerns occur due to continuous physical and chemical processes with soils, rock outcrops and the atmosphere leading to different sources of natural and man-made air pollution to water resources system.

9.4.1.1 *Acid Rain – Greenhouse Effect*

The phenomenon of acidic rainfall has gained increased attention in recent years. The prime constituents of acid precipitation are sulfur and nitrogen acids. Hydrochloric acid, carbonic acid, ammonia, calcium, iron, aluminum and various organic acids can also be present in acid rain (Assaad and Jordan 1994).

Natural airborne acids and their precursors can be products of geothermal emissions, volcanoes, wind-generated materials, or biological processes. Natural phenomena generate acids, including nitric oxide from lightning, and sulfurous gases from volcanic eruption and anaerobic decomposition.

Industrial sources of acids (SO_x, NO_x, CO_x) are linked to man-made emissions of aerosols (CFCs, "chlorofluro-carbons") which are carried upward, react with water in the atmosphere and precipitate into soils to be reached into ground water. The principal sources of acids are emissions from the combustion of hydrocarbon fuels, which are used by public utilities, industrial processes, residential heating, commercial boilers, and in vehicles. In normal conditions, rain is slightly acidic. It had a pH of 5.5 to 6.0 (as measured in the Greenland ice) before the industrial revolution. Acid deposition can be wet (acid rain) and/or dry deposition (Jordan and Weder 1995).

Wet and dry depositions have been recognized as processes by which acidic material is removed from the atmosphere (Fig. 9.6). In wet deposition, acidic substances and their precursors are suspended and/or dissolved in rain, snow, dew, frost, or hail (pH of 4–4.5). The lowest reported pH of rain was 2.4, at the Pitlochry measurement station (Scotland, April 10, 1974). In dry deposition, gaseous and particulate matter are transferred to natural surfaces by gravitational setting, turbulent exchange, and vegetation uptake.

Carbon dioxide and methane gases act as an insulating blanket around the earth, allowing incoming solar radiation to warm the earth's surface and reducing radiation of heat through the atmosphere into space.

9.4.1.2 *The Ozone Layer*

The *ozone layer* (17–24 km thick) is a region of high concentration of ozone molecules (O_3) which is produced by the action of ultraviolet rays upon ordinary oxygen molecules (O_2). Wave lengths shorter than 0.3 μm are completely absorbed by the ozone layer in the upper atmosphere. Excessive ultraviolet radiation will destroy all exposed bacteria tissues and plants. Therefore, the presence of the ozone layer is important for the continuous existence of the biosphere.

Chlorofluorocarbons (CFCs) are important halocarbons, which are compounds formed by halogens (fluorine, chlorine, bromine and, iodine) and have many applications, such as aerosol propellants, refrigerants, solvents, and fire extinguishers. The first CFCs were synthesized in 1928 and production increased sharply after that, but production was decreased recently due to concern of ozone (Rowland 1990).

The ozone layer could also be disrupted by mankind. In 1971, concern was raised about the possible effects of supersonic flights on the ozone layer. Later, in 1974, Molina and Rowland, together with Crutzen (1971), received the Nobel Prize for Chemistry 1995 for their studies in this field as they identified the potential effect of (CFCs) on stratospheric ozone.

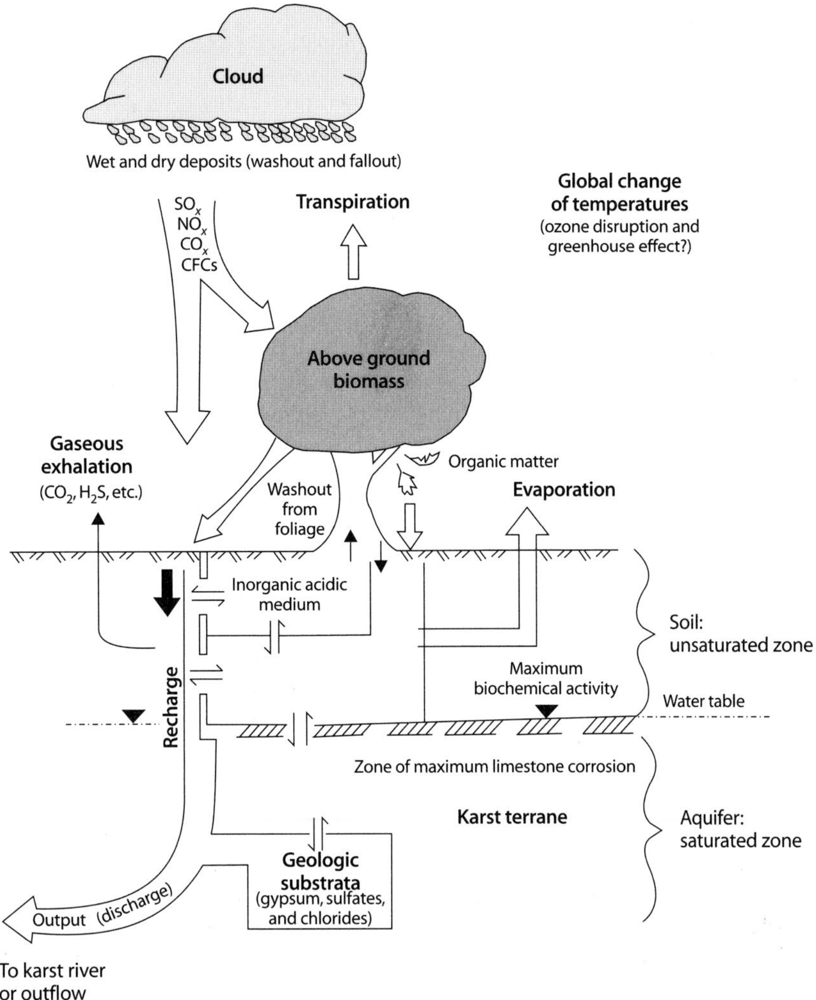
Cloud
Wet and dry deposits (washout and fallout)
SO_x
NO_x
CO_x
CFCs
Transpiration
Global change
of temperatures
(ozone disruption and
greenhouse effect?)
Above ground
biomass
Gaseous
exhalation
(CO_2, H_2S, etc.)
Organic matter
Evaporation
Washout
from
foliage
Inorganic acidic
medium
Soil:
unsaturated zone
Maximum
biochemical activity
Recharge
Water table
Zone of maximum limestone corrosion
Karst terrane
Aquifer:
saturated zone
Geologic
substrata
(gypsum, sulfates,
and chlorides)
Output (discharge)
To karst river
or outflow

Fig. 9.6.
A flow diagram of the hydrological cycle of acid rain (adapted from Kramer et al. 1986; figure was previously modified by Assaad and Jordan 1994)

Ozone depletion – A reduction in the ozone concentration of the stratosphere has been taking place since the mid-1970s both as a small, worldwide depletion and as a severe seasonal depletion localized over Antarctica. There is also a strong localized depletion, commonly known as the ozone hole, centered over Antarctica and surrounding regions. This phenomenon results from the destruction of a high percentage of the regional stratospheric ozone (more than 50%) that occurs due to: (1) the presence of halocarbons in the stratosphere, (2) isolation by the Antarctic polar vortex, and (3) high altitude ice crystals clouds ("polar stratospheric clouds"). It must be also recognized that natural volcanic eruptions have likewise an impact on the atmosphere and lithosphere.

The Antarctic polar vortex forms a natural barrier in the stratosphere at a latitude about 70°, which isolates polar air from the rest of the world during winter and part of the spring. In the presence of sunlight during Antarctic spring, chemical reactions occurring on the surface of ice crystals in stratospheric clouds, involving free chlorines from the CFCs, promote the destruction of molecular ozone.

Ozone depletion leads to an increase in the UV-B radiation at the earth's surface. There is an inverse relation between ozone and UV-B radiation, which has been established through radioactive transfer models, and good-quality spectral measurements (Diaz et al. 2000; World Mineralogical Organization 1999; Rowland 1990).

The "*greenhouse effect*" and the effect of the depletion of ozone layers in the higher atmospheres could have an effect on climate change and also to karstification. However, the depletion of the ozone layer and the increase of CO_2 (25% during the last 30 years), together with CH_4 (nearly 1% increase per year) and NO_x (nearly 0.2% increase per year) may lead to a warming climate and shift the warm climate zone to the Northern Hemisphere rather than the Southern Hemisphere (Assaad and Jordan 1994).

Eruptions of volcanoes (e.g. St. Helena 1980; El Chichen 1984), degassing of permafrost regions where the deeply frozen ground does not completely thaw during the summer (tundra) or deforestation in Africa, South America and elsewhere may possibly influence the greenhouse effect. (An international disciplinary research program on the Geo-Atmo-Hydro-Cryo-Biosphere may clarify the above problem.)

9.4.1.3 *Radon Gas*

Radon, ^{222}Rn, which is a cancer-causing radioactive gas, comes from the natural (radioactive) decay of uranium in soil and sand and tends to migrate readily in air or water. As it has a relatively short half-life (3.8 days) this migration is limited. Radon emanation and migration in the earth and in the atmosphere have been the subjects of numerous studies. Areas containing materials with high concentrations of radium, such as granitic rocks and uranium minerals, would be expected to create elevated radon concentrations in soil-gas and ground-water area (Soliman et al. 1998).

Radon gas is found in soils, and it typically moves through the ground, in the air, and into homes through cracks and other breaks in foundations. Although the primary source of radon is from soil gas, it sometimes enters buildings through the sewage pipes, or in the water, where it can be released into the air when water is used for showering and other household uses.

Radon levels in outdoor air, indoor air, and ground water differ greatly. Concentrations of radon are measured by various methods, such as an LR-115 plastic track-detector or radon emanometer. According to the U.S. Geological Survey, normal outdoor air averages about 0.2 pCi l^{-1}; indoor air averages about 2 pCi l^{-1}; and radon in soil air varies from 20 to more than 100 000 pCi l^{-1}; and the normal amount of radon dissolved in ground water may vary from about 100 to nearly three million pCi l^{-1} (Otton et al. 1993; USGS, http://www.energy.cr.usgs.gov/radon/georadon.html).

9.4.2 Sources of Pollution in Surface Water

9.4.2.1 *General*

Environmental concerns associated with water result from natural events and human activities. Although natural events, including floods, droughts, and changes to water quality, they may be beneficial to the environment. Many human water uses require changes to the natural flow of water through the construction of dams, canals, and by the pumping of ground water. These changes although bring benefits to people, they affect natural environments and habitats. Municipal, industrial, or agricultural uses of water may cause other environmental concerns as well (American Geological Institute 2002).

9.4.2.2 *Mine waste*

Mining can produce spoils, or unneeded soil, sediment, and rock moved during the mining process, and tailings, or solid waste left over after the processing of ore. These wastes may be piled on the land surface, used to fill low areas, used to restore the land to pre-mining contours, or placed in engineered landfills with leachate-collection systems. Mine wastes can generate leachate as rainwater passes through them. If sulfide minerals are present, sulfuric acid can be generated, and the resulting drainage can be acidic. Disposal of mine waste is a large issue, because an estimated 2.3 billion tons of mine wastes are generated annually in the United States. Leachate produced by unneutralized or uncontained mine wastes can be a threat to ground water and surface water (USGS 2002).

9.4.2.3 *Acid Mine Drainage (AMD)*

Surface and underground mining may disrupt patterns of natural ground-water flow and expose rocks containing pyrite or other sulfide minerals to oxygenated water. This can result in the production of acid water, which then drains from the mine. AMD is one of the earliest recognized sources of water pollution and has been the focus of research for decades. Acid mine drainage is a problem for the coal industry, as well as for other mining industries. Neutralization of acid mine drainage with lime and/or limestone results in generation of a waste slurry (sludge) containing the precipitates from the neutralization reactions as well as unreacted reagents (USGS 2002).

A lead and zinc mine was active for 25 years in Shullsburg, Wisconsin. The ground-water table was lowered below the mine levels by pumping. Sulfide minerals in the rock were subjected to oxidation along fractures in the rock and in mine workings. Contact of the resulting sulfuric acid with the dolomite host rock neutralized the sulfuric acid and produced soluble sulfate minerals. When the mining ceased due to economic factors, the dewatering pumps were shut down and the mine workings were flooded. Ground water from the mine workings contained high concentrations of sulfate (up to 3 500 mg l^{-1}), iron (up to 20 mg l^{-1}), and zinc (up to 18 mg l^{-1}). As a result, ground-water quality of a number of nearby water wells was adversely affected (Hoffman 1984).

9.4.3 Sources of Pollution to Aquifer Systems

One of the factors of ground-water contamination that makes it so serious is its long-term nature, as wastes buried long ago takes decades to be discovered. Although many ground-water contamination sites are small, some of the long-term sites are fairly extensive due to the long time period over which contamination has been migrating away from their source.

9.4.3.1 *Ground-Water Contamination*

Ground-water contamination originates from a variety of sources and creates problems with widely varying degrees of complexity. Sources of ground-water contamination include: gasoline stations, lumber-treating facilities, electronics manufacturers, food producers, and Federal weapons facilities. When contaminants leak or spill on the ground, gravity moves them downward to the water table, where even a small quantity of some chemicals can create a very large plume of contaminated ground water. There are technical difficulties in cleaning up the ground water stored in aquifers because of the following reasons (Macdonald and Kavanaugh 1994): (*a*) *physical heterogeneity* of the subsurface and the difficulty of determining pathways by which contaminants will spread through different types of rocks; (*b*) *presence of non aqueous-phase liquids (NAPLs)* such as oil, gasoline, and other solvents that do not dissolve readily in water. As NAPLs move underground, it may leave small immobile globules trapped in the porous materials of the subsurface and cannot be easily flushed from the subsurface with conventional ground-water cleanup systems; (*c*) *diffusion of contaminants* into inaccessible regions, such as aquifers that contain small pore spaces, are difficult to flush with conventional ground-water cleanup systems; (*d*) *adherence of contaminants* to subsurface materials by physical attraction or chemical reactions, is a phenomenon known as sorption. It is very difficult to remove the sorbed contaminants, because desorption is a slow process.

9.4.3.2 *Man-Made Wastes*

There are numerous hazards to ground water from man-made wastes, as well as from natural sources. Experiments show that bacteria and viruses generally do not move more than a few hundred feet in soil, whereas dissolved products during biodegradation of wastes may move freely and increase salt concentrations of ground water. Agriculture can contaminate water with dissolved constituents, nutrients, and pesticide residues. Leaching from landfills may include chemicals, oils, metals and other constituents (Macdonald and Kavanaugh 1994).

Demand for primary hard minerals increases each year. The United States alone uses about 1.5 billion tons of aluminum ore, 1 billion tons of phosphate ore; and 100 billion tons of copper ore.

Environmental effects of ground-water pollution are of great concern all over the world. Water quality requirements and limitations associated with its uses should take into consideration the bacterial characteristics and chemical constituents. The U.S. Public Health Service (U.S. EPA as well) has developed standards for physical, chemical and bacterial quality of drinking water (Soliman et al. 1998; Table 9.3).

9.4.3.3 *Regulations Establishing Drinking Water Quality Criteria*

Standards have been set forth by the Federal government for the minimum drinking water quality for human consumption. The Federal Office of Drinking Water has established recommended maximum contaminant levels (RMCLs) for contaminants in water. The RMCLs, which are health-based standards derived from toxicological data, are health related goals and are not enforceable drinking water standards. However, the Federal Primary Drinking Water Standards have established maximum contaminant levels (MCLs), which are federally enforced. These standards cover only a few of the potential contaminants that may affect water supplies.

The Drinking Water Standards and Health Advisories tables are revised periodically by U.S. EPA's Office

Table 9.3. Limiting concentrations of mineral constituents for drinking water

Constituent	Limits (ppm)
Mandatory limits	
Primary Drinking Water Standards (U.S.EPA)	
Fluoride (F)	1.0
Lead (Pb)	0.1
Selenium (Se)	0.05
Hexavalent chromium (Cr^{6+})	0.05
Arsenic (As)	0.05
Nonmandatory limits (but recommended)	
Secondary Drilling Water Standards	
Iron (Fe) and manganese (Mn) together	0.3
Magnesium (Mg)	125
Chloride (Cl)	250
Sulfate (SO_4^{2-})	250
Copper (Cu)	3.0
Zinc (Zn)	15
Phenols	0.001
Total solids, desirable	500
Total solids, permitted	1 000

of Water on "as needed" basis. All related tables may be obtained from the Office of Science and Technology homepage (http://www.epa.gov/OST).

Table 9.4 shows the drinking water standards of the summer edition 2000 and the following is the explanation of the abbreviations used:

- STWR: Secondary Drinking Water Regulations
- MCL: maximum contaminant level
- LAL: lead action level

Authorities studied legislation and regulatory actions to save the ground-water resources from being polluted due to man's activities and to improve the economy through waste management (Soliman et al. 1998; Macdonald and Kavanaugh 1994). Some types of ground-water pollution which result from man's activities, can be summarized as follows:

a Urban wastes
  - Municipal dumps and sanitary landfills have long been recognized as potential sources of ground-water pollution. Primary pollutants are BOD (biological oxygen demand is the amount of oxygen required to biologically oxidize the water contaminants to carbon dioxide (CO_2)), COD (chemical oxygen demand), iron, chloride and nitrate. Leachate originates as ground water, or surface-water drainage.
  - The analysis of roadside ground water and shallow well-water samples revealed the effects of high chloride content on plants and animals. In some areas, the pollution of ground water by road salts, resulted from salt storage piles and road drainage.
  - The widespread use of individual water supplies and sewerage systems (septic tanks and seepage pits) may cause ground-water contamination in areas with no sewers.

b Industrial wastes
  - Waste disposal: disposal of industrial wastes and its relation to ground-water pollution has been the subject of study, because of increasing threats to ground water in many nations of the world. Chloride concentration may greatly increase in ground water of an area due to infiltration from disposal ponds or from an adjacent river. The contaminated ground water can be toxic to crops and unpotable for humans.
  - Specific waste disposal operations include radioactive waste, burial grounds, landfills and dumps, sewage treatment and waste storage ponds, disposal wells and sewage-storm water tunnels.
  - Metal wastes (e.g. cadmium and chromium) are found as a toxic contaminant in some areas. The revealed path coincides with the direction of ground-water flow.
  - Oxidation and leaching connected with coal mining produce high iron and sulfate concentrations and low pH in ground water. In some oil and gas wells, along with the natural joints and fractures of the rocks, permit acid mine drainage to move downward from strip mines into underlying aquifers, thereby increasing the iron and sulfate content of the water. Acid mine drainage can be controlled by neutralization, reverse osmosis, stream-flow regulation, deep-well disposal, land reclamation, revegetation, pumping and drainage, mine sealing, etc. (see Sec. 9.3.2).

c Agricultural wastes
  - Various agricultural sources of pollution include animal wastes, fertilizers, pesticides, plant residues, and saline wastewaters.
  - Livestock operations and field-spread manure can be sources of pollutants. High BOD waste runoff (common from feedlots) is located without regard to soil inventory and topographic characteristics.
  - Pesticides and herbicides are well known as plant toxicants and may easily contaminate soils and ground water.

Ground-water pollution and environmental factors: The unsaturated zone above the water table attenuates almost all of the foreign bodies that are potential pollutants of the underlying ground water. Environmental factors that tend to reduce the pollution of ground water from wells and springs include:

1. a sufficient clay in the path of pollutants to favor retention or sorption of pollutants,
2. a gradient beneath a waste site away from nearby wells, and
3. a great distance between wells and wastes.

9.4.4 Pollution to Karstic Aquifers

9.4.4.1 *Scope*

Karst regions, areas underlain by limestones, dolomite, marble, gypsum, and salt, constitute about 25% of the land surface of the world. They are areas of abundant resources including water supplies, limestone quarries, minerals, oil, and natural gas. Many karst terrains make beautiful housing sites by urban development. However, since people have settled on karst areas, many problems have developed; for example, insufficient and easily contaminated water supplies, poor surface water drainage, and catastrophic collapse and subsidence features. By experience we have learned that each karst area is complex, and that special types of investigation are needed to help us better understand and live with them. In addition, urban development in these areas requires spe-

Table 9.4. National interim water standards (after U.S. Environmental Protection Agency 2000)

	Contaminant/standard	Critical oxygen	Maximum contaminant level (mg l^{-1}, (µg l^{-1}), except as noted)
Inorganic chemicals	Contaminant		
	Arsenic		0.005 (MCL)
	Barium		2 (MCL)
	Cadmium		0.005 (MCL)
	Chromium (total)		0.1 (MCL)
	Fluoride		4 (MCL)
	Lead		0.015 (MCL, LAL)
	Mercury		0.002 (MCL)
	Nitrate (as N)		10
	Selenium		0.05 (MCL)
	Silver		0.05 (50)
	Standard		
	Chloride		250 (STWR)
	Color		15 units (STWR)
	Copper		1.0 (1 000) (STWR)
	Corrosivity		Noncorrosive
	Foaming agents MBAS (methylene-blue active substances)		0.5 (STWR)
	Hydrogen sulfide		Not detectable
	Iron		0.3 (STWR)
	Manganese		0.05 (50) (STWR)
	Odor		3 (threshold no.) (STWR)
	Sulfate		250
	Total residue (TDS)		500 (STWR)
	Zinc		5 (5 000) (STWR)
Organic chemicals	Contaminant		
	Chlorinated hydrocarbons: Endrin (1,2,3,4,10,10-hexachloro-6,7-expoxy-)		0.0002
Radium-226 and radium-228, and gross alpha particle radioactivity	1. Combined radium-226 and radium-228		5 pCi l^{-1}
	2. Gross alpha particle activity (including radium-226 but excluding radon and uranium)		15 pCi l^{-1}
Radionuclides	Tritium	Total body	20 000 pCi l^{-1}
	Strontium-90	Bone marrow	8 pCi l^{-1}

cial sets of rules and regulations to minimize potential problems from present and future development.

The American Geological Institute produces the *Environmental Awareness Series* in cooperation with its member societies and others to provide a nonechnical framework for a better understanding of environmental geoscience (American Geological Institute 2002).

9.4.4.2 *Karstic Erosion by Ground Water*

Mandel (1965) stated that in the saturated zone of calcareous aquifers, the process of erosion by solution proceeds at a very slow rate. Throughout the aquifer, an intricate system of solution channels develops. The dominant characteristic is their direction towards the outlet.

Most limestones are not aquifers until karstification takes place, but some younger limestones behave as porous media even after karstification, therefore there is flow along fractures, joints, solution cavities as well as through the matrix or mass of the limestone and chalk; generally however, the direction of ground-water flow is controlled by fractures and bedding planes. Gravity causes downhill movement along the most conveniently oriented fractures and bedding planes. The preferential directions of flow channels do not necessarily reflect the most recent geological events (Bogli 1980).

9.4.4.3 *Karstic Corrosion by Ground Water*

In his discussion of the concept of "karst corrosion", Jakucs (1977) stated that the dissolution of limestone by water may be the result of one or any of the combination of the following distinct processes:

1. Carbonate dissolution of limestones
   Calcite dissociates into (Ca^{2+} and CO_3^{2-}) when dissolved in water. The dissolution is expressed by the following reaction:

   $$CaCO_3 \leftrightarrow Ca^{2+} + CO_3^{2-}$$

2. Dissolution of limestones
   After water becomes saturated with $CaCO_3$, a reduction of CO_2 concentration can cause precipitation of dissolved $CaCO_3$ as calcareous oozes, stalactites, calcareous tufa, etc.).

Cholnoky (1940) stressed the role of CO_2 in the soil. He stated that in the soil there is a continuous process of decay, of slow oxidation, resulting in the formation of CO_2 gas.

9.4.4.4 *Transport of Intestinal Pathogens by Subterranean Karst Systems*

Soils contain microorganisms that could be pathogenic to humans or to plants. Rock matrix and water are in direct contact in karst systems where the water flows through the solution channels of irregular dimensions and directions.

The subterranean water courses are one of the characteristics of the karst that are of interest to geologists, hydrogeneticists and epidemiologists, concerning the question of whether intestinal pathogenic bacteria (the main causative agents of typhoid and other diseases), can be transported by rivers over large karst areas (Emili 1969).

9.4.5 Protection of Water in Karst Against Pollution

Because hydraulic conductivity and water-flow velocity can be high in karst systems, the flow velocity of pollutants is also high and therefore ground water can be polluted very quickly in different pathways and directions in different velocities. The velocity of water and the migration of pollutants depend greatly on the spatial distribution of faults and fractures in the karst system.

The method for protection of ground water in limestone regions differs from that in unconsolidated water-bearing rocks (Petrik 1969). In karst terrains, rain water passing into the subsurface can carry contaminants without filtration as in porous rocks. The velocity of flow of the ground water can be high in the karst areas (on the order of several hundreds or thousands of meters per day; whereas in porous media, velocities may be several meters per day and never more than 100 m d^{-1}). Therefore, the duration of flow in the karst aquifers can be too short to allow mechanical and biological processes of purification, especially after periods of heavy rains. At such times, springs in the region may yield water, and the water may contain high concentrations of coliform bacteria and other contaminants.

In karst areas, strict regime of protection of ground water should be seriously considered. The number of industries that potentially discharge contaminants should be limited to the coastal regions and near the lowest reaches of streams. Continuous mechanical and biological treatment of wastewater, and adherence to established water quality requirements for all kinds of discharged wastewater should be enforced.

Delay time for protection zones: Porous and permeable rocks are the more extensive contacts of the contaminant within the rock matrix and relatively lead to longer delay time than that in karstic aquifers. In karst systems, contaminants may bypass the unsaturated zone (or soil) where the physicochemical and microbiological attenuation processes are most; and directly enters the ground-water system.

Petrik (1969) discussed protection of fractured or karstic aquifers against pathogens (bacteria and viruses) and rapidly degradable chemicals in the catchment areas (maximum security area) with an estimated delay time of 60 days and for more than 30 m. The first protection area (*I*) has a delay time of 10 to 25 years or 1 to 2 km (*R*). The second protection area (*II*) may be extended to the boundary of recharge area (Van Wageningh 1985; Fig. 9.7).

Computer models installed for the movement and behavior of pollution underground can be constructed with the consideration the knowledge of attenuation processes and delay factors.

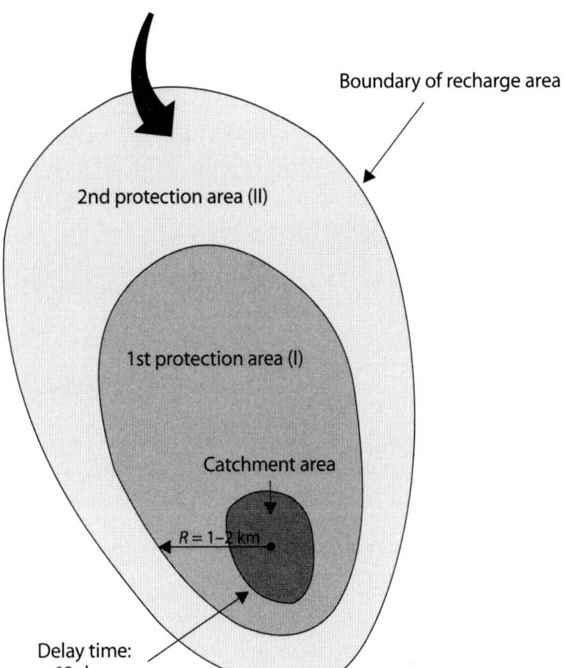
Boundary of recharge area
2nd protection area (II)
1st protection area (I)
Catchment area
R = 1–2 km
Delay time:
60 days

Fig. 9.7. Ground-water protection areas (after Van Wageningh 1985)

9.5 Dye Tracing Techniques

9.5.1 Scope

Tracers are substances which are added to water in powder to determine its spatial and temporal distributions. Tracers are divided into insoluble (solid) and soluble. Insoluble tracers include bran, sawdust, chaff, yeast fungus, *Lycopodium* spores, and different bacteria. Soluble tracers include dyes, radioactive isotopes, optical brighteners and inorganic salts. Soluble tracers are much preferable than the insoluble ones because of considerably better tracing characteristics (solubility, potentials of detection in high dilution, and simple sampling). The most important characteristics of a tracer is its concentration sensitivity that is the lowest concentration detected with accuracy (Milanović 2000).

9.5.2 Highlights in Karst History

(1) The use of tracers for investigation of "lost waters" dates back to the first years A.D. Tracing of ground-water movement was first recorded by the Jewish historian Josephus Flavius (A.D. 37). In the history of the Jewish War, he recorded the probable source of the Jordan and that Tetrach of Trachonitis used a tracer (chaff) to trace an underground stream. (2) In 1856, Frenchmen Abby Paramelle made the first attempt to study the extent of karstification and to identify the path of ground-water movement in karst. (3) In 1878, the first large, quantitative experiments were performed by injecting sodium fluorescein and potassium chloride into sinkholes near the Danube. In November 1908, large amounts of sodium chloride were injected into sinkholes in the Danube near Fridingen. (4) In 1926, the first plant spores (*Lycopodium*) were used for tracing. The advantage of *Lycopodium* was that the spores did not dissolve in water, but instead formed an emulsion of solid bodies. Due to their small size, the spores remain suspended in water.

Modern dye studies: Experimentation, research, and emphasis on tracing methods resulted in the "Specialist Conference on the Tracing of Subterranean Waters" in Graz, Austria from March 28–April 1, 1966. One hundred and twenty-five participants presented results of their work.

In 1975, J. Zotl and W. Back, through assistance of the Marshall Plan for central Europe, injected commercial salt into the Lurbach system (LaMoreaux 1991).

9.5.3 Dye Tracers

Tracer dyes are safe depending on the quantity used; they work effectively in many hydrogeologic settings, some can be used in acidic waters and the destruction of fluorescent dyes by sunlight does not preclude their use in surface water. Some of the fluorescent dyes used are the most practical tracers because they are non-toxic to people and to the ecosystem and are capable to be analyzed quickly, economically, and quantitatively (Zhou et al. 1997). Table 9.5 gives an outline of types of tracers.

Fröhlich et al. (1987) studied the implications of isotopic tracers for ground-water dating.

The tracers have different "half-lives" that range from hours and days to several years

In karst areas, sinkhole cave streams, or surface streams, which sink into the subsurface are obvious points for dye introduction into the ground-water system. These locations are well suited to studies such as delineating recharge areas for springs. However, these sites may be inappropriate for characterizing water movement from a waste site several hundreds of feet away. Many surface streams recharge aquifers or springs. It is simple to introduce a tracer dye into a surface stream and then sample appropriate wells, springs, or other features for the dye. Many stream channels and road ditches flow only during and shortly after major storm events. These features can be used for dye introduction if the dye is flushed into the ground-water system with water introduced from a fire hydrant, tanker truck, or nearby pond (Aley 1999).

Table 9.5. Types of tracers (after ASTM D 5717-95)

Labels		
	Natural	Flora and fauna (chiefly but not exclusively microorganism)
		Ions in solution
		Environmental isotopes
		Temperature
		Specific conductance
	Introduced	Dyes and dye-intermediates
		Radiometrically detected substances
		Salts and other inorganic compounds
		Spores
		Fluorocarbons
		Glasses
		A wide variety of organic compounds
		Biological entities (bacteria, viruses, yeasts)
		Effluent and spilled substances
		Organic particles, microspheres
		Inorganic particles (including sediment)
		Temperature
		Specific conductance
		Exotica (ducks, marked fish, etc.)
Pulses significantly above background of base-flow levels		
	Natural	Discharge (charge in stage or flow)
		Temperature
		Turbidity
	Introduced	Discharge
		Temperature

Backhoe trenches can often be constructed adjacent to waste sites and used as a point to introduce dye. The rate at which water will leak from such trenches should be determined prior to any dye introduction, and the trench should not be used if infiltration rate is as small as 1.63 l min^{-1} m^{-2} of trench bottom. (Aley 1999).

Monitoring wells are often poor points for dye introduction, yet sometimes they are the only means of introducing dye. Many monitoring wells have their screened openings at lower elevations than the elevations most desirable for introducing tracer dyes.

Additionally, when wells or for that matter EDIPs (EDIP Programme "Environmental Design of Industrial Products", created by Professor Leo Alting, from "IPT/IPU" and a group of major enterprises in Denmark, and supported by the Danish EPA; Alting et al. 1996) are used for introduction of dye, some residual dye will remain in the well or boring for a long period of time. The use of a monitoring well for introduction of dye can reduce the utility of the well for monitoring purposes. Finally, EDIPs are usually much less expensive than monitoring wells, and the EDIPs can be abandoned and sealed with concurrence of the regulatory agency after the tracing work has been completed (Aley 1999).

Tracer methods have been widely used since the 1960s to determine ground-water flow direction, velocity, recharge, discharge, residence time in aquifers, and hydraulic connection between surface and subsurface water or between different flow systems of ground-water aquifers, etc. It is necessary to specify very precisely the geological-hydrological model used for the application of tracers, and to select the optimal tracers at the optimal site for input and output (Jordan and Weder 1995).

Five critical factors to successful ground-water tracing are summarized as follows (Aley 1999):

1. Selection of appropriate dyes and adequate quantities of dyes and water. (Never assume that a pound of one dye equals a pound of another.)
2. Selection of appropriate types of samples. In most cases primary sampling should rely on an activated-carbon sampler rather than on water samples. Activated-carbon samplers routinely maximize the detection of tracer dyes and minimize the number of samples, sampling efforts, and project costs.

3. Procedures, which insure that no dye is lost or destroyed in samples prior to analysis.
4. Instruments and methods that will quantify dye concentrations, distinguish among dyes, and adequately deal with fluctuations in background and interference.
5. Study designs that adequately address and credibly answer all probabilities.

Qualitative dye-tracing with fluorescent dyes is the most common method used because the dyes are readily available and can be easily detected at low concentrations. Detection of fluorescent tracers is carried out by ultra violet light/quonto-lamp (UV). Qualitative dye tracing with various fluorescent dyes and passive dye detectors, consisting of activated coconut charcoal or surgical cotton, can be used to identify point-to-point connections between ground-water recharge, (e.g. sinkholes, underground streams, and karst windows) and discharge (e.g. water-supply springs and wells). Results of qualitative tracing can be used to confirm the direction of ground-water flow inferred from water-level contour maps, and to help delineate the recharge area draining to a spring or well.

Quantitative dye tracing carried out by colorometry, requires automatic samplers, discharge measurements, and fluorometric analysis to quantify passage of the dye cloud. Repeated, quantitative dye-traces between the same recharge and discharge points under different flow conditions, help to estimate the arrival time, peak concentration, and persistence of a soluble conservative contaminant at a supply spring or well, on the basis of discharge and the quantity of spilled contaminant (Käss 1992).

9.5.4 Isotopic Tracers in Karst Aquifers

Isotopic tracers may be either natural or artificial isotopes. The environmental (natural) isotopes may be either radioactive or non radioactive (e.g. tritium (^3H), deuterium (D), oxygen (^{18}O), carbon (^{13}C, ^{14}C), silicon (^{32}Si)).

Isotopes of hydrogen in the water molecule (^2H, ^3H) and oxygen (^{18}O) are considered "ideal" isotopic tracers because their migration is almost identical with the movement of ground water in aquifers. Care of using high concentration of tritium should be taken to avoid aquifer contamination; too low a concentration may conceal its effect (Moser and Rauert 1980).

Carbon-14 is used to determine the non-radioactive loss by ion exchange (especially in limestone and karstic aquifers). β-spectrometry is used for unstable radioactive environmental isotopes (e.g. ^3H, ^{32}Si, ^{14}C, etc.), whereas mass spectrometry is used for stable isotopes (e.g. ^2H, ^{18}O, ^{13}C, etc.) and γ-spectrometry for radioactive artificial isotopic tracers (e.g. ^{131}J – the radioactive isotope of the element iodium of half life 8.1 days; this means a short half life for short "travel"/"residence"/"transit" times of ground water in the aquifer). The mean residence time of water in the aquifer should be given precisely by using radioactive environmental isotopes. An example was given by Yurtsever (1979), who presented the application of environmental isotopes in karstic aquifers according to the following equation:

$$C_0(t) = \int_0^{\infty} C_i(t - \Gamma) f(\Gamma) e^{-\lambda t} \delta t$$

where $(t - \Gamma)$ is the mean residence time/transit time; $f(\Gamma)$ is the transit time distribution function of water in the aquifer system. C_o is the concentration of the radionuclide in the output (tracer output concentration); C_i is the concentration of the radionuclide in the input (tracer input concentration); $e^{-\lambda t}$ is the radioactive decay correction factor, and λ is the decay constant. The transmit time distribution function of a tracer may be described in the following equation:

$$f(\Gamma) = 1/\Gamma_{tov}\, e^{1/T_{tov}}$$

where T_{tov} is the turnover time of the aquifer system. N.b.:

- "Γ" involves the radioactive decay;
- The expression "travel"/"residence"/"transit" indicates the time between input and output passing the aquifer.

In karstic aquifers, the following equation may be also given:

$$T_{tov} = \frac{V}{Q} = \frac{\text{Volume of water in the system}}{\text{Discharge rate}}$$

The tritium output concentration from a given tritium input concentration can be computed by using the above equation for assumed values of the parameter T_{tov}. The resulting curves give an estimate of the turnover time of the ground water particularly in karstic aquifer system (e.g. 15 or 25 years). Accordingly, the volume of water in the whole karst aquifer system can be calculated (Jordan and Weder 1995).

In most of the tracer experiments, one can use wells for input and output or for intake and sampling respectively. Under special conditions, a single well can be used for applying a combined injection and detection of a γ-radiating tracer in situ. The flow direction and the water/tracer velocity (the velocity of the tracer plume, which moves away from the injection point) may be estimated by turning the injection detection unit (Fig. 9.8). If the hydraulic gradient is known (using piezometers), the filtration coefficient (K_f) can be calculated by Darcy's law:

$$V_f = K_f i \ (\text{m s}^{-1})$$

$$K_f = V_f / i$$

where V_f is the filtration velocity; K_f is the filtration coefficient; and i is the hydraulic gradient ($\Delta h/\Delta l$).

9.5.5 Quantitative Analysis of Tracer Tests

A tracer test is a valuable tool in hydrogeological investigations in loose and fractured rock or karst terrains as well. Tracer tests can become a very handy tool in a site investigation, however it is extremely important for the hydrogeology of a site or area to be accurately described, because a thorough understanding of stratigraphy and structural geology is the basis for interpretation of a tracer study. The results provide information on the aquifer characteristics between the tracer injection point and the tracer recovery point.

Depending on the type of test and the scale of investigation, the test data reflect the properties of either conduit system, or fracture system, or both. For example, if the input location is in a sinkhole, the transport characteristics of conduits are most likely examined (neglecting the effect of the transport through the unsaturated zone). With a forced-gradient tracer test between two boreholes, test data more likely represent the fracture

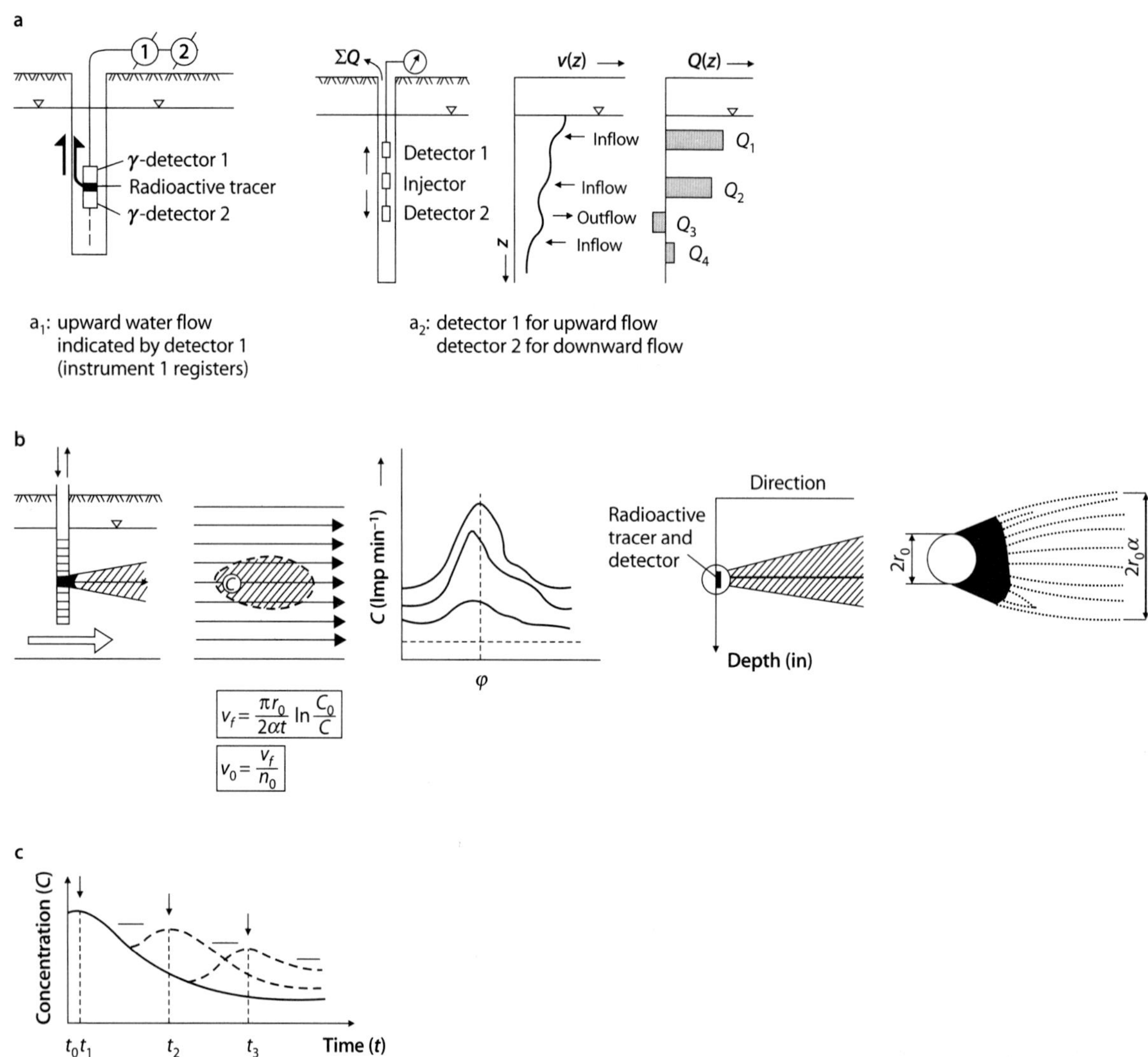
a
γ-detector 1
Radioactive tracer
γ-detector 2
ΣQ
Detector 1
Injector
Detector 2
v(z)
Q(z)
Inflow
Inflow
Outflow
Inflow
z
Q_1
Q_2
Q_3
Q_4
a_1: upward water flow indicated by detector 1 (instrument 1 registers)
a_2: detector 1 for upward flow detector 2 for downward flow
b
C (Imp min⁻¹)
φ
$V_f = \frac{\pi r_0}{2\alpha t} \ln \frac{C_0}{C}$
$V_0 = \frac{V_f}{n_0}$
Direction
Radioactive tracer and detector
Depth (in)
$2r_0$
$2r_0\alpha$
c
Concentration (C)
$t_0 t_1$
t_2
t_3
Time (t)

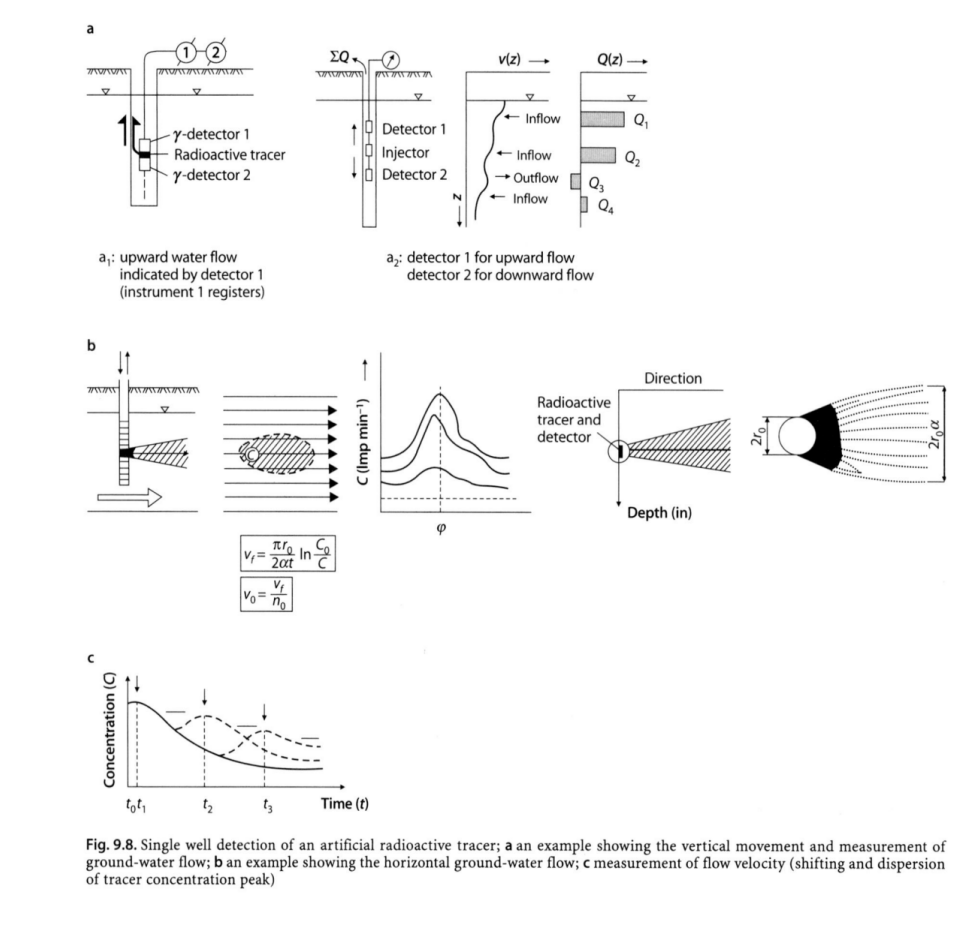

Fig. 9.8. Single well detection of an artificial radioactive tracer; **a** an example showing the vertical movement and measurement of ground-water flow; **b** an example showing the horizontal ground-water flow; **c** measurement of flow velocity (shifting and dispersion of tracer concentration peak)

system if the boreholes encounter fractures. Tracer tests, with the input in boreholes and the recovery measured at a spring, may be influenced by system fractures and conduit systems.

Parameters determined from a tracer test can be used to characterize the aquifer on the scale of the experiment. Analysis of the breakthrough curve will not be able to overcome problems related to poor design of tracer tests nor of inadequate implementation of procedures during the tests (refer to Mull et al. 1988 for procedures and techniques).

9.5.5.1 *Tracer-Breakthrough Curves*

Quantitative interpretation of tracer-breakthrough curves provides parameters controlling the tracer transport and flow conditions in the aquifer. The intended quantitative analysis must be taken into account in planning the tracer test. An adequate quantitative interpretation of tracing tests depends on the following factors:

1. Conservative behavior of the tracer;
2. Thorough inventory of sampling locations;
3. Adequate quantity of tracer injected;
4. Appropriate injection technique;
5. Sufficient monitoring frequency at sampling locations;
6. Precise discharge measurements at sampling locations; and
7. Sufficient length of time for monitoring.

These factors may be achieved through good design, implementation, and persistence. Various problems, which tend to arise when the above factors are not considered in the design of a tracer study, may include no tracer recovery, incomplete tracer recovery, or aliasing of the tracer breakthrough curve. These problems may lead to some fundamental questions regarding the tracer study. If none or only some of the injected tracer mass was recovered, what caused incomplete recovery? What was the mean residence time for the tracer in the aquifer? What were the mean and apparent tracer velocities assuming advection only? How significant was longitudinal dispersion in the aquifer? To what extent do the sorption characteristics of the tracer affect the recovery? Is adequate amount of tracer injected?

In terms of contaminant transport, answers to these questions are essential. Some of the questions can only be answered by making best professional interpretations of the tracer-breakthrough curve. Others may be answered by careful numerical analysis of the breakthrough curve. For example, in instance of insufficient sampling frequency or cessation of sampling prior to total mass recovery, good interpolation/extrapolation algorithms may be used to fill gaps in the data. However, problems aliasing may not be addressed by such efforts while extrapolation of data beyond real sampling times may not provide realistic values.

A typical tracer-breakthrough curve is shown in Fig. 9.9. Transport parameters pertinent to analysis of the breakthrough curve at a sampling point are:

- T_L: elapsed time to the arrival of the leading edge of the tracer-breakthrough curve;
- T_p: elapsed time to the peak concentration C_p of the tracer-breakthrough curve;
- T_c: elapsed time to the centroid of the tracer-breakthrough curve;
- T_t: elapsed time to the tailing edge of the curve.

The dispersion and mixing of the tracer in the receiving water takes place in all three dimensions of the medium. If a complete mixing at each sampling point is assumed, then the mean travel time of the tracer is the difference in elapsed time of the centroids of the tracer breakthrough curves defined upstream and downstream:

$$t_c = T_{c(n+1)} - T_{cn}$$

where n is the sampling location. Similarly, the travel times of the leading edge, peak concentration, and tailing edge are, respectively:

$$t_L = T_{L(n+1)} - T_{Ln}$$

$$t_p = T_{p(n+1)} - T_{pn}$$

$$t_t = T_{t(n+1)} - T_{tn}$$

9.5.5.2 *Estimation of Hydraulic Parameters of Karst Conduits*

Hydraulic parameters for karst conduits and fractures can be estimated by the method of moments. Moment analysis is accomplished by determining the area under the tracer-breakthrough curve, weighed by the discharge hydrograph.

Assume that the spring discharge (Q_i) and tracer concentrations (C_i) are measured at time t_i and the time interval is Δt_i, the mass of tracer recovered over the period of $\Delta t_i(Q_i C_i \Delta t_i)$ is plotted against time t_i. The zeroth order moment of the recovered mass μ_0 is computed by:

$$\mu_0 = \sum_{i=1}^{n} Q_i(C_i - C_0)\Delta t_i \qquad (9.1)$$

where n is the number of sampling interval which is equal to the total number of samples minus 1; C_0 is the

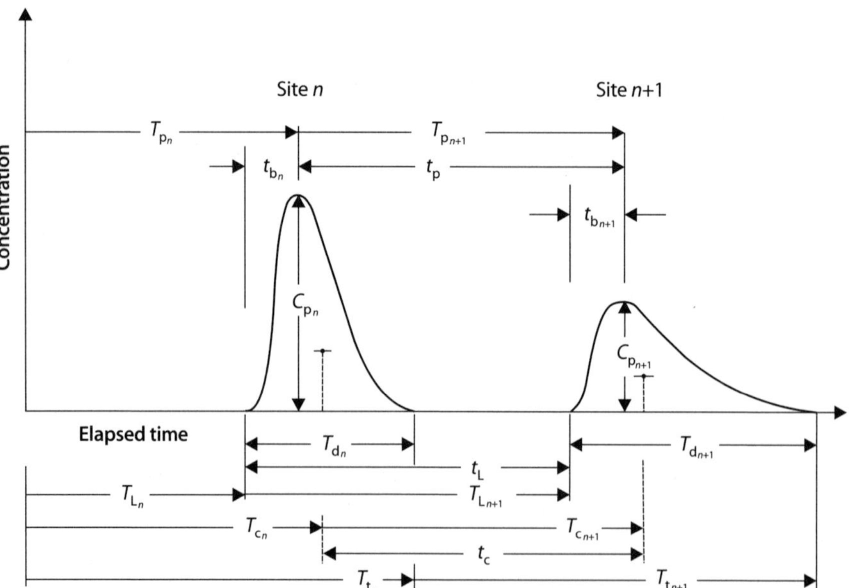

Concentration
Site n
Site n+1
Elapsed time

Fig. 9.9. Tracer breakthrough of curves along a tracer streamline from an instantaneous tracer injection (Kilpatrick and Wilson 1989)

background tracer concentration, measured at the time of injection. The zeroth order moment is equal to the total recovered mass of tracer.

The first moment (μ_1) is the centroid of the area under the recovered mass-time curve, which is expressed by:

$$\mu_1 = \sum_{i=1}^{n} t_i Q_i (C_i - C_0) \Delta t_i \tag{9.2}$$

Then, the $\bar{t}/t$ mean residence time of the tracer traveling to the sampling point, is the ratio of μ_1 and μ_0, i.e. $t = \mu_1 / \mu_0$.

The second moment (μ_2) represents the spreading or mixing in the recovered mass, which is:

$$\mu_2 = \sum_{i=1}^{n} (t_i - \bar{t})^2 Q_i (C_i - C_0) \Delta t_i \tag{9.3}$$

The standard deviation (σ) is calculated by $(\mu_2/\mu_0)^{1/2}$.

The mean travel time is the length of time required for the centroid of the tracer mass to traverse the entire length of the aquifer system. It can be used to calculate the mean velocity of ground-water flow (v) by $x/\bar{t}$, where x is the measured straight-line distance between the input and sampling point. A straight-line assumption for karst conduit is unrealistic because of its sinuosity. A correction factor of 1.5 is recommended and a parameter 'x' placed by 'x_s' where $x_s = 1.5x$ (Zhou et al. 1997).

The mean residence time allows for a rough estimation of the volume of water in the conduit or fracture (*Vol*) traversed by the tracer cloud (Atkinson 1977):

$$Vol = \sum_{i=1}^{m} Q_i \Delta t_i \tag{9.4}$$

where m is the number of monitoring intervals for spring discharge until the mean residence time.

With the knowledge of the volume and length of the conduit system, the cross-sectional area (Area) can be estimated by:

$$\text{Area} = \frac{Vol}{x_s} \tag{9.5}$$

By assuming a cylindrical karst conduit, its diameter is estimated by:

$$\text{Diameter} = 2\sqrt{\frac{\text{Area}}{\pi}} \tag{9.6}$$

9.5.6 Evaluation of Dynamic Dispersion in Karst Aquifers

Similar to hydraulic conductivity, the dispersion coefficient is another scale-dependent parameter. A dispersion means spread, which is the integrated result of mechanical dispersion and molecular diffusion. The dispersion coefficient is a measure of the rate at which concentrated solutes spread out along their flow path, and can be calculated from the standard deviation of the tracer-breakthrough curve. With the assumption of uniform flow and constant velocity for the entire duration of the tracer test, An equation was presented in 1968 (Day 1975) to calculate the dispersion coefficient (D_{tracer}) in open channels:

$$D_{\text{tracer}} = \frac{\bar{u}^2 \sigma^2}{2\bar{t}} \qquad (9.7)$$

An alternative method was applied in 1971 (Day 1975) to "open-channel flow" and "closed-conduit flow" as well. The dispersion coefficient is given by:

$$\left[t \ln\left(\frac{A_{\text{p}}}{Ct^{0.5}} \right) \right]^{0.5} = \frac{x_s}{2(D_{\text{tracer}})^{0.5}} - \frac{\bar{u}t}{2(D_{\text{tracer}})^{0.5}} \qquad (9.8)$$

The constant of proportionality A_{p} can be estimated from Day (1975):

$$A_{\text{p}} = C_{\text{p}}\sqrt{t_{\text{p}}}$$

The first term on the right-hand side of Eq. 9.8 is the *y* intercept, while the second term on the right-hand side is the gradient of the line. Either term on the right-hand side allows for solution for dispersion coefficient when a plot of the left-hand side against early-time data reasonably falls as a straight line (Day 1975).

More complicated multi-dispersion model (MDM) has also been used to evaluate tracer-breakthrough curves for large-scale tracer tests where convection and dispersion processes dominate (Käss 1998). MDM is an extension of a one-dimensional convection-dispersion model. As shown in Fig. 9.10, the resulting breakthrough curve is a composite outcome of different flow paths. The concentration contributed by an individual flow path is calculated by:

$$C_i(t) = \frac{M_i}{Q_i} \frac{1}{t_{0_i}\sqrt{4\pi P_{D_i}\left(\frac{t}{t_{0_i}}\right)^3}} \exp\left[-\frac{\left(1 - \frac{t}{t_{0i}}\right)^2}{4P_{D_i}\left(\frac{t}{t_{0_i}}\right)} \right] \qquad (9.9)$$

where

C_i = tracer concentration
M = tracer mass
Q = discharge
t_0 = mean residence time
P_D = dispersion parameter ($P_D = D / \bar{u}x = \alpha / x$)
D = dispersion
v = mean velocity
α = dispersivity
i = index of the flow path

The measured concentration is the superposition of all the individual paths, i.e.:

$$C(t) = \sum_{i=1}^{N} C_i(t) \qquad (9.10)$$

9.6 Waste Management, Rules and Regulations

9.6.1 Discussion

As population increases, the burden of disposing society's wastes increases. The land, the atmosphere, and the oceans present the only possible sites to receive these wastes, and therefore a number of current U.S. laws impose constraints on these disposals.

The land option for disposal is leads to a lot of argument because of the physical and chemical complexity of the medium, the wide range of regional differences, and the long history of multiple land use in many regions that has reduced availability of land for disposal of wastes. Land is often in short supply, fills a wide variety of needs, and serves as a source of diminishing mineral and useable ground-water resources.

The assessment and reassessment of environmental impacts for a marine discharge occurs during both the planning and the operation stages. The overall effects of waste discharge in the ocean could be determined by studying the various physical, chemical, and biological processes, which should be classified through a range of space and time scales.

Kildow (1984) emphasized that the necessity of managing waste materials by recycling, treatment, storage or dispersal, often produced clashes among conflicting interests. The toxic chemicals and pathogens in many wastes are of major concern in waste management although they constitute only a small part of the waste. For many types of wastes it is not feasible to destroy all pathogens or to separate toxic chemicals for disposal elsewhere. However, the amount of toxic chemicals in wastes can often be reduced by waste-specific types of treatment.

The following chemicals were banned from production and use because of scientific evidence or public suspicion of harm to the environment and public health:

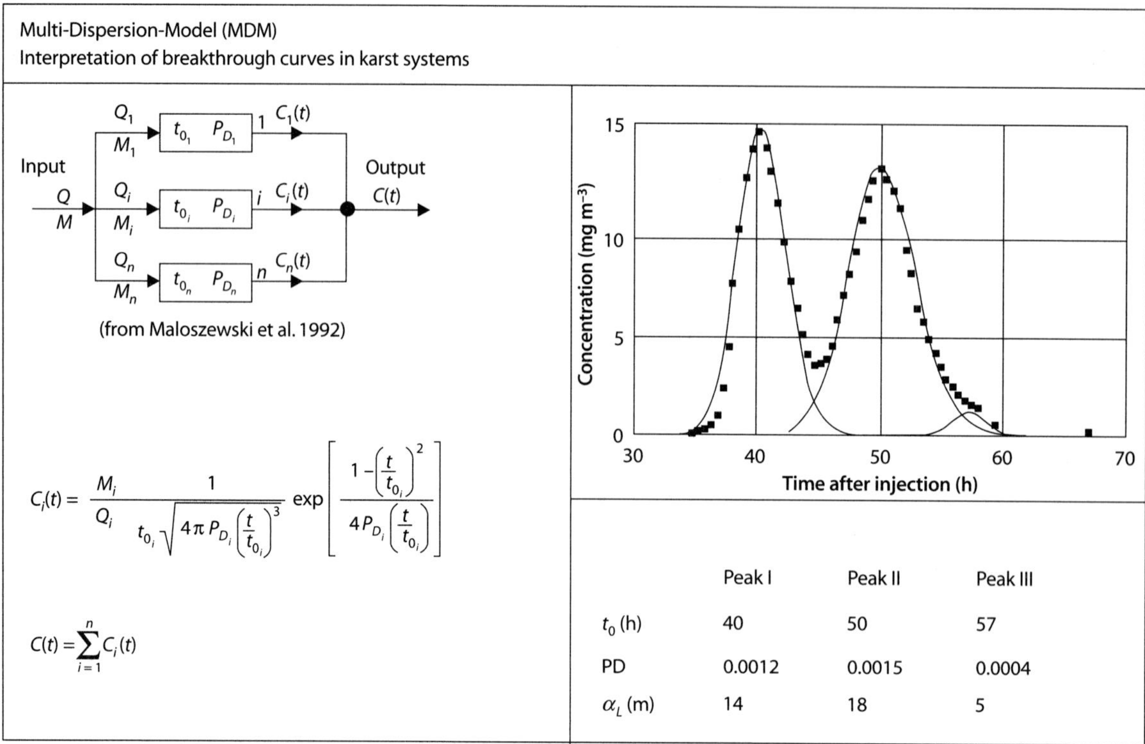
Multi-Dispersion-Model (MDM)
Interpretation of breakthrough curves in karst systems
Input
Output
(from Maloszewski et al. 1992)
Concentration (mg m⁻³)
Time after injection (h)
Peak I
Peak II
Peak III
t_0 (h) 40 50 57
PD 0.0012 0.0015 0.0004
α_L (m) 14 18 5

Fig. 9.10. Components of MDM

1. DDT because of the perceived effects on non-target organisms,
2. PCBs because of the potential effects on public health,
3. Fluorocarbons because of the potential for degradation of ozone in the atmosphere

The American Chemical Society (1990) discussed concerns for safe disposal of chemical wastes and U.S. EPA defined legal and regulatory requirements in the USA for handling the hazardous wastes in a responsible way. A list of a waste management system is shown in Table 9.6.

The Resource Conservation and Recovery Act (RCRA) of 1976 was the first national law to address hazardous waste disposal issue. RCRA was directed primarily at industrial generators of hazardous waste, but the Environmental Protection Agency (U.S. Environmental Protection Agency 1986), which implements the law, was required by the U.S. Congress to regulate all generators, including laboratories.

9.6.2 Identification of Wastes and Determination of Hazards

The U.S. Environmental Protection Agency (1986) considered the following two questions when dealing with hazardous waste management system:

1. Is this material a waste?
2. Is this waste a "hazardous waste"?

Data current as of the Federal Register dated February 15, 2002 retrieved by the electronic code of regulations (e-CFR), discussed in detail the following solid waste characteristics: ignitability (40 CFR-section 261.21); corrosivity (40 CFR-section 261.22); reactivity (40 CFR-section 261.23); and toxicity (40 CFR-section 261.24). Table 9.7 contains the U.S. EPA definitions of hazardous wastes, presented by the American Chemical Society (1990) and modified according to 40 CFR-section 26121-24 (2002) as follows:

- The hazardous waste management regulations apply to materials only when they become wastes and only if they are deemed hazardous under specific evaluation criteria. The waste regulations apply to anything that could (in the absence of legal prohibitions) be discarded in the trash, as a liquid, semi-solid, compressed gas, or solid. Such discarded wastes must be evaluated to determine if they are hazardous wastes or otherwise regulated.
- Wastes that are hazardous because they appear on one of the four hazardous waste lists, "listed hazardous wastes", are namely wastes from non-specific sources (F-list), wastes from specific sources (K-list), certain discarded commercial products (U-list), and

Table 9.6. List of a waste management systems

The laboratory professional	The waste manager	The waste handling operator
Planning	Oversight	DOT regulations
Alternatives	Training	RCRA permitted facilities
Minimization	Audit	Transportation
Experiment	Interpretation of regulations	Disposal
Waste handling	Collection	
Labeling	Storage	
Segregation	Packaging	
Accumulation	Manifest	

"acutely hazardous" discarded commercial products (P-list). The F- and K-lists are for general process wastes, the U- and P-lists are for reagent chemicals. The P-list wastes, such as cyanide, are more rigorously regulated than the U-list wastes.

- If a waste is not on the lists of hazardous wastes developed by EPA, generators are required to determine if the waste processes one or more of the four hazardous characteristics – ignitability, corrosivity, reactivity, and toxicity. Such wastes are called characteristic hazardous wastes.
- All states have laws governing the transportation and disposal of discarded materials called "special wastes" or "liquid industrial wastes". Several states regulate the disposal of waste oils, such as vacuum pump oils. For example, "used oil" is not a hazardous waste in most states if it is recycled or burned for energy recovery. Wastes regulated by states are required to be manifested and transported by a licensed transporter.

9.6.3 EPA Rules and Regulations

The following rules and regulations are presented by EPA (RCRA and OSWER, U.S. Environmental Protection Agency 1986):

- Most state regulations are nearly identical to the Federal regulations concerning accumulation and storage periods for wastes and accumulated waste management; the major difference being satellite storage. Some states do not recognize the concept of satellite accumulation points. In these states, all wastes must be accumulated in a central area that is subject to all accumulation regulations.
- Hazardous waste containers in a satellite accumulation area must be labeled with the words "hazardous wastes" or other identifying words. The accumulation start date must be marked on each container when it enters the central accumulation area. Before transporting wastes, the containers must be marked with a mandatory hazardous-waste declaration, the generator's name and address, and the shipping manifest document number. Containers also must be marked and labeled according to regulations with the Department of Transportation (DOT) proper shipping name, the UN/NA identification number, and the hazard class label, as well as other marking and labeling requirements.

  Improper or incomplete labeling and marking can lead to regulatory compliance citations from environmental and transportation agencies. It can cause wastes to be rejected by operators of disposal sites, thus significantly increasing the already high costs of transportation and disposal. If improper labeling results in improper disposal, organizations can be held liable for costs of remediation.
- State and Federal waste management laws generally forbid the treatment of significant quantities of hazardous wastes unless the treatment facility has obtained a permit. The Federal regulations, however, do allow some treatment of hazardous wastes without a permit under very controlled circumstances. Wastes that are hazardous only on the basis of their corrosive characteristics may be neutralized by the addition of bases or acids, as appropriate, producing a waste that is no longer hazardous.
- Record keeping is a vital part of the waste-management process because it records all that anyone ever needs to know about the program. Considerable care needs to be taken in compiling and maintaining these records. EPA requires that all hazardous-waste records be kept for three years, but copies of all manifests and other documentation available should be retained for an indefinite time.

9.6.4 Federal Laws in the USA and Regulatory Standards

The most important Federal laws in the USA that protect ground water include:

- Clean Water Act
- Safe Drinking Water Act
- Clean Air Act
- Comprehensive Environmental Response, Compensation, and Liability Act
- Federal Insecticide, Fungicide, and Rodenticide Act
- Toxic Substances Control Act
- Coastal Zone Management Act
- Forest Land Management Planning Act
- Ocean Dumping Ban Act
- Shore Protection Act
- Oil Pollution Act

Table 9.7. U.S. EPA definitions of hazard solid waste characteristics (after the American Chemical Society 1990, updated by Assaad after e-CFR on Feb, 15th 2002)

Characteristic hazardous wastes are defined in 40 CFR Sections 261.21–261.24. Specific tests can be used to determine if a waste possesses any of the following characteristics:	
Ignitability	A solid waste exhibits the characteristic of ignitability if the waste exists in any of the following forms: – a liquid, other than an aqueous solution containing less than 24% alcohol by volume, with a flash point below 60 °C (140 °F); – a non-liquid, which under standard conditions is capable of causing fire through friction, absorption of moisture, or spontaneous chemical changes and, when ignited, burns in a manner that creates a hazard; – an ignitable compressed gas (refer to 49 CFR Section 173.300), which includes gases that form flammable mixtures at a concentration of 13% or less in air; or – an oxidizer such as a permanganate, inorganic peroxide, or nitrate, that readily stimulates combustion of organic materials (refer to 49 CFR Section 173.151 for definition).
Reactivity	A solid waste exhibits the characteristics of reactivity if the waste – is normally unstable and readily undergoes violent change without detonation; – reacts violently with water; – forms potentially explosive mixtures with water; – generates, when mixed with water, toxic gases, vapors, or fumes in a quantity sufficient to present danger; – is a cyanide- or sulfide-bearing waste that generates toxic gases, vapors, or fumes at a pH between 2 an 12.5; – is capable of detonation or explosive reaction when subject to a strong initiating source or if heated in confinement; – is readily capable of detonation, explosive decomposition, or reaction at standard temperature and pressure; or – is an explosive, as defined in 49 CFR Sections 173.51, 173.53, 173.88.
Corrosivity	A solid waste exhibits the characteristic of corrosivity if the waste: – is aqueous and has a pH less than or equal to 2, or greater than or equal to 12.5 using EPA specified or approved test methods; or – is a liquid and corrodes steel (SAE 1020) at a rate greater than 6.35 mm (0.250 inch) per year at a test temperature of 55 °C (130 °F) (EPA SW-846); – has the EPA hazards waste number of D002.
Toxicity	A solid waste exhibits the characteristic of toxicity when EPA-defined test procedures indicate that an extract derived from the waste contains certain toxicants. Effective September 5, 1990, EPA will require toxicity to be tested using the toxicity characteristic leaching procedure (TCLP), which simulates the leaching of materials in a landfill into the surrounding ground water. The toxicants to be tested are: Arsenic, Barium, Benzene, Cadmium, Carbon tetrachloride, Chlordane, Chlorobenzene, Chloroform, Chromium, o-, m-, and p-Cresol, 2,4-D, 1,4-Dichlorobenzene, 1,2-Dichloroethylene, 1,1-Dichloroethylene, 2,4-Dinitrotoluene, Endrin, Heptachlor (and its hydroxide), Hexachlorobenzene, Hexachlorobutadien, Hexachloroethane, Lead, Lindane, Mercury, Methoxychlor, Methyl ethyl ketons, Nitrobenzene, Pentachlorophenol, Pyridine, Selenium, Silver, Tetrachloroethylene, Toxaphene, Trichlorethylene, 2,4,5- and 2,4,6-Trichlorphenol, 2,4,5-TP (Silvex), Vinyl chloride This list will be expanded in the future as additional testing is completed by EPA.

9.6.5 An Editorial Issue on USA Regulations

Freeze and Cherry (1989) discussed the legalization and regulation of ground-water contamination and corrective measures. The legislation (especially the Federal CERCLA and RCRA Acts) has resulted in an increased awareness of ground-water contamination issues in the USA as well as in other industrial and development countries and greatly increased expenditures on site investigation, ground-water monitoring, and remediation. Most of the legislation in the USA, designed to protect ground-water quality, failed to present regulations as a comprehensive, logical, practical, politically acceptable, cost-efficient, simple to administer, and fair criteria.

Most of the legislation was designed to combat pollution from managed point sources such as municipal landfills and industrial waste-management facilities, although the greatest threat to ground-water quality may result from non-point sources associated with agricultural fertilizers, herbicides, and pesticides; and from unmanaged point sources such as machine manufacturing and repair shops, dry-cleaning shops, photo-processing plants, electronics plants, etc.

The following criticism may be stated as exceptions in application of regulations: the administration of regulations is often rigid although there is a need for site-specific interpretation when a variance from the letter of the law, but not the spirit, might well be in order; e.g. rules given for saturated systems at a site with a very thick unsaturated zone, or rules intended for aqueous contamination migrating from a surface source being applied where contaminants are actually migrating from a dense, non aqueous-phase liquids (DNAPL) pool situated deep in the ground-water system.

Recommendations:

1. It is recommended that technical personnel should recognize that the attorneys operate in a different world from scientists and engineers because the attorneys represent their clients' interests.
2. It might be useful for environmental legislation to allow a negotiation approach rather than a standardized method of approach.
3. Regulatory agencies must be willing to defend technically sound siting decisions against political pressures. On the other hand, the political system must begin to examine what types of benefits can be offered to communities to offset the social costs of hosting waste-management facilities.

References

Aley T (1999) Groundwater tracing handbook – a handbook prepared for the use of clients and colleges of the Ozark Underground Laboratory. Protem, Missouri

Aller L, Bennett TW, Hackett G, Petty RJ, Sedoris H, Nielsen DM, Denne JE (1989) EPA 600/4-89/034 – handbook of suggested practices for the design and installation of groundwater monitoring wells. Environmental Monitoring Systems Laboratory, Las Vegas, Nevada, National Water Well Association, Dublin, Ohio 43017, 2:33–43

Alting L, Jorgensen J, Wenzel H (1996) The environmental dimension of the product. An introduction to the company management. Danish Environmental Production Agency and Confederation of Danish Industries, Copenhagen

American Chemical Society (1990) The Task Force on RCRA. Department of Government Relations and Science Policy (Waste management manual for laboratory personnel, pp 1–13)

American Geological Institute (AGI) (2002) Waters. Environ. Awareness Series, pp 8–10, in print

Assaad FA, Jordan H (1994) Karst terranes and environmental aspects. Environmental Geology 23:228–237

ASTM (1994) ASTM designation: D5521-94, standard guide for development of groundwater monitoring wells in granular aquifers, pp 348–362

ASTM (1995a) ASTM designation: D5092-90, standard practice for design and installation of groundwater monitoring wells in aquifers, pp 74–87

ASTM (1995b) ASTM designation: D 5717-95, standard guide for design of groundwater monitoring systems in karst and fractured-rock aquifers, pp 1–17

Atkinson TC (1977) Diffuse flow and conduit flow in limestone terrain in the Mendip Hills, Somerset (Britain). J Hydrol 35:93 (reprinted by permission of Elsevier)

Bear J (1993) Modeling flow and contaminant transport in fractured rocks. In: Bear J, Tsang CF, Marsily G (eds) Flow and contaminant transport in fractured rock. Academic Press Inc., California, pp 1–38 (adapted by permission of Academic Press)

Bogli A (1980) Karst hydrogeology and physical speleology. Springer-Verag, Berlin Heidelberg New York

Cholnoky J (1940) A mesztufa vagy travertino Kepzodestrol (On the formation of calcareous tufa or tavertine). Matematikai es Termeszettudomanyi Ertesito, Budapest, no. 3

Crutzen PJ (1971) Ozone production rates in an oxygen, hydrogen, nitrogen-oxide atmosphere. J Geophys Res 76:311–327 (adapted by permission of Journal of Geophysical Research, AGU)

Day TJ (1975) Longitudinal dispersion in natural channels. Water Resour Res 11(6):909–918 (reprinted by permission of the American Geophysical Union)

Diaz SB, Morrow JH, Booth CR (2000) UV physics and optics. In: de Mora S, Demers S, Vernet M (eds) Remote sensing for site characterization: the effects of UV radiation in the marine environment. Cambridge University Press, Cambridge, pp 45–71 (reprinted by permission of Cambridge University Press)

Emili H (1969) Possibility of transport of intestinal pathogenic germs by subterranean karst rivers. Yugoslavian Academy Press, Zagreb, Yugoslavia, Krs-Jugoslavije, Carsus Jugoslavije, pp 465–467

Freeze RA, Cherry JA (1989) What has gone wrong? Ground water. In: Rowland FS (ed) Stratospheric ozone depletion by chlorofluorocarbons. Ambio 19(6–7):281–292 (ewag@ambio.kva.se), adapted by permission of Pearson Education Inc., Upper Saddle River, NJ

Fröhlich K, Franke T, Gellermann DH, Jordan H (1987) Silicon-32 in different aquifer types and implications for groundwater dating. Proc. of an international symposium of the use of isotope techniques in water resources development. Organized by the international Atomic Energy Agency in cooperation with the United Nations Educational, Scientific and Cultural Organization, Vienna

Heath RC (1984) Groundwater regions of the United States. USGS, U.S. Government Printing Office, Washington, D.C. (Geological Survey Water-Supply Paper 2242)

Hoffman JI (1984) Geochemistry of acid mine drainage on the aquifers of southeastern Wisconsin and regulatory implications. Proc. of the Natural Water Association Conference on the Impact of Mining on Groundwater, August 24–27, Denver, Colorado. National Water Well Association, Dublin, Ohio, pp 146–161 (www.ngwa.org and wellowner.org)

Jakucs L (1977) Morphogenetics of karst regions – variants of karst evolution. John Wiley & Sons, New York, pp 26–53

Jordan H, Weder HJ (1995) Hydrogeologie, 2nd edn. Leipzig, Stuttgart

Käss HW (1992) Geohydrologische Markierungstechnik. Gebrüder Borntraeger, Berlin Stuttgart

Käss W (1998) Tracing technique in geohydrology. A. A. Balkema, Brookfield

Kildow JT (1984) Report of the panel on sludge management and public policy. In: Auerbach SI (ed) Disposal of industrial and domestic wastes, land and sea alternatives. National Academy Press, Washington D.C., pp 1, 10–73

Kilpatrick FA, Wilson JF Jr (1989) Measurements of time of traces in streams by dye-tracing techniques of water resources of the United States Geological Survey. (book 3, chap A9)

Kovski JR (1989) Physical transport process for hydrocarbons in the subsurface. Proc. of the Second International NWWA Conference on Groundwater Quality Research. Oklahoma State University Printing Services, Stillwater, Oklahoma, pp 127–128

Kramer JR, Anden AW, Smith RA, Johnson AH, Alexander RB, Ochlent G (1986) Streams and lakes. In: Committee on Monitoring Assessments of Trends in Acid Deposition (ed) Long-term trends. National Academy Press, Washington, pp 231–249

Kuehn F, Hoerig B (2000) The use of remote sensing in waste disposal site investigation. In: Kuehn TK, Hoerig B (eds) Remote sensing for site characterization – methods in environmental geology. Springer-Verlag, Berlin, pp 33–43

Macdonald AJ, Kavanaugh MC (1994) Study of groundwater cleanup alternatives – restoring contaminated groundwater: an achievable goal? Environ Sci Technol 28(8):362A–368A

Mandel S (1965) A conceptual model of karstic erosion by groundwater. Proc. of the Dubrovnik Symposium, Yugoslavia. In: Hydrology of fractured rocks, AIHS-UNESCO, II:662–664

Milanović PT (2000) Geological engineering in karst – dams, reservoirs, grouting, ground-water protection, water tapping, tunneling. Zebra Publishing Ltd., pp265–267

Moser H, Rauert W (1980) Isotopenmethoden in der Hydrologie. Institut fur Radiohydrometrie der Gesellschaft für Strahlen- und Umweltforschung, Neuherberg bei München, Gebrüder Borntraeger, Berlin Stuttgart (http://www.schweizerbart.de)

Mull DS, Liebermann TD, Smoot JL, Woosley LII Jr (1988) Application of dye-tracing techniques for determining solute-transport characteristics of groundwater in karst terranes. U.S. Environmental Protection Agency

Otton K, Gundersen CS, Schumann RR (1993) The geology of radon. USGS (http://energy.cr.usgs.gov/radon/georadon.html)

Petrik M (1969) Protection of water in the karst against pollution. Yugoslavian Academy Press, Zagreb, Yugoslavia (KRS-Jugoslavije, Carsus, Jugoslavije, pp 560–561)

Rowland FS (1990) Stratospheric ozone depletion by chloroflurocarbons. Ambio 19:281–292 (ewag@ambio.kva.se)

Soliman MM, LaMoreaux PE, Memon B, Assaad FA, LaMoreaux JW (1998) Kinds of waste and physiography of waste disposal sites. In: Environmental hydrogeology. Lewis Publishers, CRC Press LLC (chap 5, pp 103–135)

U.S. Environmental Protection Agency (EPA) (1986) RCRA Ground water monitoring technical enforcement guidance document. Office of Waste Programs Enforcement, Office of Solid Waste and Emergency Response, OSWER-9950.1

U.S. Environmental Protection Agency (EPA) (1989) Handbook of suggested practices for the design and installation of ground-water monitoring wells (600/4-89/034, 1989)

U.S. Environmental Protection Agency (EPA) (2000) Mineral constituents and standards of drinking water

USGS (2002) Acid mine drainage treatment, techniques and costs. USGS Office of Surface Mining, Washington, DC (E-mail: getinfo@osmre.gov)

Van Waegeningh HG (1985) Protection of the ground water quality in porous permeable rocks. In: Matthess G, Foster SD, Skinner AC (eds) Theoretical background of hydrogeology and practice of groundwater protection zones. Heise, Hannover (International contributions to hydrogeology, vol. 6, pp 111–113)

Villaume JF (1985) Investigations at sites contaminated with dense, non-aqueous phase liquids (DNAPLs). Ground Water Monit Rev 5(2):60–74

World Mineralogical Organization (WMO) (1999) Scientific assessment of ozone depletion. United Nations Environmental Program. In: de Mora S, Demers S, Vernet M (eds) Remote sensing for site characterization, the effects of UV radiation in the marine environment. Cambridge University Press, Cambridge, pp 45–71 (reproduced with the permission of Cambridge University)

Yaniga PM, Warburton (1984) Discrimination between real and apparent accumulation of immiscible hydrocarbons on the table: a theoretical and empirical analysis. Proc. of the Fourth National Symposium on Aquifer Restoration and Groundwater Monitoring. National Water Well Association, Dublin, Ohio, pp 311–315 (www.ngwa.org and www.wellowner.org)

Yurtsever Y (1979) Environmental isotopes as a test in hydrogeological investigations of southern regions of Turkey. In: Gunay G (ed) International seminar on karst hydrology. University of Hacettepe, Ankara, pp 269–287

Zhou W, Wheater HS, Johnston PM (1997) State of the art of modeling two-phase flow in fractured rock. Environ Geol 31(3/4):157–166

Selected References

Choubey VM, Ramola RC (1997) Correlation between geology and radon levels in groundwater, soil and indoor air in Hilangana Valley, Garhwal Himalaya, India. Environ Geol 32(4):258

Drew D, Hötzl H (eds) (1999) Karst hydrogeoloy and human activities – impacts, consequences and implications. International Association of Hydrogeologists, A.A. Balkema, Rotterdam, Brookfield, pp 3–5

EPA/600/R-02/003, (Feb. 2002) A lexicon of cave and karst terminology with special reference to environmental karst hydrology. U.S. Environmental Agency, Washington, D.C. (Supercedes EPA/600/R-99/006, 1/'99)

EPA/600/R-02/001 (May 2002) The Qtracer2 Program for tracer-breakthrough curve – analysis for tracer tests in karstic aquifers and other hydrologic systems U.S. Environmental Protection Agency, Washington, D.C. (Supersedes EPA/600/R-98/156a and 156b, 2/'99)

Fetter CW (1999) Contaminant hydrogeology, 2nd edn. University of Wisconsin-Oshkosh, Prentice Hall, Upper Saddle River, New Jersey, pp 18–33, 45–55

Freeze RA, Cherry JA (1979) Ground water. Prentice Hall Inc., Englewood Cliffs, New Jersey, pp 45–61, 152–163

Ground-Water Monitoring and Reclamation (Fall 2002): www.waterloohydogeologic.com

LaMoreaux PE (1991) History of karst hydrogeological studies. Proceedings of the International Conference on Environmental Changes in Karst Areas – mI.G.U.-U.I.S. – Italy 15–27 Sept 1991, Quaderni del Dipartmento dl Geografia no. 13, 1991, Universita dl Padova, pp 215–229 (P.E. LaMoreaux and Associates Inc., P.O. Box 2310, Tuscaloosa., AL 35403)

LaMoreaux PE (1996) Environmental and legal aspects of karst areas. In: Proc. of International Conference on "Karst-fractured aquifers-Vulnerabilty and Sustainability". Katowice-Ustron, Poland. Wyawnictwo University. Slaskiego ul. Bankowa 12B, 40-007, Katowice

LaMoreaux PE, Wilson BM, Memon BA (eds) (1982) Guide to the hydrology of the carbonate rocks. Carsologica Sinica 1(2):158–166

Molina MJ, Rowland FS (1974) Stratospheric sink of chlorofluor-methanes: chlorine atom-catalyzed destruction of ozone. Nature 249:810–812

Palmer CM, Peterson JL, Behnke J (1992) Introduction to general groundwater geochemistry. In: Principles of contaminant hydrogeology. Lewis Publishing Inc., Michigan (chap 6, pp 100–103)

Stensland GJ, Whelpdale DM, Ochlert G (1986) Precipitation chemistry. In: Committee on Monitoring Assessments of Trends in Acid Deposition (ed) Acid deposition, long-term trends. National Academy Press, Washington

Appendix 9.A · A Study of Stormy Water Runoff

P. E. LaMoreaux and Associates, Inc. (PELA), 1997

PELA is currently performing an assessment of potential ground-water contamination by highway stormwater runoff in karst areas under contract to the Federal Highway Administration (FHWA). The primary goal of this project is to develop and test a method for treating highway runoff draining into sinkholes. A secondary goal is to identify sensitive karst areas in the United States (Fig. 9.A.1).

Although many studies have addressed the impacts of stormwater and highway runoff on surface water, relatively little attention has been directed toward assessing its impact on ground water, especially karst areas. Dissolution of bedrock (usually limestone or dolomite) in karst areas results in terrane characterized by sinkholes, sinking streams, underground (cave) streams and springs. Ground water in these settings is potentially more susceptible to contamination because polluted surface runoff may pass directly into the subsurface with little or no filtration by soil. In karst areas ground water can flow through relatively large features and conduits within the bedrock transporting contamination rapidly from points of recharge (such as sinkholes) to distant cave streams, water wells, springs, and surface streams.

PELA evaluated potential sites for pilot testing runoff treatment technology in each of the fifteen states participating in the research: Arkansas, Florida, Illinois, Indiana, Kentucky, Maryland, Minnesota, Missouri, New York, Oregon, Pennsylvania, Tennessee, Texas, Virginia and Wisconsin.

Based on results of laboratory testing of various materials, PELA designed a pilot system using peat, sand, and limestone to remove the contaminants by sedimentation, filtration and absorption (Fig. 9.A.2). A sinkhole draining the I-40/I-640 interchange in eastern Knoxville, TN was selected for field testing the contaminant-removal effectiveness of the prototype treatment system. Originally, stormwater runoff from about 60 acres (0.24 km^2) of the highway interchange and adjacent land was directed through ditches and culverts to a small detention basin which was designed to allow natural filtration of runoff which had been flowing into the "old sinkhole." A new sinkhole then collapsed within the basin, allowing contaminated water from this site to pass through two small karst windows, finally being discharged approximately 420 feet (128 m) from the site at Holston Spring.

PELA's objective in installing the filter inside of this new sinkhole is to lower the level of contaminants in water flowing directly from the interstate into the sinkhole thereby reducing contamination of ground water. The filter upon which construction is soon to begin is projected by the FHWA to be a standard for similar situations throughout the country.

More detail on the project is in a recent article *"Highway Stormwater Runoff in Karst Areas – Preliminary Results of Baseline Monitoring and Design of a Treatment System for a Sinkhole in Knoxville, TN."* PELA professionals Dr. Barry F. Beck, Thomas S. Green, Brad Stephenson and Zhou Wanfang are the authors of the article published in the proceedings from the Sixth Sinkhole and Karst Conference. It is currently available upon request at our website, www.pela.com.

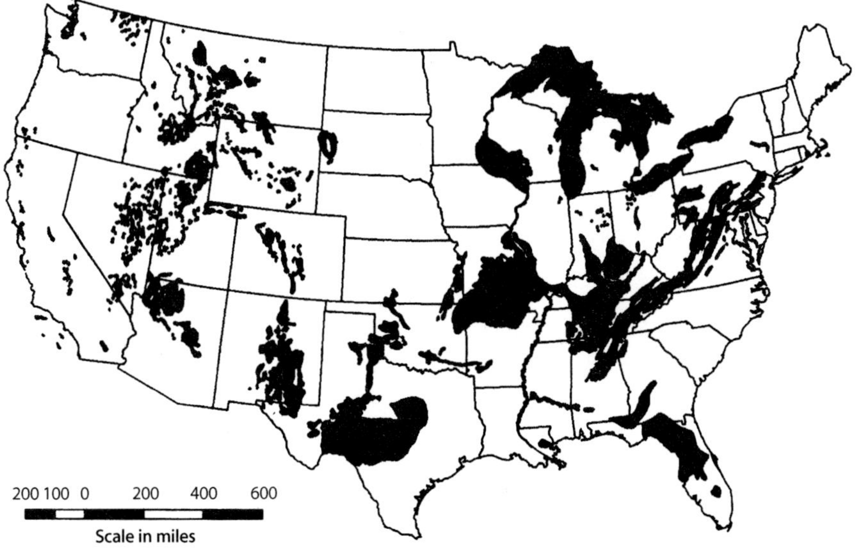
200 100 0
200
400
600
Scale in miles

Fig. 9.A.1.
To determine where the results of PELA's research might be useful, the FHWA asked PELA to create a map of the United States showing locations where karst terrane impacts the land surface. This map will also be helpful for many other studies of karst terrane

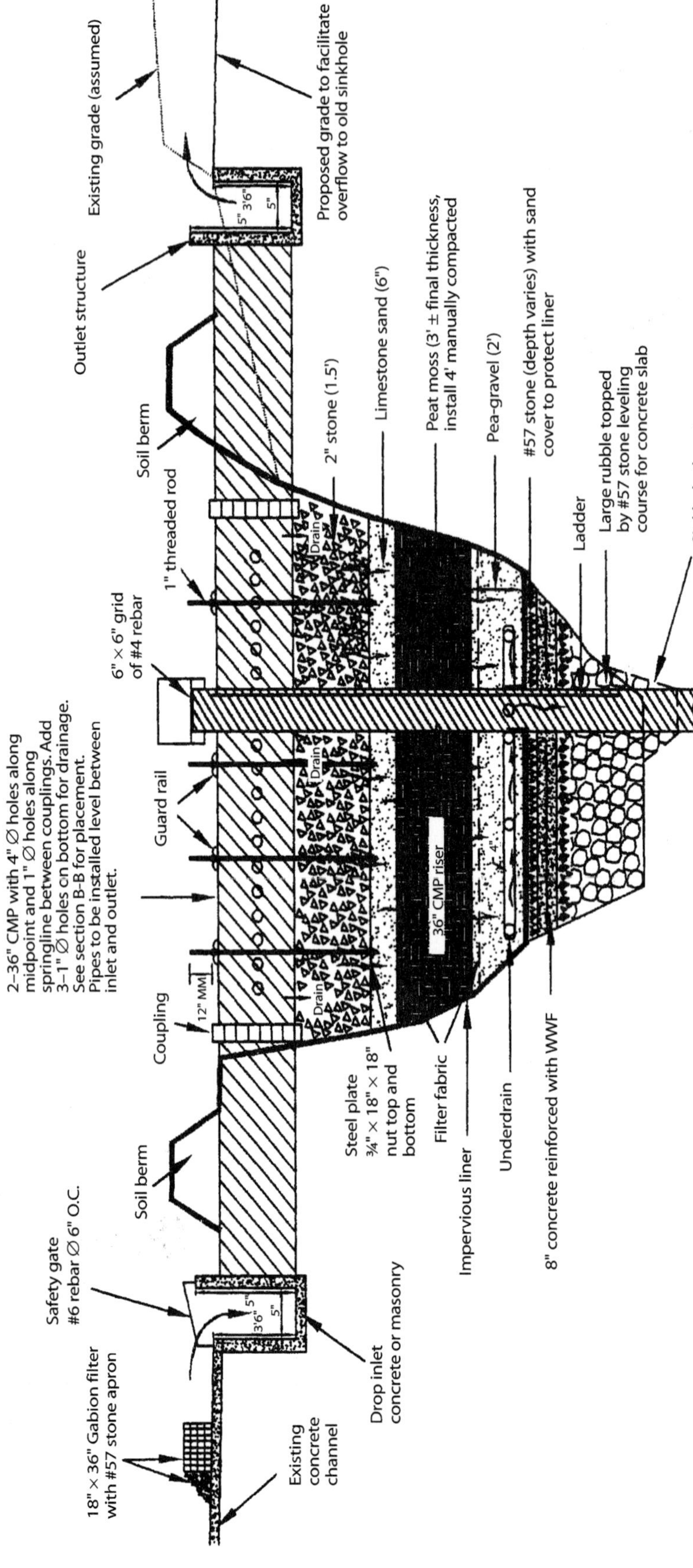

Existing grade (assumed)
Proposed grade to facilitate overflow to old sinkhole
5"
3'6"
5"
Outlet structure
Soil berm
1" threaded rod
6" × 6" grid of #4 rebar
Guard rail
2–36" CMP with 4" ∅ holes along midpoint and 1" ∅ holes along springline between couplings. Add 3–1" ∅ holes on bottom for drainage. See section B-B for placement. Pipes to be installed level between inlet and outlet.
12" MM
Coupling
Soil berm
Safety gate #6 rebar ∅ 6" O.C.
18" × 36" Gabion filter with #57 stone apron
Existing concrete channel
Drop inlet concrete or masonry
Drain
Drain
Drain
36" CMP riser
4"
2" stone (1.5')
Limestone sand (6")
Peat moss (3' ± final thickness, install 4' manually compacted
Pea-gravel (2')
#57 stone (depth varies) with sand cover to protect liner
Ladder
Large rubble topped by #57 stone leveling course for concrete slab
Sinkhole throat
Steel plate ¾" × 18" × 18" nut top and bottom
Filter fabric
Impervious liner
Underdrain
8" concrete reinforced with WWF

Fig. 9.A.2. PELA's proposed filter is designed to remove contaminants which are currently entering the ground water through this sinkhole

Part IV

Case Studies

Chapter 10

A New Approach on the Nubian Sandstone Aquifer of the Western Desert of Egypt

F. Assaad

10.1 Introduction

The Egyptian government decided to overcome the problem of having more than 95% of the population residing along the River Nile, an area that encompasses 1705 km^2 through the Egyptian territory (LaMoreaux 1964, 1976). The remaining 5% of the Egyptian population live in the Egyptian deserts that constitute more than 95% of Egypt.

The New Valley project of the Western Desert of Egypt was considered as a long-term project as it deals with one of the greatest ground-water reservoirs in the world. The project was begun through cooperation of the U.S. Overseas Mission, U.S. State Department, and UAR, Cairo, Egypt. It was designed as a detailed study of the hydrogeologic characteristics, including sedimentation, stratigraphy, and structure of the Nubian Aquifer system, which included a detailed test drilling program and monitoring. The report and recommendations for these investigations were published by the U.S. Geological Survey (LaMoreaux 1959). The studies included the training of geologists, well drillers, chemists, and engineers in carrying out work on this largest ground-water project in the world.

The New Valley is a part of the Western Desert of Egypt that covers an area of approximately 90 000 km^2 and comprises several depressions, including: Kharga, Dakhla, Farafra and Siwa, a total area of 3 000 km^2 (Fig. 10.1). The Western Desert is one of the hottest and driest places in the world and is essentially a plateau with extensive areas of rubby rock surface, covered in some places by long swaths of sand dunes. The Kharga Oasis is the capital of the New Valley. The eastern plateau of the Western Desert is capped by limestones of Eocene age, whereas the desert floor is covered by a series of parallel belts of sand dunes, being extensive in length and trending generally in a southeast direction. The oases are extensively low areas of several meters below the plateau; some areas, which reach below, mean sea level.

10.1.1 Subsurface Geology

10.1.1.1 *Lithology*

Lithological studies and electric log correlations were obtained for more than 500 wells drilled in the Kharga and Dakhla Oases. In the Kharga Oasis there are five correlating water-bearing zones intercalated by local impermeable shaly beds, probably interconnected at greater distances. Therefore, it is believed that the Nubian sandstone behaves as a single aquifer during its long period of ground-water development. Faulting, jointing and folding of the shaly sediments have developed a very extensive preferential vertical and horizontal leakage among the water-bearing sandstones of the Nubian System (Shazly et al. 1959). To the south of Beris Oasis (Beris Well 20), there are only three water-bearing zones that could be correlated (Fig. 10.2). In general, the water-bearing zones are overlain by a cap rock formed of variegated shales, reddish to violet in color indicating oxidizing conditions during deposition (Fig. 10.3a). The Nubian sandstone section to the south of Kharga Oasis proportionally decreases with decrease of the cap rock and vice versa. This fact helped to anticipate the depth to the basement when knowing the thickness of the penetrated cap rock. It has been determined that an empirical relation is established between the thickness of the cap rock and the depth to the basement rock in a specific area (Fig. 10.3b).

Thin streaks of carbonaceous shale in the lower parts of the Nubian section were noticed through drilling Zone B, and were followed upward by hematitic material (Zone D), therefore denoting oscillations in the sea level because of the changes in the oxidation-reduction potential during the deposition of the Nubian sandstone under relatively unstable conditions. High angularity of milky quartz pebbles, present in thin laminae at various depths in this area showed little effect of transportation, whereas the presence of orthoclase grains further emphasizes the nearness of the source rocks, for example, Zone D in Beris Well 15. The lowermost water-bearing zones (A and B) were missing in Beris Well 20

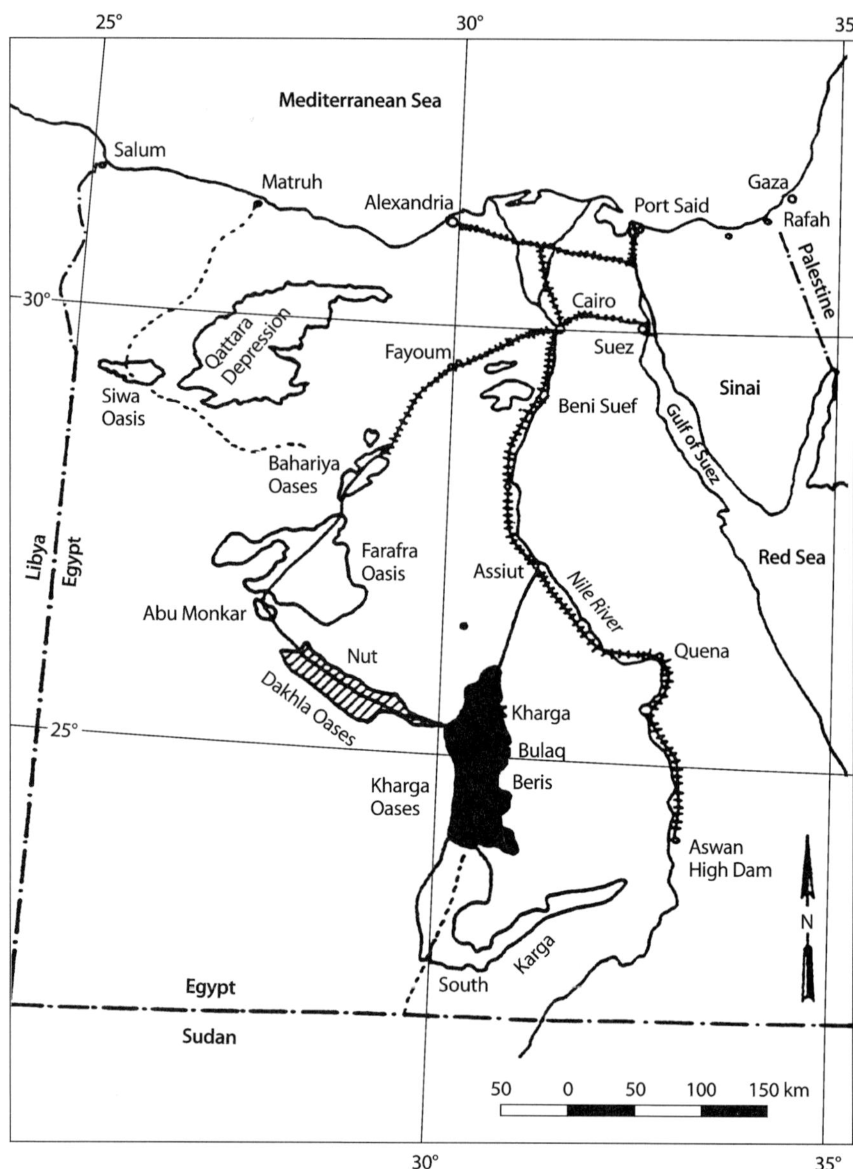

25°
30°
35°
Mediterranean Sea
Salum
Matruh
Alexandria
Port Said
Gaza
Rafah
Palestine
30°
Cairo
Qattara Depression
Fayoum
Suez
Siwa Oasis
Sinai
Beni Suef
Gulf of Suez
Bahariya Oases
Farafra Oasis
Assiut
Nile River
Red Sea
Libya
Egypt
Abu Monkar
Nut
Quena
Dakhla Oases
Kharga
Bulaq
25°
Beris
Kharga Oases
Aswan High Dam
N
Karga
South
Egypt
Sudan
50 0 50 100 150 km
30°
35°

Fig. 10.1.
A Location map of the New Valley, Western Desert, Egypt

due to nondeposition where the encountered area had been positive during the invasion of the early Mesozoic sea and possibly during late Paleozoic. The Nubian section became gravelly southward (at Beris Well 20), indicating that the sea was shallowing and a beach environment had been prevailing during deposition (Assaad 1988).

The deposition of the Nubian sandstone, which lies unconformably on the granite basement, is post-tectonic as it took place over the uplifted basement, which outcrops in Abu Bayan area south of Kharga Oasis.

It might be mentioned that the granite rocks in the middle area of Abu Bayan area is of different specific gravity where the coarse granite gives a minimum gravimetric value and the fine-grained granite in the periphery gives a maximum value, therefore, excluding the old concept of weathered granite outcropping in Abu Bayan.

10.1.1.2 *Stratigraphy*

The Nubian sandstones are considered to be wind transported, deposited in a beach or a shallow water, nearshore marine environment and range in age from Lower Carboniferous to Upper Cretaceous. They are overlain by impervious variegated shales and are underlain by the basement rocks (Figs. 10.4 and 10.5).

Stratigraphically, the age of variegated shales may be determined from the upper phosphate beds of Lower Maestrichtean outcrops north of Kharga Oasis and hence the variegated shales may be considered as Pre-Maestrichtean Age (Assaad and Barakat 1965). Also, the recovery of a complete plant leaf fossil from a core sample of a carbonaceous shale taken from El-Zayat

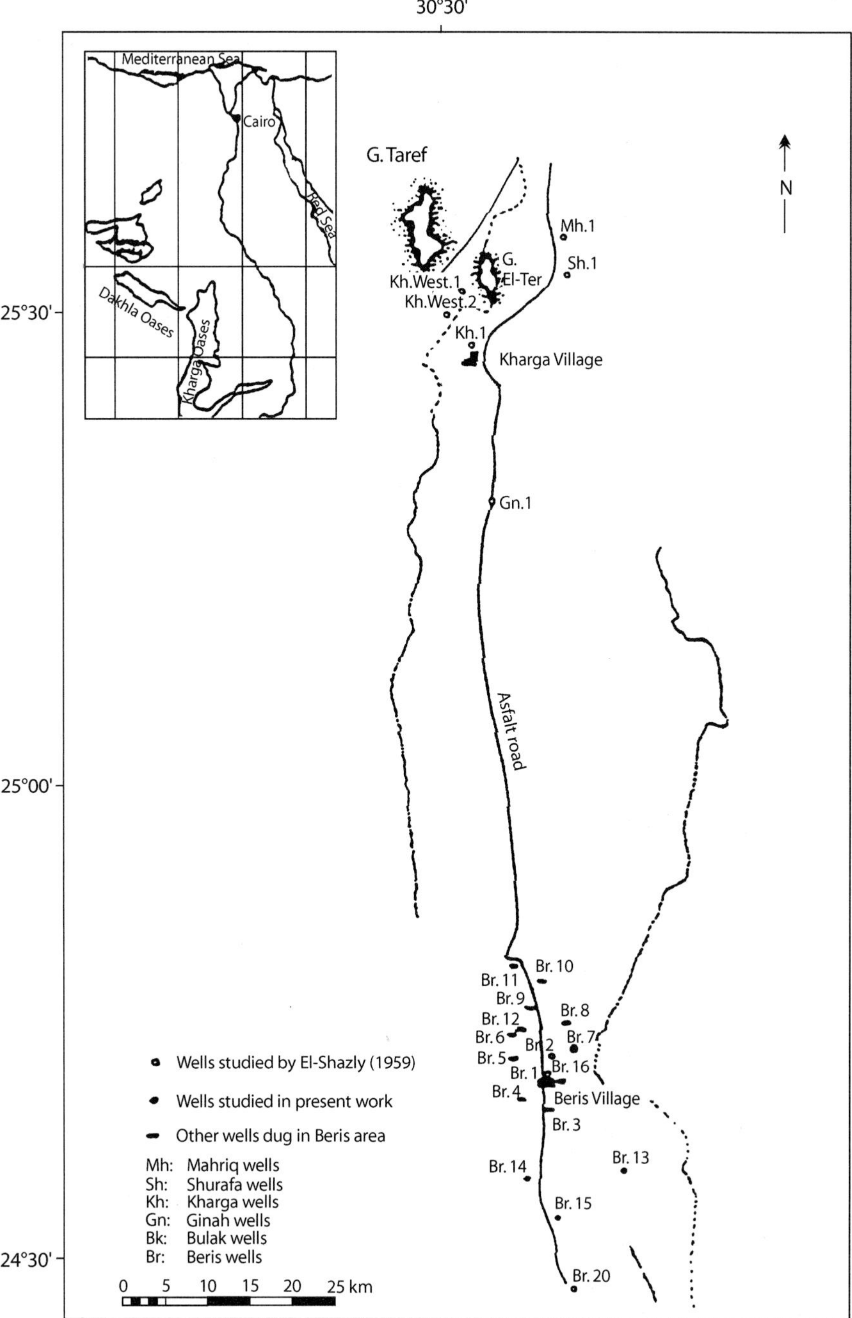
30°30'
25°30'
25°00'
24°30'
Mediterranean Sea
Cairo
Red Sea
Dakhla Oases
Kharga Oases
G. Taref
N
Mh.1
Sh.1
G.
El-Ter
Kh.West.1
Kh.West.2
Kh.1
Kharga Village
Gn.1
Asfalt road
Br. 10
Br. 11
Br. 9
Br. 12
Br. 8
Br. 6
Br. 2
Br. 7
Br. 5
Br. 1
Br. 16
Br. 4
Beris Village
Br. 3
Br. 13
Br. 14
Br. 15
Br. 20
Wells studied by El-Shazly (1959)
Wells studied in present work
Other wells dug in Beris area
Mh: Mahriq wells
Sh: Shurafa wells
Kh: Kharga wells
Gn: Ginah wells
Bk: Bulak wells
Br: Beris wells
0 5 10 15 20 25 km

Fig. 10.2. Locations of wells in Beris area, Kharga Oasis, Western Desert, Egypt

Water Well 2 (midway between Kharga and El Dakhla Oases) at a depth of 630 m, indicates the top of Lower Cretaceous bed that is overlain by Upper Cretaceous Nubian section (Assaad 1988). A surface geological section in the Eastern Desert of Egypt emphasizes this result (Shukri and Said 1944).

In the Sudan, about 150 km south of the capital Khartoum, the Nubian sandstone formations of late mid-Tertiary extends towards the Kharga and Dakhla Oases to the north.

10.1.2 Structural Geology

The Pre-Cambrian basement rocks outcrop at Djebel Oweinat in the southwest of the Western Desert. These rocks which form a parallel series of folded and faulted structures, have occurred owing to epeirogenic movements in a NE/SW trend based upon geophysical surveys (Fig. 10.6). These faults were formed during the Cretaceous period, but most important is a major fault

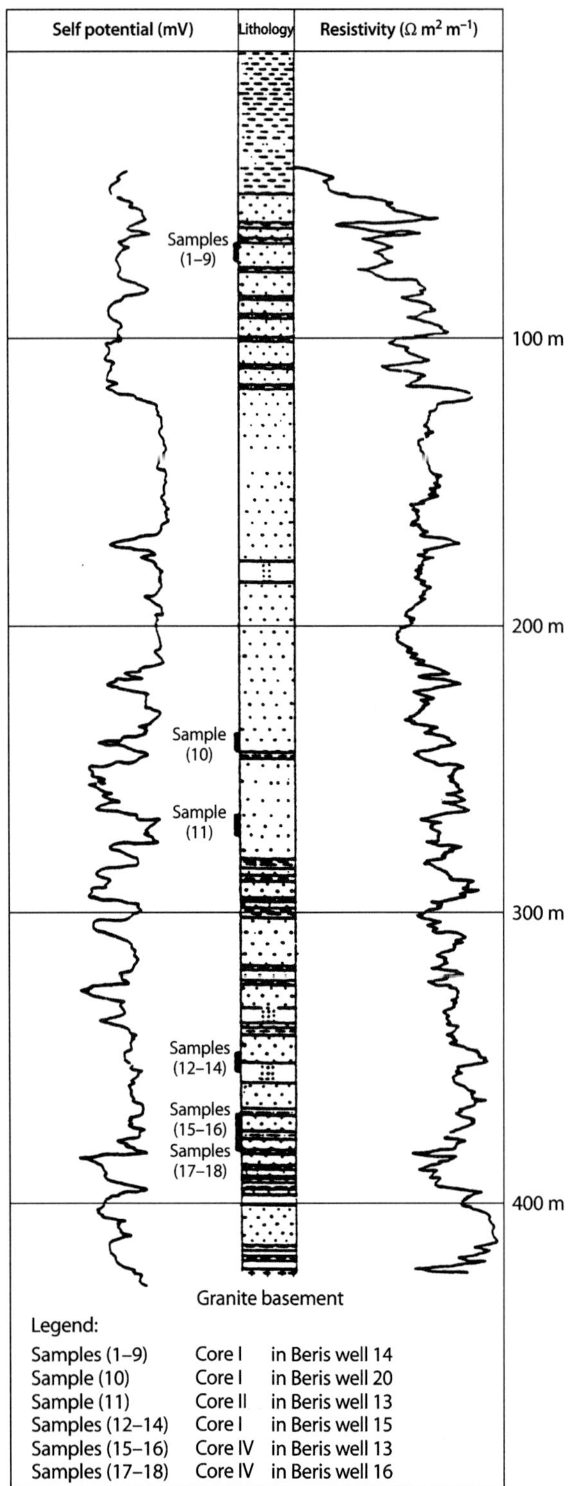
Self potential (mV)
Lithology
Resistivity (Ω m² m⁻¹)
Samples
(1–9)
100 m
200 m
Sample
(10)
Sample
(11)
300 m
Samples
(12–14)
Samples
(15–16)
Samples
(17–18)
400 m
Granite basement
Legend:
Samples (1–9) Core I in Beris well 14
Sample (10) Core I in Beris well 20
Sample (11) Core II in Beris well 13
Samples (12–14) Core I in Beris well 15
Samples (15–16) Core IV in Beris well 13
Samples (17–18) Core IV in Beris well 16

Fig. 10.3a. A composite well log of Beris area, south of Kharga Oases)

that extends from the Republic of Chad to Mount Oweinat, southwest of the Kharga Oasis. A series of east-west faults were also formed to the south of Kharga Oasis during the Post-Cretaceous period and some ready the western bank of the River Nile (Ezzat 1966).

A great anticlinal structure of a northeastern-southwestern trend exerts a significant impact on groundwater movement and extends from Bahariya and Farafra Oases southwest to the Tebesti Mountains of Chad. Two other anticlines of the same trend include one east of the south of Kharga area parallel to the western bank of the Nile, south of Aswan, and a second found between Kharga and Dakhla Oases.

To the east of Kharga Oasis a NE/SW synclinal structure exists between two anticlines. Another syncline trends north-south between Quena and Luxor. It turns to the northwest-southeast from Quena to Meniya further to the north (Fig. 10.7).

The Kharga depression is on an anticline where its main axis extends north and south and coincides with a major fault that parallels the main asphalt road.

10.1.3 Petrophysical and Petrographical Studies

Petrophysical studies were performed on cuttings and core samples from wells south of Beris Oasis (Assaad and Philip 1969). This data provides information on the environment of deposition of the Nubian sandstone. It is summarized as follows:

a *Mechanical analysis (sieving)*, using a Taylor shaker, showed that the cuttings are of an average median diameter of 1.31 mm (very coarse sand). The core samples gave a range between 0.15 mm (fine sand) and 1.80 mm (very coarse sand) with an average of 0.58 mm (coarse sand size). This indicates that the core samples contain more fine-grained material that acts as a binding matrix in the framework of the sediments. The sediments are well sorted and most of the samples show sorting coefficient values less than 2.5 (well sorted) with an average of 1.69. The core samples, by comparison, (poorly sorted) gave inclusive graphic standard deviation values (1.21∅). The sediments on the whole are more or less symmetrical (–0.07) with some tendency to be coarse skewed (–0.30). The sediments are found to be mesokurtic to leptokurtic (Folk and Ward 1957). The interrelation of the size parameters when drawn in the form of scatter plot diagrams show that the decrease in mean size of the sediment is associated with better sorting, more symmetry, and leptokurtosis (Figs. 10.8 and 10.9). These conditions can be accounted for, by assuming that transportation resulted in the removal of the coarser material from the sediment, that was originally coarser, relatively less sorted, coarse skewed and platykurtic. Shukri and Said (1944) came to the conclusion that the Nubian sandstones were wind transported, deposited on a beach or on a shallow

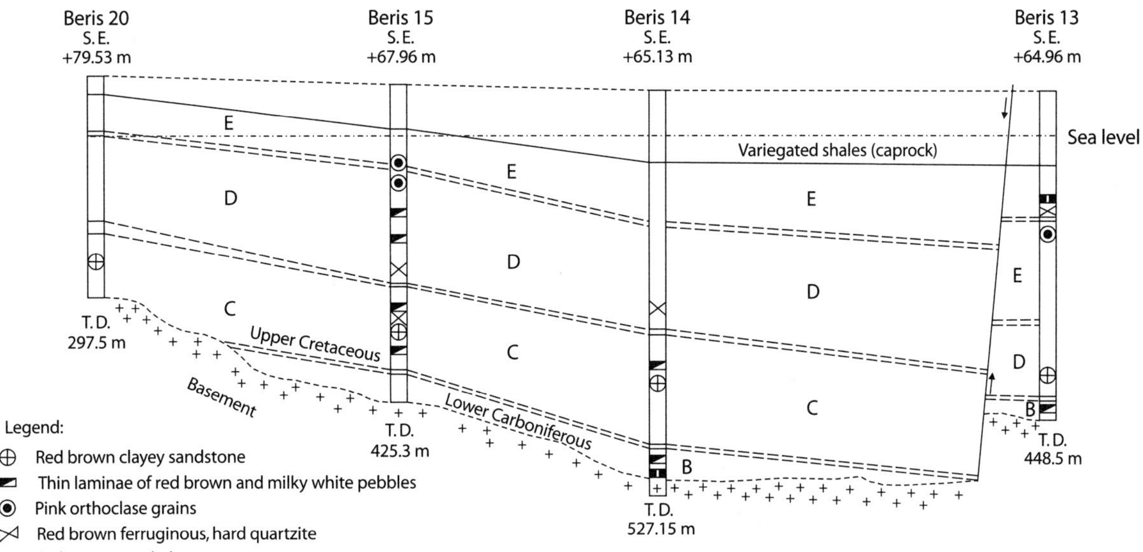

Beris 20
S.E.
+79.53 m
Beris 15
S.E.
+67.96 m
Beris 14
S.E.
+65.13 m
Beris 13
S.E.
+64.96 m
Sea level
Variegated shales (caprock)
E
D
C
B
T.D.
297.5 m
T.D.
425.3 m
T.D.
527.15 m
T.D.
448.5 m
Upper Cretaceous
Basement
Lower Carboniferous
Legend:
Red brown clayey sandstone
Thin laminae of red brown and milky white pebbles
Pink orthoclase grains
Red brown ferruginous, hard quartzite
Carbonaceous shale

Fig. 10.3b. A subsurface geology section showing mineral inclusions

water near-shore marine environment. In samples studied, however, the wind effect could be seen in the removal of the coarser ends of the distribution curve. Sorting is more or less the same in all the symmetry classes, as characteristic of a beach environment (Assaad and Philip 1969).

The results from mechanical analysis is an aid to design of gravel packing where a consolidated gravel ring is placed around the slotted production tubing to avoid casing damage from corrosive effects (Assaad and Philip 1969).

Clarke (1962) gave results of long-term field experiments in Kharga and Dakhla corrosive waters showing a preference to steel filters over aluminum.

b *Porosity percentages* were obtained using the hydrostatic method (using the bulk volume apparatus). Porosity ranged between 15.3 and 28.6% with an average of 20.3%. The difference is related to the amount of argillaceous matrix or the ferruginous cementing material that binds the sandstone grains. Porosity percentages were plotted against mean size (*Mz*) and against inclusive graphic standard deviation (σ_i). The results showed that the porosity increases with increase in mean size and better sorting.

c *Horizontal and vertical permeability values* were determined for core samples and range from 2 to 3700 millidarcy (and from 2 to 901 millidarcy, respectively. Table 10.1 shows the values of porosity and permeability of core samples taken from Kharga and Dakhla water wells together with their natural artesian discharge (Assaad and Philip 1969).

d Petrographic examination of thin sections were prepared from the core samples recovered from Beris wells and can be considered as a type sample for the corresponding water zones south of Kharga Oasis. The recovery percentages of core samples range between 12 and 86% depending on the degree of lithification. This study deals with lithified Nubian sandstone.

The examined sandstones fall into three types that are not related to the depth of the sample:

1. Siliceous quartzarenites in which the chalcedonic or crystalline silica forms the cementing material. Microcrystals of magnetite and hematite are found along the boundaries of the terrigenous quartz grains.
2. Ferruginous quartzarenites in which the cementing material is formed by the growth and contact of the microcrystals of iron oxides.
3. Poorly sorted argillaceous quartzarenites in which the amount of argillaceous matrix is as much as 38% of the rock. The matrix is usually reorganized by the recrystallization of hydrothermal solution leading to secondary quartz overgrowths that may include few iron oxides, microquartz, and muscovite flakes. Quartz grains may show orientation, with their long axes parallel to the elongation of the mica flakes that may result in a banded appearance.

The siltstones mainly have an argillaceous matrix in which developing fine crystals of iron oxides are embedded. In some cases, iron oxides fill fractures in the rock denoting their formation in a late stage in the diagenetic history of the rock.

Figures 10.10–10.14 show petrographic thin sections taken in different cores that were recovered from differ-

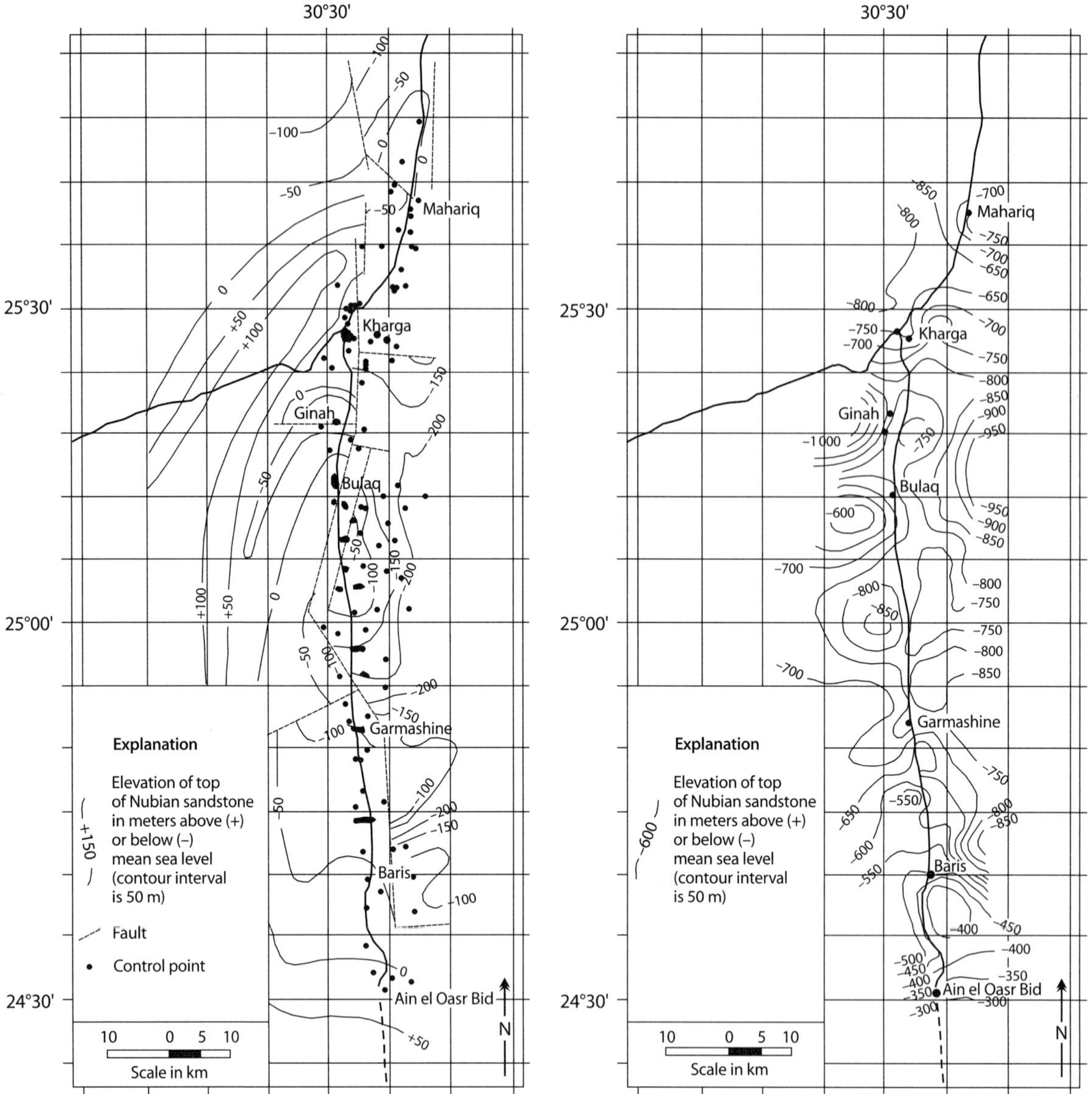
30°30'
25°30'
25°00'
24°30'
Mahariq
Kharga
Ginah
Bulaq
Garmashine
Baris
Ain el Oasr Bid
N
Explanation
Elevation of top of Nubian sandstone in meters above (+) or below (–) mean sea level (contour interval is 50 m)
+150
Fault
Control point
10 0 5 10
Scale in km
30°30'
25°30'
25°00'
24°30'
Mahariq
Kharga
Ginah
Bulaq
Garmashine
Baris
Ain el Oasr Bid
N
Explanation
Elevation of top of Nubian sandstone in meters above (+) or below (–) mean sea level (contour interval is 50 m)
-600
10 0 5 10
Scale in km

Fig. 10.4. Top of Nubian sandstone aquifers, Kharga area

Fig. 10.5. Top of basement, Kharga area

ent aquifer zones in Beris Wells 13, 14 and 15. Microscopic examination of thin sections showed that lithification of the studied rocks is the result of a process of reorganization, mainly by recrystallization of an argillaceous matrix that was deposited in between the terrigenous quartz sand grains. It was found that the secondary overgrowths on quartz grains cause a decrease in the porosity with increasing depth. The decrease in porosity in the upper 1 000 m was primarily due to mechanical compaction whereas the dissolution of quartz was more effective below such depth as evidenced by the increase of quartz overgrowths. Pressure solution is more pronounced in the fine-grained sandstones than in the coarse. Finer sediments examined from Beris Oasis wells usually contain a good proportion of matrix and the quartz grains are seldom in contact. The source of silica responsible for the overgrowth was mainly found in the clay matrix, in addition to that derived from pressure solution.

Sphericity and roundness of the quartz grains are a function of grain size, increasing from silt to medium sand. Roundness of the grains, within the same grade size, is found to be more or less the same in all samples examined from different depths (or ages) whereas its increase in roundness is accompanied by a similar increase in the index of sphericity. Roundness and sphericity of the grains from the topmost core in Beris Well 13 (Zone D) and that of Beris Well 14 (Zone E) of Upper

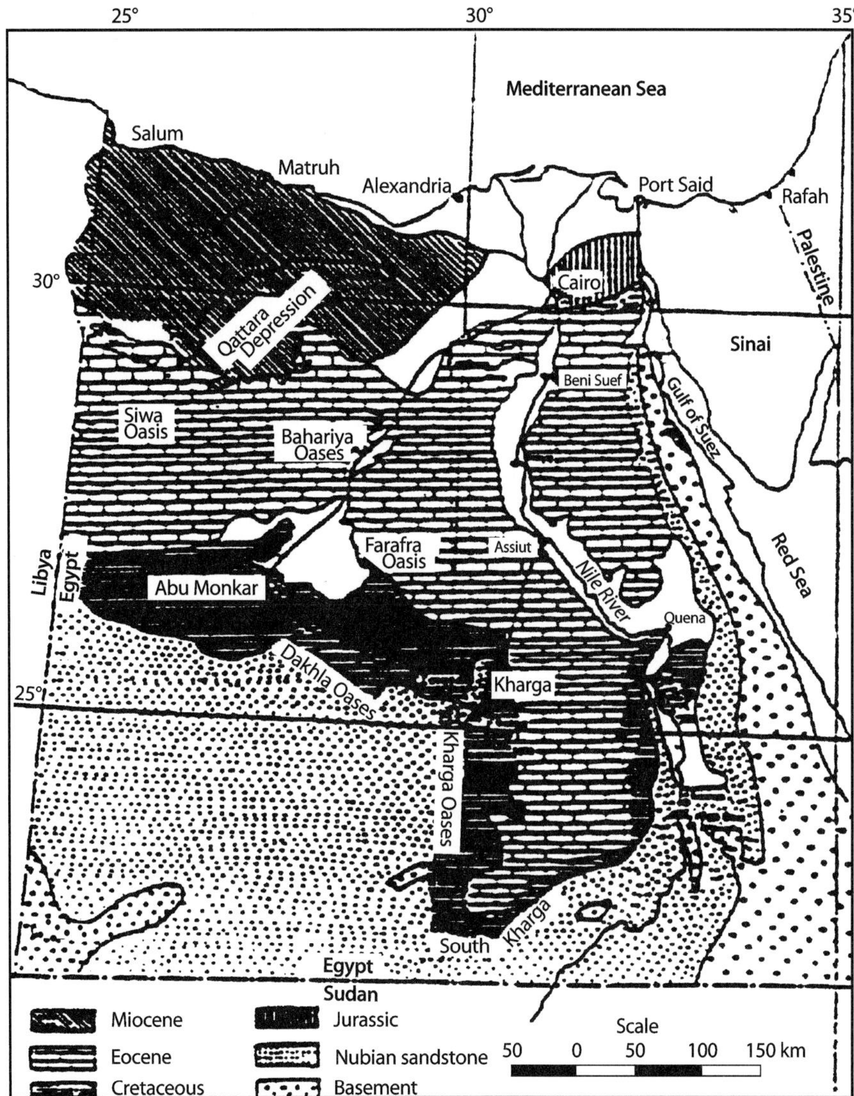
25°
30°
35°
Mediterranean Sea
Salum
Matruh
Alexandria
Port Said
Rafah
Palestine
Cairo
30°
Qattara Depression
Sinai
Beni Suef
Gulf of Suez
Siwa Oasis
Bahariya Oases
Red Sea
Farafra Oasis
Assiut
Libya
Egypt
Abu Monkar
Nile River
Quena
Dakhla Oases
Kharga
25°
Kharga Oases
South Kharga
Egypt
Sudan
Miocene
Eocene
Cretaceous
Jurassic
Nubian sandstone
Basement
Scale
50 0 50 100 150 km

Fig. 10.6. A surface geology map of the Western Desert of Egypt (after Soliman, internal Egyptian Governmental report)

Cretaceous were compared with those forming the framework of Zone B in both Beris Well 13 (Core IV) and Beris Well 15 (Core II). Both cores in Zone B are located about 20 m above the basement rocks and are considered as of Paleozoic age. The quartz grains studied from the Cretaceous and Paleozoic Nubian sediments possess more or less the same rounding and sphericity (Table 10.2; Assaad 1988).

The presence of a good portion of fines act as a matrix for the sand grains in the examined rocks, in addition to the fact that the mean rounding index for quartz grains of the four grade sizes – coarse silt, very fine, fine, and medium sand – is more or less the same, falling in the subangular class, which makes it difficult to assume wind as the transporting agent for the rocks. Such rocks would be ascribed more readily to fluviatile transportation of a changing current strength, which leads to rapid variation in grain size (e.g. Core IV of Beris Well 13). The environment of deposition might have been a shallow marine environment, in which deposition at certain periods was rapid enough to cause the rocks to stay in a poor sorting condition.

10.2 The Ground-Water Reservoir

The ground-water reservoir extends beneath the Libyan and northern Sudanese Sahara and varies in thickness from 400 m to the far south of Kharga Oasis, 800 m around Kharga village, 1 700 m in Dakhla Oasis, about 2 000 m in the Bahariya Oasis and about 600 m beneath the Quattara depression to the north. The thickness of the Nubian sandstone decreases in the north of the Quattara depression where the contact between the fresh ground water and the sea water of the Mediterranean has been traced.

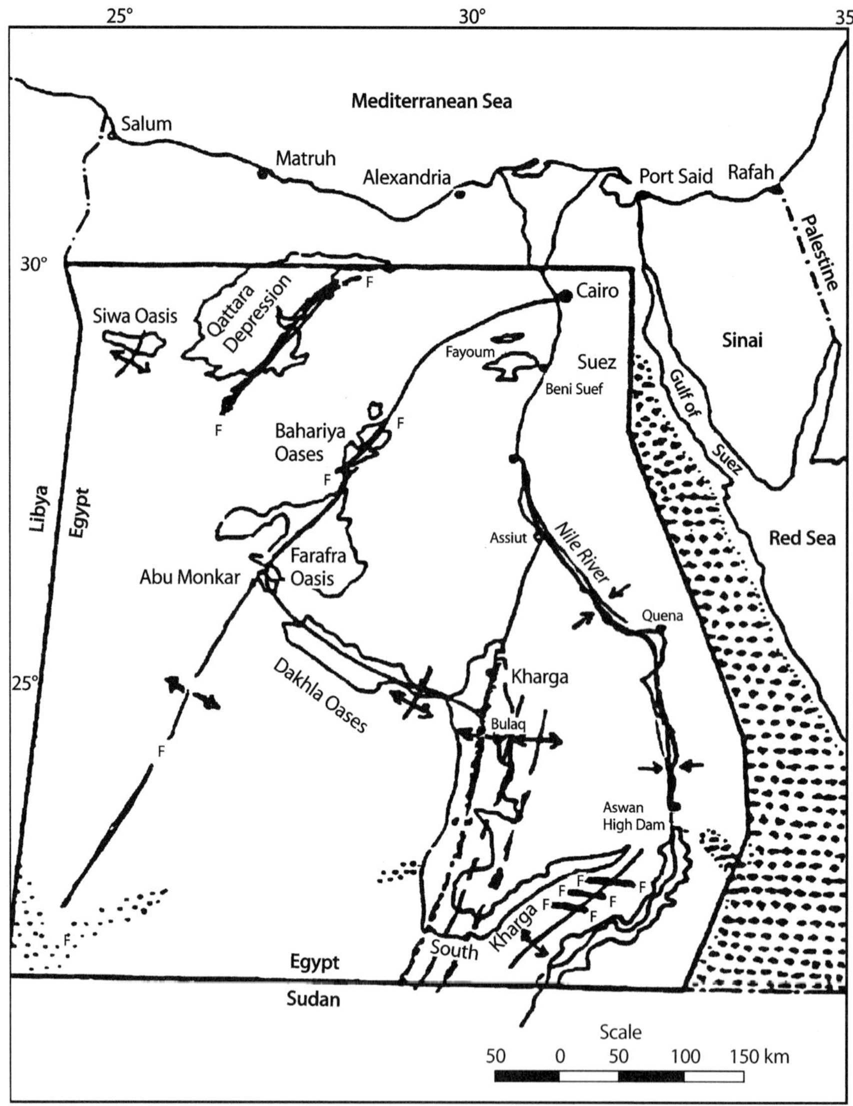
25°
30°
35°
Mediterranean Sea
Salum
Matruh
Alexandria
Port Said
Rafah
Palestine
30°
Cairo
Siwa Oasis
Qattara Depression
F
Fayoum
Suez
Beni Suef
Sinai
Gulf of Suez
Bahariya Oases
Libya
Egypt
Assiut
Nile River
Red Sea
Farafra Oasis
Abu Monkar
Quena
Kharga
25°
Dakhla Oases
Bulaq
Aswan High Dam
South Kharga
Egypt
Sudan
Scale
50 0 50 100 150 km

Fig. 10.7. A general structural map of the Western Desert of Egypt (modified from Ezzat 1966)

All oases of the Western Desert have been centers of ground-water discharge from springs and wells for many thousands of years. These long periods of discharge have influenced the regional flow system. Figure 10.15a,b shows that the ground-water flow was from the southwest and that the ground-water discharge was creating distinct cones of depressions in the piezometric surface (LaMoreaux et al. 1985). The velocity of the ground-water flow was estimated as 15 m per year and the storage capacity of the Nubian aquifer system underlying the Western Desert was estimated to be in the order of 240×10^{12} m^3. During the late 1980s the system total outflow, which includes discharges by wells and springs (about 340 wells and 1380 springs), was estimated in the order of 450 million $m^3 yr^{-1}$ (Ezzat 1966).

The shale intercalations among the aquifer zones are lenticular and therefore can only act as local confining layers. Also, faulting, folding and jointing cause extensive horizontal and vertical leakage through the aquifer zones of the Nubian systems.

Shazly et al. (1959) stated that ground water in the lowermost strata overlying the basement rock in Kharga and Dakhla depressions are renewable from rainfalls on northern Sudan. During the Pluvial Period (10 000–15 000 years ago) floods prevailed in the uppermost formations where their waters are not renewable. A mixture of both types of water could be found in intermediate formations.

In general, the Nubian aquifer is fresh water bearing throughout the whole section except for the very northern part, which is highly saline. The water salinity in the oases ranges between 200 and 500 ppm.

Geochemical studies of the GARPAD (General Authority for Reclamation Projects and Agricultural Development), defined that the production casings

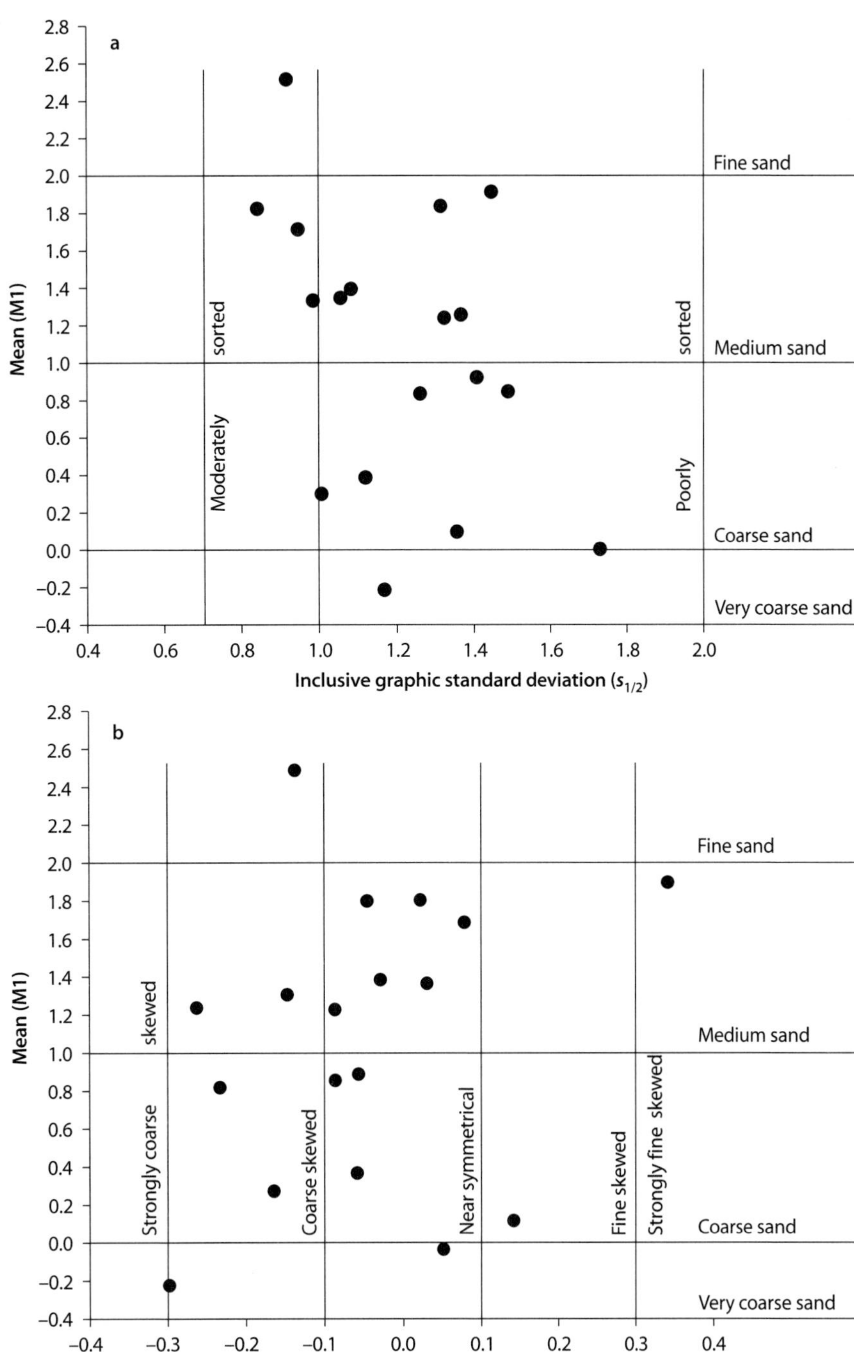
a
Mean (M1)
Inclusive graphic standard deviation ($s_{1/2}$)
Moderately sorted
Poorly sorted
Fine sand
Medium sand
Coarse sand
Very coarse sand
b
Skewness (Sks)
Strongly coarse skewed
Coarse skewed
Near symmetrical
Fine skewed
Strongly fine skewed

Fig. 10.8. Scatter plot diagrams; **a** mean diameter vs. inclusive graphic standard deviation; **b** mean diameter vs. skewness

of Monel 400, stainless steel or chrome-nickel (Fig. 10.16) were best used to avoid corrosion effects of the ground water due to the presence of dissolved carbon dioxide and hydrogen sulfide that increase the acidity of aquifers and also due to the difference in potentiality that result from the oxidation-reduction processes between the different aquifer waters (chloride, sulfate, and bicarbonate waters) and the production casings pipes. The corrosion effect generally occurs at a depth of 600 m, approximately (Clark 1962, 1963).

10.3 The Analogue Rc-Integrator Model

This analogue model was first applied in the late 1960s for the main oases of the New Valley project (the Kharga and Dakhla Oases). It basically depends on the trans-

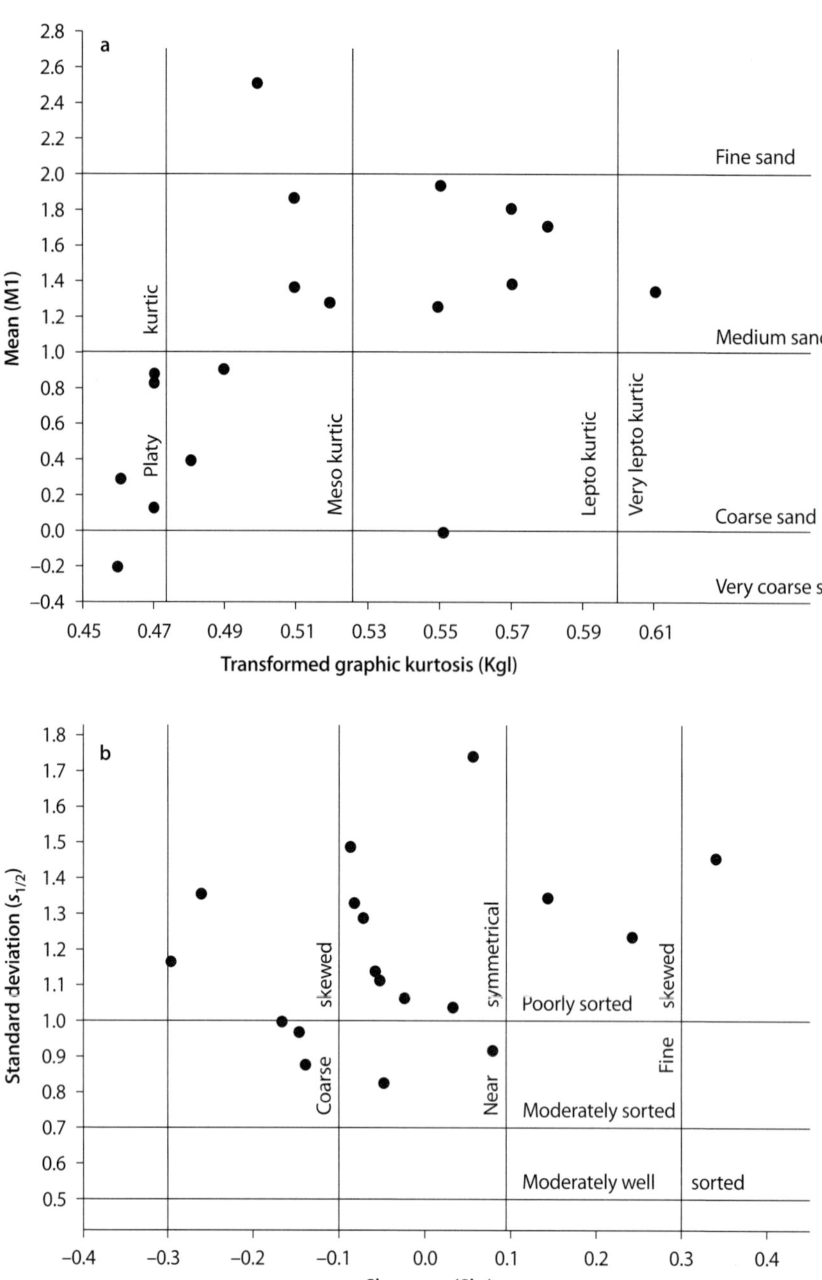
a
Mean (M1)
Transformed graphic kurtosis (Kgl)
Fine sand
Medium sand
Coarse sand
Very coarse sand
Platy kurtic
Meso kurtic
Lepto kurtic
Very lepto kurtic
b
Standard deviation ($s_{1/2}$)
Skewness (Sks)
Coarse skewed
Near symmetrical
Fine skewed
Poorly sorted
Moderately sorted
Moderately well sorted

Fig. 10.9. Scatter plot diagrams; **a** mean diameter vs. transformed graphic kurtosis; **b** standard deviation vs. skewness

Table 10.1. Petrophysical analysis on core samples of the Nubian sandstone in some wells of Kharga and Dakhla Oases

Water well	Region	Discharge (m^3 day^{-1})	Porosity (%)	Permeability (millidarcy, H2)	Permeability (millidarcy, V)	Depth of core sample (m)
Bustan	Kharga	1240	13.5	1400	1460	726–728
Bulak	Kharga	3070	30.0	937	Fractured	463–466
Garmashine	Kharga	2110	Fractured	Fractured	Fractured	434–440
Asmant	Dakhla	1690	28.5	1350	990	295–301
Balat	Dakhla	2740	12.5	3.0	–	396–402
Kalamone	Dakhla	2060	34.1	3485	3070	217–223

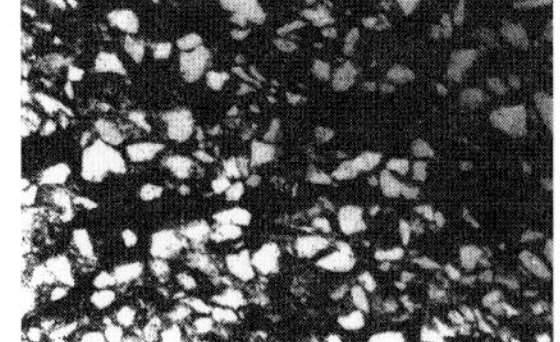

Fig. 10.10.
Ferruginous very fine quartzarenite, iron oxides in the form of microcrystals in the matrix and enclosed by silica overgrowths in quartz grains, streaks of hematite cause banding of the rock (Slide 4, Core I, Beris Well 13; ordinary light × 100)

Fig. 10.11.
Siliceous medium quartzarenite showing silica overgrowths in optical continuity on quartz grains marked by iron oxides, and a later stage with different orientation. Iron oxides partly fill intergranular spaces (Slide 15, Core II, Beris Well 13; nicols partly crossed × 100)

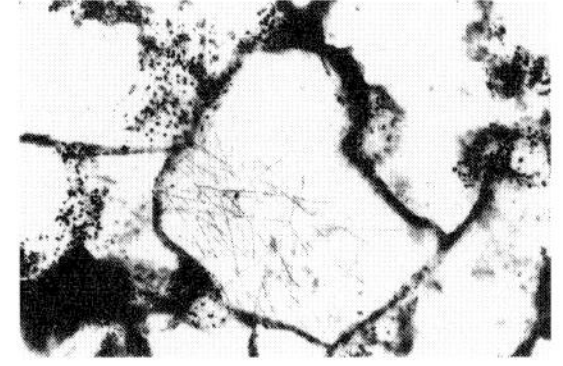

Fig. 10.12.
Feruginous medium quartzarenite. Hematite microcrystals enclosed within quartz grains by silica overgrowths, and act as cement when dense to fill intergranular space. Inclusions of rutile needles are seen in the quartz grain (Slide 62, Core I, Beris Well 15; ordinary light × 120)

Fig. 10.13.
Siliceous medium quartzarenite showing chalcedonic layers surrounding quartz grains. An earlier stage of deposition of silica in optical continuity is marked by microcrystals of iron oxides (Slide 42, Core I, Beris Well 14; ordinary light × 100)

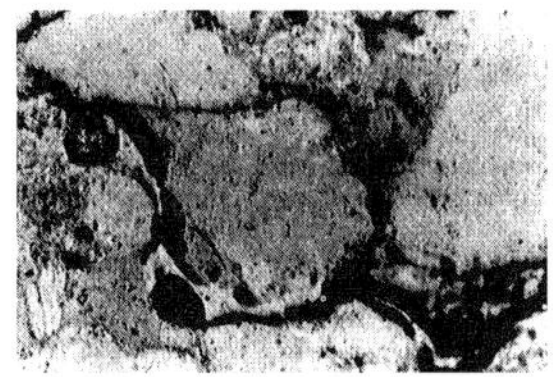

Fig. 10.14.
Feruginous quartzarenite showing silica overgrowths on the quartz grains and a "silica sphere" partly of crystalline silica. Cementing material of hematite (Slide 41, Core I, Beris Well 14; partly crossed nichols × 100)

missibility and permeability maps of the Western Desert of Egypt. It can be used as a key to many questions regarding the balance of underground waters and the regime of their exploitation (Radoslav-Rakar 1968).

Because of the decline of the regional flow system due to the long-lasting exploitation of ground water, it was found necessary to construct the model comprising a larger territory of approximately 300 km from the pumping centers, involving the larger area outside the Kharga and Dakhla Oases.

The boundary conditions on the contour of a model are given as the potential, corresponding to the piezometric pressures in nature or to the current flow adequate to the water flow through the given border.

A general analogue model of the Western Desert, comprising the territory of 700 000 km^2, was constructed to give contour conditions for the models of the Kharga and Dakhla Oases. This model was completely elaborated as a one-layered environment. The detailed model of the oases-comprising territory of 43 200 km^2 worked out as a double-layered environment – each of the layers separately showing the intermediate layer. The lower, which is under the constant artesian conditions of flow and contains the deep wells, has been constructed to be capable of simulate pumping from programmed flow wells. The upper layer consisting of shallow and self-flowing wells has the possibility of transition to water table conditions, because it is apt to widen the depression during the long period of exploitation.

Salem (1970) constructed two regional one layer Rc analogue models for the sandstone aquifer system of the Western Desert. The first model was set to simulate the artesian condition, while the second one represented the water table condition with a vertical, low hydraulic conductivity value so that an elapsed period of time would occur between the earlier artesian effect and the development of water table conditions. Cause effect response of the aquifer system was studied under artesian and water table conditions as a result of two pumping programs at the different areas of the Kharga and Dakhla Oases for a time period of 50 years.

Table 10.3 shows the computed results given by the analogue model designed for the New Valley project. The permissible amounts of the discharge of wells from each of the two oases and its related flow of electric current are also given in Table 10.4.

10.4 The Digital Model

A digital model for the evaluation of ground-water resources in the Kharga-Dakhla Oases area where a detailed numerical model, based on the integrated finite difference method, was made.

This model determined the maximum quantities of ground water to be extracted to support long-term development of integrated agriculture in the studied area. The model simulated a two-layer aquifer system connected by vertical leakage.

The ground-water model studies of the Nubian aquifer system in the Western Desert indicated that additional quantities of water in the order of 790 million m^3 yr^{-1} could be extracted from the New Valley oases of Egypt. Economical evaluation for such an extraction plan is still required for irrigated agriculture in these areas.

Table 10.2. Comparison (%) between the roundness and sphericity of quartz grains of the Cretaceous and Paleozoic sediments in Beris wells (Assaad and Philip 1969)

	Very fine sand				Fine sand				Medium sand			
	Br. 13 Core I Zone D	Br. 14 Core I Zone E	Br. 13 Core IV Zone B	Br. 15 Core II Zone B	Br. 13 Core I Zone D	Br. 14 Core I Zone E	Br. 13 Core IV Zone B	Br. 15 Core II Zone B	Br. 13 Core I Zone D	Br. 14 Core I Zone E	Br. 13 Core IV Zone B	Br. 15 Core II Zone B
	Cretaceous		Paleozoic		Cretaceous		Paleozoic		Cretaceous		Paleozoic	
Sphericity												
Low	14	41	20	11	9	17	12	16	4	10	11	22
Medium	51	45	44	58	35	52	55	34	39	41	23	22
High	35	14	36	31	56	31	33	50	57	49	66	66
Roundness												
Very angular	3	–	–	–	–	–	–	–	–	–	–	–
Angular	42	33	16	20	48	31	42	52	38	40	21	61
Subangular	47	39	72	29	48	46	54	18	56	41	57	31
Subrounded	8	28	12	51	4	23	4	30	6	16	22	5
Rounded	–	–	–	–	–	–	–	–	–	3	–	–

10.5 The River Nile of Egypt

The history and evolution of the River Nile were presented by Said (1993) in his book, *The River Nile*. A quick review is given below as an attempt to find the relation of the waters in the Nubian massif with that of the Western Desert of Egypt.

The present-day river is complex and is the result of the interconnection of several independent basins by rivers, which developed during the last wet period, which affected Africa after the retreat of the ice of the last glacial age some 10 000 years ago (Holocene Epoch). Prior to this period, the basins, which constitute part of the present river, were disconnected, forming internal lakes. During the wet climate, these basins overflowed their banks and became connected to other basins, all of which stand out in the longitudinal section of the river as flat stretches or landings that are connected with rivers of very steep slopes (Said 1993).

In the equatorial plateau, the southern basins of lakes Victoria, Albert and Kioga are connected by the swift rivers, whereas to the north of these lakes are the enormous Sudd and central Sudan basins which extend for a distance of 1 800 km from the capital of South Sudan (Juba) to Khartoum, the capital of North Sudan (Said 1993).

The Nubian swell, which extends from 85 km north of Khartoum to Aswan, represented for a long time a barrier that separated the African basin from the Egyptian Nile and the Mediterranean Sea. It was only in relatively recent time that this barrier was breached by the natural river (Said 1993). The Nubian massif thus forms the bridge across which the Nile waters have access to the sea and hence the name given by Said (1993) for the River Nile as the Egyptian Nubian Nile, which is known for its rapids and cataracts.

10.5.1 Evolution of the River Nile

During the evolution of the Neonile, which is the latest set of events that took place through the history of the Nile, is estimated to have occurred some 70 000 years ago. This set of events was associated with the following two periods:

1. The late glacial period: During this period, the lake plateau received considerably less rains; the equatorial forest had disappeared; the Sudd region was dry; and Egypt was also arid and the desert was abandoned. During the glacial period, there was the arrival of two rivers into Egypt with an Ethiopian connection and are named beta and gamma Neoniles. The two rivers tapped their water from the Ethiopian Highlands. The sluggish beta and gamma Neoniles carried large quantities of silt, which were piled up along their banks in southern Egypt. The older beta Neonile could be more than 25 000 years B.P. In the north at Quena, there occur silts that could well represent the topmost part of the beta Neonile. The age of the younger gamma Neonile is dated between 20 000–12 000 years B.P. and its sediments carry rich archeological material of late Paleolithic age.
2. The Holocene epoch (10 000 years B.P.): It followed the retreat of the ice sheets of the former glacial pe-

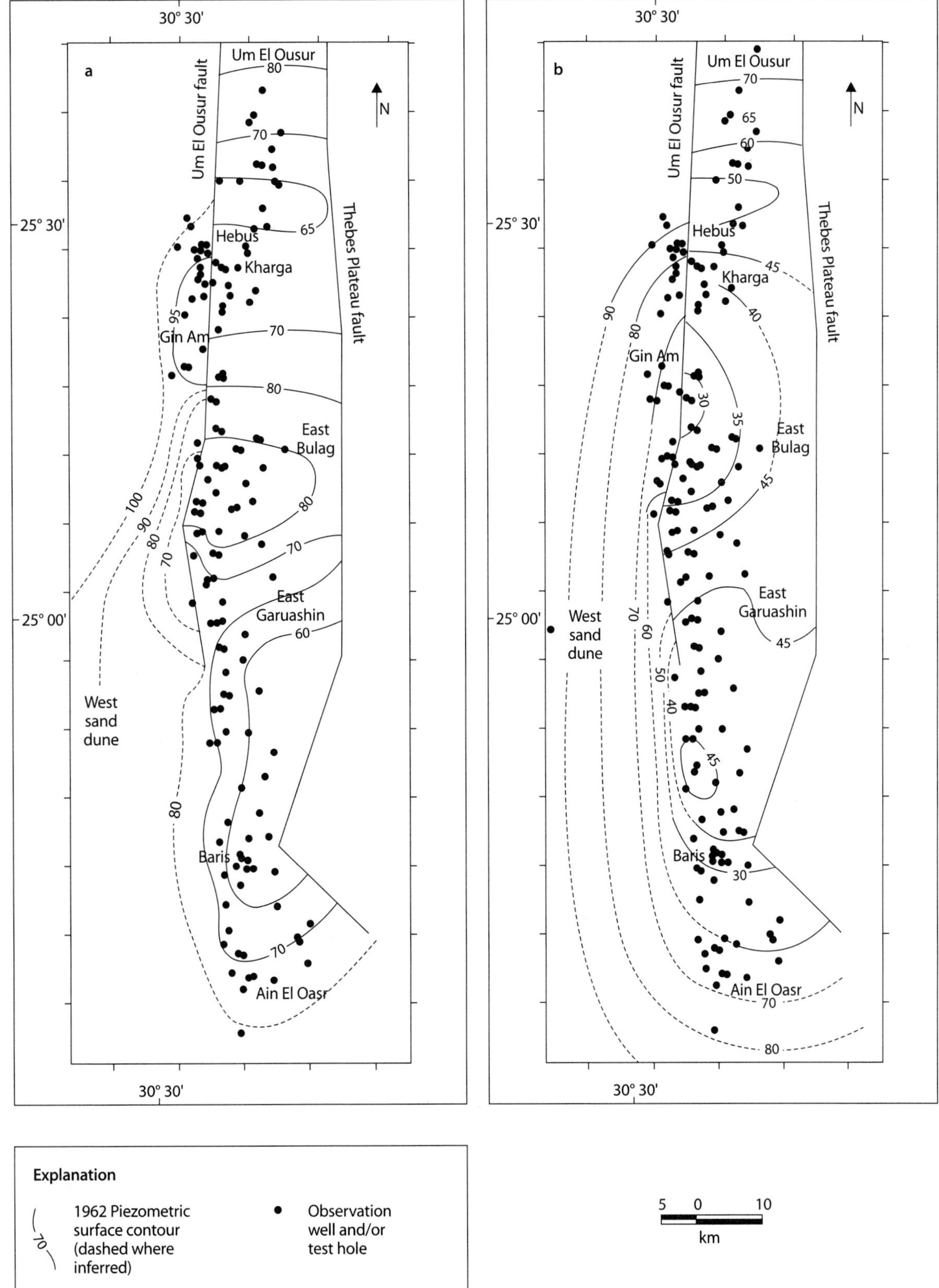

a
30° 30'
25° 30'
25° 00'
Um El Ousur
Um El Ousur fault
Thebes Plateau fault
N
Hebus
Kharga
Gin Am
East Bulag
East Garuashin
West sand dune
Baris
Ain El Oasr
b
Explanation
1962 Piezometric surface contour (dashed where inferred)
Observation well and/or test hole
5 0 10
km

Fig. 10.15. a A piezometric map of the Kharga area for 1962; **b** a piezometric map of the Kharga area for 1970 riod which caused the modern river (delta Neonile or the Perennial Nile) broke into Egypt and was accompanied by a period of increased rainfall on the equatorial lake plateau, thus increasing the flow of the Nile.

With the advent of the Holocene epoch, the forcing factors, which brought about the early rains of the equatorial lake plateau, became operational on the Ethiopian Highlands and on the plains of northern Sudan and southern Egypt. The regimen of the modern river, therefore, owes its origin to the Holocene wet phase and its silt started to build up to the north of Aswan forming the famous agricultural layer of the fertile land of Egypt.

Table 10.3. Computed results by the analogue model, designed for the New Valley Project, 1965

Estimated no. of producing years	Amount of discharge (gal day^{-1})
20	50×10^6
40	40×10^6
60	30×10^6
100	25×10^6

10.5.2 The River Nile Basin

The term "basin" was given to the path of the River Nile as it is surrounded from the east, south and west by a crescentic form of the basement rocks. These rocks were connected with those of the Arab Peninsula before the formation of the Red Sea during the Post-Miocene time.

The present River Nile basin is in the northeast of Africa and runs through six African countries from south to north as follows: Tangunice, Kenya, Oglhanda, Ethiopia, Sudan and Egypt. It extends for about 6 000 km from Lake Victoria at the equator to the Mediterranean Sea in the north.

Recent drilling in the Nile Valley confirms that the Nile was probably eroded on a line of faulting and rifting in late Pliocene from Luxor to Cairo.

The structural relation of the basement rocks and the hydrology of the River Nile basin were important as the faulting and folding structures of the basement rocks

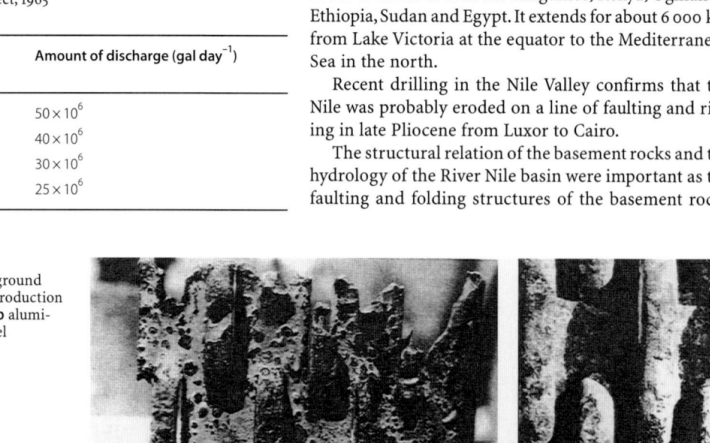

Fig. 10.16. Corrosive effect of ground water on different production pipes; **a** mild steel; **b** aluminum; **c** stainless steel

Table 10.4. Permissible amounts of discharge of the ground water in the oases

Amount of discharge	Kharga or Dakhla or Bahariya or Farafra Oases	Siwa Oasis	South of Kharga
$m^3 d^{-1}$	2×10^6	0.5×10^6	4×10^6
gallon d^{-1}	527×10^6	136×10^6	$1\,054 \times 10^6$
Ampere ms^{-1}	97.8×10^{-3}	48.9×10^{-3}	195×10^{-3}

and the associated fractures of the overlying Nubian sandstone formation greatly control the direction of flow in the Nubian aquifer system in the Western Desert of Egypt. The post cretaceous east/west faults that extend from Aswan to the south of Kharga and the northeast-southwest major fault that extends between Djebel Oweinat and the Tebesti Mountains of the Republic of Chad in the southwest are good examples. There are also two sets of E/W and N/S faulting structures in the vicinity of Nasser Lake (Issawi 1970; Fig. 10.17). One of the EW faults was the cause of the earthquakes that occurred 10 years after the full operation of Aswan High Dam and is known to have been seismically active since its inception and up to at least Roman time, having therefore no connection with the weight of the water column in Lake Nasser (Said 1993).

Actually, the River Nile started its relation with the Nubian sandstone formations at the mid-area of the Sudan (at Dowin Village) where it penetrates these formations for about 150 km from the capital Khartoum and extends to the north at Kharga and Dakhla Oases of the Western Desert of Egypt. The River Nile in the mid-area of the Sudan loses some of its water through the Nubian sandstone as it moves from the east to the west according to the decrease of the surface water elevations in this direction, knowing that the ground-water flow attains the same direction (Ezzat 1966).

The regional relief map on top of the basement rocks as well as the drilling results of two wells south of Aswan up to Tushka Village further to the south showed that there had been an old ground water Nile basin. Its axis of northeast-southwest is parallel to the West Bank of this part of the River Nile.

Salem mentioned an old path of the River Nile that had been filled with sediments thousands of years ago and that it might be connected to the Kharga Oasis. Many lakes of Quaternary age formed along the Western bank of the River Nile denoting the old path of the River Nile, which was meandering through its younger stages. The accumulation of lake deposits in the Kharga depression is an indication of their presence. The River Nile only reached south of the Sudan in early Paleolithic (50 000 B.C.). It pushed its path to the depression of the Kharga Oasis in Pre-Oligocene times while captured in Wadi Quena (Sandford 1929). Later in late Pliocene times, the River Nile found its way from Luxor to the Nile Delta after the tectonic movements that took place in Oligocene-Miocene times (Ezzat 1966).

10.6 Environmental Concerns

The New Valley area, which is an arid region of 3 000 km^2 (approximately 3 million feddans) that can be cultivated, is a part of the Egyptian deserts that cover 97% of the whole territory.

Sand dunes are well known in the Western Desert of Egypt and cause a real problem in transportation and settlement of local inhabitants. Old Ginah village, 20 km south of Kharga Oasis, was buried in the past by the moving sand dunes from the north to west. In the present, the moving sand dunes appearing 6 km from Kharga Village on the road between Kharga and Assiut could be stopped by either fixing wind barriers or constructing underground tunnels (see Appendix 10.A.1: Local photos from Western Desert of Egypt).

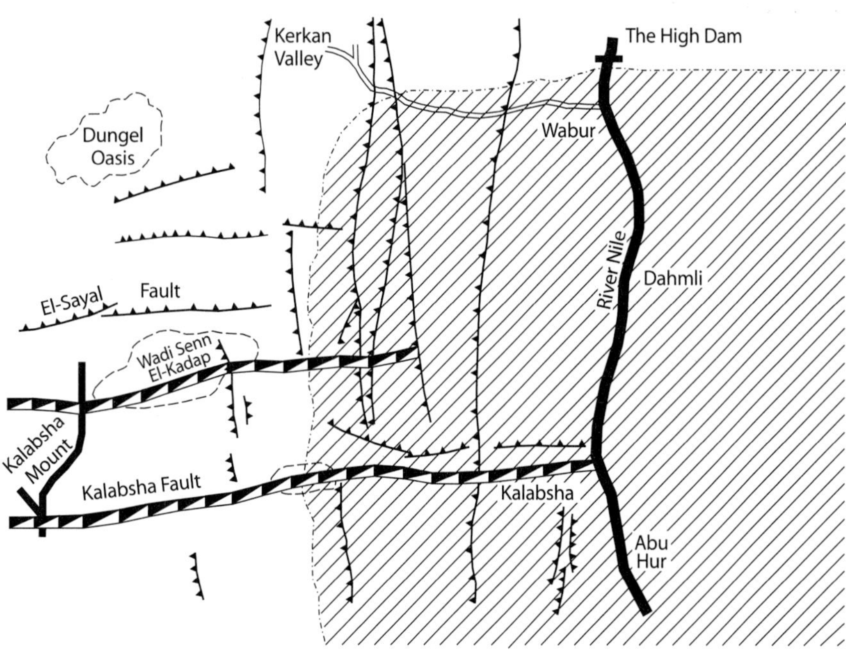

Kerkan Valley
The High Dam
Dungel Oasis
Wabur
River Nile
Dahmli
El-Sayal
Fault
Wadi Senn El-Kadap
Kalabsha Mount
Kalabsha Fault
Kalabsha
Abu Hur

Fig. 10.17. Faulting system in Nasser Lake and its vicinity (after Issawi 1970)

10.7 Local Activities

It might be interesting to mention that fine implements were found nearby old buried springs where mankind of the Recent Stone Age had used for hunting. Nowadays, the inhabitants of the old villages are still using the old arts from the topsoil layer which they treat to form nice jars of different colors and from the leaves of palm trees, they hand-made baskets of different shapes and sizes (see Appendix 10.A.1).

10.8 Conclusions

The geological and hydrological study of the River Nile basin and its surroundings can lead to a better understanding of the relation between the surface hydrology of the Nile and the flow of the ground water in the Nubian sandstone aquifer of the Western Desert of Egypt.

Several lakes that were filled with clays and silt deposits were formed during the Quaternary Age within the old paths of the River Nile in the area between mid-Sudan and the Kharga Oasis and were considered as intermediate passages for the surface waters to reach the underground Nubian aquifer of the Kharga Oasis and hence the name, "old ground-water path of the Nile." The River Nile in the mid-area of Sudan loses some of its water in the Nubian aquifer as the surface elevations are much higher than that of the Nubian ground water further to the west.

In Aswan, the east/west faults of the basement rocks on the western bank of the Nile may extend to the area south of Kharga causing leakage of some of its waters in Nasser Lake (the high dam lake south of Aswan) to the Nubian aquifer far to the west.

The geologic survey of the Western Desert showed that the basement rocks and the overlying Nubian sandstone formations are folded in the northeast/southwest direction which greatly control the direction of the ground-water movement from the south and southwest through the lowermost section of the Nubian formation (Lower Carboniferous beds?) and accordingly drilling of deep wells is recommended in selected locations of the Western Desert for carrying out more precise age dating based on radioisotopes.

Regional hydrological studies should be carried out by the United Nations and the EPA of the USA to answer many of the hydrological hypotheses around the great River Nile basin of Africa.

References

Assaad FA (1988) Hydrogeological aspects and environmental concerns of the New Valley Project, Western Desert, Egypt, with emphasis on the southern area. Environ Geol Water S 12(3):141–161

Assaad FA, Barakat MG (1965) Geological results of the Assuit-Kharga Well. J Geol 9(2):81–87

Assaad FA, Philip G (1969) Mechanical analysis, porosity and permeability studies on the Nubian sandstone, south of Beris, Kharga Oasis, Western Desert, Egypt. J Geol 13:37–48

Clarke FE (1962) Evaluations and control of water well corrosion problems in Kharga and Dakhla Oases, Western Desert, Egypt, UAR. U.S. Geol. Survey, Open File Report, Cairo

Clarke FE (1963) Appraisal of corrosion characteristics of the Western Desert well water, Egypt, UAR. U.S. Geol. Survey, Open File Report, Cairo

Ezzat MA (1966) Geological study research of the Nile basin and its relation with the ground-water path. The Arabian Engineering Conference, Jordan, August 1966. Egyptian General Desert Development Organization (EGDDO), Cairo

Folk RL, Ward WCA (1957) A study in the significance of grain size parameters. J Sediment Petrol 27:3–26

Issawi B (1970) The structural system in Nasser Lake and its vicinity. Al-Ahram Newspaper, Cairo

LaMoreaux PE (1959) Report on and recommendations for ground-water investigations, New Valley Project, Western Desert of Egypt. Admin. Report, U.S. Geol. Survey, in cooperation with Egypt and the USOM, UAR, Cairo

LaMoreaux PE (1964) A review of the New Valley Project, Western Desert of Egypt with special reference to the development of a quantitative consultant's study. General Desert Development Organization (GDDO), Cairo

LaMoreaux PE (1976) Geology and ground water in Kharga Oasis with respect to long-range ground-water development. General Desert Development Organization (GDDO), Cairo

LaMoreaux PE, Memon BA, Idris H (1985) Ground-water development, Kharga Oases, Western Desert of Egypt: a long-term environmental concern. Environ Geol Water S 7(3):129–149

Radoslav-Rakar EE (1968) Basis for the analogue model of Kharga and Dakhla Oases (electrical part). Industroprojekt, Department for Exploration of Mineral Resources, Zagreb, Yugoslavia, pp 1–12

Said R (1993) The River Nile: geology, hydrology and utilization. Pergamon Press Inc., Tarrytown, New York, pp 1–5, 28–55

Salem MH (1970) Study of the hydrologic parameters of the Nubian sandstone aquifer with reference to the productivity of pattern for well development in Kharga Oasis, Egypt. General Desert Development Organization (GDDO), Cairo, pp 223–240

Sandford KS (1929) The Pliocene and Pleistocene deposits of Wadi Quena and the Nile Valley between Luxor and Assuit. Q J Geol Soc London 75:493–548

Shazly MM, Shata A, Farag IAM (1959) The subsurface geology of el-Kharga Oasis. EGDDO, Cairo (special report)

Shukri NM, Said R (1944) Contribution to the geology of the Nubian sandstone, part 1: Field observations and mechanical analysis. Cairo University, Cairo (Bulletin of the Faculty of Science 25:149–172)

Soliman MM, LaMoreaux PE, Memon B, Assaad F, LaMoreaux JW (1998) Environmental hydrogeology. Lewis Publishers inc. (CRC)

Appendix 10.A

Local pictures in different areas of the Western Desert of Egypt, 1962 (Fig. 10.A.1.)

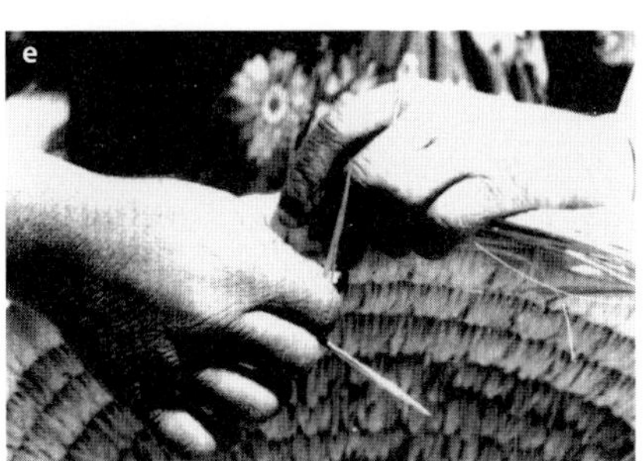

Fig. 10.A.1. Local photos from Western Desert of Egypt; **a** Kharga-Assiut road and the problem of moving sand dunes; **b** brown clay jar of New Valley; **c** fine impliment, used for hunting in the Recent Stone Age; **d** "doom trees" of the New Valley area; **e** palm leaf basket, handmade by inhabitant of New Valley; **f** workers digging a shallow well, using the "percussion" method

Chapter 11

Sulfate and Chloride Karstification and Its Economical Significance

F. Reiter · H. Jordan · H. Molek

11.1 Introduction

Easily soluble rocks, such as sulfatic and chloridic salts, show a wide spectrum of karstification and distribution, especially in central Europe (Upper Permian Zechstein and also Triassic rocks). Surrounding older rocks of Variscan orogeny, (e.g. gypsum, anhydrides, halites, and potassium salts) are subsurface deposits, which are in contact with ground water. Very intensive karstifications, e.g. sinkholes, depressions, subsidence and landslides, in the vicinity of worked-out salt mines are found active in the present. Therefore, they are a permanent danger for engineering, mining, and public affairs.

Figure 11.1 is a schematic cross section showing karstification in marginal areas of Mesozoic basins (Weber 1930). In general, it is possible to distinguish three kinds of karstification in sulfatic and chloridic rocks (Table 11.1).

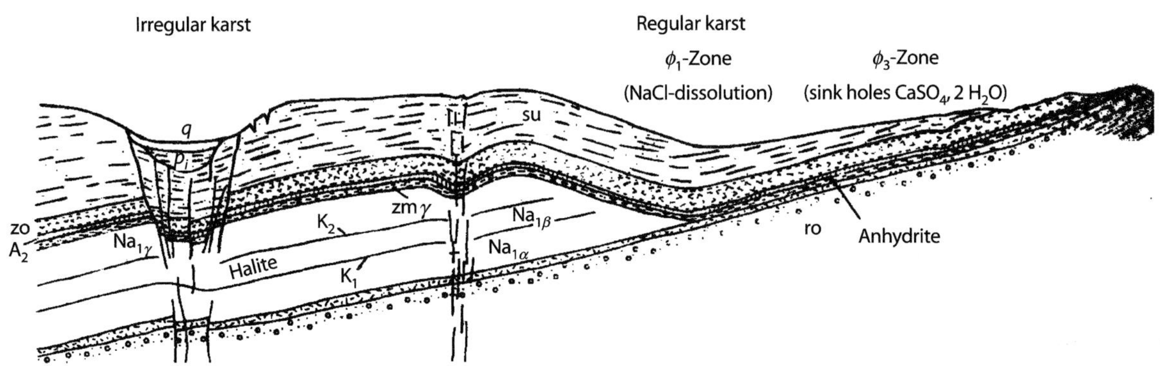
Irregular karst
Regular karst
ϕ_1-Zone
(NaCl-dissolution)
ϕ_3-Zone
(sink holes $CaSO_4$, 2 H_2O)
q
su
zo
A_2
$Na_{1\gamma}$
K_2
zmγ
$Na_{1\beta}$
$Na_{1\alpha}$
Halite
K_1
ro
Anhydrite

Fig. 11.1. Schematic cross section showing karstification in marginal areas of Mesozoic basins (Weber 1930); *su*: Lower Triassic sandstone and siltstone; *zo*: Upper Permian (Zechstein); A_2: upper anhydrite; *Na*: halite; *K*: potassium deposits; *ro*: Lower Permian

Table 11.1. Types of sulfatic and chloridic karst

Type	Overburden	Hydrogeological conditions	Examples		Rocks
			On surface	Subsurface	
Naked karst	Soluble rocks	Percolation zone; oscilating ground water; chloridic rocks are solved	Karren Clints Dolines Sinkholes	Caves Caverns	Gypsum Anhydrite
Covered karst	Insoluble rocks (permeable or impermeable)	Soluble rocks in contact with ground water (chloridic rocks are mostly solved)	Dolines Sinkholes	Caves Caverns	Gypsum Anhydrite (partially chloridic rocks)
Deep karst	Insoluble rocks	Soluble rocks below watercourse	Depressions Subsidence-troughs Sinkholes	Caverns	Salt rocks Halite Potassium salt Anhydrite

There are natural phenomena of karstification; depressions and subsidence are found in mm-scale whereas sinkholes are found of 1 to 3 m in diameter. Man-made phenomena are mainly caused by salt mining of the 19th century or water use and management. The latter are bigger and have diameters of >100 m and subsidence of >dm yr^{-1}. Therefore, it is necessary to investigate all these phenomena in-depth with regard to safety and restoration. This is often very expensive, but in the 20th century there has not been any victim of karstic disasters in the ex-German Democratic Republic (GDR).

11.2 Fundamentals of Karstification

In central Europe limestone underlies karstification, but it is less important than the saliferous rocks from the economic point of view (see Bögli 1978; Zötl 1974) because of humid conditions. The solubility factor of karstic rocks is as follows: limestone : anhydride / gypsum : rock salt = 1 : 100 : 10 000.

Sulfates: Anhydride ($CaSO_4$) and gypsum ($CaSO_4 \cdot 2H_2O$) are most important. The transformation from anhydride to gypsum is connected with a diminution of the total volume (tripestone). The solubility depends on the temperature. In presence of ions, such as Na^+, Cl^-, in the salt deposits, the solubility increases by about four times and mixed corrosion progresses under these circumstances (Table 11.2).

A high rate of sinkhole and subsidence activity can be concluded from high NaCl-concentration in the ground water.

Chlorides: Halite and potassium salts are directly soluble. A high content of potassium salts in combination with halite increases the solubility.

Geomechanical aspects of karstification: Sulfatic rocks react to stress by forming joints and fissures. Consequently, water can penetrate and dissolve the salt rock (Fig. 11.2).

The combination of solutions and dissolutions lead to the formation of caves and sinkholes. Chloridic rocks react to stress by a kind of plastic deformation. There are no joints and fissures and the solution starts from "above" in form of a "salt mirror" (plane) or "salt slope" (angular). This kind of solution mostly covers a large area connected with the effects of subsidence and depressions.

11.3 Geomechanical Models

Sulfatic karst: In general, sinkholes have different shape and scale. The sinking velocity is discontinuous and reaches 10^{-1} mm a^{-1} (annum or year) to m min^{-1}, depending on the overburden and depth; the deeper the caverns the bigger the sinkholes. Figure 11.3 shows models of subsidence and fractured forms in sulfatic karst.

Table 11.2. Solubility of anhydrite and gypsum in presence of NaCl

NaCl (g l^{-1}) in water	0.00	172	200	244	292.8	358.5
$CaSO_4$ (g l^{-1}) in solution	2.04	7.87	8.23	8.20	6.14	7.09

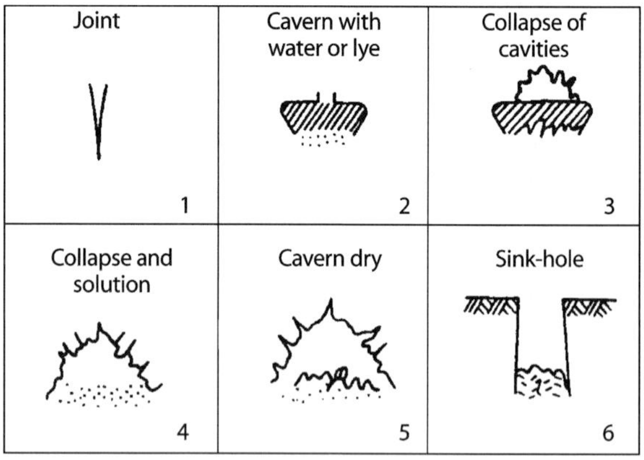

Joint 1	Cavern with water or lye 2	Collapse of cavities 3
Collapse and solution 4	**Cavern dry 5**	**Sink-hole 6**

Fig. 11.2. Origin of sinkholes in sulfatic rocks (after Kempe 1970)

The hazard potential of an (*H*) area can be estimated by statistical methods as follows:

$$H = \frac{n}{F - t} \tag{11.1}$$

where:
n = amount of sinkholes
F = area (km^2)
t = time scale (a)

The "critical diameter" is an important factor of sinkholes. It indicates the hazard potential of buildings.

In addition to that, suffusion can be observed in sulfatic karst at subsidence velocities of n–10 … n–10^3 mm a^{-1} (Fig. 11.4). Smaller landslides at slopes can also be observed which are caused by small sinkholes, suffusion and erosion.

Chloridic karst: In humid climate zones chloridic karstification occurs under the conditions of deep karst, where mostly (1) the configurations of caves are not known, (2) the corrosion develops discontinuously and is old in most cases (of Tertiary and older age), and (3) the overburden is destroyed and looks like a mosaic. Fig-

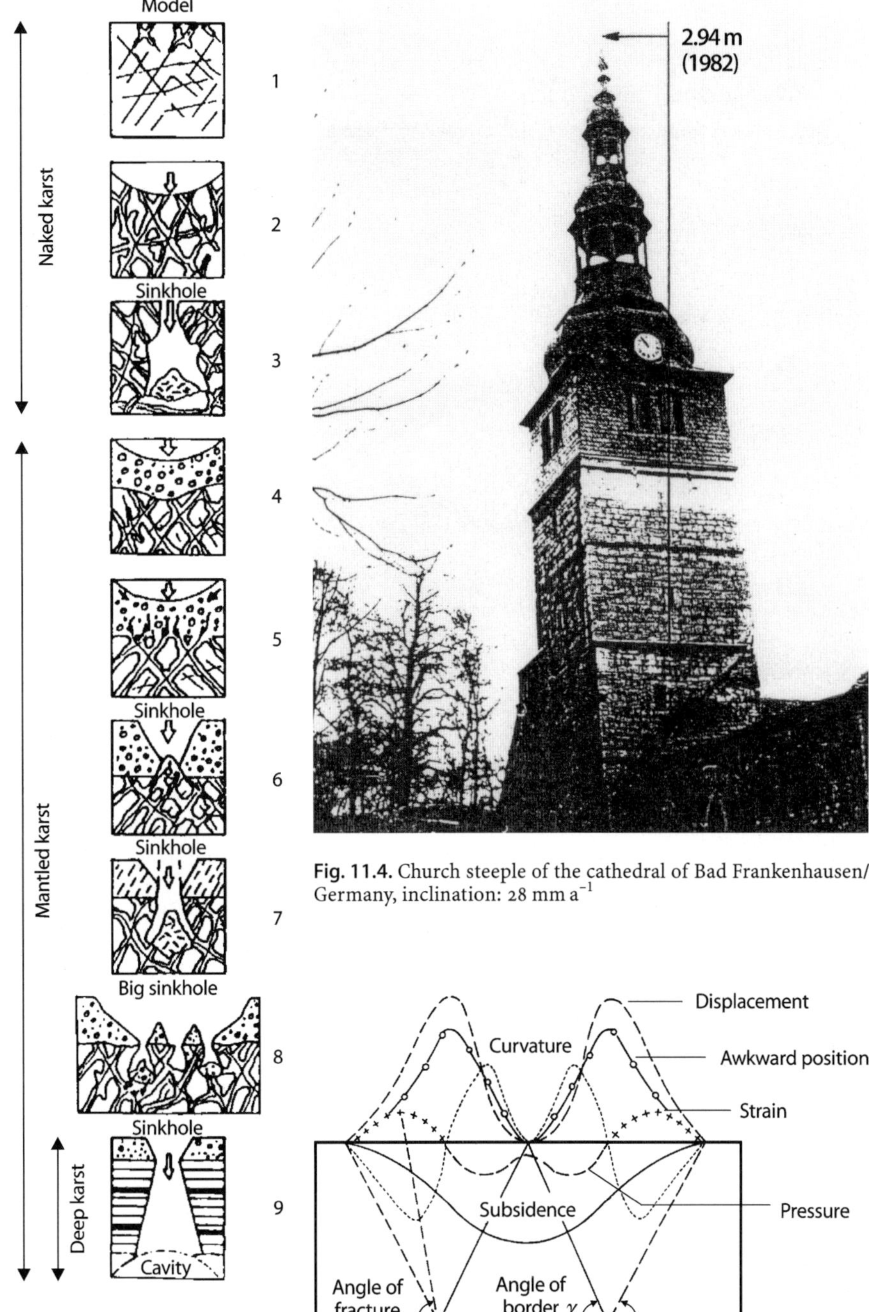
Model
1
Naked karst
2
Sinkhole
3
4
5
Sinkhole
6
Mantled karst
Sinkhole
7
Big sinkhole
8
Sinkhole
Deep karst
9
Cavity
2.94 m
(1982)
Displacement
Curvature
Awkward position
Strain
Subsidence
Pressure
Angle of fracture
Angle of border γ
β
γ_i
γ_e
Cavity

Fig. 11.3. Models of subsidence and fractured forms in sulfatic karst

Fig. 11.4. Church steeple of the cathedral of Bad Frankenhausen/ Germany, inclination: 28 mm a^{-1}

Fig. 11.5. Movement above horizontal solutions of chloridic karst; β – fracture angle, γ_i – interior angle, γ_e – exterior angle, $\gamma_i = \gamma_e$

ure 11.5 shows the movement above horizontal solutions of chloridic karst; β – fracture angle, γ_i – interior angle, γ_e – exterior angle, $\gamma_i = \gamma_e$.

These kinds of corrosion result in depressions of different forms. Depressions are deformations, which are caused by the deficiency in mass balance due to corrosion with subsidence velocities of some mm a^{-1} to more than mm d^{-1}.

The most endangered zones lie in the marginal zones. These are horizontal movements and marginal dislocations spreading over several miles and some meters in depth. They can easily be observed by air and space photography.

Fig. 11.6a. Forms of subsidence areas; fissuring

Fig. 11.6b. Forms of subsidence areas; graben

Fig. 11.6c. Forms of subsidence areas; sinkhole

Fig. 11.6d. Forms of subsidence areas; collapse of building

Table 11.3. Collapse of buildings caused by sinkholes

H (%)	*e* (1 = 100%)	*d* (m)	*E*/a	a/*E*
0.01	0.2	1	8.23×10^{-4}	1215
		5	11.0×10^{-4}	910
		10	15.25×10^{-4}	660
0.05	0.2	1	41.1×10^{-4}	243
		5	55.0×10^{-4}	182
		10	76.0×10^{-4}	132
0.1	0.1	1	41.1×10^{-4}	243
		73	5138.0×10^{-4}	
		53	10190.0×10^{-4}	

H = Number of sinkholes; *d* = diameter of sinkholes; *e* = density of buildings; *a* = year; *E* = collapse

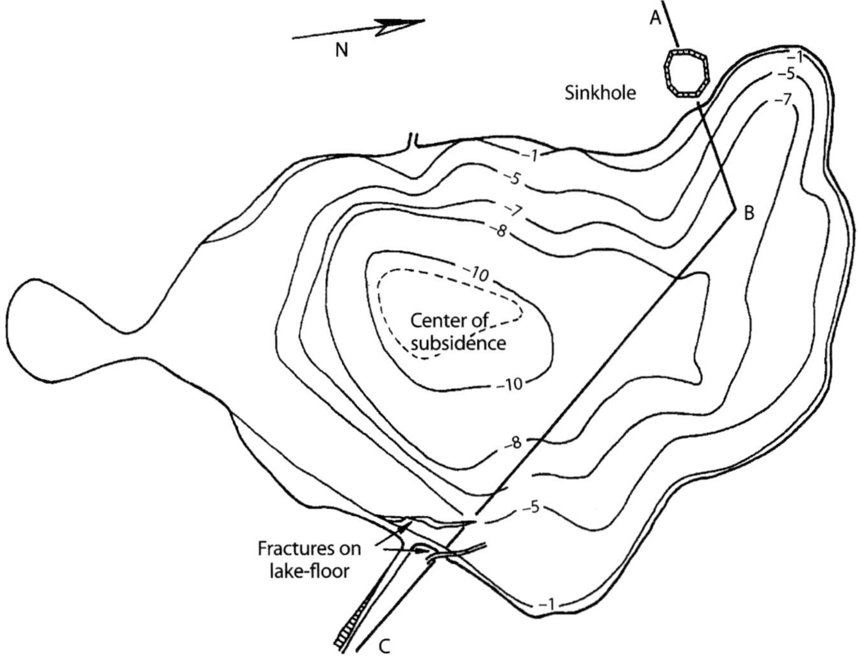
N
A
Sinkhole
-1
-5
-7
B
-1
-5
-7
-8
-10
Center of subsidence
-10
-8
-5
Fractures on
lake-floor
-1
C

Fig. 11.7a. Depression in chloridic karst with marginal dislocation and sinkhole (depth of karstic tube = 250 m); ground plane

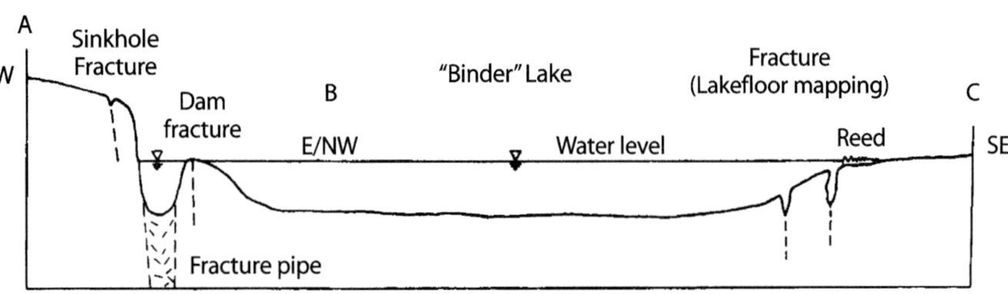
A
W
Sinkhole
Fracture
Dam
fracture
B
E/NW
"Binder" Lake
Water level
Fracture
(Lakefloor mapping)
Reed
C
SE
Fracture pipe

Fig. 11.7b. Depression in chloridic karst with marginal dislocation and sinkhole (depth of karstic tube = 250 m); cross section

Sinkholes in chloridic rocks are bigger than in sulfatic ones (diameter >30 m, depth >10 m).

It is supposed that these sinkholes originated in connection with inhomogenities in salts and overburden, aquifers and aquitards as well (Fig. 11.6a–d, Table 11.3, Fig. 11.7).

11.4 Conclusion

Sulfatic and chloridic karstification is an important factor as well as economical, in central Europe.

This case study presents principal and methodical aspects together with examples on the types of sulfatic and chloridic karst, geomechanical models and forms of subsidence areas.

References

Bögli A (1978) Karsthydrographie und physische Speläologie. Springer-Verag, Berlin Heidelberg New York

Kempe S (1970) Beiträge zum Problem der Speläogenese im Gips unter besonderer Berücksichtigung der Unterwasserphase. Z Höhle 21(3):126–134

Weber H (1930) Zur Systematik der Auslaugung. Z Deut Geol Ges Berlin 82:179–196

Zötl J (1974) Karsthydrologie. Springer-Verlag, Wien

Chapter 12

Occurence of DNAPL near an Interceptor Well – Pump and Test Treatment for Remediation

D. S. Green · B. A. Memon · P. E. LaMoreaux

12.1 Introduction

A dense, non-aqueous phase liquid (DNAPL) was detected during routine maintenance of an interceptor (pumping) well at a chemical manufacturing facility. The well is one of 10 interceptor wells at the site, and is screened at the base of an alluvial aquifer. Preliminary analysis indicated that the DNAPL was composed of a mixture of liquids (including chlorobenzene) and dissolved solid-phase organic compounds (including DDT). The location of the DNAPL indicated a potential for migration offsite.

Fluvial channel-fill deposits are the predominant coarse clastic facies at this site. Gravel and coarse-grained sand units were deposited in the central portion of meandering channels cut by paleostreams. Because these highly permeable units are often found in association with decreasing elevation of the underlying basal clay, these units provide preferential flow paths for high-density fluids. Permeability varies greatly, due to the heterogeneous and anisotropic nature of the porous media, and because of the internal variability and lenticular geometry of fluvial sand bodies. A thorough understanding of the local hydrogeologic framework is critical to describing the occurrence of DNAPLs in the subsurface.

This investigation was initiated to identify preferential routes of contaminant migration near the source area and the interceptor well system. A conceptual model was developed to aid in understanding the processes and conditions affecting the occurrence of the DNAPL. The model is also intended to facilitate the identification of data necessary to evaluate potential remedial alternatives.

12.2 Background

The site investigated is a chemical manufacturing facility that began operating in the 1950s. Ground-water monitoring in the early 1980s identified the need for a corrective action program for the uppermost (alluvial) aquifer. As part of the program, an interceptor well system was installed. The system was designed to reverse the hydraulic gradient in the alluvial aquifer near the southern property boundary and pump contaminated ground water to the on-site treatment system. The western end of the line of interceptor wells (P-1 through P-5) is shown in Fig. 12.1. Continuous pumping began in 1987.

Discharge rates at all of the interceptor wells are currently lower than when the system was first placed online (in mid-1987). The total flow from the system has been reduced by about 30% from the original rate of about 2 million gallons (7.57 million liter) per day in early 1988. The reversal of hydraulic gradient along the southern property boundary has been maintained throughout this period.

In December 1990, interceptor well P-2 was bailed and a dark brown liquid, intermixed with sediment, was first recovered. Preliminary chemical analysis indicated that the liquid was comprised primarily of chlorobenzene (specific density: 1.1058 at 20/4 °C; aqueous solubility: 500 mg l^{-1} at 20 °C (Montgomery 1991)) and *p,p*'-DDT, with minor amounts of other pesticides. Based on field observations and the physical and chemical properties associated with the constituents identified, the material was designated a DNAPL and this investigation was initiated. This DNAPL is observed regularly during maintenance of well P-2, the only well at the site in which this material has been detected.

The probable surface source of the DNAPL recovered in well P-2 is an area of historic waste disposal about 750 feet (230 m) north of the well. Effluent containing wastes and by-products from the manufacture of pesticides was disposed into an unlined pit in this area from the 1950s to the mid-1960s.

Dense, non-aqueous phase liquids (DNAPLs) are fluids that are denser than water and are immiscible with water. The principles governing the movement of DNAPLs in the subsurface are described by Schwille (1988), the Waterloo Center for Groundwater Research (1992), Cohen and Mercer (1993), and Gorelick et al. (1993). Chlorinated solvents, including chlorobenzene, are the most common DNAPL contamination problems at sites today (Cherry et al. 1993).

The fraction of DNAPL with a positive pressure, and which is available to flow into a well, is free-phase or

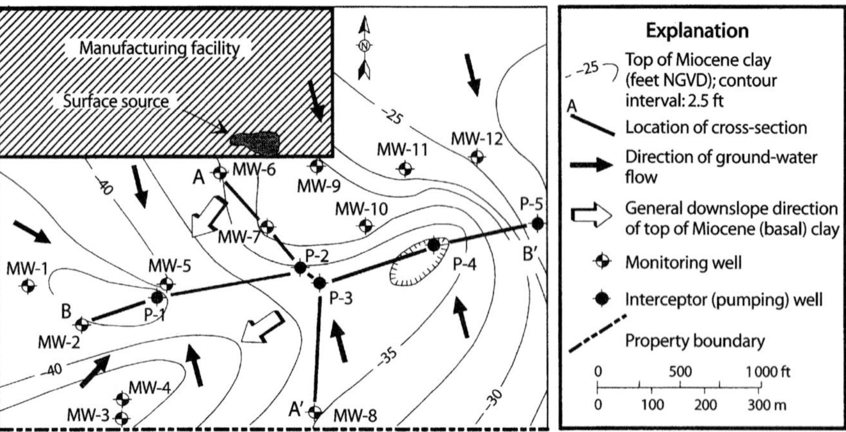
Manufacturing facility
Surface source
MW-1
MW-2
MW-3
MW-4
MW-5
MW-6
MW-7
MW-8
MW-9
MW-10
MW-11
MW-12
P-1
P-2
P-3
P-4
P-5
A
A'
B
B'
-25
-30
-35
-40
Explanation
Top of Miocene clay (feet NGVD); contour interval: 2.5 ft
Location of cross-section
Direction of ground-water flow
General downslope direction of top of Miocene (basal) clay
Monitoring well
Interceptor (pumping) well
Property boundary
0 500 1000 ft
0 100 200 300 m

Fig. 12.1. Area of investigation

mobile DNAPL. Residual components are left behind the advancing front of DNAPL as droplets or ganglia within the pores of the aquifer. Capillary tension, or negative immiscible-phase pressure, holds the immiscible phase liquid in the pore spaces. Residual DNAPL typically occupies from 1 to 25% of pore space (Cohen and Mercer 1993). Residual immiscible phase liquid cannot flow under gravitational forces alone.

Residual, lenses, and pools of DNAPL constitute sources for dissolved-solute contaminant plumes. The plumes are comprised of the dissolved-phase components of the DNAPL in the saturated zone.

12.3 Methodology

Previous investigations have been performed to define the geology and hydrogeology of the site. The water quality portions of these investigations were designed to address the miscible phase contamination of the ground water. In this investigation, the lithologic framework of the subsurface was emphasized because of its importance to the identification of preferential routes of DNAPL migration.

Data reviewed included lithologic descriptions of samples from wells, geophysical logs recorded in boreholes drilled during the installation of monitoring wells, results of chemical analyses of ground-water samples, and previous reports and documentation of hydrogeologic conditions. Hydrogeologic cross sections and structure maps were prepared to aid in the interpretation of subsurface conditions and identification of potential migration pathways near the source area and interceptor system.

12.4 Hydrogeology of the Alluvial Aquifer

The uppermost deposit at the site is a surficial clay that acts as a semi-confining unit for the underlying alluvial aquifer. The alluvial aquifer consists of fluvial deposits of Pleistocene to Recent sand and gravel that include minor (intermediate) clay lenses (Fig. 12.2). In general, grain size in this interval decreases upward from gravel and coarse-grained sand to very fine-grained sand and clay. The sand deposits are typically yellowish-orange, medium- to coarse-grained, and are predominantly comprised of moderately sorted, subangular to subrounded quartz grains. Coarser sand at the base of the unit often contains subrounded quartz and chert gravel. A paleochannel, comprised of gravel and coarse-grained sand deposits, trends northeast-southwest along a trough-like feature eroded into the underlying basal clay approximately coincident with the P-series interceptor wells. The thickness of the alluvial aquifer ranges from about 35 feet (10.7 m) in well MW-8, south of the main paleochannel, to over 70 feet (21.3 m) in well P-1, near the center of the main paleochannel.

The lower boundary of the alluvial aquifer is an unconformity at the top of a clay of Miocene age. As a potential barrier to downward migration of any DNAPL to the underlying Miocene aquifer, the configuration of the top of the Miocene clay is of particular significance. The minimum thickness of the Miocene clay is 22 feet (6.7 m), and the top of the clay occurs at depths ranging from 67.5 to 98 feet (20.6 to 29.9 m) below land surface. Figure 12.1 shows the configuration of the top of the Miocene clay. The inclination and direction of dip of the top of the Miocene clay were calculated using the three-point method. The direction of dip of the top of the clay ranges from south 2° west in the area immediately north of interceptor well P-2, and changes its direction westward to the north 65° west, in the area around the surface source area. The gradient ranges from 0.002 in the broad, flat area south of the surface source area, to 0.014 in the area immediately north of well P-2. These figures should be used only as a guide to the general direction and magnitude of dip, since the top of the Upper Miocene clay is an erosional surface and can display significant topographic relief locally.

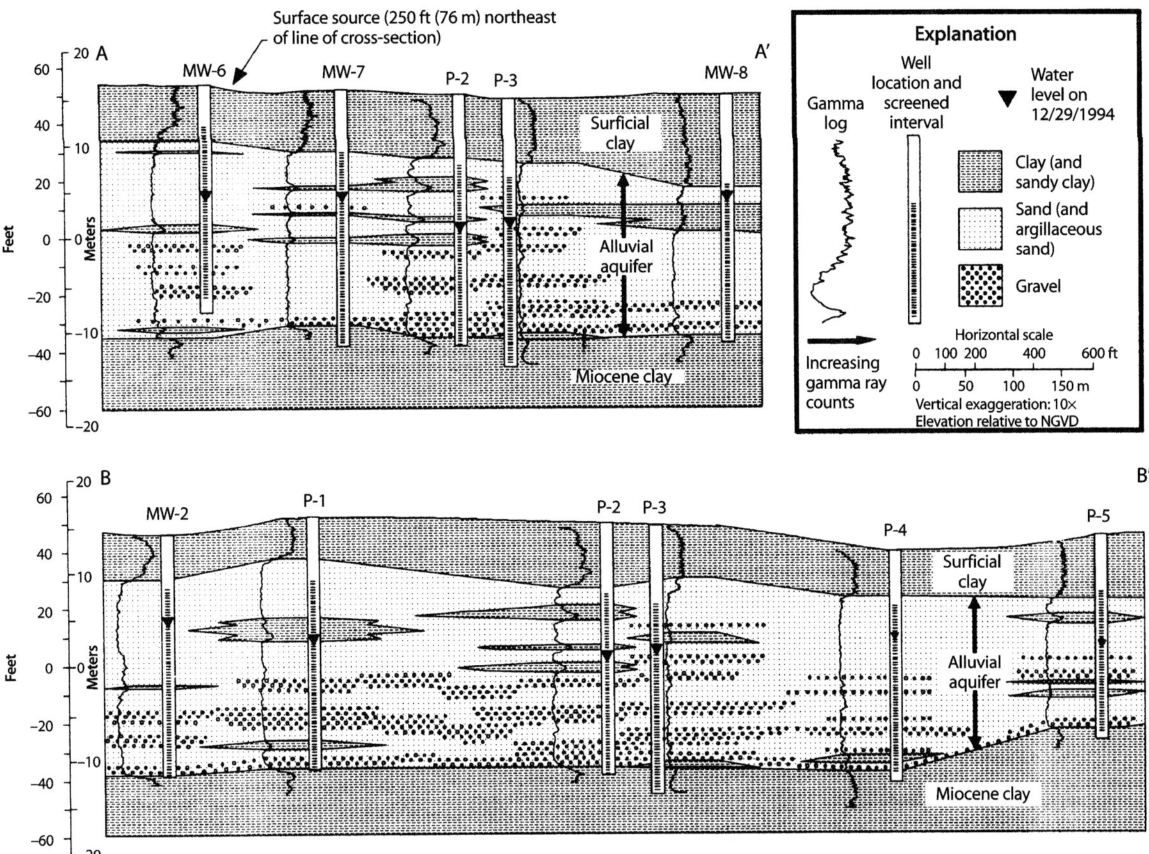
Surface source (250 ft (76 m) northeast of line of cross-section)
A
A'
MW-6
MW-7
P-2
P-3
MW-8
Surficial clay
Alluvial aquifer
Miocene clay
Feet
Meters
Explanation
Gamma log
Well location and screened interval
Water level on 12/29/1994
Clay (and sandy clay)
Sand (and argillaceous sand)
Gravel
Increasing gamma ray counts
Horizontal scale
0 100 200 400 600 ft
0 50 100 150 m
Vertical exaggeration: 10×
Elevation relative to NGVD
B
B'
MW-2
P-1
P-2
P-3
P-4
P-5
Surficial clay
Alluvial aquifer
Miocene clay

Fig. 12.2. Hydrogeologic cross sections A-A' and B-B'

The depth to ground water ranges from about 30 to 75 feet (9.1 to 22.9 m) below land surface in the interceptor wells, and from about 25 to 45 feet (7.6 to 13.7 m) below land surface in other parts of the area of investigation. Seasonal fluctuation of the water table near the source area is slightly more than 1 foot (0.3 m). Transmissivity of the alluvial aquifer ranges from 17 811 to 97 881 gallons per day per foot (221 to 1 216 $m^2 d^{-1}$).

Evaluation of water levels measured during periods of both relatively high and low water levels indicate the ground-water gradient in the alluvial aquifer near the source area ranges from 0.002 to 0.004. This small value indicates that the ground-water surface slopes gently in this area of relatively low topographic relief. The predominant direction of ground-water flow in the alluvial aquifer is southeastward (toward the interceptor well system).

Descriptions of alluvial facies models and the various sedimentary bodies associated with them are described by Allen (1965, 1970), Miall (1981), Reading (1978), Scholle and Spearing (1982), and Reineck and Singh (1980). The sand-rich deposits that comprise the alluvial aquifer at this site are characterized by blocky, relatively uniform natural gamma ray log responses, especially in the lower portion of the aquifer. These sediments are interpreted as predominantly fluvial channel-fill deposits, with associated point bar lateral accretion deposits. Gravel (up to 2 inches (5 cm) in diameter) and coarse-grained sand were deposited in the central portion of winding channels cut by paleostreams. Vertical accretion deposits, such as clay lenses, are deposited as sheet-like flood plain/backswamp deposits or as plugs in abandoned channels. The occurrence of these fine-grained deposits increases in the upper portion of the aquifer. A wide range of both horizontal and vertical permeabilities is the result of the complex heterogeneous sand-body geometry produced by fluvial systems.

In general, the downward increase in grain size at this site corresponds to an increase in permeability in the alluvial aquifer. In alluvial systems, gravel is typically deposited immediately above the surface of erosion either as a pebble pavement or a series of lens-shaped beds (Allen 1970). These basal, highly permeable sediments thicken southwestward at this site in conjunction with decreasing elevation of the top of the Miocene clay (an erosional surface) and form a preferential flow path for high-density fluids. Gravel also occurs at other intervals in the system, as later streams deposited stacked or multi-story sequences.

12.5 Discussion and Conceptual Model

Systematic ground-water monitoring at the site includes analysis of samples for chlorobenzene. As chlorobenzene is a major component of the DNAPL recovered from interceptor well P-2, trends in chlorobenzene concentrations in ground water (miscible phase) provide clues to the movement of DNAPL. Also, specific conductance profiles of ground water in wells in the study area were used to establish a baseline for monitoring changes. While specific conductance values represent the concentration of inorganic constituents of ground water, this information is used to provide a general indication of ground-water contamination and may prove to be a useful tool in estimating and monitoring the extent of DNAPL migration at this site.

Chlorobenzene levels in all wells at the site declined sharply after the interceptor well system was placed online in 1987. Concentrations continued to gradually decline, at significantly lower rates – a trend consistent with hypothetical examples of contaminant removal from aquifers provided in Mackay and Cherry (1989). An exception is the anomalously high concentration detected in well MW-7 (about 500 feet (152 meters) downgradient from the surface source) in February 1989, and the erratic pattern of values reported in this well from August 1988 to February 1989. Also, chlorobenzene levels increased slightly in interceptor well P-2 in early 1991, shortly after DNAPL was first observed in the well (Fig. 12.3).

The elevated concentrations of chlorobenzene in ground water at well MW-7 suggest the presence of immiscible-phase DNAPL near this well. The extremely high value recorded in February 1989, 1.5 years after initiation of pumping of the interceptor well system, may indicate that an advancing front of free-phase DNAPL was near well MW-7 at that time (DNAPL was detected by direct visual examination, in well P-2 in December 1990, or 1.8 years after the elevated concentration was detected in MW-7).

A conceptual model was developed to aid in investigative and remedial efforts. The model integrates site-specific information to provide a simplified view of the complex processes involved. A sketch of the initial conceptual model for this investigation is provided in Fig. 12.4. In this model, free-phase DNAPL is believed to have moved through the surficial clay underlying the waste disposal site and entered the unsaturated zone. The highly permeable basal alluvial deposits form zones of preferential flow, while the Miocene clay is the lowermost barrier to downward migration of DNAPLs. The shape of the miscible phase plume in the diagram (Fig. 12.4) represents the increase in concentrations of contaminants with depth within the alluvial aquifer. This is consistent with the densities of compounds identified in the DNAPL, and with the trends in specific conductance profiles recorded in previous investigation in wells downgradient from the surface source.

The vapor density of dry air at 20 °C and 760 mm mercury is 1.204 g l^{-1} (Montgomery 1991). Values for vapor density for the potential DNAPL components, which are liquid at normal temperatures range from 3.47 to 7.42 g l^{-1}, and indicate that any vapors volatilizing from the DNAPL will sink toward the water table. Solvent vapor in the unsaturated zone contaminates ground water by transfer of some vapor mass to the saturated zone (Cherry et al. 1993).

The water table is below the base of the surficial clay in the source area, and the DNAPL probably migrated vertically through the unsaturated zone, leaving residual DNAPL in the pore spaces. Water infiltrating through the unsaturated zone contributes to the miscible phase plume by carrying dissolved contaminates downward, and by dissolving contaminants from the residual DNAPL underneath the surface source.

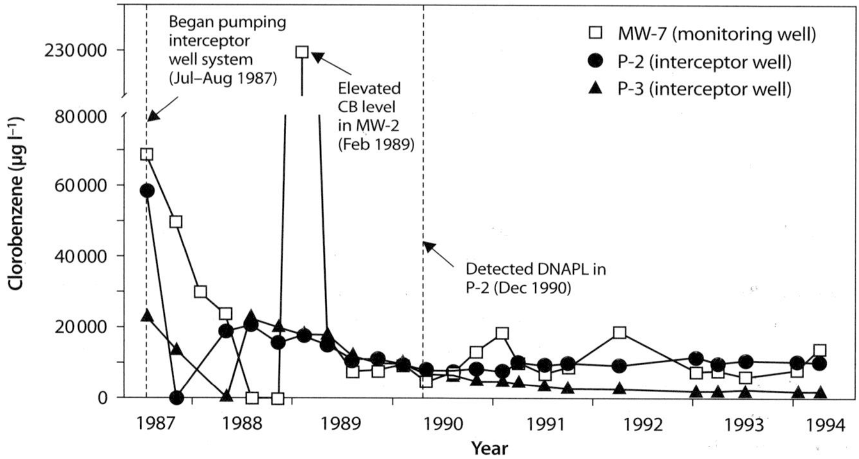
Began pumping interceptor well system (Jul–Aug 1987)
Elevated CB level in MW-2 (Feb 1989)
Detected DNAPL in P-2 (Dec 1990)
MW-7 (monitoring well)
P-2 (interceptor well)
P-3 (interceptor well)
Clorobenzene (µg l⁻¹)
230000
80000
60000
40000
20000
0
1987
1988
1989
1990
1991
1992
1993
1994
Year

Fig. 12.3. Chlorobenzene concentrations in ground water (July 1984–April 1994)

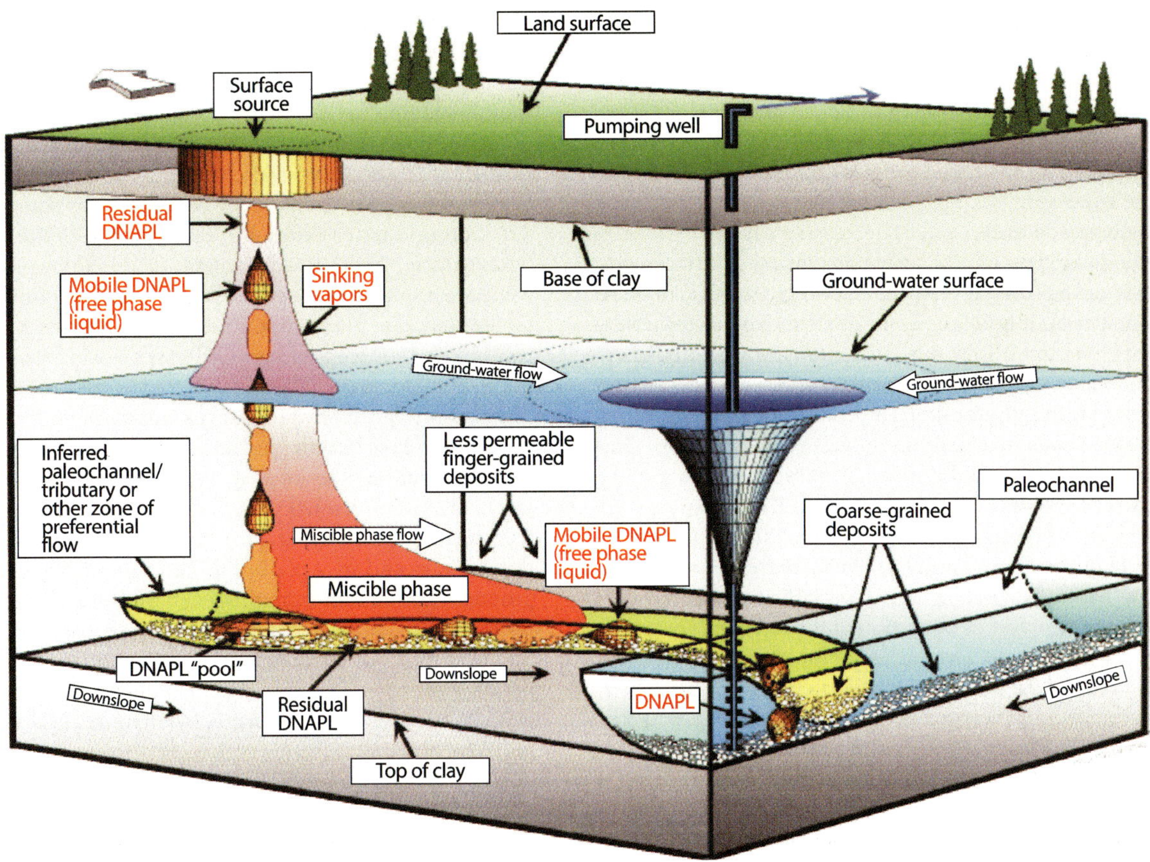
Land surface
Surface source
Pumping well
Residual DNAPL
Mobile DNAPL (free phase liquid)
Sinking vapors
Base of clay
Ground-water surface
Ground-water flow
Ground-water flow
Inferred paleochannel/ tributary or other zone of preferential flow
Less permeable finger-grained deposits
Paleochannel
Coarse-grained deposits
Miscible phase flow
Mobile DNAPL (free phase liquid)
Miscible phase
DNAPL "pool"
Downslope
Downslope
DNAPL
Downslope
Residual DNAPL
Top of clay

Fig. 12.4. Conceptual model of migration of DNAPL to pumping well

After moving downward, the DNAPL then formed a pool beneath the surface source, either at the base of the alluvial aquifer or on an intermediate clay lens within the aquifer. Existing data do not allow the delineation of the location and configuration of any closed topographic lows in the top of the basal clay, which may promote the accumulation of DNAPL in pools. However, in this initial conceptual model, a pool is postulated to have formed south of the surface source in a broad, relatively flat portion of the top of the Miocene clay.

A DNAPL pool is considered likely because of the relatively short period of time between detection of DNAPL in well P-2 after drilling and initial pumping (DNAPL was detected in P-2 5.3 years after the well was drilled and 3.3 years after continuous pumping began) compared to the period of time since the waste disposal area (the surface source) was first used (over 30 years). The DNAPL remained relatively stationary and formed a pool beneath the surface source, at the base of the alluvial aquifer or possibly on an intermediate clay lens within the aquifer. Some DNAPL may have moved slowly downslope along the top of the Miocene clay toward the southwest, until continuous pumping began at the interceptor well system in 1987.

The broad, relatively flat area in the top of the Miocene clay between the surface source and well P-2 is evident in Fig. 12.1. A small paleochannel in this area may provide a pathway for DNAPL migration. This feature is not a well-defined paleochannel, but may instead be contiguous coarse-grained, permeable deposits that provide a zone of preferential flow for the DNAPL. This hypothetical feature is illustrated in Fig. 12.4 by the small channel perpendicular to the larger, established (mapped) southwestern-trending paleochannel.

P-2 is the interceptor well nearest the surface source area (about 750 feet (229 m)) and is also the well at which the highest discharge rates were maintained during the early operation of the system. During the first year of operation (1987 to 1988), well P-2 was pumped at an average rate of 345 gallons per minute (21.8 l s^{-1}), compared to an average rate of 134 gallons per minute (8.5 l s^{-1}) for each of the other pumping wells during the same period. Also, the hydraulic gradient between the surface source and well P-2 was increased by pumping at nearby well P-3, from which ground water was discharged at an average rate of 118 gallons per minute (7.4 l s^{-1}) during the first year of operation.

The direction of ground-water flow controls the movement of the miscible phase, or contaminant plume, however, it is generally not a significant factor in migration of DNAPL. According to Cohen and Mercer (1993), the effect on DNAPL movement by the hydrodynamic force due to hydraulic gradient increases with: (1) decreasing gravitational pressure due to reduced DNAPL density and thickness; (2) decreasing capillary pressure due to the presence of coarse media, low interfacial tension, and a relatively high contact angle; and, (3) increasing hydraulic gradient. Some or all of these criteria were met near well P-2. While the density and thickness (height) of the DNAPL (the subsurface source) are not known, the gravitational pressure on the free-phase DNAPL was lessened by the low gradient in the relatively flat area south of the surface source (Fig. 12.1). Capillary pressure was decreased by the large pore spaces in the gravel and coarse-grained deposits near the base of the alluvial aquifer. The increase in the prevailing hydraulic gradient was especially pronounced during the first year of operation of the interceptor system, when pumping rates were higher for all interceptor wells.

To date, the DNAPL identified in well P-2 has not been detected in other pumping wells, including well P-3, probably because of the influence of the higher pumping rate at P-2. Also, at well P-3, a sandy clay unit occurs immediately above the top of the Miocene clay. Upgradient from P-3, in the general direction of P-2, the configuration of this sandy clay is not known. This sandy clay unit at P-3, while not a part of the Miocene clay, may alter the migration pathways near the well and prevent or impede the migration of DNAPL from the P-2 area to well P-3.

12.6 Executive Summary

1. In December 1990, a brownish-black substance was observed in material bailed from the bottom of interceptor (pumping) well P-2. Laboratory analysis indicates that the substance is comprised primarily of chlorobenzene and DDT. Based on the physical and chemical properties of these constituents, the material therefore appears to be a DNAPL (dense, nonaqueous phase liquid), consisting of a multi-component mixture of liquids and dissolved solid-phase organic compounds.
2. The likely surface source of the DNAPL which has been detected in well P-2 is an area of historic waste management activities about 750 feet north of well P-2.
3. The alluvial aquifer near well P-2 is a complex sequence of interlayered sand, silt, gravel, and clay, under semi-confined conditions. The sediments are of Pleistocene to Recent age and were deposited in a fluvial environment.
4. Ground-water monitoring in the early 1980s identified the need for a corrective action program for the alluvial aquifer at the site. Interceptor (pumping) wells, including well P-2, were installed in the uppermost (alluvial) aquifer near the southern property boundary in the mid-1980s. Continuous pumping began in July 1987 to intercept potentially contaminated ground water before the water flowed offsite.
5. Ground water in the alluvial aquifer flows southeastward across most of the site. South of the line of interceptor wells, the natural gradient is reversed by continuous pumping, and ground water flows toward the interceptor wells (Fig. 12.1).
6. The depth to ground water ranges from about 30 to 75 feet (9 to 23 m) below land surface in the interceptor wells, and from about 25 to 45 feet (7 to 14 m) below land surface in other parts of the primary area of investigation (Area A, Fig. 12.1). In the flood plain (in the eastern end of Area B, Fig. 12.1) the depth to ground water in non-pumping wells and temporary piezometers is occasionally less than 10 feet (3 m).
7. The base of the alluvial aquifer is the top of the Upper Miocene clay. This clay occurs at depths ranging from 27 to 98 feet (8 to 30 m) below land surface at the Ciba plant site. The elevation of the top of clay ranges from –10 to –60 ft (–3 to –18 m) NGVD.
8. The hydraulic conductivity of the Upper Miocene clay ranges from 3.2×10^{-11} to 5.2×10^{-8} cm s^{-1}. The Upper Miocene clay is present throughout the area of investigation and forms a barrier to downward migration of any DNAPL to the underlying Upper Miocene aquifer.
9. The configuration of the top of the Upper Miocene clay defines the potential pathways and plays an important role in the movement of DNAPL at this site because: (*a*) the top of the clay is an irregular surface which has been eroded by meandering paleostreams; and, (*b*) the paleochannels formed by these processes of erosion and deposition commonly contain substantial coarse-grained material (gravel), which comprise the most permeable deposits at the site.
10. The trough formed by the southwest-northeast trending paleochannel in the southwest portion of the area of investigation (near well MW-4) is the most significant feature regarding potential migration of DNAPL in Area A.
11. Migration of DNAPL from Site 1 eastward or southeastward to the area east of well P-4 is not likely, due to the increase in elevation of the top of the Upper Miocene clay immediately east of well P-4.
12. Additional information is needed to: (*a*) characterize the DNAPL mixture, including a comprehensive identification of constituents and quantification of the concentrations of constituents comprising the mixture; (*b*) delineate the extent of DNAPL, especially

the potential southwestward migration of DNAPL; and, (*c*) characterize lithologic units of low permeability that influence the direction and rate of migration of DNAPL in the area, including the Upper Miocene clay at the base of the alluvial aquifer, and intermediate clay lenses within the aquifer. A subsurface investigation is recommended to address items *b* and *c*.

13. A detailed plan should be formulated for the proposed field investigation. The plan should be designed to satisfy the objectives described above. The plan should include detailed procedures for collecting, handling, and analyzing samples. The plan should also identify data quality objectives to support potential remediation options.

12.7 Conclusions

Evaluation of data in this investigation shows that a DNAPL entered the alluvial aquifer at or near the former waste disposal area. It migrated through coarse-grained, permeable deposits, along the tops of relatively impermeable lithologic units (including ultimately the top of the Miocene clay), to the bottom of interceptor well P-2. Small, lenticular clay units within the alluvial aquifer near the surface source can serve as transitory barriers to downward migration of DNAPL. Depending on the configuration of the surface of a clay unit, DNAPL will either form a lens and become trapped on the clay, or will spill over the edge of the clay and continue migrating downward, possibly in a stair-step manner. Mobility of the DNAPL was enhanced by the pumping of the interceptor well system, and particularly the pumping of well P-2. The movement of DNAPL southwestward from well P-2, down the paleochannel, may be mitigated by continued pumping of the interceptor well system.

Based on hydrogeologic conditions, including changes in the hydraulic gradient by the pumping of the interceptor wells, the conceptual model indicates potential pathways of future migration of the DNAPL at this site. Of these, the most important is the northeast-southwest trending trough in the top of the Miocene clay and the associated main paleochannel near well MW-3, because: (*a*) the trough plunges southwestward (offsite); (*b*) gravel deposits are thickest in the trough; and (*c*) the trough is downslope from both the surface source and well P-2.

This investigation has identified basic characteristics of the occurrence of the DNAPL, including the probable source area and likely pathways of migration. Additional information is needed to: (*a*) further characterize the DNAPL mixture; (*b*) delineate the extent of migration of the DNAPL, especially toward the southwest; and (*c*) further characterize lithologic units, including the Miocene clay at the base of the alluvial aquifer and intermediate clay lenses within the alluvial aquifer, that influence the direction and rate of movement of DNAPL.

A subsurface investigation is recommended to address items *b* and *c*. Ground water should be monitored for components of the DNAPL and the results compared to predicted concentrations (based on calculations using the detailed chemical characterization of the DNAPL). Plume tracking and concentration trend analysis for constituents associated with the DNAPL may be used to refine the relationship between the measurement of miscible-phase components in the ground water and the proximity of immiscible-phase DNAPL.

References

Allen JRL (1965) A review of the origin and characteristics of recent alluvial sediments. Sedimentology 5:89–191

Allen JRL (1970) Physical processes of sedimentation. Allen & Unwin, London

Cherry JA, Feenstra S, Mackay DM (1993) Developing a conceptual framework and rational goals for ground-water remediation at DNAPL sites (draft). Proc. of Subsurface Restoration Conference, Third International Conference on Ground-Water Quality Research, Dallas, Texas, June 21–24, 1992

Cohen RM, Mercer JW (1993) DNAPL site evaluation. Lewis Publishers, Boca Raton, Florida

Gorelick SM, Freeze RA, Donohue D, Keely JF (1993) Ground-water contamination – optimal capture and containment. Lewis Publishers, Boca Raton, Florida

Mackay DM, Cherry JA (1989) Ground-water contamination: pump-and-treat remediation. Environ Sci Technol 23(6): 630–636

Miall AD (1981) Analysis of fluvial depositional systems. AAPG Fall Education Conference in Calgary, Canada, August 9, 1981 (AAPG Education Course Note Series 20)

Montgomery JH (1991) Ground-water chemicals field guide. Lewis Publishers, Chelsea, Michigan

Reading HG (ed) (1978) Sedimentary environments and facies. Elsevier, New York

Reineck HE, Singh IB (1980) Depositional sedimentary environments, with reference to terrigenous clastics, 2nd edn. Springer-Verag, New York

Scholle P, Spearing A (eds) (1982) Sandstone depositional environments. American Association of Petroleum Geologists, Tulsa, Oklahoma (Memoir 31)

Schwille F (1988) Dense chlorinated solvents in porous and fractured media, model experiments (English translation by J. F. Pankow). Lewis Publishers, Chelsea, Michigan

Waterloo Center for Groundwater Research (1992) Site characterization and remediation of dense, immiscible phase liquid contaminants (DNAPLs) in porous and fractured media. Notes from Short Course presented in Chicago, Illinois, November 2–5, 1992

Part V

Technical Applications in the Field and Project Performance

Chapter 13

Laboratory Tests For Soils

13.1 Introduction

Dirt, ground, earth, and soil are remarkably useful loose stuff that forms at the interface of earth's rocky crust and the atmosphere. The term soil is a layer of weathered, unconsolidated material on top of bedrock (a term used for rock beneath soil). Soil is a mixture of mineral particles, organic matter, chemicals, air, and water that supports life. The texture of the soil is determined by the proportions of sand, silt, and clay; the term "loam" refers to a medium-textured soil composed of sand, silt, and clay as well as organic matter. Loamy soils are usually well drained and fertile.

Old soils are commonly more developed and less fertile than young ones because most of the nutrients to plants provided by the organic matter in soils have been leached. The oldest known soils are in Australia in a secluded rainforest canyon. In the United States, the oldest soils lie upon terraces of the Sierra Nevada Mountains in California. The topsoil (horizon "A") is characterized by the downward movement of water and the accumulation of decomposed organic matter. Some of the dissolved soil materials in water enter the ground and moves to deeper levels. Leaching may make the "A" horizon pale and sandy, but the uppermost part is often darkened by humus (decomposed plant material). The "B" horizon, or zone of accumulation, is a soil layer characterized by the accumulation of material moved down from the "A" horizon. The "C" horizon is incompletely weathered material, lying below the "B" horizon. The parent material is commonly subjected to physical and chemical weathering from frost action, roots, plant acids, and other agents (see Chap. 2).

Soil supports plant growth and represents the living reservoir that buffers the flow of water, nutrients, and energy through an ecosystem. Water either percolates to the ground water, runs over the land surface to a stream or lake, or moves laterally through the soil to a surface body. The water quality of the soil largely determines the chemical and biological characteristics and flow dynamics of the water passing through it.

Soils have many uses in addition to food, fiber, and fuel production. They play a major role in recycling carbon to the atmosphere and nitrogen in the soil, storing water for plant use, filtering surface waters, and in disposal of solid and liquid wastes. Soils are also the base beneath most of our homes and roads as well as an important source of building materials, such as adobe and bricks. Wetlands, a general term for marshes, swamps, and other areas, permanently wet and/or intermittently water-covered, are particularly good water filters. Wetlands, typically occur at the mouths of river valleys, along low-lying coasts, and in valleys, help maintain and improve the water quality of rivers and other water bodies by removing and retaining nutrients, processing chemical and organic wastes, and reducing sediment loads to receiving waters.

Greenhouse gases, such as carbon dioxide and methane, act as insulating blankets around the earth, allowing incoming solar radiation to warm the earth's surface and reducing radiation of heat back through the atmosphere into space.

Soil texture, structure, water-holding capacity, porosity, organic matter content, and depth are some of the properties that determine soil quality. Texture, structure, and strength (soil resistance to deformation and collapse) are especially important in construction applications. The size and relative abundance of sand, silt, and clay particles in a soil determine whether its texture is coarse, medium, or fine. Medium-textured soils have the most desirable engineering properties.

In unsaturated soils, compaction is the most obvious and simple way of increasing the stability and supporting capacity. On the other hand, water reduces the compaction potential of soil because a high water concentration can serve as an internal lubricant. The same soil that is difficult to compact may be easy to shear (low shear strength).

Most buildings, roads, dams, and pipelines are built on soils. A well-drained, sandy or gravelly soil provides the most trouble-free base for roads and buildings. The physical and chemical properties of soils are critically important for construction and engineering applications. Clay, on the other hand, is a universal constituent of soils and its type has a significant impact on land use, e.g. expanding clays (known as smectites) swell as they absorb water and are very desirable for sealing lagoons or dams, because they remain swollen when wet and prevent water seepage. However, because expanding clays shrink and crack as they dry, they cause major damage to foundations and roadbeds.

The consequences of soil mismanagement are severe and sometimes irreversible. Erosion, salinization, the depletion of organic matter and nutrients in agricultural soils, and soil contamination all result from mismanagement.

Contamination of soil and water resources has been a by-product of gathering, transporting, processing, storing, using, and disposing of the chemicals on which modern society depends (Loynachan et al. 1999).

The following sections discuss the methodology of different analyses that help define the physical characteristics of soils according to the specifications given by the American Standards for Testing and Materials (ASTM).

13.2 Particle Size Analysis of Soils

13.2.1 Scope

The methodology of the particle size analysis is based on guidance from ASTM D-421 (dry sample preparation), ASTM D-2217 (wet sample preparation) and ASTM D-422 (test procedure) of the particle size analysis that covers the quantitative determination of the distribution of particle sizes in soils and of soil constants.

A representative oven-dry quantity of material is obtained of adequate mass, depending on the maximum particle size. A sample of 500 g is used for large particles (gravels and pebbles), about 100 g for sandy soils, and approximately 65 g for silty or clay soils. The sample is prepared by use of the quartering method or a sample splitter.

The distribution of particle sizes larger than the 75 µm (retained on the no. 200 sieve) is determined by sieve analysis, while the distribution of particle sizes smaller than 75 µm is determined by a sedimentation process using a hydrometer, which is usually a type designated by ASTM as 152H. The hydrometer is calibrated for use with 0 to 60 g of soil in a 1 000 ml soil-water mixture (for solid particles of soil which have a specific gravity (G_s) of 2.65 g cm^{-3}). This hydrometer is widely used in the present.

Another hydrometer, the 151H "reads" directly the specific gravity of the soil-water suspension and requires using about 50 g of soil to produce the 1 000 ml soil-water suspension.

13.2.2 Wet Preparation of Soil Samples (ASTM D-2217)

ASTM D-2217 describes the process for the wet preparation of soil samples (as received from the field) for particle size analysis and determination of soil constants.

There are two procedures for carrying out this method:

1. The first provides for a wet separation of the field sample(s) on no. 10 (2.00 mm) sieve, or no. 40 (425 µm) sieve, or both, as needed. It is used for plasticity tests and particle size analysis when the coarse-grained particles of the sample(s) are soft and pulverize readily, or when the fine particles are very cohesive and tend to resist removal from the coarse particles. The procedure can be summarized as follows:
   - Dry the sample(s) as received from the field using one of the following three methods: (*a*) samples can be dried at ambient temperature in air; (*b*) samples can be dried in an oven in which the temperature does not exceed 60 °C; or (*c*) the sample can be dried by use of any warming device that will not raise the temperature of the sample above 60 °C.
   - Any aggregates of particles of the dried sample should be broken thoroughly using the mortar and rubber-covered pestle or other suitable device, then a representative portion will be selected by the method of quartering or by use of a sampler.
   - Weigh the selected portion of the sample and separate this material into two portions using the no. 10 sieve and set aside the portion passing for later use. Place the material retained on the no. 10 sieve in a pan, cover with water, soak for several hours, wash the material on the no. 10 sieve, and then dry the material retained at a temperature not exceeding 60 °C.

     For determination of soil constants, proceed with the above steps substituting a no. 40 sieve for the no. 10 sieve.
2. The second procedure requires that samples be shipped from the field to the laboratory in sealed containers to maintain all their natural moisture. Samples that contain only particles passing the no. 10 sieve may be tested in the particle size analysis without first washing on the no. 10 sieve. Those samples containing particles passing the no. 40 sieve may be used in the tests to determine soil constants without first washing on the no. 40 sieve. This procedure can be summarized as follows:
   - Select and weigh a representative portion of the moist sample estimated to contain 50 g of particle passing no. 10 sieve for silty and clayey soil, or 100 g for sandy soil. For samples containing particles not passing the no. 10 sieve, select and weigh a representative sample estimated to contain the required amounts of particles and not passing the no. 10 sieve. Determine the moisture content at ~110 ±5 °C.

- Soak the moist sample and wash on a no. 10 sieve as previously described. After washing, dry the material retained on the no. 10 sieve in oven at a temperature of ~230 ±9 °F (~110 ±5 °C), weigh, and retain for the particle size analysis.

  For determination of soil constants, select a representative portion of the moist sample estimated to contain sufficient particles passing through the no. 40 sieve to make the required tests.

13.2.3 Dry Preparation of Soil Samples (ASTM D-421)

The soil sample(s), as received from the field, is exposed to the air at room temperature until thoroughly dried. Aggregates of soil particles should be broken down into separate grains in a mortar with a rubber-covered pestle. A representative test sample is selected by the method of quartering or by the use of a sample splitter.

13.2.4 Test Procedure of Particle Size Analysis (ASTM D-422)

13.2.4.1 *Sieve Analysis Method*

Sieve analysis is the most widely used method for obtaining the grain-size distribution. This method is carried out by passing the materials through a stacked set of 20.3 cm brass sieves in a special vibration machine. The sieve openings are designated by size in thousandths of a millimeter and by mesh number. A suggested series of sieves includes the following mesh (sieve) numbers: 10 (2.0 mm), 16 (1.190 mm), 20 (0.840 mm), 30 (0.590 mm), 40 (0.420 mm), 60 (0.250 mm), 80 (0.180 mm), 100 (0.149 mm), 120 (0.125 mm) and 200 (0.074 mm) (Driscoll 1986). All the sieves should be stacked with progressively finer sieves toward the bottom of the stack (see Chap. 5).

Samples must first be dry and any clods (aggregates of grains) should be broken down to separate all particles. A representative sample is obtained by quartering or by a sample splitter, then dried and weighed (100 g). The weight is recorded before pouring the sediment into the top sieve. The set of sieves is shaken with a mechanical shaker for 15 minutes. The sample material retained in the top sieve is transferred to a large sheet of paper, then to the weighing pan, and the weight is recorded to two decimals. This step is followed by adding the material retained on the second sieve to that already in the weighing pan on the balance. The weight of the accumulated samples is successively determined until the finest material from the bottom pan is weighed and recorded. The accumulated weight should be equal to the weight of the original sample, within ±2% of error. The cumulative percent retained on each sieve is calculated by dividing the cumulative weight retained by the total weight of the sample. The cumulative percent can then be plotted on a semi-log diagram.

13.2.4.2 *Hydrometer Test Method*

The hydrometer method determines the percentage of dispersed soil particles remaining in suspension after specific periods of time. It is based on the density of the suspension in water. The density of the suspension changes progressively as finer particles settle. Hydrometer analyses are performed by use of the standard method for particle size analysis of soils issued by the ASTM (American Standards for Testing and Materials 1997). The method for hydrometer analyses is given below:

1. Prepare a dry sample of 50 g of soil particle sizes (clays) from the no. 200 (0.075 mm) sieve, and place the sample in a 250 ml beaker. Cover it with 125 ml of sodium hexametaphosphate solution (40 g of salt per liter of distilled water). Stir until the soil is thoroughly wetted, and let it stand for at least 16 hours (overnight).
2. Next, stir with a glass rod for 10 minutes then transfer the sample from the beaker into a special dispersion cup. Wash any residue from the beaker with distilled water (using a syringe) until the cup is about 2/3 full. Disperse the sample by stirring for one minute.
3. Immediately after dispersion, wash the sample into a glass sedimentation cylinder and add distilled water until the total volume is 1 000 ml.
4. Place a rubber stopper in the open end of the cylinder and rotate it upside down and back for one minute while shaking vigorously to complete the agitation of the slurry.
5. Take the first hydrometer reading after two minutes, and then place the sedimentation cylinder into a water bath of 20 °C. Insert the hydrometer about 45 seconds before taking the next reading. The readings are taken at the following elapsed time intervals: 5, 15, 30, 60, 240, and 1 440 minutes.

13.2.4.3 *Hydrometer Readings and Measurements*

The temperature of the water bath should be measured each time the hydrometer is read. The hydrometer should be removed immediately after each reading (which is usually taken at the top of the meniscus formed by the liquid on the stem), and then placed with a spinning motion in distilled water. The following calculation is given using the 152H model of hydrometer (graduated in gram per liter):

$$\text{Partial percent finer } (P) = \frac{100}{W_o}(R_c - C_d + m) \quad (13.1)$$

where:

P = partial percent finer or the percentage of soil remaining in suspension at the level at which the hydrometer measures the density of the suspension

W_o = oven-dry weight (g) used for hydrometry analysis

R_c = composite correction for hydrometer reading (N.B.: Three corrections are considered: (1) Soil hydrometers are calibrated at 20 °C as a standard temperature, and values shown on the scale are computed using a specific gravity of 2.65 at this temperature. (2) Variations in temperature from this standard temperature produce inaccuracies in the actual hydrometer readings and a correction temperature (m) should be used. (3) Also, hydrometers are graduated by the manufacturer to be read at the bottom of the meniscus formed by the liquid on the stem and readings should be taken at the top and a meniscus correction (C_m) of 0.5 g l^{-1} can be added for routine testing)

C_d = dispersing agent correction

m = temperature correction (Table 13.1).

$$\text{Total percent finer} = P\,\frac{W_s - W_1}{W_s} \quad (13.2)$$

where:

W_s = total oven dry weight (g) of sample used for combined analysis of sieve and hydrometer tests

W_1 = oven dry weight (g) of sample retained on no. 200 sieve

13.2.4.4 *Computations*

1. Hygroscopic moisture correction (C_H)
   The hygroscopic moisture correction factor is the ratio between the weight of the oven-dried sample, and the weight of the air-dried sample before oven drying. It is a number less than one, except when there is no hygroscopic moisture.

$$C_H = W_s / W_a \quad (13.3)$$

where:

C_H = hygroscopic moisture correction factor

W_s = mass (g) of the oven-dried soil

W_a = air-dry mass (g) before drying

Table 13.1. Temperature correction factor (m)

°C	°F	Correction	°C	°F	Correction
14.0	57.2	−0.9	24.5	76.1	+0.9
14.5	58.1	−0.8	25.0	77.0	+1.0
15.0	59.0	−0.8	25.5	77.9	+1.1
15.5	59.9	−0.7	26.0	78.8	+1.3
16.0	60.8	−0.6	26.5	79.7	+1.4
16.5	61.7	−0.6	27.0	80.6	+1.5
17.0	62.6	−0.5	27.5	81.5	+1.6
17.5	63.5	−0.4	28.0	82.4	+1.8
18.0	64.4	−0.4	28.5	83.3	+1.9
18.5	65.3	−0.3	29.0	84.2	+2.1
19.0	66.2	−0.2	29.5	85.1	+2.2
19.5	67.1	−0.1	30.0	86.0	+2.3
20.0	68.0	0.0	30.5	86.9	+2.5
20.5	68.9	+0.1	31.0	87.8	+2.6
21.0	69.8	+0.2	31.5	88.7	+2.8
21.5	70.7	+0.3	32.0	89.6	+2.9
22.0	71.6	+0.4	32.5	90.5	+3.0
22.5	72.5	+0.5	33.0	91.4	+3.2
23.0	73.4	+0.6	33.5	92.3	+3.3
23.5	74.3	+0.7	34.0	93.2	+3.5
24.0	75.2	+0.8			

Table 13.2. Specific gravity correction factor (*Gc*)

Specific gravity	Correction factor
2.95	0.94
2.90	0.95
2.85	0.96
2.80	0.97
2.75	0.98
2.70	0.99
2.65	1.00
2.60	1.01
2.55	1.02
2.50	1.03
2.45	1.05

For use in equation for percentage of soil remaining in suspension when using hydrometer 152H.

2. A correction factor (*Gc*) for different specific gravities of soil particles should be applied to the reading of the hydrometer 152H, as values shown on its scale are computed using a specific gravity of 2.65 g cm^{-3} (Table 13.2).

13.2.4.5 *Application of a Hydrometer Method (Hydrometer 152H)*

The following is an example of calculations involved in the hydrometer method (American Standards for Testing and Materials 1997):

- Original weight of sample = 100 g
- The weight of clay and silt particles passed through sieve no. 200 = 77.29 g
- The weight of sample retained on sieve no. 200 = 22.7 g
- Using only 50 g (W_o) of clay and silt particles for hydrometer test:

  $W_s = (50 \times 100) / 77.29 = 64.09$ g

  and the weight of sample retained on sieve no. 200 should be 14.09 g
- *Reading after 2 minutes:* $R_c = 42$ g l^{-1}. The partial percent finer = 82% and the total percent finer = 63.96%. Therefore, the actual total percent coarser retained on sieve no. 200 = 77.29 – 63.96 = 13.33%.

  The cumulative percent coarser retained at 2 minutes interval is 13.33 + 22.71 = 36.04%.
- *Reading after 5 minutes:* $R_c = 39.0$ g l^{-1}. The partial percent finer = 78.0%. The total percent finer = 60.84%. The actual percent coarser retained on sieve no. 200 = 63.96 – 60.84 = 3.12%, and the cumulative percent coarser is 36.04 + 3.12 = 39.16%.
- The *diameter of a particle* corresponding to the percentage indicated by a given hydrometer reading can be calculated according to Strokes' law:

$$\text{Particle diameter}\,(D) = \frac{K_c}{\sqrt{L/T)}}\ (\text{mm}) \qquad (13.4)$$

where:

L = effective length in mm. Table 13.3 shows values of effective depth, based on hydrometer and sedimentation cylinder of specified sizes.

T = interval time in minutes from the beginning of sedimentation.

K_c = correction for computing diameter of particle (Table 13.4).

Then the diameter D after 2 minutes is:

$$D = 0.01344\sqrt{(9.6 \times 10)/2} = 0.0931\,\text{mm}$$

Using the hydrometer analysis data sheet (Fig. 13.1), the cumulative percent finer can be plotted on a semi-log diagram (Fig. 13.2).

13.3 Specific Gravity Method (D-854)

The specific gravity of a soil is expressed in different forms. The most commonly used form is the specific gravity of solids (G_s) applied for soils finer than the no. 200 sieve. It is defined as the ratio of the mass of a unit volume of a material at a stated temperature to the mass in air of the same volume of gas-free distilled water at the same temperature. In case of testing soils containing soluble salts, it is necessary to use other liquids (such as kerosene) in lieu of distilled water.

Procedure: A representative sample of approximately 50 g (oven-dry) is placed in a dish, mixed with sufficient distilled water to form a slurry, placed in a volumetric flask of a capacity of 500 ml (picnometer), and filled half-full with distilled water. The entrapped air may be removed by boiling the suspension gently for at least 10 minutes while occasionally rolling the flask to assist in the removal of air. The flask and contents are allowed to cool, preferably overnight, before filling to 500 ml with gas-free water and weighing. The soil is oven dried to a constant weight at a temperature of 110 ±5 °C and then allowed to cool in a desiccator. The soil is weighed to the nearest 0.01 g.

Table 13.3. Values of effective depth (L) based on hydrometer and sedimentation cylinder of specified sizes

Hydrometer 151H		Hydrometer 152H			
Actual hydrometer reading	Effective depth (cm)	Actual hydrometer reading	Effective depth (cm)	Actual hydrometer reading	Effective depth (cm)
1.000	16.3	0	16.3		
1.001	16.0	1	16.1	31	11.2
1.002	15.8	2	16.0	32	11.1
1.003	15.5	3	15.8	33	10.9
1.004	15.2	4	15.6	34	10.7
1.005	15.0	5	15.5	35	10.6
1.006	14.7	6	15.3	36	10.4
1.007	14.4	7	15.2	37	10.2
1.008	14.2	8	15.0	38	10.1
1.009	13.9	9	14.8	39	9.9
1.010	13.7	10	14.7	40	9.7
1.011	13.4	11	14.5	41	9.6
1.012	13.1	12	14.3	42	9.4
1.013	12.9	13	14.2	43	9.2
1.014	12.6	14	14.0	44	9.1
1.015	12.3	15	13.8	45	8.9
1.016	12.1	16	13.7	46	8.8
10.17	11.8	17	13.5	47	8.5
1.018	11.5	18	13.3	48	8.4
1.019	11.3	19	13.2	49	8.3
1.020	11.0	20	13.0	50	8.1
1.021	10.7	21	12.9	51	7.9
1.022	10.5	22	12.7	52	7.8
1.023	10.2	23	12.5	53	7.6
1.024	10.0	24	12.4	54	7.4
1.025	9.7	25	12.2	55	7.3
1.026	9.4	26	12.0	56	7.1
1.027	9.2	27	11.9	57	7.0
1.028	8.9	28	11.7	58	6.8
1.029	8.6	29	11.5	59	6.6
1.030	8.4	30	11.4	60	6.5
1.031	8.1				
1.032	7.8				
1.033	7.6				
1.034	7.3				
1.035	7.0				
1.036	6.8				
1.037	6.5				
1.038	6.2				

Table 13.4. Values of K_c for computing diameter of particle in hydrometer analysis

Temperature	Specific gravity of soil particles								
(°C)	2.45	2.50	2.55	2.60	2.65	2.70	2.75	2.80	2.85
16	0.01510	0.01505	0.01481	0.01457	0.01435	0.01414	0.01394	0.01374	0.01356
17	0.01511	0.01486	0.01462	0.01439	0.01417	0.01396	0.01376	0.01356	0.01338
18	0.01492	0.01467	0.01443	0.01421	0.01399	0.01378	0.01359	0.01339	0.01321
19	0.01474	0.01449	0.01425	0.01403	0.01382	0.01361	0.01342	0.01323	0.01305
20	0.01456	0.01431	0.01408	0.01386	0.01365	0.01344	0.01325	0.01307	0.01289
21	0.01438	0.01414	0.01391	0.01369	0.01348	0.01328	0.01309	0.01291	0.01273
22	0.01421	0.01397	0.01374	0.01353	0.01332	0.01312	0.01294	0.01276	0.01258
23	0.01404	0.01381	0.01358	0.01337	0.01317	0.01297	0.01279	0.01261	0.01243
24	0.01388	0.01365	0.01342	0.01321	0.01301	0.01282	0.01264	0.01246	0.01229
25	0.01372	0.01349	0.01327	0.01306	0.01286	0.01267	0.01249	0.01232	0.01215
26	0.01357	0.01334	0.01312	0.01291	0.01272	0.01253	0.01235	0.01218	0.01201
27	0.01342	0.01319	0.01297	0.01277	0.01258	0.01239	0.01221	0.01204	0.01188
28	0.01327	0.01304	0.01283	0.01264	0.01244	0.01255	0.01208	0.01191	0.01175
29	0.01312	0.01290	0.01269	0.01249	0.01230	0.01212	0.01195	0.01178	0.01162
30	0.01298	0.01276	0.01256	0.01236	0.01217	0.01199	0.01182	0.01165	0.01149

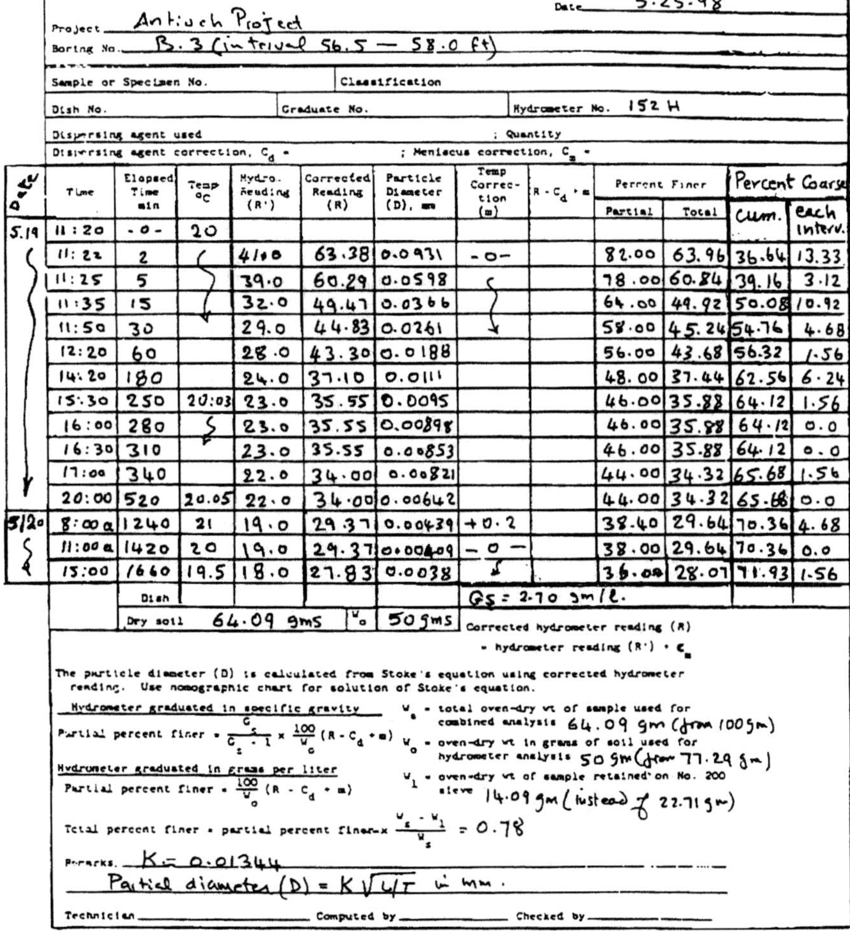

Date 5.25.98

Project Antioch Project

Boring No. B.3 (interval 56.5 — 58.0 ft)

Sample or Specimen No. | Classification

Dish No. | Graduate No. | Hydrometer No. 152 H

Dispersing agent used ; Quantity

Dispersing agent correction, C_d = ; Meniscus correction, C_m =

Date	Time	Elapsed Time min	Temp °C	Hydro. Reading (R')	Corrected Reading (R)	Particle Diameter (D), mm	Temp Correction (m)	R - C_d + m	Percent Finer Partial	Percent Finer Total	Percent Coarse cum.	Percent Coarse each interv.
5.19	11:20	-0-	20									
	11:22	2		41.0	63.38	0.0931	-0-		82.00	63.96	36.64	13.33
	11:25	5		39.0	60.29	0.0598			78.00	60.84	39.16	3.12
	11:35	15		32.0	49.47	0.0366			64.00	49.92	50.08	10.92
	11:50	30		29.0	44.83	0.0261			58.00	45.24	54.76	4.68
	12:20	60		28.0	43.30	0.0188			56.00	43.68	56.32	1.56
	14:20	180		24.0	37.10	0.0111			48.00	37.44	62.56	6.24
	15:30	250	20:03	23.0	35.55	0.0095			46.00	35.88	64.12	1.56
	16:00	280		23.0	35.55	0.00898			46.00	35.88	64.12	0.0
	16:30	310		23.0	35.55	0.00853			46.00	35.88	64.12	0.0
	17:00	340		22.0	34.00	0.00821			44.00	34.32	65.68	1.56
	20:00	520	20.05	22.0	34.00	0.00642			44.00	34.32	65.68	0.0
5/20	8:00a	1240	21	19.0	29.37	0.00439	+0.2		38.40	29.64	70.36	4.68
	11:00a	1420	20	19.0	29.37	0.00409	-0-		38.00	29.64	70.36	0.0
	15:00	1660	19.5	18.0	27.83	0.0038			36.00	28.07	71.93	1.56

Dish | Gs = 2.70 gm/l.

Dry soil 64.09 gms | W_o 50 gms

Corrected hydrometer reading (R) = hydrometer reading (R') + C_m

The particle diameter (D) is calculated from Stoke's equation using corrected hydrometer reading. Use nomographic chart for solution of Stoke's equation.

Hydrometer graduated in specific gravity

$$\text{Partial percent finer} = \frac{G_s}{G_s - 1} \times \frac{100}{W_o}(R - C_d + m)$$

Hydrometer graduated in grams per liter

$$\text{Partial percent finer} = \frac{100}{W_o}(R - C_d + m)$$

W_s = total oven-dry wt of sample used for combined analysis 64.09 gm (from 100 gm)

W_o = oven-dry wt in grams of soil used for hydrometer analysis 50 gm (from 77.29 gm)

W_1 = oven-dry wt of sample retained on No. 200 sieve 14.09 gm (instead of 22.71 gm)

$$\text{Total percent finer} = \text{partial percent finer} \times \frac{W_s - W_1}{W_s} = 0.78$$

Remarks. K = 0.01344

Partial diameter (D) = $K\sqrt{L/T}$ in mm.

Technician ______ Computed by ______ Checked by ______

Fig. 13.1. Results of hydrometer analysis of a borehole sample (B-3)

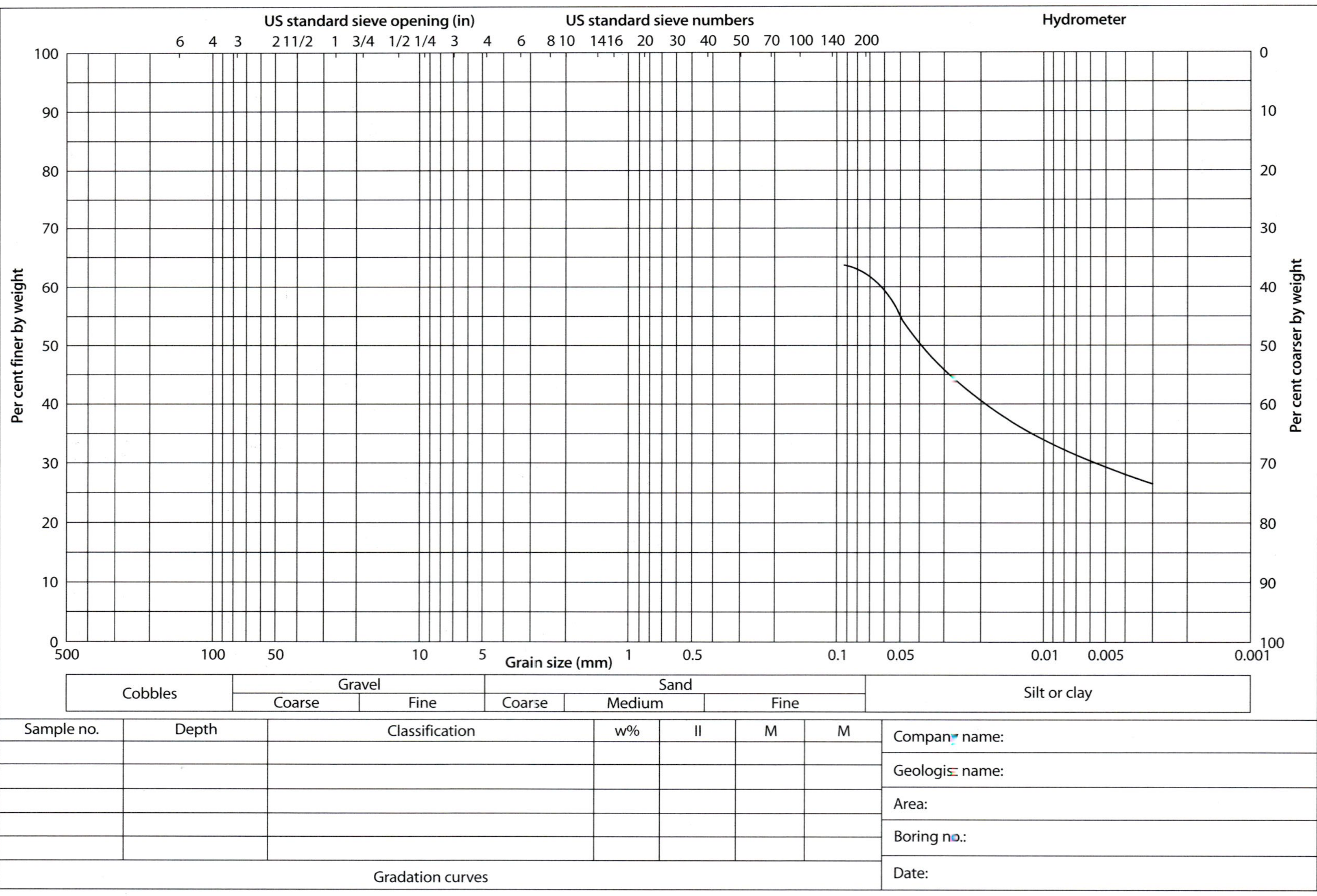
US standard sieve opening (in)
6 4 3 2 1 1/2 1 3/4 1/2 1/4 3
US standard sieve numbers
4 6 8 10 14 16 20 30 40 50 70 100 140 200
Hydrometer
Per cent finer by weight
100 90 80 70 60 50 40 30 20 10 0
Per cent coarser by weight
0 10 20 30 40 50 60 70 80 90 100
500 100 50 10 5 1 0.5 0.1 0.05 0.01 0.005 0.001
Grain size (mm)
Cobbles
Gravel
Coarse
Fine
Sand
Coarse
Medium
Fine
Silt or clay
Sample no.
Depth
Classification
w%
ll
M
M
Company name:
Geologist name:
Area:
Boring no.:
Date:
Gradation curves

Fig. 13.2. A cumulative size distribution curve of sample B-3

The specific gravity at a temperature T°C is then computed using the following formula:

$$G_s = \frac{W_s F_c}{(W_s + W_{bw} - W_{bws})} \qquad (13.5)$$

where
- W_s = weight of oven-dried soil sample (g)
- F_c = correction factor based on the density of water T°C
- W_{bw} = weight of pycnometer filled with water (g) at a temperature of T°C
- W_{bws} = weight of pycnometer filled with water and soil sample (g) at a temperature of T°C
- T°C = room temperature

An example for the determination of the specific gravity is shown in Fig. 13.3.

13.4 Atterberg Limits

The Atterberg limits are water contents, which define the limits of the various stages of consistency for a given soil. The Atterberg limits include the liquid limit (*LL*), plastic limit (*PL*) and the shrinkage limit (*SL*) of a soil. The principal stages from an engineering standpoint are shown in Fig. 13.4. The liquid limit (*LL*) and the plastic limit (*PL*) define the upper and lower limits, respectively, of the plastic range of a soil. The numerical difference between these two limits expresses the range of water content through which a soil behaves plastically and is termed the plasticity index (*PI*). The shrinkage limit (*SL*) defines the lower limit of the semi-solid range of a soil.

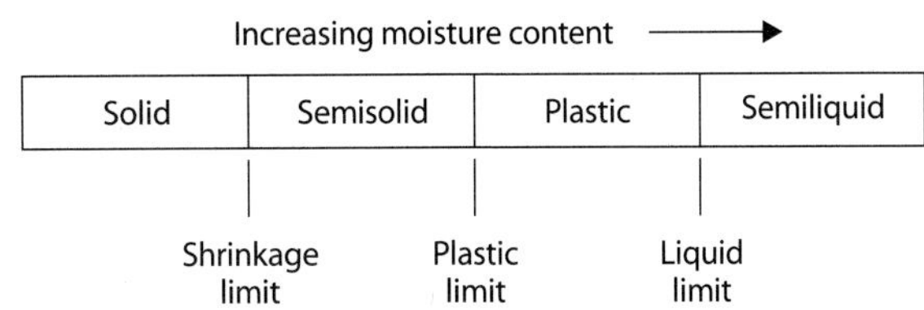
Increasing moisture content
Solid
Semisolid
Plastic
Semiliquid
Shrinkage limit
Plastic limit
Liquid limit

Fig. 13.4. Stages of consistency (after EM 1110-2-1906, 30 Nov 1970)

A sample weight of 150–200 g of the soil (finer than the no. 40 sieve) should be sufficient to perform all these tests.

13.4.1 Liquid Limit Test (ASTM D-4318-84)

The liquid limit of a soil is the water content, expressed as a percentage of the weight of oven-dried soil, at which two halves of a soil pat separated by a groove of standard dimensions will close at the bottom of the groove along a distance of 1.27 cm under the impact of 25 blows in a standard liquid limit device (Fig. 13.5).

Remarks: The following remarks should be considered while performing the liquid limit test:

1. The material should first be mixed thoroughly with distilled water until it has a water-content just above the liquid limit (a consistency requiring between 15

Fig. 13.3. Specific gravity test results of solids in Sample P1

Date: Dec 12, 96

Project: Chestnut Ridge

Boring no. P.1; Depth 8.5–10.0 ft

Specific gravity of solids (c_s)

Sample or specimen no.			01			
Flask no.			4			
Temperature of water and soil, T (°C)			22 °C			
Dish no.			4			
Weight in grams	Dish + dry soil		62 g			
	Flask		162.75 g			
	Dry soil	W_s	50 g			
	Flask + water at T (°C)	W_{bw}	659.5 cc			
	$W_s + W_{bw}$					
	Flask + water + immersed soil	W_{bws}	690.09 g			
	Displaced water, $W_s + W_{bw} = W_{bws}$					
Correction factor		K	0.9996			
$(W_s K) + (W_s + W_{bw} - W_{bws})$		c_s	2.58			

Fig. 13.5.
Grooving of a liquid limit specimen

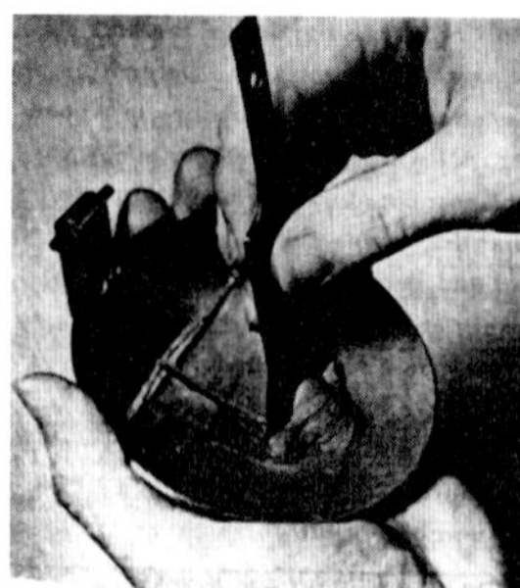

and 25 blows to cause closure of the groove). This soil mixture is used for both the liquid and plastic limits.

2. A weight of 50–80 g of the mixed specimen is placed in the brass cup and a groove is formed by a grooving tool while holding it perpendicular to the cup.
3. The brass cup is then connected to the liquid limit device and turned on. The blows are counted until the two halves of the soil pat come in contact at the bottom of the groove along a distance of 1.27 cm. A record of the number of blows is required to close the groove.
4. Remove 5 to 10 g specimen of the soil pat, and determine the water content in percent, computed to one decimal point, as follows:

$$w = \frac{W}{W_s} \times 100 \qquad (13.6)$$

where:
w = water content (%)
W = weight of moisture (weight of wet soil (W_w) – weight of dry soil (W_s)) in g
W_s = weight of oven-dried soil (g)

5. Transfer the soil sample remaining in the cup to the mixing dish; Wash and dry the cup and the grooving tool and repeat steps 2, 3, and 4 for three additional portions of the specimen for which the water content has been adjusted by drying. The water content must be sufficient to produce a noticeable variation in the number of blows required to close the groove within the above-mentioned limits.
6. The water content can then be plotted on a semi-log graph paper vs. the number of blows. The best straight line (or flow line) is drawn through the four plotted points (Fig. 13.6). The liquid limit is then identified as the water content corresponding to the intersection of this straight line and the 25 blow line on the graph.

13.4.2 Plastic Limit Test (ASTM D-4318-84)

The plastic limit of a soil is the water content expressed as a percentage of the weight of oven-dried soil, at which the soil begins to crumble when rolled into a thread 3 mm in diameter. The material used to determine the plastic limit test must be taken from the same mixture that was used to determine the liquid limit; 20 grams of material is required for the plastic limit test and the following procedure is performed: (*a*) take 2 to 5 g of the material remaining from the liquid limit test at any stage of the drying process, shape into a ball, then into an ellipsoidal mass. Roll the material, under the palm of the hand, against a hard surface using enough pressure to roll the soil into a thread of 3 mm in diameter; (*b*) continue rolling the thread until the soil has dried to the point where the 3 mm rolled thread will break into numerous pieces as shown in Fig. 13.7.

The plastic limit and plasticity index are computed as follows:

$$\text{Plastic limit}\,(PL) = \frac{W}{W_s} \times 100 \qquad (13.7)$$

$$\text{Plasticity index}\,(PI) = LL - PL \qquad (13.8)$$

13.4.3 The Shrinkage Limit Test (ASTM D-427)

The shrinkage limit of a soil is the water content, expressed as a percentage of the weight of the oven-dried soil, at which further loss in moisture will not cause a decrease in its volume. It is typically assumed to represent the amount of water required to fill the voids of a given cohesive soil at a minimum void ratio obtained by drying (usually oven). As part of the shrinkage limit test, the shrinkage ratio (R) and linear shrinkage (Ls) are also determined. The shrinkage ratio is defined as the ratio between a given volume change above the shrinkage limit and the corresponding change in water content. The linear shrinkage is defined as the decrease in one dimension of a soil mass, expressed as a percentage of the original dimension when the water content is reduced from a given value to the shrinkage limit

Liquid and plastic limit tests For use of this form, see EM 1110-2-1906					
Project No. 525401			Date Nov 5, 1999		
Boring no. 1, Depth 8.5–10.0 ft			Sample no. P.1		
Liquid limit determination					
Run no.	1	2	3	4	
Weight of wet soil (g)	7.76	7.43	5.68	8.9	
Weight of dry soil (g)	4.48	4.01	3.12	5.1	
Weight of moisture (g)	3.28	3.42	2.56	3.8	
Water content (%)	73.2	85.3	81	75.8	
No. of blows	33	11	16	28	

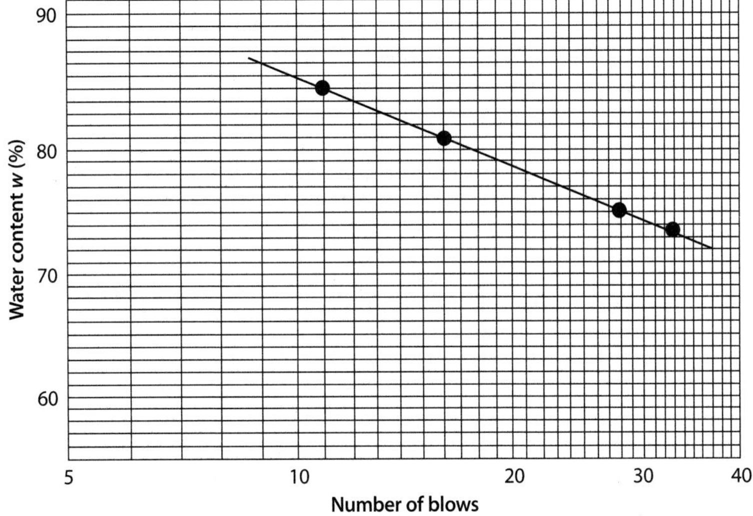
90
80
70
60
Water content w (%)
5
10
20
30
40
Number of blows

LL 76%

PL 40.7

PI 35.3

Remarks:

Plastic limit determination				
Run no.	1	2		
Weight of wet soil (g)	1.62	2.16		
Weight of dry soil (g)	1.15	1.54		
Weight of moisture (g)	0.47	0.62		
Water content (%)	41.0	40.3		
Average plasticity	40.7			

Fig. 13.6. Atterberg limit determination

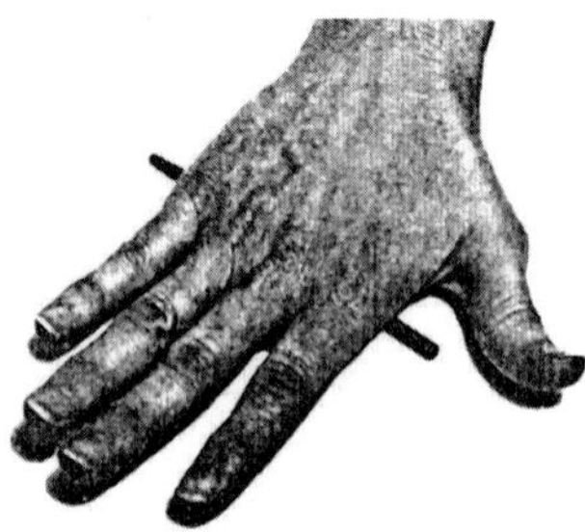

After EM 1110-2-1906
30 Nov 70

After EM 1110-2-1906
30 Nov 70

Fig. 13.7. Plastic limit testing (after EM 1110-2-1906, 30 Nov 1970)

(EM-1110-2-1906). The following steps should be followed while performing the shrinkage limit test (ASTM D-427):

1. Select approximately 30 g of soil from the thoroughly mixed portion of the original material passing the no. 40 (425 µm) sieve. The material obtained in accordance with test method D-421.
2. Place the soil in an evaporating dish (140 mm in diameter) and mix thoroughly with distilled water producing a soil with a consistency above the liquid limit (ASTM D-4318). Coat the inside surface of the shrinkage dish about 44 mm in diameter and about 12 mm in height, with a thin layer of petroleum jelly or similar lubricant to prevent the adhesion of the soil to the dish. Record the weight (in g) of the lubricated shrinkage dish and wet soil (Fig. 13.8). Allow the wet soil to air-dry until a definite color change takes place and then oven-dry it to a constant weight. Record the oven-dried weight as the weight of the dish and dry soil. Determine and record the weight of the empty dish.
3. Determine the volume of the shrinkage dish as follows:
   a Place the shrinkage dish in a shallow pan (of about 20 by 20 by 5 cm) to catch any mercury overflow.
   b Fill the shrinkage dish to overflowing with mercury and remove the excess mercury by pressing a glass plate firmly over its top.
   c Determine the volume of mercury held in the shrinkage dish either by means of a glass graduate (a capacity of 25 ml and graduated to 0.2 ml) or by dividing the measured weight of mercury by the mass density of mercury (13.55 mg m^{-3}).
   d Record the volume (V_w) of the shrinkage dish in cubic centimeters (= the volume of the wet soil).
4. Place an amount of the wetted soil in center of the shrinkage dish and determine the weight of the dish and soil. Then wet the soil according to the procedure of test method D-427 and determine the weight of the wet soil in grams (W_W).
5. Allow the soil pat to dry in air then oven-dry it at 110 ±5 °C (230 ±9 °F) and determine and record the weight of the dry soil (W_D). Calculate the initial water content as a percentage of the dry weight:

$$w = \frac{W_w - W_d}{W_d} \times 100 \tag{13.9}$$

6. Determine the volume of the dry soil pat by removing the pat from the shrinkage dish and immersing it in a glass cup full of mercury (5 3/4 in diameter and 1 2/3 in height) as given in the procedure ASTM D-427.
7. Measure the volume of the mercury displaced into the evaporating dish either by means of the glass graduate or by dividing the measured weight of mercury by the mass density of mercury and then record the volume in cubic centimeters of the dry soil pat (V_d).

   Calculate the shrinkage limit (SL) as a water content of the soil as a percentage of the dry soil mass:

Shrinkage limit (SL)

$$= w - \frac{(V_w - V_d)\rho_w}{W_w} \times 100 \tag{13.10}$$

$$\text{Shrinkage ratio}\,(R) = \frac{W_d}{V_d \times \rho_w}$$

where:

w = water content (%) of wet soil pat
V_w = volume of wet soil pat (cm^3)
V_d = volume of oven-dried soil pat (cm^3)
W_s = weight of oven-dried soil pat (g)
ρ_w = approximate density of water equal to 1.0 g cm^{-3}

13.4.4 Void Ratio

A soil mass is considered to consist of particles enclosing voids of varying sizes. The voids may be filled with air, water, or both. In soils engineering calculations, some of the important relations are used such as, unit weights,

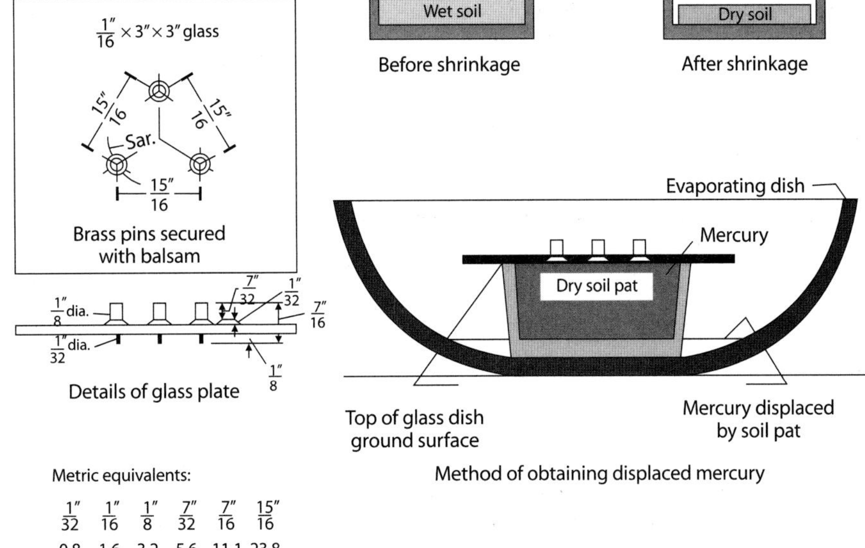
1″/16 × 3″×3″ glass
15″/16
15″/16
Sar.
15″/16
Brass pins secured with balsam
1″/8 dia.
1″/32 dia.
7″/32
1″/32
7″/16
1″/8
Details of glass plate
Metric equivalents:
1″/32 1″/16 1″/8 7″/32 7″/16 15″/16
0.8 1.6 3.2 5.6 11.1 23.8
Wet soil
Before shrinkage
Dry soil
After shrinkage
Evaporating dish
Mercury
Dry soil pat
Top of glass dish ground surface
Mercury displaced by soil pat
Method of obtaining displaced mercury

Fig. 13.8.
Apparatus for determining the volumetric change of subgrade soils

void ratio, porosity and degree of saturation. The quantities used to compute these relations are the weight and volume of the wet specimen, the weight of the same specimen after oven-drying and the specific gravity of the solids (Engineering and Design – Laboratory Soil Testing 1970).

The void ratio (R_V) is the ratio of the volume of voids to the volume of solid particles in a given weight of soil. It can be determined by the volumetric method which can be computed from linear measurements of a specimen in the form of a volumetric cylinder; the inside volume of which is the volume of the wet soil specimen (V_W).

The volumetric method consists of computing the total volume of soil from linear measurements of a regularly shaped mass (as a cylinder or parallelelepiped) as follows:

- *Dry weight of specimen*

$$W_s = W_W / (1 + 0.01W) \tag{13.11}$$

where:
W_W = wet weight of specimen
W = moisture or water content of specimen

- *Wet unit weight*

$$\gamma_W = (W_W / V_W) \times 62.4 \text{ (per 1000 kg m}^{-3}) \tag{13.12}$$

where:
V_W = volume of wet specimen (in cm^3)

- *Dry unit weight*

$$Y_s = (W_s / V_W) \times 62.4 \text{ (per 1000 kg m}^{-3}) \tag{13.13}$$

Void ratio (R_V) can be computed by the following formula:

$$R_V = (V_W - V_s) / V_s \tag{13.14}$$

where
V_s = volume in cm^3 of solids = W_s / G_s
G_s = specific gravity of solids ($g\ cm^{-3}$)

13.5 Permeability of Granular Soils under Constant Head (ASTM D-2434)

According to Darcy's law for flow of water through soil, permeability is defined as the rate of discharge of water (Q) at a temperature (t) of 20 °C under conditions of laminar flow through a unit cross-sectional area (A) of a soil medium under a unit hydraulic gradient ($\delta h/\delta l$: the loss of hydraulic head per unit distance). The coefficient of permeability ($\bar{k}$) has the dimensions of a velocity and is usually expressed in centimeters per second. The permeability of soil depends primarily on the size and shape of the soil grains, the void ratio of the soil, the shape and arrangement of the voids, and the degree of saturation (see Chap. 8).

A standard test method (ASTM D-2434) is applied to determine the coefficient of permeability for the laminar flow of water through granular soils. The test is performed on a representative sample of air-dried granular soil, containing less than 10% of material passing the 75 μm (no. 200) sieve. The constant-head test is used principally for coarse-grained soils (clean sands and gravels) with $\bar{k}$ values greater than approximately 10×10^{-4} cm s^{-1} (ASTM 1997).

Specimen cylinders are obtained by using a permeameter, which should be fitted with the following:

1. A porous disk at the bottom with a permeability greater than that of the soil specimen, but with openings sufficiently small (less than 10% finer size) to prevent movement of the particles;
2. Manometer outlets for measuring the loss of head or the difference in piezometer readings, $\Delta h = h_1 - h_2$.
3. A spring-loaded porous disk at the top of the cylinder.

Measurements: The following initial measurements in centimeters or square centimeters should be provided for the permeameter cylinder (Fig. 13.9):

- The inside diameter (D);
- The distance between manometer outlets (L);
- The height of the specimen $\Delta h = h_1 - h_2$ (measured at four symmetrically spaced points from the upper surface of the top plate of the permeameter cylinder to the top of the upper the lower porous plate;
- The cross sectional area A of specimen (cm^2).

The coefficient of permeability $\bar{k}$ (cm s^{-1}) can be determined as follows:

$$\bar{k}_{20\,°\mathrm{C}} = (QL)\,/\,(A\,\Delta h) = (\Delta h L)/(t\Delta h) \qquad (13.15)$$

where:
Q = quantity of flow of water discharged (cm^3)
t = elapsed time of discharge (s)

The permeability should be corrected to 20 °C by multiplying $\bar{k}$ by the ratio (R_T) of the viscosity of water at the test temperature to the viscosity of water at 20 °C (Table 13.5):

$$\bar{k}_{20\,°\mathrm{C}} = \bar{k} \times R_T \qquad (13.16)$$

Computation: An example of computation to calculate permeability is given below. The test was conducted at 20 °C. The soil was fine grained and clayey.

- Δh = 12 cm
- Inner diameter of manometer tubes = 0.6 cm
- Distance L = 2.4 cm
- t_1 = 15 min

a Time interval 11:15–11:30 A.M.:
- Manometer no. 1 head h_1 = 36.5 cm
- Manometer no. 2 head h_2 = 12.60 cm

Then:

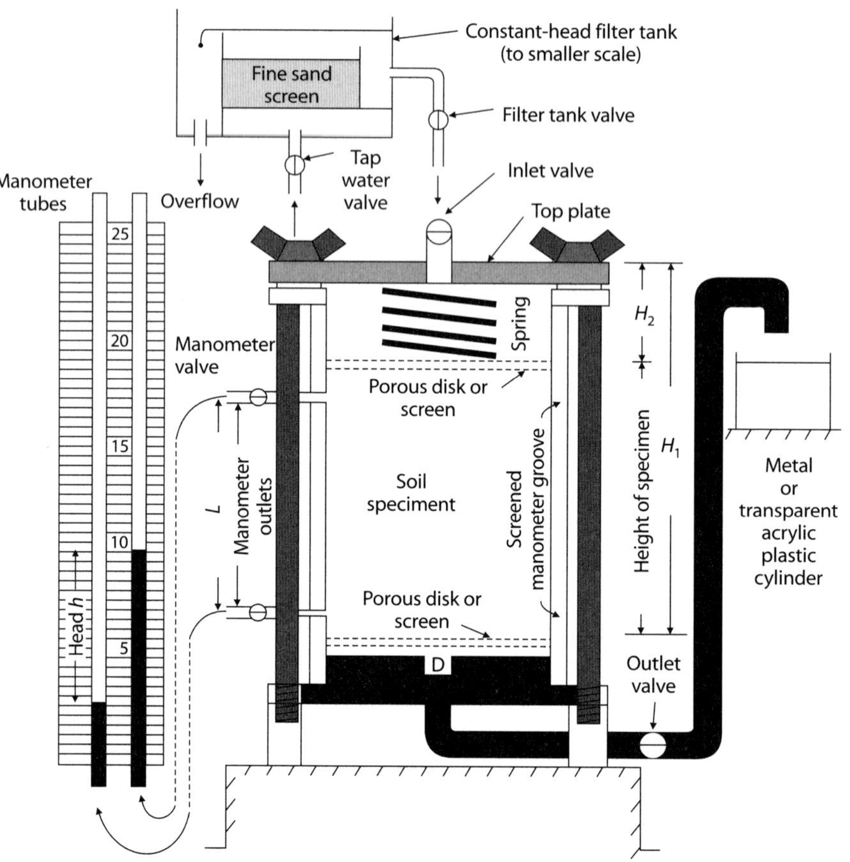
Constant-head filter tank
(to smaller scale)
Fine sand
screen
Filter tank valve
Tap
water
valve
Inlet valve
Manometer
tubes
Overflow
Top plate
25
20
15
10
5
Manometer
valve
Spring
H_2
Porous disk or
screen
H_1
Soil
speciment
Screened
manometer groove
Height of specimen
Metal
or
transparent
acrylic
plastic
cylinder
L
Manometer
outlets
Head h
Porous disk or
screen
D
Outlet
valve

Fig. 13.9.
Constant head permeameter

Table 13.5. Correction factor R_T for viscosity of water at various temperatures

Temperature (°C)	Temperature (1/10 °C)									
	0	1	2	3	4	5	6	7	8	9
0.0	1.783	1.777	1.771	1.765	1.759	1.753	1.747	1.741	1.735	1.729
1.0	1.732	1.717	1.711	1.705	1.699	1.694	1.688	1.682	1.676	1.670
2.0	1.664	1.659	1.654	1.648	1.643	1.638	1.632	1.627	1.622	1.616
3.0	1.611	1.606	1.601	1.596	1.590	1.585	1.580	1.575	1.570	1.565
4.0	1.560	1.555	1.550	1.545	1.540	1.535	1.531	1.526	1.521	1.516
5.0	1.511	1.507	1.502	1.498	1.493	1.488	1.484	1.479	1.475	1.470
6.0	1.465	1.461	1.457	1.452	1.448	1.443	1.439	1.435	1.430	1.426
7.0	1.421	1.417	1.413	1.409	1.404	1.400	1.396	1.392	1.388	1.383
8.0	1.379	1.375	1.371	1.367	1.363	1.359	1.355	1.351	1.347	1.343
9.0	1.339	1.336	1.332	1.328	1.324	1.320	1.317	1.313	1.309	1.305
10.0	1.301	1.298	1.294	1.290	1.287	1.283	1.279	1.276	1.272	1.269
11.0	1.265	1.262	1.258	1.255	1.251	1.248	1.244	1.241	1.237	1.234
12.0	1.230	1.227	1.223	1.220	1.217	1.213	1.210	1.207	1.203	1.200
13.0	1.197	1.194	1.190	1.187	1.184	1.181	1.178	1.175	1.171	1.168
14.0	1.165	1.162	1.159	1.156	1.153	1.150	1.147	1.144	1.141	1.138
15.0	1.135	1.132	1.129	1.126	1.123	1.120	1.117	1.114	1.111	1.108
16.0	1.106	1.103	1.100	1.097	1.094	1.091	1.089	1.086	1.083	1.080
17.0	1.077	1.075	1.072	1.069	1.067	1.064	1.061	1.059	1.056	1.053
18.0	1.051	1.048	1.045	1.043	1.040	1.038	1.035	1.033	1.030	1.027
19.0	1.025	1.022	1.020	1.017	1.015	1.012	1.010	1.007	1.005	1.002
20.0	1.000	0.998	0.995	0.993	0.990	0.988	0.986	0.983	0.981	0.979
21.0	0.976	0.974	0.972	0.969	0.967	0.965	0.962	0.960	0.958	0.955
22.0	0.953	0.951	0.949	0.647	0.944	0.942	0.940	0.938	0.936	0.933
23.0	0.931	0.929	0.927	0.925	0.923	0.920	0.918	0.916	0.914	0.912
24.0	0.910	0.908	0.906	0.904	0.901	0.899	0.897	0.895	0.893	0.891
25.0	0.889	0.887	0.885	0.883	0.881	0.879	0.977	0.875	0.873	0.871
26.0	0.869	0.867	0.866	0.864	0.862	0.860	0.858	0.856	0.854	0.852
27.0	0.850	0.848	0.847	0.845	0.843	0.841	0.839	0.837	0.836	0.834
28.0	0.832	0.830	0.828	0.826	0.825	0.823	0.821	0.819	0.818	0.816
29.0	0.814	0.812	0.810	0.809	0.807	0.805	0.804	0.802	0.800	0.798
30.0	0.797	0.795	0.793	0.792	0.790	0.788	0.787	0.785	0.783	0.782
31.0	0.780	0.778	0.777	0.775	0.774	0.772	0.770	0.769	0.767	0.766
32.0	0.764	0.763	0.761	0.759	0.758	0.756	0.755	0.753	0.752	0.750
33.0	0.749	0.747	0.746	0.744	0.743	0.741	0.739	0.738	0.736	0.735
34.0	0.733	0.732	0.731	0.729	0.728	0.726	0.725	0.723	0.722	0.720
35.0	0.719	0.718	0.716	0.715	0.713	0.712	0.711	0.709	0.708	0.706
36.0	0.705	0.704	0.702	0.701	0.699	0.698	0.697	0.695	0.694	0.693
37.0	0.691	0.690	0.689	0.687	0.686	0.685	0.683	0.682	0.681	0.679
38.0	0.678	0.677	0.675	0.674	0.673	0.672	0.670	0.669	0.668	0.666
39.0	0.665	0.664	0.663	0.661	0.660	0.659	0.658	0.656	0.655	0.654
40.0	0.653	0.652	0.650	0.649	0.648	0.647	0.646	0.644	0.643	0.642
41.0	0.641	0.639	0.638	0.637	0.636	0.635	0.634	0.632	0.631	0.630
42.0	0.629	0.628	0.627	0.626	0.624	0.623	0.622	0.621	0.620	0.619
43.0	0.618	0.616	0.615	0.614	0.613	0.612	0.611	0.610	0.609	0.608
44.0	0.607	0.606	0.604	0.603	0.602	0.601	0.600	0.599	0.598	0.597
45.0	0.596	0.595	0.594	0.593	0.592	0.591	0.590	0.588	0.587	0.586
46.0	0.585	0.584	0.583	0.582	0.581	0.580	0.579	0.578	0.577	0.576
47.0	0.575	0.574	0.573	0.572	0.571	0.570	0.569	0.568	0.567	0.566
48.0	0.565	0.564	0.564	0.563	0.562	0.561	0.560	0.559	0.558	0.557
49.0	0.556	0.555	0.554	0.553	0.552	0.551	0.550	0.549	0.548	0.548

Computed from *Smithsonian Physical Tables*, 8th edn., Table 170. Correction factor R_T is found by dividing the viscosity of water at the test temperature to the viscosity of water at 20 °C.

Table 13.6. Correlation chart of screen opening and sieve sizes

Geologic material grain-size range	Johnson slot no.	Gauze no.	Tyler			U.S. standard	
			Sieve no.	Size of openings (inches)	(mm)	Sieve no.	Size of openings (inches)
Clay and silt		–	400	0.0015	0.038	400	0.0015
	–	–	325	0.0017	0.043	325	0.0017
	–	–	270	0.0021	0.053	270	0.0021
	–	–	250	0.0024	0.061	230	0.0024
	–	–	200	0.0029	0.074	200	0.0029
Fine sand	–	–	170	0.0035	0.088	170	0.0035
	–	–	150	0.0041	0.104	140	0.0041
	–	–	115	0.0049	0.124	120	0.0049
	6	90	100	0.0058	0.147	100	0.0059
	7	80	80	0.0069	0.175	80	0.0070
	8	70	65	0.0082	0.208	70	0.0083
	10	60	60	0.0097	0.246	60	0.0098
Medium sand	12	50	48	0.0116	0.295	50	0.0117
	14	–	42	0.0138	0.351	45	0.0138
	16		35	0.0164	0.417	40	0.0165 (1/64)
	18	40	–	0.0180	0.457	–	0.0180
	20		32	0.0195	0.495	35	0.0197
	23		28	0.0232	0.589	30	0.0232
Coarse sand	25	30	–	0.0250	0.635	–	0.0250
	28		24	0.0276	0.701	25	0.0280
	31		–	0.0310	0.788	–	0.0310 (1/32)
	33		20	0.0328	0.833	20	0.0331
	35	20		0.035	0.889		0.0350
	39		16	0.039	0.991	18	0.0394
Very coarse sand	47		14	0.046	1.168	16	0.0469
	56		12	0.055	1.397	14	0.0555
	62		–	0.062	1.590	–	0.0620 (1/16)
	66		10	0.065	1.651	12	0.0661
	79		9	0.078	1.981	10	0.0787
Very fine gravel	93		8	0.093	2.362	8	0.0931
	94		–	0.094	2.390	–	0.094 (3/32)
	111		7	0.110	2.794	7	0.111
	125		–	0.125	3.180	–	0.125 (1/8)
	132		6	0.131	3.327	6	0.132
Fine gravel	157		5	0.156	3.962	5	0.157
	187		4	0.185	4.699	4	0.187 (3/16)
	223		3 1/2	0.221	5.613	3 1/2	0.223
	250		–	0.250	6.350	1/4	0.250 (1/4)
	263		3	0.263	6.680	–	0.263
	312		2 1/2	0.312	7.925	5/16	0.312 (5/16)
	375		0.371	0.371	9.423	3/8	0.375 (3/8)
	438		0.441	0.441	11.20	7/16	0.438 (7/16)
	500		0.525	0.525	13.33	1/2	0.500 (1/2)

Fig. 13.10.
Results of measurements for a permeability test

Project : 2000
Location : Antiuch
Boring : B4

Permeameter measurements:
Internal diameter (D) = 0.6 cm
ΔH = H1 – H2 = 12 cm
Area = πr2 = 0.28 cm2
L = 2.4 cm
Q = 9.6 cc (ΔH.πr2)

Date Sampled : 2.20.95
Date of Test : 2.25.95
Depth of Sample : 16.5–19.0 ft

Sample characteristics:
w = 19.20 % (Ww – Ws / Ws × 100)
Ww = 150 gm
Ws = 125.84 gm.
t°c = 2°c

Description of Sample:
Silty sandstone that includes very fine clayey detritals and constitutes 7% of the whole sample.

Test	h_1 cm	h_2 cm	Δh cm	t	$\bar{K}$ cm/sec	
1	36.5	12.60	23.9	15'	1.3×10^{-3}	$\bar{K}_{av}$ = 1.35×10^{-3} cm/sec
2	43.4	19.8	23.6	15'	1.36×10^{-3}	

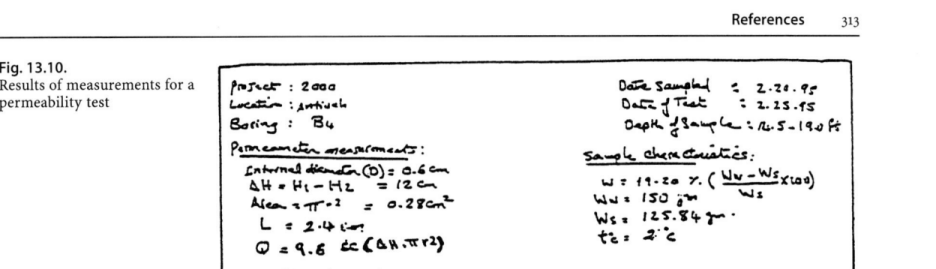

$$\Delta h = h_1 - h_2 = 23.9 \text{ cm}$$

$$\bar{k}_{20°C} = (QL) / (A t \Delta h) = (\Delta h L)/t\Delta h)$$
$$= (12 \times 2.4) / (900 \times 23.9) = 28.8 / 21\,510$$
$$= 1.34 \times 10^{-3} \text{ cm s}^{-1}$$

b Time interval 11:30–11:45 A.M.:
- Manometer no. 1 head $h_1 = 43.4$ cm
- Manometer no. head $h_2 = 19.8$ cm

Then:

$$\bar{k}_{20°C} = (12 \times 2.4) / (900 \times 23.6) = 28.8 / 21\,240$$
$$= 1.36 \times 10^{-3} \text{ cm s}^{-1}$$

and

$$\bar{k}_{AV} = 1.35 \times 10^{-3} \text{ cm s}^{-1}$$

Figure 13.10 shows the permeability test results. Table 13.6 shows the correlation chart of screen openings and sieve sizes.

References

American Standards for Testing and Materials (ASTM) (1997) Annual book of ASTM standards. ASTM, West Conshohocken, Pennsylvania (Section 4, 04-08: Construction; soil and rock); ASTM D421 (85) and ASTM D2217 – Standard practice for dry and wet preparation of soil samples and for particle size analysis and determination of soil constants, pp 8–9; 192–194; ASTM D422 (63) – Standard method for particle-size analysis of soils, pp 10–16; ASTM D427 (93) – Standard method for shrinkage factors of soils by the mercury method, pp 21–29; ASTM D4318 (95a) – Standard test method for liquid limit, plastic limit, and plasticity index of soils, pp 522–532; ASTM D2434 (68) – Standard test method for permeability of granular soils (Constant Head), pp 202–206

Driscoll FG (1986) Sediment sieve analysis in groundwater and wells. Johnson Filtration Systems Inc., St. Paul, Minnesota (chap 12, pp 405–412)

Engineering and Design – Laboratory Soil Testing (1970) Engineering manual EM 1110-2-1906. Department of the Army Office of the Chief of Engineers (4a – Appendix V: Grain size analysis; 4b – Appendix IV: Specific gravity; 4c – Appendix III and II: Water content – general, unit weights and void ratio; 4e – Appendix VII: Permeability tests)

Loynachan TE, Brown KW, Cooper TH, Milford MH (1999) Sustaining our soils and society. American Geological Institute, Alexandria, Virginia, pp 7–10, 34–35, 40

Chapter 14

Project Performance

14.1 Introduction

A successful project has specific objectives, a work schedule and a time limit for completion, assigned staffing, and adequate funding. The project should be completed on schedule and produce a technically and editorially correct report (Waste Management of North America Inc. 1989; Green 1991; Moore 1991; U.S. Geological Survey 1991, 1959–60).

The objective of a project is to solve one or more specific problems. If the objectives are clear, an appropriate approach can be devised and each step in the project can be defined. If the objectives are not clear, the project can lack focus and the report will fail to satisfy the needs it was designed to address. Indefinite objectives commonly result in wasted time, collection of irrelevant data, and neglect of critical details.

A *definite time limit* is needed for completion of a project. Undefined projects of any length can result in late reports. Accordingly, project work schedules should be designed so that parts of the projects are devoted solely to report preparation, review, and approval.

It has been our experience that the report planning and sequential preparation of segments of the final report should be undertaken "early on" in the execution of a project and not left until the last because they are too routine or simple and under the ruse that the material is obvious, easily accumulated and can be done anytime. Experience has shown that the best reports have resulted from planning and begun early in project execution.

Key staffing must preferably be full time and continuous for efficient project management. The transfer or loss of the project manager before the project is completed will result in lost continuity and delay or the abortion of the project and/or the report. A project manager that begins a project with a thorough understanding of purpose, scope, and objectives, a good set of administrative documents is most likely to complete the project on time, on budget, and with positive results.

Adequate funding is essential for project success. Managers must avoid underestimating costs to make the project more attractive to potential cooperators or clients. Cost cutting can result in substandard reports, overdue reports, and dissatisfied clients or cooperators. Therefore, good project management is imperative for a successful project.

Project progress must be reviewed on a regular schedule. The review should be conducted periodically, and a written summary of the review should be prepared and reviewed by key project and supervisory personnel. Elements that comprise a successful project are:

1. A project proposal that includes (or reflects)
   - Clear objective
   - Adequate planning
   - Detailed work plan
2. Reasonable goals
3. Adequate budget
4. Most problems anticipated
5. A technically capable staff
6. Frequent project reviews
7. A good report outline
8. A technically correct and readable report
9. Adequate supervision and quality control
10. Outside services that are on time
11. Sufficient and continuous funding
12. Completion of the report on time and within budget

Appendix 14.A – Sample forms (required for a project).

14.1.1 Project Proposal

A project proposal is a plan to address a specific problem or problems. The proposal should outline the technical objectives, the period of time needed to achieve the objectives, and the manpower and funding necessary to complete the work. A proposal should be clear and concise and should address the: "what, why, where, when, and how of the project". It should follow a standard format and contain enough information to allow the client to evaluate the proposal and report plan (Waste Management of North America Inc. 1989; Green 1991; Moore 1991). A project proposal should consider the following:

Project Contract – Most projects are governed by a contract that provides authorization for the contractor and legally dictates the requirements or work elements that must be completed on an agreed schedule and budget. Appendix 14.C shows an example of contract agreement.

Title – The project title should relate to the purpose, scope, and location of the proposed study. Ideally, the title should closely resemble the title of the proposed principal report resulting from the study. The title should be concise yet informative.

Problem – An explanation should be provided as to why the project deserves the commitment of time and money. The project must produce results worthy of funding. The need for the study must be greater than just the satisfaction of intellectual curiosity.

Objectives – Relate the proposed technical results to the expressed need for those results. The objective should be specific. This is one of the most important factors in evaluating the project proposal.

Approach – Describe how and by what means the objectives will be addressed. If standard approaches and methods are used, a brief description will suffice. If the approach is innovative and untested, a more detailed description may be needed.

Relation to long-term plans – Tell how problems or needs are addressed by a project, related to client or agency objectives.

Benefits – Show how the results of the project will be of benefit to the client or agency or to the science or issue(s).

Reports – Describe the planned reports. State probable title or titles of reports, outlets, and milestone dates. Important milestones include the preparation of report outlines, report writing, colleague review, submittal of the report for approval, and anticipated date of approval. All report activities should be planned for completion by the end of project funding. Finally, for some reports or books the market for the final product should be identified and evaluated (Appendix 14.B.1 – An example of project work elements).

Work plan – Schedule starting and ending dates for each work element. Remember that some elements might be concurrent, whereas others must be completed in proper sequence (Appendix 14.B.2 – An example of time accounting project management).

Personnel – List personnel needs by specialty and time needed. Note that all personnel must be available at the time needed in the work schedule. Also, indicate the possible need for outside advisors and consultants.

Project costs – With adequate reference to plans, schedule, and personnel, itemize costs for each work element. Be certain that the budget is adequate for all planned project activities for the anticipated period of study, including all costs associated with publishing the reports. If the proposal for a project is modified, increased or reduced, the project planning documents *must* reflect these changes (Appendix 14.B.3 – An example for distribution of work among geologists).

14.1.2 Project Planning

The key to successful project management is through planning. Planning allows the project manager or management team to establish appropriate milestones or target dates to monitor progress, anticipate problems, and to develop corrective actions in advance of need. If the project is planned in detail before it is undertaken and if the plans are revised as necessary during the project, the final report should be relatively easy to produce and the schedule will be met. In fact, report planning is best carried out as an integral part of the initial planning phase of the project.

A preliminary report outline should be developed to assure that all technical requirements are met. The outline should be reviewed by management and the client to ensure that there is a common understanding of the goals. Questions on the objectives and scope of the project should be resolved before any fieldwork begins. In some cases, this takes place during proposal negotiations.

An experienced project manager can anticipate areas where problems may arise or where field or laboratory results may require changes in the project. Problems should be discussed immediately with the client, who will not appreciate surprises at a later date.

14.1.2.1 *Project Scope and Objectives*

A project is a series of related activities with specific objectives, a beginning date, and an end date. The major elements of project planning are the project proposal, which should include a detailed work plan, and a report outline. The steps that should be followed in planning the project are as follows:

1. Define the project objectives.
2. Select an approach to accomplish the objectives.
3. Decide on the major milestones for the project.
4. Establish dates to begin and end milestones.
5. Select and assign staff to accomplish work.
6. Carry out the project.
7. Prepare a quality technical report on time.

A project can be successful only when the project manager has thoroughly planned all foreseeable aspects of the project before the project begins. Project objec-

Fig. 14.1. Art for cooking a report

tives must be specific, deadlines must be realistic, and difficulties must be anticipated.

14.1.2.2 *Project Deliverables*

The most important part of project planning is a thorough understanding of the scope of work, the nature of the deliverables and the client's expectations. The best time to clarify objectives is before the project starts. Once this understanding is reached, detailed plans can be prepared for executing the project. The list of deliverables is the natural starting point of the review because they are what the client expects to receive, such as text, graphics, CD-ROMs, solid models, photos, etc.

In many projects there is opportunity for multiple report preparation and release. A series of short progress reports; a technical report on some aspect of work; a new concept, fossil, mineral, or method are examples of topics that would justify a supplemental report. Again, if this type of progress report is considered, there must be the necessary administrative approval and change in project documentation.

14.1.2.3 *Project Budget*

Once the technical requirements have been determined, the budget can then be developed. In some cases, the client specifies the total budget project; in other cases, the budget is developed to fit the technical requirements. In this case, the budget is presented to the client as part of the proposal for review and approval. The detailed project budget includes a breakout of anticipated costs for each activity. This budget then specifies the level of staff effort and other resources that can be used to complete the required work.

14.1.2.4 *Project Schedule*

The project schedule should be developed in agreement with the client. The project manager then examines the technical plan, available staff, and budget and determines the amount of time that should be devoted to each activity. This schedule should be detailed enough to show all required activities and milestones, including separate periods for report-writing, review, and revision. On complex projects, several tasks may be executed simultaneously. In this case, interdependencies among the tasks must be taken into account on the schedule.

14.1.2.5 *Project Staffing*

The schedule and budget define the level of effort that can be expended to perform the project. Before any work begins, the manager must determine the types of service needed to execute the project. Services needed, such as drilling, logging or sampling should be scheduled to ensure that they will be available when required. Laboratories, for example, could be alerted as to the timing to expect samples for analysis.

The most important resource is the staff that will perform the work. In most offices, several projects are being carried out at the same time. This means that the projects may be in competition for the same staff. Early planning of staffing needs, allows the manager to go to management with a clear picture of staff resource requirements. Management can then take whatever steps are needed to provide the resources or at least to advise the project manager of any anticipated difficulties so that contingency plans for alternate arrangements can be made. This is the ideal situation, but it can only work if all projects are well planned, the organization is not over-extended, and enough flexibility exists for coping with unanticipated situations.

14.1.2.6 *Report Outline*

This report is typically the only product of a project that is seen by the client, and in most cases, it determines the success or failure of the project.

An outline of the report should be prepared at project initiation. The scope of work and other client technical requirements are the basis for the final report, so preparing an outline is straightforward. The report outline should be thematic, that is, it should contain a topic sentence describing the entire report and one for each report section. The outline should be carried to a level as detailed as possible. The outline is also useful in testing the manager's understanding of the project scope. If several similar projects are to be performed, it may be efficient to use a standard report format that may vary only in recommendations, data, and hydrologic description.

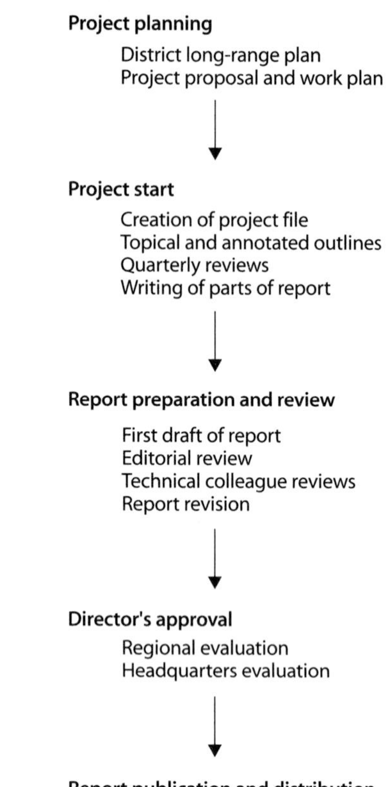
Project planning
District long-range plan
Project proposal and work plan
Project start
Creation of project file
Topical and annotated outlines
Quarterly reviews
Writing of parts of report
Report preparation and review
First draft of report
Editorial review
Technical colleague reviews
Report revision
Director's approval
Regional evaluation
Headquarters evaluation
Report publication and distribution

Fig. 14.2. A progressive chart showing steps in project and report quality assurance

14.1.3 Project and Report Quality Assurance

An orderly plan or system is needed to direct the project and the preparation of a report from conception through completion. This system, which is used in USGS offices, has evolved during many years (Green 1991; Moore 1991). For an example of the steps in a quality assurance system to guide the project and report see Fig. 14.2.

14.1.4 Types of Projects

The scientist or engineer may be called on to plan several types of projects. In consulting, the most common are short-term projects (less than 6 months) that have a budget of less than U.S.$100 000. Clients, for example, may be Federal, State, or local government agencies; insurance companies; industrial firms; or financial or legal firms and management districts.

14.1.4.1 *Short-Term Projects*

For many consultants, short-term single-purpose projects are often done with a very low margin of profit and consequently, must be run very efficiently. These projects may take only a day or two or may last several weeks. Usually, there is a single, well-defined objective. A typical project of this sort may require document review, a limited amount of field and laboratory work, data interpretation and evaluation, and a brief final report.

Projects of this type are often performed by a single staff member, who can draw upon very specific inputs from various staff specialists. Projects of this type require careful attention to planning and monitoring of progress and expenditures. In many firms, these projects are the bread and butter of the work-load and help to keep staff members productive between larger projects.

14.1.4.2 *Long-Term Projects*

Projects that last several months to several years present more of a management challenge. These projects are best run by breaking them into short-term tasks or milestones that must be met during the course of the project. The greatest danger of a long-term objective project of a busy organization is that work on it will be delayed to meet short-term needs, "solve crises". This commonly results in operating at panic speed for a short time near the completion date of the project and can result in major problems of quality and cost overruns.

14.1.4.3 *Open-Ended Project*

An open-ended project is the most difficult to manage as this type of project has no fixed completion date and often has one or more objectives that do not have clear criteria for completion. Fiscally, they are often performed as level-of-effort projects up to a ceiling amount. To be successful, it is necessary to define interim objective phases or milestones with an associated schedule, budget, and report with detailed recommendations for succeeding phases.. This approach has the advantage that progress can be clearly demonstrated during the course of the project, which may make it easier to obtain additional funding.

14.1.5 Summary of Project Planning

1. The inclusion of benefits, work plan, and summary in the project proposal greatly enhances the client's ability to focus on key issues and to grasp quickly the importance of the work proposal.
2. The work plan is an essential part of project planning. It is an excellent way to design the sequence and duration of work elements.
3. The major causes of project failure are:
   - A poorly prepared proposal
   - Unspecified objectives and tasks
   - Cost cutting
   - Failure to reduce the scope of the project if full funding not obtained
   - Not adhering to sound principals of cost estimation
   - No report outline
4. The major steps in project planning are:
   - Defines objectives
   - Prepare a detailed project proposal
   - Plan the budget
   - Prepare a detailed work plan
   - Write a report plan

14.2 Project Management

Management is used to achieve the project objectives. Management begins with a well-prepared proposal. Well-managed projects will achieve the objectives and produce an excellent report on time. Without management, the project will probably exceed budget and produce a late report (Moore 1991; U.S. Geological Survey 1991, 1959–60).

14.2.1 Management by Objectives

Management by objectives (MBO) is a major technique used by government agencies and the private sector to monitor project progress. MBO was first used in 1954 and has been used successfully at General Motors, Ford Motor Company, and General Mills. MBO defines the project objectives and provides a mechanism to monitor progress. MBO defines the following: what must be done, how it must be done, how much it will cost, what constitutes satisfactory performance, how much progress is being made, and when action should be taken to revise the project objectives and schedule.

The major steps that are needed to set up a MBO system are:

1. The supervisor and project manager meet to discuss the objectives and approach for the project.
2. The supervisor and the project manager agree on the objectives, tasks, approach, deliverables, work plan, and report.
3. The project manager strives to accomplish the objectives agreed upon.
4. The supervisor and project manager meet on a regular schedule to evaluate what was accomplished. They review milestones, revise the schedule, correct problems, evaluate report progress, funding and plans for the next meeting.

A major element of project management is a periodic review of progress. Written and oral reports on work progress may also be needed periodically. Opportunities for review are staff meetings, technical seminars, and briefings for coordinators.

An essential part of the review is to compare project progress with the work plan. Emphasis should be placed on project findings, report progress, accomplishments, needs for assistance, financial status, and plans for the next milestones. Some of the advantages of regular project review are listed below:

1. The project is kept on schedule and focused on objectives.
2. Needs for modifying project objectives are identified.
3. Personnel, technical, and financial problems are identified.
4. Guidance and assistance are provided for the project manager.
5. Technical quality control is provided.
6. Morale is maintained.
7. Managers, supervisors, and coordinators are educated.
8. The report is kept on schedule.

A project management file should be established by the project manager early in the project to maintain records and to document progress on project activity and planned reports. The file should be kept current. The following items should be included in the file:

1. Project proposal and description
2. Work plan, including milestone dates
3. Budget
4. Topical and annotated outline for report
5. Lists of report illustrations and tables
6. List of references for bibliographic citations
7. Quality review summaries
8. Report drafts and review comments
9. Summary of meetings with coordinator(s) on the project
10. All pertinent correspondence
11. News releases
12. Newspaper articles on the project

14.2.2 Position Descriptions and Performance Standards

Most consulting firms and government agencies use position descriptions and performance standards to provide employees with a better understanding of the work demands and requirements of the job. It should be a valuable aid for evaluating performance, giving promotions, and other rewards. Before starting to write performance standards, the employee's immediate supervisor should prepare the employee's position description and other documents relevant to the job (e.g. management by objectives forms, work plans, and accomplishment forms). The supervisor should then identify the elements of the job, write task statements for each element, designate critical elements, and develop performance standards for each task. The task statement is written in the following format to describe:

- What the employee does
- Where the work is to be done
- How the work is to be done

Task statements are written in the present tense with an action verb to describe what the employee is doing. For example, a task statement for a hydrologist might be as follows: "Performs computations and analysis of data (what) to prepare data for scientific interpretation and public release (why) by applying established analytical methods and procedures, applying computer techniques, selecting appropriate software programs, following instructions, and consulting with other knowledgeable staff members (how)." After the task statements have been written for each element, the supervisor designates critical elements. A critical element is an element that is sufficiently important to the overall success in the job that performance below the fully successful level results in unacceptable overall performance and requires remedial action. Elements not designated as critical elements are required elements. Performance standards should address one or more of the following criteria:

- Quantity
- Quality
- Timeliness
- Manner of performance

14.2.3 Project Controls

Project controls allow the project manager to monitor progress. The controls can provide the manager with the information needed to anticipate problems and to take preventive or remedial actions. Quality assurance is a special type of control that can help to guarantee that all project work is performed to appropriate technical standards. It may also provide the documentation needed to demonstrate in courts, licensing hearings, or in client reviews that the work was performed in accordance with professional standards, practices, and procedures. As liability questions become increasingly important, quality assurance takes on greater importance.

Projects performed for Federal agencies require frequent progress reports. Many clients are beginning to require reports on complex projects to ascertain that the project stays "on track." In some companies, internal management also requires this sort of reporting.

The types of project controls and management reports commonly required are discussed below. These project control techniques are very useful to the project manager, particularly on complex or long-term projects where parallel activities are involved. Computer graphics used to assist the project control process are described.

14.2.3.1 *Work Schedules*

Project schedules show progress as a function of time. Every project, no matter how simple, has a schedule. This includes beginning and completion dates. From these two dates, the time schedule for the entire project may be developed. The project manager must calculate back from the project end date using reasonable estimates of durations for each task or activity to determine intermediate schedule points. Milestone charts are schedules commonly required in proposals and in monthly or other regularly scheduled project management reports on government projects. The milestone chart shows actual progress against planned progress.

A common problem in many projects is not allowing enough time for report preparation, review, revision, and production. Failure to plan for these activities is a common reason for late completion of projects. If client review and response are required before final report delivery, it is important to show this on the project schedule. After the schedule is developed, project and support staff can be alerted to expect various activities at specific times.

DISTRICT HEAD
ESCAMBIA CO. PROJECT
PHASE I
PHASE II
PHASE III
COMPLETE OUTLINE OF REPORT
COMPLETE WELL INVENTORY
COMPLETE FIELD WORK
13
FRI
TO DO
DONE
U.S. GOV. PROP.
FILE

Fig. 14.3.
Assign and meet dead lines

14.2.3.2 *Staffing Projections*

Staffing projections are routinely made during the planning stages of projects. These are projections of the rate at which manpower will be expended in performing the work required for the project. More sophisticated versions can show staffing broken into labor grades to make cost calculations easier. Total hours expended are routinely compiled at least weekly in many firms; these data are readily compared to the projection. Cumulative staffing expenditure is one important piece of management information commonly required in management reports.

14.2.3.3 *Cost Projections*

The budget can be handled in much the same way as manpower data. Projected spending rates can be prepared from the initial project budget, together with the projection of staffing expenditures, with cumulative expenditures calculated and plotted. Comparison of actual and cumulative costs with projected costs gives a good idea of the financial progress of the project.

14.2.3.4 *Technical Progress*

Technical progress is much more difficult to quantify than numerical measures like cost or man-hours. Many management reports ask for an estimate such as "percent complete" or the equivalent. If this estimate is to be meaningful, it must be independent from accumulated costs or accumulated man-hours. Some necessarily qualitative measure of the amount of "work" required for a project must be qualified. This is always a highly subjective measure and is hardly a reliable indicator for decision making, although it can be useful when compared to the more quantitative indicators discussed above.

14.2.3.5 *Federal Requirements*

Most large (greater than U.S.$1 million) Federal projects in the USA require that the project be managed according to the Federal Cost/Schedule Control System (C/SCS) requirements, as outlined by the U.S. Department of Energy (DOE) or an equivalent system developed by other agencies. These requirements demand a high level of accountability, a very specific management information system, detailed cost and staffing tracking, and a well-defined set of management reports, which are due monthly, quarterly, and annually. These reports also require summary statements of technical work accomplished during the reporting period, work planned for the next period (s), problems encountered, problems anticipated, remedial actions taken and planned, and projected expenditures. Details of C/SCS requirements are found in the appropriate government orders and require a specialist trained in meeting the requirements.

14.2.3.6 *Quality Assurance*

There are many levels of quality assurance (QA) that may be applied in project management. The most rigorous level is that developed in the nuclear industry for facilities that may affect health and safety. This level requires full compliance with the 18 elements of a quality assurance program as spelled out in the standard NQA-1, accepted by the Nuclear Regulatory Commission. Similar programs are required for the design and manufacture of aerospace and military hardware. For nonnuclear projects, lower levels of quality assurance implementation are required. The lowest levels useful to a project manager call for independent review of technical work products (such as draft reports) and control of documents.

Many people equate quality control (QC) with quality assurance (QA). This misconception covers only one role of QA. A proper QA program provides assurance that work was performed according to established procedures by qualified people and that those facts are clearly documented. Procedures for performing work apply to drilling, sampling, and testing in the field; reducing and analyzing data in the office; using calibrated equipment and validated computer codes; and preparing and reviewing reports describing the work and findings. In many firms, written procedures exist for performing field and laboratory activities; formal procedures for data interpretation and writing are much less common.

One procedure that should be formally adopted in all organizations performing technical work is the review of the document. Internal review is essential to protect against litigation and liability and, in fact, is an integral part of sound science and engineering. Several levels or types of review exist, and all have their place in project management. The lowest level is editorial review, which is a check for spelling, typographical, and syntax errors. More important is the basic technical review, in which a knowledgeable professional not involved in the work or the report reviews it for technical content. All data entry and calculations should be checked independently prior to colleague review. This reviewer should also check the interpretations made by the author. The next review is the management level, where the management reviews the report to ensure that contract requirements were satisfied, that it is consistent with other work products or other information, and that it does not conflict with company or agency policies. Major technical reports, covering significant research, field, or laboratory investigations may need a peer review, especially if the findings of the project are at, near, or beyond the recognized state of the art. The peer review requires that recognized independent experts in the field, often drawn from academic or government facilities, perform a thorough review of the data, analysis, and interpretations. This level of review is not common in the consulting world but is similar to the refereeing process used for journal publications.

14.2.3.7 *Progress Evaluation*

The ability to evaluate progress and to recognize the need for remedial actions is extremely valuable to the project manager. Because very few projects run smoothly from start to finish with no problems or surprises, this is the only way to avoid disaster. A supervisor often measures the success of the project by the ability to recognize problems and put corrective actions into play.

Progress evaluation requires the comparison of project accomplishments and status with the project plans. This means that progress evaluation can only be as good as the existing plans. As previously discussed, the project manager must prepare plans before the start of work as carefully and in as much detail as possible. These plans must include intermediate targets, or milestones, that will be met along the course of the project. The final report, then, is only one of the milestones. The simplest form of progress evaluation is to compare the accomplishment at each milestone with the schedule. This, however, will only tell part of the story. Equally important is an analysis of actual expenditures against projected budget or planned staffing. Meaningful analysis usually requires that the plans, including the schedule and budget, are updated whenever conditions change.

An early slip in milestone completion means that one of two things must happen: (1) the final completion date for the project must be adjusted, and (2) the lost time will need to be made up on later milestones in the project, allowing the original completion date to be met. This may require negotiations with the client, or, more commonly, finding ways to shorten future project activities. This may be done by an accelerated expenditure of staffing or by a reduction in scope or both. It can easily be seen that the earliest possible recognition of the need for action will provide the broadest choice of possibilities for remediation.

The most useful skill a successful project manager must have is direct involvement (hands-on) to recognize upcoming problems. On very large, complex projects, computer-assisted analysis can be useful, but more commonly, a simpler analysis of staffing and cost accumulation rates will provide ample early warning. For most projects, weekly management data should be available. Less timely data can seriously handicap a project manager and permit variances from plans to get out of control.

14.2.3.8 *Data Bases*

Data base programs exist to permit the compilation, manipulation, and management of large amounts of data. They combine filing and tabulation features with various types of display techniques. They are designed to permit additional data to be added at appropriate places with a minimum disruption to the data set. The best known of these is probably Geographic Information System (GIS). These software packages are more useful for both technical data analysis and compilation where very large amounts of data are generated or must be examined and for management purposes.

14.2.4 Monitoring Progress

Frequently, reports are used to monitor project progress. Many computer programs are available to assist the project manager in both planning and monitoring progress on the project; examples are Super Project Plus by Computer Associates and Harvard Project by Management Software Publishing. These programs can be used for simple or complex multidisciplinary projects.

Progress reports have two advantages:

1. They are tools that allow the project manager to visualize the relation or interdependency of various project tasks, staffing requirements, needed services, and funding.
2. They provide a concise mechanism for reporting progress to the project staff, managers, and clients.

These reports allow the project manager to define the project work elements (milestone) and to define who will do the job. There are four basic types of progress reports: milestones; PERT (program evaluation and review technique); bar graphs (Gantt); and quarterly progress review.

A method frequently used to monitor progress of long-term projects is the quarterly review of the project progress (every 3 months). The summary is presented orally and in written form. Items that are discussed in the review are progress on milestone, difficulties, roadblocks, and plans for the next quarter. PERT, milestone, and bar graphs can be used to describe planned and actual progress. A list of action items should be prepared after each review.

Milestone graphs are very useful for analyzing and presenting project information. Tables are prepared listing milestones, starting dates, and completion dates. The report is a list of all milestones for the project, including the final report. An example of a milestone chart is given in Table 14.1 (Moore 1991).

The chart provides a means of comparing actual progress against planned completion. Departure from the planned completion dates is a fact of life in almost all projects. There are many reasons for departures, such as reduction in funding, transfer of personnel, lack of management review, inadequate planning, and delay in obtaining drilling equipment.

PERT is a graphic report technique used extensively by government agencies and the private sector. PERT identifies the tasks and specifies how these tasks relate and depend on one another. The objective of PERT is to plan and control large and complex projects in the easiest and most efficient manner. It is easily adapted to design hydrologic and geologic projects. The method that is used to apply PERT to a project is:

1. List project tasks
2. Determine the duration for each task
3. Determine available resources (staffing, equipment, and materials)
4. List costs
5. Graph activities (network)
6. Compute the latest allowable time
7. Add slack time
8. Determine the critical path (the longest path through the project network). Delays in a critical task will delay the completion of the project

Figure 14.4 shows an example of a PERT chart (Moore 1991).

14.2.5 Project Completion

When is a project complete? Is it when the final report has been submitted to the client? When it has been accepted by the client, or when all payment has been received? All of these may be correct in part, and perhaps all are also wrong to some extent. The good project manager will conclude each project with an analysis of the project. This should include an examination of the tech-

Table 14.1. Milestone chart (after Moore 1991; adapted by permission of the author)

Milestone description (task)	Jan	Mar	May	Jul	Sep	Nov
Proposal	#	o	@			
Work plan	#	o				
Report outline		#	o			
Test drilling and sampling		#		#		
Analysis of data		#			o	@
Preperation of report		#			o	
Review of report					#	o
Approval					#	o
Publication						o
Post mortem						o

Start task; o planned completion; @ actual completion.

nical, financial, and commercial success (or failure) of the project. Each project should be a learning experience for the manager and the organization. In this way, the process should become more efficient over time, and specific areas in need of improvement can be identified. These may include modifications in the accounting system, tracking of time and material expenditures, or internal communication procedures. If the organization is unwilling or incapable of making changes, the project manager can take these problem areas into account when planning the next project.

14.2.5.1 *Completion Criteria*

Many projects have clearly defined end-points. The most common end-point is the final report. When a project does not end with the final report, level-of-effort reports will be necessary. Discussions are sometimes required with the client to decide on an acceptable end of the project. For the project manager in a consulting firm, the project is not really complete until the billing has been completed and has been paid in full. Often a project manager must follow the project for months after all technical work has been completed and until comments have been received and answered by submitting a revised version of the report. This is a requirement of the project manager who has had constant contact on the work of the project.

The clearest criterion of completion is completion of the assignments made in the contract and statement of work. Technical work has been completed when the client has accepted all reports and other deliverables and has certified that the contract has been fulfilled. At this point, no further costs can be incurred on that project. This limitation is precisely the reason that it is necessary to get written approval or direction from the client when the statement of work is modified during the course of contract.

The project manager has the additional responsibility of ensuring that all costs have been accumulated for the project, all are justified expenditures on the contract, and that the billing reflects all true costs. Billing costs must be expeditiously handled for the benefit of the client as well as the contractor. In some firms, this last step

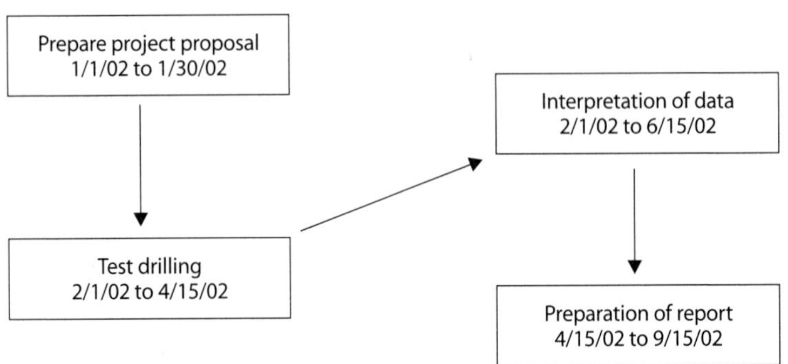
Prepare project proposal
1/1/02 to 1/30/02
Test drilling
2/1/02 to 4/15/02
Interpretation of data
2/1/02 to 6/15/02
Preparation of report
4/15/02 to 9/15/02

Fig. 14.4. An example of a PERT chart (computer programs available)

Bar (graph) charts can be used to display the projects tasks in graphic form over time. It is a way of viewing information displayed on the PERT chart.

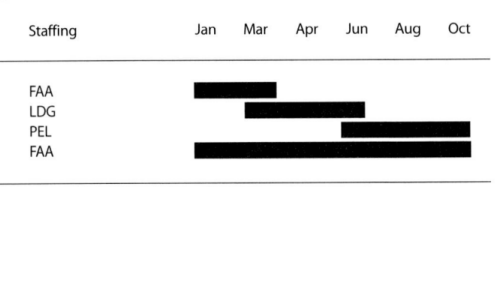

Milestone or task	Staffing	Jan	Mar	Apr	Jun	Aug	Oct
Proposal	FAA						
Test drilling	LDG						
Analysis of data	PEL						
Preparation of report	FAA						

is left to the accountant, who prepares the actual bill and sends it to the client. The project manager's responsibility may extend to collecting payment from the client. If the client does not remit in a timely fashion, the manager may be the one to remind the client of these responsibilities.

14.2.5.2 *Analysis after Completion*

Analysis after project completion is essential for the project manager and his supervisors to improve management skills, for the organization to analyze project results, and for the evaluation of the management system. A truly useful analysis must go well beyond the stage of placing blame, as often happens. Many times, weaknesses in the organization, such as priority setting, staff allocation, management support, un-experienced preliminary budgeting, and scheduling are recognized in the analysis as systematic problems.

Problems that the analysis reveals generally fall into two categories: weakness in planning and weakness in execution. Weaknesses in planning generally result from a lack of sufficient planning or from the planner's inexperience. Weaknesses in execution are more often from communication, either with the client or with the subcontractors, resulting from over-commitment of staff resources or a lack of skills among the technical staff.

14.2.6 Roles and Responsibilities

Client service can be improved through better review and communication. Steps that can be taken to improve the report submitted to the client are noted below.

The division manager or equivalent is responsible for discussing progress and/or new work with clients. The project manager is responsible for filling out the project assignment forms and project spreadsheets. The project manager or designated client contact is responsible for communicating with the client regarding all aspects (technical, schedule, budget) of the project. It is imperative that, if there is an increase in work effort, the client will be informed as soon as possible. The project manager must not undertake tasks beyond the project scope without client authorization. The client contact is responsible for daily client communications. The client contact should notify the client regarding the scheduled arrival date of deliverables. Courtesy calls to monitor client satisfaction should be conducted. The project manager is responsible for completing assignments consistent with client goals. The project staff should be aware of the overall schedule and project budget, including allotted hours. If the project manager cannot stay within the budget, he or she must inform the supervisor immediately so that a response can be made in the budget or the client can be alerted. The client does not like unpleasant surprises. The following is a checklist that could be used for reports and correspondence:

- Is the date at the top of the letter correct?
- Are the addressee's name and title correct?
- Is the addressee's company name spelled correctly?
- If the document is to be mailed overnight, the address should include a street number and name, not a post office box number. The address should not contain both a street address and a post office box number.
- Should the document be labeled "Privileged and Confidential, Prepared at the Request of Counsel"?
- Does the salutation match the name of the addressee?
- Is the letter format correct?
- Does the letter require courtesy copies to anyone?
- Should the courtesy copies be blind or noted?
- Are the courtesy copies going to the correct people?
- Should the people receiving the courtesy copies also receive enclosures?
- If the document is a letter contract or a professional services agreement, are there two originals being transmitted to the addressee?

14.2.7 Summary of Project Management

1. Project management begins with proper project planning and succeeds with implementation of the work plan. Well managed projects achieve objectives and produce excellent reports on time.
2. Poorly managed projects exceed the project budget and result in late or weak technical reports.
3. The project manager is responsible for:
   - identifying milestones and completion dates
   - defining services needed, equipment needs, and manpower
   - providing detailed progress reports
4. Management by objectives keeps the project on schedule and focused on objectives.
5. A project file should be started at the beginning of the project and maintained throughout the life of the project. The file should contain the up-to-date proposal, quarterly reviews, work plan and milestones, budget, expenditures, report topic and annotated outline, and press statements.
6. Three useful types of management charts are a milestone, PERT, and Gantt.
7. Project review should place emphasis on findings, progress of field studies, reports, needs for assistance, plans for next quarter, and report review.
8. Each project should conclude with an evaluation of the success and failure of the project.
9. The main criterion that brings repeat business is a quality report on time that meets objectives, is well organized, and is readable by the intended audience.

14.3 AIPG Bylaws and Code of Ethics

The American Institute of Professional Geologists (AIPG) was primarily adopted December 11, 1989, with modifications adopted October 1998. The institute consists of members and adjuncts who subscribe to the Code of Ethics of the institute. Members of the institute are the geological scientists who meet the institute's standards of education, experience, and integrity, as each are defined in the bylaws. Adjuncts of the institute are either students who are pursuing a course of study in the geological sciences or others who have a vocational or general interest in the geological sciences (American Institute of Professional Geologists 2000).

The institute presented several activities and services to its certified members who carry the "competence", "integrity", and "ethics", that guide their representation, conduct to protect the public from unprofessional practices, monitor governmental and other activities affecting the geological sciences, and communicate with the public.

The institute is a not-for-profit membership corporation organized under the laws of the State of Colorado and comprises different articles and sections that control its bylaws including membership registration, membership meetings, management, officials, committees, and financial responsibilities.

AIPG Code of Ethics: The Code of Ethics applies to all professional activities of members and adjuncts, wherever and whenever they occur. The title "member" where used in this Code of Ethics includes adjuncts. A member is not relieved of an ethical responsibility by virtue of his or her employment, because the member has delegated an assignment to a subordinate, or because the member was not involved in performing services for compensation.

There are several rules and obligations fore members to attain the highest standard of personal integrity and professional conduct; members of the institute should pursue honesty, integrity, loyalty, fairness, etc and they should observe and comply with the requirements and intent of all applicable laws, codes, and regulations. Also, a member should be aware of any decision or action by an employer, client, or materially affect the public health, safety, or welfare. Besides, members should respect the rights, interests, and contributions of their professional colleagues and should give credit for work done by others in the course of a professional assignment, and should not knowingly accept credit due another.

AIPG disciplinary procedures: Complaints against members of the institute are very carefully considered by the Ethics Committee chairman, care of the executive director. In case of conflicts of interest, the facts of each interest should be well studied in order to determine the nature of the conflict to others.

14.4 Project/Site Safety Precautions

A site safety plan must be prepared (or reviewed) by a qualified safety person for each project. As soon as possible when project work commences, safety requirements must be written, posted, distributed to all assigned project personnel, and discussed with them. Emergency situations may require verbal safety instructions and use of standard operating procedures until specific safety protocols can be written. For any project, the plan must include health and safety considerations for all activities required at the site. The safety plan must be periodically reviewed to keep it current and technically correct.

Project offices, laboratory and field conditions vary greatly from area to area and from project to project. The responsible supervisor, therefore, must recognize that it is necessary to properly orient a newly assigned professional to a task.

The type of natural and physical conditions and requirements to be expected from working in the Nubian Desert, part of the Sahara in Egypt, is considerably different than conditions encountered in the semi-humid gulf coast in the United States, even though the geology of the two areas is similar. In the Nubian Desert area there are few aerial photographs, fewer maps, no communication facilities, few roads, many natural hazards, including shifting sand dunes and no water, gasoline stations, grocery stores, restaurants, or hotels. In contrast to the gulf coastal plains, all of the above are readily available.

A supervising professional, therefore, has a great responsibility to provide the project and site conditions which will allow the most effective assignment of professional manpower.

At a minimum, the site safety plan must

- evaluate the risks associated with the site and with each operation to be conducted;
- identify key personnel and alternates responsible for both site safety and response operations;
- address levels of protection to be worn by personnel during various site operations;
- designate work area (exclusion zone, contamination reduction zone, and support zone), boundaries, size of zones, distance between zones, and access control points into each zone;
- determine the number of personnel and equipment needed in the work zones during the initial entries and/or subsequent operations;
- establish site emergency procedures. For example, escape routes, signals for evacuating work parties, emergency communications (internal and external), procedures for fire and/or explosion, etc.;

- determine location and make arrangements with the nearest medical facility and medical life squad unit for emergency medical care for routine injuries and toxicological problems;
- implement a program for periodic air, personnel monitoring, and environmental sampling;
- train personnel for any non-routine site activities.
- implement control procedures to prevent access to the site by unauthorized personnel.

Two forms are given in Appendix 14.A to show the required information for safety in a site.

14.5 Search for References

Government, municipal, and university libraries are the main and most important sources for obtaining geological and hydrological references for field geologists and hydrogeologists before starting a project and while in the process of preparing a final technical report. Libraries normally maintain selected microfiche references, including agencies dealing with aerial photography, climatological data, the Federal Register and Index, Code of Federal Regulations, list of Sections Affected, and U.S. Environmental Protection Agency Symposia (Moore 1991; U.S. Geological Survey 1991; 1959–60).

In the United States, the Dewey Decimal Classification (DDC) is the system followed by a majority of libraries, including nearly all public libraries and school libraries. The DDC is a hierarchical system issuing the decimal principal for the subdivision of knowledge, as represented in publications. Each group is the successive division of knowledge and is divided to the base of ten.

The GEOREF is the database of the American Geological Institute (AGI) and it covers worldwide technical literature on geology and geophysics. GEOREF corresponds to the printed publications: Bibliography and Index of North American Geology, Bibliography of Theses in Geology, Geophysical Abstracts, Bibliography and Index of Geology Exclusive of North America, and the Bibliography and Index of Geology. GEOREF organizes and indexes papers from over 4500 serials and other publications representative of the interests of the eighteen professional geological and earth science societies that are members of AGI.

Libraries that are available for field hydrogeologists are usually at USGS, universities and State Geological Survey libraries as well. Library computer retrieval systems may also be available in some larger consulting companies and may consist of several internal and external networks, which may help as an access to University Library Computer Catalogue System, Western Union Multidisciplinary Databases and Telecommunications (telex and cablegram), and the U.S. Geological Survey EROS Satellite Imagery Data Center. Librarians may be very helpful for those who want to use variable references.

The National Water Data Exchange (NAWDEX) Assistance Center is another system data base which has two sources of retrieval systems at the USGS, namely the Water Data Sources Directory (WDSD) and the Master Water Data Index (MWDI); both can be used by applying certain data retrieval commands.

A summary of main potential sources can be summarized as follows (Moore 2002):

- *Climatic data* – National Climatic Data Center in Battery Park, Aschville (NC) collects and catalogs nearly all U.S. weather records.
- *Topographic data sources* – USGS Branch of Distribution and Earth Science Distribution Center (800-USA-Maps) have map data in both graphical and digital form.
- *Aerial photographs* – Earth Resources Observation System (EROS) data center USGS Sioux Falls (SD) (605-594-6151), aerial photography obtained by the USGS and other Federal agencies and Landsat satellite imagery.
- *Geophysical maps* – USGS Denver (CO) has aeromagnetic maps, magnetic delineation, landslide information, and earthquake data.
- *Hydrologic information reports* – Water Data Information CoordinationProgram (703-648-6810) of the USGS in Reston (VA) has publications on recommended methods for water data acquisition and guidelines for determining flood frequency.
- *Computerized on-line database* – DIALOG (800-dialog) provides access to over 420 databases from many disciplines, including GEOREF, book reviews, biographies, and access to newspapers, journals and other sources; Earth Science Data Directory (ESDD) at USGS (703-648-7112) contains geologic, hydrologic, cartographic and biologic information.
- *Hydrologic Web Sites* – World Wide Web (www) became an important source for information as it provides various professional opinions and documents on geology and hydrogeology.
- *Government and university libraries* – USGS libraries in Reston (VA), Menio Park (CA), and Denver (CO), USGS web site (www.usgs.gov), EPA libraries in Washington, (DC) and regional and research offices in Cincinnati (OH), Athens (GA), Las Vegas (NV), and Ada (OK).

The following is a list of some hydrogeologic information sites:

- Aerial photographs and maps: www.aerotoplia.org
- American Geological Institute: www.agi.org

- American Geophysical Union: www.agu.org
- American Institute of Hydrology: www.aih.org
- American Society for Testing and Materials: www.astm.org
- American Water Resources Association: www.usaec.army.mil
- Environmental Protection Agency: www.epa.gov
- Geoscience Information Society: www.geoinfo.org
- Ground-water Information: www.groundwater.com
- International Association of Hydrogeologists: www.iah.org

References

American Institute of Professional Geologists (AIPG) (2000) A publication of bylaws and code of ethics. The Professional Geologist 37(4):20–35

Green JH (1991) WRD project and report management guide. U.S. Geological Survey, Department of Interior, Reston, Virginia

Moore JE (1991) A guide for preparing hydrologic and geologic projects and reports. American Institute of Hydrology, Minneapolis, MN; Kendall/Hunt Publishing Company, Dubuque, Iowa (Cartoons reprinted by permission of Sidney Harris)

Moore JE (2002) Field hydrogeology – A guide for site investigations and report preparation. CRC Press LLCC, Lewis Publishers, New York, pp 43–44

U.S. Geological Survey (USGS) (1959–60) USGS documents. Department of Interior, Reston, Virginia (The Water Resources Division of the USGS, Project Execution and Report Preparation)

U.S. Geological Survey (USGS) (1991) USGS documents. Department of Interior, Reston, Virginia (USGS National Training Center)

Selected References

Moore JE, Chase EB (1982) Water resources division project and report management guide. U.S. Geological Survey Open-File Report 85-634

Moore JE, Aronson DA, Green JH, Puente C (1988) Report planning and review guide. U.S. Geological Survey Open-File Report 88-320

U.S. Geological Survey (1958) Suggestions to authors of the reports of the U.S. Geological Survey, 5th edn. U.S. Government Printing Office, Washington D.C.

U.S. Geological Survey (1978) Suggestions to authors of the reports of the U.S. Geological Survey, 6th edn. U.S. Government Printing Office, Washington D.C.

U.S. Geological Survey (1986) Water Resources Division publications guide, vol I: Policy and text preparation. U.S. Geological Survey Open-File Report 87-205

Waste Management of North America Inc. (1989) Site assessment manual. Oak Brook, Illinois, pp 1.1–1.5, 2.1–2.16

Appendix 14.A · Sample Forms (Required for a Project)

Fig. 14.A.1.
Active proposal file

Active Proposal File

1. Company Reference Number ____________
2. Title of Proposal ____________
3. PELA Agent ____________
4. Request for Proposal No. ____________
5. Date Received ____________
6. Date Due ____________
7. Company/Agency ____________
8. Street Address ____________
9. P.O. Box ____________
10. City ____________
11. State and Zip Code ____________
12. Area Code/Phone No. ____________
13. Name of Contact ____________
14. Title of Contact ____________
15. Referenced By ____________
16. OS/6 ID No. ____________
17. Comments ____________

Fig. 14.A.2.
Safety plan

Safety Plan

Date ________________ Project number ________________

Project manager ________________

Site description

Date ________________

Location ________________

____

Type: Spill ( ) Fire ( ) HW site ( ) Other ________________

Status ________________

Project objectives ________________

____

Site size ________________

Surrounding population ________________

Buildings/homes ________________

Topography ________________

Receiving water ________________

Weather ________________

Unusual features ________________

____

____

Site history ________________

____

____

____

____

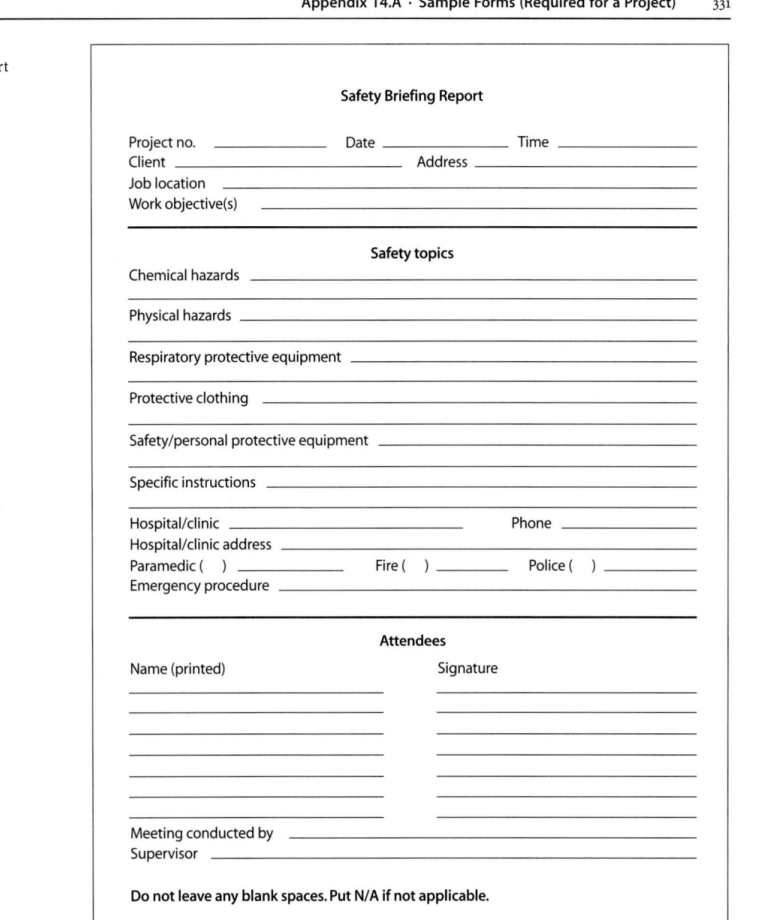

Fig. 14.A.3.
Safety briefing report

Safety Briefing Report

Project no. ______________ Date ______________ Time ______________
Client ____________________________ Address ____________________________
Job location ____
Work objective(s) ____

Safety topics

Chemical hazards ____
____
Physical hazards ____
____
Respiratory protective equipment ______________________________
____
Protective clothing ____
____
Safety/personal protective equipment ____________________________
____
Specific instructions ____
____
Hospital/clinic ____________________________ Phone ______________
Hospital/clinic address ____
Paramedic (   ) ______________ Fire (   ) ______________ Police (   ) ______________
Emergency procedure ____

Attendees

Name (printed)	Signature
______________________	______________________
______________________	______________________
______________________	______________________
______________________	______________________
______________________	______________________
______________________	______________________
______________________	______________________

Meeting conducted by ____
Supervisor ____

Do not leave any blank spaces. Put N/A if not applicable.

Attn:
Client:
Address:

Remit results to:

Project name	Project location	Page	Of
Project no.	Project contact	Project tel. no.	
Sampler(s) name(s)			

Sampling Date	Sampling Time	Sample identification	Sample type: Water	Sample type: Soil	Sample type: Other	Number of containers	Type of containers (P)lastic, (G)lass, (O)ther	Preservative (S)odium hydroxide, (I)CED, (N)itric, (H)ydrochloric, (O)ther	Required analysis						Field parameters: pH	Field parameters: SC (µmhos cm^{-1})	Field parameters: Temp. (°C)

Relinquished by:	Date:	Time:	Received by:	Relinquished by:	Date:	Time:	Received by:	Remarks:

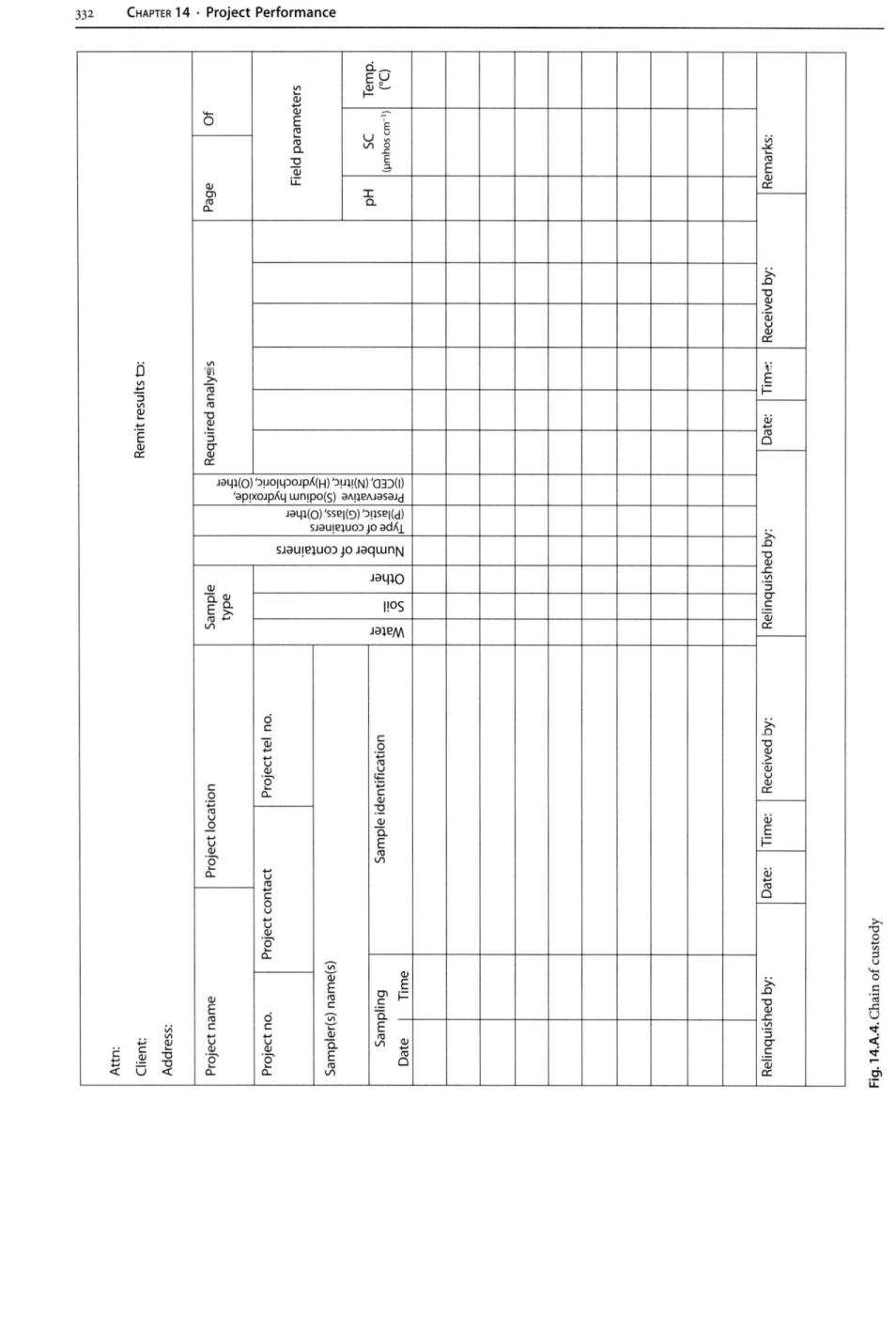

Fig. 14.A.4. Chain of custody

Fig. 14.A.5.
Request for leave

Request for Leave

Employee name: ______________________________

Type of leave requested:

Annual leave ______________________________

Sick leave ______________________________

Compensatory time ______________________________

Leave without pay ______________________________

Other (identify) ______________________________

Date(s) requested:

From ____________________ To ____________________

Comments:

____

____

____

Approval:

____________________	____________________
Supervisor	Verification of earned time available by personnel
____________________	____________________
Operations	Executive vice president (compensatory time only)

Appendix 14.B · Project Work Elements and Management Graphs

Appendix 14.B.1 Work Elements Graph

Figure 14.B.1 is a typical project diagram showing work elements to be accomplished as a part of the contract. It divides the project into specific work elements and illustrations by a series of boxes. It includes three major divisions of efforts: (1) data collection, (2) data analysis, (3) report preparation.

This graph illustrates a summary of graphic work efforts giving a prospective of work required, leading up to the completion of report(s) for the project.

Appendix 14.B.2 Time Accounting Graphs

Figure 14.B.2 shows scheduling of work and some examples of charts that will aid in development of project analysis and allow the professional geologists to more closely and effectively manage a project.

Types of information identified, includes hydrogeologic characterization, water quality, sources, contamination .and report preparation.

Dates are arbitrarily chosen that represent emphasis given to different elements of work.

Appendix 12.B.3 Cost Accounting Graphs

Figure 14.B.3 illustrates professional manpower assignment for 3 principal geologists (1, 2, 3) and their responsibilities for project work elements, estimate of time required and cost. The graphs provide a management test for project manager to maintain project on schedule within budget.

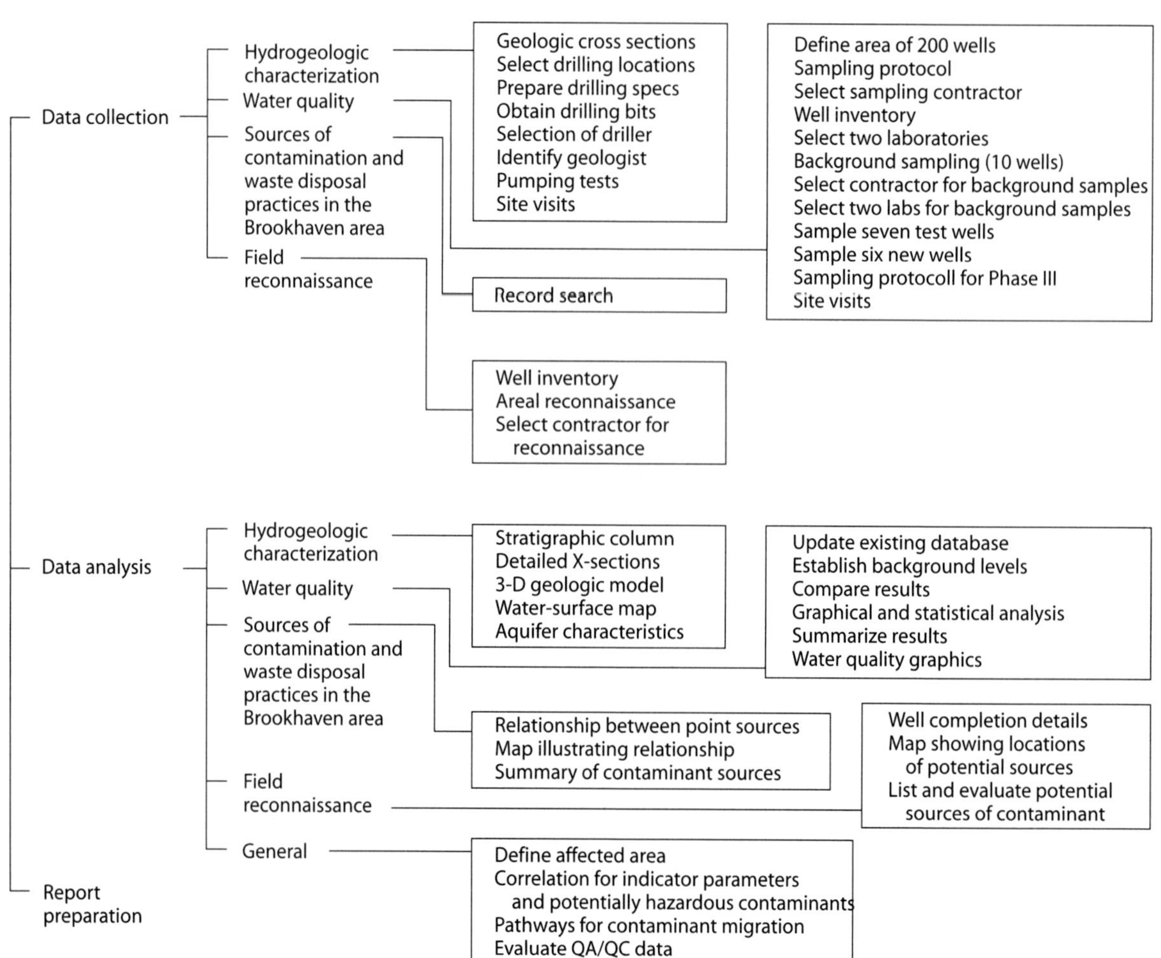
Data collection
Hydrogeologic characterization
Water quality
Sources of contamination and waste disposal practices in the Brookhaven area
Field reconnaissance
Geologic cross sections
Select drilling locations
Prepare drilling specs
Obtain drilling bits
Selection of driller
Identify geologist
Pumping tests
Site visits
Define area of 200 wells
Sampling protocol
Select sampling contractor
Well inventory
Select two laboratories
Background sampling (10 wells)
Select contractor for background samples
Select two labs for background samples
Sample seven test wells
Sample six new wells
Sampling protocoll for Phase III
Site visits
Record search
Well inventory
Areal reconnaissance
Select contractor for reconnaissance
Data analysis
Hydrogeologic characterization
Water quality
Sources of contamination and waste disposal practices in the Brookhaven area
Field reconnaissance
General
Stratigraphic column
Detailed X-sections
3-D geologic model
Water-surface map
Aquifer characteristics
Update existing database
Establish background levels
Compare results
Graphical and statistical analysis
Summarize results
Water quality graphics
Relationship between point sources
Map illustrating relationship
Summary of contaminant sources
Well completion details
Map showing locations of potential sources
List and evaluate potential sources of contaminant
Define affected area
Correlation for indicator parameters and potentially hazardous contaminants
Pathways for contaminant migration
Evaluate QA/QC data
Report preparation

Fig. 14.B.1. Project work elements

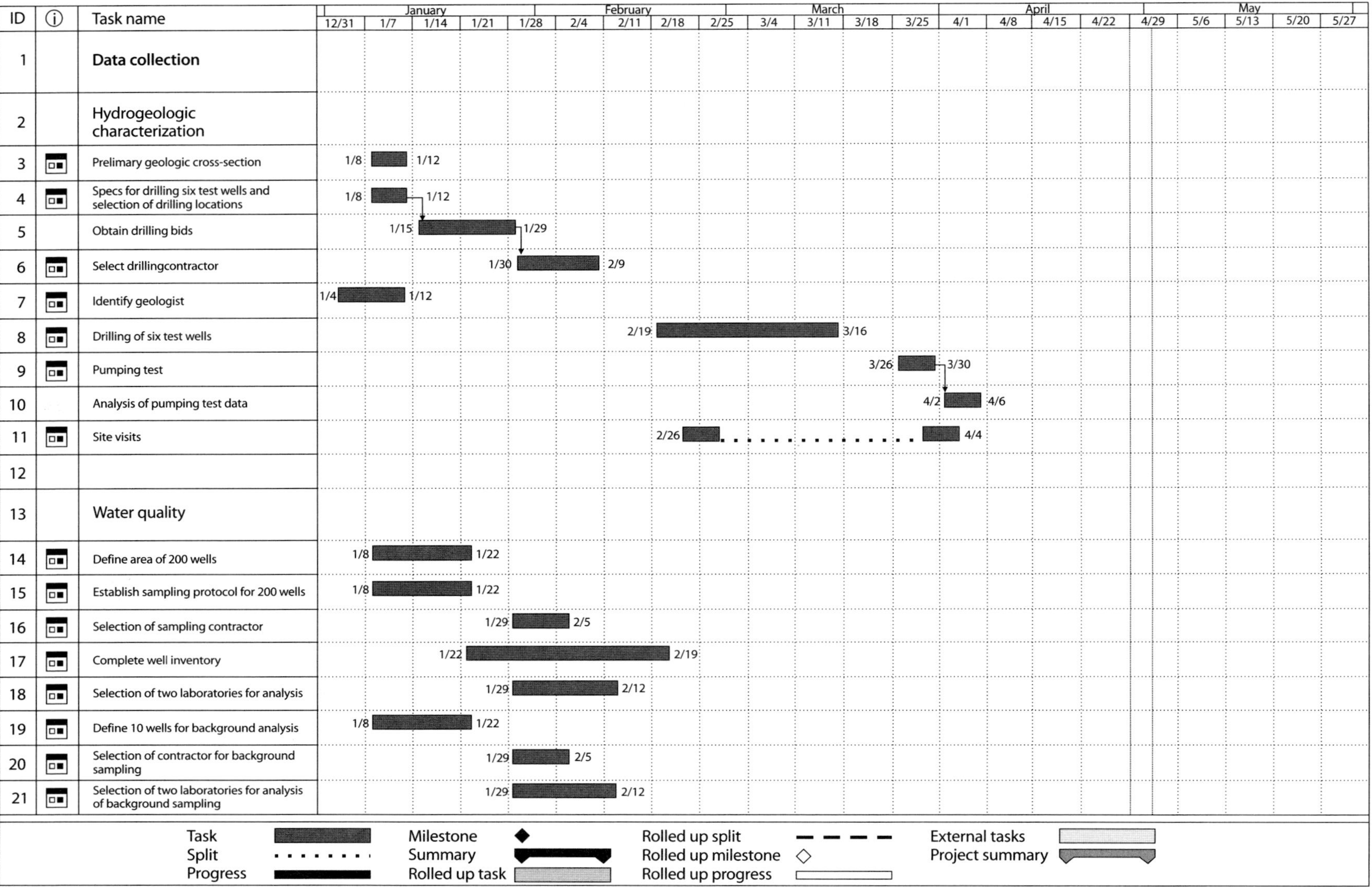

ID
Task name
January
February
March
April
May
12/31
1/7
1/14
1/21
1/28
2/4
2/11
2/18
2/25
3/4
3/11
3/18
3/25
4/1
4/8
4/15
4/22
4/29
5/6
5/13
5/20
5/27
1 Data collection
2 Hydrogeologic characterization
3 Prelimary geologic cross-section
4 Specs for drilling six test wells and selection of drilling locations
5 Obtain drilling bids
6 Select drillingcontractor
7 Identify geologist
8 Drilling of six test wells
9 Pumping test
10 Analysis of pumping test data
11 Site visits
12
13 Water quality
14 Define area of 200 wells
15 Establish sampling protocol for 200 wells
16 Selection of sampling contractor
17 Complete well inventory
18 Selection of two laboratories for analysis
19 Define 10 wells for background analysis
20 Selection of contractor for background sampling
21 Selection of two laboratories for analysis of background sampling
1/8
1/12
1/8
1/12
1/15
1/29
1/30
2/9
1/4
1/12
2/19
3/16
3/26
3/30
4/2
4/6
2/26
4/4
1/8
1/22
1/8
1/22
1/29
2/5
1/22
2/19
1/29
2/12
1/8
1/22
1/29
2/5
1/29
2/12
Task
Split
Progress
Milestone
Summary
Rolled up task
Rolled up split
Rolled up milestone
Rolled up progress
External tasks
Project summary

Fig. 14.B.2. Time accounting project management (for year 2000)

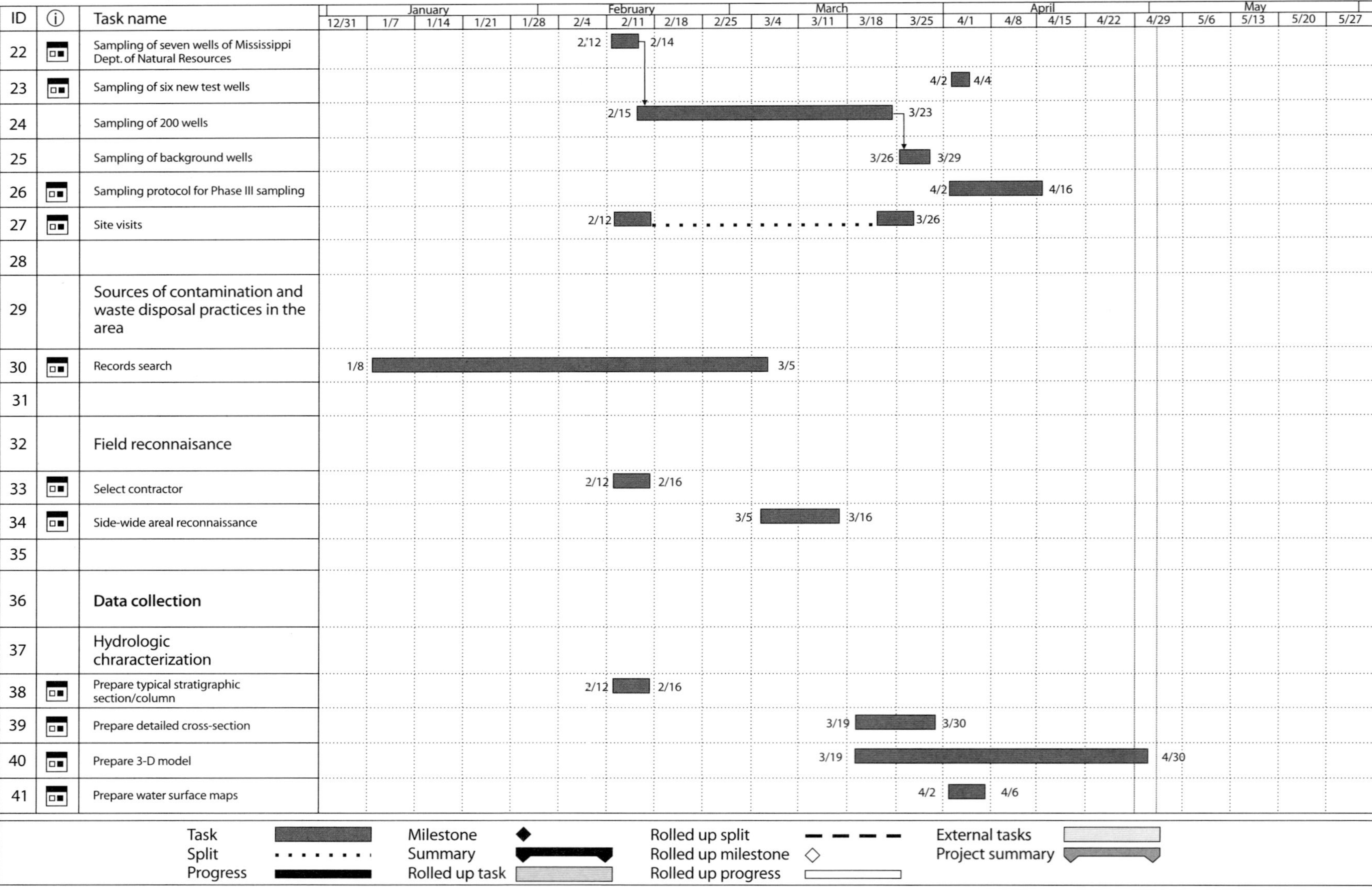

ID
Task name
January
February
March
April
May
12/31
1/7
1/14
1/21
1/28
2/4
2/11
2/18
2/25
3/4
3/11
3/18
3/25
4/1
4/8
4/15
4/22
4/29
5/6
5/13
5/20
5/27
22 Sampling of seven wells of Mississippi Dept. of Natural Resources 2/12 2/14
23 Sampling of six new test wells 4/2 4/4
24 Sampling of 200 wells 2/15 3/23
25 Sampling of background wells 3/26 3/29
26 Sampling protocol for Phase III sampling 4/2 4/16
27 Site visits 2/12 3/26
28
29 Sources of contamination and waste disposal practices in the area
30 Records search 1/8 3/5
31
32 Field reconnaisance
33 Select contractor 2/12 2/16
34 Side-wide areal reconnaissance 3/5 3/16
35
36 Data collection
37 Hydrologic chraracterization
38 Prepare typical stratigraphic section/column 2/12 2/16
39 Prepare detailed cross-section 3/19 3/30
40 Prepare 3-D model 3/19 4/30
41 Prepare water surface maps 4/2 4/6
Task
Split
Progress
Milestone
Summary
Rolled up task
Rolled up split
Rolled up milestone
Rolled up progress
External tasks
Project summary

Fig. 14.B.2. *Continued*

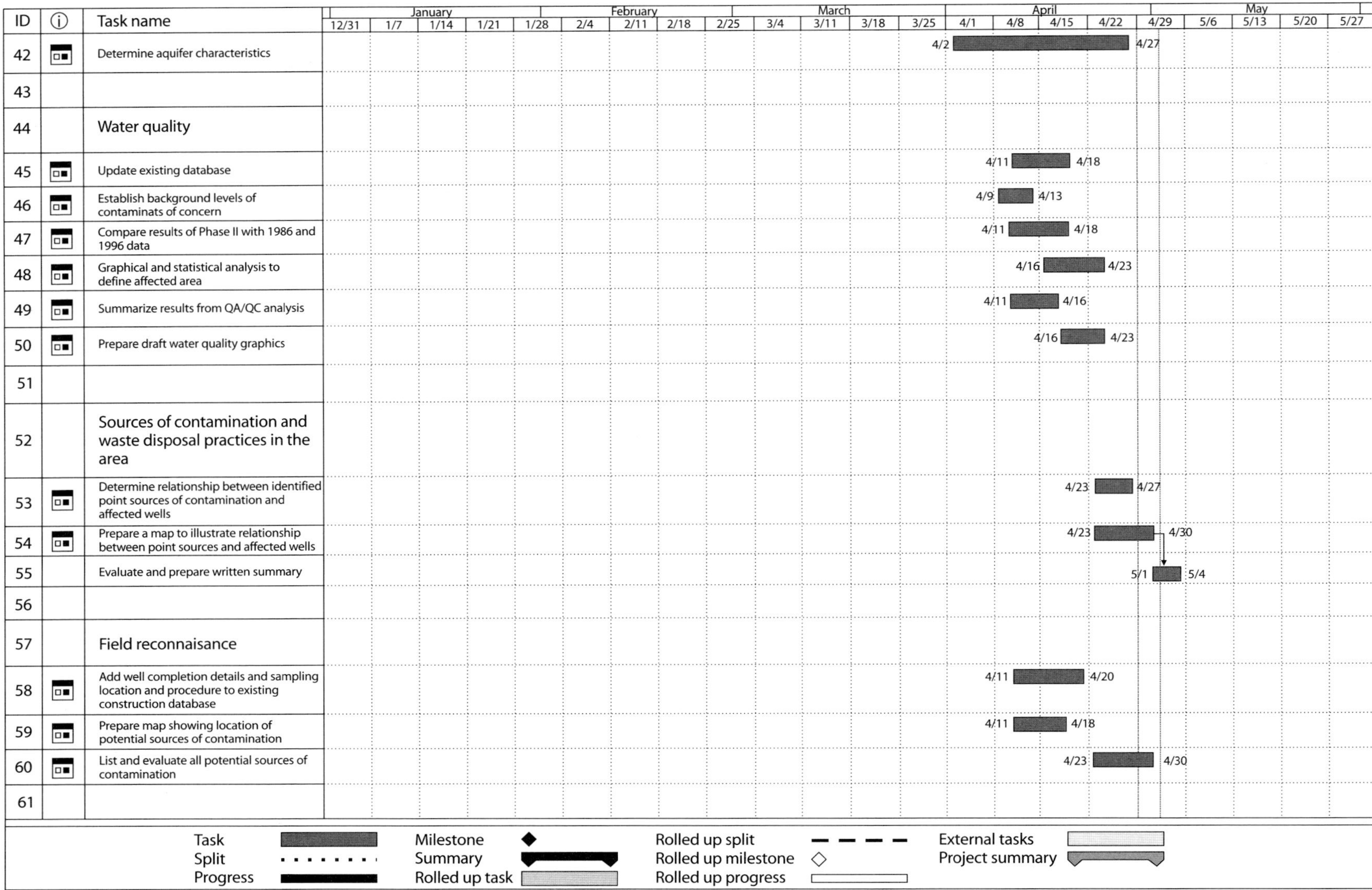
ID
Task name
January
February
March
April
May
12/31
1/7
1/14
1/21
1/28
2/4
2/11
2/18
2/25
3/4
3/11
3/18
3/25
4/1
4/8
4/15
4/22
4/29
5/6
5/13
5/20
5/27
42 Determine aquifer characteristics 4/2 4/27
43
44 Water quality
45 Update existing database 4/11 4/18
46 Establish background levels of contaminats of concern 4/9 4/13
47 Compare results of Phase II with 1986 and 1996 data 4/11 4/18
48 Graphical and statistical analysis to define affected area 4/16 4/23
49 Summarize results from QA/QC analysis 4/11 4/16
50 Prepare draft water quality graphics 4/16 4/23
51
52 Sources of contamination and waste disposal practices in the area
53 Determine relationship between identified point sources of contamination and affected wells 4/23 4/27
54 Prepare a map to illustrate relationship between point sources and affected wells 4/23 4/30
55 Evaluate and prepare written summary 5/1 5/4
56
57 Field reconnaisance
58 Add well completion details and sampling location and procedure to existing construction database 4/11 4/20
59 Prepare map showing location of potential sources of contamination 4/11 4/18
60 List and evaluate all potential sources of contamination 4/23 4/30
61
Task
Split
Progress
Milestone
Summary
Rolled up task
Rolled up split
Rolled up milestone
Rolled up progress
External tasks
Project summary

Fig. 14.B.2. *Continued*

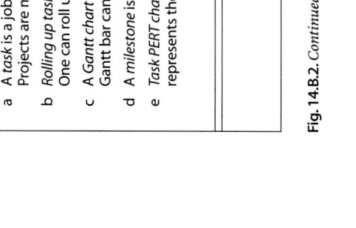

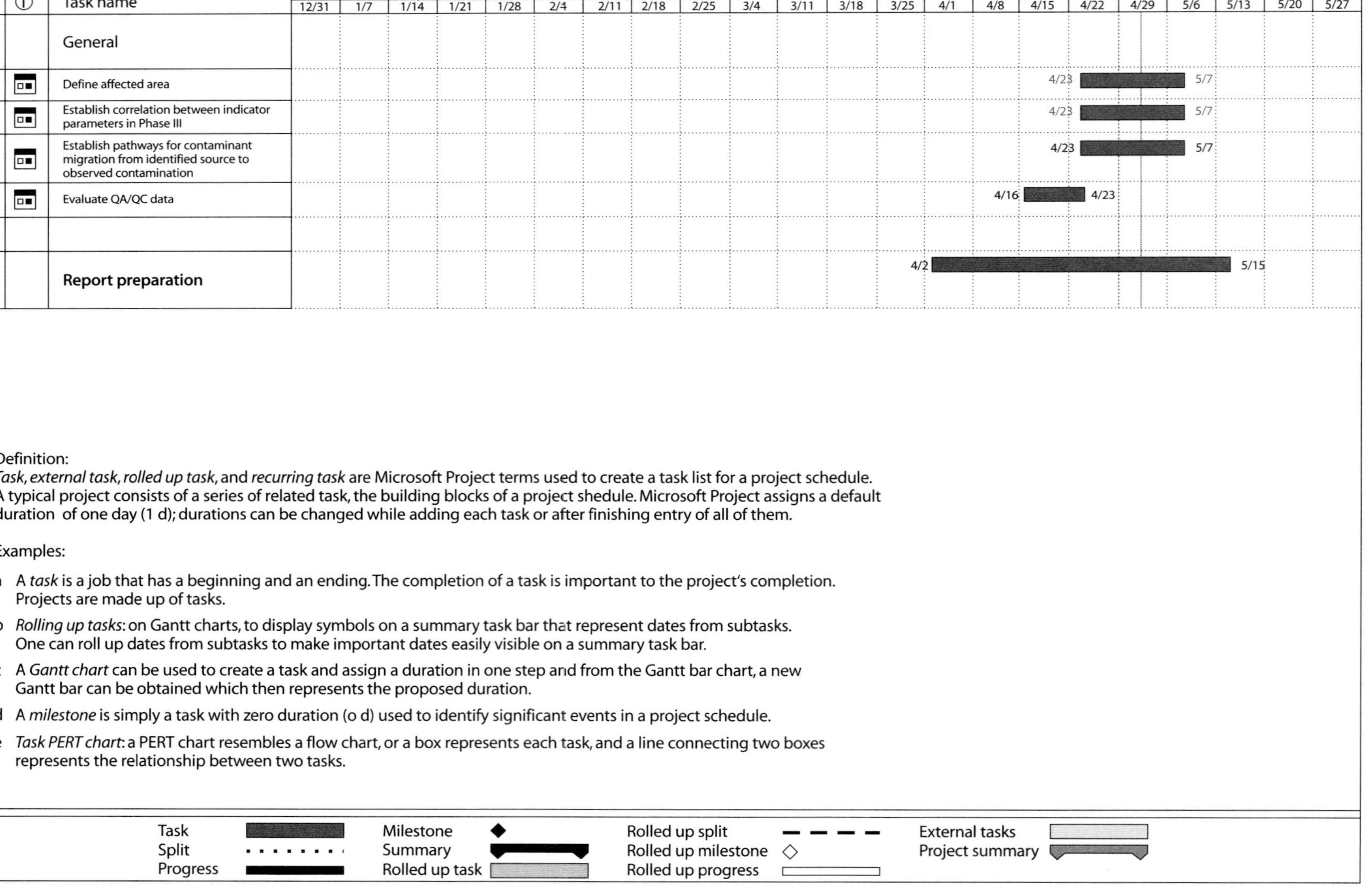
ID
Task name
62 General
63 Define affected area
4/23
5/7
64 Establish correlation between indicator parameters in Phase III
4/23
5/7
65 Establish pathways for contaminant migration from identified source to observed contamination
4/23
5/7
66 Evaluate QA/QC data
4/16
4/23
67
68 Report preparation
4/2
5/15
Definition:
Task, *external task*, *rolled up task*, and *recurring task* are Microsoft Project terms used to create a task list for a project schedule. A typical project consists of a series of related task, the building blocks of a project shedule. Microsoft Project assigns a default duration of one day (1 d); durations can be changed while adding each task or after finishing entry of all of them.
Examples:
a A *task* is a job that has a beginning and an ending. The completion of a task is important to the project's completion. Projects are made up of tasks.
b *Rolling up tasks*: on Gantt charts, to display symbols on a summary task bar that represent dates from subtasks. One can roll up dates from subtasks to make important dates easily visible on a summary task bar.
c A *Gantt chart* can be used to create a task and assign a duration in one step and from the Gantt bar chart, a new Gantt bar can be obtained which then represents the proposed duration.
d A *milestone* is simply a task with zero duration (o d) used to identify significant events in a project schedule.
e *Task PERT chart*: a PERT chart resembles a flow chart, or a box represents each task, and a line connecting two boxes represents the relationship between two tasks.
Task
Split
Progress
Milestone
Summary
Rolled up task
Rolled up split
Rolled up milestone
Rolled up progress
External tasks
Project summary

Fig. 14.B.2. *Continued*

Phase II			Geologist (1)		Geologist (2)		Geologist (3)		Total	Subcon.	Subcon.	Total
			Hours	U.S.$	Hours	U.S.$	Hours	U.S.$		#1	#2	
Data Collection	Hydrogeologic								20000			20000
		Geologic Cross-Sections	0	0	0	0	12	1620		0		1620
		Specs for Test Drilling	0	0	0	0	2	270		0		270
		Bids	0	0	0	0	1	135		0		135
		Select Drilling Contractor/Drill Holes	0	0	0	0	2	270		56000	185000	241270
		Experienced Professional Geologist	0	0	0	0	1	135			15000	15135
		Aquifer Characteristics	0	0	0	0	20	2700		41000		43700
		Site Visits	14	1890	0	0	20	2700		0		4590
	Water Quality								9000			9000
		Sampling Protocol	0	0	36	4860	0	0		0		4860
		Complete Well Inventory	0	0	32	4320	1	135		37000		41455
		Select Contractor	0	0	8	1080	2	270		0		1350
		Select Two Laboratories	0	0	8	1080	2	270		0		1350
		Sample the Seven Test Wells	0	0	0	0	0	0		2000	3500	5500
		Sample the Six New Wells	0	0	0	0	0	0		2000	3000	5000
		List Wells to be Sampled	0	0	0	0	4	540		0		540
		Establish Background Levels	0	0	4	540	4	540		5250	5000	11330
		Sample Wells(reduced parameters)	0	0	0	0	0	0		36300	14000	50300
		Visit the Site	0	0	24	3240	24	3240		0		6480
	Field Recon.								1000			1000
		Site-Wide Areal Reconnaissance	8	1080	0	0	3	405		11000		12485
		Select Contractor	0	0	0	0	2	270		0		270
Data Analysis	Hydrogeologic								21000			21000
		Stratigraphic Section	0	0	0	0	2	270		23200		23470
		Cross-Sections	0	0	0	0	2	270		0		270
		3-D Geologic Model	0	0	0	0	4	540		0		540
		Prepare a Water-Surface Map	0	0	0	0	2	270		0		270
		Aquifer Characteristics	0	0	0	0	8	1080		0		1080
	Water Quality								10000			10000
		Update Existing Database	0	0	6	810	0	0		15500		16310
		Establish Background Levels	0	0	6	810	0	0		0		810
		Compare Results Phase II	6	810	6	810	1	135		0		1755
		Graphical/Stat Analysis	0	0	6	810	0	0		0		810
		Summarize QA/QC	0	0	6	810	1	135		0		945
		Draft WQ Graphics	0	0	6	810	1	135		0		945
	Sources of Contamination								2000			2000
		Identified Point Sources	60	8100	4	540	4	540		3200		12380
		Prepare a Map	10	1350	0	0	0	0		0		1350
		Written Summary	10	1350	0	0	0	0		0		1350
	Field Recon.								10000			10000
		Construction Database	0	0	0	0	0	0		10000		10000
		Map	0	0	0	0	2	270		0		270
		Evaluate Potential Sources	0	0	24	3240	1	135		0		3375
	General		61	8235	0	0	60	8100		5000		21335
TOTALS			169	22815	176	23760	188	25380	73000	247450	225500	617905
												0
Report Prep.	I. Executive Summary		12	1620	24	3240	12	1620	14000	48000		68480
	II. Brookhave Groundwater Panel											
	III. Purpose											
	IV. Scope											
	V. Introduction											
	VI. Previous Work and Data Relied Upon											
	VII. Hydrogeologic Characterization											
	VIII. Background Water Quality Parameters											
	IX. Results of Groundwater Sampling Program											
	X. Non-Oilfield Related Sources											
	XI. Definition of Affected Area											
	XII. Conclusions											
	XIII. Recommendations											
	XIV. Bibliography											
	XV. Graphics											
	Expenses of experts			1000		1700		2000				5700
			181	24435	200	27000	200	27000				
Total Cost				25435		28700		29000	87000	295450	225500	691085

Assumptions:

Select Drilling Contractor/Drill: Based on 6 holes of 400 feet
Aquifer Tests: Based on one 72-hour pumping test, with 48-hour recovery.

Note:
Final graphics costs not included in the report total.
All costs for Panel members work have been estimated based on their input but are still subject to revision.
All costs for subcontractors have been estimated based on current knowledge and general industry costs, however, these costs may be revised.
Driller's costs are based on one 6-inch well with continuous sampling and lithologic description, and five 4-inch wells with sampling at 5 foot intervals.
Subcontracor # 1 = Performing drilling supervision, collection of samples, pumping test, well inventory and areal reconnaissance.
Subcontracor # 2 = Drilling subcontractor, geologist, and laboratory analysis.
Costs associated with report preparation will depend on the volume of data generated in the collection phase and Panelists work during the analysis phase.
Panel meetings will be billed seperately.

Fig. 14.B.3. An example for distribution of work among geologists

Appendix 14.C · Professional Services Agreement

Professional Services Agreement

between

Pipeline LLC. and Sand Pipeline LLC.

and

Consulting Company

PSA US617-XX

Table of Contents

Professional Services Agreement

This Agreement, made and entered into by and between Pipeline LLC, with general offices at 6333 Clay Street, Dallas Texas 79002 and Sand Pipeline LLC., c/o Sand Corp., 1400 Sneed Street, Dallas, Texas 79002 (each hereinafter referred to as "Company" and collectively referred to as "Companies") and Consulting Company, with general offices at 2610 Byway Rd., Huntsville, AL 35987, (hereinafter referred to as "Contractor");

Witnesseth

Whereas, Companies, and each of them, have need for certain services, hereinafter described, to be performed by an independent contractor;

Whereas, Contractor understands the types of services required by Companies and represents that it has the necessary personnel, experience, competence, and legal right to perform the services; and

Whereas, Companies desire to engage Contractor to perform the services and Contractor desires to undertake such performance under the terms, conditions, and provisions hereinafter set forth;

Now, Therfore, in consideration of the respective undertakings of the parties, and the monies to be paid hereunder, the parties have agreed and do hereby agree as follows:

1 Definitions

"Agreement" shall mean this Professional Services Agreement, including Exhibits A through D, inclusive, and such other documents as are referenced herein, as amended by any modification agreed in accordance with Section 25. For purposes of interpretation, all the parts of the Agreement shall be deemed mutually explanatory of each other, provided that the Specification shall take precedence over the Scope of Work, modifications shall prevail over the original Agreement and any modification of later date shall prevail over any modification of earlier date.

"Effective Date" shall mean that date set forth in Section 2.

"Scope of Services" or "Services" shall mean all services as set forth in Exhibit A required to be performed by Contractor under this Agreement.

"Term" shall have the meaning and be for the time set forth in Section

2 Effective Date, Notice to Proceed, and Schedule

2.1 Effective Date

The Effective Date of this Agreement shall be XXXXXXXX.

2.2 Notice to Proceed

Notwithstanding the Effective Date of this Agreement, neither Company shall have any liability whatsoever to Contractor under this Agreement or in any way related to the Services prior to issue of a written Notice to Proceed (hereinafter "NTP") to the Contractor and subject to any limitations set forth in such NTP.

2.3 Schedule

Contractor shall complete the Services in accordance with the schedule set forth in Exhibit E hereto. Time is of the essence.

3 Services

Contractor shall provide all supplies, materials, tools, equipment, labor, supervision and transportation necessary to perform the Services.

4 Price

4.1 Price

Contractor shall be paid a Price as set forth in Exhibit B in accordance with the Payment Schedule as set forth in Exhibit B. Companies shall collectively compensate Contractor in U.S. dollars, unless otherwise specifically agreed in writing by both parties.

a Companies shall collectively pay the Firm Fixed Price under this Agreement which constitutes full payment to Contractor for: (*i*) Contractor's employees' time, whether the employee works overtime or regular time or is an exempt or non-exempt employee; (*ii*) Contractor's allowance for payroll burden (i.e. payroll taxes, insurance, vacations, sick leave, holidays, excused absences, fringe benefits, etc.), (*iii*) Contractor's materials and equipment (including operating costs), and (*iv*) all overhead expenses, general and administrative expense (i.e. corporate officers, sales, public relations, personnel, law, medical, finance and accounting when not directly engaged in the Scope of Services, receptionists, janitorial, advertising personnel, rent, utilities, depreciation and maintenance of staff to provide readiness to serve), routine copies of correspondence, specifications and plans, telephone calls and postage, taxes (including real estate, income, sales, use, franchise and other taxes on Contractor or Contractor's affiliates, subsidiaries or subcontractors), insurance, profits, indemnification consideration under Section 13.1, and all costs and expenses of whatever kind except as otherwise specifically set forth in this Agreement; and

b The Price shall also include payments to all subcontractors of Contractor for the Services, and such payments shall not be a reimbursable expense.

4.2 Full Compensation

Payment by Companies for the Scope of Services set forth in this Agreement constitutes full payment to Contractor for its entire performance of the Scope of Services.

4.3 Limitation of Liability

In no event shall either Company *or Contractor* be liable *to each other* as a result of any action or inaction under this Agreement, including, without limitation, negligence, strict liability, breach of contract or warranty for any consequential, special, incidental, indirect, or punitive damages or losses of any nature whatsoever, including but not limited to loss of profits, interest, revenue, or goodwill.

5 Invoicing and Payment

5.1 Invoice Submittal

Contractor will submit its invoices for the portion of the Services performed in accordance with the Payment Schedule set forth in Exhibit B in an original and two (2) copies to:

Pipeline LLC
Sand Pipeline LLC.
xxxx Street
Dallas, Texas xxxxx
Attn: XXXX YYYY

5.2 Payment of Invoiced Amounts

Companies shall collectively, (*i*) upon acceptance of the Services, and (*ii*) receipt of an invoice, pay Contractor within twenty (20) days the approved amount (calculated as the invoiced amount, less any disputed amounts);. Companies shall collectively pay a one per cent (1%) per month carrying fee on approved amounts not remitted within thirty twenty (230) days of receipt by Companies of a complying invoice, but the approved amounts shall not be subject to such carrying fee until after such twenty (20) days. *Any portion of the* disputed amounts not paid within thirty *twenty* (230) days after *receipt by Companies, but found to be due and payable after* resolution of the dispute shall not be subject to the one percent (1%) monthly carrying fee *from the original due date of twenty (20) days after receipt by Companies* until thirty (30) days after resolution of such dispute, and then only for each month after thirty (30) days after resolution of such dispute that the disputed amount remains unpaid.

(Note: PELA wants to delete the retainage in its entirety as our subcontractors all insisting on full payment on successful completion of field work, not at end of project, as they are not involved in report preparation, etc.)

5.3 Withholding

5.3.1 Non U.S. Taxes

Companies shall not, without Contractor's consent, withhold from any invoiced amount any amount for taxes payable to any non-U.S. taxing authority.

5.3.2 Notices of Nonpayment

a If Companies receive written notice from any subcontractor, vendor or supplier of Contractor that Contractor has failed to pay such subcontractor, vendor or supplier for labor, materials, services and/or equipment related to the Services, Companies may, upon thirty (30) days notice to Contractor, withhold payment from Contractor in the amount claimed by the subcontractor, vendor or supplier as due and owing, unless Contractor notifies Companies in writing within such thirty (30) days that Contractor disputes the subcontractor's, vendor's or supplier's claim. Companies may continue to withhold such amount until Companies receive written notice from the subcontractor, vendor or supplier that such amount has been paid in full by Contractor.

b If any lien, claim, security interest or other encumbrance in favor of any subcontractor, vendor or supplier of Contractor is filed against Companies or Companies' property, or Companies' client or the client's property, and if Contractor has not caused the lien to be released and discharged, or has not filed a bond in lieu thereof which is satisfactory in all respects to Companies within five (5) days after the lien, claim, security interest or other encumbrance is filed, Companies may withhold payment from Contractor in the amount of the lien, claim, security interest or other encumbrance (and all costs, interest and other amounts which have accrued or may accrue in connection therewith) until such time as Contractor removes and secures the release of such lien, claim, security interest or other encumbrance in accordance with Section 7.7. If any such liens, claims, security interests or other encumbrances remain filed or otherwise imposed against Companies or Companies' property, or Companies' client or the client's property, at the time of completion of the applicable Scope of Services, Companies shall have the right, but not the obligation, to pay all sums necessary to obtain a release or discharge of the liens, claims, security interests or other encumbrances and deduct all such amounts from any amounts due Contractor from Companies. Contractor shall pay Companies in accordance with Section 7.7 for any amounts not deducted from amounts due Contractor.

5.3.3 Lien Release

Contractor and Contractor shall *submit to Companies within ten (10) days* to final payment for the Services as *follows*:

i an affidavit that all payrolls, bills for materials, labor and equipment, and other indebtedness connected with the Services for which Companies or Companies' property, or Companies' client or the client's property, might be responsible or encumbered have been paid or otherwise satisfied; and

ii a release and waiver of liens, claims, security interests and encumbrances arising out of the Scope of Services in the form set forth in Exhibit D for Contractor and each of its subcontractors, suppliers, and vendors whose subcontract or purchase order value exceeds U.S.$25 000.

6 Relationship of Parties

6.1 Independent Contractor

Contractor undertakes performance of the Services as an independent contractor on behalf of both Companies. Nothing herein shall create a relationship of employer and employee, joint venture, or partnership between Companies and Contractor, its agents, representatives, employees or subcontractors, for any purpose whatsoever. Neither party shall have the authority to bind or obligate the other in any manner as a result of the relationship created hereby.

6.1.1 Control and Supervision

Neither Company shall have the right to control the manner(s) or prescribe the method(s) by which Contractor performs the Services. Contractor shall be wholly responsible for supervision and the methods of performance. Contractor is entirely and solely responsible for its acts and the acts of its agents, employees, representatives and subcontractors engaged in the performance of the Services. In accordance with Section 8.7, Contractor shall provide Companies access to the Services at all times wherever in preparation or progress and shall work closely with Companies in performing Services under this Agreement, and Companies shall have the right to observe, inspect and review performance of the Services, but any observance, inspection or review of performance of Services shall not constitute or be deemed to be actual control or a right to control Contractor, its employees, agents, personnel or subcontractors.

6.1.2 Employees of Contractor

Contractor shall provide qualified personnel who shall be and remain solely the employees of Contractor, and at no time or in any manner shall said personnel be considered as or deemed to be employees of Companies, or either of them. Companies' general coordinative efforts, suggestions and procedures with respect to the Services and Companies' right of inspection, review and observation of the Services shall not make Contractor or its employees, employees of Companies, or either of them.

6.2 Agency Relationships

Contractor, its agents, employees, representatives and subcontractors shall be independent contractors and shall not be agents or representatives of Companies, or either of them.

7 Representations and Warranties

7.1 Authority and Ability to Conduct Business

Contractor represents and warrants that it has authority, licenses and qualifications to conduct business in each location where the Services are to be performed. Each party hereto represents and warrants that the person executing this Agreement on its behalf is duly authorized and empowered to do so and that all formalities necessary for its approval of this Agreement have been satisfied.

7.2 Standard of Care

Contractor represents and warrants that it will perform in a good and workmanlike manner and exercise the degree of care, skill, and diligence in the performance of the Services, in accordance and consistent with industry standards for similar circumstances and that the Services shall meet the stated requirements, standards, specifications, and procedures of this Agreement.

7.3 Administration and Staffing

Contractor represents and warrants that it will use utmost skill, efforts and judgment to further the interests of Companies, and both of them, to furnish efficient business administration and supervision, and to furnish at all times an adequate supply of workers and materials.

7.4 Authority and Infringement

Contractor represents and warrants that it has the right and authority to enter into this Agreement, to provide the Services required of it hereunder, to convey and grant all the rights of ownership as set forth in Sections 11 and 12, and that it is capable and qualified to provide the Services required of it hereunder. Without limiting the foregoing, Contractor represents and warrants that the Services and information provided to Companies by Contractor hereunder will not infringe on any third party's patent, copyright, trademark, trade secret or other intellectual property rights. Contractor shall bear and agrees to pay all costs, damages, losses and expenses (including, without limitation, attorney's fees and court costs) of every kind which Companies may incur, be required to pay or be liable for as a result of, in connection with, arising out of or related to any such infringement, and to remedy such infringement by appropriate means, including, but not limited to: (*i*) obtaining for Companies the right to continued use, reproduction, distribution, performance and display of the copyrighted, patented, trademark or otherwise infringed item; (*ii*) correction of the infringing Services and/or information such that the infringement is removed; or (*iii*) replacement of the infringing Services and/or information with equivalent non-infringing Services and/or information.

7.5 Companies Supplied Information

a Each company individually and collectively disclaims all warranties, whether express or implied, of any kind concerning information provided to Contractor by or on behalf of Companies, or either of them pursuant to or in furtherance of the services provided pursuant to this Agreement, including, but not limited to, any warranty that the information is accurate, correct, complete, fit for any particular use or can be used without infringing any patent, copyright, trademark, or other intellectual property rights of third parties under the intellectual property rights of the world.

b Notwithstanding anything in this Agreement to the contrary, Companies acknowledge that the amounts of money stated in Exhibit B were based on information provided to Contractor by or on behalf of Companies, and, to the extent that the information about field conditions varies from the information provided, Contractor may bring the variances to the attention of Companies, and may request for the services and the amounts of money stated in Exhibit B to be changed.

7.6 Accuracy

Contractor represents and warrants that all Services and information presented to each Company for acceptance are complete, accurate, authentic, and fit for the particular purpose(s) for which Companies, or either of them, utilizes it. Contractor waives any claim or defense that Companies, or either of them, has any responsibility or liability for Services performed or should have been performed by Contractor under this Agreement.

7.7 Invoices

Contractor represents and warrants that all amounts reflected on invoices submitted by Contractor for payment are accurate, just, due and owing under the terms of this Agreement, and that all Services for which Contractor seeks payment are free and clear of liens, claims, security interests and encumbrances arising in favor of Contractor and its subcontractors, vendors, suppliers and other persons or entities able to make a claim by reason of having provided labor, materials or equipment relating to the Services or any portion thereof. Contractor agrees and represents that in submitting an invoice, Contractor waives and releases all liens, claims, security interests and other encumbrances arising in favor of Contractor by reason of having provided labor, materials or equipment relating to the Services or any portion thereof, to the extent of such invoice. Contractor agrees to remove immediately any lien, claim, security interest or other encumbrances against Companies, or either of them, property of Companies, or either of them, or the affiliates of any of them, or the client or the client's property of the Companies, or either of them, arising in favor of Contractor or its subcontractors, vendors, suppliers or other persons or entities by reason of having provided labor, materials or equipment related to the Services.

7.8 Year 2000 Compliance

Contractor warrants that any and all hardware, software and firmware product delivered (as a component of a system, part of a piece of equipment, or as a stand alone item) under this Contract shall be able to:

a accurately process date data (including but not limited to accepting input, providing output and calculating comparing and sequencing) from, into and between the Twentieth and Twenty-First Centuries, including (but not limited to) leap year calculations;

b operate accurately, without interruption, and without any change in performance on and in respect of any and all dates before during and/or after January 1, 2000;

c respond to and process two digit year input without creating any ambiguity as to the century; and

d store and provide date input information without creating an ambiguity as to the century, provided that such hardware, software and/or firmware is operated in accordance with the manufacturer's recommendations, (a copy of which shall be provided to and explained to the Purchaser).

7.9 Violation of Law and Litigation

Contractor represents and warrants that it is not in violation of any applicable law which individually or in the aggregate, would affect its performance of any obligation under this Agreement. There are no legal or arbitration proceedings or any proceeding by or before any court or governmental authority now pending or (to its best knowledge) threatened against it which, if adversely determined, could reasonably be expected to have a material adverse effect on its financial condition, operations, prospects or business as a whole, or ability to perform all its obligations under this Agreement.

7.10 No Breach

Contractor represents and warrants that none of the execution and delivery of this Agreement, the consummation of the transactions herein contemplated or compliance with the terms and provisions hereof and thereof will conflict with or result in a breach of, or require any consent under, its charter or bylaws or any applicable law, or any agreement or instrument to which it is a party or by which it is bound or to which it or any of its respective assets are subject, or constitute a default under any such agreement or instrument.

7.11 Investigation

Contractor represents and warrants that it has:

I. full experience and proper qualifications to perform the Services;
   - i examined thoroughly the requirements of any project agreements furnished to Contractor which are applicable to the Services to be performed by Contractor and has become familiar with their terms; and
   - ii ascertained the nature and location of the facility, and other general conditions and laws (including labor laws) that might affect its performance of the Services or the cost thereof.

8 Responsibilities

8.1 Other Contractors of Companies

Contractor shall not be responsible for construction means, methods, techniques, sequences, procedures, or safety precautions and programs in connection with services performed by other contractors of Companies, or either of them. In addition, Contractor shall not be responsible for the failure of any other contractor, subcontractor or vendors (other than a subcontractor, supplier or vendor of Contractor), or other project participant to fulfill contractual or other responsibilities to the Companies, or either of them, or to comply with Federal, State, or local laws, ordinances, regulations, rules, codes, orders, criteria, or standards unless provided for in the Scope of Services.

8.2 Labor, Materials and Equipment

Subject to Section 4 herein, Contractor shall furnish and pay for all labor, materials, tools, equipment, transportation and supervision incident to and necessary for Contractor to perform the Services, and shall make all payments to any subcontractors of Contractor.

8.3 Permits

Contractor shall not be responsible for procuring permits, certificates, and licenses required for any construction or operation of the facility or project for which the Scope of Services is being performed (other than those required pursuant to Section 9) unless such responsibilities are specifically assigned and agreed upon in the Scope of Services.

8.4 Progress Reports

Contractor shall furnish such progress reports, schedules, financial and cost reports and other reports concerning the Scope of Services in progress as Companies may from time to time require.

8.5 Personnel; Travel; Compliance with Companies' Rules

Contractor shall provide qualified personnel to perform the Services. Contractor agrees that its employees may be required to travel to foreign and domestic locations in connection with the Services. Contractor shall require all of its employees to observe all rules and regulations of each Company, including, but not limited to plant badges, parking and entrance facilities, safety, fire, drug/ alcohol, and smoking regulations.

8.6 Access to Services

Contractor shall provide each Company access to the Services at all times wherever in preparation or progress in order to inspect the Services. Any inspection, observation, or review by Companies, or either of them, of the performance of the Services or any portion thereof shall not prejudice, be a waiver, or be deemed to be a waiver of any of its rights hereunder or of its rights to reject defective Services.

9 Compliance with Laws

9.1 Contractor Conduct

The Services provided by Contractor shall comply with applicable regulatory requirements including, without limitation, all Federal, State, and local laws, rules, ordinances, resolutions, regulations, orders, codes, criteria and national and local standards, export and import laws and regulations, issued or promulgated by units of government and regulatory bodies with jurisdiction over any aspect of the Services and/or project for which the Services are sought. Contractor shall not act in violation of the U.S. Foreign Corrupt Practices Act, and in connection therewith shall not make any payments, loans, or gifts, directly or indirectly, to or for the use or benefit of any official employee, agency or instrumentality of any government, political party or candidate thereof, or any other person or entity, the payment of which would violate the laws or policies of the United States, or the country or countries in which the Services are performed, in whole or in part. Contractor shall possess or procure all permits, certificates, and licenses necessary to allow Contractor to perform the Services at all locations of performance and shall ensure that Contractor's subcontractors have all permits, certificates, and licenses necessary for such subcontractor, vendors and suppliers to perform such Services, except those permits, certificates and licenses that are project specific and normally acquired by owner or developer. Contractor shall answer promptly and in reasonable detail any questionnaire or other written or oral communications, to the extent the same pertain to compliance with this Section 9, whether such questionnaires or communications are from Companies, or either of them, their (its) outside auditors, or other representatives.

9.2 Employment Practices

Contractor agrees that it shall be at all times during the term of this Agreement, in full compliance with all applicable Federal, State and local statutes, rules and regulations, orders and guidelines, relative to Contractor's employment of employees and agents of Contractor, in the jurisdictions where any portion of the work is performed. Contractor represents and warrants that it does not and will not maintain any segregated facilities or engage in any discriminatory practices. If applicable or unless otherwise exempted, Contractor shall obtain certifications from its subcontractors that they are and shall be at all times during performance of covered Services in full compliance with all of the above to the extent that such statutes, rules and regulations, orders and guidelines are applicable.

9.3 Correction of Non Complying Services

In the event any Services hereunder fail to comply with all applicable Federal, State and local laws, rules, orders, ordinances, codes, resolutions, criteria, regulations, local and national standards, issued or promulgated by units of government and regulatory bodies as required by Section 9.1 and Contractor shall correct such noncomplying Services or portion thereof as necessary to comply with the above. Contractor shall bear the costs of correction of such noncomplying Services and Companies shall not be required to pay for such corrective Services. In the event that Companies determine that Contractor is either not capable of reperforming the corrections or not capable of performing such corrections in time to meet Companies' requirements, Companies may, at Contractor's expense, have the Services corrected by a third party.

10 Taxes and Contributions

Contractor assumes full responsibility for and agrees to pay all contributions and taxes payable under all applicable wage, employment, social security, unemployment compensation, income and other tax laws as to all of its employees, including Seconded Personnel, engaged in the performance of Services hereunder, and to pay any and all sales, use, or other taxes levied on general office, engineering and drafting supplies, materials, equipment, and services consumed, used, provided or performed by Contractor hereunder. Contractor agrees to pay and the Price includes all taxes, excises, duties and other imposts imposed on the Services, materials and work product to be provided or delivered to the Companies and each Company.

11 Confidential Information

11.1 Confidential Information

Contractor acknowledges that all information, including but not limited to, data, drawings, recordings, tracings, specifications, calculations, diaries, memoranda, manuals, correspondence, documentation, computer software, plans, programs, plants, processes, products, costs, equipment, routes, vendors, personnel, operations, customers, reports, studies, designs, know how, trade secrets, communications written or oral, of any form or media, related to the Companies, or either of them, the owner of the proposed facilities or the proposed facilities themselves whether received from or on behalf of the Companies, or either of them, whether marked or not, is proprietary and confidential to each Company ("Confidential Information"). Confidential Information shall not include information which:

i at the time of disclosure or thereafter becomes a part of the public domain through no wrongful act or omission or noncompliance with this Section 11 by Contractor; or
ii is subsequently disclosed to Contractor by a third party, and which the third party did not acquire under an obligation of confidentiality; or
iii was in the possession of Contractor prior to entering into this Agreement and which was not previously disclosed to Contractor as Confidential Information of Companies, or either of them.

11.2 Protection of Confidential Information

Contractor shall not use or disclose (except to the extent reasonably required to perform Services and then only in compliance herewith) any Confidential Information of each Company. Contractor shall protect such information at least to the same extent as Contractor would protect the same or similar information owned by Contractor. If necessary to perform the Services, Contractor may disclose Confidential Information to third parties, but only on a confidential basis satisfactory to Companies and with the prior written consent of Companies. All Confidential Information of either Company disclosed to or used or acquired by Contractor in connection with the Services shall be and remain the exclusive property of the disclosing Company.

11.3 Developed Information

Contractor acknowledges that all information developed, derived, or created hereunder which is based on, or developed, derived or created from, Confidential Information of either Company, shall be Confidential Information of the disclosing Company.

11.4 Return of Information

Contractor shall deliver to the disclosing Company all Confidential Information provided or disclosed to or used or acquired by Contractor, including all information developed, derived, or created therefrom, or portions thereof, upon the earlier of:

i cessation of the need for the information for performance of Services; or
ii request of either Company; or
iii completion of the Services for which it was provided, disclosed, used or acquired; or
iv termination, suspension, or expiration of this Agreement.

Contractor may retain a single copy of all information upon which its Services are based for record purposes only. In the event Contractor releases Confidential Information to a third party, Contractor shall retrieve and deliver to the disclosing Company all such released Confidential Information, including any and all copies of the Confidential Information and all information developed, derived, or created therefrom, upon the earlier of:

i cessation of the need for the information for performance of Services; or
ii Companies' request; or
iii completion of the Services for which it was provided, disclosed, used or acquired; or
iv termination, suspension, or expiration of this Agreement.

11.5 Limited Access

Contractor agrees to restrict the knowledge of all Confidential Information to Contractor's employees and personnel who are directly connected with the performance of the Services and have need of such knowledge.

12 Ownership of Information, Inventions, Discoveries, Intellectual Property Rights, Services and Work Product

12.1 Ownership of Information and Inventions

The parties intend and agree that all rights, title and interest in and to all Confidential Information of each

Company and all other information, whether written or otherwise, including but not limited to data, drawings, recordings, tracings, specifications, calculations, diaries, memoranda, manuals, correspondence, documentation, computer software, plans, programs, plants, processes, products, costs, equipment, routes, vendors, personnel, operations, customers, reports, studies, designs, know how, trade secrets, communications written or oral, of any form or media, developed and created by any party or subcontractor in the performance of the Services shall be the exclusive property of the Company providing the same. Contractor further agrees that any and all inventions or discoveries developed during performance of and arising out of the Services under this Agreement, including improvements and modifications, whether or not patentable, and any applications for Letters Patent issuing thereon, including inventions or discoveries made by Contractor or its employees in performance of this Agreement, shall be the exclusive property of Companies. Contractor agrees and does hereby assign, grant, transfer and convey to Companies, their successors and assigns, Contractor's entire right, title, interest and ownership in and to such Confidential Information, information, inventions, discoveries, modifications, and improvements, including, without limitation, the right to secure patent or copyright registration. Contractor confirms that Companies and their successors and assigns shall each own an equal and undivided interest in Contractor's right, title and interest in and to, including the right to manufacture, use, reproduce, distribute by sale, rental lease or lending or by other transfer of ownership, to perform publicly, and to display, all such Confidential Information, information, inventions, discoveries, modifications, and improvements, whether or not such items constitute all "work made for hire" as defined in 17 U.S.C. Section 201(b).

12.2 Registration and Protection of Intellectual Property Rights

Contractor agrees to take all actions and cooperate as is necessary and agrees to execute any documents that might be necessary to perfect each Company's ownership of patent, copyright and other rights in such Confidential Information, information, inventions, discoveries, modifications, and improvements, and to obtain any registrations. Each Company, individually and collectively, shall have the right to file and prosecute, at its expense and at its sole discretion, all patent applications on any such inventions or discoveries, and Contractor agrees for itself and its employees to execute and deliver, or have executed and delivered to Companies any and all documents, including assignments, which a Company or the Companies shall deem necessary in order to apply for, prosecute and obtain Letters Patent for said discoveries, patent applications based thereon and Letters Patent issuing thereon. Contractor agrees on behalf of itself and its employees to furnish each Company or the Companies full assistance in the preparation, filing and prosecution of any such patent applications, including patent interference proceedings relating thereto, and to protect and enforce said patents and to assist in any proceedings and litigation in connection therewith, such assistance to be furnished by Contractor at Companies' expense with Companies reimbursing Contractor at a price to be agreed of the invention or discovery.

12.3 Third Party Rights

In the event any information covered by Section 12.1 includes intellectual property rights, proprietary information, copyrighted information of a third party, or any information or property requiring a license to use, manufacture, sell, reproduce, distribute by any means, perform publicly or display such material, Contractor shall secure the necessary copyright, license or release to allow Companies, or either of them, to use, manufacture, sell, reproduce, distribute, perform publicly and display such information.

12.4 Ownership of Work Product and Services

Each Company shall have an undivided interest in the Services work product and materials to be provided by the Contractor, regardless of to whom the same may be actually physically delivered.

13 Indemnification

Contractor agrees to indemnify, defend and save Companies, and each Company, harmless from any loss, cost or expense (including arbitration/court costs and reasonable attorney fees) ("Losses") claimed by third parties for property damage and bodily injury, including death, to the extent determined to be caused by *breach of this Agreement, violation of law or* the negligence or willful misconduct of Contractor, its agents, employees or Contractor's affiliates, *except to the extent determined to be caused by the negligence or willful misconduct or violation of law by breach of this Agreement, violation of law or Company or Companies.*

14 Insurance

Contractor shall maintain in effect during the Term of this Agreement insurance of the types and in the amounts in accordance with the provisions as described at Exhibit C.

15 Notice

Any notice, demand, or request required by or made pursuant to this Agreement shall be deemed properly made if made in writing and delivered by hand delivery, telefax and confirmed by first class mail, postage prepaid, or deposited in the United States Mail, postage prepaid, to the respective addresses and personnel specified below ("Notice Representative"):

If to Companies:

LLC/Sand Pipeline LLC.
xxxx Slade Street
Dallas, Texas 79002
Attn: XXXX XXXX
With copies to:General Counsel at the same address above

If to Contractor:

Consulting LLC
yyyy Slade Blvd.
Huntsville, AL 39401
Attn: XXXX yyyy
With copies to: Corporate Counsel at the same address above

The parties may change the address where or the individual to whom notice is to be given by providing notice of such change pursuant to this Section 15. Nothing contained in this Section shall be construed to restrict the transmission of routine communications between representatives of Contractor and Companies.

16 Not Used

17 Not Used

18 Termination of Agreement

18.1 Termination for Cause

Each Company may, in the event of bankruptcy, dissolution or other similar acts; failure to provide reasonable assurance of future performance; failure to complete any of the Services at a stipulated time; or for any other *material* default by Contractor to perform in accordance with the terms hereof, upon seven *ten (10)*7 days written notice, *said written notice to detail the respect in which Contractor is failing to comply with the terms of this Agreement,* terminate, in whole or *Contractor shall have ten (10) days after receipt of notice in which to remedy such defect, of if the defect cannot be cured within that timeframe, to commence diligently to remedy the defect. In the event that Contractor does not comply with the provisions of 18.2, then Company may immediately terminate this Agreement.*

18.2 Termination Without Cause

Each Company shall have the right for its convenience and without cause to terminate or suspend, in whole or in part, Contractor's performance of Services under this Agreement, upon written notice to Contractor. Contractor shall, upon receipt of a Company's notice of termination or suspension, immediately (unless directed otherwise in Company's notice of termination or suspension) terminate or suspend performance of the Services as directed, but only to the extent specified in Companies' notice of termination or suspension. Upon receipt of such notice of termination or suspension, Contractor shall not incur any further costs until directed otherwise by such Company. Companies shall pay Contractor such sum as is reasonable and equitable for the Services authorized and performed to the point of termination or suspension under this Section, and for which Companies had not previously paid Contractor. In the event of termination under this Section 18, Companies shall also pay Contractor for all reasonable demobilization and cancellation costs incurred by Contractor in connection with the termination.

18.3 Continuation of Services Not Terminated or Suspended

Termination or suspension of the Scope of Services, in part, shall not diminish Contractor's liability or obligation to continue prosecution of Services of that portion not terminated or suspended under this Agreement.

18.4 Companies' Rights

If Companies elect to terminate this Agreement pursuant to Section 18.1, then Companies may employ any other person, firm or corporation (the "Replacement Contractor") to finish the Services in accordance with the terms of this Agreement and all subcontracts (subject to all obligations under such subcontracts) as may be assigned to such Replacement Contractor pursuant to Section 18.4.1(c) by whatever method that Companies may deem expedient. Companies may make such expenditures as in Companies' sole judgment will best accomplish the timely completion of the Services. Contractor, if so requested by Companies, shall provide Companies and any Replacement Contractor, at Contractor's expense, with the right to continue to use any and all patented and/or proprietary information that Contractor has rights to use, if any, (subject to reasonable proprietary restrictions) which Companies deem necessary to complete the Services. Upon such termination, Contractor shall not be entitled to receive any further payments under this Agreement except for payments of Services performed in accordance with the terms of this Agreement prior to such termination.

18.4.1 General Obligations

If Companies elect to terminate this Agreement pursuant to Section 18.1, then Contractor shall, in addition to any other rights and remedies Contractor may be entitled, at Companies' request and at Contractor's expense, perform the following services relative to the Services so affected:

a cease all further Services, except such Services as Companies may specify in the termination notice for the sole purpose of protecting that part of the Services already executed;
b terminate all subcontractors, except those to be assigned to Companies pursuant to Section 18.4.1(c);
c assign to Companies or to any Replacement Contractor, without any right to compensation, title to all Services not already owned by Companies, together with all subcontractors and other agreements or agreement rights (including warranties) as may be designated by Companies, and assign to Companies to the extent assignable all issued governmental approvals, patents and other proprietary rights, if any, then held by Contractor pertaining to the Services;
d deliver to Companies all design and other information as may be reasonably requested by Companies for the completion of the Services; and
e supply any proprietary components needed for the completion of the Services that are not available from other persons on reasonable terms.

18.4.2 Payment Obligations

18.4.2.1 *Companies Expenses*

If Companies terminate this Agreement pursuant to Section 18.1, Companies shall determine the total reasonable and necessary expenses incurred by or accrued by Companies in connection with the termination of this Agreement (including all legal fees and expenses) and the completion of the Services, including all amounts charged by any Replacement Contractor to finish the Services based on the obligations such Replacement Contractor assumes under this Agreement and under any of Contractor's subcontracts or other contractual agreement(s) that Companies elect to have assigned to such Replacement Contractor pursuant to Section 18.4.1(c), and additional reasonable and necessary overhead incurred and accrued by Companies to effect such takeover and to complete the Services.

18.4.2.2 *Contractor Charges*

Companies shall pay Contractor (*i*) any unpaid portion of the price attributable to the Services executed by Contractor prior to the date of termination, and (*ii*) the value of any unused or partially used material furnished by Contractor that are taken over by Companies and have not already been paid for as part of the price paid to Contractor. Any sums due to Companies from Contractor accruing prior to the date of termination or as a consequence of termination shall be deducted from the amount to be paid to Contractor pursuant to the foregoing. If the total expenses incurred by Companies in completing the Services as set forth in Section 18.4.2.1 exceed the balance of the price unpaid at the time of Contractor's default less the amounts determined under (*i*) and (*ii*) above, then Contractor shall be liable for and shall pay to Companies upon written demand by Companies the amount of such excess or any other amounts incurred by Companies pursuant to Section 18.4.2.1. Any such amount payable by Contractor may be deducted by Companies from any portion of the price or other amounts due to Contractor under these Sections 18.4.2.1 and 18.4.2.2.

19 Uncontrollable Forces

19.1 Uncontrollable Forces

Neither Companies (or either of them), nor Contractor shall be considered to be in default of this Agreement if delays in or failure of performance shall be due to uncontrollable forces the effect of which, by the exercise of reasonable diligence, the nonperforming party could not avoid. The term "Uncontrollable Forces" shall mean any event which results in the prevention or delay of performance by a party of its obligations under this Agreement and which is beyond the control of the nonperforming party. It includes, but is not limited to, fire, flood, act of God, earthquakes, "named" storms, lightning, epidemic, war, riot, civil disturbance, sabotage, and judicial restraint, but notwithstanding anything to the contrary herein, the term "Uncontrollable Forces" specifically excludes the impacts of any weather event not a named storm. For the purposes of this Agreement, a "named" storm shall be a weather event to which the National Weather Service assigns a unique name.

19.2 Continuance of Performance

Neither party shall be excused from performance if nonperformance is due to Uncontrollable Forces which are removable orremediable (at a reasonable cost) and which the nonperforming party could have, with the exercise of reasonable diligence, removed or remedied with reasonable dispatch.

19.3 Notice

The nonperforming party shall, within a reasonable time, but not later than seven (7) calendar days, of becoming aware of being prevented or delayed from performance by an Uncontrollable Force, give written notice to the other party describing the circumstances, Uncontrollable Forces preventing continued performance, the removal or remedial actions taken or to be taken to mitigate damage to the other party, and a plan to return performance to compliance with this Agreement.

19.4 Burden of Proof

In the event that the parties are unable in good faith to agree that an event of Uncontrollable Force has occurred, the parties shall submit the dispute for resolution pursuant to Section 31 and the party claiming such event shall have the burden of proof as to whether such event (*a*) has occurred, (*b*) was not a result of such party's or its subcontractor's fault or negligence, and (*c*) could not have been avoided by due diligence or the use of reasonable efforts by such party or its subcontractors.

20 Governing Law and Forum

This Agreement, its interpretation and any disputes relating to, arising out of or connected with this Agreement, shall be governed by the laws of the State of New York, without regard to its conflicts of law provisions. Any dispute relating to, arising out of, or connected with this Agreement shall be filed and maintained in New York, New York in accordance with Section 31 hereof, or, if not in arbitration pursuant to Section 31 hereof, in the State or Federal Courts located in New York, New York.

21 Waiver

No waiver of any provision of the Agreement shall be of any force or effect unless such waiver is in writing, expressly stating to be a waiver of a specified provision of the Agreement, and is signed by the party to be bound thereby. Either party's waiver of any breach or failure to enforce any of the provisions of the Agreement, at any time, shall not in any way limit or waive that party's right thereafter to enforce or compel strict compliance with this Agreement or any portion or provision or right under this Agreement.

22 Severability

The invalidity, illegality, or unenforceability of any provision of this Agreement, or the occurrence of any event rendering any portion or provision of this Agreement void, shall in no way affect the validity or enforceability of any other portion or provision of the Agreement. Any void provision shall be deemed severed from the Agreement and the balance of the Agreement shall be construed and enforced as if the Agreement did not contain the particular portion or provision held to be void. The parties further agree to reform the Agreement to replace any stricken provision with a valid provision that comes as close as possible to the intent of the stricken provision. The provisions of this section shall not prevent the entire Agreement from being void should a provision which is the essence of the Agreement be determined to be void.

23 Assignment and Rights of Affiliated Companies

23.1 Contractor Assignment

Contractor shall not assign or transfer, in whole or in part, any rights or obligations under or interest in (including, but without limitation, monies that are due) this Agreement without the prior written consent of Companies.

23.2 Companies Assignment

Companies, or either of them, may assign this Agreement, in whole or in part, to an affiliate or subsidiary, joint venture or partner, or to a third party who is under contract to Companies, or either of them, or at some subtier level contract to Companies, or either of them. Companies shall notify Contractor of such assignment ten (10) calendar days prior to executing such assignment. Upon assignment to a third party, Contractor will be provided written assurance by the assignor and the assignee that Contractor will be afforded all the rights, privileges and protections as provided under this Agreement.

23.3 Subcontracting by Contractor

Contractor may, upon approval by Companies, which approval may be withheld for any reason, subcontract any portion of the Services to a subcontractor. In no case shall Companies' approval of any subcontract relieve Contractor of any of its obligations under this Agreement. Contractor may have portions of the Services performed by its affiliated entities or their employees, in which case Contractor shall be responsible for such Services and Companies shall look solely to Contractor as if the Services were performed solely by Contractor.

24 Successors and Assigns

The provisions of this Agreement shall inure to the benefit of and be binding upon the successors, assignees, and representatives of the parties hereto.

25 Modification

This Agreement may be modified during the Term of this Agreement only by written modification, which expressly provides that it is a modification of this Agreement and is signed by duly authorized representatives of both parties.

25.1

In the event this Agreement is modified, such modification shall be priced at the fixed hours rates set forth in Exhibit B. The Fixed Hourly Rate shall include compensation for: (*i*) Contractor's employees' time, whether the employee works overtime or regular time or is an exempt or non-exempt employee; and (*ii*) Contractor's allowance for payroll burden (i.e. payroll taxes, insurance, vacations, sick leave, holidays, excused absences, fringe benefits, etc.), overhead, general and administrative expense (i.e. corporate officers, sales, public relations, personnel, law, medical, finance and accounting when not directly engaged in the Scope of Services, receptionists, janitorial, advertising personnel, rent, utilities, depreciation and maintenance of staff to provide readiness to serve), routine copies of correspondence, specifications and plans, telephone calls and postage, taxes (real estate, income, and franchise on Contractor or Contractor's affiliates, subsidiaries or subcontractors), insurance, profits, indemnification consideration under Section 13, and all costs and expenses of whatever kind except as otherwise specifically set forth in this Agreement.

26 Inconsistencies

In the event of any conflict between this Agreement and any Exhibits attached hereto, the terms and provisions of the Agreement shall control. In the event of any conflict among the Exhibits or documents appended thereto, the Exhibit or appended document of the latest date shall control.

27 Survival

The following Sections shall survive termination of this Agreement: 4 (Compensation); 7 (Representations and Warranties); 8 (Responsibilities); 9 (Compliance with Laws); 10 (Taxes and Contributions); 11 (Confidential Information); 12 (Ownership of Information, Inventions, Discoveries and Intellectual Property Rights); 13 (Indemnification); 16 (Consequential Losses); 17 (Limitation of Liability); 20 (Governing Law); 21 (Waiver); 22 (Severability); 26 (Inconsistencies); 29 (Public Releases); and 31 (Dispute Resolution).

28 Non-Exclusive Rights

This Agreement is not exclusive and Companies retain the right, at its sole discretion, to acquire the same or similar services from others without any obligation to Contractor.

29 Public Releases

Nothing contained herein shall permit or be deemed to permit use by Contractor of the name of either Company or owner's name or any circumstances pertaining to this Agreement or the facilities being developed in connection herewith, directly or indirectly, in the form of advertising or in a press release without the prior receipt of Companies' written approval.

30 Drug and Alcohol Free Work Place

The parties desire to provide a safe and productive work environment. The parties believe that the use, possession and/or distribution of illegal/unauthorized drugs and alcohol present a serious threat to the safety of employees, visitors and others at the site, or other premises owned, leased or occupied by Companies, or either of them. Contractor shall ensure that its employees know they will be in a drug free environment, and that their person and possessions, including vehicles, are subject to random search and drug testing.

30.1 Contractor's Drug Free and Alcohol Free Plan

Contractor shall submit within seventy-two hours of signing of this Agreement its Drug Free Work Place and Testing plan for review by Companies.

30.2 Search and Testing

In addition to the requirements of Contractor's Drug Free Plan, all Contractor's and Contractor's subcontractor's employees involved in performance of any Services hereunder must agree to:

1. while on or entering the site or other premises owned, leased, or occupied by Companies, or either of them, search of personal and professional possessions including but not limited to: automobiles, trucks, briefcases, lunchboxes, and person for illegal drugs; and
2. drug testing at any time while on site or other premises owned, leased or occupied by Companies, or either of them.

30.3 Removal of Contractor Personnel from Services Under this Agreement

Contractor personnel refusing to consent to search and/or drug testing will be denied access to and/or removed from the work site and shall at Companies' request be removed from performance of any Services under this Agreement. Contractor personnel found to have illegal substances or alcohol in their possession while on premises of the Companies, or either of them, or testing positive as a result of a test conducted on premises of the Companies, or either of them, upon the request of Companies, will be removed from any further performance of Services under this Agreement.

31 Dispute Resolution

31.1 Negotiation of Disputes and Disagreements

In the event of any claim, dispute, disagreement, or controversy arising out of or relating to the implementation or performance of this Agreement, which the parties hereto have been unable to settle or agree upon within a period of thirty (30) days after the dispute or disagreement arises, each party shall nominate a senior officer of its management to meet at a mutually agreed time and place not later than forty five (45) days after the dispute or disagreement has arisen to attempt to resolve such dispute or disagreement. Should a resolution of such dispute or disagreement not be obtained within fifteen (15) days after the meeting of senior officers for such purpose, either party may then by notice to the other submit the dispute to arbitration in accordance with the provisions of this Section 31.

31.2 Arbitration Resolution

Any claim, dispute or controversy arising out of or relating to this Agreement, shall be submitted to binding arbitration by the American Arbitration Association for arbitration in New York, New York, in accordance with the Construction Industry Arbitration Rules then in effect. There shall be three arbitrators, with each party selecting one; the third arbitrator, who shall be the chairman of the panel, shall be selected by the two-party-appointed arbitrators. The claimant shall name its arbitrator in the demand for arbitration and the responding party shall name its arbitrator within thirty (30) days after receipt of the demand for arbitration. The third arbitrator shall be named within thirty (30) days after the appointment of the second arbitrator. The American Arbitration Association shall be empowered to appoint any arbitrator not named in accordance with the procedure set forth herein. Each arbitrator will be qualified by at least ten (10) years experience in construction, engineering, and/or the electric utility industry. The decision of the arbitrators shall be final and binding upon the parties without the right of appeal to the courts. The award rendered by the arbitration shall be final and judgment thereon may be entered by any court having jurisdiction thereof. The costs and expenses of the arbitration (including reasonable attorney's fees) will be borne by the losing party, unless the arbitrators determine that it would be manifestly unfair to honor this Agreement of the parties and determine a different allocation of costs.

31.3 Continuation of Services

Pending final resolution of any dispute, whether or not submitted to arbitration hereunder, Companies and Contractor shall continue to fulfill their respective obligations hereunder.

32 Headings

Headings and titles of sections in this Agreement are included herein for convenience of reference only and shall not constitute a part of the Agreement for any other purpose and will not affect in any way the meaning or interpretation of this Agreement.

33 Entire Agreement

This Agreement as executed by authorized representatives of Companies and Contractor, constitutes the entire Agreement between the parties with respect to matters herein and there are no oral or written understandings, representations or commitments of any kind, express or implied, not expressly set forth herein.

In witness whereof, the parties hereto have executed this Agreement this day and year signed.

Company:

Pipeline LLC.

____

Signature:

____

Name:

____

Title:

____

Date:

Company:

Sand Pipeline LLC.

____

Signature:

____

Name:

____

Title:

____

Date:

Contractor:

Consulting LLC

____

Signature:

____

Name: Jimmy Dean

____

Title: President

____

Date:

Index

A

B

C

D

E

F

H

M

N

O

Q

R

S

U

V

W

Y

Z

THE YEAR YO
WERE BORN

D1756198

1953

A fascinating book about the year 1953 with information on:
Events of the year UK, Adverts of 1953, Cost of living, Births, Deaths, Sporting events, Book publications, Movies, Music, World events and People in power.

THE BEANO
2d
EVERY THURSDAY
No. 530. SEPT. 13th, 1952.
Biffo the BEAR
PROFESSOR SCREWTOP INVENTOR
THANKS, PROFESSOR!
HO! HO!
NOW I'LL EAT SOME!
JUMP
REVENGE
GO GET HIM!
HA! HA! HA!
JUMPIN' HEDGEHOGS! OOOH!
THE PAPER WITH "ALI HAHA"—HO! HO! HO! HE! HE! HE!

INDEX

UK EVENTS OF 1953

January

1st The first TV detector van, used to track down users of unlicensed television sets, begins operation in the UK.

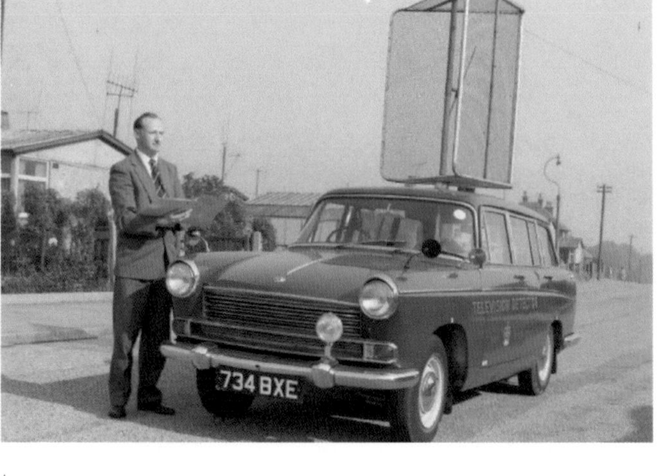
734 BXE

COMMER

5th Samuel Beckett's "En Attendant Godot" premieres in Paris.

6th The Broadcasting Council for Wales meets for the first time.

14th Ralph Vaughan Williams's Sinfonia Antarctica is given its first performance in Manchester.

28th 19-year old Derek Bentley is hanged in Wandsworth Prison, London, controversially convicted of the murder of a police officer. He was pardoned on 30th July 1998.

31st The lives of 133 people were lost when the car ferry Princess Victoria sank in a ferocious gale off the Co Down coast on January 31, 1953. Not one woman or child on board survived, and it is regarded as "a generation's Titanic" — but very little is known about the tragedy outside Northern Ireland and Scotland.

February

1st The North Sea flood of 1953 kills hundreds of people on the east coast of Britain. A corvette and a submarine sink at their moorings in HM Dockyard Sheerness.

February

3rd | Kathleen Ferrier, already suffering from terminal cancer, gives a critically acclaimed performance on the first night of a new production of Gluck's Orfeo ed Euridice at the Royal Opera House.

4th | On the afternoon of Wednesday, the 4th of February, 1953, the wartime rationing of “sweets” in the United Kingdom finally came to a complete end.

6th | During the second performance of Orfeo at Covent Garden, Kathleen Ferrier's left femur gives way; she completes the performance before going to hospital for treatment.

9th | Fraserburgh life-boat John and Charles Kennedy capsizes on service: six crew killed.

10th | Ice Dance Championship at Davos won by Jean Westwood & Lawrence Demmy Great Britain.

28th | Francis Crick and James Watson discover the chemical structure of DNA-molecule (double-helix polymer).

March

4th | Tommy Taylor, 21-year-old centre forward, becomes Britain's most expensive footballer in a £29,999 transfer from Barnsley to Manchester United.

5th | 6th British Film and Television Awards (BAFTAS): "The Sound Barrier" Best Film.

16th | Josip Tito, the leader of Yugoslavia visits the UK, the first Communist leader to do so.

24th | Queen Mary, consort of the late King George V dies in her sleep at Marlborough House.

25th | The 10 Rillington Place murders are uncovered in London.

28th | 107th Grand National: Bryan Marshall wins aboard Irish 8-year old Early Mist; first of 3 consecutive GN victories for trainer Vincent O'Brien.

31st | The funeral of Queen Mary takes place at St George's Chapel, Windsor Castle.

April

1st | BBC Television introduces its iconic Watch with Mother brand for children's programming; it runs for 20 years.

WATCH
WITH
MOTHER

April

13th Ian Fleming publishes his first James Bond novel, Casino Royale.

15th Britain awards the George Medal to 22-year-old American airman Reis Leming who rescued 27 people in last winter's floods in East Anglia.

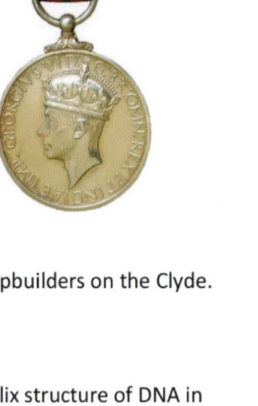

16th The Queen launches the Royal Yacht Britannia at John Brown & Company shipbuilders on the Clyde.

24th Prime Minister Winston Churchill receives a knighthood from the Queen.

25th Francis Crick and James D. Watson publish their description of the double helix structure of DNA in the paper "Molecular structure of Nucleic Acids".

May

1st The BBC brings into service television transmitters at Pontop Pike (County Durham) and Glencairn (Belfast) to improve coverage prior to the Coronation broadcast.

2nd Blackpool F.C. win the FA Cup final with a 4–3 victory over Bolton Wanderers, who have been 3–1 ahead until the final quarter of the game. Stan Mortensen scores a hat-trick, but the 38-year-old winger Stanley Matthews is instrumental in winning the game for Blackpool, who have never won a major trophy before.

25th Whitsun bank holiday; many businesses postpone the holiday for a week.

26th In the 1953 Coronation Honours, Herbert Howells receives a CBE and Benjamin Britten is appointed a Companion of Honour.

June

1st The Times exclusively carries James Morris's scoop of the conquest of Mount Everest by a British expedition on 29 May.

June

2nd The coronation of Elizabeth II took place on 2nd June 1953 at Westminster Abbey in London. Elizabeth II acceded to the throne at the age of 25 upon the death of her father, George VI, on 6 February 1952, being proclaimed queen by her privy and executive councils shortly afterwards. The coronation was held more than one year later because of the tradition of allowing an appropriate length of time to pass after a monarch dies before holding such festivals. It also gave the planning committees adequate time to prepare for the ceremony. During the service, Elizabeth took an oath, was anointed with holy oil, was invested with robes and regalia, and was crowned queen of the United Kingdom, Canada, Australia, New Zealand, South Africa, Pakistan, and Ceylon (now Sri Lanka).
The Coronation of Queen Elizabeth II is televised in the UK on the BBC Television Service. Sales of TV sets rise sharply in the weeks leading up to the event. It is also one of the earliest broadcasts to be deliberately recorded for posterity and still exists in its entirety today.

6th The Epsom Derby is won by Pinza, the only Derby victory for Gordon Richards at his 28th attempt, days after becoming the only jockey to be made a knight. The Queen's horse, Aureole, finishes second.

9th Kathleen Ferrier writes to the secretary of the Royal Philharmonic Society, thanking them for the award of the Gold Medal; it is thought to be the last letter she ever signed in person.

23rd Prime Minister Winston Churchill, 78, suffers a stroke at a dinner for the Italian Prime Minister Alcide De Gasperi. On 27 June the public are told that he is suffering from fatigue.

25th John Christie, a 54-year-old Londoner, is sentenced to death for the murder of his wife Ethel Christie. A total of eight bodies have been found at Christie's home, 10 Rillington Place in Notting Hill, including those of the wife and daughter of Timothy Evans who had been hanged in 1950 for his daughter's murder.

26th Eskdalemuir enters the UK Weather Records for the highest rainfall in a 30-minute period with 80mm, a record that will remain for at least sixty years.

30th First roll-on/roll-off ferry crossing of the English Channel, Dover–Boulogne.

July

4th Wimbledon Women's Tennis: Maureen Connolly wins 3rd leg of her Grand Slam beating fellow American Doris Hart 8-6, 7-5.

July

10th British Open Men's Golf, Carnoustie: In his only Open Championship appearance, Ben Hogan prevails by 4 strokes over Dai Rees, Antonio Cerdá, Peter Thomson and Frank Stranahan.

15th John Christie is hanged at Pentonville Prison, where a crowd of some two hundred people stand to wait for the notice of execution to be posted.

18th The Quatermass Experiment, first of the Quatermass science-fiction serials by Nigel Kneale, begins its run on BBC Television. Set in the near future against the background of a British space programme, it tells the story of the first manned flight into space, supervised by Professor Bernard Quatermass of the British Experimental Rocket Group. Originally comprising six half-hour episodes, it was the first science fiction production to be written especially for a British adult television audience. Previous written-for-television efforts such as Stranger from Space (1951–52) were aimed at children, whereas adult entries into the genre were adapted from literary sources, such as R.U.R. (1938 and again in 1948) and The Time Machine (1949). The serial was the first of four Quatermass productions to be screened on British television between 1953 and 1979. It was transmitted live from the BBC's original television studios at Alexandra Palace in London, one of the final productions before BBC television drama moved to west London.

20th The Good Old Days, filmed at the Leeds City Varieties, begins its 30-year run on BBC Television.

August

19th The England cricket team under Len Hutton defeat Australia to win The Ashes for the first time in nineteen years.

20th Iranian coup d'état ("Operation Boot"): Overthrow of the democratically elected Prime Minister of Iran by Iranian military in favour of strengthening the rule of Shah Mohammad Reza Pahlavi with the support of the United States and UK.

29th Michael Tippett's Fantasia Concertante on a Theme of Corelli is first performed in Edinburgh.

30th Myxomatosis reaches the UK, first being illegally introduced onto an estate in West Sussex. Myxomatosis is a disease caused by Myxoma virus, a poxvirus in the genus Leporipoxvirus. The natural hosts are tapeti (Sylvilagus brasiliensis) in South and Central America, and brush rabbits in North America. The myxoma virus causes only a mild disease in these species, but causes a severe and usually fatal disease in European rabbits. Myxomatosis is an excellent example of what occurs when a virus jumps from a species adapted to it to a naive host, and has been extensively studied for this reason. The virus was intentionally introduced in Australia, France, and Chile in the 1950s to control wild European rabbit populations.

September

16th 1st movie in Cinemascope "The Robe" based on the book by Lloyd C. Douglas, directed by Henry Koster and starring Richard Burton and Jean Simmons premieres.

19th Sir Hubert Parry's 1916 setting of William Blake's "Jerusalem" first appears as a permanent feature of the Last Night of the Proms (televised).

September

26th | End of post-war sugar rationing.

October

3rd | Ryder Cup Golf, Wentworth: San Snead wins 6 of 7 matches to lead US to 6th consecutive Cup win, 6½-5½ over Great Britain.

4th | British runner Jim Peters sets world marathon record 2:18:34.8 in the Turku Marathon in Finland.

9th | British Prime Minister Winston Churchill approves Guyanese Constitution.

14th | Great Britain performs nuclear test at Emu Field, Australia.

19th | Opening of the Covent Garden opera season, with a production of Wagner's Die Walküre.

27th | Arbroath life-boat Robert Lindsay capsizes on service: six crew killed.

November

1st | The first production Blue Danube atomic bomb, the first British-developed and -built nuclear weapon, is delivered to the Bomber Command stockpile at RAF Wittering, concluding the High Explosive Research project to develop it.

2nd | The Samaritans telephone counselling service for the suicidal is started by Rev. Chad Varah in London.

5th | Terence Rattigan's "Sleeping Prince" premieres in London

11th | The current affairs series Panorama launches on the BBC Television Service. It is now the best longest-running programme in British television history.

12th | Writers Frank Muir and Denis Norden introduce the dysfunctional family of The Glums into comedy series Take It from Here and they become the most popular segment of the show.

17th | Italian cargo steamer Vittoria Claudia sinks after collision with French motor vessel Perou in the English Channel, killing twenty Italian sailors.

20th | The Piltdown Man, which was discovered in 1912 and thought to be the fossilised remains of a hitherto unknown form of early human, exposed as a hoax.

November

25th Match of the Century: England v Hungary football match at Wembley Stadium results in a 6–3 defeat suffered by the England national football team against Hungary, ending a 90-year unbeaten home run against sides from outside the British Isles.

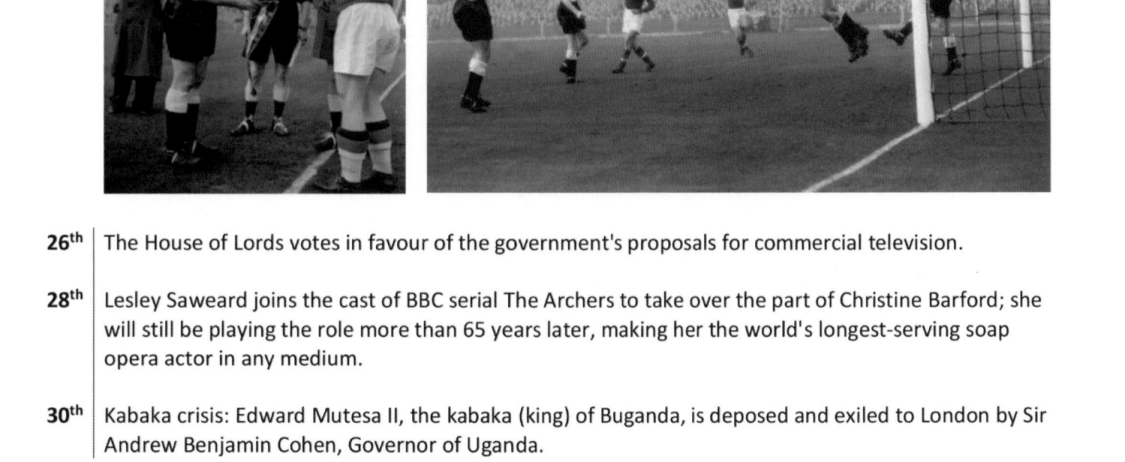

26th The House of Lords votes in favour of the government's proposals for commercial television.

28th Lesley Saweard joins the cast of BBC serial The Archers to take over the part of Christine Barford; she will still be playing the role more than 65 years later, making her the world's longest-serving soap opera actor in any medium.

30th Kabaka crisis: Edward Mutesa II, the kabaka (king) of Buganda, is deposed and exiled to London by Sir Andrew Benjamin Cohen, Governor of Uganda.

December

1st Matchbox toy vehicles are introduced by Lesney Products of London. Matchbox is a popular toy brand which was introduced by Lesney Products in 1953, and is now owned by Mattel, Inc, which purchased the brand in 1997. The brand was given its name because the original die-cast "Matchbox" toys were sold in boxes similar to those in which matches were sold. The brand grew to encompass a broad range of toys, including larger scale die-cast models, plastic model kits, slot car racing, and action figures.

10th Winston Churchill wins the Nobel Prize in Literature "for his mastery of historical and biographical description as well as for brilliant oratory in defending exalted human values".

11th Pilkington Brothers take out their first patent for the float glass process developed by Alastair Pilkington. Between 1953 and 1957, Alastair Pilkington and Kenneth Bickerstaff invented the float glass process, a revolutionary method of high-quality flat glass production by floating molten glass over a bath of molten tin, avoiding the costly need to grind and polish plate glass to make it clear. Pilkington then allowed the Float Process to be used under licence by numerous manufacturers around the world.

Look inside—
—then compare!
SEE WHY DU MONTS DO MORE
You need not be an expert to see for yourself the reason for Du Mont's outstanding performance. This is television's most precise instrument, built with more tubes, extra-size parts, and a solid, orderly design that reflects expert engineering and painstaking craftsmanship.
Look at the Du Mont chassis. Compare it with others.
Then you will know why owning a Du Mont is full assurance of long years of satisfaction.
The SHERBROOKE by DU MONT
19-inch tube; AM and FM radio; 3-speed automatic phono. Cabinet of fine mahogany veneers or blond finish.
Styled by Herbert Rosengren.
DUMONT
First with the finest in Television

Lucozade

the sparkling
GLUCOSE
drink

LUCOZADE
The
Sparkling Glucose Drink
ACIDOSIS · PEEVISH APPETITE · NAUSEA
EXHAUSTION · PREGNANCY SICKNESS · SHOCK
LUCOZADE LTD. BRENTFORD · MIDDX.

TIME FOR LUCOZADE!

In hot summer days when your energy flags and you feel 'all in'—then is the time for delicious Lucozade! This sparkling drink contains Glucose, nature's great energiser, in the most delicious form imaginable. It is instantly refreshing, wonderfully sustaining. Lucozade replaces your vitality *quickly* and *pleasantly*. Keep a supply handy—and drink Lucozade regularly!

2/6d. plus 3d. bottle deposit (returnable). Also in handy size at 8d. plus 2d. bottle deposit.

Lucozade is used by Doctors and Nurses in Clinics, Hospitals and Nursing Homes.

Lucozade REFRESHES AND SUSTAINS

LUCOZADE LTD., GREAT WEST ROAD, BRENTFORD, MIDDX.

royds

James Aloysius Hansom knew a good thing
In 1834 His Design for a "Patent Safety Cab" Sold for a Fortune!
James Hansom, of London, was a prominent Victorian architect—but his most distinctive contribution to the London scene was not a building but the familiar two-wheeled "hansom cab." This unique conveyance replaced almost all other public vehicles, and remained a common sight for nearly three-quarters of a century. Mr. Hansom's original design was briefly sketched out in 1834—and was promptly purchased by a coach maker for 10,000 pounds sterling!
HUNTER
"First over the Bars"
Blended Whiskey
If you know a good thing in whiskey...
you'll try HUNTER and discover why it will be your whiskey ever afterwards. For Hunter is light enough for you to sip it straight yet hearty enough to hold its own in a highball.
Today's great blend for today's good tastes. Why not try Hunter!
Hunter-Wilson Distilling Co., Inc., Louisville, Ky. Blended Whiskey 86.8 Proof. 65% grain neutral spirits.

Carried unanimously The new Commer light 'pick-up' is the handiest, most economical of all general purpose vehicles

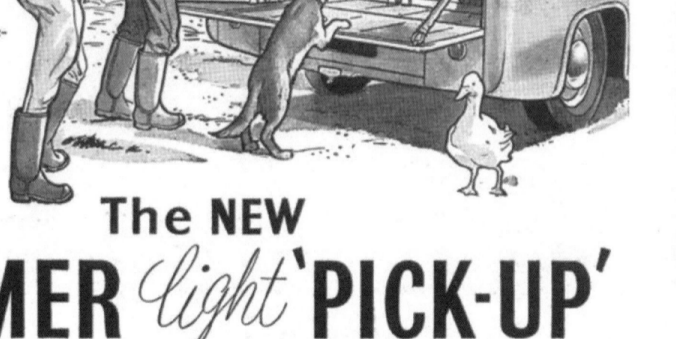

A versatile light open truck with ample power, the new Commer light 'pick-up' is smart, attractive and fast. A willing worker, strong, reliable and capable of operating either on highway or rough country track, it will give you years of trouble-free service.

The NEW COMMER *light* 'PICK-UP'

Tilt and Tonneau Cover available at extra cost

A PRODUCT OF THE ROOTES GROUP

COMMER CARS LIMITED LUTON BEDFORDSHIRE EXPORT DIVISION: ROOTES LTD. DEVONSHIRE HOUSE PICCADILLY LONDON W.1

n21

Meet the Mayflower price tag
It says a good deal!
It says the Mayflower gives you more for your money than any other cooker in the same price range.
It grills or toasts on its big eye-level grill. Warms plates on a removable rack, too.
Boils or simmers or steams or fries on four big automatic-lighting burners, 2 very fast, 2 just fast – set well above the clever deep-spillage tray so that nothing can burn on to the cooker.
Roasts and bakes in its big 20 lb turkey-size oven. Oven roof removes for easy cleaning.
Styled to fit flush into any 20" space to give that "built-in" look. Big storage compartment. Finished in gleaming white vitreous enamel, chrome fittings, grey fascia.
And the Mayflower, like all new Main appliances, is easily convertible from town gas to natural gas. Around £39 (fixing extra.) See the Mayflower at your Gas Showroom or dealer TODAY!
Main
Main leads with High Speed Gas—by a good deal!
R & A MAIN LIMITED, ENFIELD, MIDDLESEX
13
Lucozade
the sparkling GLUCOSE drink
replaces lost energy
Lucozade
is used by
DOCTORS AND NURSES IN
CLINICS HOSPITALS
NURSING HOMES & SCHOOLS
LUCOZADE

IMPORTED
Seagram's
V.O.
CANADIAN WHISKY
Known by the Company it Keeps
Seagram's VO

At Santa Barbara...Smart Guests agree on PM
THE DIVIDEND WHISKEY!
A dividend in TASTE!
A dividend in VALUE!
You'll prefer PM over
whiskies costing up to $1.00 more!
And the difference you save . . .
buys you up to
4 EXTRA DRINKS!
Enjoy today's magnificent PM —the dividend whiskey!
PM

ARRIVE IN STYLE!
Clothes get there fresh, unwrinkled–
BY CAR, PLANE OR TRAIN!
ANOTHER VINYLFILM
GOODYEAR
VINYLFILM
"A"–FIRMTEX TRAVEL BAG (OPEN)

AMAZING
COFFEE DISCOVERY!
INSTANT
MAXWELL
HOUSE
Coffee
Not a powder! Not a grind! But millions of tiny
"FLAVOR BUDS" of real coffee . . . ready to burst instantly
into that famous MAXWELL HOUSE FLAVOR!
Utterly unlike old-style "instants" . . .
just as quick but tastes so different!
100% Pure Coffee—No Fillers Added!
See how the Flavor Buds "come to life" in your cup!
Reach for the jar with the stars on top!
The only instant coffee with that GOOD-TO-THE-LAST-DROP flavor!

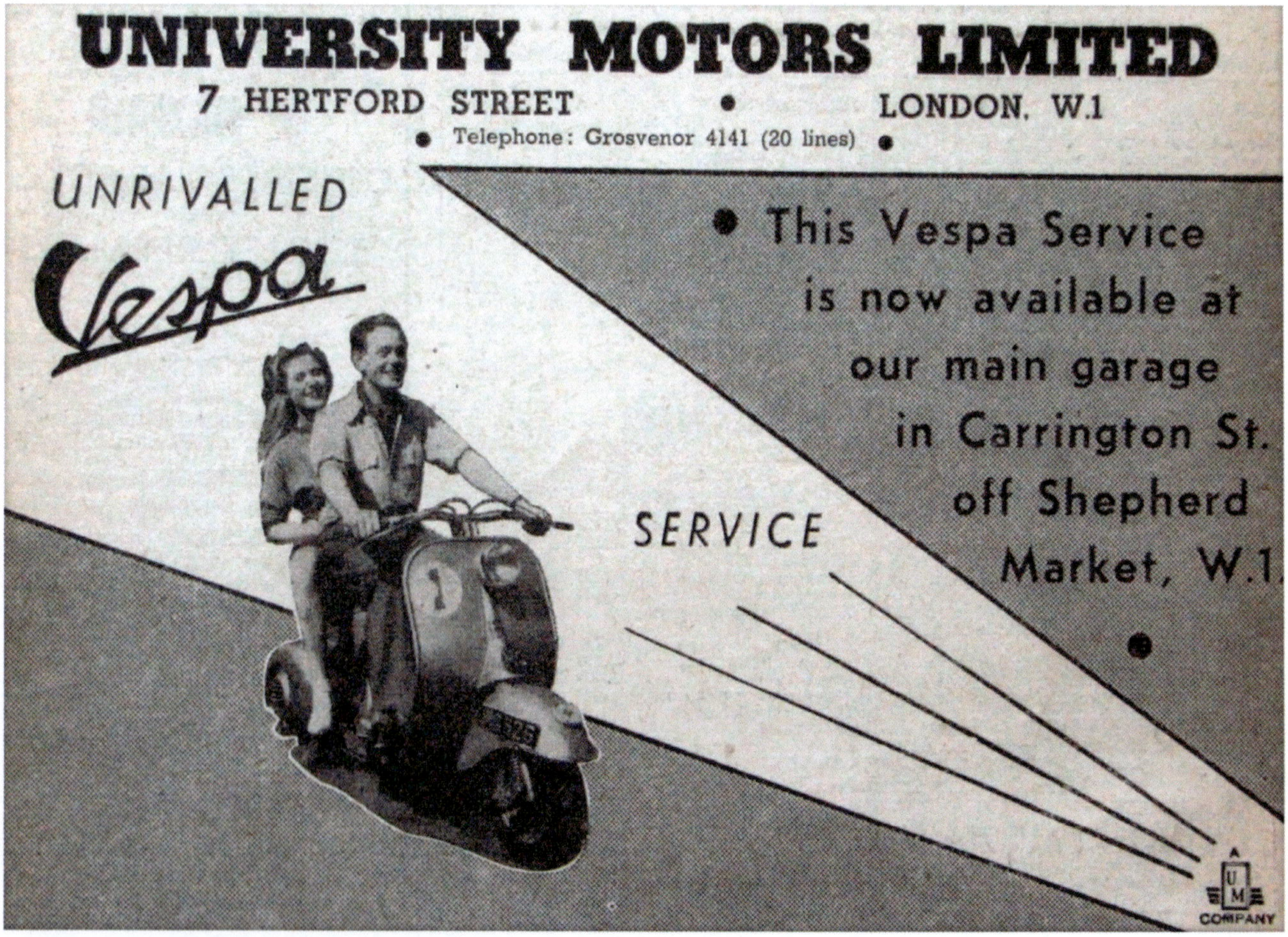

UNIVERSITY MOTORS LIMITED

7 HERTFORD STREET • LONDON, W.1

• Telephone: Grosvenor 4141 (20 lines) •

UNRIVALLED

Vespa

SERVICE

• This Vespa Service is now available at our main garage in Carrington St. off Shepherd Market, W.1.

•

A U M COMPANY

"You'll all go for
MARSHMALLOW
CRISPY SQUARES"
—SAYS HOWDY DOODY
"We're sure wild about this
homemade candy treat!"
ANDY DEVINE
GUY
MADISON
As Wild Bill and Jingles, Guy and Andy co-star in Kellogg's "Wild Bill Hickok" radio and TV shows.
© KAGRAN
MAKE 'EM EASY — in 9 Minutes
They're so good for TV snacks—for special holiday treats—for sweetenin' up lunch boxes—that whole platterfuls of Marshmallow Crispy Squares disappear almost as fast as you can make 'em!
That's fast! Even the kids can make a big batch in 9 minutes. (10, if they're slow-pokes!)
You probably already have a box of Kellogg's Rice Krispies—(the world's only talking cereal)—in your kitchen right now. If you have marshmallows, too, your youngsters are all set for some "real fun" this very minute! If you need one or the other, better see your grocer soon.
¼ cup butter or margarine
½ teaspoon vanilla flavoring
½ pound marshmallows (about 2½ dozen)
5 cups of Kellogg's Rice Krispies
1. Cook butter and marshmallows over boiling water until syrupy, stirring frequently.
2. Add vanilla; beat thoroughly.
3. Measure Rice Krispies into buttered large bowl and pour on marshmallow mixture, stirring briskly.
4. Press into buttered shallow pan; cut into squares when cool. Yield: 24 squares, about 2 inches each (13 x 9 pan).
Five other exciting variations:
Chocolate Marshmallow Squares
Peanut Marshmallow Squares
Coconut Marshmallow Squares
Peppermint Stick Marshmallow Squares
Raisin Marshmallow Squares
(Recipes for these five variations on the package)
Kellogg's
RICE KRISPIES
Kellogg's
RICE KRISPIES AND MARSHMALLOWS
"Rice Krispies" is a trade-mark (Reg. U.S. Pat. Off.) of Kellogg Company for its oven-popped rice.

BY DAY
and
BY NIGHT
The Motor Cycle, 29 January 1953
Year in, year out, the Matchless Factory works at maximum pressure to meet the insatiable world demand for Matchless Motor Cycles
Model G9 The Super Clubman
498 c.c. O.H.V. Vertical Twin
MATCHLESS
Clubman
MATCHLESS MOTOR CYCLES · PLUMSTEAD ROAD · LONDON, S.E.18 · ENGLAND

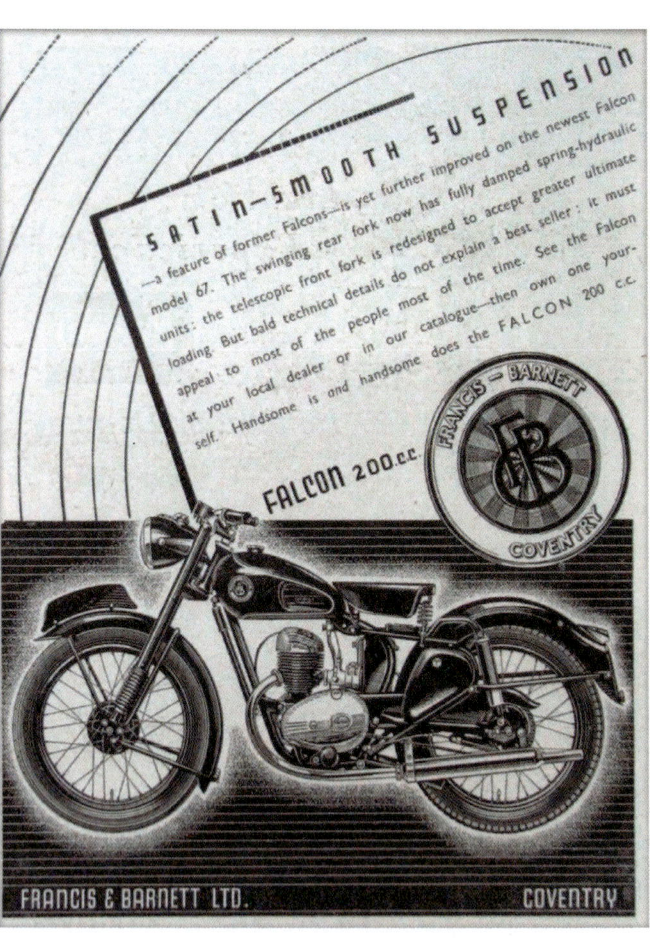

SATIN-SMOOTH SUSPENSION
—a feature of former Falcons—is yet further improved on the newest Falcon model 67. The swinging rear fork now has fully damped spring-hydraulic units: the telescopic front fork is redesigned to accept greater ultimate loading. But bald technical details do not explain a best seller: it must appeal to most of the people most of the time. See the Falcon at your local dealer or in our catalogue—then own one yourself. Handsome is and handsome does the FALCON 200 c.c.
FALCON 200 c.c.
FRANCIS — BARNETT
COVENTRY
FRANCIS & BARNETT LTD.
COVENTRY

See the new 1½ LITRE MG MAGNETTE SALOON
at the Motor Show!
MG Safety fast in airsmoothed style
This sensational new M.G. Saloon combines the best features of contemporary design with really brilliant sports car performance. Powered by a 1½ litre o.h.v. push-rod engine fitted with twin S.U. carburetters, it develops nearly 60 b.h.p. and will carry you safely and smoothly at 80 m.p.h. and more. If you want quite remarkable performance, the beauty of airsmoothed styling, and spacious luxury for the whole family, you will find that there is no car like the M.G. Magnette. Come and see it at the Motor Show, Earl's Court.
SEE ALSO THE new
T.F. SERIES MG MIDGET
— the zippiest model ever!
A new sloping bonnet, headlamps enclosed in the wings, and a smart new bow-fronted radiator, give the M.G. T.F. an even sportier look than before. Don't miss this chance of seeing this latest Midget
BMC
THE MOTOR SHOW
EARL'S COURT
OCTOBER 21-31, 1953
THE M.G. CAR CO. LIMITED, SALES DIVISION, COWLEY, OXFORD

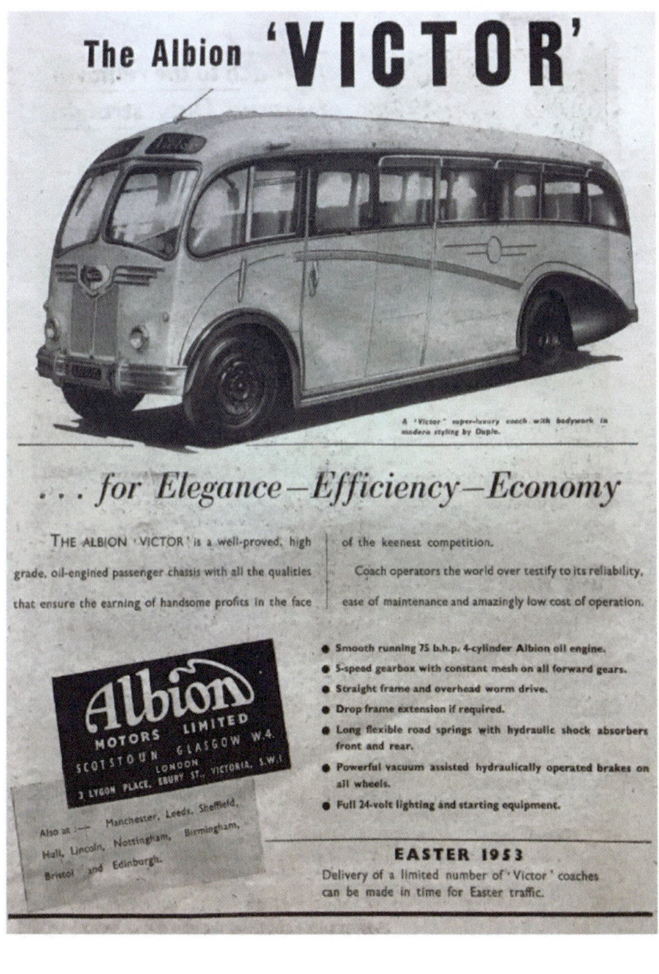
The Albion 'VICTOR'
A 'Victor' super-luxury coach with bodywork in modern styling by Duple.
. . . for Elegance—Efficiency—Economy
THE ALBION 'VICTOR' is a well-proved, high grade, oil-engined passenger chassis with all the qualities that ensure the earning of handsome profits in the face of the keenest competition.
Coach operators the world over testify to its reliability, ease of maintenance and amazingly low cost of operation.
Smooth running 75 b.h.p. 4-cylinder Albion oil engine.
5-speed gearbox with constant mesh on all forward gears.
Straight frame and overhead worm drive.
Drop frame extension if required.
Long flexible road springs with hydraulic shock absorbers front and rear.
Powerful vacuum assisted hydraulically operated brakes on all wheels.
Full 24-volt lighting and starting equipment.
Albion
MOTORS LIMITED
SCOTSTOUN GLASGOW W.4.
LONDON
3 LYGON PLACE, EBURY ST., VICTORIA, S.W.1
Also at :— Manchester, Leeds, Sheffield, Hull, Lincoln, Nottingham, Birmingham, Bristol and Edinburgh.
EASTER 1953
Delivery of a limited number of 'Victor' coaches can be made in time for Easter traffic.

CHATSWORTH HOUSE
Essentially
ENGLISH
SMITHS
DE LUXE
With the passage of time, the great masterpieces of our ancestor's architectural craftsmanship have become an integral part of the English scene . . . Today, Smiths English Watches owe their fine quality, flawless accuracy and beauty to the same characteristically English pride of workmanship that played so great a part in creating the homes of the past.
RICHARD & TUCKER NUNN · LTD
THE HOUSE FOR SMITHS WATCHES & CLOCKS
108 HATTON GARDEN · LONDON EC1
MANCHESTER: 107 Market Street.
GLASGOW: 64 Douglas Street.
LEEDS: 34 Trinity Street.

GLUCYDUR BALANCE
NIVAROX SPIRAL
NON-MAGNETIC
17 JEWELS
5+
TITUS PRICES INCREASE SALES
TITUS ADVERTISING INTERESTS THE CLIENT
TITUS RANGE OF WATCHES MEANS EASIER SALES
TITUS QUALITY ATTRACTS THE CLIENT
SELL TITUS
YOUR PROFITS WILL DOUBLE
AGENTS WANTED
TITUS
GENEVE
FABRIQUE SOLVIL DES MONTRES PAUL DITISHEIM S.A.
GENÈVE
Rue du Rhone 27
SUISSE

The
'HATTON'
LADIES' WATCH
BY
AMIDA S.A.
RETAIL PRICE
£6.13.6
INCL. PURCHASE TAX
The
'HATTON'
GENT'S WATCH
BY
AMIDA S.A.
RETAIL PRICE
£6.13.6
INCL. PURCHASE TAX
Sole Concessionaires for Great Britain:
ANDREW & CO. LTD.
102 HATTON GARDEN, LONDON, E.C.1
Phone: HOLBORN 0165 - 0166
Grams: ANDREWCLOX, LONDON

AUREOLE
Since 1868 reliable lever watches
AUREOLE WATCH CO LA CHAUX DE FONDS

COST OF LIVING 1953

A conversion of pre-decimal to decimal money

The Pound, 1971 became the year of decimalization when the pound became 100 new pennies. Prior to that the pound was equivalent to 20 shillings. Money prior to 1971 was written £/s/d. (d being for pence). Below is a chart explaining the monetary value of each coin before and after 1971.

Symbol	Before 1971	After 1971
£	**Pound (240 pennies)**	**Pound (100 new pennies)**
s	Shilling (12 pennies)	5 pence
d	**Penny**	**¼ of a penny**
¼d	Farthing	1 penny
½d	**Halfpenny**	**½ pence**
3d	Threepence	About 1/80 of a pound
4d	**Groat (four pennies)**	
6d	Sixpence (Tanner)	2½ new pence
2s	**Florin (2 shillings)**	**10 pence**
2s/6d	Half a crown (2 shillings and 6 pence)	12½ pence
5s	**Crown**	**25 pence**
10s	10-shilling note (10 bob)	50 pence
10s/6d	**½ Guinea**	**52½ pence**
21s	1 Guinea	105 pence

Prices are in equivalent to new pence today and on average throughout the UK.

Item	1953	Inflation Adjusted
Wages, average yearly	**£375.00**	**£10,650.00**
Average house price	£1,881.00	£38,704.00
Ford Anglia car	**£511.00**	**£10,608.00**
Gallon of petrol	4s 6½d	£4.60
20 Cigarettes	**3s 7d**	**£3.70**
Bread (loaf)	7½d	63p
Sugar 1lb	**7½d**	**63p**
Milk 1 pint	7d	60p
Butter ½lb	**1s 8d**	**£1.70**
Cheese 1lb	2s 2d	£2.20
Potatoes 1lb	**2d**	**17p**
Eggs 1 Dozen	4s 3½d	£4.40
Beer Bottled (Pint)	**1s 10d**	**£1.90**
Oranges 1lb	10d	85p

Prices are an average throughout the United Kingdom and not per city.

Telephone calls
Only 16% of households had a telephone in 1953.

The cost of installing a telephone was £5. You paid a quarterly rental of £3.

The rental charge included 100 free calls per year. Telephone calls were charged on a different basis from today. There were two types of call 'local' or 'trunk' calls. Local calls were within the local exchange area.

Local calls
For local calls it didn't matter how long you were on the phone as the charge was for a single call. In spite of this people used the telephone for short functional calls. Most took less than two minutes. Charges for local calls in 1955 were:

Distance	Cost	in today's money
Up to 5 miles	2d	15p
5 to 7½ miles	4d	29p
7½ to 12½ miles	6d	44p
12½ to 15 miles	8d	58p

Trunk calls
For a Trunk call you needed to contact the operator and ask her (it was usually a her) to dial the number for you. Trunk calls were charged per 3-minute duration. The operator worked out the charge. There was a cheap rate period from 6pm to 10.30pm every day.

Posting letters
At the beginning of the 1950s, it cost just 2½d (1p) to post a letter in the UK. The GPO (General Post Office) increased the cost to 3d in 1957.

Sending a postcard home from your holidays was cheaper. It cost 2d before 1957, then 2½d

E R
POSTAGE REVENUE
2½

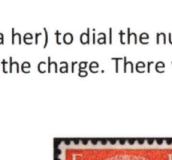

Television
Televisions were expensive in the 1950s and you could only view programmes in black and white. There was also just one BBC channel. Commercial TV started in 1955, so viewers had a choice of two channels. Most deserted the BBC for ITV.

Bush TV32 14" television costs 60 guineas, about £1300 in today's money.
Regentone A133 radio costs 19 guineas about £400 today.

Qualcast push lawn mower was 94shillings around £80 today.

Hoover washing machine was £49 17s about £1,000.

Hoover cylinder vacuum cleaner was £20 4s 3d about £400.

Some shops priced more expensive items in guineas. A guinea is one pound and one shilling or £1.05.

The inflation adjusted prices are based on the Consumer Price Index (CPI).

Groceries

People bought a lot of canned and tinned produce in the 1950s. It was a trend that began in the 1930s. They had also developed a taste for breakfast cereals and instant coffee.

These are some typical groceries people bought in the 1950s and the approximate prices.

Canned/bottled meat and fish
Maconochie's steak pudding - 16oz - 1s 10d
Chef herring in tomato - 14oz - 1s 7d
Heinz fish and meat pastes - medium size - 1s 2d

Canned fruit and fruit juices
Smedley's rhubarb - size A2 - 1s 1½d
Smedley's golden plum - size A2½ - 1s 5½d
Anderson, Richards Sunkist Californian pure lemon juice - 6oz - 9d

Canned vegetables
Crosse & Blackwell beans in tomato - per tin - 10d
Smedley baked beans - per tin - 10d
Heinz baked beans in tomato - 5oz - 5½d
Heinz spaghetti in tomato with cheese - 16oz - 10½d
Bachelor's garden peas - A1 - 1s 1d
Bachelor's processed peas (dwarf) - A1 - 6d

Soups
Heinz tomato - 15½oz - 1s 1½d
Crosse & Blackwell cream of vegetable - tin - 1s
Sauces and pickles

These are some classic sauces. You can still buy most of them today.

HP sauce - 7oz - 10½d
Daddies sauce - 7oz - 10½d
Chef tomato ketchup - medium - 1s
G Mason OK sauce - 9oz - 1s 4½d
Maconchies's Pan Yan pickle - 11oz - 1s 5d
Crosse & Blackwell Branston pickle - 11½oz - 1s 4½d
Colman's mustard - 4oz - 1s 4½d
Heinz Salad Cream - medium - 1s 4½d

Hot drinks
Nescafé instant coffee - medium - 2s 9d
Lyons Chico [instant coffee with chicory and glucose] -¼lb - 2s 4d
Lyons Bev [liquid coffee similar to Camp] - family size - 2s 1½d
Maxwell House instant coffee - 2oz - 2s 8d
Cadbury's Bourne-Vita - ½lb - 2s 9d
Brooke Bond PG Tips tea - 1lb - 6s 8d

Prices may vary depending on which county you lived.

BRITISH BIRTHS

John Gibb Marshall born 11th January 1953 and died 2nd November 2020 better known by the stage name John Sessions, was a Scottish actor and comedian. He was known for comedy improvisation in television shows such as Whose Line Is It Anyway? as a panellist on QI, and as a character actor in numerous films, both in the UK and Hollywood. John Sessions attended RADA in the late 1970s, studying alongside Kenneth Branagh; the two would work together on many occasions later in their careers. His name change occurred when he became a performer, owing to the presence of a John Marshall already on the Equity register. In 1989, he starred in his own one-man TV show, John Sessions. Filmed at the Donmar Warehouse in London, the show involved Sessions performing before a live audience who were invited to nominate a person, a location and two objects from a selection, around which Sessions would improvise a surreal performance for the next half-hour.

Norman John Pace was born on the 17th February 1953 in Dudley, Worcestershire and is an English actor and comedian, best known as one half of the comedy duo Hale and Pace with his friend and comic partner Gareth Hale. As straight actors they also fronted the original TV dramatization of Dalziel and Pascoe, and in 1989 they guest-starred together in the Doctor Who serial Survival. Also, in 1989, Hale and Pace won the Golden Rose of Montreux. In 2007 they appeared in the Christmas special of Extras, called The Extra Special Series Finale, playing themselves. In 2018 he was acting in the comedy TV series Benidorm with Gareth Hale. Norman Pace later took a direction towards theatre and starred in Chicago (Adelphi), Breakfast with Jonny Wilkinson and Our Man in Havana at the Nottingham Playhouse. In summer 2010 he appeared as the detective in a touring production of the Peter Gordon comedy Murdered to Death. In 2016 he toured with The Rocky Horror Show and in 2017 the new production of Hairspray.

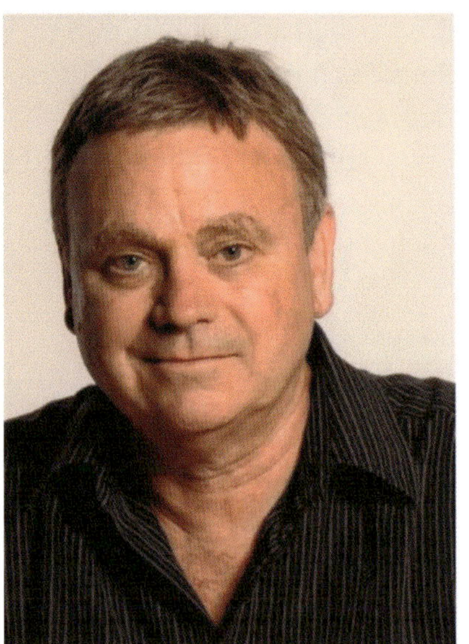

Sir Anthony Charles Lynton Blair KG was born 6th May 1953 and was a British politician who served as Prime Minister of the United Kingdom from 1997 to 2007 and Leader of the Labour Party from 1994 to 2007. In 1997, the Labour Party won its largest landslide general election victory in its history. Blair became the country's youngest leader since 1812 and remains the party's longest-serving occupant of the office. His government held referendums in which Scottish and Welsh electorates voted in favour of devolved administration, paving the way for the establishment of the Scottish Parliament and Welsh Assembly in 1999. He was also involved in negotiating the Good Friday Agreement. Blair oversaw British interventions in Kosovo (1999) and Sierra Leone (2000), which were generally perceived as successful. During the War on Terror, he supported the foreign policy of the George W. Bush administration and ensured that the British Armed Forces participated in the War in Afghanistan from 2001.

Graeme James Souness was born 6th May 1953 and was a Scottish former professional football player, manager, and is a current pundit on Sky Sports. Souness' career began as an apprentice at Tottenham Hotspur under Bill Nicholson. He signed professional forms as a 15-year-old in 1968. Frustrated at a lack of first-team opportunities, the teenage Souness reputedly informed Nicholson he was the best player at the club. Souness made one first-team appearance for Spurs, in a UEFA Cup tie as a substitute. Spurs sold Souness to Middlesbrough for £30,000 in 1972. He made his first appearance for Middlesbrough on 6th January 1973 in a 2–1 league defeat to Fulham at Craven Cottage. His first goal came on 11 December 1973 in a 3–0 league victory over Preston North End at Ayresome Park. Souness' playing career is best remembered for his seven seasons at Liverpool, where he won five League Championships, three European Cups and four League Cups.

Ian John McKay, VC born 7th May 1953 and sadly passed away 12th June 1982 and was a British Army soldier and a posthumous recipient of the Victoria Cross, the highest award for gallantry in the face of the enemy that can be awarded to British and Commonwealth forces. McKay left school at seventeen and in August 1970 enlisted in the Army, training as a paratrooper. Posted to the 1st Battalion, the Parachute Regiment (1 Para) in early 1971, he served in Northern Ireland, Germany, and the United Kingdom. By April 1982 he was platoon sergeant of 4 Platoon, B Company, 3rd Battalion, The Parachute Regiment, and deployed with his unit for service in the Falklands War. He was killed during the Battle of Mount Longdon, when the deed described below took place, for which he was awarded the Victoria Cross.
McKay's medals were sold by his wife around the year 2000, and his VC is now on display in the Lord Ashcroft Gallery at the Imperial War Museum, London.

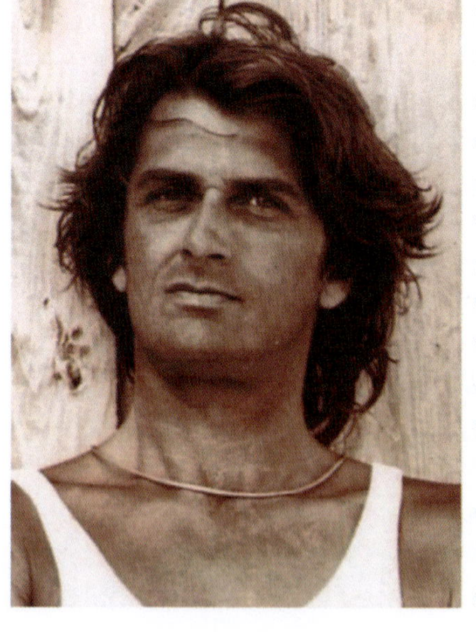

Michael Gordon Oldfield was born 15th May 1953 and is a British musician, songwriter, and producer best known for his debut studio album Tubular Bells (1973), which became an unexpected critical and commercial success and propelled him to worldwide fame. Though primarily a guitarist, Oldfield is known for playing a range of instruments, which includes keyboards, percussion, and vocals. He has adopted a range of musical styles throughout his career, including progressive rock, world, folk, classical, electronic, ambient, and new age music. Oldfield took up the guitar at age ten and left school in his teens to embark on a music career. From 1967 to 1970, he and his sister Sally Oldfield were a folk duo The Sallyangie, after which he performed with Kevin Ayers. In 1971, Oldfield started work on Tubular Bells which caught the attention of Richard Branson, who agreed to release it on his new label, Virgin Records. Its opening was used in the horror film The Exorcist and the album went on to sell over 2.7 million copies in the UK.

Victoria Wood CBE born 19th May 1953 and passed away 20th April 2016 and was an English comedian, actress, lyricist, singer, composer, pianist, screenwriter, producer and director. Wood started her career in 1974 by appearing on, and winning, the ATV talent show New Faces. She established herself as a comedy star in the 1980s, winning a BAFTA TV Award in 1986 for the sketch series Victoria Wood: As Seen on TV (1985–87), and became one of Britain's most popular stand-up comics. In April 1993, Wood began a seven-month tour of the UK. In 1994, Wood starred in the one-off BBC 50-minute programme based on her 1993/94 stage show Victoria Wood: Live in Your Own Home. In October 1997, Wood released a compilation of 14 of her songs titled Victoria Wood, Real Life the Songs. In early 2015, Wood took part in a celebrity version of The Great British Bake Off for Comic Relief and was crowned Star Baker in her episode.

Michael Denzil Xavier Portillo was born 26th May 1953 and was is a British journalist, broadcaster and former politician. His broadcast series include railway documentaries such as Great British Railway Journeys and Great Continental Railway Journeys. First elected to the House of Commons in a 1984 by-election, Portillo served as a junior minister under both Margaret Thatcher and John Major, before entering the Cabinet in 1992 as Chief Secretary to the Treasury, before being promoted to Secretary of State for Employment in 1994.
Since leaving politics, Portillo has pursued his media interests by presenting and participating in a wide range of television and radio programmes. Portillo's passion for steam trains led him to make the BBC documentary series Great British Railway Journeys, beginning in 2010, in which he travels the British railway networks, referring to various editions of Bradshaw's Guide. The success of the show led Portillo to present series about railway systems in other countries.

Hilary Robert Jones MBE was born 19th June 1953 and is an English general practitioner, presenter and writer on medical issues, known for his media appearances, most especially on television. He has written for News of the World (and The Sun on Sunday) magazines. Jones became the TV-am doctor from May 1989 and has featured regularly on GMTV since 1993, where he was the health and medical advisor. In 2010, GMTV was replaced by Daybreak and Lorraine, where Jones continued to work as Health Editor. In 2014, Daybreak was replaced by Good Morning Britain, with Jones transferring to the show. As part of this role, he reports on emerging medical news stories as well as informing the public about various medical problems such as weight issues, contraception, surgery and cancer. Jones has been appearing on the programme throughout each morning during the coronavirus pandemic. In 2013, Jones appeared on The Chase Celebrity Special. He and the other members of the team defeated "The Chaser", Paul Sinha.

Alan Sunderland born 1st July 1953 and was an English former footballer who played as a forward in the Football League for Wolverhampton Wanderers, Arsenal and Ipswich Town. He was also capped once for England. In November 1977, he joined Arsenal for £220,000. Whilst at Highbury he switched from being within the role of a midfielder to that of a centre forward. Sunderland became a regular starter for the club, playing in the 1978 FA Cup Final, which Arsenal lost to Ipswich Town. Sunderland's most famous moment came in the 1979 FA Cup Final. During the game Arsenal had gone 2–0 up against Manchester United, with goals from Brian Talbot and Frank Stapleton, and looked set for victory with only five minutes remaining. However, United scored twice in three minutes, with goals from Gordon McQueen and Sammy McIlroy, and extra time loomed. In the very last minute of the match, Arsenal pushed forward in a desperate counter-attack. Liam Brady fed Graham Rix on the left wing, and his cross was converted by Sunderland at the far post to make the score 3–2, and win the cup.

Nigel Ernest James Mansell CBE was born on 8th August 1953 and was a British former racing driver who won both the Formula One World Championship (1992) and the CART Indy Car World Series (1993). Mansell was the reigning F1 champion when he moved over to CART, becoming the first person to win the CART title in his debut season, and making him the only person to hold both the World Drivers' Championship and the American open-wheel National Championship simultaneously.

His career in Formula One spanned 15 seasons, with his final two full seasons of top-level racing being spent in the CART series. Mansell is the second most successful British Formula One driver of all time in terms of race wins with 31 victories, (behind Lewis Hamilton with 103 wins), and is seventh overall on the Formula One race winners list, behind Hamilton, Michael Schumacher, Sebastian Vettel, Alain Prost, Ayrton Senna and Fernando Alonso.

Labatt's

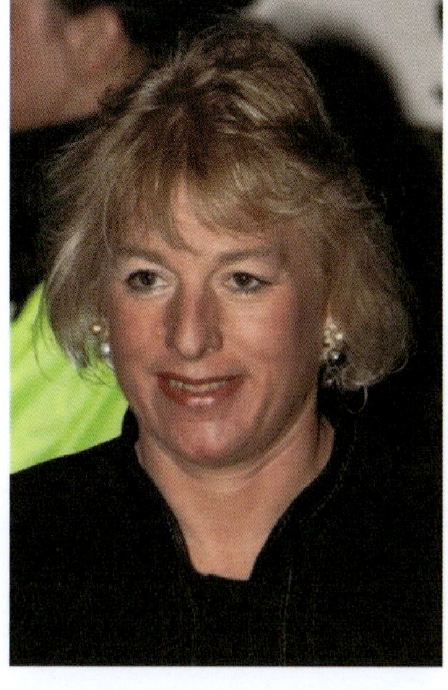

Carol Jane Thatcher born 15th August 1953 and is an English journalist, author and media personality. She is the daughter of Margaret Thatcher, the British prime minister from 1979 to 1990, and Denis Thatcher. Thatcher began her career as a journalist in Australia, working on the Sydney Morning Herald from 1977 to 1979. She became a TV reporter at Channel Seven, also in Sydney, and later a reporter on its news morning show, 11AM. On her return to Britain, she worked as a presenter for LBC, BBC Radio 4, TV-am and wrote travel articles for The Daily Telegraph. Due to her mother's high-profile political position, many newspapers refused to publish work with her by-line. In November 2005 Thatcher was selected to appear with a number of fellow celebrities on the ITV television show I'm a Celebrity...Get Me Out of Here! The format of the show meant that she would be forced to spend at least a week in the Australian rainforest with a minimal supply of food in basic living conditions. Ultimately, she emerged as the fifth series winner and second 'Queen of the Jungle'.

Diane Julie Abbott MP born 27th September 1953 and is a British politician who has been the Member of Parliament (MP) for Hackney North and Stoke Newington since 1987. A socialist member of the Labour Party, she served in Jeremy Corbyn's Shadow Cabinet as Shadow Home Secretary from 2016 to 2020. Abbott is the first black woman elected to Parliament, and the longest-serving black MP in the House of Commons. A supporter of Jeremy Corbyn's bid to become Labour Leader in 2015, Abbott became Shadow Secretary of State for International Development, then Shadow Health Secretary, and eventually Shadow Home Secretary. As a key Corbyn ally, she supported his leftward push of the Labour Party. She unsuccessfully attempted to be the Labour candidate for the 2016 London mayoral election, and backed the unsuccessful Britain Stronger in Europe campaign to retain UK membership of the European Union. After the 2019 general election, Abbott left the Shadow Cabinet

Leslie Dennis Heseltine born 12th October 1953 and is an English television presenter, actor, and comedian. In 1982, Dennis joined as one of the teams on Russ Abbot's Madhouse and The Russ Abbot Show before forming a comedy partnership with fellow impressionist Dustin Gee, which in turn led to a series of their own, The Laughter Show. Following Gee's sudden and unexpected death in January 1986, Dennis carried on The Laughter Show as a solo performer and became the third host of Family Fortunes for a 15-year run between 1987 and 2002. It was at a recording of an episode of Family Fortunes in 1997 that Dennis was surprised by This Is Your Life. In 2017, Dennis played the role of Uncle Fester on the UK tour of the musical production of The Addams Family. In 2019, Dennis performed with the Royal Shakespeare Company in Restoration plays The Provoked Wife and Venice Preserved. In November/December 2021, Dennis performed as Sir Joseph in the English National Opera Performance of HMS Pinafore at the London Coliseum.

James Cameron Davidson OBE born 13th December 1953 and is an English stand-up comedian. He hosted the television shows Big Break and The Generation Game. Davidson found his way into show business when, as a regular in a pub in Woolwich, he stepped in after the pub's regular comedian had not turned up. He then became a regular on the London comedy circuit, and first auditioned unsuccessfully for Opportunity Knocks in 1975. His audition for New Faces was more successful, and he proceeded to win the show by one point, coming second in the overall contest. He starred in TV sitcoms Up the Elephant and Round the Castle (1983–1985) and Home James! (1987–1990). His one-man show for Thames Television, Stand Up Jim Davidson (1990).

On 3rd January 2014, a year after being arrested and without being charged, he became a housemate in the show's 13th series. On 29th January 2014, he left the Big Brother house as the winner.

BRITISH DEATHS

Mary of Teck (Victoria Mary Augusta Louise Olga Pauline Claudine Agnes; 26 May 1867 – 24 March 1953) was Queen of the United Kingdom and the British Dominions, and Empress of India, from 6th May 1910 until 29th January 1936 as the wife of King-Emperor George V. At the age of 24, she was betrothed to her second cousin once removed Prince Albert Victor, Duke of Clarence and Avondale, but six weeks after the announcement of the engagement, he died unexpectedly during an influenza pandemic. The following year, she became engaged to Albert Victor's only surviving brother, George, who subsequently became king. Before her husband's accession, she was successively Duchess of York, Duchess of Cornwall, and Princess of Wales. After George's death in 1936, she became queen mother when her eldest son, Edward VIII, ascended the throne; but to her dismay, he abdicated later the same year in order to marry twice-divorced American socialite Wallis Simpson.

John Reginald Halliday Christie born 8th April 1899 and died 15th July 1953, known to his family and friends as Reg Christie, was an English serial killer and alleged necrophile active during the 1940s and early 1950s. He murdered at least eight people—including his wife, Ethel—by strangling them in his flat at 10 Rillington Place, Notting Hill, London. The bodies of three of Christie's victims were found in a wallpaper-covered kitchen alcove soon after Christie moved out of Rillington Place during March 1953. The remains of two more victims were discovered in the garden, and his wife's body was found beneath the floorboards of the front room. Christie was arrested and convicted of his wife's murder, for which he was hanged. Two of Christie's victims were Beryl Evans and her baby daughter Geraldine, who, along with Beryl's husband, Timothy Evans, were tenants at 10 Rillington Place during 1948–49.

Dylan Marlais Thomas born 27th October 1914 and died 9th November 1953 and was a Welsh poet and writer whose works include the poems "Do not go gentle into that good night" and "And death shall have no dominion"; the "play for voices" Under Milk Wood; and stories and radio broadcasts such as A Child's Christmas in Wales and Portrait of the Artist as a Young Dog. He became widely popular in his lifetime and remained so after his death at the age of 39 in New York City. By then he had acquired a reputation, which he had encouraged, as a "roistering, drunken and doomed poet".

Thomas came to be appreciated as a popular poet during his lifetime, though he found earning a living as a writer was difficult. He began augmenting his income with reading tours and radio broadcasts. His radio recordings for the BBC during the late 1940s brought him to the public's attention, and he was frequently used by the BBC as an accessible voice of the literary scene.

SPORTING EVENTS 1953

1953 County Cricket Season

The 1953 County Championship was the 54th officially organised running of the County Championship. Surrey won the Championship title.

On 16th May 1953, the match between Surrey and Warwickshire finished within the first day, with Surrey winning by an innings and 49 runs.

Surrey won seven consecutive titles from 1952 to 1958. Surrey won 23 of its 28 county matches in 1955, the most wins by any team in the County Championship and a record which can no longer be beaten (as fewer than 23 matches have been played each season since 1993). Surrey have won the County Championship 19 times outright (and shared once), a number exceeded only by Yorkshire, with their most recent win being in 2018.

1845
SURREY
COUNTY CRICKET CLUB

Position	Team	Played	Won	Lost	Drawn	No Dec	1st inn lead match L	1st inn lead match D	Points
1	Surrey	28	13	4	10	1	0	7	184
2	Sussex	28	11	3	13	1	1	8	168
=3	Lancashire	28	10	4	10	4	1	8	156
=3	Leicestershire	28	10	7	11	0	3	6	156
5	Middlesex	28	10	5	11	1	1	5	150
=6	Derbyshire	28	9	7	9	3	2	5	136
=6	Gloucestershire	28	9	7	10	2	2	5	136
8	Nottinghamshire	28	9	10	8	1	4	1	128
9	Warwickshire	28	6	7	14	1	2	11	124
10	Glamorgan	28	8	4	14	2	0	6	120
11	Northamptonshire	28	6	3	15	3	2	7	114
=12	Essex	28	6	7	13	2	1	6	100
=12	Yorkshire	28	6	6	13	3	1	6	100
14	Hampshire	28	6	11	11	0	2	4	96
15	Worcestershire	28	5	12	10	1	1	2	72
16	Kent	28	4	14	8	2	1	3	64
17	Somerset	28	2	19	6	1	0	3	36

1952–53 in English football

The 1952–53 season was the 54th completed season of The Football League.

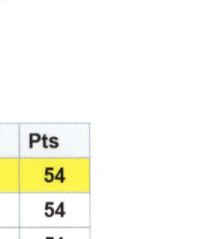

Arsenal won their second league title of the post-war era, finishing ahead of runners-up Preston North End on goal average - denying their nearest rivals a first league title since they won the first two English Football League titles more than 60 years earlier. Wolverhampton Wanderers bounced back after two disappointing seasons to finish third, three points short of the title. They finished one point ahead of their local rivals West Bromwich Albion. Defending champions Manchester United, in a period of transition as the team captained by Johnny Carey started to make way for a younger generation of players finished eighth.

Pos	Team	Pld	HW	HD	HL	AW	AD	AL	Pts
1	Arsenal	42	15	3	3	6	9	6	**54**
2	Preston North End	42	15	3	3	6	9	6	**54**
3	Wolverhampton Wanderers	42	13	5	3	6	8	7	**51**
4	West Bromwich Albion	42	13	3	5	8	5	8	**50**
5	Charlton Athletic	42	12	8	1	7	3	11	**49**
6	Burnley	42	11	6	4	7	6	8	**48**
7	Blackpool	42	13	5	3	6	4	11	**47**
8	Manchester United	42	11	5	5	7	5	9	**46**
9	Sunderland	42	11	9	1	4	4	13	**43**
10	Tottenham Hotspur	42	11	6	4	4	5	12	**41**
11	Aston Villa	42	9	7	5	5	6	10	**41**
12	Cardiff City	42	7	8	6	7	4	10	**40**
13	Middlesbrough	42	12	5	4	2	6	13	**39**
14	Bolton Wanderers	42	9	4	8	6	5	10	**39**
15	Portsmouth	42	10	6	5	4	4	13	**38**
16	Newcastle United	42	9	5	7	5	4	12	**37**
17	Liverpool	42	10	6	5	4	2	15	**36**
18	Sheffield Wednesday	42	8	6	7	4	5	12	**35**
19	Chelsea	42	10	4	7	2	7	12	**35**
20	Manchester City	42	12	2	7	2	5	14	**35**
21	Stoke City	42	10	4	7	2	6	13	**34**
22	Derby County	42	9	6	6	2	4	15	**32**

1952–53 Scottish Division A

The 1952–53 season was the 80th season of competitive football in Scotland and the 56th season of the Scottish Football League. Rangers won the title with a 1–1 draw in their last match, away to Queen of the South. Rangers equalised with 17 minutes to go and thereby won the league on goal average from Hibernian, thus preventing Hibs from winning their third title in a row.

Pos	Team	Pld	W	D	L	GF	GA	GR	Pts
1	Rangers	30	18	7	5	80	39	2.051	**43**
2	Hibernian	30	19	5	6	93	51	1.824	**43**
3	East Fife	30	16	7	7	72	48	1.500	**39**
4	Heart of Midlothian	30	12	6	12	59	50	1.180	**30**
5	Clyde	30	13	4	13	78	78	1.000	**30**
6	St Mirren	30	11	8	11	52	58	0.897	**30**
7	Dundee	30	9	11	10	44	37	1.189	**29**
8	Celtic	30	11	7	12	51	54	0.944	**29**
9	Partick Thistle	30	10	9	11	55	63	0.873	**29**
10	Queen of the South	30	10	8	12	43	61	0.705	**28**
11	Aberdeen	30	11	5	14	64	68	0.941	**27**
12	Raith Rovers	30	9	8	13	47	53	0.887	**26**
13	Falkirk	30	11	4	15	53	63	0.841	**26**
14	Airdrieonians	30	10	6	14	53	75	0.707	**26**
15	Motherwell	30	10	5	15	57	80	0.713	**25**
16	Third Lanark	30	8	4	18	52	75	0.693	**20**

1952–53 Scottish Division B

The 1952–53 Scottish Division B was won by Stirling Albion who, along with second placed Hamilton Academical, were promoted to the Division A. Albion Rovers finished bottom.

Pos	Team	Pld	W	D	L	GF	GA	GD	Pts
1	Stirling Albion	30	20	4	6	64	43	+21	**44**
2	Hamilton Academical	30	20	3	7	72	40	+32	**43**
3	Queen's Park	30	15	7	8	70	46	+24	**37**
4	Kilmarnock	30	17	2	11	74	48	+26	**36**
5	Ayr United	30	17	2	11	76	56	+20	**36**
6	Morton	30	15	3	12	79	57	+22	**33**
7	Arbroath	30	13	7	10	52	57	−5	**33**
8	Dundee United	30	12	5	13	52	56	−4	**29**
9	Alloa Athletic	30	12	5	13	63	68	−5	**29**
10	Dumbarton	30	11	6	13	58	67	−9	**28**
11	Dunfermline Athletic	30	9	9	12	51	58	−7	**27**
12	Stenhousemuir	30	10	6	14	56	65	−9	**26**
13	Cowdenbeath	30	8	7	15	37	54	−17	**23**
14	St Johnstone	30	8	6	16	41	63	−22	**22**
15	Forfar Athletic	30	8	4	18	54	88	−34	**20**
16	Albion Rovers	30	5	4	21	44	77	−33	**14**

1953 Five Nations Championship

The 1953 Five Nations Championship was the twenty-fourth series of the rugby union Five Nations Championship. Including the previous incarnations as the Home Nations and Five Nations, this was the fifty-ninth series of the northern hemisphere rugby union championship. Ten matches were played between 10th January and 28th March. It was contested by England, France, Ireland, Scotland and Wales. England won its 14th title.

Table

Position	Nation	Games				Points			Table points
		Played	Won	Drawn	Lost	For	Against	Difference	
1	England	4	3	1	0	54	20	+38	**7**
2	Wales	4	3	0	1	26	14	+12	**6**
3	Ireland	4	2	1	1	54	25	+29	**5**
4	France	4	1	0	3	17	38	−21	**2**
5	Scotland	4	0	0	4	21	75	−54	**0**

Results

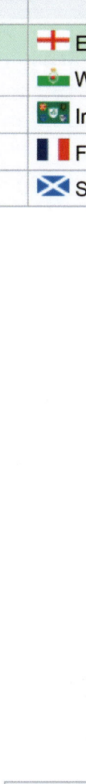

France	11–5	Scotland
Wales	3–8	England
Ireland	16–3	France
Scotland	0–12	Wales
Ireland	9–9	England
England	11–0	France
Scotland	8–26	Ireland
Wales	5–3	Ireland
England	26–8	Scotland
France	3–6	Wales

Nation	Venue	City	Captain
England	Twickenham	London	Nim Hall
France	Stade Olympiqu Yves-du-Manoir	Colombes	Guy Basquet
Ireland	Lansdowne Road	Dublin	Des O'Brien
Scotland	Murrayfield	Edinburgh	Peter Kininmonth/Arthur Dorward
Wales	National Stadium/St. Helens	Cardiff/Swansea	John Gwilliam

The Masters 1953

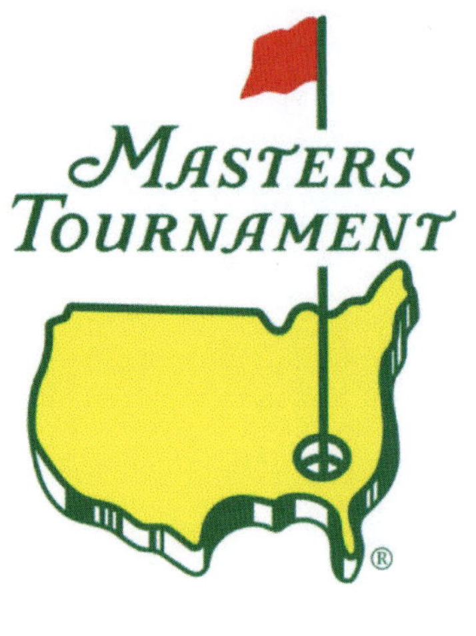
MASTERS
TOURNAMENT

The 1953 Masters Tournament was the 17th Masters Tournament, held April 9th–12th at Augusta National Golf Club in Augusta, Georgia.

Ben Hogan shattered the Masters scoring record by five strokes with a 274 (−14), which stood for 12 years, until Jack Nicklaus' 271 in 1965. Hogan shot four rounds of 70 or better, and went on to win the U.S. Open by six strokes in June and the British Open by four in July. Through 2020, it remains the only time these three majors were won in the same calendar year.

Hogan, age forty, finished five strokes ahead of runner-up Ed Oliver to win his second Masters, the seventh of his nine major titles. This win was commemorated five years later in 1958 with the dedication of the Hogan Bridge over Rae's Creek at the par-3 12th hole.

Hogan was the first Masters winner over age forty; a few months older than Hogan, Sam Snead won the next year at 41.

Place	Player	Score	To par	Money (US$)
1	Ben Hogan (c)	70-69-66-69=274	−14	4,000
2	Ed Oliver	69-73-67-70=279	−9	2,500
3	Lloyd Mangrum	74-68-71-69=282	−6	1,700
4	Bob Hamilton	71-69-70-73=283	−5	1,400
T5	Tommy Bolt	71-75-68-71=285	−3	900
	Chick Harbert	68-73-70-74=285		
7	Ted Kroll	71-70-73-72=286	−2	700
8	Jack Burke Jr.	78-69-69-71=287	−1	650
9	Al Besselink	69-75-70-74=288	E	600
T10	Julius Boros	73-71-75-70=289	+1	523
	Chandler Harper	74-72-69-74=289		
	Fred Hawkins	75-70-74-70=289		

Augusta National Golf Club, sometimes referred to as Augusta or the National, is one of the most famous and exclusive golf clubs in the world, located in Augusta, Georgia, United States. Unlike most private clubs which operate as non-profits, Augusta National is a for-profit corporation, and it does not disclose its income, holdings, membership list, or ticket sales.

Founded by Bobby Jones and Clifford Roberts, the course was designed by Jones and Alister Mackenzie and opened for play in 1932. Since 1934, the club has played host to the annual Masters Tournament, one of the four major championships in professional golf, and the only major played each year at the same course. It was the top-ranked course in Golf Digest's 2009 list of America's 100 greatest courses and was the number ten-ranked course based on course architecture on Golf week Magazine's 2011 list of best classic courses in the United States.

Cheltenham Gold Cup 1953

Knock Hard was an Irish Thoroughbred racehorse who won the 1953 Cheltenham Gold Cup. He showed good form on the flat, winning the Irish Lincoln Handicap and finished second in the Irish Cesarewitch and the November Handicap. As a steeplechaser he was a fast but unreliable jumper who fell when well fancied in both the King George VI Chase and the Cheltenham Gold Cup in the 1951/52 National Hunt season.

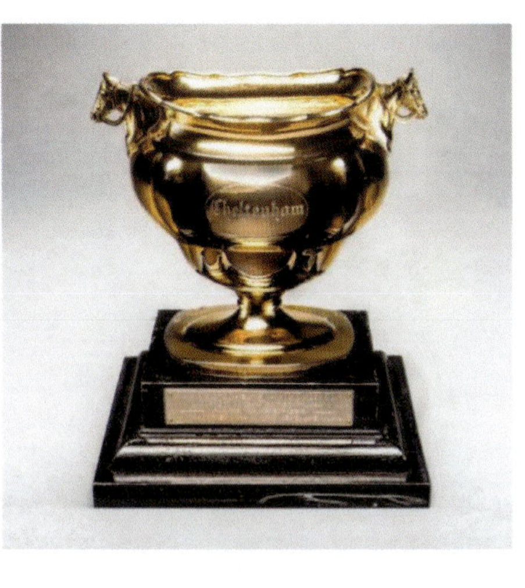
Cheltenham

In the following year his early form was inconsistent but he then won the Great Yorkshire Chase before defeating a strong field in the Gold Cup. His subsequent form deteriorated and he was retired to become a hunter in England.

Triple Crown

2,000 Guineas 1953

Nearula was an Irish-bred British-trained Thoroughbred racehorse and sire, best known for winning the classic 2000 Guineas in 1953. Trained in Yorkshire, he was the top-rated British two-year-olds of 1952 when he won the Middle Park Stakes. In the following year he won the 2000 Guineas and the St James's Palace Stakes over one mile and the Champion Stakes against older horses over ten furlongs. He won two further races as a four-year-old before being retired to stud, where he had some success as a sire of winners before dying at the age of ten.

The Derby 1953

Pinza was a Thoroughbred racehorse and sire. In a career which lasted just over a year– from July 1952 until July 1953– he ran seven times and won five races. He was the best British colt of his generation in 1953, when he won The Derby and the King George VI & Queen Elizabeth Stakes. He was then retired to stud, where he had little success. Pinza ran against older horses in the third running of the King George VI & Queen Elizabeth Stakes at Ascot, starting the 2/1 favourite in a field of thirteen which included the winners of the Prix de l'Arc de Triomphe (Nuccio) and the Washington, D.C. International Stakes (Worden). He produced what was described as a "brilliant burst of speed" to win by three lengths, again beating Aureole, with Worden third. Pinza was being prepared for a run in the St Leger when he sustained a tendon injury in training. He was unable to race again and was retired to stud at a valuation on £220,000.

St Leger 1953

Premonition was a British Thoroughbred racehorse and sire. In a career which lasted from autumn 1952 until July 1954 he ran fourteen times and won eight races. He won the Classic St Leger as a three-year-old in 1953, a year in which he also won the Great Voltigeur Stakes and was controversially disqualified in the Irish Derby. He won the Yorkshire Cup as a four-year-old in 1954 before being retire to stud, where he made very little impact as a stallion. In the Derby at Epsom, Premonition started 5/1 joint-favourite with Pinza in a field of twenty-seven runners. He was never in contention at any stage and finished unplaced behind Pinza and the Queen's colt Aureole

1953 British Grand Prix

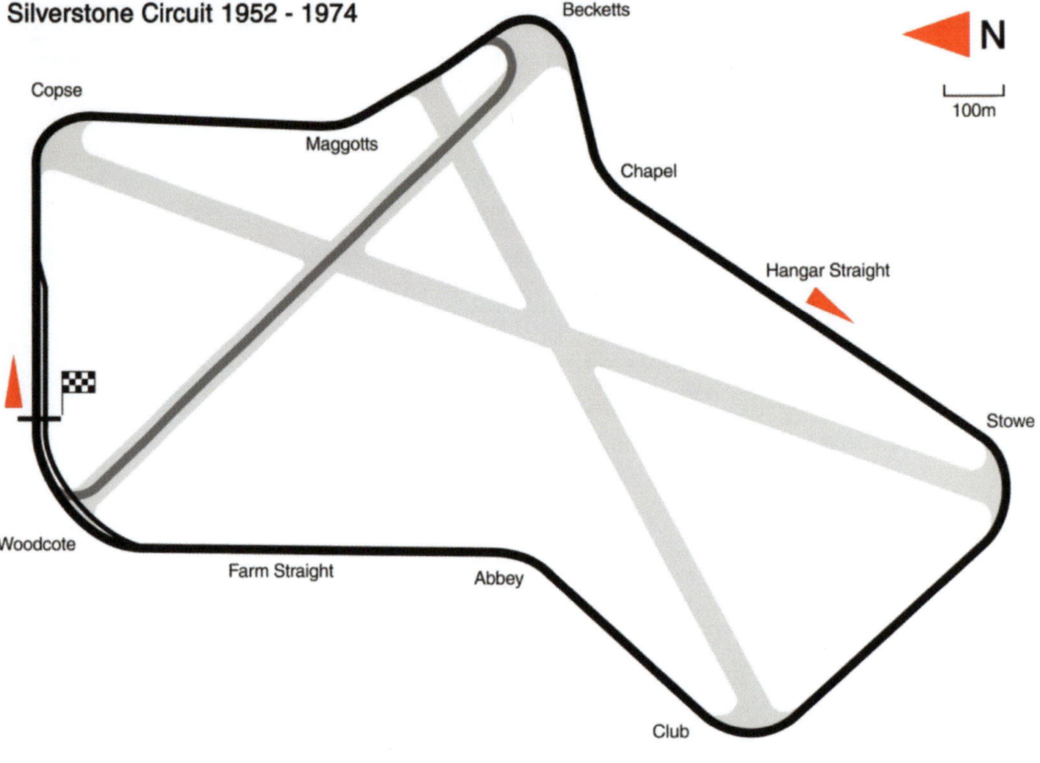
Silverstone Circuit 1952 - 1974
Becketts
N
100m
Copse
Maggotts
Chapel
Hangar Straight
Stowe
Woodcote
Farm Straight
Abbey
Club

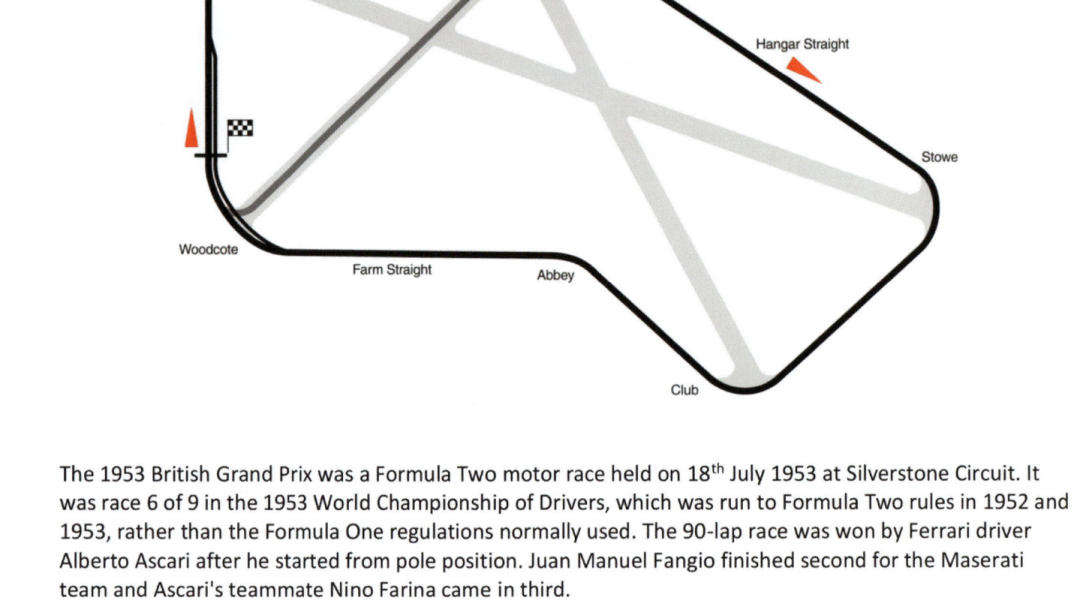

The 1953 British Grand Prix was a Formula Two motor race held on 18th July 1953 at Silverstone Circuit. It was race 6 of 9 in the 1953 World Championship of Drivers, which was run to Formula Two rules in 1952 and 1953, rather than the Formula One regulations normally used. The 90-lap race was won by Ferrari driver Alberto Ascari after he started from pole position. Juan Manuel Fangio finished second for the Maserati team and Ascari's teammate Nino Farina came in third.

Final Placings

Pos	No	Driver	Constructor	Laps	Time/Retired	Grid	Points
1	5	**Alberto Ascari**	**Ferrari**	90	2:50:00	1	**8.5**
2	23	**Juan Manuel Fangio**	**Maserati**	90	+ 1:00	4	**6**
3	6	**Nino Farina**	**Ferrari**	88	+ 2 Laps	5	**4**
4	24	**José Froilán González**	**Maserati**	88	+ 2 Laps	2	**3.5**
5	8	**Mike Hawthorn**	**Ferrari**	87	+ 3 Laps	3	**2**
6	25	Felice Bonetto	Maserati	82	+ 8 Laps	16	
7	10	Prince Bira	Connaught-Lea-Francis	82	+ 8 Laps	19	
8	16	Ken Wharton	Cooper-Bristol	80	+ 10 Laps	11	
9	20	Peter Whitehead	Cooper-Alta	79	+ 11 Laps	14	
10	9	Louis Rosier	Ferrari	78	+ 12 Laps	24	

Includes 0.5 points for shared fastest lap

1953 Wimbledon Championships

The 1953 Wimbledon Championships took place on the outdoor grass courts at the All England Lawn Tennis and Croquet Club in Wimbledon, London, United Kingdom. The tournament was held from Monday 22nd June until Saturday 4th July 1953. It was the 67th staging of the Wimbledon Championships, and the third Grand Slam tennis event of 1953. Vic Seixas and Maureen Connolly won the singles titles.

Men's Singles

In the 1953 Wimbledon Championships – Gentlemen's Singles, second seed Vic Seixas defeated the unseeded Kurt Nielsen in the final, 9–7, 6–3, 6–4, to take the Gentlemen's Singles tennis title. Frank Sedgman was the defending champion, but was ineligible to compete after turning professional.

Women's Singles

Maureen Connolly successfully defended her title, defeating Doris Hart in the final, 8–6, 7–5 to win the Ladies' Singles tennis title at the 1953 Wimbledon Championships.

Men's Doubles

Ken McGregor and Frank Sedgman were the defending champions, but were ineligible to compete after turning professional. Lew Hoad and Ken Rosewall defeated Rex Hartwig and Mervyn Rose in the final, 6–4, 7–5, 4–6, 7–5 to win the Gentlemen' Doubles tennis title at the 1953 Wimbledon Championship.

Women's Doubles

Shirley Fry and Doris Hart successfully defended their title, defeating Maureen Connolly and Julia Sampson in the final, 6–0, 6–0 to win the Ladies' Doubles tennis title at the 1953 Wimbledon Championships.

Mixed Doubles

Frank Sedgman and Doris Hart were the defending champions, but Sedgman was ineligible to compete after turning professional. Hart partnered with Vic Seixas, and they defeated Enrique Morea and Shirley Fry in the final, 9–7, 7–5 to win the Mixed Doubles tennis title at the 1953 Wimbledon Championships.

Frank Sedgman

Maureen Connolly

BOOKS PUBLISHED IN 1953

A Pocket Full of Rye is a work of detective fiction by Agatha Christie and first published in the UK by the Collins Crime Club on 9th November 1953, and in the US by Dodd, Mead & Co. the following year. The UK edition retailed at ten shillings and sixpence (10/6) and the US edition at $2.75. The book features her detective Miss Marple. Like several of Christie's novels (e.g., Hickory Dickory Dock and One, Two, Buckle My Shoe) the title and substantial parts of the plot reference a nursery rhyme, in this case "Sing a Song of Sixpence". Miss Marple travels to the Fortescue home to offer information on the maid, Gladys Martin. She works with Inspector Neele until the mysteries are revealed.

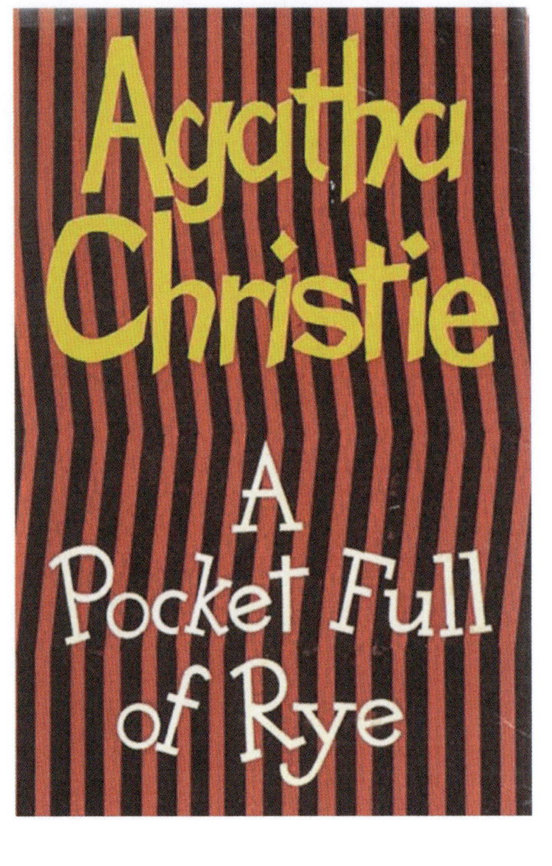
Agatha
Christie
A
Pocket Full
of Rye

Two reviewers at the time of publication felt that "the hidden mechanism of the plot is ingenious at the expense of probability" and that the novel was "Not quite so stunning as some of Mrs Christie's criminal assaults upon her readers". Christie's overall high quality in writing detective novels led one to say "they ought to make her a Dame". Writing later, another reviewer felt that the characters included an "exceptionally nasty family of suspects" in what was "Still, a good, sour read."

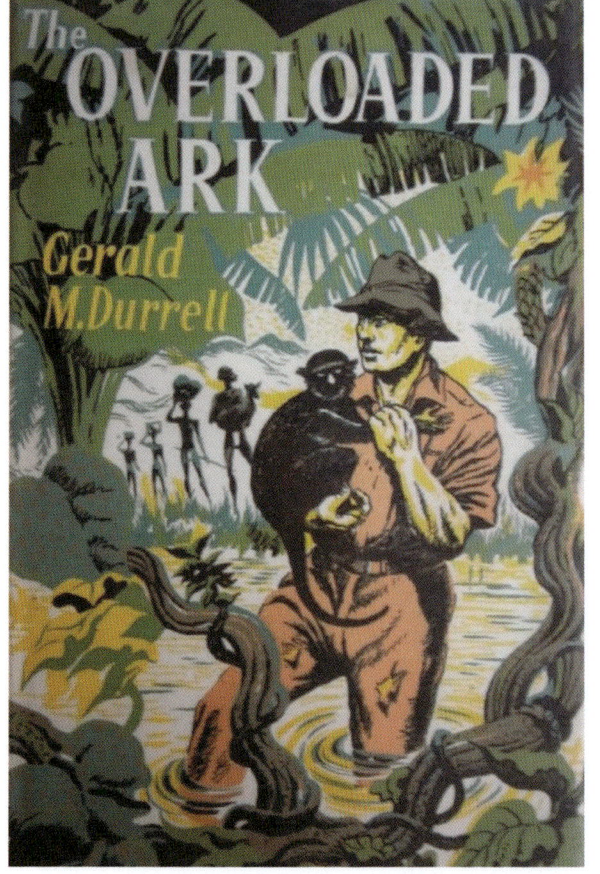
The
OVERLOADED
ARK
Gerald
M.Durrell

The Overloaded Ark first published in 1953, is the debut book by British naturalist Gerald Durrell. It is the chronicle of a six-month collecting trip, from December 1947 to August 1948, to the West African colony of British Cameroon – now Cameroon – that Durrell made with aviculturist and ornithologist John Yealland.

Their reasons for going on the trip were twofold: "to collect and bring back alive some of the fascinating animals, birds, and reptiles that inhabit the region", and secondly, for both men to realise a long-cherished dream to see Africa.

Its combination of comic exaggeration and environmental accuracy, portrayed in Durrell's light, clever prose, made it a great success. It launched Durrell's career as a writer of both non-fiction and fiction, which in turn financed his work as a zookeeper and conservationist.

The Bafut Beagles and A Zoo in My Luggage are sequels of sorts, telling of his later returns to the region.

Casino Royale is the first novel by the British author Ian Fleming. Published in 1953, it is the first James Bond book.

The story concerns the British secret agent James Bond, gambling at the casino in Royale-les-Eaux to bankrupt Le Chiffre, the treasurer of a French union and a member of the Russian secret service. Bond is supported in his endeavours by Vesper Lynd, a member of his own service, as well as Felix Leiter of the CIA and René Mathis of the French Deuxième Bureau. Fleming used his wartime experiences as a member of the Naval Intelligence Division, and the people he met during his work, to provide plot elements; the character of Bond also reflected many of Fleming's personal tastes. Fleming wrote the draft in early 1952 at his Goldeneye estate in Jamaica while awaiting his marriage. He was initially unsure whether the work was suitable for publication, but was assured by his friend, the novelist William Plomer, that the novel had promise. Within the spy storyline, Casino Royale deals with themes of Britain's position in the world, particularly the relationship with the US in light of the defections to the Soviet Union of the British agents Guy Burgess and Donald Maclean.

CASINO
ROYALE
A WHISPER OF LOVE
A WHISPER OF HATE
by
IAN
FLEMING

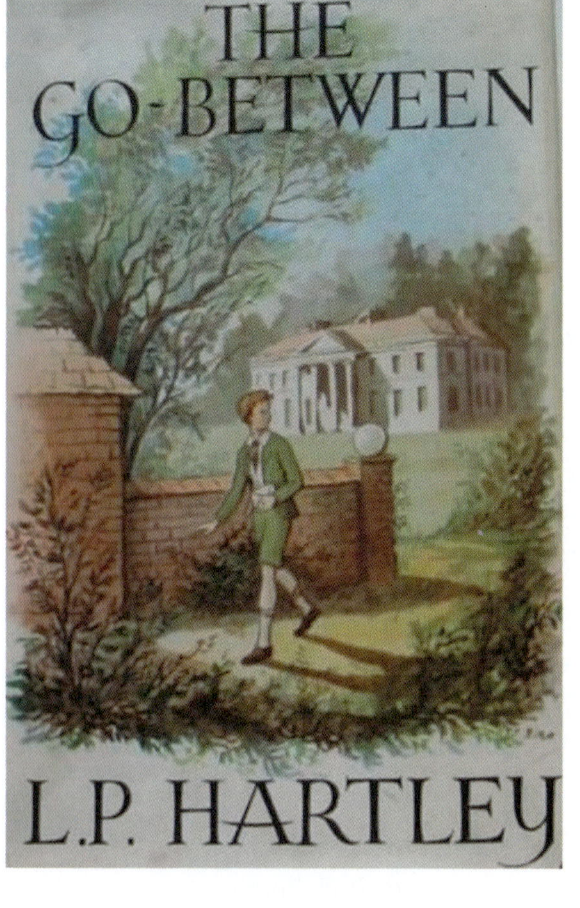
THE
GO-BETWEEN
L.P. HARTLEY

The Go-Between is a novel by L. P. Hartley published in 1953. His best-known work, it has been adapted several times for stage and screen. The book gives a critical view of society at the end of the Victorian era through the eyes of a naïve schoolboy outsider. In the book's prologue, Leo Colston chances upon a diary from 1900, the year of his thirteenth birthday, and gradually pieces together a memory that he has suppressed. Under its influence, and from the viewpoint of what he has become by the midpoint of "this hideous century", Leo relives the events of what had once seemed to him its hopeful beginning. The importance of his boarding school's social rules is another theme running through the book and complicates Leo's interaction with the adult world. "Curses" of his devising had routed boys who were bullying Leo at school and had given him the reputation of a magician, something that he came to half-believe himself. As a result, he is invited as a guest to spend the summer at Brandham Hall, the country home of his school friend, Marcus Maudsley. There the socially clumsy Leo, with his regional accent, is a middle-class boy among the wealthy upper class. Though he does not fit in, his hosts do their best to make him feel welcome, treating him with kindness and indulgence, especially their daughter Marian.

The Silver Chair is a children's fantasy novel by C. S. Lewis, published by Geoffrey Bles in 1953. It was the fourth published of seven novels in The Chronicles of Narnia (1950–1956); it is volume six in recent editions, which are sequenced according to Narnian history. Like the others, it was illustrated by Pauline Baynes and her work has been retained in many later editions.

THE CHRONICLES OF NARNIA • 6
THE
SILVER
CHAIR
C. S. LEWIS
ILLUSTRATED

The novel is set primarily in the world of Narnia, decades after The Voyage of the Dawn Treader there but less than a year later in England. King Caspian X is now an old man, but his son and only heir, Prince Rilian, is missing. Aslan the lion sends two children from England to Narnia on a mission to resolve the mystery: Eustace Scrubb, from The Voyage of the Dawn Treader, and his classmate, Jill Pole. In England, Eustace and Jill are students at a horrible boarding school, Experiment House.

The Silver Chair is dedicated to Nicholas Hardie, the son of Colin Hardie, a member of the Inklings with Lewis.

The Silver Chair was adapted and filmed as a BBC television series of six episodes in 1990.

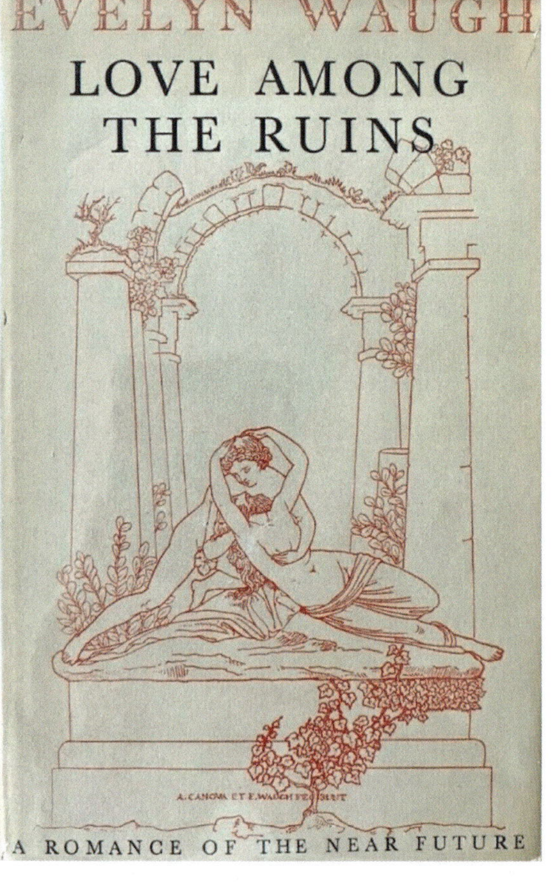
EVELYN WAUGH
LOVE AMONG
THE RUINS
A ROMANCE OF THE NEAR FUTURE

Love Among the Ruins: A Romance of the Near Future is a 1953 novel by Evelyn Waugh. It is a satire set in a dystopian, quasi-egalitarian Britain.

The protagonist, Miles Plastic, is an orphan who, at the beginning of the story, is finishing a prison term for arson. Crime is treated very leniently by the state, and conditions in prison are actually quite superior to those among the population at large, leading to an understandably high recidivism rate. Upon release, Plastic goes to work at a state-run euthanasia centre. The centres are not restricted to the terminally ill and are so popular that Plastic's sole responsibility is to stem "the too eager rush" of perfectly healthy but "welfare weary" citizens. Plastic soon falls in love with Clara, a bearded woman who is a "priority case" at the centre. However, she does not wish to die (she was sent there by her department) and the two begin a romance. One day, however, she suddenly disappears, and when he finds her, she has a rubber jaw replacing her formerly bearded face. Distraught, Plastic sets his former prison on fire, and, unidentified as the perpetrator of the crime, becomes elevated in status as the prison's only "successfully rehabilitated inmate."

MOVIE'S 1953

TITANIC
CLIFTON
WEBB · STANWYCK · WAGNER
BARBARA
ROBERT
AUDREY
THELMA
BRIAN
RICHARD
DALTON · RITTER · AHERNE · BASEHART

Titanic. Unhappily married and uncomfortable with life among the British upper crust, Julia Sturges takes her two children and boards the RMS Titanic for America. Her husband, Richard, also arranges passage on the doomed luxury liner in order to allow him to have custody of their two children, Annette and Norman. Meanwhile, Annette begins a romance with a young American college student and tennis player, Gifford Rogers. Unfortunately, their family problems soon seem minor when the Titanic strikes an iceberg. As the Titanic is in her final moments, Richard and Norman find each other. Richard tells a passing steward that Norman is his son and then tells Norman that he has been proud of him every day of his life.

Box office: Budget $1,805,000 (estimated)

Filming locations:
Stage 4, 20th Century Fox Studios - 10201 Pico Blvd., Century City, Los Angeles, California, USA

Run time is 1h 38mins

Trivia

During the boarding of the lifeboats, Norman changes seats with a woman who arrives at the last moment when the boat was completely full. This was inspired by the action of a Mexican passenger in first class named Manuel Uruchurtu, who did the same thing to a woman from second class who was refused a seat on the lifeboat. After he gave up his seat to her, he asked her to travel to Mexico, if she survived, and tell his wife what happened. His body was never found.

To ensure authenticity, the producers recruited a former captain of the Queen Elizabeth as a technical consultant, and no background music was played during the feature film. The only music heard was that of the musicians aboard the ship.

Some of the original survivors of the RMS Titanic were invited to a tear-filled special screening of the film in New York.

Goofs

The iceberg is shown, correctly, hitting the right (Starboard) side of the ship. But in the underwater shot, we see the iceberg cutting into the Titanic's left (Port) side.

Early scenes during the sinking show the engineering areas experiencing severe listing, whilst the lounge where passengers are playing cards has no tilt whatsoever.

Trying to buy a ticket at the last minute, Richard Sturges is told that the voyage has been sold out since March. In fact, it wasn't even close to sold out.

Crewmembers on the Titanic did not wear Royal Navy uniforms.

ALAN JEAN VAN
LADD ARTHUR HEFLIN
GEORGE STEVENS'
PRODUCTION OF
SHANE
Color by Technicolor
Costarring
BRANDON DE WILDE with JACK PALANCE
BEN JOHNSON · EDGAR BUCHANAN
GEORGE STEVENS
A. B. GUTHRIE, Jr.
JACK SHER
JACK SCHAEFER
A PARAMOUNT PICTURE

Shane. A gunfighter who refers to himself simply as Shane (Alan Ladd) seeks respite from gunslinging by taking a job as a farmhand on the homestead of a Wyoming family—Joe (Van Heflin) and Marian (Jean Arthur) Starrett and their eight-year-old son Joey (Brandon De Wilde). However, a conflict has developed between homesteaders and cattle baron Rufus Ryker (Emile Meyer), who wants to drive away the homesteaders and take over their land for grazing his cattle. Rufus brings in gunflighter Jack Wilson (Jack Palance) from Cheyenne, and things grow even more heated ...in more ways than one.

When originally released theatrically in the UK, the BBFC made cuts to secure a 'U' rating. All cuts were waived in 1986 when the film was granted an 'PG' certificate for home video.

Filming locations: Grand Teton National Park, Wyoming, USA

Budget: $3,100,000 (estimated)

Run time is 1h 58mins

Trivia

Jack Palance had problems with his horse during filming. When Shane and Jack first look each other over at the Starrett Ranch, Palance was supposed to dismount for a minute, then remount his horse. He could not remount, so the director had Jack dismount his horse slowly, then ran the film in reverse for the remount.

The scene where Alan Ladd practices shooting in front of Brandon De Wilde took 119 takes to complete.

The first gunshots in the film are when Shane shows Joey how to fire a revolver. To enhance the dramatic effect of the shooting, the sounds of the gunshots were elevated by firing a gun into a garbage pail. The echoed reverberations made the gunfire sounds much louder. George Stevens' intention was to startle the audience with the first firing of a gun.

Goofs

In the opening scene when Shane rides a horse down the hill, Teton Pass Highway is visible in the background.

At Grafton's Supply Store, Joe Starrett is flipping through "Sears and Roebuck" "Catalogue 112". Catalogue 112 is dated 1905; some 20 years after Shane takes place.

At the end of the big gun fight when Shane and Joey are talking outside of Grafton's bar Shane calls him Jimmy.

Shane clearly misses the third man in the showdown - he fires level instead of up at the balcony, but the next shot shows him almost standing and firing in the right direction. In the following shot he's crouching again.

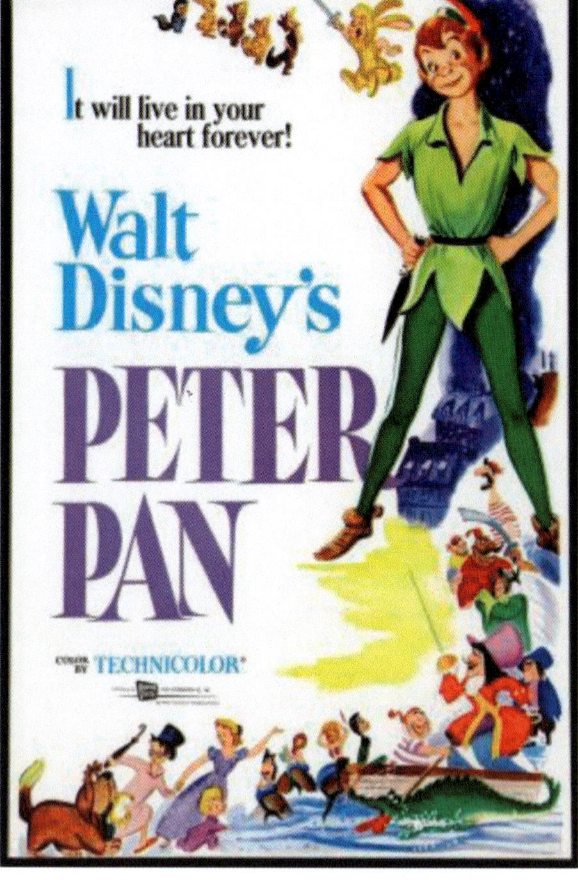
It will live in your heart forever!
Walt Disney's
PETER PAN
TECHNICOLOR

Peter Pan. Based upon Sir James M. Barrie's 1904 play about the boy who refuses to grow up, the film begins in the London nursery of Wendy, John, and Michael Darling, where three children are visited by Peter Pan. With the help of his tiny friend, the fairy Tinkerbell, Peter takes the three children on a magical flight to Never Land. This enchanted island is home to Peter, Tink, the Lost Boys, Tiger Lily and her Native American nation, and the scheming Captain Hook who is as intent on defeating Peter Pan as he is from escaping the tick-tocking crocodile that once ate a hand of his that Peter Pan cut off--and loved the taste of so much.

A message appears during the credits: "Walt Disney Productions is grateful to the Hospital for Sick Children, Great Ormond Street, London, to which Sir J.M. Barrie gave his copyright of Peter Pan."

Box Office:

Budget: $4,000,000 (estimated)
Cumulative Worldwide Gross: $1,865,056

Run time 1h 17mins.

Trivia

Though the film was a modest success, Walt Disney himself was dissatisfied with the finished product, feeling that the character of Peter Pan was cold and unlikable. However, experts on J.M. Barrie praise this as a success, as they insist that Pan was originally written to be a heartless sociopath.

In the originally-planned version, Nana travelled with the children to Neverland. It also had a much darker ending.

In the original play, Hook loses his right hand, but the Disney artists felt that would limit his actions too much, and switched the hook to the left hand.

J.R.R. Tolkien was a Peter Pan fan. Neverland and the Lost Boys had a definite impact on Middle-earth; Peter Pan himself particularly influenced the elves.

Goofs

Smee tells Hook that the cook told him that the first mate told him that he heard that Pan had banished Tinkerbell but technically Smee is the first mate.

When the children are in the nursery being tucked into bed, Wendy's pillow changes from being striped to being white and then striped again.

One of the mermaids' hair colour in the mermaid lagoon keeps changing. The one with upturned clam shells has black hair when she's first seen. Then a minute later it changes to blonde and another minute later it is red.

Roman Holiday. Princess Anne embarks on a highly publicized tour of European capitals. When she and her royal entourage arrive in Rome, she begins to rebel against her restricted, regimented schedule. One-night Anne sneaks out of her room, hops into the back of a delivery truck and escapes her luxurious confinement. However, a sedative she was forced to take earlier starts to take effect, and the Princess is soon fast asleep on a public bench. She is found by Joe Bradley, an American newspaper reporter stationed in Rome. He takes her back to his apartment. The next morning Joe dashes off to cover the Princess Anne press conference, unaware that she is sleeping on his couch. Once he realizes his good fortune, Joe promises his editor an exclusive interview with the Princess.

Filming locations: Cafe Rocca, Via della Rotonda 25, Pantheon, Rome, Lazio, Italy.

Box office: Budget $1,500,000 (estimated)

Run time 1h 58mins

Trivia

After filming, Gregory Peck informed the producers that, as Audrey Hepburn was certainly going to win an Oscar (for this, her first major role), they had better put her name above the title. They did and she did.

When Gregory Peck came to Italy to shoot the movie, he was privately depressed about his recent separation and imminent divorce from his first wife, Greta Kukkonen. However, during the shoot he met and fell in love with a French woman named Veronique Passani. Following his divorce, he married her, she became Veronique Peck, and they remained together for the rest of his life.

In the 1970s, both Gregory Peck and Audrey Hepburn were approached with the idea of a sequel, but the project never came to fruition.

Goofs

When the princess and Joe Bradley stand in front of the magistrate after the scooter incident, her blouse is dirty and so is her face. When they come out of the police station, her blouse is spotless and so is her face. She could conceivably have washed her face in the interim, but there would not have been an occasion in 1953 to clean and dry a blouse that quickly.

When Ann is sitting on the banister in front of the clock tower, her cone has a large scoop of gelato, but when Joe arrives a moment later and sits beside her, the gelato is almost gone.

When Bradley and Princess Ann are emotionally holding each other in the car, at one point you can see it raining outside the passenger side window. But on the following shot when she gets out the car it is not raining nor are there any signs that it was raining.

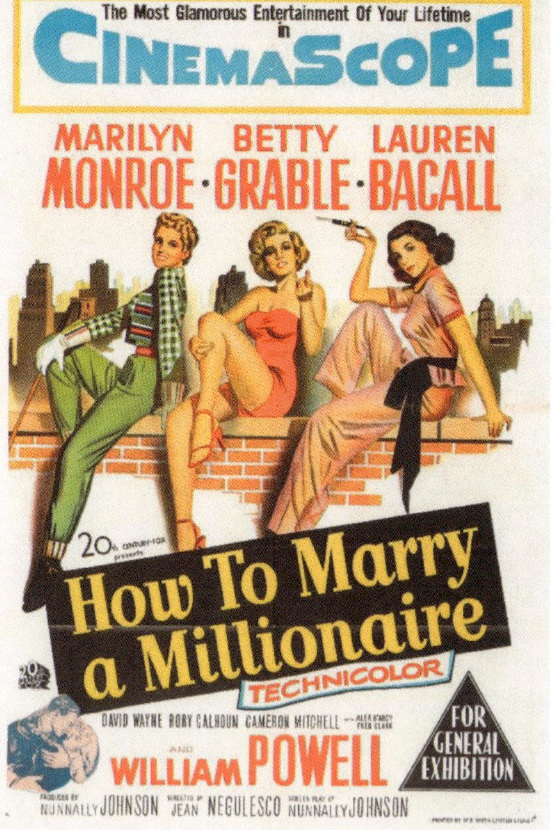
The Most Glamorous Entertainment Of Your Lifetime
in
CinemaScope
MARILYN BETTY LAUREN
MONROE · GRABLE · BACALL
20th Century-Fox presents
How To Marry a Millionaire
TECHNICOLOR
DAVID WAYNE RORY CALHOUN CAMERON MITCHELL
AND
WILLIAM POWELL
FOR GENERAL EXHIBITION
NUNNALLY JOHNSON JEAN NEGULESCO NUNNALLY JOHNSON

How To Marry a Millionaire. Three New York models, Shatze, Pola and Loco set up in an exclusive apartment with a plan.... tired of cheap men and a lack of money, they intend to use all their talents to trap and marry three millionaires. The trouble is that it's not so easy to tell the rich men from the hucksters - and even when they can, is the money really worth it?

How to Marry a Millionaire is one of the brightest and wittiest comedies of the fifties and certainly quite an eyeful when you've got three leads of the calibre of Lauren Bacall, Marilyn Monroe, and Betty Grable. These three lovely girls, following the cue from Lauren Bacall, chip in and get a long-term lease on a swank apartment where the owner has had to leave the country because of income tax problems. The post-World War II years saw a lot of that happening. The idea is to set up a mantrap, put up a good front in the hopes of attracting men with wealth.

Box Office: Budget: $1,870,000 (estimated)

Run time 1h 35mins

Trivia

Lauren Bacall's character, Schatze, says, "I've always liked older men . . . Look at that old fellow what's-his-name in "The African Queen (1951)." Absolutely crazy about him." She is referring to her then real-life husband, Humphrey Bogart.

When Pola (Marilyn Monroe) is modelling the red swimsuit, the description given of the outfit is: "You know, of course, that diamonds are a girl's best friend." Marilyn Monroe sings the number "Diamonds Are a Girl's Best Friend" in "Gentlemen Prefer Blondes (1953)," which was released the same year as this film.

Hollywood legend has it that Marilyn Monroe, who had already rocketed to major stardom in Gentlemen Prefer Blondes (1953), was befriended during filming by Betty Grable, who offered her this encouragement: "Honey, I've had mine. Go get yours."

Goofs

When Pola, who repeatedly demonstrates that she is completely blind without her glasses by bumping in to everything, answers the door to Loco and Hanley she is able to find both the door and the door handle first time, even though she isn't wearing her glasses.

One of the motorcycles that stop Loco and Brewster on the bridge changes design from when it is seen starting up to when it pulls over the car.

Lauren Bacall is shown with a cigarette holder in the movie's poster, yet she never uses a cigarette holder in the movie itself.

Loco is single, yet during the sequence when the girls are sleeping, she is wearing a wedding ring.

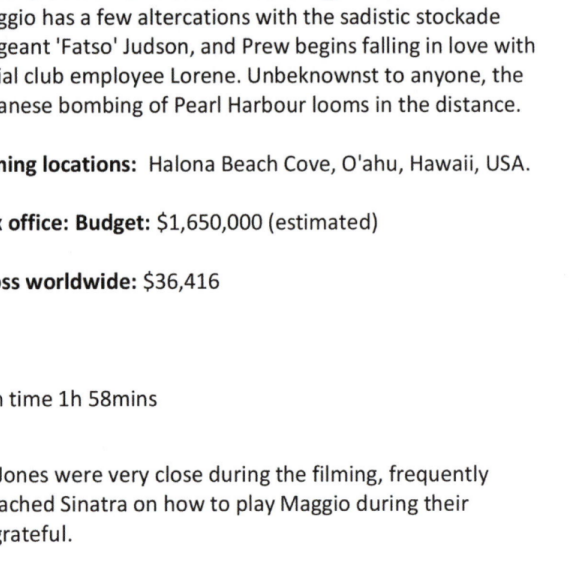

From Here to Eternity. It's 1941. Robert E. Lee Prewitt has requested Army transfer and has ended up at Schofield in Hawaii. His new captain, Dana Holmes, has heard of his boxing prowess and is keen to get him to represent the company. However, 'Prew' is adamant that he doesn't box anymore, so Captain Holmes gets his subordinates to make his life a living hell. Meanwhile Sergeant Warden starts seeing the captain's wife, who has a history of seeking external relief from a troubled marriage. Prew's friend Maggio has a few altercations with the sadistic stockade Sergeant 'Fatso' Judson, and Prew begins falling in love with social club employee Lorene. Unbeknownst to anyone, the Japanese bombing of Pearl Harbour looms in the distance.

Filming locations: Halona Beach Cove, O'ahu, Hawaii, USA.

Box office: Budget: $1,650,000 (estimated)

Gross worldwide: $36,416

Run time 1h 58mins

Trivia

Montgomery Clift, Frank Sinatra and author James Jones were very close during the filming, frequently embarking on monumental drinking binges. Clift coached Sinatra on how to play Maggio during their soberer moments, for which Sinatra was eternally grateful.

The now classic scene between Burt Lancaster and Deborah Kerr in the rushing water on the beach was not written to take place there. The idea to film with the waves hitting them was a last-minute inspiration from director Fred Zinnemann.

In the scene where Burt Lancaster and Montgomery Clift play drunk sitting on the street, Clift actually was drunk, but Lancaster was not.

Deborah Kerr and Burt Lancaster were romantically involved during filming.

Goofs

In one scene, Donna Reed holds a filtered cigarette. The movie takes place during World War II, and they didn't make filtered cigarettes until the 1950s.

At the beginning of the scene in which Buckley first talks to Prewitt about his situation, Prewitt's line, "You know anything in army regulations says I gotta box?"- has obviously been dubbed over a different line - his mouth movements don't match those words.

Throughout the film, the hairs on Prewitt's chest are plainly visible when the top of his shirts are open, but when he's shown without a shirt in Alma's house, all his chest hair has been shaved, which was the usual practice in 1950s Hollywood films.

JANE RUSSELL
MARILYN MONROE
HOWARD HAWKS'
Gentlemen Prefer Blondes
TECHNICOLOR
CO-STARRING
CHARLES COBURN

Gentlemen Prefer Blondes. Entertainers Dorothy Shaw and Lorelei Lee head for Europe on an ocean liner and encounter several mishaps and adventures on the way. For Lorelei, the trip will provide a necessary break from her fiancé Gus Edmond Jr. whose very rich father disapproves of their relationship. In fact, Gus' father convinced that Lorelei is just after a rich husband and sends a private detective on the trip to keep an eye on her. As for Dorothy she attracts many beaus, including the US Olympic team! All of this and several song and dance numbers along the way.

Filming locations: MGM Studio Borehamwood London, England.

Box office
Budget: $2,260,000 (estimated)

Run time 1h 31mins

Trivia

In the "Ain't There Anyone Here for Love?" sequence, Jane Russell's fall into the pool was an accident. When Howard Hawks saw the dailies, he kept it in the film.

This was Jane Russell's only film with Marilyn Monroe. They got along well. According to Russell's 1985 autobiography, she called Monroe "Blondl" and was often the only person on the set who could coax Monroe out of her trailer to begin the day's filming.

Originally bought by Fox as a vehicle for Betty Grable. After the success of Niagara (1953) (which featured Marilyn Monroe), however, the studio believed they had a more potent and far less expensive sex symbol than Grable (who was earning around $150,000 per picture vs. Monroe's $18,000).

Marilyn Monroe wears a gold lamé evening dress previously worn by Ginger Rogers in Dreamboat (1952).

Goofs

The "Two Little Girls From Little Rock" number ends with Dorothy near stage right and Lorelei near stage left. As the girls leave the stage, Dorothy is near stage left and Lorelei is near stage right.

When the ship is shown docking, the tops of the funnels have a wide red band but, seconds later, when the whistle is shown blowing, they are entirely black.

In the later part of the movie when both Marilyn and Jane are talking, Marilyn has bright red lipstick and then a few seconds later it was a faint pink as if it didn't get colourized.

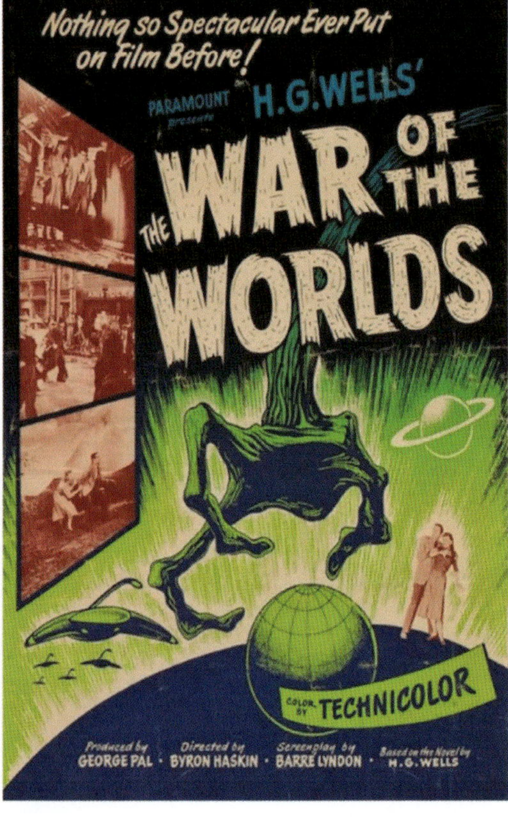
Nothing so Spectacular Ever Put on Film Before!
PARAMOUNT presents
H.G. WELLS'
THE WAR OF THE WORLDS
COLOR BY TECHNICOLOR
Produced by GEORGE PAL · Directed by BYRON HASKIN · Screenplay by BARRE LYNDON · Based on the Novel by H.G. WELLS

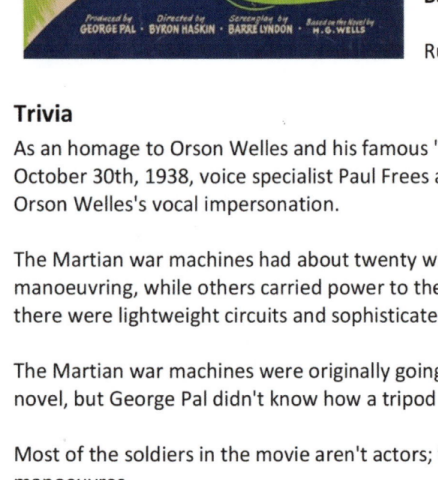

The War Of The Worlds. The film begins with a voiceover (Sir Cedric Hardwicke) telling the audience that greedy eyes are watching the blue planet. They envy our water, clean air and abundance of resources. The race of beings watching the blue planet had considered moving to another planet in the Solar System but were unable because every other planet is uninhabitable. The voice also tells us that WWI and a WWII have already occurred, but that there is going to be another kind of war, the war of the worlds. At a time when the Earth and Mars were closest to each other in orbit, the Mars beings begin to attack. A strange fireball streaks across the southern California skies and lands in a gully in the San Gabriel mountains east of Los Angeles. Firemen quickly extinguish the fire that has broken out, but authorities are puzzled by the long, cylindrical object that fell to earth and started the fire. The object attracts tourists--and also the attention of Dr. Clayton Forester (Gene Barry) of the Pacific Technical Institute.

Box office:
Budget: $2,000,000 (estimated)

Run time 1h 25mins

Trivia

As an homage to Orson Welles and his famous "War of the Worlds" radio broadcast, on Sunday evening, October 30th, 1938, voice specialist Paul Frees appears on-screen as a radio reporter and does his famous Orson Welles's vocal impersonation.

The Martian war machines had about twenty wires running to each one. Some were for suspension and manoeuvring, while others carried power to the various lights and mechanisms. This was produced before there were lightweight circuits and sophisticated radio controls.

The Martian war machines were originally going to be walking tripods as they were depicted in H.G. Wells' novel, but George Pal didn't know how a tripod would walk and instead went with the flying machines.

Most of the soldiers in the movie aren't actors; they're actual National Guard troops going through real manoeuvres.

Goofs

The Northrop YB-49 "Flying Wing" is shown carrying an atom bomb to destroy the Martians. This movie was made in 1953, two years after the last YB-49 made its final flight (April 26, 1951). The aircraft was ordered to be scrapped December 1, 1953.

The sound and the flash from the atomic bomb explosion arrive at the bunker at the same time. The sound should have arrived several seconds after the light.

The narrator incorrectly pointed out that Jupiter is a rocky molten lava planet with extremely high atmospheric pressure. What he was actually describing was the characteristics of the planet Venus - Jupiter has no surface. Also, Mars' nearest neighbour is actually Earth, not Jupiter.

Marilyn Monroe and Niagara a raging torrent of emotion that even nature can't control!
20th CENTURY-FOX presents
Niagara
TECHNICOLOR
MARILYN MONROE · JOSEPH COTTEN · JEAN PETERS
CHARLES BRACKETT · HENRY HATHAWAY · CHARLES BRACKETT, WALTER REISCH, RICHARD BREEN

Niagara. Polly and Ray Cutler finally get to go on their long-delayed honeymoon - they've been married three years - and arrive in Niagara Falls to find that the Loomises - Rose and George - are still in what is supposed to be in their cabin. Rose Loomis is a sultry blond who catches the eye of every man around. Husband George is older and keeps to himself a great deal. The Cutlers take a different cabin but when they go off to visit the falls, Polly sees Rose passionately kissing another man. Rose and her lover are out to kill George and run off together, but things don't quite go as planned and Polly soon finds herself kidnapped and in a boat racing to the edge of the Falls.

Filming locations:
Rainbow Tower, Niagara Falls, Ontario, Canada.

Box office:
Budget $1,250,000 (estimated)

Run time 1h 32mins

Trivia

Even though she had a starring role, Marilyn Monroe was still under contract to "20th Century-Fox" as a stock actor at a fixed salary, so she actually made less money than her make-up man did.

During filming of the shower scene, director Henry Hathaway had to keep yelling at Monroe to keep away from the shower curtain and away from the lights as she insisted on being naked (as she was under the bed sheets at the beginning of the film). To pass the censors of the time, the scene was darkened in post-production.

First of three huge hits for Marilyn Monroe in 1953 - the others being "Gentlemen Prefer Blondes (1953)" and "How to Marry a Millionaire (1953)." The trio grossed over $25,000,000, making it Monroe's most successful year of her film career.

Goofs

Polly is lifted off the rock by a large Sikorsky H-19. In the next scene we see a different helicopter, a tiny Bell H13 parked outside the hut where the next scene takes place.

After Rose gets strangled in the bell tower, the overhead shot shows her holding the green scarf, and it is next to her shoulder. In the next overhead shot, in a closeup, her arm is outstretched and the green scarf is an arm's length away from her shoulder.

Crossing into Canada. Customs checkpoint. Entering in a single car drive flanked by curbs. Rear projection driving away shows a double drive behind them, no official standing on the left as in previous scene, and booth closer to driver side when was previously closer to passenger side.

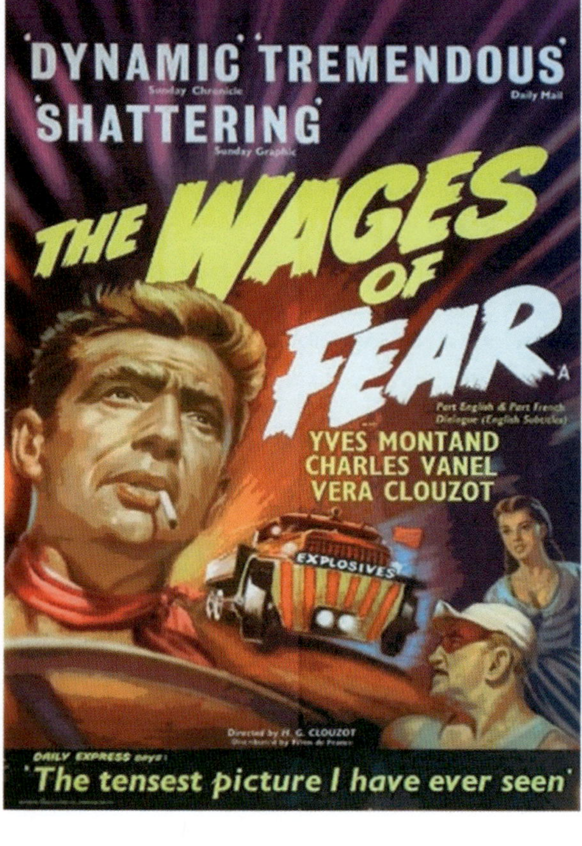
'DYNAMIC' 'TREMENDOUS'
Sunday Chronicle
Daily Mail
'SHATTERING'
Sunday Graphic
THE WAGES OF FEAR
A
YVES MONTAND
CHARLES VANEL
VERA CLOUZOT
EXPLOSIVES
Directed by H. G. CLOUZOT
DAILY EXPRESS says:
'The tensest picture I have ever seen'

The Wages Of Fear. Begging for work, to find the money and break out of the dusty and God-forsaken town of Las Piedras, four stranded men--the tough Corsican, Mario; the nihilistic French gangster, Jo; the Italian workhorse, Luigi, and the mysterious German, Bimba--accept a suicide mission. As the flames of a raging fire threaten to consume the facilities of the unscrupulous Southern Oil Company, the desperate men will have to complete a seemingly simple but severely hazardous mission. Now, the risk-takers must drive two trucks loaded with highly unstable nitro-glycerine over hundreds of kilometres of rugged mountain roads to the oilfield. And in this tortuous and nerve-wracking journey, the slightest vibration can blow both the drivers and their hulking lorries to smithereens, as, more and more, the unrelenting heat and a silent undercurrent of rivalry get the best of them. In other words, the scarred adventurers are taking their lives into their hands. Does fortune favour the bold?

Run time 2h 11mins

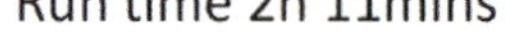

Trivia

Filming began on 27 August 1951 and was scheduled to run for nine weeks. Numerous problems plagued the production, however. The south of France had an unusually rainy season that year, causing vehicles to bog down, cranes to fall over and sets to be ruined. Director Henri-Georges Clouzot broke his ankle. Véra Clouzot fell ill. The production was 50 million francs over budget. By the end of November, only half the film was completed. With the days becoming shorter because of winter, production shut down for six months. The second half of the film was finally completed in the summer of 1952.

This was the first film to win both the Golden Palm at the Cannes Film Festival and the Golden Bear at the Berlin Film Festival.

Was the fourth-highest-grossing film of the year in France.

Goofs

At least one truck has a sign saying 'no smoking' within 50 feet of the truck, but they are smoking near the trucks all the time and even in the cabs. Mario is also smoking while the charge to explode the boulder is being set up.

When Bimba is shaving in the cab of the truck, he has the right side of his face covered in shaving cream, but when he turns to talk to Luigi the right side of his face is clear of shaving cream.

Although the platform has survived two heavy trucks being driven on it, it collapses completely in splinters when one cable is broken. The hole caused in the rotten floor by the first truck seems to disappear when the second one comes.

THE STAR-SPANGLED, LAUGH-LOADED SALUTE TO OUR P.W. HEROES!
Paramount presents
"Stalag 17"
WILLIAM HOLDEN·DON TAYLOR·OTTO PREMINGER
BILLY WILDER

Stalag 17. It's a dreary Christmas 1944 for the American POWs in Stalag 17. For the men in Barracks 4, all sergeants, have to deal with a grave problem - there seems to be a security leak. The Germans always seem to be forewarned about escapes and in the most recent attempt the two men, Manfredi and Johnson, walked straight into a trap and were killed. For some in Barracks 4, especially the loud-mouthed Duke, the leaker is obvious: J.J. Sefton, a wheeler-dealer who doesn't hesitate to trade with the guards and who has acquired goods and privileges that no other prisoner seems to have. Sefton denies giving the Germans any information and makes it quite clear that he has no intention of ever trying to escape. He plans to ride out the war in what little comfort he can arrange, but it doesn't extend to spying for the Germans. As tensions mount and mob mentality takes root, it becomes obvious Sefton will have to find the real German agent in their midst, which he finally does.

Box office: Budget $1,661,530 (estimated)

Run time 2h 00mins

Trivia

Charlton Heston was originally considered for the role of Sgt. J.J. Sefton, but when the script was altered to make the character less heroic, he was dropped in favour of someone more suitable for the role. Kirk Douglas stated he was next in line and declined the part, making William Holden the third choice. Douglas came to rue his decision, saying it was the biggest mistake of his career.

This film was one of the biggest hits of Billy Wilder's career. He expected a big piece of the profits. The studio accountants informed him that since his last picture "Ace in the Hole (1951)" lost money, the money that picture lost would be subtracted from his profits on this film. Wilder left "Paramount" shortly after that.

The role of Sefton was originally written for Charlton Heston. But as the role evolved and became more cynical, William Holden emerged as the director's choice. Holden was asked to see the play on which the movie was based. He walked out at the end of the first act. He was later convinced to at least read the screenplay.

Goofs

As is common in many older World War II movies, the SS men sent to transport Dunbar to Berlin are wearing the iconic black SS uniforms that were discontinued as duty wear in 1939, 5 years before the setting of the film. Additionally, the uniform of one of them has a cuff title with just the numeral "2." Cuff titles were only worn by combat units, such as the Waffen-SS, and contained unit names and/or symbols. Worn on a general duty SS man this cuff title makes no sense and refers to no known SS organization.

The German machine gun team that shoots the escaping prisoners in the beginning of the film, us an American M1919 .30 calibre machine gun, instead of a German MG-42.

When Dunbar climbs out of the water tank he nudges two icicles that move. If they were real icicles they would have broken.

Yippeeeee! It's the Big Bonanza
in Musical Extravaganza!
DORIS
DAY
HOWARD
KEEL
WARNER BROS'
SKY-HIGHEST
SMILE-WIDEST
WILD'N WOOIEST
MUSICAL
OF 'EM ALL!
Calamity Jane
TECHNICOLOR
BRAND NEW SMASH HITS BY THE STAGE LOAD!
ALLYN McLERIE PHILIP CAREY DICK WESSON

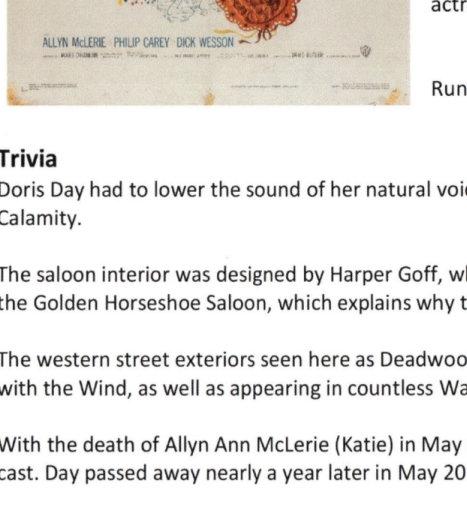

Calamity Jane. It's the late nineteenth century in Deadwood, located in the Dakota Territory. Jane Canary - better known as Calamity Jane or Calam for short - is a sharp shooter who takes it upon herself to protect the area, especially the stagecoach, from the marauding Sioux. Her skill and fearlessness are matched only by Wild Bill Hickok, with whom she has a friendly rivalry, but who she still considers her best friend. Calam shows no signs of femininity, despite being in love with a soldier, Lieutenant Danny Gilmartin. Despite having been saved before by Calam, Danny only sees her as one of the guys and has no idea that she loves him. There is a dearth of females in the area, and as such, Harvey Miller or Milly for short, the proprietor of the local saloon called the Golden Garter, brings in actresses to perform whenever he can to entertain the men who are starved for female companionship. So, when Milly's latest attempt to bring in an actress doesn't turn out quite the way he expects, Calam takes it upon herself to bring in the most famous Chicago actress, Adelaid Adams, to keep the peace in Deadwood.

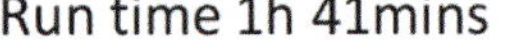

Run time 1h 41mins

Trivia

Doris Day had to lower the sound of her natural voice, in order to sound gruffer to play the rough and ready Calamity.

The saloon interior was designed by Harper Goff, who also designed for Disneyland including the interior of the Golden Horseshoe Saloon, which explains why they look so similar.

The western street exteriors seen here as Deadwood City had earlier been used as war-torn Atlanta in Gone with the Wind, as well as appearing in countless Warner Brothers Westerns.

With the death of Allyn Ann McLerie (Katie) in May of 2018, Doris Day was the sole surviving member of the cast. Day passed away nearly a year later in May 2019, at age 97.

Goofs

The woman who plays Frances Fryer's date for the Ft. Scully ball is also seen in the chorus line for the Adelaid Adams finale in Chicago and then again with the group of ladies catching the wedding bouquets at the end of the movie.

After leaving the ball at the fort, we cut to a shot of Calamity's bare back as she is undressing. Once she gets the dress off she is shown wearing undergarments that clearly cover most of her back.

When Calamity rides into the Indian camp to rescue Dan, she fires seven shots from her six-shooter in such rapid succession she would have had no time to reload.

At the beginning of the movie during the stagecoach scene, tire tracks are visible behind the coach.

MUSIC 1953

Artist	Single	Reached number one	Weeks at number one
1953			
Al Martino	Here in My Heart	14th November 1952	9
Jo Stafford	You Belong To Me	16th January 1953	1
Kay Starr	Comes A-Long A-Love	23rd January 1953	1
Eddie Fisher	Outside of Heaven	30th January 1953	1
Perry Como	Don't Let the Stars Get in Your Eyes	6th February 1953	5
Guy Mitchell	She Wears Red Feathers	13th March 1953	4
The Stargazers	Broken Wings	10th April 1953	1
Lita Roza	(How Much Is) That Doggie in the Window?	17th April 1953	1
Frankie Laine	I Believe	24th April 1953	9
Eddie Fisher	I'm Walking Behind You	26th June 1953	1
Frankie Laine	I Believe	3rd July 1953	6
Mantovani	The Song from Moulin Rouge	14th August 1953	1
Frankie Laine	I Believe	21st August 1953	3
Guy Mitchell	Look At That Girl	11th September 1953	6
Frankie Laine	Hey Joe	23rd October 1953	2
David Whitfield	Answer Me	6th November 1953	1
Frankie Laine	Answer Me	13th November 1953	8
David Whitfield	Answer Me	11th December 1953	3

The UK Singles Chart is the official record chart in the United Kingdom. Record charts in the UK began life in 1952 when Percy Dickins from New Musical Express (NME) imitated an idea started in American Billboard magazine and began compiling a hit parade. Prior to this, a song's popularity was measured by the sales of sheet music. Initially, Dickins telephoned a sample of around 20 shops asking for a list of the 10 best-selling songs. These results were then aggregated to give a Top 12 chart published in NME on the 14th November 1952. The number-one single was "Here in My Heart" by Al Martino.

According to The Official Charts Company and Guinness' British Hit Singles & Albums, the NME is considered the official British singles chart before 10th March 1960. However, until 15th February 1969, when the British Market Research Bureau chart was established, there was no universally accepted chart. Other charts existed and different artists may have placed at number one in charts by Record Mirror, Disc or Melody Maker. Alternatively, some considered BBC's Pick of the Pops, which averaged all these charts, to be a better indicator of the number-one single.

Al Martino

" Here In My Heart"

HERE IN MY HEART
GRANADA
AL MARTINO
ORCHESTRA UNDER
THE DIRECTION OF MONTY KELLY

"Here in My Heart" is a popular song, written by Pat Genaro, Lou Levinson, and Bill Borrelli, and published in 1952. A recording of the song by Al Martino made history as the first number one on the UK Singles Chart, on the 14th November 1952. "Here in My Heart" remained in the top position for nine weeks in the United Kingdom, setting a record for the longest consecutive run at number one, a record which, over 50 years on, has only been beaten by eight other tracks - Bryan Adams's "(Everything I Do) I Do It for You" (16 weeks), the Wet Wet Wet version of The Troggs' "Love Is All Around" (15 weeks).Mario Lanza, at the height of his popularity in the early 1950, had also planned to record this song, but changed his mind when asked not to by Martino, so his recording would not be overlooked.

Jo Stafford

"You Belong To Me"

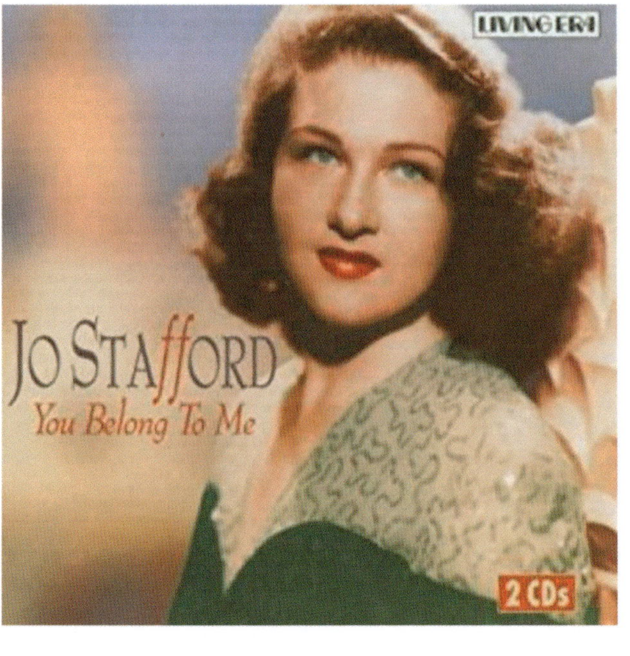
LIVING ERA
JO STAFFORD
You Belong To Me
2 CDs

"You Belong to Me" is a romantic popular music ballad from the 1950s. It is well known for its opening line, "See the pyramids along the Nile". The song was published in Hollywood on 21st April 1952, and the most popular version was by Jo Stafford, reaching No. 1 on both the UK and US singles charts. The Stafford version appeared in the first ever UK singles chart of 14th November 1952 (then a top 12) and reached number 1 for a single week on 16th January 1953, its tenth week on chart. It thus became only the second record to top the chart, and remained on it for a total of 19 weeks. Stafford was to re-record "You Belong to Me" twice, both in the 1960s. The first of these later recordings was made on 13th January 1963, and issued in January 1964 on a stereo Capitol LP, The Hits of Jo Stafford On 14th May 1969.

Kay Starr

" Comes Along A Love"

Capitol
ASCAP
10511
Vocal with Orchestra
COMES A-LONG A-LOVE
KAY STARR
with Orchestra Conducted by Harold Mooney
2213

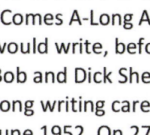

"Comes A-Long A-Love" was a hit single for American singer Kay Starr. The song was released in 1952 and was written by the former Tin Pan Alley song writer Al Sherman. The melody was adapted from the final part of the overture to Gioachino Rossini's opera Semiramide. "Comes A-Long A-Love" was the last hit song Sherman would write, before handing the reins over to his sons, Bob and Dick Sherman, who were just beginning their song writing careers. The song was first published on 9th June 1952. On 27th September 1952, Starr's version of "Comes A-Long A-Love" charted on the Billboard Best Selling Pop Singles chart, where it reached No. 9. Outside, the US, the track also topped the then fledgling UK Singles Chart in January 1953 for a week, becoming only the third chart topper in that listing.

Eddie Fisher

"Outside of Heaven"

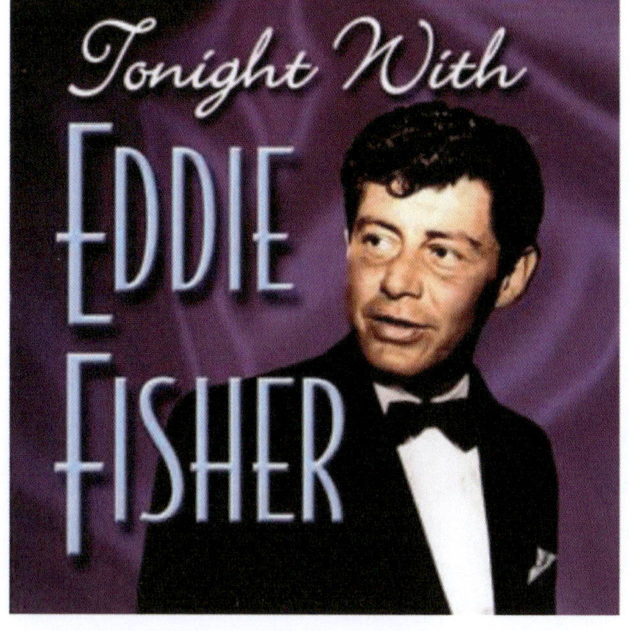

Tonight With
EDDIE
FISHER

"Outside of Heaven" is a popular music song written by Sammy Gallop and Chester Conn. A recording by Eddie Fisher with Hugo Winterhalter's orchestra and chorus was made at Manhattan Centre, New York City, on 19th July 1952. In America, the recording made No. 8 on the Billboard charts. Fisher's version reached No. 1 on the UK Singles Chart in 1953. "Outside of Heaven" was the first UK hit for Fisher, and only the fourth single to top the, then fledgling, UK chart.

On the UK's sheet music sales chart, "Outside of Heaven" first charted on 13 December 1952, peaking at No. 2 in a 23-week chart run. There, Fisher's was amongst the first issued recordings of the song, in November 1952, alongside versions by Vera Lynn, Margaret Whiting and David Carey.

Perry Como

" Don’t Let The Stars Get In Your Eyes”

"Don't Let the Stars Get in Your Eyes" is a country song about a man away from home who is worried that his paramour may unwittingly stray from their relationship. The song was recorded in many different styles by many artists. It was written by Winston L. Moore (whose stage name was Slim Willet) and published in 1952.

HERE IN MY
HEART
GRANADA
AL MARTINO
ORCHESTRA UNDER
THE DIRECTION OF MONTY KELLY

Perry Como's recording of the song became a No. 1 hit in both the US and UK. In the UK, "Don't Let the Stars Get in Your Eyes" first entered the sheet music charts on 17th January 1953. The song peaked at No. 1 on 7th February its fourth week on chart, staying there for a week. In total, it spent 16 weeks on the sheet music charts. The first recording to be issued in the UK was a British recording by Dennis Lotis in December 1952.

Guy Mitchell

“She Wears Red Feathers”

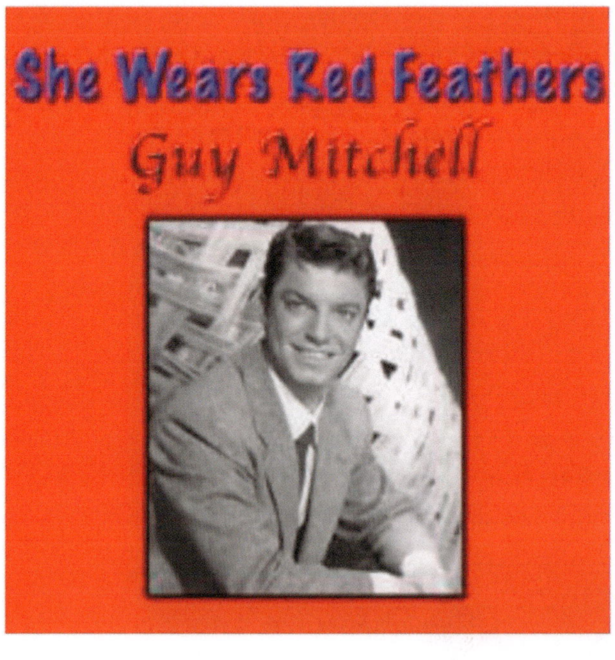
She Wears Red Feathers
Guy Mitchell

"She Wears Red Feathers" is a popular song, which was written by Bob Merrill and published in 1952. The best-known recording of the song was made by Guy Mitchell in 1952 and was a No. 1 single in the UK Singles Chart in March 1953 for four weeks. It was only the sixth single to reach the top spot in the UK. In the UK, Mitchell's single first charted on February 13, 1953, and reached No. 1 in its fifth week. It was the only charting recording of the song. "She Wears Red Feathers" first appeared on the UK's sheet music charts on 21st February 1953, and peaked at No. 3. February 1953 saw the only three recordings of the song issued in the UK: these were by Guy Mitchell, The Ray Ellington Quartet with The Peter Knight Singers, and Donald Peers with The Kordites. In May, Mitchell's version was issued on the new 45rpm format, having initially only been available on 78rpm.

The Stargazers

" Broken Wings”

"Broken Wings" is a 1953 popular song that was written by John Jerome and Bernhard Grun. The most successful version of the song was produced by Dick Rowe and recorded in the UK by vocal group The Stargazers in 1953. It was the first record by any UK act to reach number one in the UK Singles Chart (all previous number one singles were by American artists), and was the first of two number-one UK hits for the group, the other being "I See the Moon", a year later. Coming just a few months after the launch of the singles chart, it was the first hit for the group, entering the New Musical Express listings on 7th February 1953. It dropped out of the chart on 14th February, before returning the week after for a run which would see the single reach number one on 10th April for a single week. The Stargazers were consequently the first group to reach number one in the UK singles chart.

THE
STARGAZERS
BROKEN WINGS

Jo Stafford

"(How Much Is) That Doggie in the Window?

Lita Roza
How much is that Doggie

"(How Much Is) That Doggie in the Window?" is a popular novelty song. It was written by Bob Merrill, and first published on 25th September 1952 as "The Doggie in the Window". On 27th January 1953, it was published in New York as "How Much is That Doggie in the Window?". The song was loosely based on the folk tune "Carnival of Venice" and the song "Oh, Where, Oh, Where, has my Little Dog Gone?"

The recording by Lita Roza was the one most widely heard in that country, reaching No. 1 on the UK Singles Chart in 1953. It distinguished Roza as the first British woman to have a No. 1 hit in the UK chart, and was also the first song with a question in the title to reach the top spot.

Frankie Lane

" I Believe"

"I Believe" is a popular song written by Ervin Drake, Irvin Graham (a pseudonym used by Irvin Abraham), Jimmy Shirl (a pseudonym for Jack Mendelsohn) and Al Stillman in 1953. The most popular version was recorded by Italian-American singer Frankie Laine, and spent eighteen weeks at No. 1 on the UK Singles Chart. Laine's recording spent eighteen non-consecutive weeks at the top of the UK Singles Chart. It entered the listings on 3rd April 1953, and first reached No. 1 in its fourth week on chart, spending nine weeks at the top. On 26th June, it was replaced at No. 1 for a week by "I'm Walking Behind You" by Eddie Fisher featuring Sally Sweetland, but returned to the top spot on 3rd July for another six weeks. On 14th August, it was again replaced at the top for a week. On 21st August, "I Believe" returned to No. 1 for its final run at the top, for three weeks, totalling eighteen weeks.

LAINE
Frankie
I BELIEVE

Eddie Fisher

"I'm Walking Behind You"

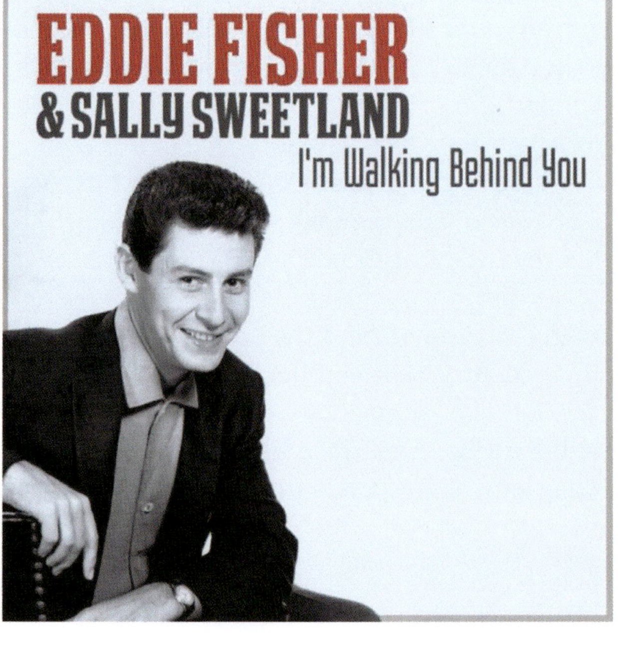
EDDIE FISHER
& SALLY SWEETLAND
I'm Walking Behind You

"I'm Walking Behind You" is a popular song which was written by Billy Reid and published in 1953. The recording by American singer Eddie Fisher was a No. 1 hit in both the US and UK Singles charts. In the UK, the Fisher recording was issued by EMI's His Master's Voice label (catalogue number B 10489) in May 1953. It first entered the UK chart for the week ending 16th May 1953, and reached No. 1 on 26th June, its sixth week on the listings. The single spent a week at No. 1, and 18 weeks on chart in total. Fisher's single entered the Billboard Best Selling Singles chart on 9th May 1953, and reached No. 1 on 25th July 1953, staying there for two weeks. It also reached No. 1 on the Billboard charts for Most Played by Jockeys (on 11th July, for three weeks) and Most Played in Juke Boxes (on 27th June, for seven weeks).

Mantovani

" The Song from Moulin Rouge"

"It's April Again" (also known as "The Song from Moulin Rouge" and "Where Is Your Heart") is a popular song that first appeared in the 1952 film Moulin Rouge. It became a No. 1 hit in the UK Singles Chart when recorded by Mantovani. In the United Kingdom, the version by Mantovani and his Orchestra, recorded on 6th March 1953, was the only hit version of the song. On this recording, produced by Frank Lee at Decca, the plaintive accordion theme was played by Henry Krein. Released the same month, it entered the UK singles chart on 23rd May 1953, and reached No. 1 on 14th August its twelfth week on chart, for a single week.

MADE IN ENGLAND
DECCA
THE SUPREME RECORD
THE DECCA RECORD Co. LTD
N
THE SONG FROM THE
MOULIN ROUGE
MANTOVANI AND HIS
ORCHESTRA
DR.17664
F.10094
CAMPBELL CONNELLY & CO

It was the first instrumental recording to top the UK charts, spending a total of 23 weeks on the listings.

Guy Mitchell

"Look At That Girl"

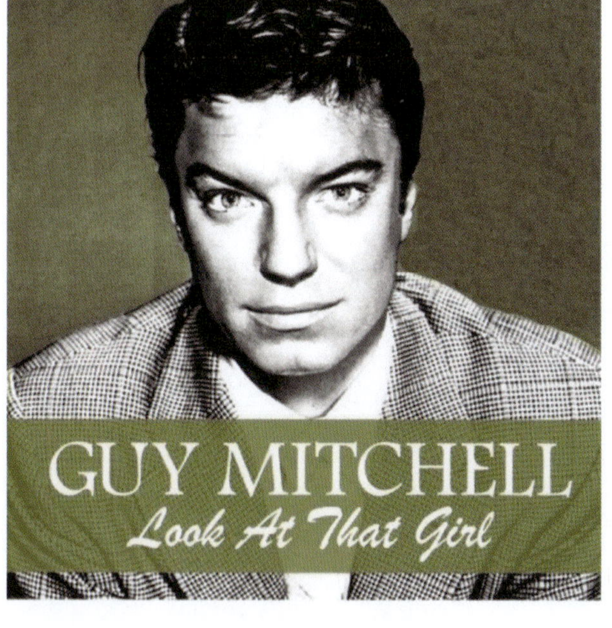
GUY MITCHELL
Look At That Girl

"Look at That Girl" is a 1953 popular song, which was written by Bob Merrill. The song was recorded by Guy Mitchell and produced by Mitch Miller, giving Mitchell his second number one on the UK Singles Chart, where it spent six weeks at the top. The single entered the UK Singles Chart on 28th August 1953, and reached No. 1 on 11th September where it stayed for six weeks. In total, it spent fourteen weeks on the singles chart. On the UK's sheet music charts, "Look at That Girl" entered the listings on 22nd August 1953, and peaked at No. 6. The first recordings issued were in July 1953, by Frankie Vaughan with Ken Mackintosh and his Orchestra, and Guy Mitchell. The following month saw a cover by Dennis Lotis and The Stargazers, while a version by Victor Silvester and his Ballroom Orchestra was released in October.

Frankie Lane

" Hey Joe!"

"Hey Joe!" is a 1953 popular song written by Boudleaux Bryant. A contemporary cover version by Frankie Laine was a hit on the Billboard chart, and also reached No. 1 in the UK Singles Chart. In the UK, Laine's recording was an even bigger success. Released by Philips in August 1953, it entered the New Musical Express singles chart on 16th October 1953. "Hey Joe!" reached No. 1 on the UK Singles Chart the following week, 23rd October. It was Laine's second UK chart topper, but unlike his record-breaking hit "I Believe", "Hey Joe!" only stayed on the chart for eight weeks, including two at No. 1. On 23rd October Laine had three singles in the chart, which at that time consisted of only twelve positions. The following week, Laine's third No. 1 hit in the UK, "Answer Me", entered the chart, giving him a third of all the records on the listing.

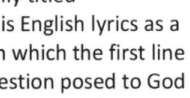

PHILIPS
Electrical Limited
A Product of Philips
PHILIPS
B21094H
AA 21094 1H
P.B.172
78 r.p.m. Green
HEY JOE!
FRANKIE LAINE
with PAUL WESTON and His
Orchestra and The Norman
Luboff Choir
(Carl Fischer—Piano)
ROBBINS MUSIC CO LTD

David Whitfield

"Answer Me"

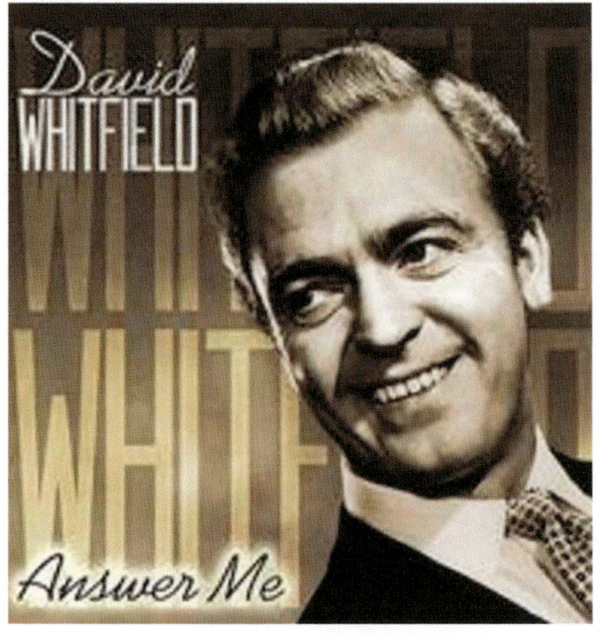
David
WHITFIELD
Answer Me

"Answer Me" is a popular song, originally titled "Mütterlein". Sigman originally wrote his English lyrics as a religious-themed song, "Answer Me", in which the first line reads 'Answer me, Lord above', as a question posed to God about why the singer has lost his lover. This lyric was recorded by Frankie Laine in Hollywood on 22nd June 1953. British light operatic tenor David Whitfield recorded the song on 23rd September the same year. Despite competition from other recordings of "Answer Me", only the two versions by Whitfield and Laine appeared on the UK Singles Chart. Both were released in the UK in October 1953. On 13 November 1953, for the first time in UK Singles Chart history, one version of a song was knocked off the top spot by another version of the same song, when Frankie Laine's "Answer Me" made No. 1 in its third week on chart, deposing Whitfield's version after a week.

WORLD EVENTS 1953

January

3rd	Frances Bolton and her son, Oliver from Ohio, become the first mother and son to serve simultaneously in the U.S. Congress.
4th	Operation Bretagne ends, with French victory over the Viet Minh in Vietnam.
5th	Two Dutch passenger ships collided in the Red Sea. It is the 'Willem Ruys' and 'Orange'. The collision occurred at the height of Port Sudan. No deaths or injuries.
7th	US President Harry Truman announces American development of the hydrogen bomb.
9th	Korean ferryboat "Chang Tyong-Ho" sank off Pusan killing 249.
10th	Bollingen Prize for poetry awarded to Archibald MacLeish.
13th	"Doctors' plot": The state newspaper Pravda publishes an article alleging that many of the most prestigious physicians in the Soviet Union, mostly Jews, are part of a major plot to poison the country's senior political and military leaders.
14th	The CIA-sponsored Robertson Panel first meets to discuss the UFO phenomenon.
15th	Georg Dertinger, foreign minister of East Germany, is arrested for spying.
17th	Australian Championships Women's Tennis: In an all-American final Maureen Connolly wins 1st leg of her Grand Slam; beats Julia Sampson 6-3, 6-2. Australian Championships Men's Tennis: In an all-Australian final Ken Rosewall wins his first Grand Slam title; beats Mervyn Rose 6-0, 6-3, 6-4.
19th	71.1% of all television sets in the United States are tuned into I Love Lucy, to watch Lucy give birth to Little Ricky, which is more people than those who tuned into Dwight Eisenhower's inauguration the next day. This record has yet to be broken.
20th	Dwight D. Eisenhower is sworn in as the 34th President of the United States.
22nd	The Crucible, a historical drama by Arthur Miller written as an allegory of McCarthyism in the United States, opens on Broadway.
24th	Leader of East Germany Walter Ulbricht announces that agriculture will be collectivized in East Germany.
27th	The Canadian Dental Association approves the use of fluoride in drinking water.
31st	The North Sea flood of 1953 kills 1,836 people in the southwestern Netherlands (especially Zeeland), 307 in the United Kingdom, and several hundred at sea, including 133 on the ferry MV Princess Victoria in the Irish Sea.

February

1st The surge of the North Sea flood continues from the previous day. The 1953 North Sea flood was a major flood caused by a heavy storm at the end of Saturday, 31st January 1953 and morning of the next day. The storm surge struck the Netherlands, north-west Belgium, England and Scotland.

3rd J Fred Muggs, a chimpanzee, becomes a regular on NBC's Today Show.

5th Walt Disney's feature film Peter Pan premieres.

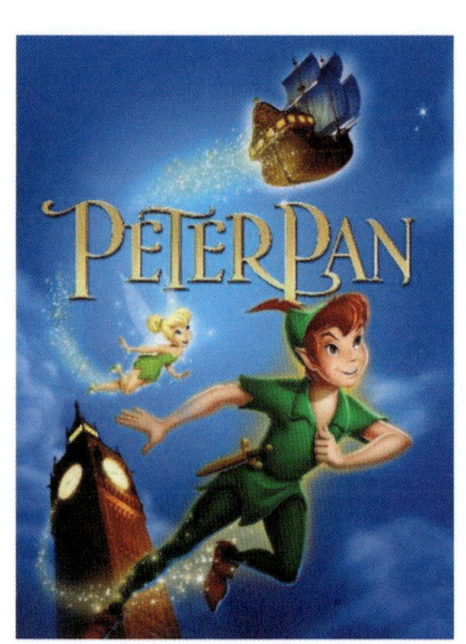
PETER PAN

6th Ian Craig makes Test Cricket debut at 17 yrs. 239 days, youngest Aussie.

9th Charlie Spencer, English soccer defender and manager (2 caps; Newcastle United; mgr. Grimsby Town 1937-51), dies at 53

11th The Soviet Union breaks diplomatic relations with Israel, after a bomb explosion at the Soviet Embassy, in reaction to the 'Doctors' plot'.

14th Actress Agnes Moorehead (52) weds actor & film director Robert Gist (35)

16th John "Brad" Bradbury, British ska drummer and record producer (The Specials), born in Coventry, England (d. 2015).

February

18th Derek Pellicci, English-born Australian rock drummer (Little River Band - "Help Is On The Way"), born in London, United Kingdom.

19th Georgia approves the first literature censorship board in the United States.

20th August A. Busch buys St. Louis Cardinals MLB club from Fred Saigh for $3.75 million; pledges not to move the team from St. Louis, Missouri.

21st "Maggie" closes at National Theatre NYC after 5 performances.

22nd Nitroform Products Company plant in Newark was destroyed by an explosion.

25th Jacques Tati's film, Les Vacances de M. Hulot, is released in France, introducing the gauche character of Monsieur Hulot.

26th Allen Dulles officially promoted from deputy director to become the 5th Director of the Central Intelligence Agency.

10th Golden Globes: "The Greatest Show on Earth", Gary Cooper, & Shirley Booth win.

28th Greece, Turkey, and Yugoslavia sign the Balkan Pact.

March

1st Joseph Stalin suffers a stroke, after an all-night dinner with Soviet Union interior minister Lavrentiy Beria and future premiers Georgy Malenkov, Nikolai Bulganin, and Nikita Khrushchev. The stroke paralyzes the right side of his body and renders him unconscious until his death on 5th March.

American golfer Babe Zaharias wins a controversial Sarasota Women's Open by 7 strokes as playing partner Louise Suggs refuses to sign the scorecard after Zaharias given a beneficial ruling.

3rd Boston Braves, who own Milwaukee minor league franchise, block St Louis Browns attempt to shift their franchise to Milwaukee.

5th 6th British Film and Television Awards (BAFTAS): "The Sound Barrier" Best Film.

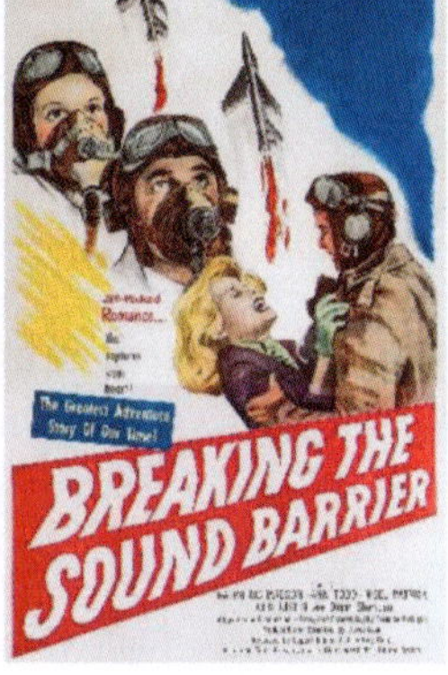
BREAKING THE SOUND BARRIER

March

6th Georgy Malenkov succeeds Joseph Stalin, as Premier and First Secretary of the Communist Party of the Soviet Union.

8th The Thieves World, which has been transformed into the Russian mafia, are freed from prisons by the Malenkov regime, ending the Bitch Wars.

9th Draft Treaty establishing the European Political Community, never brought into effect.
Joseph Stalin's funeral is held in Moscow after four days of national mourning.

13th The United Nations Security Council nominates Dag Hammarskjöld from Sweden as United Nations Secretary General.

14th Nikita Khrushchev is selected General Secretary of the Communist Party of the Soviet Union.

15th LPGA Titleholders Championship Women's Golf, Augusta CC: Patty Berg wins her 5th Titleholders title by 9 strokes from Betsy Rawls.

17th The first nuclear test of Operation Upshot–Knothole is conducted in Nevada, with 1,620 spectators at 3.4 km (2.1 mi).

18th The Yenice–Gönen earthquake affects western Turkey, with a maximum Mercalli intensity of IX (violent), causing at least 1,070 deaths, and $3.57 million in damage.

19th The 25th Academy Awards Ceremony is held (the first one broadcast on television).

25th Dr. Jonas Salk announces that he has successfully tested a vaccine to prevent polio, clinical trials began the next year.

26th "Ugetsu", Japanese film directed by Kenji Mizoguchi, starring Masayuki Mori, Machiko Kyō and Kinuyo Tanaka, is released.

28th 7th Tony Awards: "The Crucible" (Outstanding Play) & "Wonderful Town" (Outstanding Musical) win.

31st US Department of Health, Education & Welfare established.

April

1st West Indian cricket batsmen Frank Worrell (237), Clyde Walcott (118) and Everton Weekes (109) all make centuries in 1st innings of drawn 5th Test v India in Kingston, Jamaica.

3rd American magazine "TV Guide" publishes 1st issue, features on the cover the new born baby of actors Desi Arnaz and Lucille Ball, Desi Arnaz Jr.

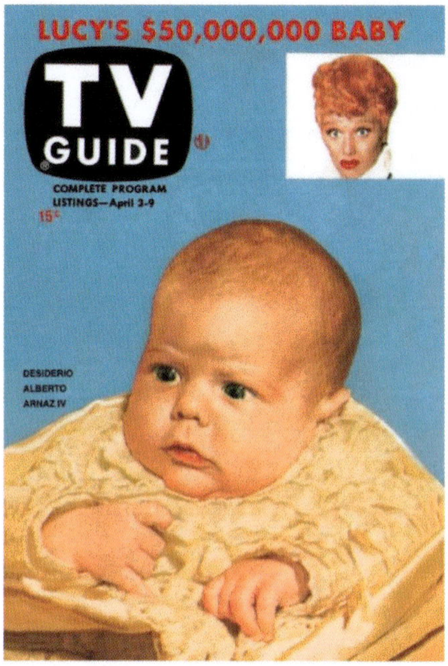

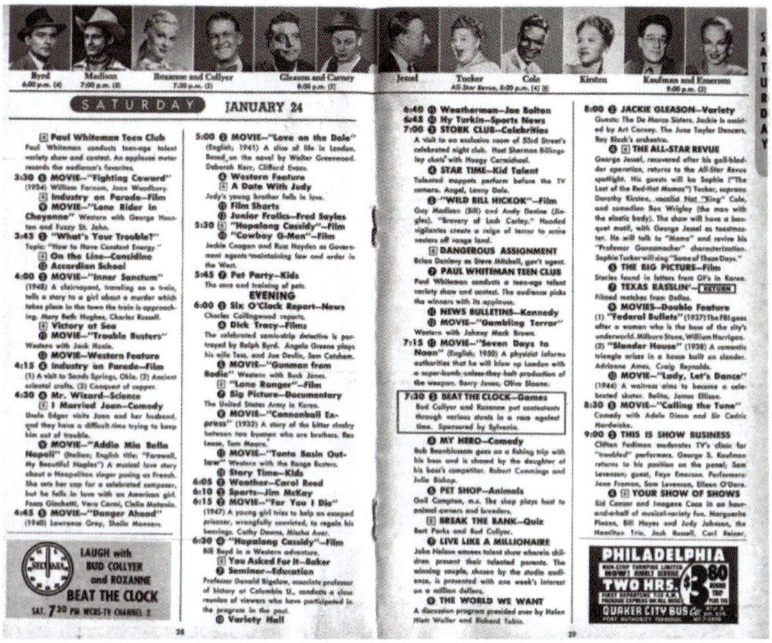

7th UN General Assembly begins session that will elect Dag Hammarskjöld of Sweden as Secretary-General.

8th Jomo Kenyatta convicted of involvement with the Mau Mau rebellion and sentenced to 7 years jail in Kenya.

10th "House of Wax" 1st colour 3-D movie, premieres in New York.

11th US Department of Health, Education and Welfare created.

12th 17th US Masters Tournament, Augusta National GC: Ben Hogan shatters the Masters scoring record by 5 strokes with a 274 (−14) to finish 5 strokes ahead of runner-up Ed Oliver; Hogan's second Masters.

13th 1st game of Milwaukee Braves, they beat Cincinnati Reds 2-0.

16th British royal yacht Britannia launched by Queen Elizabeth II.

Stanley Cup Final, Montreal Forum, Montreal, Quebec: Montreal Canadiens beat Boston Bruins, 1-0 for a 4-1 series win.

17th Mickey Mantle hits a 565' (172 m) HR in Washington, D.C.'s Griffith Stadium.

April

20th Frank Sinatra and arranger Nelson Riddle began their first recording sessions together at Capitol Records, which results in some of the defining recordings of Sinatra's career.

23rd "Shane", directed by George Stevens and based on the 1949 novel by Jack Schaefer, starring Alan Ladd and Jean Arthur, is released.

25th Francis Crick and James Watson's discovery of the double helix structure of DNA is published in "Nature" magazine.

27th 1st general elections in British Guiana, won by the People's Progressive Party with Cheddi Jagan first person of Indian descent to be elected head of government outside South Asia.

Wrestler Freddie Blassie coins term "Pencil neck geek".

29th The first U.S. experimental 3D-TV broadcast showed an episode of Space Patrol on Los Angeles ABC affiliate KECA-TV.

6th Cannes Film Festival: "The Wages of Fear" directed by Henri-Georges Clouzot wins the Grand Prix du Festival International du Film.

30th Little-Bigger League changes its name to Babe Ruth League.

May

2nd 79th Kentucky Derby: Hank Moreno aboard Dark Star wins in 2:02. In the Derby on 2nd May, Dark Star started at odds of 25/1, with Native Dancer, unbeaten in eleven races, going off the 3/5 favourite. Apart from the crowd at the track, the race attracted a huge television audience, with three-quarters of American viewers tuning in to the coverage. Dark Star broke quickly from a wide draw and was sent into the lead at the first turn by his twenty-three-year-old jockey Hank Moreno, staying clear of the "bumping and pushing" further back in the field, in which the favourite was badly affected. As the field turned into the straight, Dark Star broke away from his nearest challenger, the Eddie Arcaro-ridden Correspondent, to open a clear lead. Native Dancer produced a powerful late run, but Dark Star held on to win by a head. The winning time was 2:02.0. After the race, Moreno confessed to being surprised by Dark Star's effort, saying that he had "hoped to run third".

4th Pulitzer Prize for Literature awarded to Ernest Hemingway for "The Old Man & The Sea".

5th Aldous Huxley first tries the psychedelic hallucinogen mescaline, inspiring his book The Doors of Perception.

7th Cole Porter's musical "Can-Can" opens at the Shubert Theatre, NYC; runs for 892 performances.

9th Australian Senate election, 1953: The Liberal/Country Coalition Government, led by Prime Minister Robert Menzies, holds their Senate majority, despite gains made by the Labour Party, led by H. V. Evatt. This is the first occasion where a Senate election is held without an accompanying House Of Representatives election.

10th The town of Chemnitz, East Germany becomes Karl Marx Stadt.

11th Waco tornado outbreak: An F5 tornado hits in the downtown section of Waco, Texas, killing 114.

Winston Churchill criticizes US Secretary of State John Foster Dulles' domino theory.

15th The Standards and Recommended Practices (SARPS) for Aeronautical Information Service (AIS) are adopted by the ICAO Council. These SARPS are in Annex 15 to the Chicago Convention, and 15 May is celebrated by the AIS community as "World AIS Day".

In his first world heavyweight title defence, Rocky Marciano KOs former champion Jersey Joe Walcott in the 1st round at Chicago Stadium.

WORLD'S HEAVYWEIGHT CHAMPIONSHIP
CHICAGO STADIUM
May 15, 1953
15-ROUNDS
ROCKY MARCIANO
VS
JOE WALCOTT
PRESENTED BY
The INTERNATIONAL BOXING CLUB

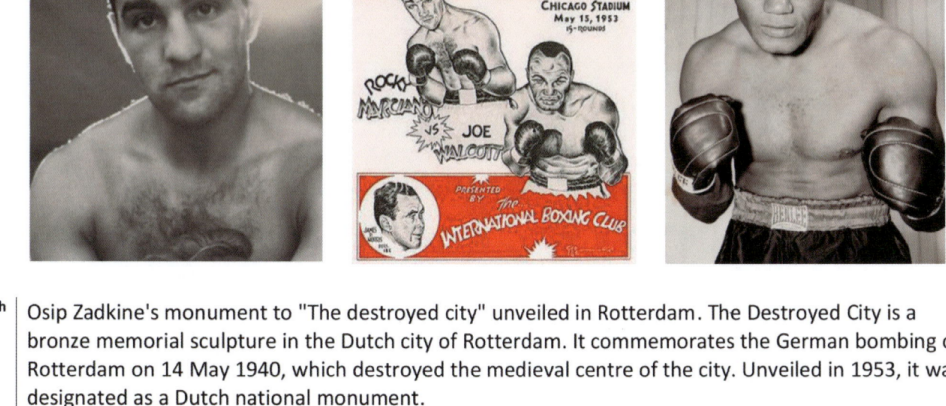

15th Osip Zadkine's monument to "The destroyed city" unveiled in Rotterdam. The Destroyed City is a bronze memorial sculpture in the Dutch city of Rotterdam. It commemorates the German bombing of Rotterdam on 14 May 1940, which destroyed the medieval centre of the city. Unveiled in 1953, it was designated as a Dutch national monument.

18th American Jacqueline Cochran becomes the first woman to break the sound barrier. In 1953, eager to make the transition to jet aircraft, Cochran became the first woman to break the sound barrier, piloting an F-86, and that year set world speed records for 15-, 100-, and 500-km courses. Her autobiographical The Stars at Noon, written with Floyd B. Odlum (her husband from 1936), appeared in 1954.

19th Nuclear explosion in Nevada (fall-out in St George, Utah).

22nd President Eisenhower signed legislation today reaffirming the Federal Government's ownership of offshore oil lands in the outer Continental Shelf.

23rd 78th Preakness: Eric Guerin aboard Native Dancer wins in 1:57.8.

24th Pope Pius XII publishes encyclical Doctor Mellifluus.

May

25th On 25th May 1953, during the Operation Upshot-Knothole test series at the Nevada Test Site, now known at the Nevada National Security Site (NNSS), a milestone occurred in ordnance development. A 280-mm cannon, nicknamed Atomic Annie, fired the first and last nuclear projectile as part of the Grable test.

26th A Convair CV-240-4 passenger plane, registered PH-TEI, was destroyed in an accident at Amsterdam-Schiphol Airport ... And 2 persons on the ground were killed.

27th Dutch social democratic/Dutch Liberal Party win municipal elections.

28th Melody is a 1953 American animated short film shot in 3D and produced by Walt Disney Productions and directed by Ward Kimball and Charles A. Nichols. Originally released on 28th May 1953, this film was the first in a proposed series of animated cartoon shorts teaching the principles of music, called Adventures in Music. However, only one other entry in the series was produced, Toot, Whistle, Plunk and Boom, which was released later that same year.

THE SCREEN'S FIRST ANIMATED CARTOON IN
3-DIMENSION
WALT DISNEY
PRESENTS
MELODY
FIRST OF THE "ADVENTURES IN MUSIC" SERIES
Color by TECHNICOLOR
Distributed by RKO RADIO PICTURES, INC.

Walt Disney
ANIMATION STUDIOS

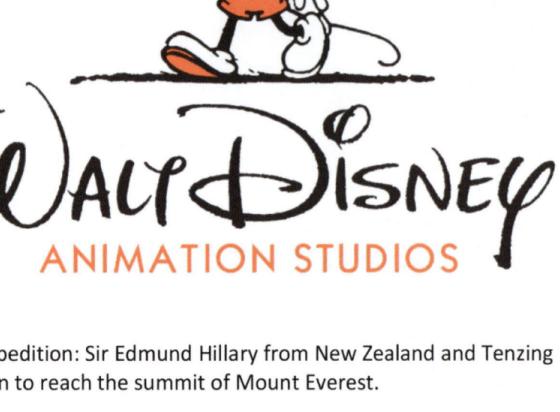

29th 29th May 1953 British Mount Everest expedition: Sir Edmund Hillary from New Zealand and Tenzing Norgay from Nepal become the first men to reach the summit of Mount Everest.

30th Indianapolis 500: Labelled "Hottest 500" due to high temperatures, Bill Vukovich wins first of 2 consecutive Indy 500 victories; Carl Scarborough drops out of race, and later dies of heat prostration.

French Championships Men's Tennis: Ken Rosewall of Australia wins his 2nd Grand Slam title, beating American Vic Seixas 6-3, 6-4, 1-6, 6-2.

French Championships Women's Tennis: Maureen Connolly beats fellow American Doris Hart 6-2, 6-4 for the 2nd leg of her Grand Slam.

31st Lebanese president Camille Shamun disbands government.

June

1st Uprising in Plzeň: Currency reform causes riots in Czechoslovakia.

4th Pittsburgh pirates trade outfielder Ralph Kiner & catcher Joe Garagiola go to Chicago Cubs.

5th Denmark adopts a new constitution.

US Senate rejects China People's Republic membership to UN.

7th Italian general election: the Christian Democracy party wins a plurality in both legislative houses.

Flint–Worcester tornado outbreak sequence: A single storm-system spawns 46 tornadoes of various sizes, in 10 states from Colorado to Massachusetts, over 3 days, killing 246.

8th On the second day of the Flint–Worcester tornado outbreak sequence, a tornado kills 115 in Flint, Michigan; it will be the last to claim more than 100 lives, until the 2011 Joplin tornado.

9th On the third day of the Flint–Worcester tornado outbreak sequence, a tornado spawned from the same storm system as the Flint tornado the day before hits in Worcester, Massachusetts, killing 94.

11th "Amos 'n Andy" TV Comedy, also radio from '29; last aired on CBS.

13th US Open Men's Golf, Oakmont CC: Ben Hogan wins a record-tying 4th US Open title, 6 strokes ahead of runner-up Sam Snead.

388 YDS
5
5
BRAE

Ben Hogan

Sam Sneed

June

13th 85th Belmont: Eric Guerin aboard Native Dancer wins in 2:28.6.

14th Elvis Presley graduates from L: C. Humes High School in Memphis, Tennessee.

15th NY Yankees first baseman Johnny Mize is 93rd MLB player to get 2,000 hits.

16th Despite Johnny Mize 2,000th hit, NY Yankees lose ending an 18-game winning streak and also ending St Louis Brown 14 game losing streak.

17th Workers' Uprising in East Germany: The Soviet Union orders a division of troops into East Berlin to quell a rebellion.

83

18th Tachikawa air disaster: A United States Air Force Douglas C-124 Globemaster II crashes just after take-off from Tachikawa Airfield near Tokyo, Japan, killing all 129 people on board in the worst air crash in history up to this time, and the first with a confirmed death toll exceeding 100.

19th Julius and Ethel Rosenberg are executed at Sing Sing Prison in New York for conspiracy to commit espionage.

The Baton Rouge bus boycott begins in the Southern United States.

20th LPGA Western Golf Open Women's Golf, Capital City Club: Louise Suggs defeats Patty Berg, 6 & 5 in the final.

25th 86°F in Anchorage, Alaska. The Hottest ever recording in Alaska. Since been broken in 2006 and again in 2019 hitting 90 degrees.

26th Lavrentiy Beria, one of the trio of Russian leaders after Stalin's death and the former secret police chief, is ousted from power and arrested.

28th US Open Women's Golf, CC of Rochester: Betsy Rawls wins an 18-hole Sunday playoff by 6 strokes over runner-up Jackie Pung.

31st 1st Chevrolet Corvette manufactured.

July

3rd	First ascent of Nanga Parbat in the Pakistan Himalayas, the world's ninth highest mountain, is made by Austrian climber Hermann Buhl alone on a German–Austrian expedition.
	Wimbledon Men's Tennis: American Vic Seixas wins his only Wimbledon singles title with a 9-7, 6-3, 6-4 over Dane Kurt Nielsen.
4th	Wimbledon Women's Tennis: Maureen Connolly wins 3rd leg of her Grand Slam beating fellow American Doris Hart 8-6, 7-5.
5th	Phillies pitcher Robin Roberts hurls his 28th consecutive MLB complete game in a 2-0 win over Pittsburgh.
7th	PGA Championship Men's Golf, Birmingham CC: Walter Burkemo wins 2 & 1 from Felize Torza in the Tuesday final; his lone major title.
	Che Guevara sets out on a trip through Bolivia, Peru, Ecuador, Panama, Costa Rica, Nicaragua, Honduras, and El Salvador.
8th	US stops aid to Persia.
9th	1st helicopter passenger service (NYC).
10th	British Open Men's Golf, Carnoustie: In his only Open Championship appearance, Ben Hogan prevails by 4 strokes over Dai Rees, Antonio Cerdá, Peter Thomson, Frank Stranahan.
14th	First US national monument dedicated to a black American, to preserve the boyhood home of agricultural scientist and inventor George Washington Carver in Newton County, Missouri.

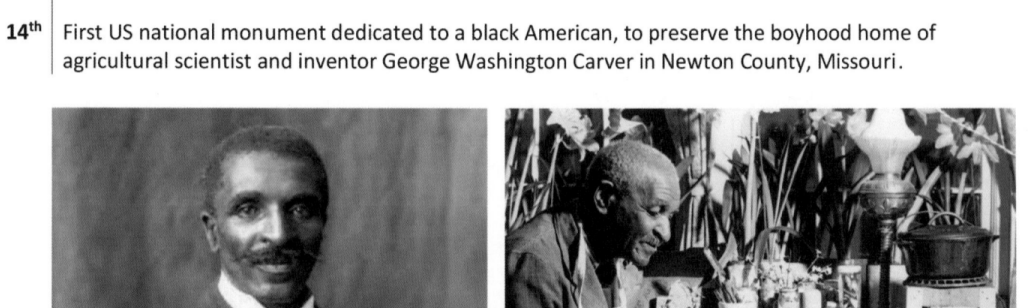

15th	China First Automobile Work, present day of FAW Group, a truck, bus and automobile product and sales in China, was founded in Changchun.
17th	USMC R4Q NROTC crash: the greatest recorded loss of United States midshipmen in a single event results from an aircraft crash near NAS Whiting Field.
19th	WAKR (now WAKC) TV channel 23 in Akron, OH (ABC) begins broadcasting.

July

20th The United Nations Economic and Social Council votes to make UNICEF a permanent agency.

23rd Howard Hawks's musical film Gentlemen Prefer Blondes, starring Marilyn Monroe and Jane Russell, is released by 20th Century Fox.

JANE RUSSELL
MARILYN MONROE
in
HOWARD HAWKS'
Gentlemen Prefer Blondes
Colour by TECHNICOLOR
CHARLES COBURN
DIAMONDS ARE A GIRL'S BEST FRIEND
BYE BYE BABY
LITTLE GIRL FROM LITTLE ROCK
WHEN LOVE GOES WRONG
AIN'T THERE ANYONE HERE FOR LOVE?
Produced by SOL C. SIEGEL
Directed by HOWARD HAWKS
Screenplay by CHARLES LEDERER

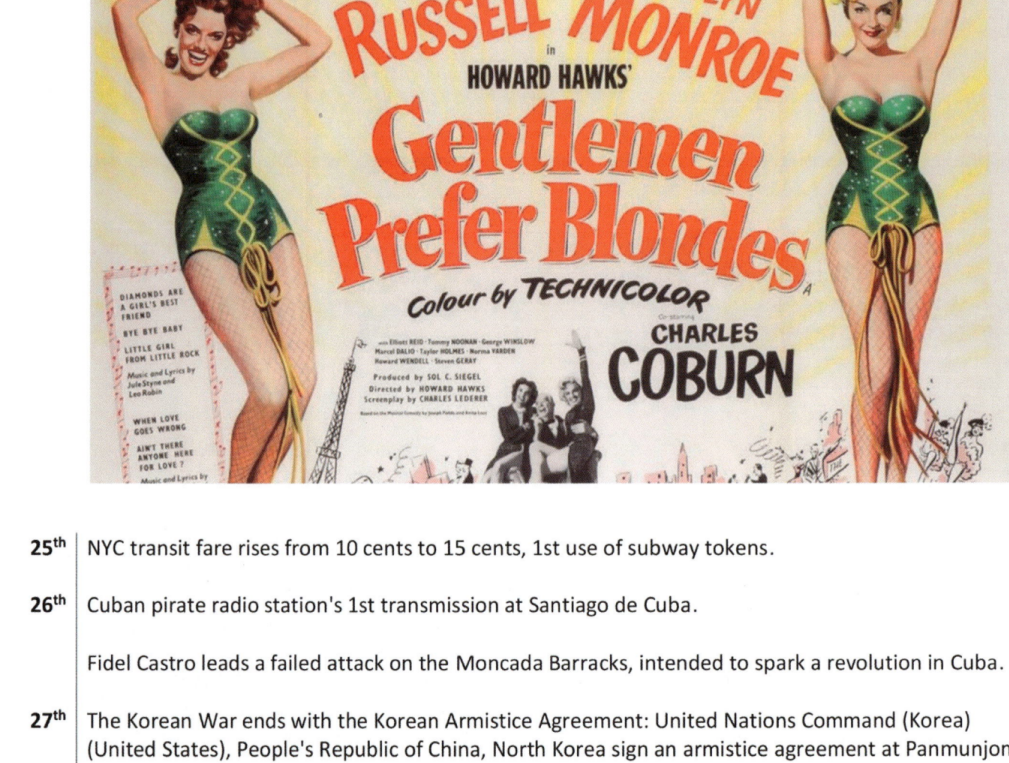

25th NYC transit fare rises from 10 cents to 15 cents, 1st use of subway tokens.

26th Cuban pirate radio station's 1st transmission at Santiago de Cuba.

Fidel Castro leads a failed attack on the Moncada Barracks, intended to spark a revolution in Cuba.

27th The Korean War ends with the Korean Armistice Agreement: United Nations Command (Korea) (United States), People's Republic of China, North Korea sign an armistice agreement at Panmunjom and the north remains communist while the south remains capitalist.

Vatican disallows priest holiday work in factory.

29th US bomber shot down by Soviet Air Defence Forces in the Sea of Japan, north of Vladivostok.

30th Rikidōzan holds a ceremony announcing the establishment of the Japan Pro Wrestling Alliance.

August

1st Fidel Castro arrested in Cuba.

Northern Rhodesia becomes part of Federation of Rhodesia and Nyasaland.

August

2nd	Betty Jack Davis, American country singer (with Skeeter Davis in The Davis Sisters), killed in car crash at 21.
3rd	Frank Blair becomes news anchor of "Today Show".
4th	Black families move into Trumbull Park housing project in Chicago.
5th	"From Here to Eternity" based on book by James Jones, directed by Fred Zinnemann and starring Burt Lancaster, Montgomery Clift and Frank Sinatra is released (Academy Awards Best Picture 1954).

6th	Future Baseball Hall of Fame slugger Ted Williams returns to Red Sox from military service in Korea; ends abbreviated season with .407 batting average.
7th	Eastern Airlines enters jet age, uses Electra prop-jet.
8th	Soviet leader Georgi Malenkov reports possession of hydrogen bomb.
	US & South Korea initial a mutual security pact.
9th	1st elected Prime Minister of Jammu and Kashmir, Sheikh Abdullah dismissed by the Indian government and later arrested.
10th	Pete Schoening saves members of the American K2 expedition, one of the most famous events in mountaineering history.
12th	A magnitude 7.2 earthquake devastates most of the Ionian Sea islands in Greece's worst natural disaster in centuries.

August

13th Four million workers go on strike in France to protest against austerity measures.

US President Dwight Eisenhower establishes Government Contract Compliance Committee.

14th 20th NFL Chicago All-Star Game: Detroit 24, All-Stars 10 (93,818).

15th General Omar Bradley leaves office as the Chairman of the Joint Chiefs of Staff after four years and retires from active military service.

16th Shah of Persia Mohammad Reza Pahlavi & princess Soraya flee to Baghdad & Rome.

17th Addiction: First meeting of Narcotics Anonymous in Southern California.

18th The second Kinsey Report, Sexual Behaviour in the Human Female, is published in the US.

19th Democratically elected Prime Minister of Iran Mohammad Mosaddegh is overthrown in a coup orchestrated by the United Kingdom (under the name 'Operation Boot') and the United States (under the name TPAJAX Project).

20th Russia publicly acknowledges hydrogen bomb test detonation.

14th Venice Film Festival opens. No Golden Lion awarded.

21st Marion Carl in Douglas Skyrocket reaches record 25,370 m.

23rd Former Boston Braves pitcher Phil Paine becomes first major leaguer to play in Japan; on military service with U.S. Air Force plays first of 9 games for Nishitetsu Lions.

Cyclist Arie Van Vliet becomes world champion sprinter.

Italian Ferrari driver Alberto Ascari clinches his second Formula 1 World Drivers Championship by winning Swiss Grand Prix at Bremgarten.

27th Roman Holiday", starring Audrey Hepburn, Gregory Peck, and Eddie Albert, is released.

28th "Me & Juliet" opens at Majestic Theatre NYC for 358 performances.

Nippon TV launches, becoming Japan's First Commercial Television Channel.

29th USSR explodes its first hydrogen bomb.

31st KRBC TV channel 9 in Abilene, TX (NBC) begins broadcasting.

WKBG (now WLVI) TV channel 56 in Cambridge-Boston, MA (IND) begins.

September

1st Buck Baker takes lead with 10 laps remaining to win the Southern 500 at Darlington in the most competitive event in NASCAR Grand National history; four drivers swap lead a record 35 times.

101°F highest temperature ever recorded in Cleveland.

Fokker begins building F-27 Fokker Friendship.

3rd French minister François Mitterrand, resigns due to colonial policy.

4th WGEM TV channel 10 in Quincy-Hannibal, IL (NBC) begins broadcasting.

5th US give Persian premier Zahedi $45 million aid.

6th Roy Campanella sets record for Home Runs by a catcher at 38.

7th US National Championship Men's Tennis, Forest Hills, NY: Tony Trabert beats fellow American Vic Seixas 6-3, 6-2, 6-3 to win his first of 5 major titles.

Tony Trabert

Vic Seixas

US National Championship Women's Tennis, Forest Hills, NY: In an all-American final Maureen Connolly becomes first female to achieve a Grand Slam; beats Doris Hart 6-2, 6-4.

10th The Swanson & Sons' TV dinner branded frozen meal, sold 5,000 units when it was first introduced in 1953; just one year later, the company had sold over 10,000,000 TV dinners.

11th WEHT TV channel 25 in Evansville, IN (CBS) begins broadcasting.

September

12th Brooklyn Dodgers clinch NL pennant earlier than any other team, defeating Milwaukee Braves 5-2. Brooklyn finishes season with record of 105-49.

13th Italian Ferrari driver Alberto Ascari retains Formula 1 World Drivers Championship although forced to retire (engine trouble) in season ending Italian Grand Prix at Monza; wins title by 6.5 points from Juan Manuel Fangio.

14th Nikita Khrushchev appointed First Secretary of the Communist Party of the Soviet Union, succeeding Malenkov.

15th Boxing's NBA adopts 10-pt-must-scoring-system (10 pts to round winner).

16th 1st movie in Cinemascope "The Robe" based on the book by Lloyd C. Douglas, directed by Henry Koster and starring Richard Burton and Jean Simmons premieres.

17th Ernie Banks becomes Chicago Cubs 1st black player.

19th "Hazel Flagg" closes at Mark Hellinger Theatre NYC after 190 performances.

23rd The Pact of Madrid was signed by Francoist Spain and the United States of America, ending a period of virtual isolation for Spain.

24th Rocky Marciano TKOs home town favourite Roland LaStarza in 11 at NYC's Polo Grounds to retain his world heavyweight boxing title.

25th The first German prisoners of war return from the Soviet Union to West Germany.

Primate of Poland Stefan Wyszyński, imprisoned by the communist government, was placed under house arrest in Rywałd.

26th Shortstop Billy Hunter smashes final home run in St Louis Browns history during a 6-3 loss to Chicago WS at Busch Stadium; franchise moves to Baltimore next season.

US & Spain sign defence treaty (4 US bases in Spain).

27th St Louis Browns play last game in Sportsman's Park, losing 100th game.

Typhoon destroys one third of Nagoya, Japan.

29th 1st department store to sell insurance is Carson Pirie Scott in Chicago, Illinois.

"Milton Berle Show" premieres on NBC in the US.

30th On 30th September 1953, father and son set a new depth record of 3,150 metres in the Trieste – and Auguste Piccard became the first person to explore the stratosphere and the deep ocean. The French Navy pipped the Piccard's record on 15th February 1954, reaching 4,050 metres with Georges Houot and Pierre Willm in the bathyscaphe FNRS-3.

October

1st Indian state of Andhra Pradesh partitioned from Madras.

2nd "Comedy in Music (Victor Borge)" opens at John Golden NYC for 849 performances.

3rd NY Yankees legendary centre fielder Mickey Mantle hits a grand slam off Russ Meyer; Bronx Bombers hold on to win, 11-7 v Brooklyn Dodgers in Game 5 of Baseball World Series; NY wins series, 4-2.

4th British runner Jim Peters sets world marathon record 2:18:34.8 in the Turku Marathon in Finland.

5th Earl Warren sworn in as 14th Chief Justice of US Supreme Court.

The first documented recovery meeting of Narcotics Anonymous is held.

7th Bill Veeck tells Browns stockholders he faces bankruptcy unless they drop their suit to block his move to Baltimore, they comply.

8th Birmingham, Alabama, bars Jackie Robinson's Negro-White All-Stars from playing there Robinson gives in & drops white players from his group.

9th Konrad Adenauer elected Chancellor of West Germany.

10th Roland (Monty) Burton wins the 1953 London to Christchurch air race in under 23 hours flying time.

The Mutual Defence Treaty between the United States and the Republic of Korea is concluded in Washington, D.C.

11th Pauline Robinson Bush died at the age of three from leukaemia.

12th The play The Caine Mutiny Court-Martial opens at Plymouth Theatre, New York.

Primate of Poland Stefan Wyszyński, imprisoned by the communist government, was relocated from Rywałd to Stoczek Klasztorny.

October

13th Burglar alarm-ultrasonic or radio waves patented by Samuel Bagno.

14th 1st 3 Dutch female police officers go into service.

15th John Patrick's play "Teahouse of the August Moon" premieres in New York.

16th Fidel Castro sentenced to 15 years (Havana). Although the maximum penalty for leading an uprising was 20 years, Castro was sentenced to 15, being imprisoned in the hospital wing of the Model Prison (Presidio Modelo), a relatively comfortable and modern institution on the Isla de Pinos, 60 miles off of Cuba's southwest coast.

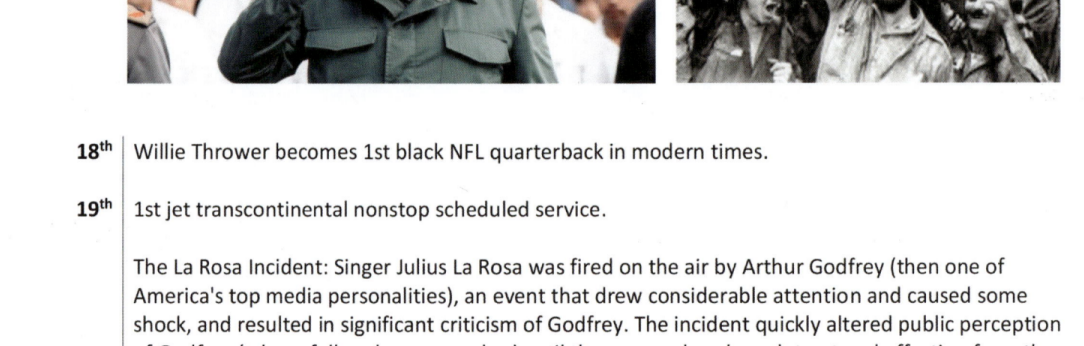

18th Willie Thrower becomes 1st black NFL quarterback in modern times.

19th 1st jet transcontinental nonstop scheduled service.

The La Rosa Incident: Singer Julius La Rosa was fired on the air by Arthur Godfrey (then one of America's top media personalities), an event that drew considerable attention and caused some shock, and resulted in significant criticism of Godfrey. The incident quickly altered public perception of Godfrey (whose folksy demeanour had until then engendered much trust and affection from the American public), materially damaging his career.

22nd Laos gains full independence from France.

23rd Alto Broadcasting System in the Philippines makes the first television broadcast in southeast Asia through DZAQ-TV. Alto Broadcasting System (ABS) is the predecessor of what would later become ABS-CBN Corporation after a being bought by the Chronicle Broadcasting Network (CBN) in 1957.

25th Coal mine in Seraing Belgium explodes, 26 die.

30th Cold War: U.S. President Dwight D. Eisenhower formally approves the top-secret document of the United States National Security Council NSC 162/2, which states that the United States' arsenal of nuclear weapons must be maintained and expanded to counter the communist threat.

Dr Albert Schweitzer & Gen George Marshall win Nobel Peace Prize.

November

1st Czech long-distance runner Emile Zatopek sets world 10,000m record 29:01.6 & 6-mile mark 28:08.4 in Stara Boleslav, Czech Republic.

Herb Thomas, driving his own No. 92 Hudson Hornet wraps up the NASCAR Grand National Championship with 14th-place in 100-mile finale at Atlanta's Lakewood Speedway; Thomas first repeat champion of the series.

2nd Pakistan becomes Islamic republic.

3rd "Tokyo Story", Japanese film directed by Yasujirō Ozu, starring Chishū Ryū, Chieko Higashiyama and Setsuko Hara, is released.

4th New baseball balk rule gives the batter option of accepting the outcome of the pitch or the balk.

5th Film "How to Marry a Millionaire" directed by Jean Negulesco, starring Lauren Bacall, Betty Grable and Marilyn Monroe, first to be filmed in CinemaScope; release delayed to allow "The Robe" to debut the format.

The Most Glamorous Entertainment Of Your Lifetime
CinemaScope
YOU SEE IT WITHOUT GLASSES!
MARILYN BETTY LAUREN
MONROE·GRABLE·BACALL
How To Marry a Millionaire
TECHNICOLOR
WILLIAM POWELL

Marilyn Monroe

Betty Grable

6th French National Meeting grants Saarland more autonomy.

9th Cambodia (aka Kampuchea) gains independence from France, within the French Union.

10th New York Giants end their tour of Japan (players got $331 of $3,000 promised).

12th David Ben-Gurion, resigns as Prime Minister of Israel.

17th The government evacuated most of the remaining residents to the mainland on 17th November 1953 because of increasingly extreme winter weather that left the island's ageing population cut off from emergency services. The evacuation was seen as necessary by both the Islanders and the government.

November

18th Anti-Revolutionary Party (ARP) accept female suffrage.

19th US VP Richard Nixon visits Hanoi.

20th Scott Crossfield in Douglas Skyrocket, 1st to break Mach 2 (1,300 MPH).

21st Authorities at the British Natural History Museum announce the "Piltdown Man" skull, one of the most famous fossil skulls in the world, is a hoax.

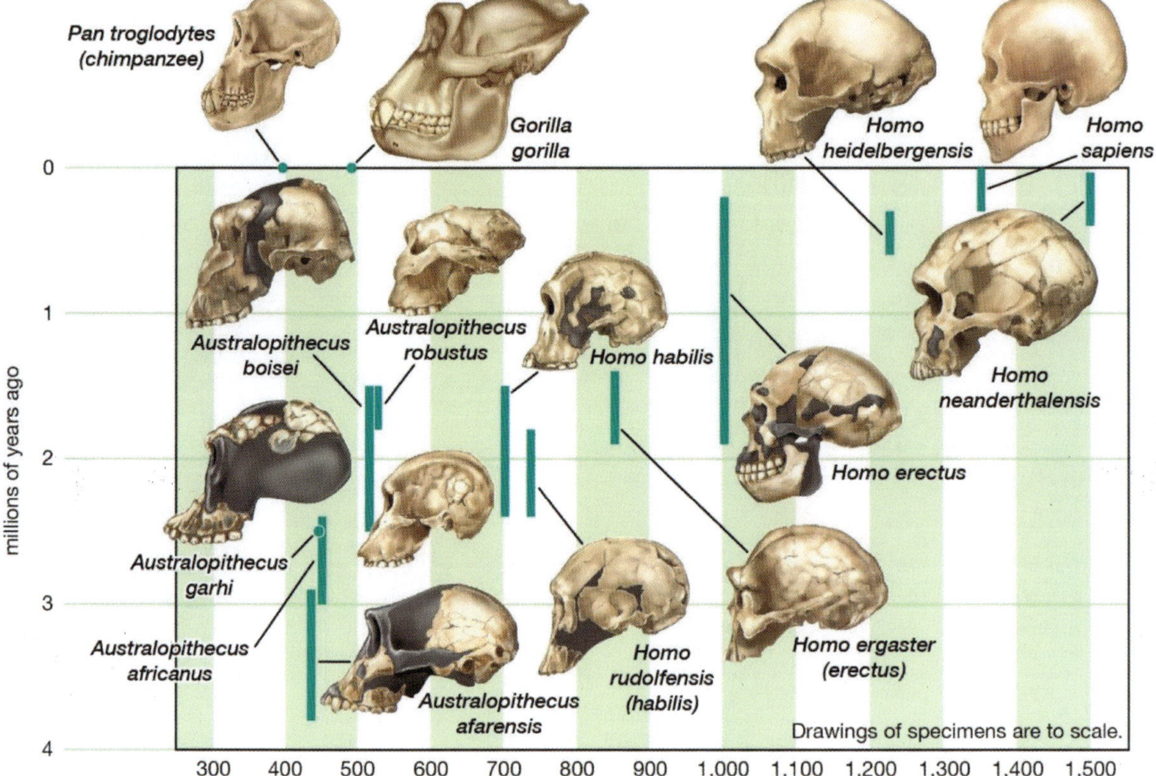

Pan troglodytes (chimpanzee)
Gorilla gorilla
Homo heidelbergensis
Homo sapiens
Australopithecus boisei
Australopithecus robustus
Homo habilis
Homo neanderthalensis
Homo erectus
Australopithecus garhi
Australopithecus africanus
Australopithecus afarensis
Homo rudolfensis (habilis)
Homo ergaster (erectus)
Drawings of specimens are to scale.
millions of years ago
0
1
2
3
4
300 400 500 600 700 800 900 1,000 1,100 1,200 1,300 1,400 1,500
brain capacity in cubic centimetres

25th "Guys & Dolls" closes at 46th St Theatre NYC after 1,200 performances.

Earthquake and tsunami strike Honshu, Japan.

26th Yamada Koun, leader of Sanbo Kyodan line of Zen, found 1st awakening.

28th CFL Grey Cup, Varsity Stadium, Toronto: Hamilton Tiger-Cats defeat Winnipeg Blue Bombers, 12-6.

29th American Airlines begins 1st regular commercial NY-LA air service.

30th French parachutist under Colonel De Castries attacks Dien Bien Phu.

Edward Mutesa II, kabaka (king) of Buganda is deposed and exiled to London by Sir Andrew Cohen, Governor of Uganda.

December

1st Hugh Hefner publishes the first issue of Playboy magazine in the United States, featuring a centrefold nude photograph of Marilyn Monroe; it sells 54,175 copies at $.50 each.

3rd Robert Wright and George Forrest's musical "Kismet" opens at Ziegfeld Theatre, NYC; runs for 583 performances, wins Tony Award for Best Musical.

US President Dwight Eisenhower criticizes Wisconsin Senator Joe McCarthy for saying communists are in the Republican Party.

6th With the NBC Symphony Orchestra, conductor Arturo Toscanini performs what he claims is his favourite Beethoven symphony, Eroica, for the last time. The live performance is broadcast across the United States on radio, and later released on records and CD.

7th A visit to Iran by American Vice President Richard Nixon sparks several days of riots, as a reaction to the August 19 overthrow of the government of Mohammed Mossadegh by the U.S.-backed Shah. Three students are shot dead by police in Tehran. This event becomes an annual commemoration.

8th U.S. President Dwight D. Eisenhower delivers his Atoms for Peace address, to the United Nations General Assembly.

9th General Electric announces all Communist employees will be fired.

10th Albert Schweitzer is given the 1952 Nobel Peace Prize.

12th 12th December 1953: Maj. Chuck Yeager flies his Bell X-1A to March 2.435, approximately 1,650 miles per hour, at Edwards Air Force Base, Calif. At Mach 2.4 at 80,000 feet the aircraft spun out of control, spinning on all 3 axes. G-forces sent Yeager's head into the canopy, cracking it and bending the control stick.

GLAMOROUS
GLENNIS

December

16th 1st White House Press Conference (President Eisenhower & 161 reporters).

17th US Federal Communications Commission approves RCA's black & white-compatible colour TV specifications.

18th KATV TV channel 7 in Little Rock, AR (ABC) begins broadcasting.

20th KID (now KIDK) TV channel 3 in Idaho Falls, ID (CBS) 1st broadcasting.

22nd Jack Dunn III, owner of Baltimore Orioles in Intl League, turns name over to newly relocated St Louis Browns.

24th Two fast express trains crash head-on killing 103 in Czechoslovakia.

25th Avalanche of lava kills 150 from Ruapehu volcano in New Zealand.

The Amami Islands are returned to Japan, after 8 years of United States military occupation.

27th National Football League Championship, Briggs Stadium, Detroit: Detroit Lions beat Cleveland Browns, 17-16 to retain title.

28th WLBT TV channel 3 in Jackson, MS (NBC) begins broadcasting.

30th The first ever NTSC colour television sets go on sale for about USD at $1,175 each from RCA.

31st Bill Shoemaker shatters record, riding 485 winners in a year.

CALENDAR 1953

January 1953

M	T	W	T	F	S	S
			1	2	3	4
5	6	7	8	9	10	11
12	13	14	15	16	17	18
19	20	21	22	23	24	25
26	27	28	29	30	31	

February 1953

M	T	W	T	F	S	S
						1
2	3	4	5	6	7	8
9	10	11	12	13	14	15
16	17	18	19	20	21	22
23	24	25	26	27	28	

March 1953

M	T	W	T	F	S	S
						1
2	3	4	5	6	7	8
9	10	11	12	13	14	15
16	17	18	19	20	21	22
23	24	25	26	27	28	29
30	31					

April 1953

M	T	W	T	F	S	S
		1	2	3	4	5
6	7	8	9	10	11	12
13	14	15	16	17	18	19
20	21	22	23	24	25	26
27	28	29	30			

May 1953

M	T	W	T	F	S	S
				1	2	3
4	5	6	7	8	9	10
11	12	13	14	15	16	17
18	19	20	21	22	23	24
25	26	27	28	29	30	31

June 1953

M	T	W	T	F	S	S
1	2	3	4	5	6	7
8	9	10	11	12	13	14
15	16	17	18	19	20	21
22	23	24	25	26	27	28
29	30					

July 1953

M	T	W	T	F	S	S
		1	2	3	4	5
6	7	8	9	10	11	12
13	14	15	16	17	18	19
20	21	22	23	24	25	26
27	28	29	30	31		

August 1953

M	T	W	T	F	S	S
					1	2
3	4	5	6	7	8	9
10	11	12	13	14	15	16
17	18	19	20	21	22	23
24	25	26	27	28	29	30
31						

September 1953

M	T	W	T	F	S	S
	1	2	3	4	5	6
7	8	9	10	11	12	13
14	15	16	17	18	19	20
21	22	23	24	25	26	27
28	29	30				

October 1953

M	T	W	T	F	S	S
			1	2	3	4
5	6	7	8	9	10	11
12	13	14	15	16	17	18
19	20	21	22	23	24	25
26	27	28	29	30	31	

November 1953

M	T	W	T	F	S	S
						1
2	3	4	5	6	7	8
9	10	11	12	13	14	15
16	17	18	19	20	21	22
23	24	25	26	27	28	29
30						

December 1953

M	T	W	T	F	S	S
	1	2	3	4	5	6
7	8	9	10	11	12	13
14	15	16	17	18	19	20
21	22	23	24	25	26	27
28	29	30	31			

PEOPLE IN POWER

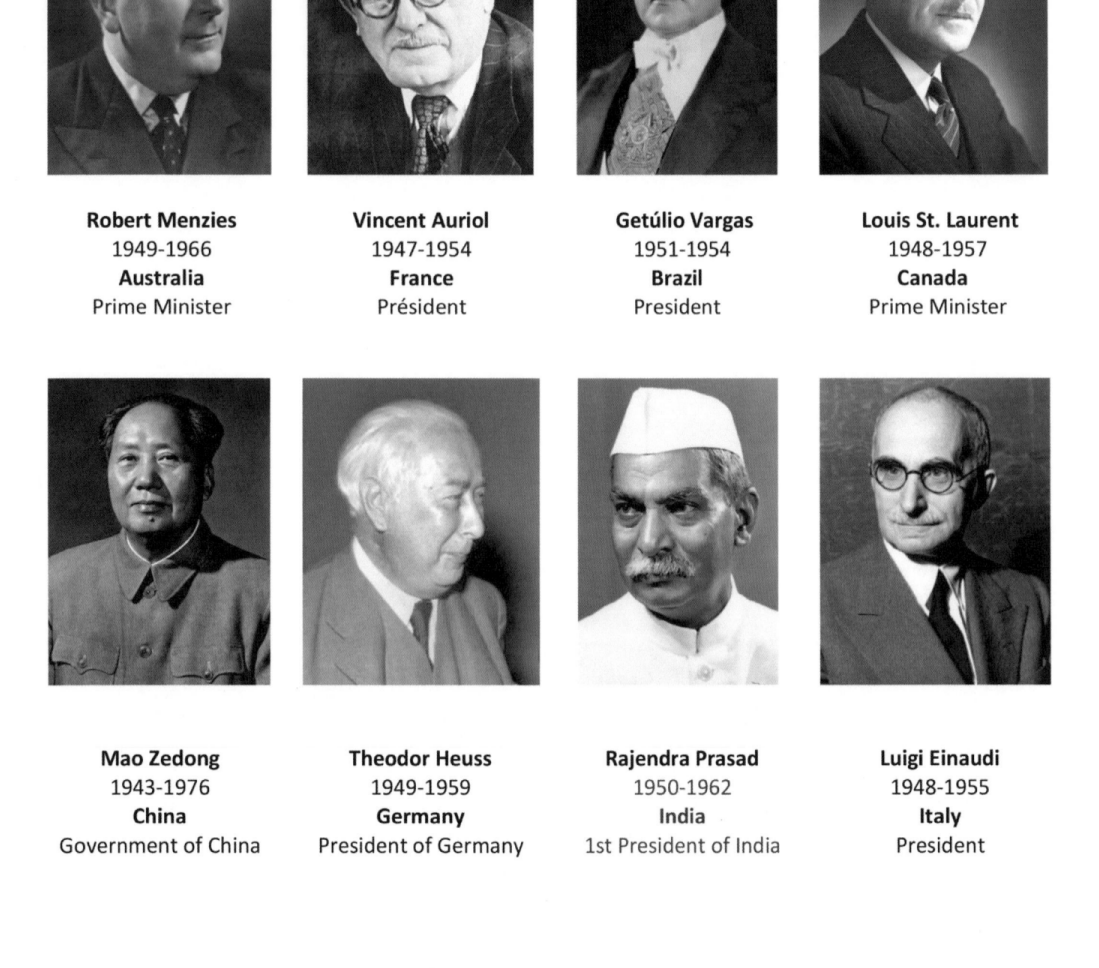

Robert Menzies
1949-1966
Australia
Prime Minister

Vincent Auriol
1947-1954
France
Président

Getúlio Vargas
1951-1954
Brazil
President

Louis St. Laurent
1948-1957
Canada
Prime Minister

Mao Zedong
1943-1976
China
Government of China

Theodor Heuss
1949-1959
Germany
President of Germany

Rajendra Prasad
1950-1962
India
1st President of India

Luigi Einaudi
1948-1955
Italy
President

Hiroito
1926-1989
Japan
Emperor

Adolfo Ruiz Cortines
1952-1958
Mexico
54th President

Nikita Khrushchev
1953-1964
Russia
Premier

D. F. Malan
1948-1954
South Africa
Prime Minister

Harry S. Truman
1945-1953
United States
President

Baudouin of Belgium
1951-1993
Belgium
King

Sidney Holland
1949-1957
New Zealand
Prime Minister

Sir Winston Churchill
1951-1955
United Kingdom
Prime Minister

Tage Erlander
1946-1969
Sweden
Prime Minister

Erik Eriksen
1950-1953
Denmark
Prime Minister

Francisco Franco
1936-1975
Spain
President

Mátyás Rákosi
1948-1956
Hungary
Hungarian Working People's Party

The Year You Were Born 1953
Book by Sapphire Publishing

Printed in Great Britain
by Amazon

19220743R00047

Printing and Binding: Stürtz AG, Würzburg